Calendula

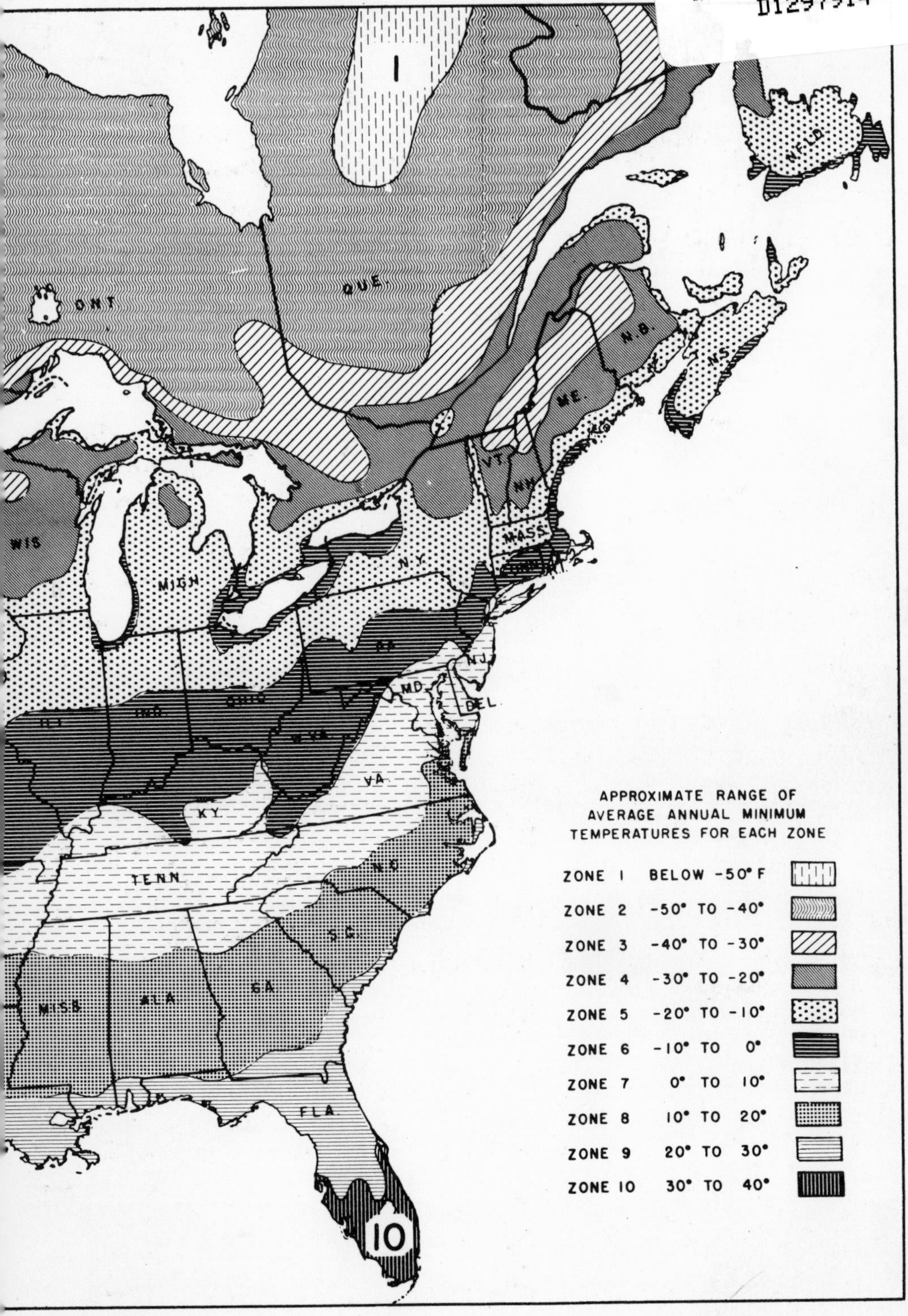
1
QUE.
ONT
N.FLD.
N.B.
N.S.
ME.
VT.
N.H.
MASS.
CONN.
N.Y.
WIS
MICH.
PA
N.J.
MD
DEL.
OHIO
IND.
ILL.
W.VA.
VA.
KY
TENN.
N.C.
S.C.
GA.
ALA.
MISS.
FLA.
10
APPROXIMATE RANGE OF
AVERAGE ANNUAL MINIMUM
TEMPERATURES FOR EACH ZONE
ZONE 1 BELOW -50° F
ZONE 2 -50° TO -40°
ZONE 3 -40° TO -30°
ZONE 4 -30° TO -20°
ZONE 5 -20° TO -10°
ZONE 6 -10° TO 0°
ZONE 7 0° TO 10°
ZONE 8 10° TO 20°
ZONE 9 20° TO 30°
ZONE 10 30° TO 40°

The Complete Book for Gardeners

THE COMPLETE BOOK FOR GARDENERS

edited by

RACHEL SNYDER

Editor-in-Chief of *FLOWER* and *GARDEN* Magazine

D. VAN NOSTRAND COMPANY, INC.

PRINCETON, NEW JERSEY   *Toronto · London · Melbourne*

EDITOR'S FOREWORD

If You Are a New Gardener with a new house and a bare lot, start at the beginning of this book and study the plot plans. One of them will suit your place and your family's needs, whether there are two or ten of you. Move on through the pages to lawns, trees, shrubs, and other plants. Follow the advice given you so that you end up with an attractive planting at lowest possible cost—a planting well organized and inexpensive to maintain.

Read the "Easy-Does-It Ideas" at the end of each chapter. They are a distillation of garden wisdom, the essence of old-timers' experience.

Read "Garden Where You Live." Locate your property on the Zone Map in front. All plants will not thrive everywhere. When you select anything as important as a shade tree, for example, you want to be sure it will grow in your area. The zone symbols help you to decide what to plant where.

Developing a good lawn requires knowledge and effort. Study the lawn chapter to get real know-how, less work, and grass that will endure.

A plan, a lawn, a tree, and a few shrubs come first. Then read on for guidance in more ambitious plantings and projects—and for information on upkeep.

Use the extensive index (with pronunciation of difficult plant names indicated) to find what you want to know: how to sow seeds, when to cultivate the soil, how to water, how to prune, what makes compost, how to use a mulch, how to cope with some pest or disease. All the business of maintenance is clearly explained in these pages. There is no need to do anything at the wrong time or the wrong way, no need for mistakes with this book in hand.

Experienced Gardeners may turn first to the sections on special plants—roses, vines, perennials, and vegetables perhaps. Here is the real fun of gardening, and this book shows you how to have it. Whatever your hobby, we think we have included it here—herbs, flowering trees, camellias, rock walls, cold frames, hybridizing, bonsai. You too can use the index to locate authoritative discussions on these and many other subjects.

Anybody who wants to attract birds, design a pool, construct a patio, build a fence, or just lay a brick walk with a few steps can also find directions in this book.

The editors of *Flower and Garden* have tried to cover here all the subjects their readers far and wide want to know about. Here are the answers to questions that have been asked over and over again. But we hope you will find this more than a reference book and that you will enjoy reading it as well, chapter by chapter.

Rachel Snyder, Editor-in-Chief
Flower and Garden Magazine

Kansas City, Missouri
January, 1964

CONTENTS

List of Illustrations

LINE ILLUSTRATIONS

PART I

FIRST THINGS FIRST

Chapter 1

A GARDEN
FOR WHERE YOU LIVE

How can I pick out the best plants for my location?

One thing about a garden cannot change: *where it is.* What you grow, your methods, your insect and disease pests, your weeds, climatic problems and possibilities—they all depend on geography. Your longitude and latitude, elevation, nearness to sea-coasts, valleys or mountains—these and other things make up your local climate and they dictate to you. You can't change them.

No matter where you live you can have a fine garden. From the start the important thing is to assess the opportunities and limitations of your own particular spot in these United States, and then pay attention to them. Peonies in Massachusetts, yes; in California, no. Gardenias in Georgia, yes; in Minnesota, no.

HOW YOU CAN LEARN
ABOUT YOUR REGION

In *Flower and Garden's* regional approach, the country is divided into four-teen basic areas. An expert from each of these areas has contributed a section about it later in this chapter. Find your own place in one of these areas and read the regional advice written for you. Then look at the zone map on the end paper of this book, and fix firmly in your mind the zone *you* are in. By these two methods you will be starting off on the right foot toward relating your yard, and what you can grow in it, with where you live.

HOW TO USE THE ZONE MAP

The zone map back of the front cover helps tell you what will grow for you. Most of the plants mentioned in this book are keyed to this map. If the book tells you, for instance, that the star magnolia is rated Zone 5, it means that it stands an excellent chance of doing well there. Look on the map to see where Zone 5 is and where you are. If you live in Zone 6, your weather is even a little warmer than Zone 5, so you can certainly expect to grow star magnolia with every promise of success. If you live in Zone 4 you are in a colder region, so you would take a risk in planting it (although it might possibly succeed). The zone rating gives the northernmost (or coldest) area where a plant is expected to be satisfactory. Each zone represents an average annual minimum temperature range of ten degrees. Find the zone you are in and commit it to memory. All you need to remember is its number.

This is a new zone map. It was published in 1960 under the title "Plant Hardiness Zone Map," after years of work by the American Horticultural Society, U. S. National Arboretum, Agricultural Research Service of the U. S. Department of Agriculture, American Association of Nurserymen, weather bureaus of the United States and Canada and many independent horticulturists. It is the latest thing of its kind available. Before this came out, nurserymen and garden books used a variety of old maps, each of them numbered or divided somewhat differently, so the situation was confused. If you see zone references in other books, pamphlets and magazines, find out to which map they refer, or you might be led astray. Every reference in this book is to this new plant hardiness zone map.

The truth is, hardiness is something more than the ability of a plant to stand cold. It is also the ability to tolerate all kinds of bad conditions—heat, drouth, too much rain, dry winds and swift changes of weather. Other things that might decide if you can grow a certain plant are the length of the growing season, and the length of the dormant season. The relative humidity of the air is another factor. But still and all, cold hardiness is the main one, which is why the new plant hardiness map is so valuable. No zone map ever devised shows perfectly every

place a plant may be grown. But it is one of the best guides you have.

Each region has its own set of plants and methods to be used. Even in severe climates there are long lists of possible trees, shrubs, vines and flowers. Gardening where you live is just as rewarding as it is anywhere else, but it is different. Once you accept this fact, you have learned something important.

If you grew up in the area where you live, you probably know (or think you know) a lot about your climate. If you've always kept a yard there you can judge how much winter protection to give certain plants, how much watering to do, what to do about pests.

But if you have recently moved to the region, you have a great deal to learn. Chances are you'll start in the new place with plants and methods you used before. It takes a few seasons to discover they no longer work so well. Northerners moved to Florida try in vain to grow tulips as they did back home.

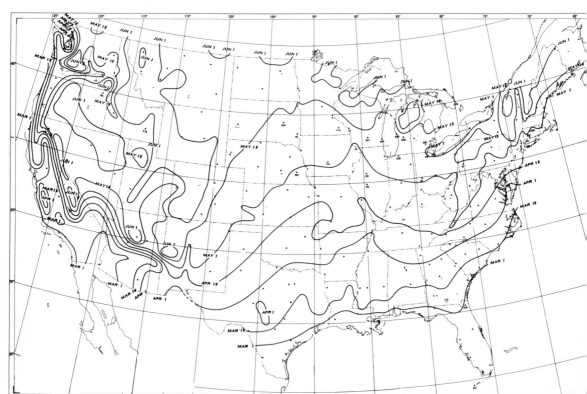

Fig. 1 Map of average last 32-degree temperatures or frost-free dates in spring, tells you when you may safely plant.   *Courtesy U. S. Department of Commerce, Weather Bureau*

Easterners moved to California are stunned to learn they don't have natural rain to grow broad lawns. Southerners moved north are disappointed with their crape-myrtles.

For local problems, you have neighbors, your agricultural extension agent (there's one in every county), and the nearby nurserymen who can help. Another, and important, place to get advice is the state extension service. All states have one. It is located at the major land grant university in each state. Part of its work is to publish bulletins to help farmers and gardeners. It has experts, too, who can answer questions. In recent years, since many people have left farms and moved to cities and suburbs, workers at extension offices and state experiment stations have been putting more and more emphasis on ornamental horticulture. Feel free to consult them, for they are definitely interested in problems of the home gardener—and there is no charge.

See Section C of Useful Miscellany for addresses in each state where you can write for bulletins and state extension help.

WHAT IS A MICROCLIMATE?

Before closing the subject of your garden's "place" in the world, think of it in one more way—the smallest sense.

You know that there is a protected sunny pocket on the south side of your house where crocuses come up and bloom in January. But on the north under the apple tree you have a clump of crocuses that hardly look through the ground until all the others in the yard have finished their bloom. One reason, perhaps, is that here is the last place where snow remains.

To use the technical name, these are examples of "microclimates" or little climates right there in your own yard, a warm one and a cool one. Look around your place and you will find other examples: the cool but protected spot at the northeast corner of

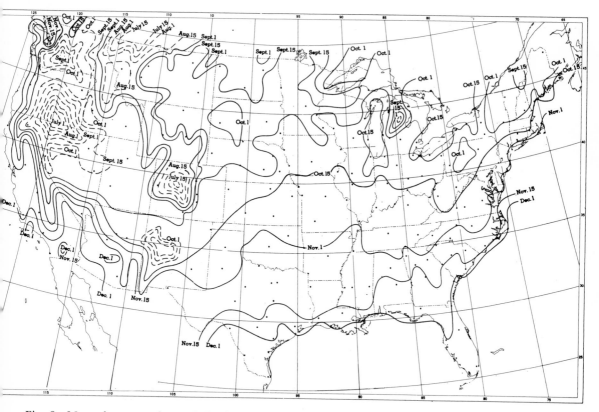

Fig. 2 Map of average dates of the first 32-degree temperatures or frosts in fall, tells you when the growing season ends. *Courtesy U. S. Department of Commerce, Weather Bureau*

5

your house, good for azaleas; the north hillside where peach blossoms do not freeze; the place for early onions and peas on a sun-warmed south slope.

The year around, keep your eyes open to what happens in your yard. Have you a big hovering tree that wards off early fall frosts as an umbrella does rain? If so, take advantage of it. Put dahlias and chrysanthemums in a sunny part of this circle of safety to get later bloom from them. Have you low places that are first to show white frost in fall, and last to show it in spring? These are the cold spots of your yard, so avoid them when you plant things you suspect are slightly tender. Have you a north or east basement window that seems always in summer to be a fountain of cool moist air? If so, outside it is an ideal spot for tuberous begonias, even in regions you may have supposed too hot for them.

These are matters so concerned with your own set of circumstances that they're beyond the scope of books, magazines, extentension bulletins or newspaper garden colums. Your own observations are the best guide.

HOW TO READ THE REGIONAL MAPS

Each of the following fourteen short articles contributed by gardening experts for their different sections of the country, is accompanied by a small sectional map to picture the area concerned. These maps help you place your area in a region—but use them with understanding.

It is important to realize that climatic boundaries are not sharply drawn. You couldn't stand astride one of them. You could go from one region into another on a day in winter or summer without telling the difference. The zones blend imperceptibly into one another. The climatic or geographic differences that give a region its own particular flavor are gradual things, hard to put your finger on, but nevertheless real; and all combined they make up a set of conditions that you know are different from those elsewhere. It is to make it possible to talk about them that they are encircled on the maps. They overlap; in many

ways they merge; and most of them have small portions that seem like misfits. So it is a good idea to read not only the piece written just for your own area, but also those for the areas nearest yours.

GARDENING IN THE NEW ENGLAND AREA

By Bernice Brilmayer

The only reliable generalization that can be drawn about gardening in New England is that for every rule there will be one or more immediate exceptions. Many shrubs are not hardy in Maine *"except* in the temperate coastal area"; herbaceous perennials do well in Connecticut *"except* in winters of little or no snow"; some fruit trees are not a good risk *"except* when planted in favorable sites."* But these capricious conditions make gardening a perpetually exciting interest and challenge.

Fig. 3

The growing seasons (number of days between last killing frost in spring and first killing frost in fall) vary from an average of 96 days in the extreme northern tip of New Hampshire to 223 days in the favored Block Island section of Rhode Island. The overall average is about 145 days—definitely calling for crops that mature in the shortest possible time. In Boston the average last spring frost date is April 13 and the first fall frost is October 29 (199 days).

The average annual minimum temperatures range from 30 degrees below to 10 above—rather a wide range. The new plant hardiness zone map indicates five different hardiness zones (Zones 3-7); only on the

6

Pacific Coast is there such wide variation. Rainfall also varies, but the annual average is 41 inches, and periods of prolonged drouth are infrequent.

In general, temperatures drop and severities increase the farther north one goes. But the coastal areas are unexpectedly temperate, particularly in southern Maine and in southern Connecticut along Long Island Sound. Even hot, dry summer weather is moderated by cool, moist air from the ocean and Sound.

In almost all of New England, apples, potatoes, and cool, short-season vegetables (lettuce, peas, root types, and those of the cabbage group) are good crops. Small fruits like strawberries and raspberries are best in more moderate areas and peaches are risky except in the warmest parts.

As far as New England weather is concerned, you cope with occasional high winds and hurricanes that break branches and beat down flower beds; freak winters like that of 1958-59, when snow did not protect the ground; and short growing seasons and cool summer temperatures that make it hard to grow heat-loving plants, sometimes even to mature biennials by the second year.

Except for part of northwestern Connecticut, New England soil is mostly acid. Apply lime for plants requiring it. Maintain fertility with applications of commercial fertilizer and added organic matter. Our soils are mostly friable, and drain well.

With proper care, you can grow most tree fruits (but dwarf trees with questionably hardy rootstocks are best in milder areas); most small fruits (but limit grapes to southern sections and up to Massachusetts); and all short-season vegetables. Special varieties of warmth-lovers like melons, peppers, eggplant, and lima beans have been bred. Start these early indoors, if possible. Among flowering plants, herbaceous perennials are reliable. Most annuals will grow for you. Select varieties of trees and shrubs according to their winter hardiness. Evergreens are widely planted, particularly the acid-loving broadleaf laurels and rhododendrons.

Most of the "general" horticultural information in this book is applicable to, or can be adapted to New England, with one possible exception. Even in midsummer, the sun is not terribly intense for many hours of the day. In my experience, most plants will take —and often need—more direct sunlight than in the greater part of the country.

GARDENING IN THE MIDDLE-ATLANTIC AREA

BY HERBERT C. BARDES

The Middle-Atlantic area can be described as a patchwork of varied geography and different soil, climate and weather conditions. You must learn to cope with—or, more usually, resign yourself to—the unpredictable changes and inconsistencies in conditions from season to season or from one year to the next within your own locality.

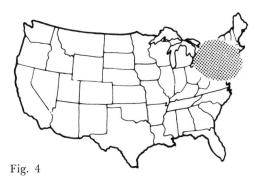

Fig. 4

In any given winter, for example, many parts of our area have spells of 10 to 20 degrees below zero, immediately followed or preceded by periods of barely freezing or well above freezing temperatures. Also, snow can be practically non-existent all winter or there can be a protective blanket of it on the ground continuously from late November to March.

In one year the summer in a particular section may have nary a day above 90 degrees, and the next summer the residents lose count of the number of days at or above 100 degrees. All of this, of course, bears heavily on the kind of plants you should select.

A significant percentage of the land area is under the moderating influence of the Atlantic Ocean; a portion is affected by the Great Lakes. Mountains and valleys influ-

7

ence the climate in many other sections of the area. Often a distance of a few miles can make a world of difference in the rate and vigor of growth, even the survival of a given species of plant.

Although weather statistics usually rate the Middle-Atlantic area as having a good annual rainfall (40-45 inches), there are many years when this moisture is delivered in a "feast or famine" pattern. Long drouths can occur, and cause trouble, in any season, but they are especially hard on plants in summer, when demands on the public water supply are highest. It has reached a point where restrictions on watering lawns and gardens are automatically announced every summer in many communities.

The length of the growing season, of particular importance to vegetable gardeners, has a wide range. In Pennsylvania alone, it spans almost 100 days; some sections of the state have an average growing season of 209 days, while in other sections it averages only 112 days. This is roughly equivalent to the range from South Carolina to Maine! In central New York the growing season ranges from 84 to 105 days. Thus the over-all Middle-Atlantic span can be as much as 125 days (84 to 209). This wide difference is, of course, caused by the great range of dates for the last spring frost and the first fall frost. In northern New Jersey, northern Pennsylvania and up into New York state, the last hard frost in spring generally occurs between May 1 and May 30. In southern New Jersey, southeastern Pennsylvania and down into Delaware and Maryland, the last frost may come along from April 1 to 30. In autumn the first black frost may strike northern or mountain sections in early September; milder sections may be free of frost until November or even early December.

In areas where the growing season is short, start seeds ahead of time indoors (especially slow-growing annuals and vegetables). In sections known for wide fluctuations of winter temperatures and snowfall, learn to mulch evergreens, roses and perennials, to protect them from soil heaving (also the anti-transpirant sprays play a role in the winter protection of broadleaf evergreens). In sections of unreliable rainfall,

plant drouth-tolerant grasses, shrubs and so on, and mulch beds and borders to conserve soil moisture.

GARDENING IN THE SOUTHEAST AREA

BY FRED J. NISBET

This is an area of gardening extremes. Subtropical plants along the Atlantic coast give way to warm, temperate plants in the Piedmont and lower mountains. These yield to almost alpine flora in the higher mountains. In parts of the upper Piedmont and lower mountains you can grow many fine plants from both South and North, an enviable situation.

Fig. 5

Soils are also variable, with sands and fine-to-coarse sandy loams common along the coast and in the "Sandhills." These, with silt loams and silts, are also found along streams. From the lower edge of the Piedmont into the mountains, clays and clay loams are usual. Acid soils predominate, but scattered alkaline areas are found.

The growing season length varies dramatically. Along the coast it ranges from 310-315 days (Alabama) to a low of about 225 days in parts of Virginia. In the Piedmont the spread varies from about 225 days to 185. The mountains have from 190 days to fewer than 170 days at high resort areas (a bit shorter than in Albany, N. Y. by way of comparison).

The average last frost date for Raleigh, N. C., and Atlanta, Georgia and the first frost date are the same, March 23—November 9. Richmond, Va., lists the average last

8

frost date as March 29; the first autumn frost November 2. Winston-Salem and Asheville have the first fall frost around October 20 and the last spring frost April 10. Savannah, Georgia has the last spring frost February 28 and the first frost of autumn on November 28.

Rainfall ranges from generally adequate (37 inches in Asheville, N. C.) to very heavy in a few small localities. More than 100 inches have been reported in parts of the Alabama coast and *above* the town of Highlands, N. C. Generally the amount is between 45 and 60 inches with distribution varying from reasonably even (notably in the "thermal belt" centering at Tryon, N. C.) to definitely wet summers and winters and dry periods in spring and fall.

Along coasts and in the Sandhills, favorite plants include azaleas (Indicas, Kurumes and some Pericats), camellias, gardenias, many of the tender evergreen viburnums, feijoa, aucuba, the hardiest palms, magnolias and yaupon (*Ilex vomitoria*). No tulips (without artificial cold treatment) and only a few daffodils do well.

In the Piedmont, azaleas are important. Kurumes, Kaempferis and Glenn Dales are generally best. Camellias, except for more tender varieties, are becoming popular. This is about the northern limit of feijoa, aucuba and *Daphne odora*. Daffodils and roses are widely grown, with this the northern limit for tea roses. Rhododendrons which stand heat (Catawba hybrids and a few English hybrids) are increasingly popular.

In the mountains nearly all azaleas except Indicas and similar tender kinds grow to perfection as well as rhododendrons, daffodils, tulips, and lilies. This is about the southern limit for firs, birches and lilacs. Roses are fine here, but only the hardiest of camellias ('C. M. Hovey,' 'Gov. Mouton') are possible.

Special cultural problems: Watering is critical in periods of extreme heat. Mulch to conserve water and reduce soil temperatures. Shade many plants (azaleas, camellias especially) in the Piedmont down to lower elevations. In regions of heavy soils use more compost to supply humus, which breaks down quickly in summer heat. Here

also drainage is often poor, so use more raised beds.

GARDENING IN FLORIDA

BY EVELYN KNAPP

Florida's peculiar geography offers a wide climatic variation which results in great diversity of plants. Except for red clays in the northwest, limestone soils in the southeastern tip and organic peats around Lake Okeechobee, the soils are light and sandy. These are of poor fertility and dry out quickly. Add organic matter and fertilizer to them regularly and they become highly productive. They are well drained except in low spots. Most are acid and require liming for many plants.

Fig. 6

Our rain is heavy, averaging 50 to 60 inches a year, much of it falling in summer. Whenever rain is deficient, give weekly watering of one inch or more. Heavy mulching is good too, to retain moisture and add humus to the soil.

During the cool months of the year you can grow a wide variety of annual flowers and vegetables. But from May through August, high temperatures and heavy rains restrict you to a few sturdy bloomers like zinnias and marigolds and tough vegetables, such as collards, okra and black-eyed peas.

Minimum winter temperatures control the distribution of plant life. The state has three distinct plant zones. *The southern zone* covers a narrow coastal belt from Vero Beach to Bradenton. This area is semitropical, having serious cold snaps only rarely. Here you can have a wealth of tropical ex-

9

otics and many fine native plants which grow nowhere else in the continental United States. Scores of palms, numerous flowering trees and shrubs and lush tropical foliage plants thrive here with little protection. So do tropical and subtropical fruits like avocado, limes, lemons, mango, papaya and others.

The central zone is bordered on the north by a line from Cedar Key to Daytona Beach. It includes the citrus belt. From December 15 through February 15, there may be several light to heavy frosts that rule out the tender tropicals of south Florida. However, many subtropicals not suited to the warmer area thrive here. Queen palms, almost as handsome as the coconuts and royals of the tropics, are hardy throughout this zone. Many flowering trees like jacaranda, tibouchina, koelreuteria and orchid trees are well adapted. So are hibiscus, calliandra, poinsettia and numerous handsome flowering shrubs. Camellias and azaleas are also at home and citrus of all types. Dogwoods, live oaks, magnolias and hollies are native to the area.

The northern zone includes the panhandle of Florida and all of the northern counties. Citrus is limited here to occasional plantings in protected spots. Killing frosts with temperatures down into the teens are expected anytime from November 20 through March 20. Magnolias, live oaks, maple, dogwood and redbud are common native trees. Camellias and azaleas are ideally adapted to both soil and climate and are the most important garden plants. Pecans, Japanese persimmon, clingstone peaches and pears help compensate for the scarcity of citrus and other subtropical fruits. Temperate bulbous plants like iris, tulips, narcissus and daffodils will grow through much of the area.

GARDENING IN THE EAST CENTRAL AREA

BY VICTOR H. RIES

The length of our growing season varies from 210 days between frosts (Evansville, Indiana, October 30 to April 2) in the southern part; to as few as 100 days (near Ona-

way, Michigan, September 14 to June 5) in the north and not much more in the higher mountains of West Virginia. Where it is shorter than 150 days, long season crops like sweet potatoes may be difficult to mature.

Fig. 7

Urban areas are usually less windy, and sometimes warmer than nearby rural areas. Altitude tends to give the same climate as areas farther north. Nearness to large bodies of water, especially the Great Lakes, tends to lengthen the growing season and lessen sudden damaging changes in temperature. The south and east sides of Lake Michigan, south side of Lake Ontario and all around Lake Erie benefit especially. The Ohio River valley is milder than nearby areas just to the north.

The average January temperature can be used as an indicator of plant hardiness. If the January average is below 25 degrees, avoid using woody plants of questionable hardiness. The average for this area varies from 12 degrees in parts of Michigan to 36 and 38 in sections of Kentucky and southern Illinois.

In much the same way, summer temperatures control the use of certain other plants. They average from 62 degrees in parts of Michigan to 78 in southern areas. If the July average is above 70 degrees, annual flowers requiring cool nights, like godetia and salpiglossis, will be difficult to grow. Delphiniums, phlox and some other hardy flowers may also fail to do well.

Rainfall must be considered, both annual and summer totals. The annual average varies from 28 inches in parts of Michigan to 48 and 50 in parts of Kentucky and western Pennsylvania. Summer rain varies from 16 inches to 28. Where summer rain is below 20 inches, watering is necessary. And if yearly rainfall is below 36 inches all evergreens, especially broadleafs, require heavy late fall watering. Remember that one side of your house may be drier than the others. Large trees and even shrubs may keep small areas dry.

Much of our section has rather open winters with the ground bare of snow much of the time. This calls for extra care in mulching and winter protection.

Considerable areas have heavy soils. You may need to drain them by installing agricultural drain tile. These same soils respond to liberal applications of organic matter to loosen and aerate them. Some are alkaline, so don't lime them. Others may be acid. All the soils respond to complete fertilizers, but few need the so-called "trace elements."

In general, most annual flowers, hardy perennials, hardy bulbs, woody trees and shrubs will thrive. Roses are satisfactory except in extreme northern parts where they need extra winter protection. Broadleaf evergreens grow in much of our section except where the January average is below 25 degrees.

Most of us can feast on our own sweet corn, tomatoes and sweet potatoes. Spring planting is best for white birch, flowering dogwood, redbud, cherries, magnolias and peaches. Most others can be planted in fall or spring. Camellias, mimosa and empress tree are doubtful except in warmer parts of the area. Hardy strains of box will grow in most sections. Evergreen vines, like English ivy, are safest on east and north exposures, protected from winter sun. The north of buildings is often safest for slightly tender plants.

Lawns should be mainly Kentucky bluegrass and its varieties. Except in the extreme southern part, zoysia is brown for a longer period than most of us wish.

GARDENING IN THE NORTHERN AREA

by Robert A. Phillips

This region has many contrasts in climate, topography, soils, vegetation and seasons.

Our winters are generally long and cold, the summers short and warm. Spring and autumn are short with fluctuating temperatures and weather. The seasons are not consistent from year to year. Some winters are mild, others bitter cold. Some have lots of snow, some very little. Summers vary from cool and damp to torrid and dry.

Fig. 8

Gardening may start as early as mid-March in the south and as late as May 1 in the far north. It may end as early as September or extend into November in some places.

Rainfall ranges from an annual average of 15 inches in the northwest to 35 inches in the south. Because of the variations and uncertainties of the seasons, you need to regulate your activities by the weather rather than the calendar. Soil varies as much as the climate. There are sand, peat and clay, and some sections of fertile loam. In the north, you may find it necessary to improve the soil, adding organic matter and fertilizers and providing for good drainage.

Generally, tender annuals like zinnias and marigolds can be seeded or set out at the beginning of May in some sections but not until the end of the month in others. Plant hardy perennials and woody plants as soon as frost is out of the ground and you can work the soil. This usually is in April, later in the far north. Spring is our main planting season. September and October are the months for fall planting.

Because of the danger of winter injury, fall planting is seldom done here but if you do it properly, you *can* plant or transplant many woody trees and shrubs in early fall. Do not attempt to fall-plant roses or fruits. Plant tulips, narcissus and other hardy

11

spring flowering bulbs in September or October to assure sufficient rooting before winter arrives. Spring flowering perennials are best planted in midseason or early fall.

Practically all the popular annuals are successful here. Our summer weather is ideal for them. Because petunias, salvias, verbenas, asters, snapdragons and others take a long time to flower, you are wise to buy them as transplants or start seed early indoors. Fall seeding of annuals won't work because of winter conditions and the need to cultivate the soil in spring.

Our region is perhaps the most favorable for perennials. Many kinds grow here successfully. This is not an ideal climate, however, for most popular biennials. Tuberous begonias do well and exceptionally fine roses can be grown if given enough winter protection.

Subzero temperatures make winter protection especially necessary. The unreliability of snow makes winter mulching mandatory on flower beds, hardy bulbs and roses from November to April. Use leaves or hay. Roses require especially heavy protection.

Because rain is insufficient in some sections and usually is not adequately distributed, you need to water. One good, deep soaking a week is right for all types of garden plants. Indeed, it is a rare year when we don't need to water.

Consult your local agricultural agent, colleges and experiment stations for exact information about recommended varieties.

GARDENING IN THE HEARTLAND AREA

BY ROSE ROSS

Climate here is understandably "continental." Drastic sudden changes go from warm to cold and vice versa. In summer the land is buffeted by hot, dry winds and parched by occasional drouths. Following some idyllic spring days may come pelting rain and hail. Sometimes the winter brings lasting snow, but more often the ground lies bare most of the season. Because of this erratic climate, gardening here is challenging and interesting—it is a transition area and

we use plants from both north and south, if we are willing to run a few risks.

Fig. 9

In winter, cold may go as low as 20 below zero in the northwest, or barely hit zero in the south. Average date for the last killing frost varies from about March 26 in southeast Missouri, to April 26 in the north. In fall we expect first killing freezes in the north and the high Ozarks about October 15, and in the rest of the region up to about the first week of November in the southeast lowlands. Thus the growing season runs from about 178 days in the northwest to 218 days in the southeast. Mulch valuable plants like azaleas that may be slightly tender in winter, and provide them with windbreaks.

Summer temperatures go as high as 110 degrees. In July, the daily average is over 90 nearly everywhere in our region. This heat makes the corn grow, but it is hard on bluegrass lawns, tuberous begonias, and delphiniums. Some annuals that prefer coolness, like godetia and nemesia, are almost impossible to grow here. But we grow fine zinnias, marigolds, petunias, dahlias, gladiolus, iris, spring bulbs, lilies—and luxuriant crops of tomatoes, sweet corn, melons, green and lima beans, and almost any other vegetable you might want.

Average rainfall ranges from more than 50 inches a year in the southeast to 32 inches in the northwest. We seldom need to water, except roses and lawns during the hottest weather. Summer mulching helps conserve moisture for shrubs, flowers and vegetables and it also lessens the effects of heat. Sometimes in spring we get periods of warm dry winds—then it is well to water emerging bulbs and perennials. Water evergreens well in November.

Our area lies in Zones 5 and 6. Some typical woody plants of the northern part (Zone 5) are flowering dogwood, slender deutzia, early forsythia, Amur privet, Boston ivy, Arnold crab, Mollis azalea and the rhododendron 'America.' In Zone 6, typical plants are Japanese maple, silk tree, common box, weeping forsythia, English ivy, American holly, and California privet. Many kinds adapted to Zone 6 are possible in the northern part too, in protected locations. Our best shade trees include ginkgo, tulip tree, Norway maple, hard maple, honey locust, sweet gum, Northern red oak, linden, white oak, pin oak, sycamore and London plane-tree.

A few of the many fruits are apples, pears, plums, peaches, sour cherries, blackberries, raspberries, grapes and strawberries. Bluegrass is best for lawns, although we can grow zoysia and bermuda. The green-up date for zoysia in the Kansas City area is about May 1. Crabgrass is a serious lawn weed—but pre-emergent controls are effective here. Cut bluegrass high—at least 2½ inches.

Wide variety of soils is found between the rolling deep prairies of the north and the stony thin, Ozark soils. We find local areas of acidity or alkalinity, but most soils are nearly neutral. Some of the deep clays need attention to drainage. County agricultural agents offer test services to help you assess soil needs.

GARDENING IN THE SOUTHERN AREA

BY MINNIE HALL BROWN

In the South, from Zone 8 down, we consider our section a gardener's paradise, because we can have color the year around. In winter we have broadleaf evergreens, such as pyracantha, cotoneaster, holly, dogwood, euonymus, several haws, thorny olive (*Elaeagnus pungens*) and others. Winter-flowering shrubs include *Camellia sasanqua* and *Camellia japonica,* which begin blooming in early fall and continue through March, and flowering quince, winter honeysuckle and oriental magnolias. Azaleas, camellias, tube-

roses, cape jasmines, crape-myrtle, tea roses and sweet olives grow to perfection here.

Fig. 10

For bedding plants we use stock, calendula, pansy, violas, petunias and others. We have many winter-blooming bulbs, including narcissus, hyacinths, snowflakes and species tulips. All of these may be planted in fall and winter. If you use seeds instead of plants, start them early enough to harden off before frost.

Our summer annuals include zinnias, portulaca, salvias, snow-on-the-mountain, dianthus, marigolds, sultanas, periwinkle, balsam, stokesia, columbine and dahlias. In fall we enjoy chrysanthemums, fall marigolds and gloriosa daisies.

Summers are rather warm—our average high runs between 80 and 85 degrees. There are short periods most years when the mercury climbs to the middle and high 90's. Periods of high humidity hit us now and then. The first frost usually comes in November and the last one in March with a growing season of about 240 to 280 days. In Shreveport we have about 48 inches of rain a year. Winds are moderate except in March and sometimes in September.

Our average winter temperature is 40 degrees but we usually have one or two periods when the low goes down briefly to 17 or 20. These periods are short. We have many balmy winter days when the temperature may reach 85 degrees. The most rain falls in January and May. The two driest months are July and September.

New Orleans and the Gulf Coast are almost tropical. Allamandas, poinsettias, bauhinia, hibiscus *rosa-sinensis* and begonias usually survive the winter.

13

If you live in the cool mountainous regions to the north in Arkansas, you can grow peonies and tiger lilies beautifully—also hybrid tulips and peegee hydrangeas which we cannot grow well in the lower south. The humidity there is lower, too. Farther south, tulips are used only as annuals, and refrigerated before planting. Other "impossibles" are coralbells, clarkia, lilac (except *Syringa vulgaris*), rhododendron and laurel.

Our soils are varied. We have a good bit of red clay which is fine for roses and lawns. We also have rich alluvial soils, loams, rocky soils and wonderful leaf mold. The river bottoms are alkaline but other soils are somewhat acid. If you plant camellias or azaleas in river sand, add acidifying materials.

Use lots of mulch in summer to keep down weed growth, cool roots, conserve moisture and add humus to the soil.

GARDENING IN THE MID-AMERICA SOUTHWEST

BY ROBERT H. RUCKER

This section is in three different hardiness zones, 6, 7, and 8, with even a part in Zone 5, so our plant material is extensive. Here is where eastern, western, northern and southern plants meet. We have representatives of all four. This wide variety plus the ever-changing growing seasons challenge our gardeners. By the same token, the many plants possible to grow, the long, warm season and the intermittent days of pleasant weather present us with many opportunities.

Our area has a growing season averaging 200 days in the northern and western parts, increasing by an added 25 or 30 days in the south and east. We expect the last spring frost from March 25 to April 15 and the first killing frost of fall from about October 25 to November 10.

The temperature range is almost unbelievably wide—from 10 degrees moving sometimes to an unseasonable high of 80 degrees in the dead of winter. From December to March we sometimes get drops of 40 to 50 degrees in 12 hours. These rapid changes are usually accompanied by strong winds, snow or freezing rain. This extreme variation is hazardous for plants. In summer the average temperature is in the 80's, occasionally reaching more than 100 degrees.

Fig. 11

Rain varies from 16 inches a year in the west to about 40 inches in the east, the average for the area being in the mid-20's. Unfortunately winter drouths are common, and together with the low temperatures, cause much damage to ornamentals. Water is a critical factor over the whole area. You will need some type of irrigation installed to guarantee success in gardening efforts. Yard enclosures like fences and walls are important to modify the effects of wind and sudden climatic change. This protection makes it possible to grow a wider variety of plants.

Most of our soils are in the sandy loam group with clay subsoils. The alkalinity increases from east to west, but never to the point of being completely toxic to plant life. All our soils usually lack humus or organic matter. You can improve them greatly by adding organic fertilizers like cottonseed meal, which is one of the best all-purpose fertilizers for garden use, and is plentiful here. Because of variable climate, you need to experiment on your own initiative to find out what will grow for you.

We grow roses well over the entire area. Good trees are northern red oak, honey locust, bald cypress, sycamore, green ash, Austrian pine, ponderosa pine, hackberry, Scotch pine, sweet gum, and silver maple, all varieties of junipers, mugho pine, arborvitae, and Arizona cypress. Prominent broadleafs are Burford holly, Chinese holly, yaupon, nandina, purple honeysuckle, euonymus, privet, pyracantha, abelia and mahonia. Flowering shrub possibilities include redbud, forsythia, lilac, spirea, magnolia, flowering quince, buddleia, vitex, crape-myrtle and weigela. Vines and ground covers are English ivy, trailing periwinkle, ajuga, honeysuckle, liriope, wisteria, bittersweet, Hall's honeysuckle, clematis. Annuals are practically unlimited, and you can choose from nearly the whole range of herbaceous perennials. Spring-flowering bulbs like tulips, daffodils, hyacinths, crocuses, all grow well here, and also the summer-blooming bulbs like cannas, caladiums, begonias, gladiolus and tuberoses.

GARDENING IN THE NORTHERN GREAT PLAINS

BY GLENN VIEHMEYER

Great Plains gardening is different. You need to recognize that fact and live with it. The fine gardens here attest to the good job that many people have done in understanding this climate and meeting its challenges. We are in an area of transition and violent weather changes. To be successful here, you need to be flexible and take general garden advice cautiously.

Fig. 12

From north to south, our growing season varies from 100 to almost 200 days as it extends through Zones 3, 4, and 5. Average last frosts range from April 15 at Dodge City, Kansas, to May 30 at Hannah, North Dakota and first frosts from October 25 to September 9. Altitudes go from less than 1,000 feet to more than 5,000 feet as the plains rise toward the Rockies. Annual rainfall varies

from as little as 10 inches in parts of the west to nearly 40 inches in the east. Temperatures may range from minus 50 degrees to over 110 degrees. To give average temperature and rainfall figures is meaningless in a region as variable as this.

Add to the climatic picture a pattern of soils and topography just as variable, and the problems of the gardener in the Plains indeed seem complex. Soils range from sterile sands of the Nebraska Sandhills, through fine textured soils of the loess regions, on to heavy clays. Soil pH values range from 4.5, very acid; to 10.0, very alkaline. In the high pH areas iron chlorosis limits the plants you can grow.

You must be an innovator who can find ways to stop wind and provide water. You'll learn by doing and through the experience of others. Work closely with your state experiment station to learn the needs of soil and plants. For the backbone of your plantings, select plants originating in this area or those from parts of the world having a similar climate, like Siberia, Manchuria and Korea. There is no place here for "softies."

The great rose family offers flowering crabs, apples, pears, apricots, plums, cherries, haws, cotoneasters and others. Many of these provide both fruit and beauty. Elms, locusts, hackberries and lindens are the best tall shade trees. From the Rockies come the pines, firs, spruces and junipers, a wealth of evergreens. We have an abundant list of shrubs, both native and from other places. Bluegrass is our best lawn grass, if you have means of watering it. The number of ultra-hardy new mums, iris, hemerocallis and other perennials and annuals is constantly growing. New and hardier roses are just around the corner, so it seems that tomorrow's gardener here is in for an exciting time.

GARDENING IN THE HIGH PLAINS

BY GENE S. HOWARD

The High Plains is here considered as the region just east of the Rockies from Montana south through Wyoming, Colorado, into northern New Mexico and northeastern Arizona. The eastern edge is near the 5000 foot level in Montana and Wyoming and progressively higher to the south. That eastern boundary is more definitely determined by the average length of the growing season —fewer than 150 days frostfree, and a rainfall of less than 20 inches. Some of the intermountain valleys to the west can also be included, as many have the same difficult conditions.

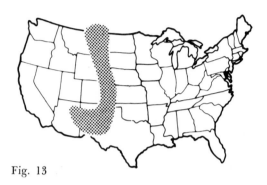

Fig. 13

Some areas near the mountains are protected by high ranges, hence have a longer season than 150 days, and are not included. The first frost in Cheyenne is generally October 2 and the last frost May 14. Great Falls, Montana, expects the first killing freeze-up September 25 and the last around May 9. September 29 is the first frost date for Flagstaff, Arizona, and the last frost date there is June 3. In Albuquerque the first frost occurs October 28 and the last around April 13.

Rainfall ranges from 6 to 20 inches a year with most places getting less than 15. The low-rain areas are classed as desert. Temperatures range from 10 to 50 degrees below zero in winter and 90 to 110 in summer. Average January temperatures range from 16 to 30 degrees above zero and average July temperatures range from 63 to 76.

Gardening is different but not unusually difficult here if you follow certain rules. Some plants, such as lilacs and tatarian honeysuckle are adaptable but many common ornamentals like pin oaks and weigela will not thrive or even survive. Gardeners in the southern part where minimum temperatures are higher, can grow some that northerners cannot, such as van houtte spiraea and Mentor barberry. Climate has more effect on plant growth and survival than soils.

Soil in the High Plains is generally fertile, well drained and slightly or moderately alkaline. You can usually improve it by adding nitrogen, phosphorus and soluble iron salts that prevent yellowing of plant leaves, a condition called chlorosis. Add organic matter at regular intervals, at least yearly, spring or fall.

Adaptable plants include some of the conifers, some of the deciduous trees and shrubs, some herbaceous perennials and many annual flowers. Due to the high altitude and strong sunshine most annuals have a brilliance here not characteristic of low altitudes. Broadleaf evergreens, as a group, are generally unadaptable. Your best guide is to look at the thrifty plants in your own location and grow those kinds, for undoubtedly they have survived from years of trial. Some new or little known plants (unavailable commercially) are adapted to the High Plains. These are growing at various experiment and research institutions of the region. If you learn of such plants, promote and request them from your nurserymen to make them commercially available. Hardy varieties of sour cherries, apples, plums and pears are reliable here. In small fruits, Manchu cherries, strawberries, currants and gooseberries are well adapted.

Our humidity is very low. This combined with the low atmospheric pressure of high altitudes causes much moisture evaporation, often three or more times the annual rainfall. Adaptable woody plants have special natural characteristics in bark and twigs, preventing loss of excess moisture during winter. Unadaptable plants often lack these defenses and are killed by drying out, not because they cannot stand the cold.

Ornamental plantings need much watering. Give water as needed, summer or winter, soaked to a depth of several inches.

Mulching may benefit some ornamentals and small fruits, to keep down weeds and conserve moisture.

GARDENING IN THE
WESTERN MOUNTAINS

by George W. Kelly

This section differs from other garden areas largely because of its limited rain or snow. True, there is enough moisture *in* the mountains, but this is not really the area we are interested in, for 80 per cent of the population here actually lives at the *foot* of the mountains. Rainfall and snow are limited, roughly, to about 15 inches a year. Because of this we have problems of too little subsoil moisture, of low air humidity and of the resulting alkaline soil. Then, because of closeness to mountains, weather is often erratic and unpredictable, especially in spring and fall.

Fig. 14

While soils vary widely, from heavy "dobie" to light and sandy, they have generally one quality in common—they lack the humus usually found in soils where rainfall is greater. This makes the addition of humus important in all our gardening.

Since lack of "normal" moisture is the outstanding characteristic, the *proper* application of additional water is another important essential. Remember that a plant needs the soil around its roots to be moist at all times, but does not want soggy soil that restricts the entrance of sufficient air. So it is necessary to water sometimes during the winter, but too-frequent surface watering appears to be as detrimental as too little watering.

The damage often occurring here to many plants that are common and indispensable in other areas is usually classed as "winter-kill." Actually, this damage is more often caused by excessively dry hot periods while plants are dormant than by severe cold. The remedy is usually protection from the hot southwest sun and from drying northwest winds. A place to the east of a building often gives the necessary protection for otherwise "impossible" plants.

The erratic weather caused by the nearness of mountains often results in plants not being hardened-off enough in fall. Sometimes it induces them to start growth during those "May-like days" in February and then they suffer during the May snows.

Our soils generally lack nitrogen and phosphorus but have plenty of potash. The alkalinity of the soils may prevent sufficient availability of iron, so chlorosis from lack of iron is common.

Many old favorites do well here. Typical are American elms, soft maples, spireas, barberries, honeysuckles, lilacs and roses. Rhododendrons, magnolias, Japanese cherries and crape-myrtle are typical of the "impossibles." Borderline plants that survive only when you give proper protection, drainage and soil, include weigelas, deutzias, Japanese maples, tulip trees and yews.

Length of the growing season depends on altitude and the amount of protection naturally offered by features like narrow canyons or hills to break the wind. For instance, Denver's first frost comes around October 14; Santa Fe's on October 19; Salt Lake City's on October 22 while their last frost dates are April 26, April 24 and April 13, respectively. Low temperature, of itself, affects only those plants from the south that are not cold resistant.

Differences in climate definitely influence the planning, planting and maintenance of gardens. Good planning takes advantage of the delightful climate, but modifies the effects of excessive wind, heat, and dust. Select plants that tolerate the "peculiar" conditions. Good maintenance makes plants feel at home and involves proper soil preparation, watering, fertilizing, pruning, mulching, good drainage and winter protection or shading.

GARDENING IN THE PACIFIC NORTHWEST

BY MARK M. TAYLOR

The mountainous, tree-covered areas of the Pacific Northwest have a stable, abundant water supply. Southwestern Oregon and northwestern California, for example, have an average annual rainfall of 18 inches; northwestern Oregon and southwestern Washington, 35 inches and northwestern Washington, 45 inches. The Cascade mountain range that bisects the three coastal states bars the spreading of this moisture to areas farther east. So trees and other plants on the western slopes of the mountains reflect the abundance of rain.

Fig. 15

The whole Pacific Northwest weather is greatly modified by the Japanese ocean current, bringing a mildness of temperature equaled, perhaps, nowhere else at this latitude. The average date of the last killing frost in the spring is April 20, the earliest in the fall, October 20, giving an average growing season of 180-200 days. As you near the actual seacoast, protected by a smaller mountain range, the weather is milder still.

The Pacific Northwest is blessed with cool nights and warm days in the summer that, with adequate moisture, cause lush growth and satisfactory conditions for ornamentals and fruit trees ranging from true tropicals and subtropical types in the southwestern section to the great apple, pear, prune, cherry and nut-growing areas of the central northwest.

Because of the abundance of natural moisture over the centuries, with the attendant lush vegetation, there has developed a soil with high humus content, largely with an acid reaction. This is most receptive to broadleaf evergreens, many of which are native here.

With this mild weather and stable moisture, it was only natural that camellias were introduced to the area already noted for its native growth of rhododendrons, azaleas and hollies.

The Northwest is a center for fruit growing and timber, and also for roses, broadleaf evergreens and lilies. Much of the nation's flax, bent and ryegrass seed come from here.

In the coastland sections, crops preferring summer coolness predominate. The naturally fertile soil consistent throughout the area promotes the growth of most temperate zone crops without special care.

GARDENING IN THE WARM SOUTHWEST

BY MARGARET TIPTON WHEATLY

Our climate ranges from subtropical ocean-scented air, to hot desert winds; in between are the winter fog-bound inland valleys with about 90 degree temperatures in summer. You can go through one zone and into another in less than an hour's drive.

Fig. 16

The frostfree season may last from practically all year long at San Diego and San Francisco to about 250 days at Salinas, California where fall frosts are expected about November 22 and the last frost of spring about March 17. In Phoenix, Arizona the average frosty season lasts from December 6 to February 15.

18

On uplands near the sea are stubborn adobe soils; closer to the shore, sandy alkaline soil with silt-loam in the inland valleys. To improve conditions for the growth of plants, use agricultural gypsum for soil softening and reduction of alkaline tendencies. Large amounts of humus are beneficial. Where manure is plentiful, use it, for it is the best source of humus.

All parts of this area have rainless summers for the most part. This means you need to give summer supplemental watering for most plants. The water you use may be alkaline if from deep wells. Even if it comes from reservoirs it may be alkaline in low rainfall years, unless the sources are fed by rivers and lakes of the high Sierra snow packs. You need to expect this alkalinity, and adjust to it in the plants you choose, or else add sulfur, gypsum or lime-sulfur to the soil to counteract it.

Where hot weather hits hard, it is as important to get plants ready for the heat of summer as for the cold of winter. We use a cold weather technique—that is, we grow plants through a period of hardening off. To accomplish this, feed plants early in the season with a *growth* strength (6-10-6) concentrated plant food, and follow it in summer and early autumn with a *dormant* strength (0 or 2-6-4) formula. This latter, lacking or being much lower in nitrogen, does not induce rapid vegetative growth, but the phosphoric acid and potash keep plants in good health and let them complete their seasonal production.

Climate differences limit plant types. Along the coast, even tender subtropicals may be grown without shelter. As the needs of plants approach tropical temperatures (as with orchids and papaya), some shelter is necessary.

On thermal (almost frostfree) "islands" found in various areas of the state as at San Diego, hardy subtropicals like citrus thrive and even tender ornamentals like Chinese hibiscus may flourish. In desert regions grapefruit and dates reach perfection. Temperatures may be *too high* for some exotic ornamental plants. Observe what your neighbors are growing; consult with your nearby nurseryman about possibilities.

Here is a practical approach to having a fine show of plants where rain is a rarity: Keep broadleaf evergreens requiring copious moisture to a minimum and then grow them only as intimate patio plants (perhaps in tubs); use living ground covers extensively to catch and conserve all possible soil moisture and to reduce the evaporation by the sun. Bring all your appropriate plants together in one area to make up a luxuriant garden in the place where you spend the most time. Plant the outer garden to such drouth-enduring kinds as tamarix and rhamnus (buckthorn) that require little attention.

Chapter 2

A PLAN FOR YOUR PLACE

Where do I start?

You start by deciding what kind of place you want. The idea is to think a lot before you dig even a little. Try to decide the kind of setting you'd like best for your house. If you can do this the result will be a planting to please your eye, meet the needs of your way of life, and save you money.

Think of low upkeep from the word go. Nothing will increase your joy as homeowner as much as being master of your property, instead of having it boss you. Every summer Saturday and Sunday should not see you, wild-eyed and hot, trying to care for an elaborate set-up you designed—or more likely didn't design—in the first cool, enthusiastic days of spring.

Let's have a look first at the kind of place your family needs. If you have children, a play area within clear view of a "working" house window will be an important part of your plan. If you are just a couple, you may want mainly an outdoor living room, pretty to look out on throughout the year, pleasant to entertain in during fine weather. If the place is yours alone, you may want a hobby or collector's garden. Perhaps you enjoy lots of outdoor work for the satisfaction it brings in a wealth of bloom or flower show prizes for your A-1 roses or peonies or chrysanthemums. In any case a cookout spot or a swimming pool may be among your requirements. Or perhaps what you want is an almost do-nothing place—very little lawn to mow, flowers that pretty much take care of themselves (there are such), no vines to tie, no hedges to clip, no borders to cultivate.

Actually, you can have a place that fulfills any or all of your desires provided you determine at the outset *what they are.*

Why not make a list? Let the family add or subtract from it. It might come out this way:

Fenced-in playground for swings and sandbox,

Flowers to cut for the house (perhaps in rows),

Doorway planting that won't outgrow the location,

Plants to attract birds,

Big tree to sit under,

Plenty of open lawn,

Plants we've seen and want—sweet gum tree, weeping willow, magnolia, wisteria, daffodils, bleeding hearts, chrysanthemums.

What we don't want (as important as what you do!)—no barbecue, no pools of any kind, no formal garden, no statues, no spraying.

Study this book. Start by checking over the headings that apply particularly to your way of thinking. You will find your answers here. Don't rush at everything at once. Easy does it. If you can get on paper a practical design for your place, you can work it out gradually year by year. Then whatever you plant will be put in the right place at the start. No hodgepodge. No big redo. Make that vision of yours become a reality.

HOW TO MAKE A MASTER PLAN

MEASURE THE SITUATION

To get the facts of your property—on which to base your plan—*measure every-*

thing, and try to be accurate. It pays in the end. A long tape measure on a reel is a big help, also someone to hold the other end and jot down the figures. If the real estate man supplied a map of your lot, you have some measurements to start with. Otherwise, get them all—property boundaries, outline of house, garage, terrace, driveway, possible shade spread of any large trees, size and extent of existing plantings of shrubs or flower beds.

If the ground slopes sharply, better get some measurements of declivities so that later on your flat plan you won't forget special treatment for those problem areas.

Get figures so you can fill in the floor plan of the house to the extent that important windows—picture and otherwise—doorways and porches, also the needs of privacy, affect plantings.

If your place is new, probably all you have now is earth, house, and sky. This gives you a free hand, and not much to measure. If you are going to improve an old place, perhaps one much overgrown, you will have the job of deciding what to save and what to get rid of fast. Just clearing out the tangles may reveal lots of worthwhile stuff, and very likely on an old place, you will have shade—perhaps too much of it. Anyway you will need to know the size of everything. A plan will give you perspective for new designing that a man's eye view, particularly if it's discouraging, can't supply.

SKETCH TO SCALE

Now with all your figures at hand, you are ready to make a workable paper plan of your place. A large piece of graph paper, printed, say in one-inch squares, is a big help. You might let each square represent a 5- or 10-foot area. Of course, you can make your own graph by ruling off a big piece of heavy paper into squares. (This plan needs to be sturdy; it's going to have lots of handling.)

Now transfer your figures into outlines on your plan. Work big, with squares large enough for you to write in clearly the names of possible trees and shrubs. For a 75- by 125-foot lot, an easy work plan might measure 15 by 25 inches.

TO HELP YOU PLAN

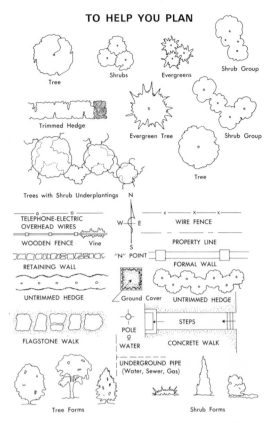

Fig. 17 Use symbols to show the various elements of your plan.

Use simple symbols like these in Figure 17 to indicate the various elements of your plan—trees, shrubs, hedges, fences, walls, walks, and all the other things. Then when you look at your plan it will instantly mean something to you.

THINK IN THREE AREAS

Usually in laying out property, it's best if you plan for three major divisions—a public or approach area, a work or utility area, and a private or living area. Study your property plan and try to decide on a convenient location for:

1. *The approach area,* on the street side extending to the front door.

2. *The work area* at the back or side entrance, reserved for the trash burner, garbage can, clothes dryer or line, vegetable garden if you want one, a storage shelter for tools, and perhaps a play area.

3. *The living area,* for the special enjoy-

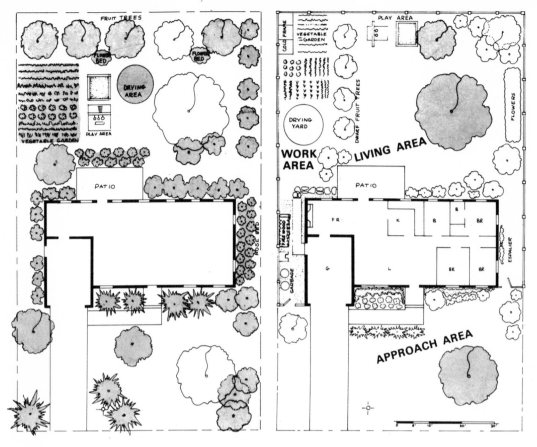

Figs. 18, 19   A plan of your place as you might draw it. Existing grounds are at left, the plan for the new landscape at right, with approach, work, and living areas decided.

ment of the family and your guests. All that can be spared from the other two areas can be allocated for outdoor living, for patio or terrace perhaps, lawn, and maybe a flower border or a little formal garden.

If you live in the country and have lots of space, you won't have to plan as carefully as people with city lots. Even so, these three divisions will still serve you well as a useful basis for organizing your yard. Everything will have a reason for being where it is.

Now let's consider each area and what you want it to do for *you*.

Your approach or public area. The size of this space between street and house depends on where the house sits on the lot. The area may be just large enough for a small open lawn to make a setting, and a pleasant doorway or "foundation" planting. Or it may be a vast sward. The goal here is

to blend your house with its surroundings and make it look hospitable.

Low evergreens and shrubs that stay small are mainly what you want near the house, although something tall next to the entrance is good if there is room. Too often plants set out at the foundation take over the house so that it seems to crouch behind them. Air and light are greatly reduced and the effect is generally unattractive.

If you buy a house where this has happened, tear out the foundation planting and throw most of it away. Transplanting big evergreens and shrubs is a hard job, usually not worth the effort, and the overpowering materials at the front door are probably far from choice. Those ratty-looking arborvitae and overgrown junipers don't belong anywhere on your place. Start over, and don't be afraid to start small. You can fill

22

1 The approach area, the part that meets the public, is hospitable and easy to care for. Low plants near the house are kinds that will stay small—dwarf boxwood, American holly, azaleas, and rhododendrons. The "island" under the oak trees is filled with azaleas, rhododendrons and pachysandra.   *Genereux*

in with some perennials—chrysanthemums, perhaps, or with annuals like cut-and-come-again zinnias while your fine new evergreens and shrubs get going. You may want some color at the front door anyway; many people do. Daffodils or hyacinths followed by petunias, or patience plants if it's shaded, make a nice picture. (Take a look at the sketches for front door plantings in this chapter, Figures 23, 24, 25.)

Your work area. What a joy this will be if it is well screened so that there is never a glimpse into it from the adjacent living area. Here's the place for a fence or thick hedge or a row of shrubs. In the work area are grouped neatly together the mechanics of your life. Coldframe, a compost bin or heap, and tool shed—the business end of the garden—can also go here near the garage or carport and turn-around. If there's

to be a vegetable or kitchen garden or an herb patch, it's nice to have it in this enclosure. Maybe you will also want the sand box and swings in the work area where it will be easy to watch the children from the kitchen and so they can tramp in and out the back door. Give some thought here as to what will work out best for you.

Your living area. More than any other part of the grounds, this should be related to the house, and easily reached through a door and seen through living and dining room windows. Here's the place for a terrace or patio. The barbecue and outdoor dining space belong here too, and the children's play yard, if this is not planned for the work area. The simplest setup for outdoor living consists of a shaded spot to sit in—maybe just a bench or a hammock under a big tree—and something serene to look

23

at. Open lawn with a border of shrubs is pleasant and easy. Don't let this area get "busy" and overplanted or so complex that you never live in it but only work there. However if you are one to whom gardening is a grand pursuit and you're keen on flowers, the living area is the place for flower beds or a formal layout of roses or a perennial border. If you want a game court, this is also the place for it.

SOME THINGS TO THINK ABOUT NEXT

With your three main areas blocked out, go over in your mind some general considerations before you begin to select your plants.

KEEPING DOWN THE UPKEEP

As you make plans and choose materials, have in the back of your mind a realistic idea of the time you want to devote to your place. Unclipped hedges or fences take less time than clipped hedges. Lawn and shrubs are less demanding than flower beds. Curved borders are easier to mow around than sharp corners. Open lawn mows faster than space that is cluttered or cut up. Edging strips of metal, wood, or brick around trees and flower or shrub beds get rid of hand clipping. Faucets placed close to where you need water save dragging the hose around. Plants that are litter-free, not dropping messy fruits or leaves, cut down cleanup time. A buttonwood tree or a mulberry near the house is a curse; a pin oak or a sweet gum a blessing. Unless you are willing to spray regularly, better not have rose beds or fruit trees. Espaliers and vines to train and tie, or anything that takes coddling—special winter protection, for instance—these all take time. So are pools which have to be drained and cleaned, and stepping stone paths, unless laid flush so you can go over them with your mower.

HOW TO SECURE PRIVACY

This can be obtained by a screen of trees, where height is needed, or by low hedges or fences. On small lots the most practical

2 English ivy frames this doorway and makes a low border against the house foundation. Box-wood accents the doorstep and house corner. *Caldwell*

3 The living area is for the enjoyment of you, your family, and guests. It reflects your own tastes and activities and is apart from the "working" sections of your yard. *Genereux*

screen is a fence of pickets, stakes or boards, painted gray or brown. Bright colors or white on a fence will make your yard seem smaller, and stained or natural wood fences are easier to maintain. If tall board fences are banned in your neighborhood, plant a hedge of shrubs or evergreens.

EXTENDING OUTDOOR PLEASURE WITH LIGHTS

In your planning, consider outdoor lights. Placed right, they make everything more beautiful at night, and steps and walks are safer if they're lighted. You are sure to want light on a terrace where you spend relaxed evening hours. If you like to work outdoors after nightfall, you'll need light in the garden to see what you're doing. If you do put in outdoor lights, install electrical outlets at the same time so you can connect work-saving tools like an electric lawn mower, edger, or hedge clipper.

"PLANTING" ON PAPER

Now tentatively select the plants. Use a pencil so you can erase. This is the hard part, easier if you have some idea of what you like, what will grow where you live, and what plants will look like in a few years. To get help, look at chapters 5 through 12 of this book. Visit the best yards around you and find out what your neighbors have grown successfully. Go to the parks, too. Make lists of possibilities.

First choose plants for the framework—the screens and backgrounds, the shade

trees, the corners of the house and the door-way. Then go on to other plants to get the effects you want. Remember to leave room for plants to grow. Resist the urge to over-plant. If things look sparse to you at first, when plants are small, fill the voids with annuals, perennials, or bulbs.

THREE BIG PROBLEMS AND HOW TO SOLVE THEM

THE SPLIT LEVEL HOUSE WITH EXPOSED FOUNDATION

Usually it consists of two parts side by side, one lower than the other, with bare foundations on the downhill sides and the upper one-story section like an afterthought.

Ways to solve: Group important shrubs or trees on the uphill side in front of and well out from the house, to give that end better balance with the larger lower portion. Set another important tree, with perhaps a few

4   The shaded outdoor dining area abounds in color from tubbed geraniums, potted marigolds, and caladiums and hostas in ground beds.
Gottscho-Schleisner

big shrubs out from it, a distance beyond the downhill wall and slightly in front of the house, to relieve the sharp line here. On hillside lots, draw contour lines on your plan to reflect the steepness and location of slopes. These will help to show you where to place terraces, shrubs for privacy and trees for a view.

THE TWO-STORY HOUSE WITH AN ADDED GARAGE

The one-story garage at one end often looks like a midget by comparison with the house, which itself may seem too high for its width or length. A tall chimney on the end opposite the garage does not help matters.

Ways to solve: Here plant sizable shrubs at the chimney end, and out from them put a fairly large tree. This will anchor the house. Place tall trees at the garage end to help restore balance taken away by the diminutive garage. Trees with rounded shapes are better than pyramidal ones in these situations.

THE DEVELOPMENT HOUSE LIKE ALL THE OTHERS

This is typically a low rectangular shape that needs interesting landscaping to keep it from looking like every other house in the neighborhood.

Ways to solve: Try a clump of small trees —flowering kinds, perhaps—near the street on the house side of the driveway. This gives an upward lift to the flat line of the house. A smaller ornamental tree in the opposite part of the front yard provides the other side of the "frame" to anyone viewing the house from the street. Low evergreens between house and street along the drive will make the yard seem more spacious. Consider adding a planter at one end of the house to break its regularity and give you a chance to use colorful flowers.

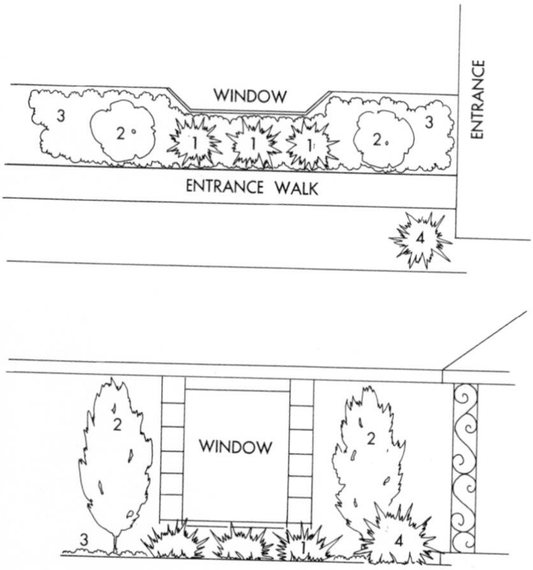

THREE LITTLE PROBLEMS AND HOW TO SOLVE THEM

HOW SHALL I PLANT OUR PICTURE WINDOW?

Is it really a picture window or does it look out on something that shouldn't be pictured? That is the first question. Far from the original purpose of framing a living picture, these windows often need special treatment.

Our picture window pictures nothing. In Figure 20 the answer is to put plants below the window. This gives something to look at from inside. The low shrubs will not need much trimming. The larger plants at each side of the window frame it and break the long flat line usually found in this type of house. Ground covers under the plants make upkeep easy, and the bulbs give spring color.

Can I point up our view? In Figure 21 the plan improves the view—a covered patio and open court—which was probably the excuse for the picture window. The planting makes the vista seem longer and borders it

Fig. 20 Planting a picture window that pictures nothing. Key to plants:
1. English yew, Japanese holly or dwarf Pfitzer juniper;
2. sweetbay magnolia or doublefile viburnum;
3. *Vinca minor*, pachysandra, or English ivy underplanted with daffodils;
4. improved yew or mugho pine.

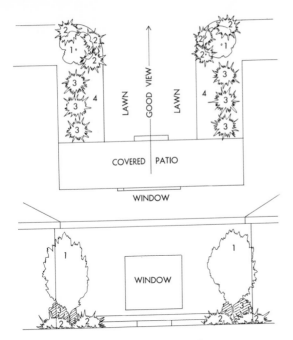

Fig. 21 Helping the view from a picture window. Key to plants:
1) Washington hawthorn or *Viburnum burkwoodi;*
2) English yew, Andorra juniper or improved yew;
3) mahonia or julianae barberry;
4) low annuals.

with pleasing shapes and colors which are uniform and orderly.

How can I get rid of an unpleasant view? In Figure 22 the problem is to screen off something you'd rather not see. Here at the front of the house the plantings must look good from both inside and out. The plants and arrangements chosen here would do that.

HOW SHALL I PLANT AROUND THE DOORWAY?

The doorway of almost any house is the most prominent part of the front. People see landscaping here closer than in any other part of the yard. Doorways are worth special effort. First, make them say welcome. Next, let them offer friendly protection from the elements and provide attractive color. Finally, plan them for easy upkeep so that they always look neat and presentable.

Figure 23 is an interesting, colorful gar-

den type of planting. The fence makes the space look wider. Study what has been done with the shade tree, flowering plants, and easily maintained ground covers.

In Figure 24 the doorway has been framed by the symmetrical use of materials. This nicely formal arrangement has lots of color and interest in the plants used.

Figure 25 creates an informal feeling by combining some of the ideas in Figures 23 and 24. The window justifies the semiformal planting between walk and house. The free-form layout of the front bed combines well with the informality of the plants chosen for the scheme.

All three plans use easy and effective ac-

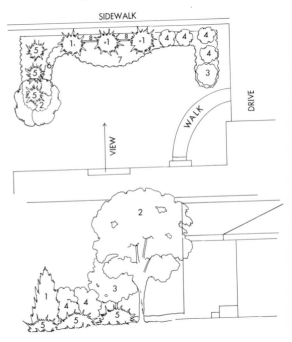

Fig. 22 Screening an unpleasant window view. Key to plants:
1. Scotch pine, hemlock, or upright yew;
2. 'Moraine' locust, hard maple or red oak;
3. flowering crabapple or Washington hawthorn;
4. *Viburnum burkwoodi* or mahonia;
5. Japanese yew, Japanese holly or Pfitzer juniper;
6. annuals;
7. *Vinca minor* or pachysandra underplanted with spring bulbs;
8. short fence sections.

Fig. 23 A garden type of doorway planting. Key to plants:

1. 'Moraine' locust, sugar maple, or red oak;
2. English yew, mugho pine, or dwarf Pfitzer juniper;
3. climbing roses;
4. perennial and annual flowers;
5. *Vinca minor* or English ivy, underplanted with daffodils.

cessories: boulders in Figure 23, tubs or pots in Figure 24, and lamp posts in Figure 25. These add interest. But choose them carefully, keeping in mind the style of the house, and do not have too many.

WHAT SHALL I SET OUT AT THE CORNERS OF THE HOUSE?

Corner plantings soften and broaden the look of a house and make it seem more comfortably settled. Vertical lines are seldom emphasized.

Figure 26 is a commonly used plan with many combinations. The main plant is both informal and interesting, since it is seen from all sides. At its base are plants that offer contrast. If a deciduous main plant is used, for instance, try evergreens below.

Figure 27 is a planting of a two-story house. It will fit many older style homes.

The large tree suggested as the main plant should be farthest from the corner. Between it and the house put a fairly large second plant.

Figure 28 shows a formal treatment using hedge or fence as a screen. Either one makes a good backdrop for roses, perennials, or annuals. The large shrub anchors the planting at the free end.

THREE WAYS WITH A SMALL BACK YARD

In the three small back yards planned here, a six-foot privacy fence has been used as the beginning. Each is planned for families with small children and a love for gardening and outdoor living. The first two plans have straight lines; the third uses curves. All are organized to separate the

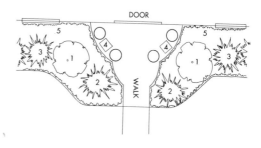

Fig. 24 Symmetrical doorway planting. Key to plants:

1. dogwood, American holly, or flowering crab;
2. boxwood, Japanese yew, or Japanese holly;
3. Japanese yew, Pfitzer juniper, or mahonia;
4. tubs of annual flowers or foliage plants;
5. English ivy or pachysandra, underplanted with daffodils.

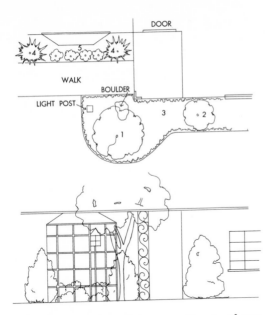

Fig. 25 An informal doorway. Key to plants:
1. 'Marshall' ash, Norway maple or flowering crabapple;
2. doublefile viburnum, sweetbay magnolia, or upright yew;
3. Sargent's juniper or *Vinca minor*;
4. leatherleaf viburnum, American holly or upright yew;
5. floribunda or grandiflora roses.

work from the living areas. Each has a paved terrace in the center of the flowers and shrubs. Unsightly places are screened off; living space is kept close to the house and accessible by all-weather paths.

THE SAME PLACE PLANTED THREE WAYS

Figures 30, 31, and 32 show how a 75- by 125-foot lot with a development kind of house has been planned in three different ways, for three different types of family living.

The first plan (Figure 30), designed for a family of four, a couple with two children, has easy upkeep, good looks, and room for lots of living. There is plenty of play space for the children, and this is placed where it can be seen from the kitchen, porch, bedroom or bathroom windows. The paved area with a grill and a table provides an outdoor dining and recreation area for the whole

family, and it is slightly separated from the children's play space, although still in view. Hedges near the grill and in the play area will keep the children from running into the swings or the grill. This plan can grow with the family. When the children no longer need swings and a slide, that area might make way for a badminton court. The walks and paved area could become a framework for a garden, after the children are grown. A six-foot fence with gates encloses the entire back yard. Existing trees are shown with the trunk cross-hatched. Other trees are shown with a small open circle at the trunk.

The second plan (Figure 31) is for a couple without children. Here the emphasis is on entertaining in the garden, plus easy maintenance ideas. In areas that are difficult to mow, this scheme uses ground covers like periwinkle instead of grass. The paved area is brick, or scored concrete. There is only one bit of clipped hedge, near the front entrance. A fence with gates is provided around the entire back yard as the best way of giving

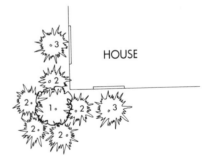

Fig. 26 A corner planting open to many variations. Key to plants:
1. hawthorn, or redbud, or dogwood;
2. English yew, or Andorra juniper;
3. mahonia, or bigleaf wintercreeper (*Euonymus*).

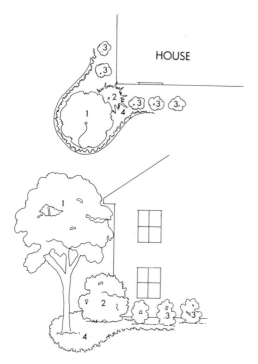

Fig. 27 A two-story house uses a high corner planting. Key:
1. 'Hopa' crab or 'Marshall' ash;
2. leatherleaf viburnum or Japanese yew;
3. star magnolia or American holly;
4. hybrid tea or grandiflora roses.

privacy and making a background for the plantings of low-growing shrubs.

The third plan (Figure 32) is a hobby garden just for the gardening enthusiast of the family. Let's say it is for you, and your hobby is roses. The plan presents a scheme for a little formal rose garden. Perhaps you ordinarily think of a formal garden as befitting only a pretentious house—but there is no reason why a modest place should not have a formal garden if one is wanted. The dot and dash line down the center shows the alignment of the garden with the rear door of the house, through which you would enter this outdoor area. The fact that the back terrace or porch—a sitting area—is slightly off the center actually helps the plan, since the best view of any formal garden is from off the axis.

The garden itself is very simple, although at first glance it may not seem so. The low wall (24 to 30 inches high and 18 inches

wide) defines the rose garden area and provides a background for the roses, but it does not restrict the view into the other parts of the garden. This garden can grow. First you would build the wall, the paved area, the pool and rose beds. Later add the arbor with climbing roses. This arbor will look best if it is kept simple. Still later you can build the semicircular area of tree roses. Or if you prefer, turn this part into an informal arrangement of perennials and shrubs.

A high garden wall near the street gives interest and provides a support for vines as well as a background for flowers and shrubs. A high fence encloses the rest of the back yard. Perennials at the west and north sides are edged with a wood or masonry curb set low enough into the grass to permit easy mowing. Or you could make a wider brick mowing strip to let you walk near the flowers soon after a rain or on a dewy morning. Small flowering shrubs build up the corner, with one vertical evergreen as an accent.

WHAT A LANDSCAPE ARCHITECT CAN DO

Maybe you have special problems and the plan just won't take shape. If you live in any

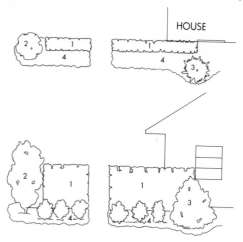

Fig. 28 This corner planting incorporates a hedge for a screen. Key:
1. juniper, yew, arbor-vitae or hemlock hedge, (or constructed fence);
2. *Viburnum carlesi,* or upright flowering crab;
3. star magnolia or American holly;
4. hybrid tea or grandiflora roses.

31

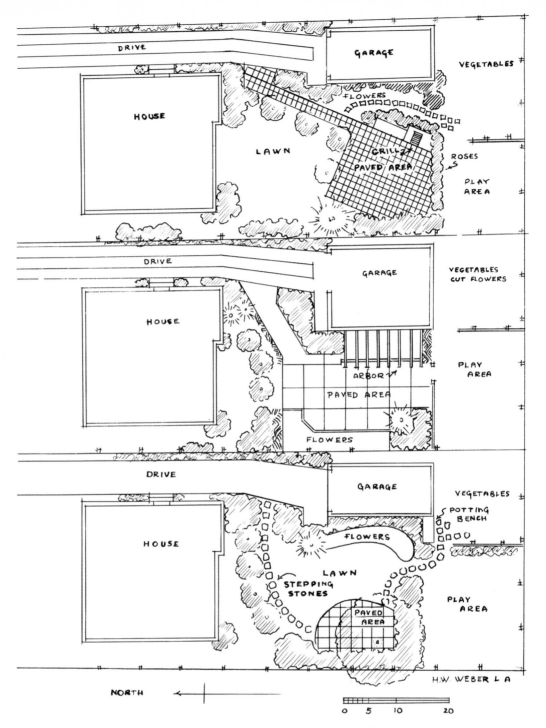

DRIVE

GARAGE

VEGETABLES

HOUSE

FLOWERS

LAWN

GRILL

PAVED AREA

ROSES

PLAY
AREA

DRIVE

GARAGE

VEGETABLES
CUT FLOWERS

HOUSE

ARBOR

PAVED AREA

PLAY
AREA

FLOWERS

DRIVE

GARAGE

VEGETABLES

HOUSE

POTTING
BENCH

FLOWERS

LAWN
STEPPING
STONES

PAVED
AREA

PLAY
AREA

H.W. WEBER L A

NORTH

0   5   10   20

Fig. 29 Three ways to develop a small back yard. *Herschel W. Weber,* landscape architect

large community you have a professional nearby who can help you—a landscape architect. He is trained and experienced in designing gardens and yards. He knows ways to place things conveniently, make upkeep easy, and add beauty. He can plan construction features in detail—walks, steps, walls, shelters, decks, or terraces—and show you

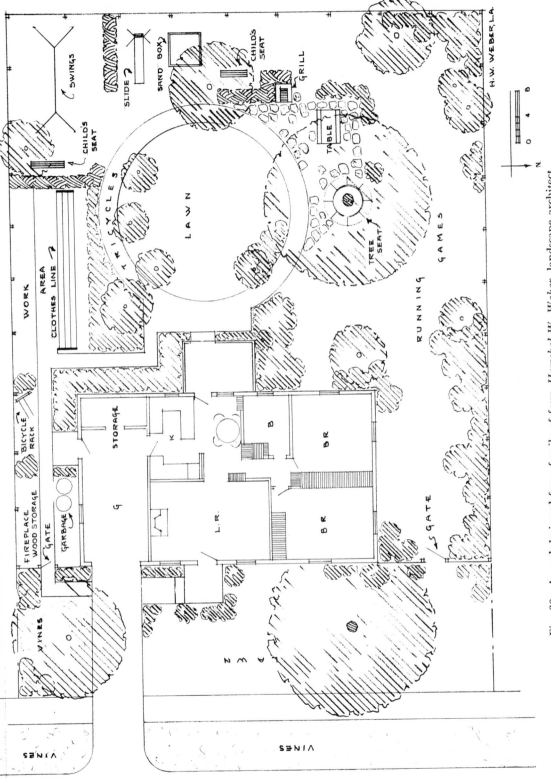

Fig. 30 A yard designed for a family of four. *Herschel W. Weber*, landscape architect

33

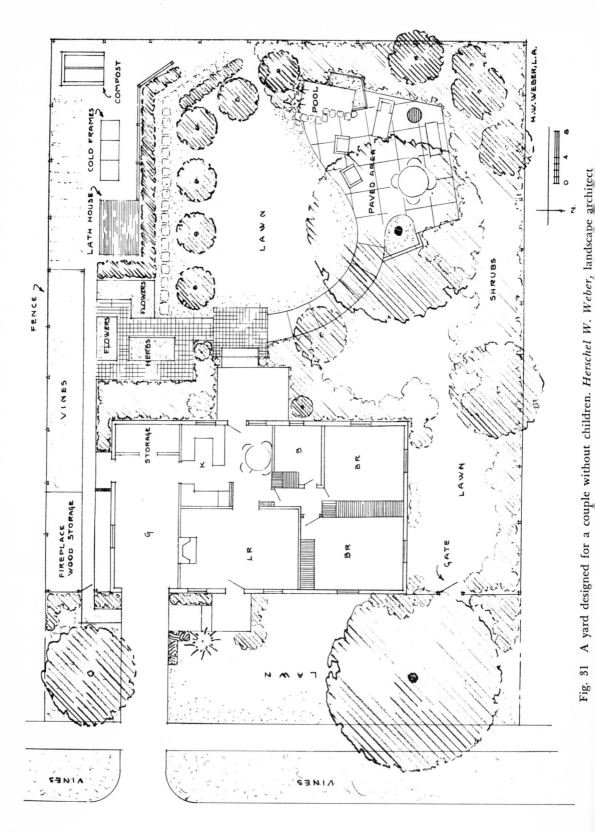

Fig. 31 A yard designed for a couple without children. *Herschel W. Weber,* landscape architect

34

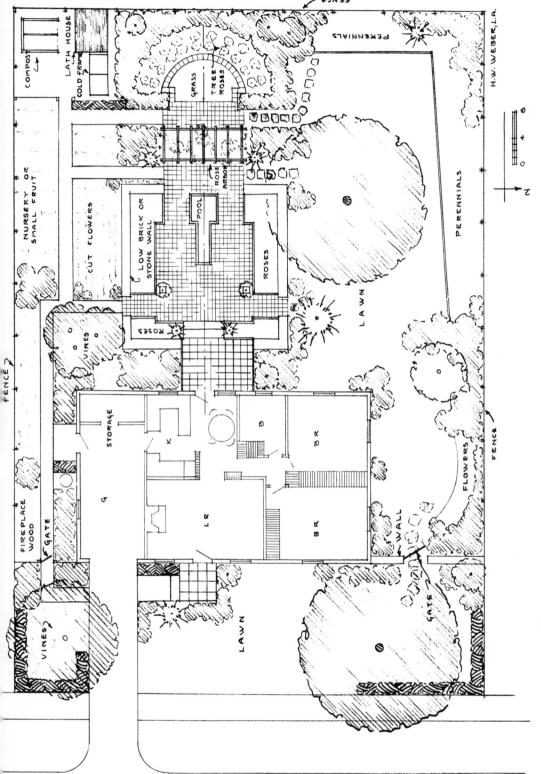

Fig. 32 A yard designed for a rose enthusiast. *Herschel W. Weber, landscape architect*

35

where to put them. If ever you are in doubt about your own judgment, you'll do well to talk to this man or woman and follow the advice given.

EASY-DOES-IT IDEAS

To see what a new bed will look like and how much it will encroach on open space, outline it first with plant stakes. For this get a bundle of fifty 3-foot green-painted wood or bamboo stakes; they'll find many later uses. Lay them along the proposed outline. Or use a garden hose. The hose makes curves nicely but is less tractable to handle than stakes.

To visualize plans for door or foundation plantings, sketch your house or take a photograph of it. Then experiment with cut-out cardboard "shrubs" that you can move around until they look right.

When you plan walks and drives, make them straight or at least direct. They'll cost less, be safer, and look better than if they're full of useless curves—and they'll take up less space.

Chapter 3

TAKE A GOOD LOOK
AT YOUR SOIL

What is this "good loam" I hear so much about?

Now that your place is planted on paper, take a good look at the soil that will soon have to support it. It's best to start with a clear view of what to expect from your soil and how to get along with it. This honest appraisal saves you time, expense, and later worry.

WHAT IS TEXTURE?

The size and arrangement of particles—that is what soil texture is about. Try this bottle test: In a round quart jar put a quarter cup of soil and a pint of water. Seal and slosh the mixture lightly for half a minute. Let it settle, then slosh it again. Set it aside and let it settle for three or four days or until the water clears (for very fine clay particles it may take a week). Compare the widths of the various layers. Coarsest sand is at the bottom. Fine sand, silt, and clay appear in that order toward the top.

If it is over half sand, you'd call it a *light sandy soil.*

If it is over half silt, with hardly any clay, it is a *heavy silt soil.*

If it has more than one-fourth clay and a large amount of silt, you'd call it a *clay soil.*

If it is about two-fifths sand, two-fifths silt and the rest clay, you have the ideal, the kind you'd call a *good loam,* and you should be thankful.

Light sandy soils are easy to work. They warm up early in spring and usually drain well. They are not especially rich, so you have to water and fertilize them often in easy doses. Plant bulbs and seeds in this kind of soil a little deeper than the instructions commonly recommend. Cover a daffodil with 5 inches of soil instead of 4, for instance.

Fig. 33 A water test helps you analyze soil texture.

To improve the soil, add organic matter (peat moss, leaf mold, compost).

Heavy silt and clay soils are cold and wet. You can't plow or spade them early in spring because they are dense and slow to dry out. Never work them when they are wet or they will make bricklike lumps. When you tap a slice of this soil with the spade and it falls apart, it is in good shape for tilling. This kind of soil often drains poorly. Cover bulbs and seeds planted here less deep than you would in an average soil. The daffodil bulb gets a soil covering of only 3 or 3½ inches instead of 4.

To improve this kind of soil, add peat moss, leaf mold or compost and sometimes vermiculite or sand and lime.

IS THERE ENOUGH HUMUS OR ORGANIC MATTER?

Humus is the life of the soil. It is practically impossible to add too much of it. The benefits of humus are so great that volumes could be (and have been) written about nothing else. Suffice it to say that organic matter (or humus) improves the texture of soils, whether they are too light or too heavy; it helps soil absorb and hold water and nutrients; and it releases a number of foods that plants use.

Humus is what makes a soil a true "loam." Without organic matter it is just a collection of assorted minerals of various sizes.

Humus comes from the decomposition of things that have been alive—plants or animals. Sometimes you can see humus. In the bottle test you made you probably saw bits of matter floating loose from the soil that obviously were not minerals. This was organic matter. You cannot see most humus because the particles are too small. You know that they are there by what they do to make plants grow better. When people see dark brown or black soil they think it is a sign of humus; sometimes this is true, but not always. In the many stages through which organic matter passes as it decomposes, it either directly or indirectly releases substances precious to plant growth. It becomes the home of countless micro-organisms that work to break down dead tissues and reduce them further into chemical forms which growing plants can use.

Places with much rainfall are more likely to have humus-rich soil than places where rain is scanty. Regions that are cool have more natural soil humus than places that are hot. By various processes, humus is constantly lost out of soil but nature is also always at work replacing it, or trying to. Man in his gardening and farming activity often does more harm than good along this line.

You can remedy a shortage of soil humus by adding compost, manures, leaf mold or peat moss. A good loam should be at least one-tenth humus. For thousands of years gardeners have added organic matter to soil, aware that it was vital to growing plants but not understanding (even to this day) the whole maze of life processes which it feeds.

WHAT IS COMPOST?

Compost is the remains of plants that have decomposed. You can make it systematically by piling up plant refuse and encouraging it to decay. Leaves, grass, plant tops, straw, old hay and sod are some of the raw materials. Use any such ingredients that are not full of disease or weed seeds. Keep out twigs and coarse prunings, or plant tops like tomato vines that take a long time to rot. Lay all this down in a layer a foot thick. Add a sprinkling of nitrogen fertilizer and a half inch of earth. Add more layers this way, as many as you want, making the top like a saucer to catch rain. Water a new compost pile at first to get it started. In three months (in warm weather) it will sink down to half its size and you can turn and mix it. In another two months it is ready to use—a moist, crumbly, dark earth.

Most gardeners simply heap the refuse of their gardens as it becomes available into two piles, one that is "working" and the other, older, that is made and ready to use. They don't bother to layer the pile, which speeds the process but does not greatly change the product. They make handling it an annual affair, emptying the pile in the fall, spreading compost on shrubs and flower borders to make way for the new harvest of leaves and refuse that comes after frost. Do it either way that suits you. There is nothing messy or offensive about a well-run compost pile, and you won't mind having it in your yard. A single forsythia bush can conceal a large pile fenced in with a circle of coarse wire or screening.

Animal manures, whether used as humus or for fertility, are not so likely to burn plants if they are first composted. You'll often see instructions telling you to use "well-rotted manure." This means manure that has been aged this way until it is odorless and shapeless. It takes a year or more.

If the ingredients of a compost—leaves, straw, plant tops—were added directly to the soil without composting, the result would be a temporary nitrogen shortage badly depriving the growing plants. You would see evidence in yellowing foliage. In this case, what happens is that soil bacteria working on the *new* plant tissues speed up activity to such a pace that they use more than their share of the natural nitrogen and phosphorus from the soil. The lesson here is that when you cultivate undecayed plant remains into the soil, it's best to add a complete fertilizer at the same time so there will be enough nourishment for both growing plants and the busy soil bacteria.

Leaf mold and peat moss. These are two forms of organic matter you can add directly to the soil. They are already composted.

Peat moss is the fibery brown, almost decayed remains of plants that are ages old. It is mined from great deposits in this country and elsewhere. You buy it in bales or large packages. Among its properties, it is able to absorb and hold astonishing amounts of water. It also is so granular that it holds air. This is why it is such a boon for either a sandy light soil or a heavy one. Moisten it before mixing it with the soil by letting water from a slow-running hose seep into an open bale. Peat moss retains its identity in the soil for a long time.

Leaf mold is the carpet from the floor of the forest. It is the accumulation of leaves that have fallen over several years and gradually broken down on their return to dust. As leaf mold they are caught before the process is quite complete. This soft flaky material is so nearly disintegrated that it takes nothing from the soil—only sinks into it as life-bringing humus. You will find it under the top layer of leaves in the woods, where,

if it's your woods, you can help yourself. Sometimes you can buy it in bags.

HOW ABOUT DRAINAGE?

Consider the way water drains from or through your soil. Heavy soils are especially likely to need improved drainage.

To check surface drainage, all you have to do is go out an hour after a good rain and see where water is standing. Mark the puddles. After the soil dries you can do something about them. For one thing, spade the ground and add humus, so water can penetrate. Next, if the ground slopes so water runs into pools with no outlets, fill the depressions and grade the surface to make the water run off gradually.

To test how water runs through your soil, dig a hole as you would to plant a rose and fill it with water. If water is still there an hour later, drainage is poor. Perhaps a hardpan layer a little farther down is keeping moisture from moving through—just like the bottom of a bathtub. Dig down to see if this is what causes the blockage, and if it is, make some drain holes through it, two or three feet apart, with a post-hole digger.

If a tight, heavy upper soil is causing the problem, the best remedy is to lay drain tiles at a $1\frac{1}{2}$- to 2-foot depth, on a bed of gravel, to lead off the water to a lower place. If much of this needs doing, you had better hire a contractor who knows this business. In small areas, you might get by if you lighten the soil with additions of fine gravel, vermiculite, sand, and humus. Use plenty of these additives to do any good, and mix them in to a depth of at least 18 inches.

Should your soil be so sandy that it drains too fast, your problems are just as bad. Fertilizer and water rush right down through it and the plants go begging. The first thing to do is add compost or something like peat moss—lots of it. If this is not help enough, the remedy is drastic—dig out soil two feet deep and spread a double layer of sod, or a five-inch layer of clay, at the bottom of the excavation. Then replace the sandy soil. Water will still rush through the soil but when it reaches the barrier, it will slow enough for plants to have a chance to use nutrients and humus in the stream.

HOW IS THE pH?

You don't have to be a chemist to know and do something about the acidity-alkalinity balance of your soil—otherwise known as the pH. It's an extremely important subject to plants you try to grow.

An acid (or sour) soil is required by such plants as rhododendron, holly, camellia, cranberry and heather. An alkaline (or sweet) soil is necessary for gypsophila, cabbage, asparagus, pyracantha, clover, lilac, iris and peony. See Section H of "Useful Miscellany" for more plant pH preferences.

For a way to study and express relative acidity or alkalinity, chemists invented the pH scale. On it, 7 is the middle point. Soil of pH 7 is neutral, neither acid nor alkaline. Numbers below 7 express acidity. Numbers above 7, alkalinity. The scale starts at 0 and goes to 14, but you hardly need to know this since practically all plants grow only in the range from pH 4 to 9. The majority grow in a still narrower range—from 6 to 7. And most are quite tolerant if the soil goes one way or the other over the mark. If you plan to grow a wide variety of plants, aim to keep your soil near pH 6.5.

You can learn the pH of your soil with a simple test you do yourself with a soil-test kit. Testing the main areas of your yard once a year or less should be often enough to tell you what you need to know.

There is another way to track down acidity-alkalinity troubles—by watching your plants. If some have all the soil nutrients they need and still show symptoms of malnutrition, the soil pH may be out of kilter. A frequent example is yellowing leaves caused by unavailability of iron. The soil may contain plenty of iron, but if it is too alkaline the iron is "locked" and will not dissolve in water. The plant cannot absorb it, so it "starves" in the midst of plenty. Those who have seen chlorotic pin oaks or birch trees in the alkaline soils of the Great Plains or the sunny West have met this phenomenon. Other elements besides iron may be unavailable under certain conditions,

and the symptoms take a variety of forms. Where you possibly can, avoid these troubles by keeping your soil pH in balance for the plants you want to grow. Of course, large ones like trees cover such space that it's practically impossible to change soil from alkaline to acid or the other way. In these cases it's best to stick to plants that can take the pH you already have.

To make a soil more acid, add sulfur. A half cup of dusting sulfur to 9 square feet will lower the pH rating about a point in a medium loam soil. Other acidifying materials are acid peat moss, pine needles, sawdust and leaf mold from certain trees like oak and beech.

To make a soil more alkaline, add lime, preferably as ground agricultural limestone. Use 50 pounds to 1,000 square feet if it is average loam. Give clay soils more, up to twice as much. Lime has another benefit on clay. It helps to open it up by making tiny particles cling together, leaving larger air and water spaces between. A year may go by before the effects of lime show. Other substances that make a soil more alkaline are wood ashes—use those from your fireplace—and ground oyster shells.

IS YOUR SOIL "NUTRITIOUS"?

The numbers on a bag of plant food refer to the proportions of the three main soil elements used by plants. If they are 12-12-12, it means that 12 per cent of the contents is nitrogen, 12 per cent is phosphorus, and 12 per cent is potash. The elements are always listed in that order. These are the nutrients likely to be in short supply, which is mainly all you need to be concerned with.

Nitrogen. This is the most important element in making plants grow. Although nitrogen is abundant in nature, it is almost always scarce in soil. One reason is that it is easily dissolved by water and washed away.

A nitrogen deficiency shows up in leaves that look yellowish, with red tinges in the veins of young ones.

This element is the center of a vital, endless natural chain of events called the nitrogen cycle. Plants containing nitrogen die; the dead tissues fall to earth where they decompose, assisted by many soil micro-organisms, until they are reduced to simpler elements again, including usable nitrogen. Then a new plant absorbs the nitrogen, starting the chain over again. If some nitrogen gets lost along the way (perhaps by escaping to the atmosphere as gas) it can be replaced by certain soil bacteria that pick nitrogen from the air and make it available to plants. Rain, snow, and lightning also bring down nitrogen to the soil from the air.

The cycle works well only where plants grow continuously and return to the soil. You can see why desert soils and those where crops are continually removed are so devoid of nitrogen, and why you have to replenish it.

Ammonium sulfate is the commonest *chemical* form of nitrogen fertilizer. *Organic* sources are cottonseed meal, fish emulsions, dried blood, and sewage sludge.

Phosphorus. This element and the use plants make of it are not completely understood, but we know that phosphorus is necessary in cell formation, and that it is a key to the blooming and seed-making of plants.

Although plants use little phosphorus compared to their use of nitrogen, most soils do not have enough to satisfy their demands. A deficiency shows up in older leaves which are spotted with yellow, and leaf stalks and veins tinged purple. Only a fraction of what phosphorus is in the soil ever becomes available to the plant. So to furnish enough, you need to apply many times more than what the plant takes out. In cultivated soil nature has no way of keeping up the level of essential phosphates, so you have to supply them.

Mineral phosphates are the commonest sources of phosphorus fertilizer—superphosphate is an example. Organic sources are guano, fish meal and bone meal.

Since phosphorus does not move around in the soil, plant roots must come to it. So to do any good mix this element in the soil where the roots are, not on the surface.

Potassium. Potash is the common name of this plentiful substance. It is essential to growth, and plants use lots of it. It seems to do a variety of jobs, all of them adding to the quality and endurance of the plant. Tissues are stiffer, firmer, and in the case of some plants like dahlias, tubers store better if there is plenty of potash in the soil. The element is needed most when plants are maturing.

A shortage shows in older leaves of plants. Leaf margins turn purple, then reddish and brittle, and crumble off.

Most potassium fertilizer comes from minerals. The commonest form of it is potassium sulfate. This leaches so easily that it tends to run right through the soil. So you make small applications of it every few months, rather than a big one once a year, especially if your soil is sandy. Wood ashes contain lots of potash and were once widely used as fertilizer. Their only disadvantage is that they are extremely alkaline. Potassium sulfate is acidifying, so it is a good form to use in alkaline soils or around acid-tolerant plants. But it is bad for soils that are already too acid. There you would use muriate of potash, which hardly changes the soil's pH.

Minor or trace elements. These are as important as the major elements but the plant needs smaller amounts of them. They are calcium (lime), magnesium, sulfur, iron, manganese, zinc, copper, boron, molybdenum and chlorine.

Your soil probably has ample amounts of these. If the pH is right, they are all available and everything is fine. If the pH is far enough off to lock some of them in the soil, then various deficiency symptoms develop. Before diagnosing a shortage, check the soil pH. When pH is in balance you seldom need to add any of these. Many of them are there as impurities in the chemical fertilizers you use.

HOW TO MAKE YOUR OWN SOIL TEST

The birthday or Christmas may come when your family lovingly presents you with a kit of test tubes, funnels and solutions for testing the soil of your yard. You can have a lot of fun with a soil-test kit, and learn a great deal about your place, if you don't take your prowess as a soil chemist too seriously.

The most important use you can make of

the kit is to check the soil pH. If you do the testing right, the kit will tell you accurately about acidity and alkalinity. Wait until soil is thoroughly warm in the spring and plants are growing. Test each section of the yard separately—the rose garden, shrub border, lawn, vegetable area. Take the soil sample four to five inches deep. Use a clean spoon and don't touch the soil with your fingers. Follow directions that come with your kit and to be absolutely sure of your findings, repeat the test a time or two.

You have a right to be skeptical about the worth of these kits for measuring major nutrients—the nitrogen, phosphorus, and potash. Soil chemistry is so complicated that even experts have trouble getting a true picture of these chemicals in a soil. Even if your analysis is accurate, it tells you little about the availability or forms of the various elements. So you have only a vague idea of how to correct deficiencies you might think you find. If valuable time and irreplaceable trees and shrubs are at stake, it is wiser to pay to have the soil tested and recommendations made by a professional soil laboratory. Ask your county agent about the procedure to follow. Sometimes state or county agencies test soil free of charge.

EASY-DOES-IT IDEAS

Before you start spading in spring, squeeze a clod of soil in your hand. If it makes a glistening tight ball, postpone the digging another day or so—it is too wet.

Autumn leaves are a no-cost conditioner for soil in your vegetable garden. Spread them thick and rototill them in before freezeup. By spring most will have melted into humus.

Save wood shavings and sawdust from the workshop for your compost pile. After a year there they become good organic matter to put around bushes and flowers.

Chapter 4

HOW TO MAKE
AN ENDURING LAWN

Will grass cover up this rough grading?

The first thing you as a new homeowner probably want is a "nice green lawn." Practically, a lawn gets your house out of the mud or dust and helps keep the inside cleaner. Esthetically, a lawn makes a soft green setting for your house, walks, shrubs, trees, and flowers, and is the natural element that unites them all.

Regretfully, it must be stated, there is no royal road to a fine lawn. Before you start, have a visit with the neighbor who runs the best lawn in the vicinity, and ask him how he does it. He can give advice that will work in your yard, too.

NO ROYAL ROAD

Before setting out with rake and grass seed, consider the condition of the ground you intend to sow. You can have a beautiful and lasting lawn only if what is underneath has been properly prepared. The building contractor should have attended to:

1. Removal of debris. No junk—boards, roofing, sacks, cans—left below ground or above it.

2. Grading. Leveled to the right slopes, with no humps or hollows. If he didn't, you'll probably have to hire somebody to do these things. Machinery is needed for the grading.

Cut off roots that are sticking up; do with tree stumps as you like. Some people put

them to use until they rot. You can always cover them with vines or use one as a pedestal for a birdbath.

If no topsoil is left after grading you have two choices. You can either buy some, from someone you trust, in hopes that it really is topsoil. Or you can go to work and improve the subsoil you have left to make a decent seedbed out of it. If you buy topsoil, put it on 5 or 6 inches deep and smooth it down. It is not cheap or easy to find.

If you want to improve the soil you have, the best means is humus and lots of it. This can be peat moss, leaf mold, sawdust, compost or manure. To do any good, put on plenty and rototill it in. If you can stand to wait a season before having a lawn, plant something like cereal rye on the rough surface, and plow it under when it's 15 inches tall to add humus. Put on a sprinkling of ammonium sulfate to make it decay in a hurry.

DOES YOUR SOIL NEED LIME?

Ask your good-lawn neighbor about this. Many areas, but not all, have acid soils that need lime. Grass needs a soil pH between 5.9 and 6.9. If your soil pH is lower than this, put on about 50 pounds of agricultural lime to each 1,000 square feet. Then add fertilizer, something like 10-10-10, at the rate of 15 to 20 pounds per 1,000 square feet, and till all this in. Finally rake and rake. Work out the clods, stones and trash. You want a smooth surface for sowing.

5 This excellent lawn was built with good soil, proper grading, fertilizer, good seed, and faithful care. There is no royal road to a fine lawn. *Vance*

This preparation goes ahead of any kind of lawn, whether you sod it, plug it or sprig it. When you are through you have a firm, even, fine textured (but not dustlike) seedbed with no hills and hollows, and it is charged with fertilizer and humus.

WHAT GRASS SEED TO USE?

Where you live determines the type of lawn you can have. The map shows the approximate division between northern and southern grasses. If you are in the band on either side of the line you are in a zone where you can probably grow some of either kind. If your climate is mild with long warm seasons you need one of the southern grasses like St. Augustine. If you live where sum-

mers are cool and winters cold, you will do better with a northern grass like bluegrass. Where there is little rainfall and not much irrigation water, sow buffalo or crested wheatgrass (especially crested wheatgrass in the North). These do not make the lush lawns produced by better grasses under irrigation. Study lawns in your locality winter and summer. Choose the kind you like best and plant that kind.

Elevation is also a factor. At high elevations, you can grow bluegrass some distance into the South, like the Blue Ridge highlands of Georgia. In river valleys and lowlands Bermuda grass grows far north, varying with the kind used. Of all the southern grasses it is most versatile and hardy, but it can become a pest if it creeps into flower beds.

44

Fig. 34 Approximate division between northern and southern grasses. In the white band you can probably grow some of either kind.

KINDS OF GRASSES FOR THE NORTH

The finest lawns in the North are made of all bluegrass, all bentgrass, or mixtures between bluegrass and a fine-leaf fescue. For utility lawns you sometimes plant a thick stand of a tall fescue.

Mixtures. The object of planting mixed grasses is to provide kinds to meet the varying conditions in your yard and make up for each other's shortcomings. Always study the label to see what is in the mix. The bulk of a good mixture should be bluegrass of one or more kinds, or red fescue of one or more kinds (for shade). Redtop is sometimes added for a quick sprouting "nurse grass," and for use in shade you'll find bentgrass or *Poa trivialis* included. Never take any mixture that has Alta or K-31 fescue in it—they are a nuisance sprinkled into a fine lawn. When you see Italian (domestic) or perennial ryegrass on a label, it's a sign of a cheap mixture made for quick results but not a permanent lawn. You may or may not want the white Dutch clover you'll find in many

mixtures. Some like it, both because of its appearance and because it withstands chinch bug invasions. But it is killed by some weed killers, so it may interfere with your use of chemical weed controls.

Bentgrass. An all-bentgrass lawn carefully tended is a thing of beauty. It is the grass of golf greens. But mixed in bluegrass lawns it is considered a weed because it makes noticeable spreading patches. In the North it crowds out other grass, but in hot damp climates it does not do well. It can take much shade, especially in the South.

Bluegrass. Kentucky bluegrass (*Poa pratensis*) is the most widely used of northern grasses. There are many commercial strains. Merion is the main one except for common bluegrass. Merion is darker green, shorter growing and more drouth tolerant than most. All bluegrasses stay green most of winter, and start growing in earliest spring. They may go dormant in the heat of summer; you have to water hard then to keep them looking good. Bluegrass grows best in full sun but a species of it, *Poa*

45

trivialis, thrives in shade and you'll sometimes find it in mixtures. It is lighter green than other bluegrass.

Red fescue. For fine lawns this is a good choice. Kinds include Chewings, creeping red fescue, Pennlawn, Illahee, and others. This grass has fine wiry leaves like bluegrass. It does well in shade and you'll find it often in mixtures with bluegrass where it is good, because the two look alike and complement each other in growing habit.

Tall fescue. For a dark green, pest- and trouble-free utility lawn, this is superb. It is for play yards and game fields, not fine lawns. The two main kinds, Alta and Kentucky 31, are coarse-leaf plants with a bunchy habit unless planted thickly. Use one kind alone. Combined with bluegrass or fine-leaf red fescues, it is conspicuous and weedy looking. Tall fescue takes lots of traffic and abuse, and tolerates heat and drouth. It grows well in California and the South, too.

Redtop. This is a bentgrass that does not creep. It comes up fast; for this reason it is found often in mixtures where it is billed as a "nurse grass" to protect seedlings of more desirable kinds. It seldom lives more than a few years.

Perennial rye. The best thing about this is that it sprouts fast and covers the ground in an emergency, but it is never a good permanent lawn. It forms bunches and clumps. Similar but with coarser leaves is common annual ryegrass (also called Italian rye) which lives only one season.

KINDS OF GRASSES FOR THE SOUTH

Here you seldom see mixtures of grasses in lawns but rather pure stands of different kinds. It is possible, however, to get seed mixtures of southern grasses.

Bermuda. This makes a fine-textured, evenly light lawn which is beautiful when it is well cared for. It grows too well, and comes up in flower beds and other places where it isn't wanted. It needs full sun and frequent mowing, watering, and feeding to make the best appearance. The common kind is usually started from seed, but special selections (like U-3, Tiflawn, and Ever-glades) are sold as plugs or sprigs. U-3 is the hardiest and grows north to Nebraska. All bermudas turn brown with the first frost and stay that way until spring. In the South it is customary to overplant bermuda in winter with something like annual ryegrass that stays green.

Zoysia. A thick lawn of zoysia makes a dark green dense springy turf that stands lots of traffic and crowds out crabgrass. It's so slow growing it does not need such frequent mowing as some grasses; but as a result it takes two seasons to get a good lawn of it after setting out plugs or sprigs. It is hardly ever started any other way except for *matrella japonica* zoysia, for which you can sometimes get seeds. Other common kinds are Meyer and Emerald. Meyer is apparently the hardiest, and grows in far north places like Iowa and Michigan. But all zoysias, even if root hardy, will turn brown at frost and stay that way until late spring.

St. Augustine. One of the most widely used Southern grasses, this makes a loose low dark green durable turf with a rather coarse texture. It spreads by creeping runners but does not often get out of hand. It's good for play yard or lawn, and grows well in shade. Start it with sod or sprigs.

Centipede. Not as coarse as St. Augustine or as fine as bermuda, this makes an easy and pretty lawn. It grows slowly and does not need frequent mowing. It does well on poor soil and needs little fertilizing but it will not grow in shade. It spreads by creeping stolons, so you start it either from plugs, sprigs, or seed. In winter it turns brown.

Carpet. This makes a wiry, loose, coarse turf popular in warm coastal regions. You can seed it but are more likely to start it by sprigs. Put it in moist shady places where you can't grow other grass. Its wiry seed spikes make it hard to mow. It turns brown in winter and won't survive freezing weather.

Dichondra. Though not a grass this round-leaf plant makes a nice bright green lawn substitute, especially in the warm Southwest. It is so low you don't have to mow it often. Start with sprigs or seed. It spreads by runners. Commonest on the West Coast, it won't survive sharp freezes, and does best where air is dry.

WHEN TO SOW SEED
AND HOW MUCH

In the North, sow grass seed in late summer and early fall. From mid-August on is about right. Measure the area to find the number of square feet so you can figure how much seed to use. Rates for commercially packaged mixtures are on the box or bag. For straight seeds purchased from bulk follow the rates in Figure 35.

To sow seed evenly, divide out the right amount for the size of the area and go back and forth spreading by hand in both directions until you use up the allotment for that space. Or, an easier way, use an accurate lawn seeder set to sow thinly, and cross the area in both directions until the needed amount is used. Don't cover bluegrass seed at all. Rake in large seeds like ryegrass or tall fescues lightly to cover them.

To help keep a new seeded lawn from washing away on slopes, cover with cheesecloth, gunny sacks or commercial mulching cloth like Erosionet. Grass grows through the cloth and it soon disintegrates.

Water with a fine spray from the hose or sprinkler so as not to wash seeds. Unless

Fig. 35

LAWNS FROM SEED

KIND OF SEED	WHEN TO PLANT	AMOUNT OF SEED (per 1,000 sq. ft.)
Bermuda	Spring	1-2 lbs.
Buffalograss	Spring	1-2 lbs. (hulled)
Creeping bent-grass	Fall	1 lb.
Crested wheatgrass (Fairway strain)	Fall	4 lbs.
Kentucky blue-grass	Fall	2-2½ lbs.
Mixed bluegrass-red fescue	Fall	2-2½ lbs.
Red fescue	Fall	2-2½ lbs.
Redtop	Fall	3 lbs.
Ryegrass (domestic and perennial)	Spring-Fall	5-10 lbs.
Tall fescue (Alta and K-31)	Fall	7-10 lbs.

rain falls, water the new seeded area once or twice a day to keep it damp, for the first

6   To keep a new seeded lawn from washing away on slopes, cover with cheesecloth or a commercial mulching cloth, as shown here. The cloth soon disintegrates.   *Better Lawn Institute*

Fig. 36

LAWNS FROM SOD, PLUGS, SPRIGS

KIND OF GRASS	TIME TO PLANT
Bermuda	Spring-summer
Buffalograss	Spring
Carpetgrass	Spring-summer
Centipede	Spring-summer
Creeping bentgrass	Early fall
Zoysia	Spring-summer
St. Augustine	Spring-summer

two or three weeks. As soon as the new grass is an inch high, you can slack up; but do not let the new grass ever really dry out.

THE FIRST MOWING

Finally you can start mowing, when grass reaches $2\frac{1}{2}$ inches high. Never let it go higher than 3 or $3\frac{1}{2}$ inches before starting to cut. These first mowings encourage permanent grasses to spread out and they prevent any "nurse" grasses you may have sown from smothering the tiny new seedlings of better kinds coming up. Mowing every five or six days guarantees that no heavy crop of clippings falls all at once to blot out young grass. The first autumn stop mowing only when winter comes. If winter weeds show up, go after them with a butcher or dandelion knife or if there are too many, wait until next spring and apply weed killers.

LAWNS FROM SPRIGS AND PLUGS

Although sprigging and plugging to start lawns is more a Southern method than a Northern one, with some lawns like bermuda and zoysia it's common wherever they grow.

Prepare the soil the same careful way as if you were seeding it. The right season is spring or early summer.

You need a special tool called a plugger to lift out plug size openings in the soil. You can probably rent or borrow one from the

7 A zoysia plugging project nearing completion, with sod strips instead of plugs laid near the crown of the slope to prevent washing. *Dudney*

place that sells the plugs. For large areas it's customary to space plugs 12 inches apart each way. To get quicker coverage you can space them closer but you'll use more, and the cost goes up. To get a faster "take" on plugs, soak or dip them in a bucketful of a weak soluble fertilizer before putting them in the planting holes. Keep a newly plugged lawn watered well the first season. Count on two seasons for a plugged lawn to fill in completely.

Sprigging is cheaper than plugging. It's almost as successful, except where a grass may be on a borderline of hardiness. Keep sprigs fresh in water while you prepare to plant. Open evenly spaced planting holes the same as for plugs.

CARING FOR AN ESTABLISHED LAWN

The better the care, the better the lawn, and vice versa. The care consists of regular mowing, feeding, watering and weed control. Sometimes there are a few extra chores, such as raking, aerating, and controlling bugs and diseases. The first step, upon which much else depends, is to do everything possible to keep lawn grasses flourishing. You do this mainly by feeding.

HOW TO FEED NORTHERN GRASSES (BLUEGRASS, BENT, FESCUES)

The easiest and best fertilizer to use on lawns is a dry chemical mixture high in nitrogen with less phosphorus and potash. The kinds made for lawns are like this, with an analysis (printed on the bag) of something like 12-6-4. This means 12 per cent nitrogen, 6 per cent phosphorus, 4 per cent potash.

The lawn needs between 3 and 4 pounds of *actual* nitrogen per 1,000 square feet each year. So if it's 12-6-4, the amount you need to use annually per 1,000 square feet is about 30 pounds (12 per cent of 30 equals 3.6 pounds actual nitrogen). You can put this on in three equal doses: one in early

spring, one in late spring, one in fall. Where summers get hot early, make the late spring feeding light, and the fall feeding proportionately heavier. If you live near the southern edge of bluegrass country, limit yourself to two feedings a year, one in spring, and a heavy one in fall. This is done to make nitrogen less likely to burn the grass or cause disease in over-stimulated mid-summer lawns. In northern states where cool seasons are long, you can make four feedings instead of three: March, May, July, and September.

If you use a lawn food containing ureaform nitrogen you don't need to worry so much about burning from heat, and you need to make only two feedings a year anywhere, because the nitrogen is released slowly and each feeding lasts longer. Some commercial lawn foods contain this new form of nitrogen. The best have half or more of the nitrogen in ureaform, and the rest as a quick-acting kind.

HOW TO FEED SOUTHERN GRASSES

Here you judge your actions by the kind of grass you have. Feed bermuda lawns lightly every month or six weeks except in winter. In spring and fall apply a regular lawn fertilizer containing nitrogen, phosphorus and potash. Use a low analysis, like 6-6-6, and apply it at a rate of 15 to 20 pounds per 1,000 square feet. The other feedings are usually with straight nitrogen (like ammonium sulfate) applied at 7 or 8 pounds per 1,000 square feet.

Fertilize centipede or carpetgrass only once a year, in spring. Feed St. Augustine and zoysia grass three times a year—in fall, spring, and early summer. Dichondra lawns benefit from frequent light feedings every two to four weeks when the weather permits them to be in active growth. Wash all fertilizer in with the hose, to keep it from burning foliage.

HOW OFTEN TO MOW ESTABLISHED LAWNS

On bluegrass lawns. Mowing at the right height helps control lawn weeds. It also

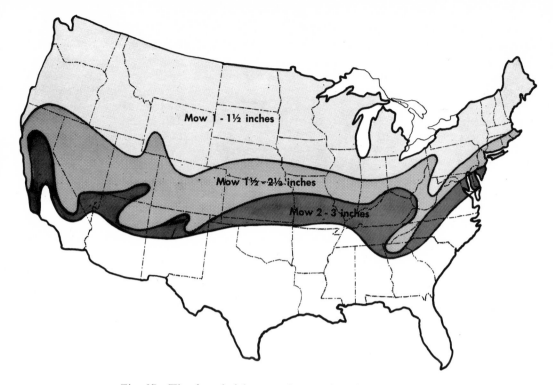

Fig. 37 The three height zones for mowing bluegrass lawns.

means a better appearance through heat and drouth. The map (Figure 37) shows three bluegrass mowing height zones. In northern states where bluegrass grows actively in summer, set the mower to cut at 1 to $1\frac{1}{2}$ inches. In the central zone mow at a medium height of $1\frac{1}{2}$ to $2\frac{1}{2}$ inches. In the south of the bluegrass country, high summer mowing is essential to health of the grass and to keep out weeds, especially crabgrass. So here mow at a height of 2 to 3 inches. Cut Merion bluegrass slightly shorter than other bluegrasses —about $1\frac{1}{2}$ to 2 inches. How frequently to mow depends on how fast the grass is growing. As a rule of thumb, cut whenever grass has grown an inch since the last time. In summer this could mean three weeks between mowings—but in spring you may mow every four or five days. The average is about once a week.

Mowing other grasses. Cut zoysia lawns about $1\frac{1}{2}$ inches high; bentgrass $\frac{3}{4}$ to 1 inch high; highland bent about $1\frac{1}{2}$ inches; bermuda a little under a half inch. Cut mixtures of bluegrass and red fescue at the bluegrass height.

HOW AND WHEN TO WATER YOUR LAWN

Normal rainfall seldom furnishes all the water a fine lawn needs. Southern lawns generally need more water than Northern ones. Lawns in the dry West need more watering than those of the high rainfall East. In many arid parts of the West you can't have a lawn unless you water it. The minimum moisture a lawn needs is about an inch a week. If this does not come down as rain, provide it with the hose. Where lawn watering is a regular chore, it's most practical to provide an underground sprinkling system when you first put down the lawn. Then you can water with a turn of the valve. For real automation you can get timers to turn on the water any day and hour without attention from you.

Where watering is only occasionally needed, your best tools are the garden hose and various sprinkling devices which you move about. Water early enough in the day to let grass dry before night. Once a week is often enough for a particular place, but

50

let the sprinkler run long enough there to give an inch of moisture. You can measure this by putting empty coffee cans under the edge of the spray. Don't move the sprinkler until cans have an inch of water in them.

HOW TO DEFEAT WEEDS

Where do lawn weeds come from? On the wind, the feet of birds, dogs, cats and people, in the topsoil you may have bought, on tools—and alas, in the seed you planted which you thought was pure lawn grass.

Broadleaf weeds like dandelions and plantain can be killed with 2,4-D. Use this or its partner 2,4,5-T very carefully. For greatest safety use an amine form. Choose a windless day and even then cover valuable plants nearby from the drift of fumes. Despite your care, sensitive plants like grapes, roses, or tomatoes many feet away may show injury. And one more warning—*never* use the same sprayer you've used for weed killer for any other purpose. This is a potent chemical and it won't wash out. Keep two sprayers, and mark the one for weed killer with red paint.

Use 2,4-D when the temperature is above 70 degrees and when plants are growing fast. For early weeds like dandelions and shepherd's purse, pick a warm day either early or late in the year, like March or October, when desirable plants nearby are nearly dormant. Remember that 2,4-D or 2,4,5-T will damage or kill clover in your lawn, if you have any. Several commercial products containing 2,4-D in dry granular form are on the market. They are more convenient and safe to use than liquid spray.

A DOZEN LAWN WEEDS AND HOW TO GET RID OF THEM

BROAD-LEAF PLANTAIN (*Plantago major*)—Found everywhere. Perennial, it prefers shade. It survives rough traffic and close mowing (because its flat leaves lie on the ground) and if it succeeds in sending up even a few wand-like seed stalks, it will spread. If you have only a few, dig them out with an asparagus or butcher knife. If the whole area is covered, dig it up and replant

grass—then watch closely for a year or two to remove young seedlings that may come up. Or spray with 2,4-D in early spring or late fall.

SHEPHERD'S PURSE (*Capsella bursa-pastoris*)—Some call it pepper grass. It appears in the spring, starting from a little rosette that stayed alive all winter. It shoots up a flower and seed stalk on the first warm days. A few in the lawn can be dug out. If you have many, treat late in fall or early in spring with 2,4-D. Early frequent mowing helps stop seeding.

CARPET WEED (*Mollugo verticillata*) —A sprawling, matted annual, sometimes confused with chickweed, but you can easily tell it by its light green leaves in little whorls at the joints of stems. Tiny white flowers come at the nodes in June. It begins to grow about when crabgrass does. Pull or dig it; or if it's too thick, spray it in early June with 2,4-D.

CHICKWEED (*Stellaria media* or *Cerastium vulgatum*)—In early spring it is blooming before bluegrass wakes up. Its little roundish light yellow-green leaves on many-branched stems form a tangled mass among the grass. It has made seeds almost before you start to mow. An annual, it comes up every year—usually from seeds that sprout in fall. You can hoe or pull it out with a rake; or if you have a bad invasion spray or sprinkle with potassium cyanate or 2,4,5-T in late fall or early spring. Weedone is one brand name under which these chemicals are sold.

CRABGRASS (*Digitaria*, several species) —You may not recognize it when it's young, but by July when finger-like seed heads appear there is no mistake. The plant has become a spreading mass, rooting at every joint that touches ground. Mowing cannot keep it from seeding, although close and frequent mowing, especially if you lift it with a rake beforehand—will cut down the amount of seed produced. Crabgrass grows only in the sun; so the best way to discourage it is to keep lawn grass growing heavily and cut high. Even this won't help when the real heat comes and lawn grasses go on vacation. Then crabgrass really takes over.

Three ways to deal with crabgrass. There are three approaches to crabgrass control.

1. Dig it out by hand, when you spot it in the lawn. This is not hard if you have only a little.

2. Use chemicals to kill the seeds when they sprout. Chemical mixtures called pre-emergents made just for this purpose are on the market. Most of them are fairly effective if you put them on exactly at the right rate and time, and in the way recommended on the package. Usually you apply these with a fertilizer spreader in early spring, three weeks or more before crabgrass germinates.

3. Use chemicals that kill the young plants. These chemicals are called post-emergents. There are many kinds. The most common one contains disodium methyl arsenate, like Scott's Clout, which seems to give consistent results over a wide area. Again, follow package directions. You will need to make two or three applications.

GILL-OVER-THE-GROUND (*Glechoma hederacea*)—Other names are creeping charley and ground ivy. This weed is perennial and its flowers are blue. It is often confused with henbit (*Lamium amplexicaule*) which is annual and has purple flowers. Both are bad pests, rooting at every joint and spreading fast. Faithful hand pulling controls it, or spray it early in spring or late in fall with 2,4-D or 2,4,5-T.

BUCKHORN (*Plantago lanceolata*)—This is a plantain—but its leaves are longer and more pointed than common plantain, and its seed and flower heads more club-like. It sometimes comes to a lawn in clover seed. Dig it out or spray with 2,4-D. Frequent lawn mowing during hot weeks when grass doesn't grow fast keeps it from going to seed.

GOOSEGRASS (*Eleusine indica*)—An annual, it grows west to Nebraska. Sometimes called crabgrass. It is the toughest, darkest grass, growing in paths and driveways where even crabgrass gives up. It bucks the lawn mower, and a husky plant is almost impossible to pull. Seeds come on finger-like stems. First keep this grass from seeding by frequent mowing; hoe or pull out young plants. A squirt of kerosene, gasoline or diesel oil on the crown usually kills it; and some crabgrass killers will get it while it is still young.

DANDELION (*Taraxacum officinale*)—A perennial, the dandelion grows practically the year around in mild climates. The best way to control dandelions is to keep grass flourishing. Keep lawn mowed high—2 to $2\frac{1}{2}$ inches. If you have only a few stragglers, dig them with an asparagus or butcher knife. Get most of the root or it soon sends up a new top. If you have lots of dandelions, spray them with 2,4-D in fall after other plants have gone dormant.

KNOTGRASS (*Polygonum aviculare*)—This is really "not grass"—it is a buckwheat, with small, long oval leaves on many-jointed stems. It grows where ground is hard—along driveways and paths, coming from seed each year. To control it, hoe or dig it out in May or June while it is young, before it seeds. Mowing does not keep it from seeding. After a plant is full grown it is hard to pull. Spraying with 2,4-D kills it, if done early.

MONEYWORT (*Lysimachia nummularia*)—Sometimes planted as a ground cover in rockeries and shady places, this plant becomes a pest when it escapes into the lawn. It has round leaves on long, creeping, rooting stems, and little yellow flowers. Where there's too much to pull by hand, spray or sprinkle it with 2,4-D or 2,4,5-T.

WILD GARLIC (*Allium* species)—Once an eastern weed, this has now reached as far west as Missouri and maybe beyond. It makes bright little clumps that rise above surrounding grass in the spring. Pinch a blade and you'll notice the onion odor. Dig it out (be sure to get it all); or spot treat it with engine oil. In very early spring you can kill it with 2,4-D.

PICK YOUR PEST CONTROL

When trouble shows up on your lawn, first find out if the cause is an insect or a disease before trying any remedies. Don't rule out dogs, spills of fertilizer, or gas or oil from the mower as possible causes.

Preventing and getting rid of insects. Perhaps the day is near when you can apply certain chemicals periodically on your lawn to prevent insect troubles. This utopia is almost here now. But the fact remains that present chemicals are so expensive, or tricky to handle, or poisonous to man and beast that most people don't want to use them until they have to. Nevertheless a step in this direction has been made by companies that put out insecticides intended to control a large number of common lawn insects, like Scott's Cope, and du Pont's Oust. Apply these according to package instructions.

Some of the chemicals you might use to control crabgrass are also powerful insecticides, so if you use those you accomplish two things at once. The bags will tell you if they control lawn insects too.

The foremost lawn insect chemicals are dieldrin, chlordane, heptachlor, diazinon and DDT. *All of these are dangerous if misused.* Observe all the warnings on the label.

Every region has insect troubles. In the North and Northeast it may be grubs, the larvae of Japanese or other beetles; in the South and East it may be chinch bugs and crickets. In the Midwest, Southwest or California it may be sod webworms or armyworms. In the South it may be ground pearls or chinch bugs.

Check Lawn Disease Before It Starts. Lawn diseases are nothing new, but as your standards go up the disease problem seems to get worse, since you are more aware of spot blights, brown patches and rusts. Two steps toward disease control are (1) good lawn care and (2) effective fungicides, put on at the right time.

Science has produced remedies called *broad-spectrum* fungicides for lawns. The name means that they control many different diseases. So you don't need to be able

LAWN INSECTS AND WHAT TO DO

Insect	What damage looks like	What insect looks like	Treat with
Ants	Unsightly mounds of dusty soil, interfere with grass growth	Brown, black or red, three-segment busy insects	Chlordane, dieldrin
Armyworms and cutworms	Grass blades are chewed	Soft gray or brown worms; adults are gray moths	Chlordane, dieldrin, heptachlor, diazinon
Chiggers	You don't see but feel these insects. They attack man, cause itchy bites, make lawn unusable	Microscopic reddish mites	Dieldrin
Chinch bugs	In hot, dry areas of lawn, scattered patches suddenly turn brown, die	$\frac{1}{8}$-inch long red or black insect with white wings and marks on back, suck juices	Dieldrin, chlordane, diazinon
Ground pearls	In the South, centipede and bermuda lawns, areas wilt, become thin, eventually die	Pinhead size yellow-white round larvae feed on roots	Water once a week and use nitrogen fertilizer to keep grass growing
Grubs	Turf browns in small or large areas; can be rolled up like carpet	Larvae of Japanese beetles, June bugs, May beetles; C-shaped white soft worms up to an inch long eat grass roots	Dieldrin, heptachlor, chlordane, diazinon
Leaf hoppers	Whitish or dried foliage, especially new grass	Tiny wedge-shaped yellow or green jumping insects	Chlordane, diazinon
Mole crickets	Roots and seedlings disturbed by burrowing runs and feeding on grass roots	Large dark crickets that jump, have short front legs	Dieldrin, heptachlor, chlordane, diazinon
Sod webworms	In late summer, turf turns straw colored, pulls up easily, in irregular patches	Brown hairy worms $\frac{3}{4}$ inch long, found in webby tunnels in soil, feed on stems, grass blades at crown. White moths lay eggs.	Dieldrin, chlordane, DDT, heptachlor, diazinon

53

LAWN DISEASES AND WHAT TO DO

Name of disease	Grasses attacked	What damage looks like	How to control it
Leaf spot, meltingout, going-out, dying-out	Bluegrass, fescue, bermuda, bentgrass, zoysia, St. Augustine, carpet	Purple-black, dark brown, light gray, tan, or yellow-brown leaf spots, with red-purple margins. Leaves turn yellow, brown, then die. Irregular areas suddenly die in hot weather. Small spots sometimes occur.	Apply broad-spectrum fungicide at 5-14 day intervals, starting in early spring.
Brown patch, large brown patch, rhizoctonia disease	Bentgrass, fescue, ryegrass, bermuda, bluegrass, centipede, zoysia, carpet, St. Augustine	Circular patches up to several feet across during hot, humid weather; first water-soaked and dark, then a light brown or bleached white. Sometimes gray-black ring of wilted "cobwebby" grass borders diseased area.	Apply broad-spectrum fungicide when night temperatures above 70°F.
Grease spot, spot blight, cottony blight	Bentgrass, fescue, bermuda, bluegrass, probably others	Round spots, several inches across with black, greasy borders. Spots turn red-brown, may streak into low areas as disease apparently spreads by mowing or flowing water. In South, small white spots, later becoming cottony are common.	Provide good drainage. Avoid overwatering. Apply broad-spectrum fungicide.
Rusts: leaf rust, crown rust, stem rust	Bluegrass (especially Merion), fescue, bermuda, bentgrass, St. Augustine	Yellow-orange, reddish or black pustules on leaves and stems. Plants may shrivel and die, or winterkill.	Water, fertilize to maintain good growth. If necessary, apply 2-3 broad-spectrum sprays 7-15 days apart.
Powdery mildew	Bluegrass, fescue, probably others	Gray-white, powdery patches in shade or poorly drained areas. Leaves may yellow, shrivel and die. Most serious on young seedlings.	Apply Acti-Dione RZ, Kromad, sulfur, Karathane WD or Mildex 1-3 times, 10 days apart.
Snow mold (gray and pink), fusarium patch, scald	Bentgrass, fescue, bluegrass, bermuda, zoysia, carpet, possibly others	Circular areas at edge of melting snow covered with a white, pink, gray or nearly black fungus growth. Dead, bleached patches may be several feet across. Do not let lawn grow long in fall. Worst in northern, humid areas.	Apply broad-spectrum fungicide (except Acti-Dione RZ), just before first snow or cold, wet period is forecast in late fall or early winter. Avoid fertilizing after Sept. 15 in northern states.
Dollar spot, small brown patch	Bentgrass, bermuda, zoysia, St. Augustine, centipede, bluegrass, fescue	Round, light brown dead spots, 2 inches across. Spots may run together. White cobwebby growth often shows when dew is present	Fertilize adequately. Apply broad-spectrum fungicide in fall and spring when disease strikes.
Fairy ring, mushrooms, toadstools, puffballs	Bluegrass, bermuda, bentgrass, probably others	Circular rings of vigorous green with ring of thin or dead grass inside. Mushrooms or puffballs may appear following wet periods. Suppress by aerating (or deep forking), watering, fertilizing.	Apply dilute monthly soil drench of Thimer, Tersan OM or Calocure, to aerated area.
Slime molds	All grasses	Small, white, gray or yellow slimy globs on grass surface. They dry to bluish-gray, black or white powder which may smother or shade grass in patches. Follows heavy rains or watering.	Rake or brush affected areas and wash down with water. If molds reappear, apply broad-spectrum fungicide.

to name the disease to do something about it. Some of these products are Tersan OM, Kromad, Thimer, and Acti-Dione RZ. In the chart they are not mentioned specifically. In each case, follow the manufacturer's directions carefully. The chart also gives a few other fungicides for special purposes.

RENOVATING AN OLD LAWN

Short of digging it all up and starting over, what can you do for an impoverished lawn full of weeds and bare spots? Actually, there is quite a bit you can do and it's worth trying if it saves you the expense and trouble of a complete doing over.

Start renovating an old lawn in the fall, August and September. First mow it as short as you can set your mower, then rake it. Rent or borrow an aerator made just for lawns or golf courses. Companies that rent power tools have them. Sometimes it is simply a spike tooth roller and you provide the power, but it works in small areas. The object is to loosen and puncture the soil without digging out all the good grass. Work this over your lawn thoroughly. Now follow with a feeding of lawn fertilizer which you spread at the rate suggested on the bag. Finally, reseed the whole lawn with the kind of grass you want to prevail in it. Set your sprinklers and water daily, unless there is rain, until the new grass is up. In the meantime keep on with your lawn mowing until winter, so the old grass does not get so tall it steals sun from the new.

The following spring, if crabgrass has been one of your problems, get out early and put on (in March as soon as snow leaves) a careful application of a pre-emergent crabgrass killer. Follow directions to the letter. If the pre-emergent is a kind that contains nitrogen fertilizer, it takes the place of a feeding; but if it has no food value, give an application of lawn food at the same time or soon after. If broadleaf weeds like dandelions have plagued your lawn, get out as soon as you see them starting to grow, and spray them with 2,4-D or apply a dry granular control with your spreader.

Pick up from here with the good lawn care described earlier in this chapter, and your lawn should be back on its feet again.

GROUND COVERS INSTEAD OF GRASS

On steep banks, rocky or wooded places, or under some trees where grass is hard to grow or mow, stop struggling. Plant a ground cover. There are dozens of little places for ground covers—under shrubs and arbors, along paths and walks, fringing foundations to prevent rain splashes and covering the feet of trees where you don't care to mow.

Choose the best ground covers for your purpose. You'll probably want them to look good the year around, and be comparatively carefree and long lived. Sometimes you'll expect them to stop banks from washing and weeds from growing, or bear up under traffic.

SIX GOOD GROUND COVERS YOU WILL ENJOY

WINTERCREEPER (*Euonymus fortunei* varieties). Zone 5. These versatile vines grow in sun or shade, any soil or exposure, and can stand light traffic. Don't put them where they are walked on continually. Space plants 12 inches apart. When established they hold steep banks.
E. f. coloratus—Fastest growing and hardiest of them, it has leaves that turn plum-purple in winter. Makes a tight cover 8 inches thick, takes two or three years to cover; permanent, few pests.
E. f. vegetus—Similar to *coloratus* but with smaller, dark green leaves all year.
ENGLISH IVY (*Hedera helix*). Zone 6. The glossy dark ivy leaves are attractive and adaptable in shade or part shade the year around. They do best where they get no traffic. By clipping stray wands, you can make neat narrow ribbons of ivy. Planted 18 inches apart it takes two to three years to cover densely, making a springy mat 6 inches thick.
H. h. baltica—Baltic ivy, is like English ivy except hardier (Zone 5), leaves are smaller and not so glossy.

55

8 Where grass is hard to mow or grow, use ground covers. English ivy carpets the niche beside paving on this shaded terrace.   *Linton*

MYRTLE (*Vinca minor*). Zone 4 or 5. Oval small glossy leaves make a 12-inch mat when established, in part shade to al-most full sun. Myrtle (also called peri-winkle) will hold a sloping bank and spreads fairly fast in moist soil. In spring, some-

9 Wintercreeper (*Euonymus*) holds the bank beside these steps and eases the task of grass trimming.

Genereux

times fall, it produces starry blue or white flowers. Set plants 12 inches apart. Covers thickly in about two years.

JAPANESE SPURGE (*Pachysandra terminalis*). Zone 5. Glossy bright green leaves are atop erect stems 8 or 10 inches high. Spreads by underground runners. Does best in semi-shade; moist humusy soil. When established will hold slopes. Set plants 8 inches apart. Makes thick cover the second year. Mulch soil with peat or compost.

HALL'S HONEYSUCKLE (*Lonicera japonica halliana*). Zone 5. This woody, trailing semi-evergreen vine grows fast for a quick cover on banks and rock piles, but it is invasive, so put it where it can't get away and run wild. Give it sun or shade, any soil. The yellow-white flowers are pleasantly fragrant. As ground cover it makes a rambling mat 10 inches thick, evergreen in the South.

FERNS, many kinds. Although most of them die down in winter, they are charming ground covers to grow in shaded places under trees, on north banks or to the north of buildings where sun never shines. Some, like hay-scented fern, weave a dense root network that binds slopes. Give them a humusy soil and water until they are established. After that ferns need nothing extra in care or site, and survive years of neglect.

Dennstaedtia punctilobula—Hay-scented fern, Zone 4, has yellow-green fronds 2 feet high that grow tightly together in a thick sod that holds soil. Give semi-shade.

Polystichum acrostichoides—Christmas fern, Zone 4, 1 to 2 feet, is an evergreen type that flourishes in humus-filled soil, in semi-shade. It spreads slowly.

Adiantum pedatum—American maidenhair fern, Zone 4, has flat graceful fronds in wheel-like arrangement, under 2 feet. Give it rich, humusy, moist soil in the shade. It combines well with broadleaf evergreen shrubs.

GROUND COVERS FOR BANKS

Banks that have slopes no greater than 45 degrees, but are too steep for lawns, can be held with ground covering plants. Success

57

10 In the warm Southwest, dichondra makes a beautiful ground cover, substituting for hard-to-grow grass.

Tatch

with such bank covers lies in a suitable soil and the care given to quick establishment of the plants. Barren soil like that sometimes exposed in highway cuts will discourage most plants. In such places, supply good soil in the planting holes. If the bank is over 10 feet long, it pays to dig a shallow gutter along the top, to lead off surface water and keep it from cascading down the bank. This prevents washouts.

Use plants that protect the soil surface the year around, not just in the growing season. The list of such plants is rather short; it contains *Euonymus coloratus, Lonicera japonica halliana* (Hall's honeysuckle), *Vinca minor,* Baltic ivy, *Pachysandra terminalis* (the last three for shade or part shade).

Among the woody plants, slightly larger possibilities are *Rosa wichuraiana,* and other creeping roses like 'Carpet of Gold,' *Cotoneaster horizontalis* and the various ground hugging junipers such as *Juniperus horizontalis procumbens,* and Sargent's juniper.

To get quick cover on steep banks, plant thickly. Mulch generously over the slope and hold it in place with netting, sacking, strings or wires woven between stakes or brush placed thinly over the ground.

Water regularly and deeply through the first season and keep weeds removed. A cedar shingle set in the ground just below each plant will make a little dike to hold back some of the water runoff until the plant can use it.

It often takes about three years to get enough cover on a difficult bank for it to hold itself without help from you. After that, however, it will be carefree and self-sustaining.

EASY-DOES-IT IDEAS

Set your hose and sprinklers over new lawn area before you finish sowing it. Then you won't have to walk on the new seeded surface and can water conveniently by just turning the faucets. This avoids uprooting seedlings by dragging the hose over them.

Mow often enough so clippings will be less than an inch long and you won't need to sweep or catch them. Short clippings won't hurt the lawn.

To see if it's really insects making brown spots on your lawn, cut the bottom out of a coffee can, push the can into turf and fill it with water. Keep it full for two to three minutes. Any bugs underneath will pop to the surface. A good way to spot chinch bugs.

TWENTY-FIVE GOOD GROUND COVERS

Name	Zone	Foliage	Berry or flower	Evergreen Deciduous	Exposure	Comment
Arctostaphylos uva-ursi Bearberry	4	Small, oval leaves on woody stems, 8 inches	Whitish flowers, persistent red berries	E	Shade where summers are hot; sun where cool	Sulks in heat. Needs perfect drainage. Cut it back in spring. Slightly acid soil.
Adiantum pedatum Maidenhair fern	4	Flat graceful fronds, wheel shaped, under 2 feet	None	D	Shade, moist humus soil	Combines well with evergreen shrubs.
Bergenia cordifolia	5	Large, glossy green foliage	Pink flowers in spring	E	Semi-shade; moist, cool	Give a gritty, lime soil.
Ceratostigma larpentae Plumbago	3	Glossy green leaves turn bronze in fall	Blue flowers in late summer	D	Sun or part shade	Late coming up in spring. Good to cover gentle slopes.
Convallaria majalis Lily-of-the-valley	3	Dark green leaves, sometimes unsightly by late summer	White fragrant bell-shaped flowers in spring	D	Shade	Any soil. Needs cool winters to produce bloom.
Cotoneaster horizontalis	5	Small, round, on low spreading stems	Small pink flowers in spring, red berries	E	Sun or light shade	Not evergreen in northern part of range.
Dennstaedtia punctilobula Hay-scented fern	4	Yellow-green fronds, two feet high	None	D	Semi-shade	Forms a thick sod, holds soil.
Euonymus fortunei coloratus Wintercreeper	5	Glossy leaves turn plum colored in fall	Rarely blooms	E	Full sun or shade	Versatile, hardy, makes 8-inch mat, covering in about three years. A greenleaf and small leaf kind available.
Fragaria vesca americana American strawberry	3	Dark green, fast spreading in mats	Small white flowers and red sweet berries in spring	D	Sun or semi-shade	Stands no traffic.
Hedera helix English ivy	6	Glossy, dark leaves on creeping stems	Rarely blooms, used as ground cover	E	Semi or full shade	Takes two or three years to cover densely; makes mat 6 inches thick.
Hedera helix baltica Baltic ivy	5	Smaller than *H. helix* and not so shiny	Seldom any	E	Semi or full shade	Similar to *H. helix* but hardier.
Juniperus horizontalis procumbens Creeping juniper	3	Long trailing branches, blue-green	None	E	Sun	Good for covering banks. Tolerates sandy or rocky soil.

60

Name		Leaves	Flowers/Fruit	Type	Exposure	Remarks
Liriope spicata Creeping liriope	6	Grass-like leaves in 8-10 inch clumps	Lilac flowers in summer; blackish fruit in fall	E	Shade or semi-shade	Best in acid soil. Forms a sod.
Lonicera japonica halliana Hall's honeysuckle	5	Trailing, oval leaves, bronzes in winter	Yellow-white, fragrant flowers in summer	E	Shade or sun	Invasive—plant where you can control it. Covers quickly; may climb trees or walls.
Lysimachia nummularia Moneywort	4 or 5	Round light green leaves on prostrate stems	Small yellow flowers in summer	$\frac{1}{2}$E	Sun or shade	May invade lawns. Stands light traffic. Roots at each joint.
Mahonia repens Creeping barberry	5	Holly-like leaves on woody, 10-inch stems	Yellow flowers, blue berries	E	Moist, cool shade	Keep from winter sun. Good under pines. Spreads underground.
Pachistima canbyi	6	Purplish in winter; dense, 10 inches high	Inconspicuous	E	Semi-shade	Needs well drained, slightly acid soil. Does not spread fast.
Phlox subulata Creeping phlox	4	Needle-like in 6-inch mounds	White, pink, red or blue flowers in early spring, showy	$\frac{1}{2}$E	Sun	'Blue Hills' has phlox-blue flowers; 'Alba' pure white. Good for rocky banks, along walls.
Polygonum reynoutria Fleecevine	5	Green leaves, stems 15 inches high, red foliage in fall	Pink blooms in fall	D	Sun	Spreads fast underground. Invasive.
Rosa wichuraiana Memorial rose	5	Glossy, small	Pink, red or white flowers	$\frac{1}{2}$E	Sun	Useful for slopes, banks. Canes take root. Spreads fast.
Sedum acre	4	Fat soft green leaves in mat 4 inches thick	Yellow flowers in spring	E	Sun or semi-shade	Trailing succulent. Good for rocky banks.
Sedum spurium	4	Dense light green, in 6-inch mat	Pink flowers in midsummer	$\frac{1}{2}$E	Sun or semi-shade	More evergreen in mild climates. Dry soil.
Thymus serpyllum Mother-of-thyme	5	Creeping, small, dark green	Purplish flowers in summer	E	Sun or light shade	Grows best where snow covers in winter; needs good drainage; stands light traffic.
Vinca minor Myrtle	4 or 5	Small oval glossy leaves make 6-inch mat	In spring, starry blue or white flowers	E	Nearly full sun to part shade	Spreads fairly fast in moist soil.
Viola species Violets	3	Dark green in 8-inch clumps	White to dark purple flowers in spring	D	Semi-shade	Some useful kinds are Confederate (*V. priceana*); Canada (*V. blanda*) and 'Royal Robe.'

Chapter 5

TREES FOR SHADE
AND BLOSSOM

What are good big trees to set out first?

The more you know about plants, the more pleasure and service they give you. You are faced with choosing from the thousands of possibilities, kinds that are just right in flower, leaf and fruit for what you want them to do, and easy to grow in the environment you have and the care you can give them.

The end is never reached in discovering new plants. Suggestions in this chapter and those to follow are only a beginning. Zone numbers given beside plant names refer to the new plant hardiness zone map (end paper of this book).

Checking the zone is one way you can tell if a plant is for you. Another way is to ask a successful gardening neighbor. What grows for him will grow for you, and he knows some that won't grow, too. A third source is a local nurseryman. He stocks plants he thinks suit your climate, and kinds you will want. But you need not stop with his selection. The whole range of plants come to your door when you shop from catalogs of nurseries that sell by mail. The commercial catalog is the fourth source of information to help you in selecting—and a most useful and interesting one, especially if it's illustrated in color.

Deciduous shade trees should be the first plants you choose.

A deciduous tree is one that loses its leaves in fall and stands bare through the winter. Where winters get cold and even in much of the South where weather is warmer, it is the principal kind of tree.

Air conditioning will never replace a good shade tree. It cools the earth in summer and warms it in winter. It slows down the wind but lets a comfortable breeze slip through. Its leafy branches absorb noise and dust and make a haven for birds. You can hang a swing from big trees or build a play house in the branches. In short, you'll have more pleasure and better living around your place if you have some good shade trees.

Before you begin to think about what kinds to plant, look at the plan for your whole yard and see how many big trees you can use and where you'll put them. The location of your neighbor's trees might change your plans too. Once a tree is planted, you won't be moving it. Make sure you set it where it does the most good to bring shade at the heat of the day.

Try to plot where the hot summer sun hits your house. Think ahead to how big the tree will grow, so you can avoid placing it where it will soon tangle with overhead wires, or interfere with paths, drives or gar-

11 *Opposite* A shade tree cools the earth in summer and warms it in winter, absorbs noise and dust, and makes a haven for birds. This towering maple shelters a group of flowering dogwoods. *Roche*

dens. Finally, put it where it flatters your house—side yards or back are usually best for large trees. If your place is about average, it has room for only two or three big trees.

If you have native trees on your lot, you are lucky. Don't even consider cutting them down. No matter what kind they are, they are far ahead of anything you can buy. You won't have to wait while they grow up, and you already know they are well adapted to your yard or they wouldn't be there.

The ideal shade tree is one that:

leafs out early,
holds leaves late in fall,
grows to the size and shape you want,
is high branched and deep rooted enough so something can grow underneath,
is free from insects and disease,
survives drouth, cold or what have you,
is neat—doesn't drop messy litter to clean up.

No one tree has all these advantages, but there are six that measure up well.

SIX IMPORTANT LARGE TREES

OAK (Quercus)

More than most trees, oaks speak of permanence. When you set out one of these you are planting for the future. There are hundreds of kinds, but nearly all grow slowly to become large and ancient trees. You'll probably have little trouble with insects or diseases. Although oaks are occasionally bothered by wilts, scales and gall insects, they seldom succumb to them. You will rarely have to pick up broken branches after storms, because oaks are strong. They send roots deep, and don't compete with your lawn or flowers for food and moisture. After they mature they make annual crops of acorns which are irresistible to squirrels and children. Most acorns are so small you won't notice them, but the large kinds (like those of the bur oak) do have to be cleaned up. All summer the foliage is dark green but in fall many oaks turn red, amber and purple. Some hold their leaves until early spring buds push them off the stem. Pin oak is one

that does. These kinds give protection to winter birds.

If you go in for the organic side of gardening, you'll prize oak leaves above all others. They are so stiff they make a springy mulch; when they rot down they make a slightly acid compost good for mulching around sour-soil plants like azaleas.

Pin oak (*Q. palustris*). To 80 feet. Zone 5. Pyramidal with lower limbs sloping earthward when young—high crowned at maturity. It is hard to grow anything underneath unless the tree is trimmed up. Small, shiny leaves turn red in fall, and stay on until late winter. Does not do well in alkaline soils.

Red oak (*Q. rubra*). To 60 feet. Zone 5. Grows fairly fast for an oak, and forms a round top with a short trunk and spreading branches. Makes thick shade. Large handsome leaves turn dark red in autumn.

Bur oak (*Q. macrocarpa*). To 100 feet. Zone 3. One of the hardiest of all the common kinds. Pyramidal when young but in age becomes rounded with spreading, irregular high limbs. Bark is furrowed and corky. Acorns are large (to $1\frac{1}{2}$ inches long) and enclosed in over-size fringed cups. Foliage in fall is not particularly colorful. This oak does well throughout the Great Plains.

White oak (*Q. alba*). To 100 feet. Zone 5. Thick trunk with spreading branches. Bright green leaves are light underneath, and turn red in fall. It is named for its whitish bark.

Scarlet oak (*Q. coccinea*). To 80 feet. Zone 5. An upright tree that has an irregular outline or when old, a broad, open crown. In fall it distinguishes itself with brilliant scarlet foliage.

MAPLE (Acer)

Compared to oaks, most maples grow fast and have greedy roots. If you are going in for a picture lawn or a show garden of roses, don't put a maple nearby. One exception to this flat statement is the hard or sugar maple, which isn't quite so greedy. Otherwise, maples are excellent as shade trees. They have pretty red buds in spring, followed by fluffy small flowers. The winged seeds that spin down in June or thereabouts are small and no bother. In summer their foliage is clean and shining, and in autumn most maples turn to glorious flame and sun colors. Their symmetrical shape and usually dark bark make them enjoyable in winter and on rainy days when they seem like silhouettes.

Sugar maple (*A. saccharum*). To 100 feet. Zone 4. The "hard" maple. It makes a symmetrical oval or round top, so strongly branched it seldom breaks in ice and wind. Fairly deep rooted and slow growing. Bark is dark gray, leaves bright green. Most beautiful in fall, when it turns to scarlet and gold. It is without serious faults except that it is susceptible to a verticillium wilt disease. Apparently it does not do well in alkaline or dry soils.

Norway maple (*A. platanoides*). To 90 feet. Zone 4. Has smooth five-lobed leaves with pointed tips. Bark is black and smooth. There is a variety with variegated green and white leaves ('Harlequin'), and another ('Schwedler's') with red leaves that turn dark green later in summer. Still a third ('Crimson King'), stays red-purple all season. In fall most of them turn yellow, and leaves hang on late. Makes dense shade.

Red maple (*A. rubrum*). To 100 feet. Zone 4. In spring it has showy red flowers, and later red seeds. In fall it is one of the first to turn red and gold. Even leaf stems are red. Summer foliage is small, dark green and shining. Upright branches form a rounded or irregular top.

Silver maple (*A. saccharinum*). To 100 feet. Zone 4. This is the riverbank maple. It is fast growing, and it stands heat and drouth well. Its trunk is short and thick, and the branches grow upward, with supple wands that arch down. The summer leaves show silver underneath when a breeze turns them, and in fall they become clear yellow. Because of the narrow angle of branching and weak wood structure these trees are bad about breaking in storms, especially when they are old. They get too big too soon for a small yard.

ASH (Fraxinus)

Some of the hardiest and toughest trees are found in this group, and they are ornamental as well. All of them have compound leaves—each leaf a structure of many smaller leaflets. In spring small male or female flowers appear with the leaves, and trees may be of different sexes. Female trees bear winged seeds in clusters that eventually fall.

White ash (*F. americana*). Usually to 80 feet. Zone 4. Makes an upright tree, usually oval. Dark green compound leaves each with up to nine large leaflets, which turn deep purple or yellow in fall.

European ash (*F. excelsior*). To 90 feet. Zone 4. Similar, but leaves are not so coarse, and are light on underneath sides. There are many varieties of this, including slow growing and dwarf kinds like *F. excelsior pendula*, weeping European ash, and *F. excelsior umbraculifera*, globeheaded European ash.

Green ash (*F. pensylvanica subinterregima*). To 60 feet. Zone 3. Fast growing tree mainly adapted from Rocky Mountains eastward, although in dry parts of the West it is often used as a street and lawn tree. It forms a neat, rounded top. There is a seedless kind called Marshall ash.

Modesto ash (*F. velutina glabra*). To 20 feet. Zone 5. Fast growing, beautiful street and shade tree with shining green foliage in summer. A round head, ability to withstand wind and adapt to any soil make this a fine choice for suburban lawns.

LINDEN (Tilia)

Sometimes called basswood, this is a widely distributed native. It has soft wood but is surprisingly tough and stands storms fairly well. Heart-shaped smooth leaves cast dense shade, and unless you trim a linden up high, you will have trouble making grass grow under it. Its seeds are winged pellets that spin like feathercocks in summer, but they are so small they never have to be cleaned up. In the fall the whole tree turns evenly gold. Most lindens grow large but not particularly fast. You can get several small kinds like *T. tomentosa* and *T. platyphyllos* for street trees. A recent introduction, the Redmond linden, is more tailored and upright than *T. americana*.

12 The honey locust casts a light shade that encourages the lawn below. 'Moraine' locust, shown here, is an improved new hybrid. *Genereux*

American linden (*T. americana*). To 100 feet. Zone 3. Usually vase-shaped with a top like an umbrella, but in the North it is smaller, more pyramidal. Leaves are large, perhaps 8 inches long.

Littleleaf linden (*T. cordata*). To 70 feet. Zone 4. Slow-growing and makes a dense rounded shape. It has fat little heart-shaped leaves of dark green, seldom larger than 3 inches across.

13   Beech trees are as beautiful in winter as in summer, because of the smooth, silvery bark.

Roche

LOCUST (Gleditsia triacanthos)

Here is a native with many good habits, and what it lacked in the beginning, plant breeders have given it. The fern-like foliage sifts the sun but does not cast dark shade. Lawn grows easily under it—also flowers. You will have little raking to do in fall, for the tiny leaflets settle into the lawn and practically disappear. Trees stand upright and are high spreading, becoming large in time, up to 100 feet. The wood is strong, and does not break easily. As natives, locusts are armed with thorns, but the cultivated kinds you'll see at the nursery are thornless. In spring they have small flowers, followed in summer by seed pods, although the choice hybrids are seedless. When they are young they grow fast.

Moraine locust. To 100 feet. Zone 4. A variety with green leaves, no thorns and no seed pods.

Sunburst locust. To 100 feet. Zone 4. A thornless kind with light yellow leaves at tips of branches, making it look as if the tree is in bloom.

CHRISTINE BUISMAN ELM (Ulmus)

Since Dutch elm disease and phloem necrosis have caused widespread destruction of American elms over much of the country, this has become the most widely recommended elm for replanting. It appears to resist both diseases—one of the very few recently introduced elm selections that does. Elms have no peer as shade trees. The Buisman elm lacks the fountain shape of the American elm when it is young. Instead, it has a central leader and develops a broad-based pyramid. As it matures the crown widens, and the tree begins to look more like the traditional street elm. It is fast growing (10 feet in four years) and wears a heavy foliage of shiny leaves. Branches are strong and withstand wind storms tenaciously.

The Buisman is a selection of smooth leaf elm (*U. carpinifolia*), which reaches a height of about 75 feet. You can grow it from Zone 5 southward, coast to coast.

68

SIX MORE LARGE TREES IF THERE IS ROOM

AMERICAN SYCAMORE (Platanus occidentalis)

Also called buttonwood. A giant often 120 feet. Zone 5. Tall, smooth, white, scal trunk is interesting all year. Broad leaves ten blight and fall in midsummer, makin mess. The one-inch round button fruits d off in fall and winter. Trees are stro break-resistant, and stand city life, dro heat and cold well. They cast a thin, h shade. The London planetree is similar does not drop leaves all summer.

EUROPEAN BEECH (Fagus sylvatica)

To 80 feet. Zone 5. Handsome, oval, lo lived trees with smooth gray bark and sh ing dark leaves on branches that hang ne to the ground. Don't try to grow anyth under them. They take large space but m magnificent specimens where they do w which is mainly east of the Mississi River. Purple-leaf, copper-leaf and colu nar forms are also to be had.

GINKGO (Ginkgo biloba)

To 80 feet. Zone 4. Fan-shaped lea graceful, thinly held on ascending branc attached to a central trunk. Grows slow but can take drouth, heat and cold. *Av using female trees*—they drop messy a smelly fruit. You can get males from n eries. In fall ginkgo turns bright yellow a leaves all drop within a few days. Good py midal and columnar forms are available.

KENTUCKY COFFEE TREE (Gymnocladus dioicus)

To 75 feet. Zone 4. Large, compound, l foliage. The leaves are so big that when tl drop in fall you'll think the tree is losing limbs too. Clusters of flowers in June, lowed by bean-like pods that hang on winter. Hardy and tolerant from the Ro ies eastward. If you don't want the pods, male trees only.

14 Redbud, which flowers with dogwood, is occasionally found in this rare white form.
Roche

15 The many kinds of flowering crabapples glow with color in spring, and again with red-yellow fruits in fall. *Genereux*

SWEET GUM (Liquidambar styraciflua)

To 80 feet. Zone 5. Where they grow well, the most beautiful trees for red-gold fall color. Star-shaped leaves, compact, on rounded tree. Ball-shaped fruits hang on into winter. Transplant when young, with earth ball. Needs soil moisture, and is seldom seen in alkaline soils.

TULIP TREE (Liriodendron tulipifera)

To 100 feet. Zone 5. Transplant with earth ball, when small. Trees grow fast, making a tall straight trunk and cylindrical outline. The wood is very brittle. Flowers enclosed in large green and orange cups or "tulips" come among the leaves in June. In fall foliage turns yellow, and in winter curious seed "cones" hang on.

SIX SMALL TREES FOR SHADE

AMUR CORK TREE (Phellodendron amurense)

To 50 feet. Zone 4. Shining, divided leaves cast light shade; they turn yellow in fall. Corky gray bark is interesting in winter, along with black berry fruits that hang on. Spreads to 30 feet, making a rounded head. Stands city conditions.

CUTLEAF WEEPING BIRCH (Betula pendula *varieties*)

To 45 feet. Zone 3. In winter the white peeling bark and hanging branches are attractive, and in summer the delicate dark green leaves make fine shade in a small yard. It grows fast if it has coolness and moisture. If your summers really warm up, place the birch on north of trees or buildings, out of hot winds. Don't attempt it in the South.

GOLDENRAIN (Koelreuteria paniculata)

Also called varnish tree. To 30 feet. Zone 5. Rounded, spreading to 25 feet, with fine-cut leaves, yellow flowers in pointed clusters in summer, followed by red-brown balloon-like pods that last until fall. Smooth, gray-

barked skeleton is attractive in winter. Withstands dry, limy soils and drouth.

HORSECHESTNUT (Aesculus hippocastanum)

To 60 feet. Zone 4. Round-headed handsome trees, sometimes with divided trunks. Flowers come above dark green foliage in May or June, erect red-white clusters followed by bristly nuts. They are strong trees and seldom break.

JAPANESE PAGODA TREE (Sophora japonica)

To 60 feet. Zone 5. Round crown spreads to 40 feet, above a short trunk. Foliage is lacy, dark green. Creamy pea-like flowers come in loose long clusters in midsummer, followed in fall by small seed pods. Does well in cities.

WEEPING WILLOW (Salix babylonica *or hybrids*)

To 45 feet. Zone 5. Rounded trees with long trailing branches that sweep in the wind. In spring twigs turn bright yellow. Do not plant near sewer lines or lateral systems—the roots will invade. Fast growing if soil is moist.

SIX SMALL TREES
FOR SPRING BLOSSOMS

FLOWERING CRAB (Malus *species and varieties*)

Flowering crabapples are the most sure-fire small trees you can get for spring flowers, no matter where you live. They form rounded symmetrical shapes. Most of them are long lived and ultra-hardy, and many are fragrant. Colors go from white to purple-pink and sizes from dwarfs like the Sargent to giants like the Siberian. Most of them spread as much as they go up, so allow space. After the flowers you'll have small red or yellow apples that make a lively show. Birds and squirrels love them. Flowers last two weeks, usually opening in May; Bech-

16 The crisp, horizontal look of flowering dogwood is as charming in your yard as in the woodlands.   *Weber*

17 Of starry aspect, the Korean dogwood blooms later than the native kind, and has strawberry-like seed fruit.   *Genereux*

tel's is a little later. Plant in full sun. Do not fertilize. Some, like 'Hopa,' make good jelly.

M. baccata, Siberian crab, to 30 feet, Zone 3, white, early.

M. floribunda, Japanese crab, to 25 feet, Zone 5, pink.

M. sargenti, Sargent crab, to 10 feet, Zone 5, small, white.

M. ioensis plena, Bechtel's crab, to 15 feet, Zone 3, double pink, late.

Hopa crab, a hybrid, to 25 feet, Zone 4, deep pink.

FLOWERING DOGWOOD
(Cornus florida)

To 25 feet. Zone 5. The pleasing horizontal spread (12 feet or more) and crisp white flowers in May make this a favorite small tree. It does best in dappled shade of taller trees. In autumn the oval leaves turn to crimson, and after they fall you can still see some of the scarlet fruit clusters hanging on. In winter the gray twigs are swollen with flower buds for the next season. Transplant while young, in spring, with earth ball. Tolerates most soils, but not the hot, dry winds of the plains. You can also get a pink flowering kind under various names like *C. rubra* and 'Cherokee Chief.'

FLOWERING PEACH (Prunus persica)

To 20 feet. Zone 5. For sheer show, the flowering peaches outdo all the other flowering fruit types. They start to bloom the first year with splashy double flowers. Like all peaches they have a short life span, and you're lucky if they last ten years for you. But then you can start over, maybe with a different variety. Plant them in spring only, full sun, and prune them heavily after they bloom. Allow space for a 20-foot spread. 'Iceberg' is a pure double white; 'Cardinal' rich double red; and 'Peppermint Stick' white with red streaks.

REDBUD (Cercis canadensis)

To 30 feet. Zone 5. In April and May, before leaves appear, rosy pink flowers shaped like little sweet peas cover the twigs and even the trunk. Redbud opens just before the dogwood and blooms awhile with it. The tree grows into a flat-topped shape that in age becomes irregular. It grows naturally under shade of high trees, but tolerates full sun, although trunks of young trees may sunscald in winter. In autumn short seed pods hang on after leaves fall. Some nurseries offer a white form and a clear pink. Takes drouth, heat, cold and quick changes all in stride and never fails to bloom.

SAUCER MAGNOLIA
(Magnolia soulangeana)

To 30 feet. Zone 5. In April and May, on bare gray branches, the waxy pink and white saucer-shaped flowers open, to last three weeks, if weather permits. Leaves are long, dark, thick and glossy. Trees become spreading, as wide as high, with low sweeping branches. Knobby seed pods appear in late summer. After leaves fall the furry buds for next year show up. You can transplant these trees when they are in bloom, but the fleshy roots do not move easily. The nursery always sells them balled and burlapped or in cans. Plant in sun or light shade. Keep new trees watered well the first summer. This is the hardiest magnolia. You can get it in color variations from white (*alexandrina*) to purple pink (*nigra*).

WASHINGTON HAWTHORN
(Crataegus phaenopyrum)

To 25 feet. Zone 5. In May, creamy white flowers in crowded clusters cover the rounded thorny trees. This is one of the last of the many hawthorns to bloom and probably the easiest because it is widely adapted climatically, and resists the cedar-apple rust which attacks other kinds. In fall when the small scarlet berries appear, you'll have

18 *Opposite* Sweet gum makes an autumn show with red-gold starry leaves and then falls bare to show the bobbing brown seed balls all winter.
Roche

more spectacular color than in the spring. The berries remain far into winter unless robins and cedar waxwings eat them. Fall foliage is red. Always transplant hawthorns in spring. Have them balled and burlapped or container grown.

SIX SMALL TREES
FOR LATER FLOWERS

GOLDENCHAIN (Laburnum watereri) (vossi)

To 25 feet. Zone 6. Wisteria-like flowers of yellow hang from the branches in June. Clover-like green leaves cover the upright branches, which spread to 10 or 15 feet. In winter the distinctive green of the twigs is eye-catching. This little tree is slightly particular where it grows. It can't stand much heat or drouth, so if your summers are that way, set this in part shade on the north side of your house and give it plenty of water, but good drainage. It does well in lime-rich soil.

JAPANESE DOGWOOD (Cornus kousa chinensis)

To 20 feet. Zone 5. An upright spreading tree with wavy foliage like *Cornus florida,* but it blooms in June. The white flower bracts are pointed at the tips, giving each cluster the appearance of a star, and a well-endowed tree the look of a heavenly galaxy. The fruit ripening in September is a fleshy pink ball looking a little like a strawberry. The leaves turn scarlet in autumn. Give full sun or semi-shade, a humusy soil and protect from hot winds.

MIMOSA (Albizzia julibrissin)

To 25 feet. Zone 6. Fast growing, round topped spreading trees once considered Southern, but they have moved a long way north. The much-divided foliage has a tropical look. In June, July and August fluffy pink blooms open above the leaves. Many times the trunks branch at the ground, and the plants usually spread wider than they are high. They volunteer from seeds, are

easily transplanted and begin blooming while only a few years old. This plant apparently can stand any amount of heat, and drouth does not seem to stop it, although you should water young ones the first two years to get them started. Give sun and any garden soil. Variety *rosea* seems to be the most hardy.

ROSE ACACIA (Robinia hispida)

To 10 feet. Zone 5. In late May and June it opens showy drooping clusters of rose-colored flowers, each shaped like a sweet pea bloom. The plant is brittle and small with locust-like foliage, armed with the thickest prickles you ever saw, and *much given to root suckering.* Kinds offered by nurseries are usually grafted on a locust of a different sort to prevent suckers from coming up all around. This plant grows in shade, in any sort of soil and can take drouth and heat. A good variety is 'Monument.'

TREE LILAC (Syringa amurensis japonica)

To 25 feet. Zone 4. A lilac in tree form with a short trunk and upright branches that form a rounded top. In June at the ends of the branches it opens large clusters of creamy flowers that are pleasantly fragrant. Foliage is of typical lilac shape, and large. It grows under toughest conditions of heat, drouth and cold.

WHITE FRINGETREE (Chionanthus virginica)

To 20 feet. Zone 5. Sometimes this is shaped like a shrub, but you can train it to a single trunk if you try. Always late in leafing out, it makes a nice little oval tree with long pointed leaves that turn bright yellow in autumn. In late May and June it displays drooping clusters of pure white very fragrant feathery blooms. It has blue seed berries in September. Tolerates weather extremes pretty well and has a wide range. It grows in gardens in Omaha, Nebraska, and Minneapolis, Minnesota, for two examples, and is native in Southeastern United States. Give it fertile light soil, sun and good drain-

19 The well-named saucer magnolia (*M. soulangeana*) is a glamorous tree in early spring, with waxen pink blooms.　　*Roche*

20 Star magnolia (*M. stellata*) bears a profusion of fragrant white and pink flowers that come early, before the leaves.　　*Roche*

TALL TREES FOR SHADE

(Use these where you have plenty of room)

Name	Zone	Height (feet)	Growth rate	Shape	Faults	Soil or exposure	Care or characteristics
Acer negundo Box elder	3	70	Fast	Broad crown	Rather weak; attracts box elder bugs	Any dry, sunny site	Resists drouth. Good for windbreaks, but not near house. Best in semi-arid regions.
A. platanoides Norway maple	4	90	Moderate to fast	Oval or rounded, dense	Shallow-rooting	Sun, any soil	Good fall coloring; some varieties have variegated or red leaves.
A. rubrum Red maple	4	100	Moderate to fast	Rounded or irregular	Shallow-rooting	Sun, any soil	Has red flowers and seeds, and dark green leaves turn red-gold in fall. Small foliage.
A. saccharinum Silver maple	4	100	Fast	Arching	Too big for small yards; breaks easily in wind storms	Sun, any soil	Tolerates heat and drouth; sometimes used in shelterbelts.
A. saccharum Sugar maple	4	100	Slow to moderate	Oval or rounded top	A wilt disease sometimes attacks it	Acid or neutral, moist soil; sun	Fairly deep rooted and strongly branched.
Carya ovata Shagbark hickory	5	100	Rapid	Oblong top	Difficult to transplant; not for small gardens	Rich, moist; sun	Fruit ripe in September. Wind resistant, tough. Very tasty nuts.
Celtis occidentalis Hackberry	3	80	Fast	Tall, high branching, open	Seedlings are a weed problem; witches' broom is a disfiguring disease	Any soil, sun	Difficult to transplant. Blue seed-berries are relished by birds.
Fagus sylvatica European beech	5	80	Moderate	Oval	Low-growing; nothing will grow underneath	Sun, any soil (mainly east of Mississippi)	Handsome year around; purple leaf, coppery, and columnar forms available.
Fraxinus americana White ash	4	80	Moderate	Upright, oval	Seed clusters may make clutter	Sun, any soil	Leaves are large, rather coarse.
F. excelsior European ash	4	90	Moderate	Upright, oval	Seeds are a bother unless you use male trees	Sun, any soil	Some slow growing and dwarf kinds are available.
F. pensylvanica subinterregima Green ash	3	60	Fast	Rounded	Seeds a bother except with male trees	Sun, any soil; tolerates drouth, wind	A seedless kind is called Marshall ash.

Name				Shape	Problems	Culture	Remarks
F. velutina glabra Modesto ash	5	20	Fast	Rounded		Sun, any soil; tolerates drouth, wind	Well adapted for small lawn or street tree; much used in the West.
Ginkgo biloba Ginkgo	4	80	Slow	Tall, ascending branches	Female trees drop messy fruit	Sun, any soil	Use male trees; good pyramidal and columnar forms are available.
Gleditsia triacanthos Locust	4	100	Fast	High and open	May be attacked by borers or leaf eating insects	Any soil, sun	Thornless, seedless kinds are available, like Moraine, Shademaster; and a yellow-tipped variety called Sunburst.
Gymnocladus dioicus Kentucky coffee tree	4	75	Moderate	Rounded, open	Late leafing out; pods of female trees may make clutter	Sun, any soil; tolerates drouth	Use male trees only if you want no pods. Enormous compound leaves.
Juglans nigra Black walnut	5	100	Moderate	Rounded, spreading	Don't plant in root distance of vegetable or flower garden; tomato and some of its relatives react unfavorably to the presence of this tree in the vicinity; foliage falls early	Fertile, well drained	Nuts ripen in October and November. Grafted kinds bear by third to fifth year. Need space.
Liquidambar styraciflua Sweet gum	5	80	Moderate	Rounded		Sun, any moist soils except heavily alkaline	Red-gold fall color is unsurpassed. Ballshaped fruits hang on all winter.
Liriodendron tulipifera Tulip tree	5	100	Fast	Tall, cylindrical	Wood is brittle, breaks easily	Sun, any soil	Transplant when small, with earth ball. Tulip-shaped flowers, June.
Platanus occidentalis American sycamore	5	120	Fast	Tall, high, open	Leaves often fall in midsummer	Any soil, sun; tolerates drouth, poor soil	A smaller, more tailored tree, closely related, is the London planetree, which holds leaves all season.
Populus alba nivea Silver poplar	4	80	Fast	Broad	Suckers must be kept down; roots run on surface; weak wood	Sun, any soil	Pretty when the wind blows.
P. nigra italica Lombardy poplar	4	100	Fast	Tall like exclamation point	Short lived; winter-kills sometimes	Sun, any soil; tolerates wetness	Clean, no seeds or fruit. Wind resistant. Plant 5-6 feet apart for dense screen.
Quercus alba White oak	5	100	Slow	Spreading		Any soil, full sun	Leaves turn red in fall. Bark is whitish.

TALL TREES FOR SHADE (continued)

Name	Zone	Height (feet)	Growth rate	Shape	Faults	Soil or exposure	Care or characteristics
Q. coccinea Scarlet oak	5	80	Slow	Upright, irregular		Any soil, full sun	Brilliant scarlet foliage in fall.
Q. macrocarpa Bur oak	3	100	Slow	Rounded, irregular when mature	Large acorns may litter a fine lawn	Any soil, full sun	Very hardy and tolerant. Fall foliage not particularly colorful.
Q. palustris Pin oak	5	80	Moderate	Pyramidal when young, then rounded	Low limbs impede growing things below	Acid or neutral soil	Leaves stay on all winter.
Q. rubra Red oak	5	60	Moderate	Rounded, spreading		Any soil, full sun	Handsome dark red coloring in fall.
Sassafras albida Sassafras	5	80	Moderate	Rounded, irregular	Not easy to transplant; suckers to be controlled	Acid, shade	Aromatic stems and roots. Colorful scarlet fall foliage. Yellow spring bloom.
Tilia americana American linden	3	100	Slow	Umbrella-shaped when mature	Dense shade and shallow roots handicap lawns	Sun, any soil	Good gold color in fall; winged seeds are interesting, small.
T. cordata Littleleaf linden	4	70	Slow	Dense, rounded	Large specimens cast heavy shade	Sun, any soil	Has small, heart-shaped leaves.
Ulmus 'Christine Buisman' Buisman hybrid elm	5	75	Moderate	Pyramidal when young		Sun, any soil	Apparently completely resistant to Dutch elm disease and phloem necrosis. Takes city conditions.
U. pumila Siberian elm (also called Chinese)	4	50	Very fast	Spreading	Invasive roots bad next to garden	Sun, any soil	Extremely hardy. Good foliage color, autumn.

LOW TREES MAINLY FOR SHADE
(Use where space is limited)

Name	Zone	Height (feet)	Growth rate	Shape	Faults	Soil, site	Comment
Aesculus hippocastanum Horsechestnut	4	60	Fast	Rounded, spreading	Casts a very dense shade	Sun, any soil	Showy flowers followed by bristly nuts.
Amelanchier canadensis Shadblow (Serviceberry)	5	40	Medium	Round top on tall slender tree	Alternate host for juniper rust	Any soil, moist	Profuse white flowers in April, May. Red berries, June, July.
Betula nigra River birch	5	60	Fast	Upright oval	Often suckers at base	Sun, any soil, moist	Trunk is usually divided; has ragged red bark.
Betula pendula varieties Cutleaf weeping birch and European birch	3	45	Medium	Hanging	Sometimes is attacked by borers, not long lived	Sun or part shade, any moist soil	Protect from intense heat. White bark develops after several years.
Carpinus betulus European hornbeam	4	50	Slow	Pyramidal, broad		Any, moist, part shade or sun	Often used for tall hedges, withstands storms; has strong wood.
Castanea mollissima Chinese chestnut	5	60	Slow	Rounded		Sandy loam	Bears when young, but two trees are needed for pollination. Not subject to chestnut blight.
Cladrastis lutea Yellowwood	4	50	Medium	Rounded, low branched		Average, sun	Showy white fragrant flowers, June. Stands drouth.
Elaeagnus angustifolia Russian olive	3	25	Fast	Irregular	Sometimes spiny	Any, sun	Fragrant flowers in spring. Silver-gray foliage. Hardy, wind resistant. Good for windbreak. Stands drouth.
Koelreuteria paniculata Goldenrain tree	5	30	Fast	Rounded, spreading		Average, sun	Withstands dry limy soils and drouth.
Phellodendron amurense Amur cork tree	4	50	Fast when young	Rounded, spreading		Average, sun	Stands city conditions. Has black berries in fall. Corky bark.
Salix babylonica or hybrids Weeping willow	5	45	Fast	Rounded, trailing	Roots may invade sewer lines	Sun, moist soil	Graceful in a breeze, winter and summer.
Sophora japonica Japanese pagoda tree	5	60	Medium	Rounded crown, spreading		Sun, any soil	Pea-like flowers appear in midsummer. Stands city conditions.

FLOWERING TREES YOU'LL PRIZE FOR BLOOMS

Name	Zone	Height	Bloom	Flower description	Shape	Sun or shade	Soil	Comment
Aesculus carnea Red horsechestnut	4	30	May, June	Pink to deep red erect, candlelike clusters	Rounded, shiny foliage	Sun or semi-shade	Average	Slightly prickly, 1½-inch fruit.
Albizzia julibrissin Mimosa (Silk tree)	6	25	July, August	Pink puffballs	Wide spreading	Sun	Average	Fast growing, heat tolerant, fairly hardy when established.
Cercis canadensis Redbud	5	30	April, May	Rose-pink, white	Flat-topped	Sun or high shade	Average	Reliable; a good combination with white dogwood.
C. chinensis Chinese redbud	6	15	April, May	Rose-purple, in small clusters	More shrubby than native redbud	Sun or high shade	Rich, sandy	Glossy foliage, turns yellow in fall. Needs drainage; is sensitive to climate extremes.
Chionanthus virginica White fringetree	5	20	May, June	Feathery, white	Upright, oval	Sun	Fertile, well drained	Needs some protection in the North.
Cornus florida Flowering dogwood	5	25	May	White or pink	Spreading, horizontal	Dappled shade	Average, moist humus	Crimson autumn color. Not for windy, hot, dry sites.
C. kousa chinensis Japanese dogwood	5	20	June	White, starry	Upright, spreading	Sun or semi-shade	Humusy	Scarlet foliage in fall; strawberry-like fruit.
Crataegus oxyacantha English hawthorn	5	15	May	White or rose-pink in large clusters	Rounded with low branches	Sun	Limy, sandy loam	Susceptible to cedar-apple rust, therefore hard to grow around junipers. Large red berries in fall. Best east of Mississippi River.
C. phaenopyrum Washington hawthorn	5	25	May	Cream-white	Rounded, thorny	Sun	Average	Transplant with earth ball; red autumn berries are showy.

Franklinia alatamaha (*Gordonia*) Franklin tree	6	20	August-October	3-inch, white cup-shaped, like single camellias	Shrubby, with upright stems	Sun	Moist, humusy	Small round fruit; autumn foliage red. Not satisfactory in extreme climates. The last tree to bloom.
Halesia monticola Great silverbell	5	40	April, May	White, drooping, in clusters	Short trunk, broad crown	Sun or semi-shade	Acid, loam	Fall color yellow. Nut-like fruit. Needs well-drained sheltered site.
Laburnum watereri (*vossi*) Goldenchain	6	25	June	Yellow, hanging in clusters	Upright	Part shade or sun	Limy, well-drained	Protect from intense heat, drouth; a north exposure may be best.
Magnolia soulangeana Saucer magnolia	5	30	April-May	White to purple-pink	Spreading, irregular	Sun, light shade	Any	Transplant with earth ball if possible; in spring.
M. stellata Star magnolia	5	15	March, April	White or pink, star-like, before leaves appear	Rounded, wide spreading	Sun	Any, with humus added	Fruit in September, October, to 2 inches long, twisted, cylindrical.
Malus baccata Siberian crab	3	30	May	White	Rounded	Sun	Average	Early, extremely hardy, large.
M. floribunda Japanese crab	5	25	May	Pink	Rounded	Sun	Average	
M. 'Hopa' Hopa crab	4	25	May	Deep pink	Rounded, upright	Sun	Average	Red fruits good for jelly.
M. ioensis plena Bechtel's crab	3	15	Late May	Double pink	Rounded	Sun	Average	Especially susceptible to cedar-apple rust. Avoid using near juniper plantings.
M. sargenti Sargent crab	5	10	May	Small white	Rounded	Sun	Average	One of the smallest kinds of crab.

FLOWERING TREES YOU'LL PRIZE FOR BLOOMS (continued)

Name	Zone	Height	Bloom	Flower description	Shape	Sun or shade	Soil	Comment
Paulownia tomentosa Princess tree	6	40	April, May	Two-inch, violet, spotted, in large clusters	Open, like catalpa	Sun	Rich loam	Often winterkills in North.
Prunus blireiana Flowering plum	5	15	May	Semi-double pink among developing purple leaves	Rounded	Sun	Average	Leaves stay purple all season.
P. persica Flowering peach	5	20	Early May	White, red, pink	Open, spreading	Sun	Average	Usually short lived, but showy.
P. serrulatus (sargenti) Flowering cherry	5	30	April, May	Double white, pale pink, to dark red	Upright, spreading in time	Sun	Rich, well drained	Less drouth-tolerant and adaptable than flowering crabs. Try variety James Veitch, double-flowering pink.
Robinia hispida Rose acacia	5	10	May, June	Rose, in drooping clusters	Spreading, open	Sun or shade	Average	May root sucker unless you use grafted variety.
Sorbus aucuparia European mountainash	3	30	May, June	Small, whitish, in clusters, showy	Pyramidal	Sun or semi-shade	Average	Fern-like leaves. Red berries in fall. For northern states.
Syringa amurensis japonica Tree lilac	4	25	June	Creamy clusters	Rounded	Sun	Any	Very tolerant of trying conditions.

82

21 Native trees—walnuts, oaks, maples, and a birch—wisely preserved by the builder of this home, have added immeasurably to the beauty of it. *Scott*

age. Northern gardeners should give it a sheltered site and winter protection.

EASY-DOES-IT IDEAS

When you plant a tree over your patio, choose a neat and tidy kind, not one that keeps you busy all summer cleaning up under it. Avoid those with messy seeds or fruit, or those that drop leaves prematurely.

Locate big trees where you get the advantage of the shade they cast—to the south or southwest of the living part of your yard.

If your space is limited, it helps to know you can grow some small flowering trees in the shade of large ones. For instance, you can have dogwoods or redbuds in the shade of your elms or oaks.

PART II

THE RIGHT PLANT
FOR THE RIGHT PLACE

Chapter 6

FLOWERING SHRUBS ARE YOUR BEST FRIENDS

What easy plants will give me lots of color?

The most color for the least effort and expense—that sums up what you get from flowering shrubs. If you want color through the year, without burdensome upkeep, shrubs are your answer. Besides flowers, most of these plants give a wide variety of color and texture of foliage. Some of them, like the smoke tree, are quite beautiful— you can use these shrubs as screens for privacy or to divide areas. For good measure many kinds also produce colorful fruit. This is a dividend for you and the birds. (See Chapter 16.) A few even rate on one more score—they stand out in the winter landscape because of picturesque structure —leaves that hang on, or uncommon twig color—the red-twig dogwood, for instance, or the kerria.

Shrubs are for the small place or the large. You can find something of a size to fit almost any spot. Substitute large shrubs for trees where you are really pinched for room. If space is what you have most of, you can let yourself go. Use tall shrubs to face down tree borders for wind control and to block out views you'd rather not see. Use them along a boundary for privacy. Make "rooms" with them around your work or living areas. Use them for bright color accents through the season among lineups of broadleaf or needle evergreens. You'll enjoy bringing the budded branches inside in January and February to force for pre-season

flowers. Later there will be many more for cutting at the regular blooming time.

The main business of taking care of flowering shrubs comes at the beginning. Give them the right location so they get what they need of sun or shade, drainage and soil. It's most important to choose them for climatic suitability. If your weather is too dry, too hot, too cold, or your soil too alkaline, too acid or whatever, you'll have trouble growing certain shrubs. It's best to find this out before you plant and choose something more suitable.

Your gardening neighbors, your nurseryman and your nursery mail catalogs are sources of knowledge about the best shrubs for you. In our suggestions, the zones referred to are ways of knowing whether a shrub is likely to do well for you. (See zone map on inside cover of this book.)

What do *you* want in a shrub? The main things are:

hardiness in your climate,
a size at maturity to fit your space,
interesting and pleasing bloom,
handsome foliage in spring, summer, and fall,
berries or seeds that add to beauty,
carefree and long life.

From our lists, you can find several that meet your requirements.

With most of these, once you've planted them, the work is practically over and you can sit back and enjoy them for the rest of your days. If you must find some chores to do, you can study ways of rejuvenating old-timers. (See Chapter 21.) On a few you may find insects or diseases that require occasional spraying.

SIX IMPORTANT FLOWERING SHRUBS

FLOWERING QUINCE (Chaenomeles japonica)

From 18 inches to 8 feet, depending on variety. Zone 5. One of the first to bloom in spring. Most kinds are scarlet, pink, or deep red; but a few like 'Charming' have salmon flowers or white ones, like 'Nivalis.' Blooms come just before leaves or along with them, appearing the full length of the spiny stems. Leaves are dark green and glossy. The plant makes thick, upright growth from the base and is one of the few shrubs grown for flowers that also makes a good clipped hedge. Use tall kinds like *C. rubra* (6 feet) in a shrub border or for a background or screen. Low kinds, like 'Knaphill,' belong

in front of the border or foundation planting, or as a low edging. It seldom gets above 18 inches high, and is that wide. In the fall, you may find fruit hanging among the branches, little apple- or pear-shaped yellow quinces. Plants tend to sucker around the base. Simply cut out the extras.

FORSYTHIA (Forsythia horticultural forms)

From 8 to 12 feet. Zone 5. Goldenbell is another name for these, probably the most common flowering shrubs in America. They bloom in April and early May, covering themselves with golden flowers before the leaves appear. Put forsythias in a shrub border where they can make large plants with upward-reaching branches. If you place one where it does not have a spread of at least 6 feet you will be constantly trimming at it, because forsythias grow fast and far. Although plants are hardy even in northern states, they are not satisfactory north of Zone 5, because flower buds too often winterkill. 'Spring Glory' has abundant light yellow flowers and is especially good for forcing indoors. 'Lynwood Gold' has bells

22 'Hills of Snow' hydrangea makes a showy midsummer shrub in partial shade.   *Taloumis*

23 *Opposite* Cornelian cherry (*Cornus mas*) rings in the new flowering season with its early blooms of gold. *Roche*

24 *Below Left* Forsythia or golden bell is probably the most widely planted flowering shrub in America and is a favorite for forcing. *Roche*

25 *Below Right* Often called the pink snowball, the *Viburnum carlesi* is unmatched for its heavenly fragrance. *Roche*

of deep yellow. 'Beatrix Ferrand' has golden flowers that, like the bush itself, reach large size, the flowers perhaps 2 inches across. Dwarf forsythia forms, like 'Arnold,' available now from a few nurseries, are better than the other varieties for small yards. Give full sun, average soil.

MOCKORANGE (Philadelphus)

To 10 feet with 5 foot spread. Zone 4. In late May the mockorange opens clusters of gleaming white flowers which in many varieties are quite fragrant. They go well in a border of mixed shrubs, but make a poor screen because of thinness at the base. You will prize the blooms for cutting. They grow upward, sometimes with irregular branches. Keep them in shape by pruning right after blooming. A maze of different kinds exist, all distinct in small ways. *Philadelphus coronarius* is the common fragrant kind, making a 10-foot arching plant with small, single, white flowers. *P. virginalis* is also common; it has fragrant double or semidouble flowers, but often makes a gangling upright bush. Among hybrids of *P. lemoinei* are named varieties such as 'Belle Etoile,' a 5-foot shrub with fragrant starlike small flowers, touched with purple at the base. Average soil suits them, and they tolerate all sorts of climatic extremes. They will grow in full sun or part shade but in too much shade they may not bloom.

LILAC (Syringa vulgaris hybrids)

To 8 feet, spreading to 6 feet. Zone 3. These are the ones called French hybrids, although the term is not always accurate. They bloom in May with pointed clusters of fragrant white, lavender, "blue," magenta, or purple florets, single and double, late and early. Use lilacs in borders, tall unclipped hedges or screens, or as specimens close to the house where you can smell the unrivaled fragrance and admire the bloom. Although plants grow large, they never get rank, so they go well at a house corner or beside a gate.

Plant lilacs in spring or fall, spring preferred. Set them in full sun two inches

deeper than they stood in the nursery. This is so they will form roots above the graft and be long lived. Many lilacs do not flower until they mature, so you may wait a few years before seeing bloom.

Caring for lilacs is an occasional thing. They need pruning every year or two to cut out at ground level some of the oldest, woodiest branches. New shoots will replace them. Around the base you will probably find suckers. A few of these you can leave for future stems, but slice most of them off below the ground with the spade, or if you like you can dig them with some roots attached to get new plants. Lilacs sometimes need protection from scale insects and borers. (See Chapter 26.) Their one climatic requirement is cold winters—so they are not practical in the South.

Good varieties: 'Vestale' (white, single); 'Paul Thirion' (magenta, double); 'Marechal Foch' (carmine-rose, single, large, early); 'Edith Cavell' (double, cream-white); 'Firmament' (blue, single); 'Ludwig Spaeth' (single, purple); 'Henri Martin' (lilac, double); 'Mme. Antoine Buchner' (lilac-pink, double).

See the chart at the end of this chapter for another type of lilac.

PINK SNOWBALL (Viburnum carlesi)

To 6 feet with a 5-foot spread. Zone 5. Indispensable! This is not the old-fashioned Japanese snowball that was attacked by aphids every spring. Carlesi is a stiff-leafed kind with light pink ball-shaped 3-inch flower heads that open early, usually in April. They have the most delightful, spicy fragrance you ever smelled.

Put this in a border of mixed shrubs or use it near a corner of the house as you would a lilac. The fragrance is something you won't want to keep at a distance. This shrub is not good as a background or screen because you can usually see right through it. Yet the plant is balanced, globe-shaped, and branched just enough to make it attractive in summer and winter. In fall the leaves turn bronze-red. All winter you can see flower buds already formed and waiting for spring. For a small yard this shrub is one of the best. Plant it in full sun or light

26 The mockorange, *Philadelphus,* bears pure white flowers in luxuriant clusters. This is the fragrant variety 'Innocence.'   *Tiemann*

27 In a large space, the doublefile viburnum is a graceful shrub. Flower clusters have two kinds of blooms, large at the rim, small in the center.   *Roche*

28 Butterfly bush, *Buddleia davidi,* may die to the ground in hard winters, but it comes up again to bloom in midsummer with fragrant white, pink, or purple spikes that attract butterflies.   *Roche*

29 Showy violet berries of buckshot size are the main attraction of the beautyberry or *Callicarpa.* Berries mature in autumn.   *Genereux*

shade. It grows in any soil and tolerates summer heat, drouth, and sudden changes.

AZALEA (Certain Rhododendron species and varieties)

From 3 to 6 feet. Zones 8 to 5 depending on kind. Where you can grow azaleas, they give more brilliant spring color than any other shrub. Orange, red, yellow, lilac, pink, and white blooms obscure the plants at flowering time, which comes from March to June. Most azaleas do not tolerate limey soils. If your soil is lime-rich, neutral, or on the alkaline side, you have to make special provisions about this or else plant something else. As you go westward, climatic conditions get more difficult for azaleas, too, although the frontier is widening. In the plains west of Kansas City they are probably more trouble than they are worth. In the far southeastern United States and the Northwest, on the other hand, conditions are close to ideal, and you can grow almost any kind you choose.

Placement is important. Select a site that gets sun for a few hours in the morning, but shade in the heat of the day. Either a northeast corner or a place on the north in open shade is good. Don't put them in dark shade or they won't bloom. Protect them from wind, both winter and summer. A north sloping site is excellent because of coolness and drainage.

You can't add too much humus for azaleas. If your soil tests alkaline, excavate a hole a foot and a half deep and a yard across and remove all the soil. Replace it with a mixture of moist acid peat moss (one part), rotted leaf mold from the woods or your compost pile (one part) and coarse river sand (one part). Add one-half cupful of ammonium sulfate, and mix it in well. If your soil tests acid, you don't need such elaborate preparations—just lighten your existing soil with liberal amounts of peat and sand.

The plant from the nursery is usually balled and burlapped, and you can move it in full bloom to be sure about color. Some varieties clash badly. Set each plant in a hole so the crown is a little above ground level, and build the bed up to it. Use 3 or 4 inches of mulch over the roots but don't pile it right around the trunk, for that might start rot. After the mulch is in place, leave it alone—don't stir or cultivate or you'll cut shallow roots.

Aside from these details about the first planting, azaleas require little care. There's scarcely any pruning to do, and pests are rare. See that the roots never suffer from drouth. If you're on the "azalea frontier," you will have to rig up winter protection like a lath tepee to give shade from winter sun and drying wind.

Azaleas make good accent plants where you want bright color: doorways, foundations, low shrubbery borders. Or naturalize them among tall open-leafed trees like pines and oaks, if you have the space.

A. mucronulatum, one of the first to flower. Rosy lavender flowers same time as forsythia, a good companion, 6 feet, Zone 5.

A. schlippenbachi, one of the earliest, showy pink flowers. Does not require acid soil, 5 to 8 feet, Zone 5.

A. calendulaceum, flame-yellow to red. Hardy, flowers in May, 6 feet, Zone 5.

A. arborescens, white with pink. Tall, to 9 feet, fragrant, June blooming, good for naturalizing, Zone 5.

A. vaseyi, shell pink. Hardy, up to 8 feet tall, flowers April, May, Zone 5.

A. nudiflorum, white to pink. Flowers in May; reaches 5 feet or taller, Zone 4.

A. roseum, rose pink, fragrant, blooms in May, 3 to 5 feet, Zone 4.

Mollis hybrids, 5 to 9 feet, May. 'Christopher Wren,' large yellow; 'Dr. M. Oosthoek,' red-orange; 'Director Moerlands,' golden yellow. Zone 6.

Ghent hybrids. In variety of colors, 5 to 9 feet, bloom after Mollis. *Daviesi,* white with yellow; 'Gloria Mundi,' orange. Zone 5.

Knaphill (including Exbury), 5 to 10 feet, blooms in May. 'Balzac,' fragrant, orange-red; 'Brazil,' orange, shapely shrub; 'Gibraltar,' copper orange; 'Golden Girl,' yellow; 'Flamingo,' pink; and 'White Throat,' white. Zone 5.

ELEVEN FLOWERING SHRUBS FOR SUPPORTING ROLES

BEAUTYBUSH (Kolkwitzia amabilis)

To 8 feet. Zone 5. Arching branches with showy pink flowers through May and June. A carefree shrub that grows in any soil and stands heat and drouth; but be sure to allow space for it to spread as wide as it is high. Good for shrub borders and screens on a large property. Plant in full sun.

BUTTERCUP SHRUB
(Potentilla fruticosa)

To 3 feet. Zone 3. A small shrub for a dooryard, a spot in front of evergreens or for a low hedge or border. From June to October it is covered with bright golden or yellow flowers. Finely cut foliage is attractive. Takes average soil, full sun. Perfect in a small yard. A good variety is 'Gold Drop,' 2½ feet, small flowered.

CRAPE-MYRTLE (Lagerstroemia indica)

To 25 feet in the South. Zone 6. To 5 feet, in north of its range. A southern tree-shrub that succeeds northward if protected like hybrid tea roses. Crape-myrtles die back in winter. Cut to live wood, they will rise again. Ruffled heads of white, red, pink, or purple flowers come on new wood in summer. Give full sun, rich soil, and a protected location close to walls or fence backgrounds or at the edge of shrubbery.

FLOWERING ALMOND
(Prunus glandulosa)

To 4 feet. Zone 4. A graceful round shrub covered before the leaves in April with small, double, pink or white flowers. Ideal for a small yard, at the edge of larger shrubs, or for a low border. Grows best in full sun but is not particular about soil or site.

KERRIA (Kerria japonica)

To 5 feet, spreads to 5 feet. Zone 5. In May, bright yellow, double flowers that come and go all summer. In winter the light green stems are distinctive. Tolerates heat, drouth, and light shade, but sometimes winterkills. Give any good garden soil. A single form is also available; it is perhaps prettier than the double, and not so common. Use it in shrub borders or for screens. Thin out suckers from the base occasionally.

PEEGEE HYDRANGEA (Hydrangea paniculata grandiflora)

To 5 feet. Zone 5. An old favorite. Robust with cone-shaped flowers appearing in midsummer and lasting to frost, changing as they age from white to pink to buff. Hydrangea does well in average soil, sun, or light shade. It will grow on the north of a house. Stands heat and drouth.

PUSSY WILLOW (Salix discolor)

To 20 feet. Zone 3. The flowers are furry, silver catkins that come out to announce spring in February or March. You can cut branches in January and force them indoors. Plant in sun or light shade and any good moist soil. Allow plenty of space. They are good for shrub backgrounds and screens, although often short-lived. A cultivated kind called French pussy willow has 2-inch pink-silver pussies; to 10 feet. Zone 5.

RED SPIRAEA (Spiraea japonica coccinea)

To 3 feet. Zone 5. In May and June, rosy red flowers appear in heads above the neat, rounded bush. They continue to bloom sparsely through the summer. Ideal for low edgings, borders, foundations, doorways, or in front of other shrubs. Give sun or light shade and average soil. Tolerates heat and dry winds, but the roots must be watered during drouth.

ROSE OF SHARON (Hibiscus syriacus)

To 10 feet. Zone 5. Also called althaea. Troublefree shrubs, upright, with hibiscus-like blooms of white, pink, blue, and variegated patterns or double forms in August and September. Blooms best in sun, but tolerates shade. Grows well in the South. Give average garden soil and water during drouths. Seeds itself profusely in flower beds, shrub borders.

SMOKE TREE (Rhus cotinus or Cotinus coggyria)

To 12 feet. Zone 4. In June, cloudlike pink or purple flowers appear, lasting for weeks. Give full sun and average soil. Use as a specimen or in a shrub background. A row makes a tall, dense screen. It grows large and is not for the small yard. The foliage is as interesting as the flowers—even more so in the purple-leaf ('Royal Purple') and bronze-leaf forms (*R. rubrifolius*).

WEIGELA (Weigela hybrids)

To 7 feet. Zone 5. At the north of Zone 5, locate in a protected place. Upright, rounded, spreading to 6 feet, producing in May and June and later in summer trumpet-shaped flowers of red, pink, and white. Give full sun and ordinary soil. Grows fast. Try 'Bristol Ruby,' ruby-red blooms on rounded, large plants; and 'Boskoop Glory,' pink blooms on 4-foot plants.

SHRUBS FOR FRAGRANCE

Among the flowering shrubs are some of the most fragrant of all plants. Here are some that perfume the air.

Burkwood viburnum, *Viburnum burkwoodi*
Butterfly bush, *Buddleia davidi*
Chaste tree, *Vitex*
Glossy abelia, *Abelia grandiflora*
Hardy buddleia, *Buddleia alternifolia*
Lilac, French hybrids, *Syringa*, Persian *S. chinensis*
Mockorange, *Philadelphus coronarius*, 'Belle Etoile'
Pink pepperbush, *Clethra alnifolia*
Rose daphne, *Daphne cneorum*
Roseshell azalea, *Azalea rosea*
Snowball, fragrant *Viburnum carlecephalum*, pink *V. carlesi*
Sweetshrub, *Calycanthus floridus*

Winter honeysuckle, *Lonicera fragrantissima*

SHRUBS FOR BERRIES

With some shrubs the berries are more showy than the flowers, or equally attractive.

Beautyberry, *Callicarpa japonica*
Bush honeysuckle, *Lonicera tatarica*
Cranberry cotoneaster, *Cotoneaster apiculata*, *Cotoneaster divaricata*
Deciduous holly, *Ilex serrata*
Golden cranberry, *Viburnum xanthocarpum*
Jetbead, *Rhodotypos scandens*
Laland firethorn, *Pyracantha lalandi*
Oregon grape-holly, *Mahonia aquifolium*
Sea buckthorn, *Hippophae rhamnoides*
Snowberry, *Symphoricarpos orbiculatus*
Viburnum opulus
Viburnum tomentosum

SHRUBS FOR FOLIAGE

A few have nothing showy about flower or fruit, but the foliage makes a fine display.

Burning bush, *Euonymus alatus compactus*, fall
Dwarf Japanese maple, *Acer palmatum atropurpureum*, spring
Golden privet, *Ligustrum vicari*, spring, summer
Heavenly bamboo, *Nandina domestica*, fall
Purple-leaf filbert, *Corylus maxima*, spring to summer
Red barberry, *Berberis* 'Crimson Pygmy,' summer to fall
Stephanandra incisa, fall

EASY-DOES-IT IDEAS

Take a short shrub, a medium height and a tall one to fill up an eyesore corner that leads nowhere. These could be flowering almond, callicarpa, and lilac.

Take an early flowering shrub, a midseason, and a late one to group in another uninteresting corner, for all-season excitement. Here you might use cornelian cherry, deutzia, and caryopteris 'Blue Mist.'

To help you compute how far apart to space two different kinds of shrubs, estimate the mature spread of each (or look them up in the chart in this chapter), add them together, and divide in half. Then dig planting holes with centers that far apart.

THIRTY-FIVE FLOWERING SHRUBS FOR YOUR YARD

Name	Zone	Height (feet)	Spread (feet)	Bloom time	Flowers or berry	Foliage	Exposure	Soil	Comment
Abelia grandiflora Glossy abelia	6	5	5	June through summer	Fragrant blush pink flowers like weigela	Dense, glossy, semi-evergreen	Sun, semi-shade	Average with humus	Not showy but pleasing. For hedges, low shrub borders. Tolerates heat and alkalinity.
Azaleas	5-8	3-6	3-6	March-June	Flamboyant orange, yellow, red, lilac, pink, white	Some deciduous kinds have red fall foliage	Semi-shade	Acid, moist, humus	Needs shade in heat of day. Not for limy soils. Accent plants for bright color.
Buddleia davidii Butterfly bush	6	8	5	July, August	White, pink, shades of purple, fragrant, on dense spikes	Vase-shaped bush with long arching canes	Sun	Light, rich	Mulch for winter with straw. Cut to ground in spring. Attracts butterflies. In the South does not die back, but prune back anyway, heavily.
Callicarpa japonica Beautyberry	6	5	5	July, August	Small pink flowers followed in fall by showy, violet berries, size of buckshot	Small arching branches, rounded bush	Sunny, warm	Average, loam	Birds relish berries. Satisfactory in Zone 5 if sheltered.
Calycanthus floridus Sweetshrub	5	4	4	April-June	Fragrant purple-brown flowers	Glossy leaves	Sun, semi-shade	Average, well-drained	Blooms, leaves and bark are all fragrant. For shrub border, or near house.
Caryopteris 'Blue Mist' Blue spiraea	4	2	3	July-September	Blue, fringed, on willowy sprays	Silvery green, low mounds	Sun	Sandy	In cold areas give winter mulch of straw or leaves. Grow it in the perennial border. Good in Great Plains area. Takes extremes.
Chaenomeles japonica (Cydonia) Flowering quince	5	1½-8	1½-4	March, April	Showy crimson, pink or white flowers	Dense, shiny	Sun	Average	Upright shrub, good for city yards. Makes good clipped hedge. Use low kinds for foundation plantings or as low edging.
Cornus mas Cornelian cherry	5	15	10	March, April	Yellow tufts thick on leafless branches; scarlet fruit in fall	Shiny, dogwood-like, on spreading branches	Sun	Average	Use in large shrub plantings (not for the small place). One of the earliest things to bloom.
C. stolonifera Red-twig dogwood	3	6	4	May, June	Small 2-inch clusters of white flowers; pea-size blue or white fruit, August, September	Dark green, dense on erect red branches	Sun, semi-shade	Average, moist	Red branches good for floral arranging, winter color. For shrub border.

Name				Blooming	Flowers	Form	Light	Soil	Remarks
Cotoneaster apiculata Cranberry cotoneaster	4	2	4	May	Small pink flowers, not showy; in fall, attractive red berries	Shiny dark green, low spreading bush	Sun	Average	For shrub border, foundation planting, rock gardens. Extremely hardy and tolerant.
C. divaricata	5	6	6	May, June	Small, not showy, pink blooms; red berries in fall	Small, glossy round, turn red in fall	Sun, semi-shade	Average well-drained	Will grow on north. Prune low at first to make it branch. For shrub border.
Deutzia gracilis Deutzia	5	3	4	May	Bell-shaped, small, white	Dense, spreading	Sun, semi-shade	Average	Use for low edgings, foundations, front of larger shrubs. Stands heat well.
Forsythia, horticultural forms Golden bell	5	10	10	April, May	Bell-shaped, yellow	Rounded, with arching branches	Sun, light shade	Average	Shrub border plant. Stands city smoke. A rapid grower, so give it space. Dwarf forms available.
Hibiscus syriacus (*Althaea*) Rose of sharon	5	10	6	August, September	Hibiscus-like flowers, white, pink, blue, variegated	Upright, tree-like	Sun, semi-shade	Average	Troublefree. Tolerates city and seashore conditions. Can even be espaliered. Water during drouths. Grows well in South.
Hydrangea paniculata grandiflora Peegee hydrangea	5	5	5	August, September	Cone-shaped flowers, white blending to pink as they age	Large, bright green	Sun, semi-shade	Average	Specimen, good for north. Tolerates heat, drouth, seashore and shade.
Hypericum Sun Gold St. John'swort	5	2	3	July, August	Showy golden flowers with tufts of stamens	Oval-shaped, low plants	Sun, semi-shade	Dry, sandy, drained	For low borders, hedges, edging. Tops may winterkill—cut them off and new growth comes from base.
Kerria japonica Kerria	5	5	5	May through summer	Bright yellow double flowers	Low rounded shrubs, light green branches	Sun, semi-shade	Average	Tolerates heat, drouth. Use in shrub border and as screen. Light green stems distinctive in winter. Single form available.
Kolkwitzia amabilis Beautybush	5	8	8	May, June	Showy pink flowers	Arching branches, spreading shrub	Sun	Average	Give space for it to spread. Use as screen or in border. Tolerates heat and drouth.
Lagerstroemia indica Crape-myrtle	6	5-25	3-?	August	Red, pink, purple or white flowers	Tree-like in South; bushy in North	Sun	Rich	Size depends on location. Much larger in South. Northward it is a small shrub, dies back each winter. Cut to live wood in spring; give protected site.

97

THIRTY-FIVE FLOWERING SHRUBS FOR YOUR YARD (continued)

Name	Zone	Height (feet)	Spread (feet)	Bloom time	Flowers or berry	Foliage	Exposure	Soil	Comment
Lonicera fragrantissima Winter honeysuckle	5	6	6	March, April	Fragrant, cream-white small flowers come before leaves	Stiff, leathery, on spreading branches	Sun, semi-shade	Average	Foliage stays on into late winter. Sometimes blooms in December or February. Will grow on north of house.
L. tatarica Bush honeysuckle	3	8	6	May, June	Dainty pink flowers followed soon by soft red berries	Blue-green leaves on upright stems	Sun or light shade	Average	Stands drouth. Makes a good screen. Grows fast. Berries attract birds.
Nandina domestica Heavenly bamboo	6	6	4	July	White flowers in clusters, dark red berries in fall	Graceful foliage in thick mound, turns red in fall	Sun, semi-shade	Average humusy	Smaller in North. Foliage stays on most of winter, even in North.
Philadelphus Mockorange	4	10	5	May, June	White flower clusters, usually fragrant	Slender branches, light green foliage	Sun, semi-shade	Average	Often thin at the base. Prune after bloom.
Potentilla fruticosa Buttercup shrub	3	3	2	June-October	Golden yellow flowers	Finely cut leaves	Sun	Average	For small yard, dooryard, front of evergreens or low border.
Prunus glandulosa Flowering almond	4	4	4	April	Small double pink or white flowers	Round graceful shrub	Sun	Average	For low borders, small yards, or the edge of larger shrubs.
Rhodotypos scandens Jet bead	5	5	5	May, June	Small, rose-like white flowers in profusion; shiny black berries last all winter	Light green on spreading branches	Sun, semi-shade	Average	Stands city conditions well. For low shrub borders, screens.
Rhus cotinus (*Cotinus coggygria*) Smoke tree	4	12	6-8	June	Cloud-like pink or purple flowers	Purple, bronze or light green	Sun	Average	Easy. Specimen, screen, or shrubbery border in large yard.
Salix discolor Pussy willow	3	20	4-6	February, March	Silver catkins	Upright, slender branches	Sun, semi-shade	Average, moist	Often short-lived. Tolerates swampy soil. To force, cut branches in January.

Name				Bloom time	Flower	Foliage	Light	Soil	Remarks
Spiraea japonica coccinea Red spiraea	5	3	3	May, June	Crimson heads of bloom	Neat rounded shrub	Sun, semi-shade	Average	Easy, little pruning needed. For foundations, borders. An improvement over Anthony Waterer. Blooms most of summer.
S. van houttei Van Houtte spiraea (Bridal wreath)	4	5	6	May	Arching sprays of white flowers	Small, green leaves on fountain-shaped bush	Sun, semi-shade	Average	Stands city conditions, seashores, drouths. Use in hedge or shrub border.
Syringa chinensis (rothomagensis) Persian lilac	3	8	6	May	Lilac-red flowers in cone-shaped clusters. Smaller than French hybrids. Fragrant.	Smaller, thinner than common lilac	Sun	Average, limy	Good for specimen, in screen or shrub row. Blooms when young.
S. vulgaris hybrids French lilacs	3	8	6	May	Fragrant clusters of white, lavender, magenta, purple; single or double	Dense, large dark green leaves	Sun	Limy	Begin to flower when mature. Not for the South. For specimen, hedge and border.
Tamarix gallica French tamarix	5	15	12	June, August	Dainty pink lacy sprays above foliage	Light green feathery on thin upright plants	Sun, semi-shade	Average	Good for shrub border or background. Sometimes dies back in winter. Tolerates seashore. Cut it back to 8 inches when you plant.
Viburnum carlesi Pink snowball	5	6	5	April, May	Fragrant pink ball-shaped flower heads	Stiff leaves turn bronze in fall; globe-shaped bush	Sun, semi-shade	Average	Early blooming, tolerates heat, drouth. A good corner plant or for the border. *V. carlecephalum* is an improved form with white blossoms.
V. tomentosum Doubleflle viburnum	5	8	8	May, June	White flat wheel-like clusters with small blooms in center; red fruit turns blue-black	Horizontal branching makes bush look layered	Sun	Average	Not for the small place. Beautiful even when not in leaf.
Vitex agnus-castus Chaste tree	6	9	5	July-September	Long spikes of fragrant blue-lavender flowers	Dark green in palm-shaped clusters	Sun	Average, well-drained	Grows fast. Sometimes dies back, but blooms on new wood. Starts growth late.
Weigela Weigela hybrids	5	7	6	May-September	Trumpet-shaped, red, pink, white flowers	Excellent clean foliage, rounded shrub	Sun	Average	Grows fast. Easy. Locate in sheltered site north of Zone 5.

Chapter 7

EVERGREENS FOR WINTER BEAUTY

What shall I plant at the front door?

Your place can be beautiful and interesting the year around if you plant evergreens. People who live in the South, California, and other areas where winters are mild are blessed with greenery regardless of the season. Gardeners in other parts are learning ways they too can have color at the door after the red-gold autumn leaves have fallen.

The mainstay of the winter garden in any climate is the evergreen tree or shrub. "Evergreen" covers two general plant types. First is the needle group—the cone-bearing kinds like pines and a few others without cones, like junipers and yews. The other is the broadleaf evergreen group, whose leaves are like those of deciduous (leaf shedding) plants except that they stay on all winter, or most of it, and are green or at least colorful.

Neither kind of evergreen stops with the foliage. Pines, spruces and firs have interesting cones. Junipers have delightful blue berries. Yews produce sparkling red fruit. Many broadleafs have spectacular flowers—rhododendrons, andromedas, camellias, and magnolias, to name a few. Others like holly have berries for dashes of color when it is needed most—in winter.

Hardly a gardener lives who knows enough about evergreens of either type. They are a good subject for a hobby specialty or at the least for extra study in nurseries, arboretums, or books written just about them. No matter where you live, there are some good evergreens you can plant in your yard.

NEEDLE EVERGREENS ARE HARDY

Some needle evergreens are among the hardiest of trees and shrubs; they will grow where almost nothing else will. Their deep, dense green feathery texture makes them ideal as backgrounds for other plants. They are good windbreaks. Many hug the ground, a habit good in rock gardens, tops of walls, or edges of steps or ramps. Most cone-bearing evergreens like pines need full sun. Hemlocks are an exception—they tolerate partial shade. Yews will grow in shade too, and where summers are sizzling they require it. White pine and Keteleer junipers also tolerate light shade.

Needle evergreens are often used in doorway and foundation plantings. Many dwarf forms are beautifully suited for that. Make sure before you plant any to find out how big they will grow. Some seem innocently small in the nursery or when you first set them out, but they rapidly grow into forest giants. They can block your doorway, obscure your house and cut off sun and air. This is a common mistake of do-it-yourself landscapers. How much better to select carefully a dwarf or slow-growing kind in the first place!

Except for tiny seedlings, these plants come balled and burlapped or in containers. Plant them spring or fall (spring preferred

30 This planting of needle and broadleaf evergreens will be as beautiful in winter as in summer. Spreading yews are at the corners; dwarf boxwood edges the walk, and rhododendrons stand near the door. A wisteria climbs high beyond the door, and euonymous rises between the windows.

Genereux

31 Young pines set close together serve here as a hedge and year-round screen.   *Roche*

in the North) and water them well the first season.

BROADLEAFS ARE VARIED

This group is complicated. No one knows how many different plants can be included in it. Because of the high interest in the subject, new kinds are continually being added to the list. Climate makes a difference between whether a plant is evergreen or not. The Mentor barberry, for example, keeps its leaves in Oklahoma but drops them before spring in northern Ohio. Pyracantha may be evergreen in one place but not somewhere else.

There is also the problem of hardiness. The more severe the winters, the shorter is the list of reliable broadleaf evergreens. Not only winters but summers may affect them. Some like the ericas will survive the test of cold but collapse in drying wind and heat. A few that keep their leaves through winter suffer so from sunburn that they are a blight on your landscape and you wish they weren't there.

If you want to be cautious about broadleaf plantings, use only the kinds guaranteed by a nurseryman in your neighborhood. If you feel more experimental, select from the catalogs some that may be strange to you, but which seem, based on all you can learn of them, likely to succeed in your yard.

Finding the right location is one secret to success with some "difficult" broadleafs. Seek a place in semishade for kalmia, leucothoe, rhododendron, and pieris. A site protected from winter sun and wind may let you grow a few that you had not thought reliable, like aucuba and skimmia.

If you want to grow some that demand acid soil, and yours is alkaline, all you can do is excavate and replace with earth of the right sort. Broadleafs usually come balled and burlapped or in containers and are best planted in spring.

SIX GOOD NEEDLE EVERGREENS FOR THE FRONT DOOR

SPREADING JUNIPER (Juniperus chinensis pfitzeriana *varieties*)

32 *Pieris japonica* and rhododendrons make a year-long pleasing picture near this foundation, with colorful flowers in spring. *Vinca minor* covers the ground. English ivy ascends the chimney wall. *Hampfler*

Zone 4 to the Gulf and coast to coast. This much-used shrub is carefree and tolerant of all kinds of conditions. It stays under 4 feet and spreads to 15 feet if permitted. In the trade it is called a "spreader." If you use pfitzers to flank a walk, set them back far enough to allow for quadrupling in size. Otherwise you'll have to shear them into lopsided hulks to permit traffic to pass. Better for doorway planting is the small version of it, called 'Compact Pfitzer.' These shrubs have good green color summer and winter, tolerate cold, heat and drouth, and are long lived. They will grow in sun or light shade.

CREEPING JUNIPER (Juniperus horizontalis douglasi 'Waukegan')

Zone 3 southward. In summer the Waukegan juniper has blue-gray foliage, but in winter the leaves turn pale purple. Plants are very low, seldom over 10 inches high, but they spread with trailing branches reaching out several feet. They are good shrubs to cover a low bank, because they follow the slope. Give them sun and any soil, even rocky or sandy.

JAPANESE SPREADING YEW (Taxus cuspidata nana)

Zone 5 southward. Usually this yew grows to 5 or 6 feet, and spreads to more than that, but you can easily keep it small by pruning. The dark green smooth needles look elegant in summer and winter. This is one shrub that does as well in shade as in sun, and perhaps better if your summers are hot. It is a good doorway shrub on the north or east side of the house, and makes a serene background for lilies and other perennials.

103

33 The mountain laurel makes a beautiful shrub similar to its relative the rhododendron with purple-pink flowers in May and June.

Roche

It grows in average soil, but does better in one containing humus. Water yews occasionally during dry spells. If you want them to produce their attractive red berries, ask the nurseryman for female shrubs with one male among the planting for pollination.

MUGHO PINE (Pinus mugo mughus)

Zone 3. Of all the pines this is the only one that stays small enough long enough to make it practical in a foundation planting or close to a doorway. For the first ten years it grows slowly. Eventually it begins to get large, going beyond 5 feet in height and width, and then you will probably have to replace it with a smaller one. It lives in any soil, and through almost any weather. As a doorway plant, it has a good rounded shape with the large needles and "candles" distinctive among smaller foliage types.

COLUMNAR YEW (Taxus media 'Hatfield')

Zone 6. The Hatfield yew is a hybrid. It grows in a compact cone shape or high pyramid with upright branches that have spreading leaves. Use it for doorway or foundation plantings where you want a shape that "lifts." Yews need pruning occasionally to keep them in bounds, and to guide their growth the way you want it, but the job is easier and the results more pleasing than with junipers.

UPRIGHT JUNIPER (Juniperus virginiana 'Canaert')

Zone 3 southward. Like other junipers, almost any climate agrees with it. It grows from Canada to the Gulf and sea to sea. The 'Canaert' is a pyramidal, compact variety with rich green foliage and many attractive blue berries. In time it will become too large for a small space, reaching perhaps to 10 or 12 feet. But it is comparatively slow growing and is one of the best junipers for a vertical accent in foundation and door plantings. You can keep it in hand for many years by persistent shearing. Give it full sun. Extremely susceptible to cedar-apple rust.

SIX GOOD NEEDLE EVERGREENS FOR LARGE SPACES

WHITE OR COLORADO FIR (Abies concolor)

Zone 4 southward, but not south of Zone 7 except in mountains. This is a forest tree growing to 50 feet or more with beautiful blue-green needles and tapered upright cones. It likes cool, moist soil, but is fairly tolerant of drouth, soil variations, heat and intense cold. It is the most valuable fir for widespread use. In the central states red spider may damage the tree in hot weather. Plant it in full sun in easy reach of the hose for the first few years.

WHITE PINE (Pinus strobus)

Zone 3 but not for the South or Southwest except in mountains. A noble tree, white pine makes a striking specimen, rising to 75 feet or more. It grows fast and has a wide spread, so give it space—10 feet each way—if you intend it to remain permanently. This is a five-needle pine—having five soft slender long needles in each little leaf bundle—giving it a fine texture unusual among pines. Cones are long and narrow. Plant white pine in full sun.

DOUGLAS-FIR (Pseudotsuga taxifolia)

Zone 4 for those raised from Rocky Mountain stock. (Pacific coast stock is not so hardy.) It makes a tall narrow tree, growing up to 40 or 50 feet in cultivation but much more than that in native forests. Branches have a horizontal or layered look, with leaves short and flat like a yew. Cones are small, rough and they hang down. The Douglas-fir is fairly tolerant of drouth and heat and can be used over a wide area. Give it full sun. You've no doubt used Douglas-fir for Christmas trees as they are one of the familiar kinds, popular because needles stay on a long time.

COLORADO SPRUCE (Picea pungens)

Zone 3 southward over a wide area but not for the South or mild Southwest except in the mountains. The blue form of this, which is the commonest kind, is often called blue spruce. It stands out and should be used with discretion. It is tolerant of drouth and is one of the best spruces in dry areas. The tree makes a narrow straight pyramid

105

up to 50 feet high, with short curved needles that are blue-green or light blue. When they get older they sometimes lose the blueness. You can get kinds with green, not blue, leaves. The cones are short and small, hanging down from sides of branches. Single specimen trees are handsome, but a row may disappoint you because of variations in the color.

AMERICAN ARBORVITAE (Thuja occidentalis)

Zone 3 southward. A long-lived tree that grows almost anywhere. Its foliage consists of flat sprays of small overlapping "needles" or scales, quite different from the look of other needle evergreens. Winter damage, dog burn, and other adversities sometimes combine to produce a ragged look that spoils the symmetry of young trees. Nurserymen have created a welter of kinds. Unless labeled "dwarf" or "globe," they are probably capable of becoming tall timber, with straight or branched trunks, up to 50 or 60 feet high. This is why you should not use ordinary arborvitae at your doorway. Give it space to become the handsome tree that it potentially is. It likes moist soil. If your winters are dry and windy, be sure to water well in the fall before freeze-up. Plant in sun or slight shade. In the South a less hardy kind, the oriental arborvitae, is used instead of *T. occidentalis.*

HEMLOCK (Tsuga canadensis)

Zone 3 southward, but it is not for the deep South, the Southwest, or dry plains with hot winds and alkaline soil. The hemlock stands out as the most airy and graceful of needle evergreens. It needs humus, and tolerates shade. Under good conditions it becomes a big tree 90 feet high, spreading to 30 or 40 feet. Needles are short, blunt, soft green, on drooping slender branches. Cones are smooth and small. If you plant it with protection while it is young, you can remove the protection in a few years and the tree will have established itself and be quite hardy.

SIX GOOD BROADLEAF EVERGREENS FOR THE FRONT OF THE HOUSE

LALAND FIRETHORN (Pyracantha coccinea lalandi)

Zone 6 southward. Here is a versatile shrub that always looks good and has the added attraction of hard bright orange berries in fall. They last most of the winter. It seems to thrive in heat and sun, and survives best in a protected location. In the very north of the range it may drop leaves before spring, but is bare only a short time. The white flowers in May and June are not spectacular. Use pyracantha at walls, where it will "climb" or espalier well; among other shrubs at the foundation or in a mixed border of shrubs for a screen or background. It gets to be 8 feet high, and the same across, but grows slowly and you can easily keep it in bounds by pruning or cutting sprays of berries for the house. Give it average soil or one on the limy side, and good drainage; transplant it while small and use extra care. An even hardier variety, 'Kasan,' Zone 5, is like it but the foliage turns more bronze in winter.

LITTLELEAF BOXWOOD (Buxus microphylla)

Zone 6. For something low and bright green at a doorway, the littleleaf box seems perfect. It grows slowly, and makes a compact mound of small leaves 2 or 3 feet high. Although it does not have the glossy dark foliage of old-fashioned boxwood, *B. sempervirens,* it has a big advantage in being more hardy. You can grow it in sun or part shade and average soil. An even hardier variation, Korean boxwood, *B. microphylla koreana,* will grow in Zone 5. It has smaller leaves and stays under 2 feet. Keep watered in winter.

JAPANESE ANDROMEDA (Pieris japonica)

Zone 6. These shapely shrubs mix well in doorway plantings with rhododendrons or shrub hollies. They can get as large as 10 feet, but seldom do. The leaves are glossy

34 *Upper Left* Oregon grape-holly, *Mahonia aquifolium,* offers leathery foliage turning purple-bronze in winter. The yellow spring blossoms are followed by blue berries.   *Roche*

35 *Upper Right* Rhododendrons produce spectacular springtime color. This is the variety 'Blue Peter.'   *Roche*

36 *Lower Left* Wintercreeper (*Euonymus fortunei vegetus*) grows fast and large; if supported it will rise to great heights. The small flowers shown here will develop pink-yellow berries.   *Roche*

37 *Lower Right* The laland firethorn or pyracantha is fine against sunny walls. It is evergreen in most places, and the orange berries are showy in fall.   *Genereux*

107

dark green. In April and May they are topped by drooping clusters of ivory-white flowers. Give a position in part shade, and an acid soil with plenty of peat moss or leaf mold. Keep moist in summer and winter.

JAPANESE HOLLY (Ilex crenata *and varieties*)

Zone 6. Most kinds stay under 5 feet. All have small dark leaves and are densely branching, making thick glossy green mounds. Their berries are black. *I. crenata* is the tallest growing and the least hardy of the group. It reaches a height of 8 to 10 feet or taller. *I. crenata convexa* (ordinarily sold as *I. convexa*) has curved shiny leaves resembling boxwood, and is a little hardier. It is slow growing and reaches about 4 feet. *I. crenata microphylla* has tiny roundish leaves only $\frac{1}{2}$ inch long or less and is the hardiest of this group. It sometimes reaches more than 5 feet in height. Use any of these near foundations or doorways. They do well in either sun or light shade, and are not particular about soil as long as it is humusy.

BURFORD HOLLY (Ilex cornuta burfordi)

Zone 6. Moderately fast growing, this holly usually stays under 6 feet. It has lacquered-looking holly-like leaves, with a pin at the tip of each. Unlike most hollies, it may set berries (red) without pollen from a male shrub—at least, it will do this in the South. Grow it in sun or part shade. It does best in an acid soil, but will tolerate a neutral one that has much humus. It takes heat and drouth well. Burford holly is good at doorways, under windows and among other evergreens. It is handsome and distinctive.

OREGON GRAPE-HOLLY (Mahonia aquifolium)

Zone 5. To 5 feet. Glossy holly-like leaves cover the rounded plants. In the spring there are bright yellow flowers, followed in summer by blue berries. In harsh winters the foliage turns bronze. There is much variation in the appearance of this shrub, which is a cousin of the barberry. Compare plants at the nursery and select those that look good to you. Be especially careful if you want three or four in a row to be uniform. They are tolerant of heat, drouth, and cold, and do best in partial shade. Although they will grow in neutral or even alkaline soil, they do better if it is acid and humusy. This is a good choice for a doorway plant or for shrub rows near the foundation.

RHODODENDRONS ARE A SPECIAL GROUP

Along with their shining mounds of evergreen leaves, they are topped in spring with trusses of lavish flowers. No other broadleaf matches them in this regard. Where they succeed they are the cream of the evergreens. Your climate and soil decide what kinds you can grow, or whether you can grow them at all. Rhododendrons as a group are a little less tolerant of hardship than most azaleas. Although they take the cold well, they can't stand drying winter winds, or drouth and heat in summer. Sudden changes are hard on them.

Assuming your climate is agreeable, you can use rhododendrons, and technically this includes azaleas,* beautifully in plantings around your house. They mingle well with other shrubs at the foundation or border. Rhododendrons are too thin for screens or backgrounds, and azalea types are too low. Azaleas make good foreground plants with rhododendrons and give fine spots of color for doorways. You can plant azaleas in full bloom, which lets you control the color combinations.

Give these plants a fully light place but out of early morning and noonday sun, where drainage is perfect and the soil is acid and full of humus. They grow well in a north exposure.

If your soil tests alkaline, dig it out and replace it with the mix described in Chapter

---

* The evergreen types of azaleas are described here. Deciduous or leaf shedding kinds, thought of as flowering shrubs, are described in Chapter 6.

38 For something small, as in a rock garden, *Erica carnea* is a pretty low evergreen with rose-colored flowers in earliest spring. This is the variety 'King George.' *Graff*

6. If the soil is already on the acid side, prepare it by lightening with liberal additions of peat moss, compost, rotted sawdust (any kind but pine), and sand. Never let roots suffer drouth. Fertilize rhododendrons with cottonseed meal ($\frac{1}{2}$ cup to a plant) or ammonium sulfate (a teaspoon to a plant) in early spring and again the first of July.

THE HARDIEST RHODODENDRONS

Catawba rhododendron (*R. catawbiense* and hybrids). Zone 5. Become large, 6- to 8-foot, spreading plants. Give these some sun to make them bloom. They have large handsome leaves. Flowers early to mid-June.
  R. roseum elegans, rosy pink.
  R. album grandiflorum, white.
  'Charles Dickens,' medium red.
  'Mrs. Charles Sargent,' deep rose.
  R. atrosanguineum, red.
Carolina rhododendron (*R. carolinianum*). Zone 5. White to rose-purple. To 3 feet, spreading to 6. Small leaves. Blooms early May.

Rosebay (*R. maximum*). Zone 4. To 6 feet. Blooms are pink to white, in June. Tolerates more shade than most.

THE HARDIEST AZALEAS THAT ARE EVERGREEN OR NEARLY SO

Gable hybrids. Zone 6. Height, 4 feet.
  'Elizabeth Gable,' pink with darker blotch.
  'Louise Gable,' pink, late.
  'Purple Splendor,' purple.
  'Stewartonian,' bright red.
Glenn Dale hybrids. Zone 7. To 5 feet.
  'Samite,' white.
  'Aztec,' red with white.
Kaempferi hybrids. Zone 6. To 6 feet.
  'Othello,' brilliant red.
'Hinodegiri.' Zone 6. Vivid crimson. Three feet high and spreads. Harsh and brilliant, not good with most other colors.
  R. poukhanense. Zone 6. Red-violet, to 6 feet. Hardy into Zone 5 but not evergreen there.

SIX BROADLEAF EVERGREENS
FOR BORDERS AND SCREENS

AMERICAN HOLLY (Ilex opaca)

Zone 6. To 75 feet, but slow growing. This native lacks some of the luster of English holly but it is far more adaptable, succeeding even where winters are bright and windy. Good specimens are beautiful, with dark green leaves that are stiff and leathery. Typical specimens rise in steep thick pyramids with foliage from the ground up, although there are rounded and spreading forms, too. In October, female trees ripen red berries, very profuse on some kinds such as 'Old Heavy Berry.' For best fruiting and thickest foliage, place American holly in full or nearly full sun. It tolerates shade but is slow and sparse there. It prefers an acid peaty soil but is fairly tolerant. To have berries you need a male tree in the vicinity. Water during drouths and don't cultivate around the roots. Cutting off branches for Christmas greens will not hurt it.

BOXWOOD (Buxus sempervirens)

Zone 6. To 20 feet. This slow-growing and long-lived shrub takes many years to reach ultimate size—a lifetime is hardly long enough. Although often sheared into hedges, boxwood makes a pleasing untrimmed form, rounded, spreading and undulating. It is so dense that you cannot see through it, and is clothed to the ground. The small oval leaves are glossy, dark and thick. A garden full of boxwood has a characteristic nostalgic odor. Water plants late in fall to prevent winter drying. It needs soil that is humusy and slightly acid. It can take full sun in summer, but to prevent sunburn in winter it's best where it gets part day shade.

ENGLISH HOLLY (Ilex aquifolium)

Zone 7. To 50 feet. The polished leaves are larger than those of the American holly, and more spiny. Tiny flowers and large red berries come in small clusters among the branches. The tree rises in a thin pyramid tightly covered with branches right to the

ground. Like other hollies it requires a peaty, acid soil, with moisture. Put a mulch over the roots but do not pile it up close to the trunk of the tree. Where it grows well, as in the far Northwest, this tree is more beautiful than American holly. It comes in many varieties of shape and habit. 'Winter Queen' and 'Brownell's Special' are good varieties. 'Silvary' has a light edge.

MOUNTAIN LAUREL (Kalmia latifolia)

Zone 5. In gardens, to about 6 feet. Dark green, shiny, leathery leaves cover the twisting stems and branches, making a rounded shrub. In May and June large clusters of purple-pink to nearly white shell-like flowers appear at ends of branches. It grows in sun or part shade, but requires an acid, humusy soil. Otherwise it is not difficult, and probably stands climatic fluctuations better than its relative the rhododendron. Plant like rhododendron, furnish with a mulch over the roots, and keep well watered.

SWEET BAY (Magnolia virginiana)

Zone 6. To 30 feet. Thick oval leaves cover this small tree. It sometimes loses leaves to the north of its range, depending on winter weather. Globular creamy-white flowers appearing in June are deliciously fragrant. This magnolia grows in sun or shade but blooms better and is more compact in sun. Any good soil suits it, and it can take drouth and heat.

SPREADING EUONYMUS (Euonymus kiautschovicus *or* E. patens)

Zone 5. To 6 feet. Permitted to grow untrimmed in a shrubbery border this makes a rounded, thick-spreading shrub with handsome glossy bright green foliage. In July and August small white ill-smelling flowers appear, so don't plant it too near the house. In fall there will be showy pink-orange berries resembling bittersweet. If planted in shade the foliage remains beautiful all winter. It does not fall until late spring and then is immediately replaced with fresh light green leaves. In sun the foliage burns in winter. This is probably the most widely grown broadleaf shrub. It grows fast, is drouth tolerant, takes any kind of soil. In the North, variety 'Manhattan' is a fine selection for good winter color.

EASY-DOES-IT IDEAS

Group acid-soil-requiring broadleaf evergreens together in a planting—things like rhododendrons, azaleas, hollies, leucothoes, and pieris. It's easier to provide for their soil needs this way than if plants are scattered over your yard.

Needle evergreens like spruce are tough and hardy, so let them stand guard over tenderer types like broadleafs. They can furnish necessary shade and ward off harmful winds. The needles even make a protective mulch just right for broadleafs.

If you're unsure about flower colors of azaleas or rhododendrons and how they will mix, select and plant them while in bloom. Then you can tell whether they are compatible.

THIRTY-SIX BROADLEAF EVERGREEN SHRUBS FOR WINTER BEAUTY

Name	Zone	Height (feet)	Flowers and fruit	Foliage	Exposure	Soil	Comment
Aucuba japonica	7	4	Bright red berries form on pollinated flowers	Large glossy leaves seem gold-sprinkled	Shade, protected	Humusy	For doorways, foundations, front of border. Slow growing.
Berberis julianae Wintergreen barberry	5	5	Small, insignificant flowers in May; black berries in fall	Leaves to 3 inches long, narrow, dark, thick; spiny	Sun	Any	Usually stays low. Makes dense shrub.
B. 'Mentor' Mentor barberry	4	7	Small flowers in May. Seldom forms berries.	Leaves an inch long, leathery, stiff spines	Sun	Any	Half evergreen in the North. Usually low. Tolerates heat and drouth.
B. triacanthophora Threespine barberry	6	4	Flowers small, whitish, followed by black berries	Long narrow leaves, bright green	Sun	Any	Graceful spreading branches have thin spines.
Buxus microphylla Littleleaf boxwood	6	3	Inconspicuous	Small bright leaves, dense plant	Sun or part shade	Any	Neither this nor its hardier variety, Korean box, has the glossy good looks of the next kind of boxwood.
B. sempervirens English boxwood	6	20	Inconspicuous	Small, oval shining dark green	Sun, part shade	Any	Long lived, slow-growing, may be sheared or left alone; favorite for hedge.
Cotoneaster dammeri Bearberry cotoneaster	6	1	Flowers white, $\frac{1}{2}$ inch; red berries are showy	Smooth, 1-inch leaves, bright green	Sun, light shade	Any	Grows low and slowly. Long trailing branches, good for planting on banks.
Daphne cneorum Rose daphne	5	1	Pink flowers in April, May; delightfully fragrant	Crowded tiny leaves with bristle-tips on low branches	Sun, but needs winter shade	Limy, with good drainage	Matlike plants have trailing or ascending branches; need mulch over roots.
Erica carnea Spring heath	6	1	Rose-red or white, in March to May; small	Leaves in whorls, needle-like, on prostrate branches	Sun	Acid, with peat and sand	Low tufted shrubs are good for rock gardens.

Name		Height	Flowers/Berries	Leaves	Light	Soil	Habit
E. vagans Cornish heath	7	1½	Pink-purple bell-shaped flowers July to October; not long lasting	Leaves a little longer than in *E. carnea*	Sun	Acid, with peat and sand	Low, spreading, many branches, broader than high.
Euonymus fortunei vegetus Bigleaf wintercreeper	6	4	Small flowers in June; pink-yellow berries, abundant in October	Leaves are broad ovals, 1½ inch long, leathery	Sun or part shade	Any	Fast growing, spreading, goes much higher if supported.
E. japonica	7	10	Pink berries	Glossy, thick, bushy	Sun	Any	Fast growing, reliable; variegated kinds are available.
E. kiautschovicus Spreading euonymus	5	6	Small white flowers in summer; pink-red berries in fall	Oval, glossy bright green	Sun or shade	Any	If planted in shade, leaves stay green all winter; in severe years they winterburn in sun.
Ilex aquifolium English holly	7	50	Small white flowers, large red berries in showy clusters	Large, polished, sometimes variegated	Sun or light shade	Acid, peat; moist	Usually dense, narrow pyramids but available in many shapes.
I. cornuta Chinese holly	6	8	Large scarlet berries	Leaves usually with five spines	Sun or shade	Acid, peat	Slow growing, compact and bushy. Needs male nearby to set berries.
I. cornuta burfordi Burford holly	6	6	Small flowers; red berries sometimes produced without pollinator	Shining, large, with pin at the tip	Sun or part shade	Acid or humusy	Fairly vigorous, makes compact rounded shrub good for doorways.
I. crenata varieties Japanese holly	6	5-10	Produce black berries	Small dark leaves, glossy	Sun or light shade	Humusy	Most stay under 5 feet. *Convexa* is a kind with curved boxwood-like leaves; *microphylla* has tiny roundish leaves.
I. opaca American holly	6	75	Small white flowers, orange-red berries appear in fall	Leathery, dark leaves, not so shiny as *I. aquifolium*	Sun or part shade	Acid, peat or humus	Tolerates wide weather extremes. Fairly fast growing when young.
Kalmia latifolia Mountain laurel	5	6	Purple-pink to nearly white flowers, showy, in May, June	Dark green, leathery, shiny	Sun or part shade	Acid, humus	Makes a rounded shrub, tolerant of weather extremes.

113

THIRTY-SIX BROADLEAF EVERGREEN SHRUBS FOR WINTER BEAUTY (continued)

Name	Zone	Height (feet)	Flowers and fruit	Foliage	Exposure	Soil	Comment
Laurus nobilis Sweet bay	8	20	Small black berries on female plants	Aromatic, stiff, $\frac{3}{4}$ inch oblong leaves	Sun	Peaty soil, moist	A favorite for shearing in any form.
Leucothoe catesbaei Drooping leucothoe	5	3	White bells along undersides of branch in April, May	Long, pointed leaves, dark green or variegated, bronze in fall.	Stands dense shade	Acid, peaty, light, well-drained	Low graceful shrubs with spreading arching branches. Twigs often reddish.
Magnolia virginiana Sweet bay	6	30	Cream-white flowers in June are fragrant	Thick oval leaves, dark	Sun or part shade	Any fertile soil	Sometimes loses leaves north of its range.
Mahonia aquifolium Oregon grape-holly	5	4	Bright yellow blooms in spring, followed by blue berries	Glossy, holly-like foliage, bronze in winter	Sun or part shade	Humusy	Tolerates heat, drouth and cold. Forms are quite varied.
M. bealei	7	8	Fragrant yellow flowers on stiff racemes. Blue fruit.	Leaflets are holly-like in 12-inch leaf groups	Part shade	Any, tolerates lime	Handsome in border or foundation planting. Protect from winter sun and wind.
Osmanthus ilicifolius Holly osmanthus	7	8	White flowered in July, fragrant, followed by blue berries	Thick, glossy leaves like holly, but arranged in opposite pairs	Sun, part shade	Acid, loamy, well-drained	For hedge, specimen, corner or background. Prune tips of young shoots to induce bushiness.
Pieris floribunda Mountain pieris	5	5	White urn-shaped flowers in April, May, on upright stems	Dark green, pointed, not particularly glossy but leathery	Part shade	Moist, humusy, slightly acid	Low shrub with erect stems, bushy, spreading.
P. japonica Japanese andromeda	6	10	Ivory-white flowers in drooping clusters in April, May	Glossy, dark green	Part shade	Acid, peaty, moist	Good for doorways and north of buildings. Surprisingly tough.
Pyracantha coccinea lalandi Laland firethorn	6	8	White flower heads in May; bright orange berries ripen in fall	Small, dark, glossy	Sun	Any, well-drained	Tolerates lime soils. North of its range may drop leaves before spring. Good against walls.

114

Plant			Flower	Foliage	Light	Soil	Remarks
Rhododendron catawbiense Catawba rhododendron	5	8	In early to mid-June, showy white, pink, red flowers	Large, dark, handsome	Part shade	Acid, humusy, well-drained	Spreading shrubs, good for north exposures. Many varieties.
R. carolinianum Carolina rhododendron	5	3	In May, white to rose-purple flowers	Small	Part shade	Acid, peaty, well-drained	Plants spread widely, perhaps to 6 feet.
R. (Azalea) Gable hybrids Gable azaleas	6	4	Flowers showy pink, purple, red	Small oval, bright green	Sun part of day	Acid peat, moist	Can be considered evergreen, though leaves may bronze or fall in severe winters.
R. (Azalea) Glenn Dale hybrids Glenn Dale azaleas	7	5	Flowers showy white to red, mixtures	Small oval, dark green	Sun part of day	Acid peat, moist	Similar to Gables, not so hardy.
R. (Azalea) kaempferi Kaempferi azaleas (Flame)	6	6	Flowers large, showy brilliant yellow to red	Oval leaves	Sun part of day	Acid peat, moist	Not evergreen north of range.
R. maximum Rosebay rhododendron	4	6	Flowers pink to white in June	Glossy, handsome	Semi-shade	Acid peat, moist	Tolerates more shade than most.
Skimmia japonica Japanese skimmia	7	3	White flowers in early spring, then showy red berry cluster	Shining leaves on rounded plant	Part shade	Peat	Male plants needed nearby to get berries. Choice for doorways.
Yucca filamentosa Adam's needle	5	2	Tall spikes of ivory flowers in early summer rise to 6 feet	Large, pointed stiff leaves, in high rosette	Sun	Any, even the poorest	Make strong accents, but use sparingly.

FOURTEEN NEEDLE EVERGREENS FOR LARGE SPACE

Name	Zone	Height (feet)	Growth habit	Foliage	Exposure	Soil	Comment
Abies concolor White or Colorado fir	4	50	Dense, upright high pyramid	Blue-green needles, fine textured	Full sun	Any moist	Tolerant after established. Tapered cones sit upright. Not for the South.
Cedrus libani Cedar of Lebanon	6	80	Stately, upright or spreading; has leading shoot	Dark or bright green, short needles	Sunny open	Any except limy	Slow growing, handsome specimens.
Chamaecyparis obtusa Hinoki false cypress	5	80	Tall, pyramidal and dense	Lustrous dark green	Sunny	Any except limy	Prefers humid climate. Makes quick screen or background.
Picea abies Norway spruce	3	75	Straight with spreading hanging branches	Dark green, lustrous	Sun	Any	Cones hang down. Fast growing, tolerant of extremes. Most beautiful when young.
P. glauca densata Black Hills spruce	3	40	Symmetrical, compact	Blue-green, small needles, fine textured	Sun	Any	Tough but prefers cool summers. Slow growing. Not for the South.
P. pungens Colorado spruce	3	50	Narrow straight pyramid	Blue-green, short curved needles	Sun	Any	Often called blue spruce. Green forms are available. Tolerant and good for dry areas.
Pinus flexilis Limber pine	3	50	Narrow pyramid when young; rounded in age	Five thin needles in each sheath; pliant branches	Sun	Any	Tough. Won't break from snow, wind. Recommended for Great Plains.
P. nigra Austrian pine	4	50	Pyramidal but sometimes flat topped in old age	Stiff, two needles in each sheath, about 5 inches long, dark green	Sun	Any	Handsome and vigorous.
P. resinosa Norway or red pine	3	60	Broad, tall pyramid	Two long flexible needles in each sheath, blue-green	Sun	Any	Fast growing.
P. strobus White pine	3	75	Broad, tall pyramid	Five soft slender needles in each bundle, fine textured	Sun	Any	Not for the South. Makes a beautiful specimen, needs large space.

P. sylvestris Scotch pine	3	40	Pyramidal when young, irregular when old	Two needles in each sheath, shorter than 3 inches, sometimes twisted	Sun	Any	Fast growing, often considered a temporary tree, as it may be short lived. Popular for Christmas tree.
Pseudotsuga taxifolia Douglas-fir	4	50	Tall, narrow pyramid	Needles short, flat, in layered effect	Sun	Any	Rocky Mountain stock is hardiest. Fairly tough and tolerant. Popular for Christmas trees.
Thuja occidentalis American arborvitae	3	60	Usually pyramidal, sometimes rounded	Flat vertical sprays of scale-like needles	Sun, light shade	Any	Some dwarf and low kinds are available. Easy and durable.
Tsuga canadensis Hemlock	3	90	Broad pyramid, graceful	Soft green small blunt needles, on drooping branches	Sun or shade	Humusy, acid to neutral	When young, is sensitive to hot dry winds and weather extremes. Difficult in the South or Southwest, and in arid plains.

FOURTEEN NEEDLE EVERGREENS FOR SMALL SPACE

Name	Zone	Height (feet)	Growth habit	Foliage	Exposure	Soil	Comment
Juniperus chinensis keteleeri Keteleer juniper	4	12	Pyramidal	Dense, bright green, feathery	Sun, light shade	Any	Shear to keep it low.
J. chinensis pfitzeriana Spreading juniper (Pfitzer)	4	4	Spreading, to 15 feet	Dark green, layered	Sun, slight shade	Any	A small-growing kind is called 'Compact Pfitzer.'
J. chinensis pfitzeriana hetzi Hetz juniper	4	4	Spreading, to 15 feet	Silvery-blue, layered	Sun, light shade	Any	Grows faster than pfitzer, denser, otherwise similar.
J. horizontalis plumosa Andorra juniper	3	1½	Low, ascending branches, spreading	Blue-green in summer; purple in winter	Sun	Any	Spreads much wider than it is high.
J. horizontalis douglasi Waukegan juniper	3	1	Low, trailing branches	Blue-gray in summer, pale purple in winter	Sun	Any	Plants spread out several feet. Tolerates poor soil.
J. sabina Von Ehron Globe (Savin)	3	4	Spreading, rounded, or fan shaped	Dark green feathery, dense	Sun, light shade	Any	Fast growing, endures city smoke.
J. scopulorum 'Silver Beauty' Rocky Mountain juniper	3	20	Pyramidal	Greenish-silver with silver tips	Sun	Any	Many other varieties available. Shear regularly to keep it small and compact.
J. virginiana canaerti Canaert juniper	3	12	Pyramidal, compact	Rich green, dense	Sun	Any	Extremely susceptible to cedar-apple rust. Has abundant blue berries.
Pinus mugo mughus Mugho pine	3	5	Rounded	Bright green, usually dense	Sun	Any	Grows slowly when young; good for doorways, foundations.

Name			Form	Foliage	Light	Soil	Remarks
Taxus cuspidata nana Japanese spreading yew	5	5	Spreading, ascending branches	Dark green, smooth needles	Semi or full shade	Any, humusy	Female plants bear attractive red berries.
T. media browni Brown's yew	6	6	Rounded, upright	Dense, dark green	Semi or full shade	Any, moist	Slow growing, sometimes used in globe form.
T. m. hatfieldi Hatfield columnar yew	6	10	Upright, cone or high pyramid	Dark green, smooth needles	Semi or full shade, or sun	Any, humusy	Needs occasional pruning to keep it in bounds.
T. m. hicksi Hick's yew	6	6	Narrow, columnar	Dark green, smooth needles	Semi or full shade, or sun	Any, moist	Use in narrow areas. By trimming you can keep it lower.
Thuja occidentalis globosa Globe arborvitae	3	3	Dwarf, globe-shaped	Bright green leaves in short fans	Sun or light shade	Any, moist	Useful for formal accents.

Chapter 8

HEDGES HAVE MANY USES

How can I get privacy for our terrace?

One good way is to plant a hedge around or on one side of it. There are many types of hedges. You can have high, low, clipped, natural, flowering, non-flowering, deciduous, or evergreen. You can have one that costs you nothing (if you beg privet cuttings from your neighbor and stick them in a trench), or you can spend a great deal on a luxury hedge of hemlock. And you can put them to all sorts of uses. Make rows to note your boundaries; make impenetrable fences to prevent trespass; screen off areas, block bad views, safeguard your privacy. Tall thick hedges help check dust and noise from roadways and they slow down the wind, too. They make good backgrounds for flowers. All the while they themselves are beautiful through the year in flower, foliage or bare twig.

First decide if you want your hedge to be clipped or natural. A clipped hedge makes a neat formal boundary—but it takes a lot of work. You must expect to trim something like euonymus at least three times a season. A natural or unclipped hedge is no trouble at all, provided it *naturally* stays the height you want. If you want an informal 3-foot hedge, don't select something like privet which requires steady clipping to keep it that low. Mentor barberry, or the dwarf hedge viburnum would be better choices. They will go on for years without getting above your limits, and you never touch them with the shears. You can find natural hedge plants to run in size from tiniest boxwood edgings to shrub rows as high as a house. If you want a hedge to produce flowers as well

as foliage, you have many plants from which to choose, but don't plan to trim them. If you do you will probably sacrifice the flowers. Things like Persian lilacs and *Spiraea van houttei,* for which the flowers are the main attraction, would flower sparsely if at all if kept clipped, and you could find better plants for foliage. If you do plant flowering hedges, locate them where you won't have to clip. That means allowing plenty of width.

If you want a hedge to keep out traffic, you have many possibilities. Some plants make such a thick and thorny barrier they would almost stop a Sherman tank, or at the least the neighborhood little league football gang. Two such hedges are trifoliate orange and Japanese barberry. Dogs, cats, and maybe rabbits are stopped by these, too. Hedges do this job as well as a fence, with less upkeep, and more attractively.

HOW TO SPACE HEDGE PLANTS

You decide this after thinking how high you want the hedge to be and what kind of plants you are using. If set close together most plants stay smaller than if they stand alone. Miniature hedges to stay low like boxwood may be set as close as 6 to 8 inches. Hedges you intend to shear like privet are also spaced fairly close, 1 to 1½ feet. Hedge plants you want to grow to 5 feet or more should go farther apart—perhaps 2 feet between virginiana junipers you want to have as a 5-foot hedge. If it's to be an informal, unclipped hedge that develops naturally, space the plants farther yet.

For a sheared hedge that will be planted

close, the best approach is to open a trench. Make it deep and wide enough so you won't have to cramp roots to get them in. To make the hedge absolutely straight, stretch a line end to end and set plants so the crowns are on it. If it's a deciduous hedge like privet, cut plants back halfway when you plant them (unless the nursery has done it already). This starts base branching, which is what you want, and it helps overcome the shock of transplanting. If it's an evergreen hedge like juniper, you don't need to cut it back.

If it's to be a natural high hedge like a row of honeysuckle shrubs, instead of a trench dig a series of individual holes two or three feet apart and plant each as you would any shrub. Space plants for low hedges close together in a staggered pattern (like footprints). This gives a good proportion of width to height. Set the plants deep and gradually fill in the depression as plants grow.

HOW TO SHEAR

Start shearing a deciduous hedge after it has made about 6 inches of growth. Leave about 3 inches of new height at each trimming. You can shear the hedge at least twice the first season. After that, plan to give three trimmings each year. When the hedge finally reaches the level you want, keep it there with your clippers. To get a professional-looking job, stretch a tight line between stakes—level, and set it at the proper height and cut along that line. The sides are as important as the top. *Develop a wide base so light can reach the lower branches.* The best hedge shape is one with a wide base, narrower top, and sides sloping symmetrically upward. A rounded top is good, too, if the shape widens toward the ground. Never let the hedge get wider at the top than the bottom or it will thin out at the base. Rigidly vertical sides are hard to maintain, and are only for very low hedges.

Trim coniferous evergreen hedges like junipers and spruces the same as you would deciduous ones, but not so drastically. They cannot put out new side branches on stems and trunks as freely as other shrubs can. If you remove too many leaves, you may damage the plant, or kill it. The best way with these is to shear them often enough so drastic cutting is never needed to keep them to size, about three times a year. To make an evergreen hedge thick and bushy, start tipping back branches while the plants are small, say 18 inches. If they were bigger than this when you got them, the nursery probably tipped them for you.

A big hedge is a formidable thing to trim unless you do it electrically. The powered hedge clipper cuts the time needed in less than half. Observe the usual precautions so you don't cut the cord or electrocute yourself. For small plantings the hand-operated shears like giant scissors are justified.

REJUVENATING AN OLD HEDGE

You can cut off and start over with old hedges of privet, mulberry, Siberian (Chinese) elm and currant. If they've grown thin, uneven, gawky at the base, this is the thing to do. Wait until early spring just before the leaf buds break, and cut them down leaving only 6 to 8 inches above ground. At the same time, feed the hedge. Dig a shallow trench along each side and sprinkle in fertilizer (like 10-10-10 or 12-12-12), a pint to 12 feet, and water it in.

Soon new growth will push out from the base of the plants, and you can start shearing and shaping the hedge as if it were brand new.

Don't try to renew a hedge of needle evergreens this way. You would kill it. The most you can remove here is about 6 inches from the top and sides (on a 4-foot hedge). For thin places and holes in these hedges, the remedy is to patch in new plants matching the others in size. In a big hedge this gets expensive or impossible. Your only other course is to dig out the whole hedge and start with new.

SIX KINDS OF UNCLIPPED HEDGES

BARBERRY (Berberis)

Mentor barberry (*B. mentorensis*). Zone 4. Makes an upright, compact hedge of 3 feet in height, $2\frac{1}{2}$ feet in width, that stays low and holds a nice shape without trimming. Thorny, it is a thick barrier. It holds dark green leaves all winter in some places; elsewhere it drops them in midwinter. Stands heat, drouth, changeable climate. Plant 18 inches apart in sun or light shade.

Dwarf red barberry (*B. thunbergi* 'Crimson Pygmy'). Zone 3. Deep red foliage on a dense low thorny plant that never gets much above 18 inches. To develop the sparkling red leaf color, grow it in full sun. Space plants 12 inches apart.

Japanese barberry (*B. thunbergi*). Zone 3. Makes a spreading spiny barrier 3 feet high and 3 feet across, thick almost to the ground. In fall it turns to shades of scarlet and covers its stems with red berries. Grows in sun or semishade, heat and drouth. Space plants 12 inches apart.

HEDGE VIBURNUM (Viburnum opulus nanum)

Zone 4. To 2 feet. The bright green leaves of this bushy little plant are viburnum-like but in size and compactness it is unlike any of its kind. It spreads as wide as high. Seldom if ever does it produce flowers or fruit. Give it a heavy soil, and put it in light shade if you wish, although full sun is good too. Space plants 12 inches apart.

HONEYSUCKLE (Lonicera)

Clavey's dwarf (*L. compacta nana*). Zone 3. Although this looks in every way like honeysuckle, it is only 4 feet high when fully grown, and spreads about as far. In spring it produces small creamy flowers, followed by red berries. In a hedge space plants 18 inches apart.

Tatarian honeysuckle (*L. tatarica*). Zone 3. For a high screen this shrub excels. It grows to be 8 feet high, and about that wide. In spring it makes rosy pink blossoms, followed soon by soft red berries that the birds devour. Give it loamy, dry soil, in sun or part shade. In an unclipped hedge space plants 4 to 5 feet apart.

LILAC (Syringa)

Persian lilac (*S. chinensis* or *rothomagensis*). Zone 3. To 8 feet high, 4 feet across. This small-leaf lilac has a twiggy habit and upright nature that make it a good light screen. In spring it produces small red-purple lilac sprays that are mildly fragrant. If you clip it you won't get the full crop of flowers. Space plants $2\frac{1}{2}$ feet apart.

Common lilac (*S. vulgaris*). Zone 3. In a large space this robust plant makes a thick wide screen, with a bonus each spring of fragrant, abundant lilac flowers. It becomes 8 feet high, 6 feet across. In a hedge row space plants 4 feet apart.

RUSSIAN OLIVE (Elaeagnus angustifolia)

Zone 3. To 15 feet. Silvery foliage graces the Russian olive in summer. Another good point is a stout constitution that makes it hardy almost everywhere. For a boundary or screen on a large place it is superb. In old age, the picturesque plants thin out at the base. They are far prettier if not trimmed. Give well drained soil and sun. Its small flowers are fragrant although inconspicuous. Sometimes thorny. It is subject to a bacterial dieback disease that seems to become more severe each year.

SPIRAEA (Spiraea)

Van Houtte spiraea or bridal wreath (*S. van houttei*). Zone 4. This familiar shrub makes a spectacular hedge in May when it wears white fountains of bloom. As a hedge it grows about 5 feet high, in graceful arching shape, spreading to 5 feet. Plant $2\frac{1}{2}$ feet apart, in sun or part shade and in any soil.

Froebel spiraea (*S. bumalda froebeli*). Zone 5. A vigorous, spreading plant that rises about 4 feet high. In May and June it has bright lively pink flowers. Foliage is tipped purple in spring, and in fall it turns autumnal colors. It needs moisture, a neutral soil, and sun or light shade. In hedges, space plants $2\frac{1}{2}$ feet apart.

39 American arbor-vitae makes a rich looking hedge. It grows fast where soil is moist and is a dense screen from top to bottom.

Genereux

40 Boxwood, the classic of all hedge plants, looks as good un-clipped as clipped. Where it is hardy, it is long-lived and needs little care. *Genereux*

41 Japanese barberry makes a tailored hedge with a minimum of clipping. Its fall foliage is an added attraction. *McFarland*

SIX KINDS OF CLIPPED HEDGES

BOXWOOD (Buxus)

True dwarf boxwood (*B. sempervirens suffruticosa*). Zone 6. To 3 feet high, 3 feet wide. For formal uses where it does well, this makes the most perfect low clipped evergreen hedge available. It is best where winters are not too cold and changeable or bright and windy, and where summers are moist and mild. Round, shiny leaves are delightfully aromatic. Space plants 1 foot apart for 2-foot hedge.

Korean boxwood (*B. microphylla koreana*). Zone 5. To 2 feet high. Evergreen leaves are smaller and not so glossy as the sempervirens boxwood, but the plant is hardier in severe winters. Space plants 8 inches apart.

EUONYMUS

Euonymus kiautschovicus (*patens*). Zone 5. You can keep dwarfed selections of this shrub under 2 feet by clipping. It is prac-tically evergreen, and develops dense branches that make it tight and compact to the ground. Leaves are glossy green, and in fall it sets on pink-orange berries. Does well in the shade and any soil. Space miniature forms 9 inches apart, large forms may require up to two feet.

E. fortunei vegetus. Zone 5. Dark evergreen leaves on stems that grow upright. Will grow up to 4 feet but can be clipped to 1- or 2-foot hedge. Has leaves 1 to 1½ inches long and whitish pink fruit in fall. Give it full sun or semishade, a lime-rich soil and space 9 inches apart.

HOLLY (Ilex)

Japanese holly (*I. crenata convexa*). Zone 6. The shiny dark green leaves resemble boxwood, but this evergreen plant is hardier than true dwarf box. Its leaves are slightly oblong averaging an inch in length and densely covering the plants. Bushes become about 3 feet high and will grow that wide if you wish them to. A variety of it called *hetzi* is hardier and similar except faster

42 One of the finest of all evergreen hedges, the yew looks good clipped or unclipped. This superbly developed example is made of hick's yew (*Taxus media hicksi*). *Genereux*

growing with a little larger foliage. Still another similar is *I. microphylla* with smaller leaves. This is the best holly for hedges. Plant it in sun or light shade, a peat-filled soil and space 18 inches apart.

KETELEER JUNIPER (Juniperus chinensis keteleeri)

Zone 4. To 8 feet. An upright juniper ideal for hedge, since it does not get cedar-apple galls or play a part in the cycle of this disfiguring plant disease. The feathery foliage is dense, bright green both winter and summer. Shearing will keep the hedge to 4 feet high, 18 inches thick. Space plants 2 feet apart and give full sun.

PEKING COTONEASTER (Cotoneaster acutifolia)

Zone 3. To 5 feet. Upright, shiny foliage on dense, spreading branches. Makes an attractive clipped hedge 3½ by 4 feet wide. The leaves turn orange in fall. Tolerates sun or shade, drouth, any soil. Space plants 2 feet apart.

PRIVET (Ligustrum amurense)

Zone 4. Makes a clipped hedge from 18 inches to 4 feet high, 2 feet thick. The olive green foliage is small and glossy. Plants stand city smoke, drouth, heat and cold, sun or semishade. It is not satisfactory in complete shade. You can start privet from cuttings, if you do it right. In spring after the first hedge trimming gather slender twigs half the thickness of a pencil and about 8 inches long. Insert them 4 inches deep base down in a shallow trench which you can keep watered. Most of them will soon be growing. Space plants 1 foot apart in the hedge row.

EASY-DOES-IT IDEAS

Want a "friendly" fence to prevent foot traffic from crossing your front yard? A barberry hedge will do the job, and be an improvement to your landscape as well.

Set crowns of hedge like privet and euonymus a little deep and don't quite fill up the planting trench. As plants grow, fill in the depression gradually. This makes the hedge branched and dense at the base, and simplifies the watering problem.

If you want a juniper hedge, and have apple, hawthorn, or crabapple trees in the neighborhood, choose the keteleer juniper instead of canaert. Otherwise you'll have a perfect setup for the cedar-apple rust disease, that disfigures both the apples and the junipers. Keteleer stays free of the disease.

THIRTY-TWO GOOD PLANTS FOR HEDGES

Name	Zone	Height (in feet)	Width	Evergreen or deciduous	Foliage	Informal or clipped	Exposure	Space (in ft.)	Comment
Berberis mentorensis Mentor barberry	4	3	2½	½E	Dark green, thorny	Unclipped	Sun or semi-shade	1½	Thick barrier, upright, compact, stays low without trimming. In some regions holds leaves in winter.
B. thunbergi Japanese barberry	3	3	3	D	Scarlet fall foliage and berries	Unclipped	Sun or semi-shade	1	Spreading spiny barrier, thick almost to ground. Withstands heat and drouth.
B. t. Crimson Pygmy Dwarf red barberry	3	1½	1½	D	Deep red, thorny, dense	Unclipped	Sun	1	Sparkling red leaf color if grown in sun.
Buxus microphylla koreana Korean boxwood	5	2	1	E	Small, pointed	Clipped	Sun or semi-shade	¾	Smaller leaves than *sempervirens* and not so glossy. Hardy in severe winters.
B. sempervirens suffruticosa True dwarf boxwood	6	3	3	E	Round, shiny dark green, aromatic	Clipped or unclipped	Sun or semi-shade	1-2	Most perfect low clipped evergreen hedge for formal uses. Requires moist, mild summers; does not tolerate extremes.
Cotoneaster acutifolia Peking cotoneaster	3	5	4	D	Shiny dense spreading; orange fall foliage	Clipped	Sun or shade	2	Makes attractive hedge 3½ feet high by 4 feet wide. Leaves turn orange in fall. Takes drouth, any soil.
Elaeagnus angustifolia Russian olive	3	15	8	D	Silver-gray willowlike	Clipped or unclipped	Sun	5	Hardy almost everywhere. Good boundary or screen. Prettier if not trimmed. Well-drained site. Fragrant small flowers.
Euonymus alatus compactus Winged euonymus	5	6	5	D	Oval, smooth green in summer, turning crimson in autumn	Unclipped	Sun or semi-shade	4	Branches have interesting bark with corky "wing" formations along twigs. Flowers and fruit are inconspicuous. Fairly slow growing.
E. fortunei vegetus Bigleaf wintercreeper	6	4	1½	E	Small dark green, leathery	Clipped or unclipped	Sun	¾	Can be clipped to 1- or 2-foot hedge. Needs limy soil. Whitish pink fruit in fall.

Name				Foliage	Clipping	Exposure		Remarks
E. kiautschovicus (patens) Spreading euonymus	5	3	3	½E	Glossy green, dense; fall berries are pink-orange	Clipped	Sun, shade	¾-2	Keep under 2 feet by clipping. Compact to the ground. Any soil.
Ilex crenata convexa Japanese holly	6	3	3	E	Shiny dark green	Clipped or unclipped	Sun or semi-shade	1½	Best holly for hedges. Prefers peaty soil. Variety Hetzi is faster growing, has larger foliage. *Microphylla* has smaller leaves.
I. vomitoria Evergreen yaupon	7	5	3	½E	Small, oval	Clipped	Semi-shade or shade	2	Red berries on females. Needs acid soil, moisture. Have male for pollinator.
Juniperus canaerti Canaert juniper	3	5	1½	E	Dark green needles	Clipped	Sun	2	Tolerates drouth. Plentiful blue berries.
J. chinensis keteleeri Keteleer juniper	4	8	2	E	Bright green, feathery, dense	Clipped or unclipped	Sun	2	Upright juniper ideal for hedge. Can be sheared to 4-foot height, 1½ feet wide. Not susceptible to cedar-apple rust.
Ligustrum amurense Amur River privet	4	1½-4	1½-2½	D	Small, glossy olive green	Clipped	Sun or semi-shade	1	Makes a clipped hedge 1 to 4 feet high, 2 feet thick. Takes city smoke, drouth, heat, cold.
L. regelianum Regel's privet	5	3	3	D	Glossy, small	Clipped	Sun or semi-shade	1½	Thick horizontal twigs. Impenetrable hedge. Stands city smoke.
Lonicera compacta nana Clavey's dwarf honeysuckle	3	4	4	D	Small, oval, deep green	Unclipped	Sun or semi-shade	1½	Small creamy flowers in spring. Red berries.
L. tatarica Tatarian honeysuckle	3	8	6	D	Small, oval, deep green	Unclipped	Sun or semi-shade	4-5	Fine for high screen. Rosy pink flowers in spring. Soft red berries. Attracts birds. Loamy dry soil.
Pachistima canbyi	6	1	1½	E	Small, dark green	Clipped or unclipped	Sun, light shade	1	Prefers acid soil, well-drained. Makes neat edging.
Physocarpus opulifolius nanus Dwarf ninebark	4	2	2	D	Small, dark green	Clipped	Sun	2	White flowers May-June. Twiggy, dense.

THIRTY-TWO GOOD PLANTS FOR HEDGES (continued)

Name	Zone	Height (in feet)	Width	Evergreen or deciduous	Foliage	Informal or clipped	Exposure	Space (in feet)	Comment
Picea pungens Colorado spruce	3	5	2½	E	Blue-green needles	Clipped or unclipped	Sun	2	Select plants for uniformity of color. Makes handsome background.
Poncirus trifoliata Hardy orange	6	5	2	D	Glossy dark green	Usually clipped	Sun or semi-shade	1½	Non-edible fruit. Green thorny branches weave impenetrable barriers.
Rhamnus species Glossy and dahurian buckthorn	3	6	3	D	Shiny	Usually clipped	Sun	3	Thorny. Dark red fruits, needs alkaline soil. Tolerates drouth.
Ribes alpinum Alpine currant	2	3	3	D	Small bright green	Clipped or unclipped	Sun, shade	2	Some states ban it because of pine blister rust disease. Brilliant red fruit.
Spiraea bumalda froebeli Froebel spiraea	5	4	3	D	Small, green, purple-tipped in spring; bronze in fall	Unclipped	Sun or light shade	2½	Give moist, neutral soil. Pink flowers, May-June. Vigorous spreading plant.
S. van houttei Van Houtte spiraea (Bridal Wreath)	4	5	5	D	Small green	Unclipped	Sun or semi-shade	2½	White fountain of bloom in May. Any soil.
Syringa chinensis (*rothomagensis*) Persian lilac	3	8	4	D	Small green	Unclipped	Sun or semi-shade	2½	Twiggy habit, upright nature. A good screen. Red-purple sprays in spring. If clipped there are less flowers.
S. vulgaris Common lilac	3	8	6	D	Large green	Unclipped	Sun or semi-shade	4	Fragrant lilac flowers in spring. Thick wide screen.
Taxus media hicksi Hick's yew	6	4	1½	E	Dark green needles	Clipped or unclipped	Semi- or full shade	1½	Red berries in late summer. Good dense background.
Thuja occidentalis American arborvitae	3	5	1½	E	Bright green fans	Clipped	Sun	2	Likes moisture. Makes good screen, background.
Tsuga canadensis Hemlock	3	5	3	E	Soft, feathery green needles	Clipped	Sun, part or full shade	2	Handsome. Needs humusy soil.
Viburnum opulus nanum Hedge viburnum	4	2	2	D	Bright green	Unclipped	Sun or semi-shade	1	No flowers or fruit. Heavy soil. Bushy plant. Compact.

Chapter 9

GRACEFUL VINES AND ESPALIERS

What can I plant for quick effect on this bare new house?

The ready answer is a vine.

Some wag once said that "doctors bury their mistakes but architects plant a vine." Although this statement points out one of the uses of vines and espaliers (as well as the frailties of doctors and architects), it is far from stating the complete case. Many vines are so decorative in their own right, you will be pleased if you plan your yard just to include them. Think then of vines as ways to emphasize your attractive architecture, to soften a line, to make delicate tracery on a fence or wall, to weave a thin veil where one is needed, or mainly for the beauty of their company.

You have a wide choice of long and short term vines. The long-lasting kinds are perennials. They are either woody or come back each year from a hardy root, and each season they become larger and more beautiful. But most of them grow slowly and take time to give the effect you want. Annual vines like morning glories have speed but not permanence. They are finished in one year; you can have them over again only by planting seeds the next season. Some vines are colorful and well worth annual replanting. On a new place where you need instant decorative effects, they are one answer.

Among perennial vines, some are evergreen. These present possibilities of winter color. English and Baltic ivy are two hardy kinds that stay green in many zones all win-

ter and are a wonderful asset to your landscape.

Wherever you plan to grow vines, give them something to climb on. It may be a brick or stone wall, a fence, trellis, tree, arbor, or a steep bank. The type of vine determines the type of support. Clingers, like Virginia creeper and English ivy, will scale solid brick, stone, or wood with rootlets or "holdfasts" that are part of the vine. All the help they need is a little moisture occasionally sprinkled on the surface until they get started. Vines with tendrils, like grapes, gourds, and passion flowers, go up any support slender enough for the tendril to wrap around—wire fences, trellises, strings, or twigs. Sometimes tendrils are disguised, as with clematis, which climbs by twisting its leaf petioles or stems. Twiners like wisteria, honeysuckle, and dutchman's pipe have stems that circle the support. Trellises for these should be slender enough so the vine can find its way but heavy enough to support its heavy mature growth. Climbing roses are not true vines but tall plants you can use as vines if you tie them. Otherwise they sprawl all over the ground.

TRELLISES FOR EACH PURPOSE

Trellises are the usual supports for vines. Make them attractive as well as practical and durable. They can be wood strips arranged on wood frames; or wire mesh stretched on pipe or wood frames. For heavy

43 A pyracantha in a superb example of informal espalier makes a bold pattern on a plain wall. In this case the branches are anchored directly to wood, and no trellis is used.   *Sibley*

vines like wisteria, grapes, roses, or espaliered trees, make them stout. Use two by fours in them. Arbors are better than trellises for the very strong growers like wisteria and grape. Light weight vines like clematis and the black-eyed susan vine require less— wire on a frame is fine for them. If the trellis is up against a house, *hinge it at the base so you can fold it down when you paint.* If the trellis goes into the ground, protect posts from rotting. The best way is to use galvanized metal pipe for the underground portion. If you set wood into the soil, treat it first with preservative, like penta or copper naphthenate (Cuprinol).

For espalier trellises, whether you make them of wood or wire, plan them to last. Where summers are hot, wood is better than wire because it won't burn the vine. Redwood is a long-lasting material. A frame for a dwarf espaliered fruit tree should have the lower horizontal piece 15 inches above ground, with the highest one 5 feet above, and the in-between ones spaced 15 inches apart. With wall nails you can espalier light

vines like English ivy in patterns on brick and stone walls.

Fences are the other favorite supports for vines. No fence—whether it be wire, stone, iron, board, picket, or stockade—is so beautiful it cannot wear a vine. For best effect, don't overplant. *Let the greater part of the fence show.* And use a vine in scale with the fence. Sweet autumn clematis (*Clematis paniculata*) billows pleasingly over large barriers like stone, iron, rail fences, and stockades. The large-flowered clematis makes a delicate tracery on ornamental iron, woven wire, or stockades. Bittersweet belongs in a rustic setting and on something strong like a country rail or stone fence. Virginia creeper climbs well on wooden fence posts and trails on rail fences.

WHAT IS AN ESPALIER?

An espalier is a shrub or tree treated like a vine and trained in a flat pattern. It takes extra work to maintain but it looks very

130

44 Dwarf fruit trees, like this young apple, are favorites for espaliers. They furnish fruit and flowers in a small space. The trellis holds it a few inches away from the brick wall.

Roche

handsome decorating an open wall. It is usually tied to a trellis which is parallel to the wall or fence, but held away from it 4 or 6 inches to allow air behind the plant.

Dwarf fruit trees are popular espaliers. They are easy to train; produce flowers and fruit in a small space; and as espaliers are easier than other fruit trees to care for. Don't espalier a fruit tree against a clean white wall, though, or your insect sprays will spoil the paint. Newly popular for espaliering is pyracantha, which can take the heat of south or west facing walls, has flowers and showy berries in fall and winter. Others sometimes used are camellias, magnolias, forsythias, yews, althaeas, flowering quince (*Chaenomeles*), Russian olive, euonymus, and viburnums. Figs are good in mild climates. In California pomegranates are possibilities.

You're in luck if you can buy an espalier already started. It's easier to continue the pattern a specialist has already laid out. To make your own espalier, start with small plants. Decide on the design and make your support follow it. You probably will choose a fan, candelabra or grid pattern. Set the plant at the middle. Don't fertilize it—you don't want it to grow fast.

Let's assume you want to form a candelabra design of two U's, one inside the other. Cut off all side shoots except two opposite ones for the branches of the outer U. Leave the central leader. Study it. Look about 6 inches above the first branches for two opposite buds you can encourage for the second U. If there are none, let the leader grow until it produces such a set. Then cut it off just above these buds. The buds will become the branches of the inner U. Train these horizontally until they are as long as you want, then carefully tie the tips so they will grow upward. In this way, you can create a candelabra of any number of branches. If you like, let the central leader grow too. Basically this is how all espaliers are created. Let only the desired branches grow, and shape and curve them as they develop by tying to the support. Strips of cloth, polyethylene film, rubber or raffia are all good tie materials. Prune fruit trees only in summer, not spring or fall—or you'll remove bloom spurs.

Sometimes espaliers grow so fast they burst out of their patterns or break down the supports. To curb them, root prune. Dig a narrow trench around plants 18 inches away from the trunks and sharply cut the roots a spade deep at least.

Cordons are special espaliers, simpler than others. They make attractive and different edgings for paths. You let only one or two branches develop, and train them to low wire or rail trellises. Fruit trees, especially apples and pears, gooseberries and currants will grow this way. If it's a one-stem cordon, cut off all but the central stem and bend this in one direction along a horizontal rail or wire tied to posts 18 inches above the ground. Space trees $2\frac{1}{2}$ feet apart and bend all in the same direction. Or leave two branches with one going each way, and space plants 5 feet apart.

You can espalier vines. English ivy is a favorite plant for this on *shaded* walls. Form it in grids, scallops or loops on wires against stone or brick. On walls, stretch wires between expansion bolts set in at the proper places. Select branches to follow each line and tie them to the wire. Cut out all others. You'll have to do this at least five times a summer, but once the pattern is set, all you do is clip off stray branches. Ampelopsis, euonymus and creeping fig are other vines to use this way. Avoid large leaf kinds like Virginia creeper which obscures the design, and rampant annuals like morning glories which grow so fast you can't keep up with them.

SIX IMPORTANT VINES

WISTERIA

Wisterias climb vigorously by twining stems to 25 feet or more. On a house they can lift shingles, and stop up or dislodge drain pipes. But for porches, pergolas, arches, arbors, and as specimens they are most beautiful. A mature vine blooming in May and June is a floral extravaganza beyond compare. The heavy long racemes of lavender, pink or white blooms have everything—even fragrance. Their light green leaves are lacy and ornamental, and in winter the bare stems often hold interesting seed pods. Although wisterias require nothing except sun and good drainage, they do need a permanent support of unusual strength, preferably an arbor.

They can take years to bloom if you get a seedling. Buy plants grown from cuttings or grafts, not seeds, to be sure they will flower immediately. Reliable nurseries sell only kinds known to have bloomed. Occasionally you can find wisteria trained in tree or shrub form for lawn specimens. Pruning either vine or tree kinds to keep them in bounds does them no harm, but wait to prune until July after their flowering. Three prunings a season may be needed to keep them in hand and flowering heavily.

Chinese wisteria *(W. sinensis)*. Zone 5. Flower clusters are not so long as in Japanese wisteria, but the florets are larger and the clusters more dense. This is the common kind that blooms a week or two earlier, before leaves open, and the flowers last until leaves are out.

Japanese wisteria *(W. floribunda)*. Zone 5. This is a kind not commonly planted, although it is a little hardier than Chinese wisteria. It has the longest clusters of flowers. They open from the base downward to the tip and come with the new leaves.

EUONYMUS

Called wintercreepers, these are evergreen vines of exceptional hardiness. The new growth has holdfasts that enable it to cling to brick, stone, tree bark, or wood. A tree or wall clothed in euonymus is beautiful. The vines also make good ground or bank covers because they spread evenly. They are slow growing until they get established. Train and lead them in the way you want them to go. They thrive in any soil, sun or shade, with little care, and can stand drouth and dry winds.

Euonymus fortunei radicans. Zone 5. It has dark evergreen leaves and is vigorous, may climb to 30 feet.

E. f. vegetus. Zone 5. The bigleaf wintercreeper, this is practically like *radicans* but has pink-orange berries in fall to add to the color. Leaves are a little bigger. Grows upright, is also used as a low shrub if clipped.

E. f. kewensis. Zone 5. Similar but has tiny leaves and is small growing.

E. f. coloratus. Zone 5. Hardiest of all, it has leaves that turn plum-colored in winter. It almost never bears fruit, but is vigorous and high climbing.

BOSTON IVY (Parthenocissus)

P. tricuspidata. Zone 5. With dark green, three-pronged leaves it covers stone, stucco, brick, and rough wood walls thickly and to great heights. It easily climbs 40 feet or more. Although sometimes accused of damaging the surface it covers, it has never been convicted. Actually by shielding the wall from driving rain and shading it from sun and heat, it probably helps preserve it. Certainly a cloak of Boston ivy makes a building cooler in summer. You won't want it on a surface you have to paint; and you may find it a nuisance if it crawls over screens and shutters.

Flowers and blue fruits that come in summer and fall are inconspicuous, but the sunset colors of the foliage in autumn are spectacular. The leaves hang on long into winter.

Give this plant a moist but well-drained soil in sun or shade. Vines may be slow to establish, but once started they grow fast.

Formerly botanists called this *Ampelopsis veitchi,* and you may find it listed as such in some catalogs.

P. t. lowi. Zone 5. This is a small growing version, good for stone gate posts, pillars, and low walls.

ENGLISH IVY (Hedera)

H. helix. Zone 6. This is true ivy, an evergreen vine highly prized for its thick, lobed, dark green leaves and its ability to climb on stone, stucco, brick, and rough wood. A sturdy old vine may ascend 90 feet or so. The clean, compact growing habit gives unlimited uses in landscaping. You can train it on wire frames in espaliers, or weave it over low wire trellises and clip stray ends to make a formal thin trimmed "hedge."

The English ivy has large glossy leaves up to 5 inches long. Where winters and summers are both mild, give it sun or part shade. Where summers are hot and winters are cold and bright, put it in full shade, as at the north of your house, otherwise leaves will burn and be unsightly. Always provide moist, humusy soil.

H. h. baltica. Zone 5. Called Baltic ivy, it looks and grows like English ivy but is hardier. It has smaller leaves and is a little less glossy. Where winters are too severe to grow it on walls, it will perhaps do well as a ground cover.

HONEYSUCKLE (Lonicera)

Although honeysuckles make no bold splash of color, they are important vines. Their dark oval foliage is attractive through a long season. In some it is almost evergreen. Their winsome flowers last through the summer, and give off a fine perfume. They climb by twining.

Gold-net honeysuckle (*L. japonica aurea-reticulata*). Zone 5. It is like Hall's except for the leaf color, which is bright gold with green veining. Leaves are useful in arrangements.

Hall's honeysuckle (*L. j. halliana*). Zone 5. *This one may grow too well.* It has the reputation of being a weed where it has gone out of control, become invasive, and smothered low plants or even trees with its rampant twining stems. Where it is carefully contained it is delightful. Its dense wiry stems have dark green leaves that turn purple-bronze in winter and stay on almost until spring. The very *fragrant* white and yellow flowers last from June to September. The plant tolerates heat, cold, drouth, wind, any soil, sun, or shade. Give it a sturdy support and large space.

Trumpet honeysuckle (*L. sempervirens*). Zone 4. Showy large flower clusters of orange and coral appear from June to September. Although this is not as rampant as Hall's, it is vigorous and high-climbing (to 20 feet). Give it a sturdy wire or wood trellis in sun or part shade. It tolerates drouth, wind, and cold, but is not as fragrant as the other honeysuckles.

CLEMATIS

For trellises, fences, lamp posts, tree stumps, and arches, there is nothing to surpass the various members of the clematis clan. The flowers are beautiful and they are easy to grow. Give them firm, thin supports, like wire or lattice.

Sweet autumn clematis (*C. paniculata*). Zone 4. This is the largest growing of them all and is one of the few clematis that succeed in the South. Although its flowers are small, they are exceedingly fine, white, and fragrant. Coming in September they are a good combination with late roses, both in the garden and in arrangements. After the flowers the seed heads appear, fluffy poms that are interesting and attractive. The lacy leaves hang on into winter and in the South they are evergreen. The vine grows fast and is long lived. Nothing ever bothers it. Give it a sunny place in well-drained soil, and a strong large trellis. It rises 25 feet if invited.

Jackman clematis (*C. jackmani*). Zone 4. Striking purple 5-inch flowers with four or five petals burst over the slender vine in June at rose time, and sparsely again through the summer. It grows almost anywhere except the deep South, and in its gentle way is quite tough. It climbs 12 to 15 feet. Cut it down halfway in early spring. It comes up again from the roots and remaining stems. This keeps all the blooms from being out of sight at the top of the vine. Locate it in limy soil where the top is in sun but the roots in shade. It tolerates drouth and dry winds, but does better if watered.

Large flowered hybrid clematis. Zones 4 or 5. These have the most beautiful flowers of the hardy vines. Although showy in flower they are not rampant growing and little pruning is needed. They make a tracery with delicate foliage, beautiful on an iron grillwork or against a white pillar. In early June they bloom heavily, then lightly through the summer. In the South and other mild climates they will not live long. In the North if you protect them by hilling up in winter, you can grow them even in Zone 3. Give them rich, well-drained lime soil, sun in the morning, and something thin to climb, from the day you set them out. Some of the many choice varieties:

'Comtesse de Bouchard,' pinkish rose.
'Crimson Star,' red 3-inch blooms
'Gypsy Queen,' deep velvety purple.

45 Sweet autumn clematis, *C. paniculata,* blooms in early autumn in a cloud of fragrant white flowers. Abundant foliage stays green long into winter. *Caldwell*

46 Grapes are among the most ornamental of vines in all seasons. Here the sun makes interesting shadows through a well-built arbor. *Roche*

'Henryi,' white 6- to 8-inch blooms.

'Lanuginosa Candida,' large white.

'Lasurstern,' large blue-purple.

'Nelly Moser,' light lavender with rose midrib.

'Ramona,' lavender blue, easy.

SIX MORE PERENNIAL VINES YOU WILL LIKE

Bittersweet (*Celastrus scandens*). Zone 3. Give this rapid-growing vine a sturdy per-manent support. Its ropelike stems weave a dense mat, reaching 10 to 20 feet upward by twining. The female vine has the berries; it needs a male pollinator nearby. The color-ful orange fruits, attractive to birds, stay on from September through the winter. Give bittersweet sun or part shade, and plenty of room.

Climbing hydrangea (*Hydrangea petio-laris*). Zone 5. Although slow growing at first, this plant moves faster when it is es-

47 The wintercreeper (*Euonymus fortunei*) covering this chimney is a vine of exceptional hardi-ness and beauty.

Genereux

48 Wisteria produces a bower of fragrant spring blooms. This white-flowering Chinese wisteria is pruned annually to control its vigorous growth. *Genereux*

tablished. Give young plants winter protection for several years. You will be rewarded with showy white flowers in July. The woody, deciduous vine may reach 40 feet, climbing by aerial rootlets on wood, stone, brick walls, or stumps and trees. Give it rich, moist soil, semishade and a north or west exposure. If well situated it will be long lived. It does not tolerate hot dry winds or drouth.

Porcelain ampelopsis (*Ampelopsis brevipedunculata*). Zone 5. A grape-like vine, this is good for sturdy wire arbors and trellises, where it climbs by tendrils, making a dense screen of bright green foliage. It grows fast in average soil and sun or semishade. In fall it has shiny berries, porcelain-like, of lavender, green, and aqua colors. Prune it halfway back each February or March, to thin and shape it. Tolerates cold, heat, and wind.

Silver lace vine (*Polygonum auberti*). Zone 5. For a big wood or wire trellis where it can twine and clamber, this is a fast growing ornamental. It will cover an overhead arbor. In September it is festooned with foamy white flowers. Each spring you will have to prune off dead wood, but the vine soon covers the loss, growing up to 25 feet in the season. Give sun or semishade in any soil.

Trumpet vine (*Campsis radicans*). Zone 4. Fast growing, this makes a heavy vine and needs space and something strong to grow on. It can fasten itself to brick or wood, but gets too big and invasive for most houses. Outbuildings, rough walls and fences are more suited. In July to September, bold red-orange trumpetlike flowers appear at the ends of branches. A hybrid variety 'Mme. Galen,' which has orange-salmon flowers 3 inches across, is an improvement on the

138

49 Morning glory is one of the best of the flowering annual vines. It will cover a large trellis with blooms of red, white, or blue in late summer. *Decker*

50 The orange or white Susans of black-eyed Susan vine (*Thunbergia*) shine out all season in sun or shade. *Morse*

species. Give trumpet vine full sun and a well-drained soil. It does best with moisture, but tolerates drouth.

Virginia creeper (*Parthenocissus quinquefolia*). Zone 4. Another common name is woodbine. For wood, stone or brick walls this native vine is a handsome thing. It may quickly climb 75 feet into trees or on walls, clinging with disks on the tendrils. Leaves are dark shining green, five-parted, and in fall they turn crimson. The shy flowers are followed by blue-black fruit. Leaves fall before winter. Give any soil, sun or part shade. Stands heat, cold, wind.

SIX ANNUAL VINES
YOU WILL ENJOY

Black-eyed susan vine (*Thunbergia alata*). Also called clock vine. Start seeds indoors early or put them in the ground where you want the vines—either way they grow fast and bloom soon. Although they grow to 10

feet they are not rampant and are a good vine for a lamp post, clothes pole, or porch pillar if given a "ladder" of some sort for the twining stems. They will also trail from a window box or hanging basket. Bright round dollar-size flowers, orange to white with maroon eyes, bloom from summer until frost. Give sun or semishade, and water during drouths.

Cup and saucer vine (*Cobaea scandens*). Dainty, interesting foliage and rose-purple flowers are features of this quick growing vine. It reaches to 20 feet and blooms from summer to frost. Start seeds indoors in March. Press them sidewise into moist soil and barely cover. Transplant outdoors to a warm sunny site when frosts are over.

Cypress vine (*Quamoclit pennata*). This slender vine with ferny foliage does not hide its support. Use it to ornament a small trellis of wire. It will climb 10 feet. Small starry scarlet to white flowers open early in morning or after sunset. Plant seeds outdoors as trees are leafing or earlier indoors in pots.

TWENTY-THREE PERENNIAL VINES FOR PERMANENT EFFECT

Name	Zone	Height (feet)	Foliage	Flowers	Uses	Exposure, Soil	Comment
Aristolochia durior Dutchman's pipe	4	30	Glossy 8-inch heart-shaped leaves, dense, twines	Purple-brown, pipe-like, in summer	Thick screen, porch or high fence	Sun, semi-shade	Needs strong support. May be slow starting. Woody.
Ampelopsis brevipedunculata Porcelain ampelopsis	5	30	Grape-like, bright green, has tendrils	Insignificant	Wire arbors, trellises, dense screen	Average soil, sun or semi-shade	Has lavender, green, aqua berries in fall.
Campsis radicans Trumpet vine	4	20	Lacy, bright green	Bold red-orange trumpets in July-September	Covers outbuildings, rough walls, fences	Sun, average soil	A hybrid variety, Mme. Galen has large orange-salmon flowers.
Celastrus scandens Bittersweet	3	20	Oval, on rope-like stems	Small, followed by red-orange berries	Covers stumps, rail fences	Sun, shade; average soil	Berries come only on female plants; need male nearby for pollination.
Clematis jackmani Jackman clematis	4	15	Compound leaves on twining petioles	Purple 5-inch flowers in June and later	For trellises, fences, iron rails	Top in sun, roots in shade; lime soil	Not long lived in the South. Other large-flowered hybrids similar, with flowers from white, mauve, pink, crimson.
C. paniculata Sweet autumn clematis	4	25	Semi-evergreen; lacy; twining petioles	Fragrant white small flowers in autumn	For large strong trellises; railings	Sun, semi-shade	Fast growing, easy; succeeds in the South. Seed heads are also attractive.
Dioscorea batatas Cinnamon vine	6	30	Shiny, dark, twining	Fragrant, white, cinnamon-scented	Heavy temporary screens, large trellises	Sun, semi-shade; average soil	Stands heat and drouth. Often invasive. Dies back in winter. North of Zone 6 dig and store tubers in winter.
Euonymus fortunei radicans Wintercreeper	5	30	Dark, evergreen, climbs by holdfasts	Seldom produced	Covers trees, stone walls, banks	Sun, shade, any soil	Vigorous, drouth tolerant.
E. f. vegetus Bigleaf wintercreeper	5	30	Dark, glossy, evergreen, larger than above kind	Flowers (small) and pinkish berries in fall	Covers trees, stone walls, banks	Sun, shade; any soil	Practically like *radicans*. Also available: *E. f. kewensis* (small leaf), and *E. f. coloratus* (purple leaf).

Name			Foliage	Flowers	Support / Use	Light / Soil	Remarks
Hydrangea petiolaris Climbing hydrangea	5	40	Rich abundant foliage, deciduous	Showy white flowers in July	Climbs stone, brick, wood walls; covers stumps, trees	Semi-shade; rich moist soil	Protect young plants in winter until established.
Hedera helix English ivy	6	90	Evergreen, dark, lobed leaves, shiny	Inconspicuous flowers and fruit	Climbs stone, stucco, brick, rough wood, by holdfasts	Semi to full shade; moist humusy soil	Clean looking and compact; a favorite for landscaping. Can be trained on wire fence.
H. h. baltica Baltic ivy	5	60	Evergreen, dark, not as glossy or large as above kind	Inconspicuous flowers and fruit	Climbs stone, stucco, brick, rough wood, by holdfasts	Semi to full shade; moist humusy soil	More tolerant of extremes than English ivy.
Lathyrus latifolius Perennial sweet pea	4	8	Blue-green, pea-like	Long stemmed, white, pink or magenta; not fragrant	Picket or wire fence	Sun, semi-shade; alkaline soil	Dies down in winter. Strong, rampant. Transplant with earth ball.
Lonicera japonica halliana Hall's honeysuckle	5	30	Dark green, on wiry, twining stems	Yellow-white flowers in summer, fragrant	Coarse walls or fences where it is well contained	Sun or shade; any soil	Grows too well sometimes. Plant where it will not escape and smother trees or shrubs.
L. sempervirens Trumpet honeysuckle	5	20	Dark green, on twining stems	Coral-orange trumpet flowers in summer	Strong wire or wood trellis	Sun, part shade; any soil	Vigorous, tolerates drouth, wind, cold.
Lycium halimifolium Matrimony vine	5	9	Dense, dark green, spiny	Purple, June to September, orange berries in fall	Rock piles, stumps, old fences	Sun, shade; any soil	Rank growing, suckers badly, may choke out other plants.
Parthenocissus quinquefolia Virginia creeper	4	75	Dark, shiny, five-parted; scarlet in autumn	Tiny flowers; blue-black fruit	Large trees, stone, wood, or brick walls	Sun, semi-shade; any soil	Stands heat, cold, wind.
P. tricuspidata Boston ivy	5	40	Dark green, three-pronged leaves; scarlet in autumn	Flowers and fruit are small, inconspicuous	Covers walls, trees; climbs by holdfasts	Sun, shade; any soil	Takes time to establish, then grows fast. Small growing kind is available (*P. t. lowi*).
Passiflora incarnata Passion vine	6	15	Bright green, heavy, with tendrils	Blue and white, thread-like petals and interesting 3-part pistil	Sturdy trellis or fence	Sun, semi-shade; any soil	Dies down in winter, reappears from root in spring, perhaps several feet away. Easily transplanted.

TWENTY-THREE PERENNIAL VINES FOR PERMANENT EFFECT (continued)

Name	Zone	Height (feet)	Foliage	Flowers	Uses	Exposure, Soil	Comment
Polygonum auberti Silverlace vine	5	25	Vigorous, twining foliage	Foamy white flowers in September	Large wood or wire trellis or arbor	Sun, semi-shade; any soil	Part of vine may winterkill; prune off dead parts.
Pueraria thunbergiana Kudzu vine	6	50	Dense, coarse, dark, fast growing	Forms purple flowers in South, but no blooms in North	On rough banks, rock piles	Sun, semi-shade; any soil	Dies to ground in North; invasive; put it away from desirable plants.
Wisteria floribunda Japanese wisteria	5	25	Large compound leaves on heavy twining trunk	Extremely long flower clusters, open with new leaves	Porches, pergolas, arbors	Sun, any well-drained soil	Need strong support; growing on houses they may damage shingles, downspouts.
W. sinensis Chinese wisteria	5	25	Similar to above kind	Clusters are shorter but florets bigger than above	Porches, pergolas, arbors	Sun, any well-drained soil	Flowers open before leaves.

TWELVE ANNUAL VINES FOR ONE-SEASON BEAUTY

Name	Height (feet)	Foliage	Flowers	Uses	Exposure, Soil	Comment
Adlumia fungosa Allegheny vine	15	Soft, airy, like bleeding-heart	White, pinkish like bleeding-heart	Cover iron fences, trellises, small trees, shrubs	Shade, protected from wind; any moist soil	Grows on shrubs without harming them. Really biennial, does not climb until second year. Then seeds and dies.
Boussingaultia baselloides Madeira-vine	20	Heavy, glossy	Filmy, white, in late summer; fragrant	Porches, trellises	Sun, moist light soil	Dig tuberous roots and store for winter. Plant like cannas.
Calonyction aculeatum Moonflower	30	Dark, heart-shaped leaves, luxuriant	Fragrant, 5-inch white, opening in evening	Porches, high trellises	Sun, moist soil	Makes quick cover. Climbs by twining.
Cardiospermum halicacabum Balloon vine	8	Delicate, fine-cut	Inconspicuous, white, followed by inflated seed pods	Medium trellises, wire fence	Sun, any soil	Sow where to bloom, when soil is warm.
Cobaea scandens Cup and saucer vine	20	Dainty, interesting, lacy	Rose-purple flowers summer to frost	For small trellises, wire fences	Sun, any soil	Start early indoors; transplant outdoors when soil is warm.
Humulus japonicus Japanese hop	30	Handsome, dark	Inconspicuous, female vines have hop seeds	For massive shade on arbor, porch, high trellis	Sun, semi-shade; any soil	Rampant, self sows. Plant in fall or early spring where to grow.
Ipomoea purpurea Morning glory	20	Soft, abundant	In late summer, flowers of red, white, pink, blue; doubles	Trellises, tree stumps, high fences, arbors	Full sun; light well-drained soil	Plant where to bloom or in pots indoors; soak or notch seed first to induce good germination.
Maurandia barclaiana Maurandia	6	Glossy, twines on slender stem	Purple-blue foxglove-like flowers all summer	Makes tracery on low trellis, screens	Sun, semi-shade; moist soil	Start seeds indoors in February; plant outside in May.
Momordica charantia Balsam-pear	15	Smooth green	Yellow, small, with warty fruit that holds scarlet seeds	Large trellises, stumps, rock piles	Sun; moist soil	Gourd-like.
Phaseolus coccineus Scarlet runner bean	15	Beanlike	Scarlet bean-shaped blooms midsummer to frost	Trellises, screens, fences, pergolas	Sun, soft loam	Plant when soil is warm; beans are edible if shelled green.
Quamoclit pennata Cypress vine	10	Slender, ferny, sparse leaves	Small starry scarlet to white flowers	Small wire trellis or iron rail	Sun, semi-shade; any soil	Notch seeds or soak them before planting.
Thunbergia alata Black-eyed susan vine	10	Small arrow-shaped leaves, dense	Round, dollar-size orange or white blooms	For posts, small trellis, porch pillar	Sun, semi-shade; any soil	Plant seeds outdoors in May; or start in pots early indoors.

Notch seeds or soak them before planting. Give sun or semishade.

Moonflower (*Calonyction aculeatum*). Use this on porches or high trellises, where you want quick cover. It twines swiftly up to 30 feet or more, making luxuriant dark heart-shaped foliage. The fragrant 5-inch white flowers open at sundown and close the next morning. They are interesting if planted near a terrace or porch where you sit in the evening. If you live in the North sow seeds indoors in March and set plants outside when weather warms. Soften seeds by nicking or soaking before planting. Give sun and moist soil.

Morning glory (*Ipomoea purpurea*). Many named varieties add to the interest of this familiar vine. It grows fast, to 20 feet or more and is good for covering trellises, arbors, high fences, and tree stumps. Plant seeds after weather is warm; soak them a day first or notch the seed with a nail file. Plant in ground where they are to bloom or in pots sunk in soil and kept watered. Pots promote flowering. Give full sun and light well-drained soil. Morning glories reach their flowering stride in late summer and continue until frost. You can get red, white, blue, muted shades, and doubles.

Scarlet runner bean (*Phaseolus coccineus*). Fast growing and colorful, this old favorite covers trellises, screens, fences, and pergolas with scarlet bloom from midsummer to frost. It climbs to 15 feet. The beans are edible if shelled green. Sow seeds outdoors in soft loam, full sun, as soon as other beans are planted. Water them during dry spells.

EASY-DOES-IT IDEAS

Need a quick screen to give privacy or shade on your new patio? Put up a temporary wire fence and plant it with morning glories. Within a few weeks you will have a bower of foliage and flowers to enjoy while permanent shrubs or trees are getting their growth.

You can train slender vines like clematis and English ivy on brick, cement or stone without benefit of trellis if you use the hold-fasts marketed commercially for anchoring vines in place. They anchor into the surface and you wrap the pliable end around the vine.

Build trellises for permanent vines so they are hinged at the bottom to fold down when painting needs to be done behind them. Then the vine does not need to be pulled down or cut off.

PLATE I. Narcissus brighten an early spring day with a reflection of sunshine. Here they bloom with hyacinths and primroses. Roche.

PLATE II. Kaufmanniana hybrid tulips and blue *Scilla sibirica* make a splash of color on the first warm days. Grossman.

PLATE III. Probably the most planted shrub in America, the forsythia or golden-bell is among the first plants to bloom. Groffman.

PLATE IV. In warm climates, the mid-day flowers, mesembryanthemums, will light
a bonfire in a sun-drenched spot. Hampfler.

PLATE V. The peony, one of the most permanent flowers, bursts with abundant blooms at iris time. This is the single variety 'Krinkled White.' Genereux.

PLATE VI. Springing from sturdy perennial roots, the oriental poppy and early daylilies flower together year after year in a carefree display. Harshbarger.

PLATE VII. No flowering shrub surpasses the lilac in beauty and sweet fragrance, and few can match it for hardiness and ease of culture. Roche.

PLATE VIII. Hybrid clematis, the large-flowering kinds, offer distinguished blooms of clear colors, on refined, self-contained vines, hardy and easy to grow over most of the country. Hampfler.

PLATE IX. In midsummer sure color comes from a mixed garden—here are anthemis, phlox, delphinium, baby's breath and double hollyhocks; and petunias in the foreground. Genereux.

PLATE X. Among annual flowers, zinnias are supremely easy to grow, and give flowers by the armful for color or landscape color through the warmest weather. Blue morning glories festoon a wall in the background. Henderson.

PLATE XI. The rose offers many forms. In the background is the yellow floribunda 'La Fontaine'; nearer is a row of the miniature 'Scarlet Gem,' and in the basket are blooms of the grandiflora 'War Dance.' Hampfler.

PLATE XII. Ferns were made for shade. In the center a cinnamon fern raises generous fronds, with silver-green Japanese ferns clustering beneath. Roche.

PLATE XIII. The white and gold trumpets of centifolium or Olympic hybrid lilies highlight the garden in July and August and drift it with sweet fragrance. Genereux.

PLATE XIV. For spectacular color, the 'Enchantment' lily, a Mid-Century hybrid, is unmatched, and it grows and spreads exuberantly. Snyder.

PLATE XV. From grapes you can reap a large harvest in small space, and the upkeep is low. This is the American variety most widely grown, 'Concord.' Staby

PLATE XVI. Strawberries, the first fruit of spring, and the most delicious of the whole year. Everbearing kinds will yield again in summer and fall. Staby.

PLATE XVII. Hardy aster or Michaelmas daisy provides soft colors in late summer and early fall, before chrysanthemums hit their stride. Dwarf varieties blanket this slope. Finnis.

PLATE XVIII. Chrysanthemums blaze with warm hues as the days grow cool and short in fall, giving the garden's last strong blooming surge of the year. Groffman.

Chapter 10

FINE PERENNIALS FOR YOUR GARDEN

What will give me lots of color for a long time?

If you really like color, grow lots of flowering plants, both perennial and annual. You'll have a rainbow in your yard, with plenty of blooms to cut for the house, right through the season. These give you more color than shrubs, because taken all together they bloom longer. If you choose well, you can have something in bloom almost all year. But flowers mean more work. There will be planting, digging, dividing, transplanting, occasional staking, and many other jobs through the season. Most people think flowers are worth the effort.

You'll find many places where flowers bring welcome color—little groups in front of shrubbery, beside a door or step. The most lavish use is in borders—long wide ribbons planted to mixed flowers, usually perennials, ranged along boundaries or in front of shrubs. Another way is in narrow edgings, often of annuals (although not always), fringing a walk, patio, foundation, pool or fountain. Besides these, you can grow them in the vegetable garden in rows, where you can cut with a clear conscience and never spoil the garden picture. Patchy beds in the middle of a lawn are bad. Leave the lawn open and put the flowers around the sides. Locate flowers where they'll do well—sun seekers, like phlox, in sun; others like hostas in shadows.

Choose kinds to grow for your climate and site, by their height and color, the time when they bloom, how well they will grow for you. By all means choose some for fragrance—especially those you'll meet often close to your house.

For flowers as for everything else in your yard, you'll want to plan in advance. Get your ideas down on paper before you turn a spadeful of soil, and then follow them. Use printed graph paper just as you did for your landscape plan—or make your own square-ruled paper.

If it's to be a long strip of flowers—a border—draw it out. Let an inch equal one foot. Be generous with size. A border of perennials looks skimpy unless it is at least 5 feet wide, and 8 or 10 feet would be better where you have room. In tiny dooryard nooks, little flower patches are appropriate. Keep flower plantings in scale with the size of your place.

List plants you'd like to use and divide them into tall, medium and low. Group them by colors if you think that helps. Put tall ones at the back, medium ones mid-way and low ones in front, and arrange colors to suit yourself. Use your best judgment when it comes to color. Bad choices can ruin everything, although many more flower colors will harmonize than you think. Consider the misfortune, though, of locating something like pink phlox next to brick red lilies! It's always safe to use white or pale yellow flowers or those with gray foliage close to bold colors. In fact, white makes other colors seem clearer and it helps to blend them. You'll especially appreciate the

51 The first great burst of color from perennials comes at bulb time in spring. Basket of gold, white candytuft, multicolored primroses, blue wood phlox, and white solomon's seal flourish together under dogwoods in flower.

Gottscho-Schleisner

white ones if you sit in the garden in the evening. White looks beautifully luminous by moonlight.

Your planting rises from the average into the distinguished if you establish a design for it. An easy way to do this is by repeating certain plants or combinations of them rhythmically along the bed. Without being geometric, give the garden some central accents of organization that come through subtly. Gray plants like artemisia, lamb's-ear, and *Veronica incana* will serve all season in this design capacity.

When you have completed the plan, go over it for mistakes. To check it make three tracings. Color one for spring, another for summer, and the third for fall—thinking of when each plant is in bloom and the color of its flowers. Fill in out-of-bloom spots with green to show foliage. These "dummies" of your garden expose errors you can easily correct before planting.

When all meets with your approval redraw the plan in ink to serve as your blueprint as you go ahead with planting.

If you grow flowers you will use three kinds—perennials, annuals, and the flowering bulbs. For annuals read Chapter 11. For bulbs read Chapter 12. For perennials, read on. For plants especially adapted to gardening in shaded places, read Chapter 15.

PERENNIALS ARE YOUR STANDBYS

Like trees and shrubs, perennials stay with you year after year. When cold comes, they die down, but as spring returns they start up again from their hardy roots. Many can stay in the same space for several years, without special replanting or attention. A few, like peonies and dictamnus, once planted are not moved. They are so long-lasting that they may outlive you. But they do need care, some far more than others if they are to look their best. Fortunately with perennials the work comes pretty evenly over the year, and not all at once.

Choose for continuous bloom. No perennials are in flower all summer. Instead, different kinds perform in relay—first basket of gold, then the iris, then phlox, then chrysanthemums. Midsummer may find a scarcity

of bloom of any kind. This is the reason that annuals like petunias, nicotiana, and marigolds are so often used *along with* perennials to carry the color procession through when perennial flowering is light.

WHAT CONSTITUTES A GOOD PERENNIAL?

A good perennial has to meet the standards you set for it—and only you can decide what they'll be. But here are a few things to consider. In the first place is it truly perennial—*through the years?* It need not be immortal, but it should last at least several seasons for you. Another good trait is the ability to stay put. This means it won't go roving all over the flower bed shouldering out other plants and becoming a weed. Naturally you want beautiful bloom from it—clear, living colors that you like, and pleasing shapes. If you grow for cut flowers, then you'll like kinds with long, strong stems. For easy upkeep, choose plants that stand up alone and won't need staking. A fairly long blooming season is desirable too and a healthy tolerance of dry weather, heat, and disease. Finally, it helps if the plant looks good even when it isn't blooming. Fine foliage is a great asset.

All of these good traits are too much to ask in any one plant, perhaps, but some perennials, like peonies, come close. Others like columbine are so lovely that you happily overlook their small faults and plant them anyhow.

PREPARE BEFORE YOU PLANT

Perennials are a long-term investment so put plenty of effort into preparation. Spade the ground 12 inches deep. Add humus (leaf mold, compost, peat moss, rotted manure), the more the better. Spread fertilizer, something like 8-8-8, a pound to 100 square feet and dig it all in at least to one spade depth. Level the bed off and let it settle a week or two while you get your plants together.

Plant by plan. Mark the places with stakes, or with a light outline of sand or fertilizer sprinkled on the ground. If your plan calls for things you can't plant until

147

52 Masses of color, a complete rainbow, are furnished by tall bearded iris late in spring. *Roche*

53 and 54 The Siberian and Japanese irises (below, left and right) extend the iris season and add diversity in bloom sizes and styles. *Adams, Kohl*

later (like bulbs that you'll add in the fall) use markers, cut-up plant stakes, perhaps, to indicate the space and fill in temporarily with annuals. In fact, identify everything you plant with markers, so you'll know what and where it is. A perennial garden takes time to establish itself. The first year or two it always looks adolescent, but as it matures it becomes more substantial and filled out. From the beginning, you'll want to water and cultivate to get rid of weeds. Never hoe deeply among perennials. Many of them—iris and phlox, for instance, have shallow roots that are easily hurt. A mulch like buckwheat hulls, peat moss, or compost will cut down on cultivating and weed pulling. When you water, let the hose run an hour without moving it, to develop deep roots. Shallow watering is almost worse than drouth!

SIX IMPORTANT PERENNIALS AND HOW TO GROW THEM

TALL BEARDED IRIS

Iris means rainbow. No other flower deserves this name so well. Among the tall bearded irises you will find masses of all the colors of the spectrum. Add to that their elegant form and texture, and a hardy disposition that lets the plant live almost anywhere. Only in the warm climates of Florida, the Gulf Coast and Southern California will it fail.

The many members of the iris group spread the blooming season over a long span. Tall bearded kinds, reaching a peak in May and June, provide the most color, the biggest blooms, and the widest variety of them all. A few kinds will sometimes bloom lightly again in fall. Before this you have had color from the fragrant netted iris (*reticulata*) which came into flower with the scillas; the dwarf irises which flower with species tulips; the median, table or intermediate irises which are halfway in size and season between dwarfs and talls. As the tall bearded flowers begin to taper off, the slender purple or white buds of Siberian irises open. Next are the spurias, usually white and yellow (but not always) and con-

siderably larger, and like the Siberians, beardless. Finally, the last strong note of the iris season is sounded by the Japanese irises (*kaempferi*) opening magnificent blue, white, orchid, and purple flowers in late June and July.

Scattered through the season are flowers from others of this numerous group—the *cristata* or crested iris, the *tectorum* or roof iris; the Louisiana iris; and later in summer the afternoon-blooming vesper iris (*dichotoma*).

You can use irises all alone, or mixed with other plants. When you have a large collection of them it's best to give them space alone. While they are blooming they make a show that stops traffic. The rest of the year the plants are just there.

You may prefer to grow iris among other flowers. The spear-like leaves make good accents in a mixed planting, so you are getting some good out of irises even when they are not blooming. Put tall bearded irises about midway in a border—neither at front nor back but where other plants can be on all sides.

Start with the tall bearded kinds. Here you can select from hundreds of good varieties. They come in sizes from 15 to 40 inches high, and the catalogs, many of which show them in beautiful color, rate their blooming times as early, midseason, and late. Look for Dykes Medal winners. This is an award the American Iris Society gives to superior varieties. You can't go wrong with any of them. Some of the catalog words will puzzle you—the "falls," which are the three lower petals, and the "standards" which are the upright ones; "self" which means the flower is all one color; "bicolor" meaning the standards are a different hue from the falls; "plicata" meaning color dotted or streaked on a white or light background. The root is called a rhizome.

Plant tall bearded irises in sun, where the ground drains well. They can stand baking in the summertime. Plant rhizomes so the root sits flat just under the soil, and the white roots extend out and down. After three or four years, clumps become crowded. When flowers seem smaller or fewer, the roots probably need dividing. Do this right

TWELVE GOOD BEARDED IRIS VARIETIES

	Color	Height (inches)	Bloom time
Argus Pheasant	Golden brown	38	Early midseason
Blue Rhythm	Medium blue, smooth	40	Midseason late
Blue Shimmer	Blue-white plicata	38	Midseason
Blue Sapphire	Silver-blue, ruffled	40	Early midseason
Cloud Cap	Large; flamingo pink	40	Midseason late
Mary Randall	Rose pink	36	Midseason
New Snow	White, ruffled	38	Midseason late
Ola Kala	Deep gold yellow, ruffled	38	Midseason
Ranger	Near crimson-red, large, fragrant	36	Late
Sable Night	Black-violet with red-tinged standards	36	Midseason
Truly Yours	Yellow falls shading to white standards, ruffled	40	Very late
Violet Harmony	Violet, ruffled	38	Early midseason

after blooming time. Dig the clump, break off the husky outer rhizomes topped with big foliage fans and save them for replanting. Throw the rest away. One single fan is enough to start a new clump, but if you're in a hurry plant three. A strong root usually produces flowers the year after it's planted.

Give them room—a clump needs 18 inches of air around it. Don't let other plants grow up to them or you're inviting the one serious trouble they have—rhizome rot. This is a bacterial disease, worse on some varieties than others but none seems immune. Leaves are water-soaked and slimy near the base, and the rhizome is full of soft, smelly mush. When you find this, dig the plant and burn all the infected parts. Soak any roots you salvage in a solution of bichloride of mercury (poison), a 7-grain tablet to a pint of tepid water, for two hours. Replant in a fresh spot. The iris borer (a moth-worm combination) is to blame for a lot of this trouble. The worm eats holes in the root, letting the bacteria get started. So if you have this trouble in your locality, spray your irises every few weeks with a DDT spray to get the borers, and start as the leaves emerge in spring.

THREE OTHER TYPES OF IRIS

Siberian iris. These need more moisture and shade than tall bearded kinds, but don't put them in deep shade. Their roots are fibrous. They can be transplanted any time, even while blooming. Once you've planted them, leave them alone. They need little attention except dividing when clumps get overgrown, every four or five years. Erect and stately, with fine foliage and slender stems—each crowned with a few perfect, small, beardless iris flowers of purple, blue, or white—these make good accents among other plants. They average 30 inches when in bloom so place them halfway back in the bed. Two of the good varieties: 'Caesar's Brother,' deep pansy violet; 'Seven Seas,' blue-violet with golden patches.

Spuria iris. These resemble Siberians, but they are taller, stiffer, and have no fountain of foliage at the base. They may grow 5 feet tall. The flowers are large and flaring, wonderful for corsages and bouquets, and usually white, yellow, and light blue colors. Place spurias toward the back of plantings, and where there's moisture. A good kind: *ochroleuca gigantea*, beardless with yellow and white falls and standards.

Japanese iris. Here are handsome flowers unlike any other irises. They are flat and wide, perhaps 8 inches across without a trace of beard but often waved or ruffled. They sit atop 3-foot stems. Colors are in the white-orchid-mauve-blue-purple range. Plants need more humus and soil acidity than other irises and more moisture at certain times. Water them copiously in spring and summer, but in winter see that they're well drained and also well mulched. Plant or divide any time after flowering. Try any of the Oregon-bred kinds called Marhigos.

PEONY

Peonies are the backbone of a garden, because they're so permanent. They can be part of a border of mixed flowers, or alone they make a summer hedge along walks or boundaries. They even mix well with your shrubs, and they will probably still be there years after the shrubs are gone. They need the rest cold winters give them which is why they are not practical in Florida, the warm Southwest, and most of the South.

This is one perennial that seems to have no faults. It gives bountiful color in the yellow-white to red range, stems good for cutting, all-season handsomeness of foliage, and a carefree and hardy constitution. Only on one point can you criticize it—its blooming time in spring is so short.

To get a longer season from peonies, plant several kinds to bloom at different times. The earliest flowers come from some of the tree peonies which are really shrubs since their woody frame does not die to the ground. At about the same time you will have the fern-leafed *Paeonia tenuifolia* blooming and the old fashioned, small, red-flowered *P. officinalis*. The beautiful new peony hybrids like 'Red Charm' are also early, blooming at this same time. Soon afterwards the single and Japanese kinds begin. On their heels come the full course of

Chinese doubles—the favorites for Memorial Day. Among these are kinds rated early, midseason, and late.

Your selection depends on how you'll use them. In a mixed garden of perennials, you need early, midseason, and late kinds. Among other flowers the singles, Japanese, or hybrids are more graceful than the Chinese doubles—and they don't have to be staked. Yet this is a matter of taste and for sheer show there's nothing like combining the doubles with iris to burst simultaneously into the most rousing color affair of the year. If you want to plant a row, it is best to have them all one kind, or at least kinds that bloom all at once, or you'll get a ragged effect.

Some people who grow herbaceous peonies to show, disbud them. They go over the plants when buds have reached the size of a pea, and nip out all except the top one. This makes an extra large bloom, one on each stem, but it has a disadvantage: the plant tends to bloom all at once and then quit, since no buds are left to come on. So unless you're interested in winning prizes, don't bother to disbud, or do it in moderation. Don't disbud the single and Japanese kinds at all, for hardly anything is gained by it.

Plant peonies where they get sun at least half the day and are well drained. Space them 3 feet apart, or 2 feet from other plants. The right time is as soon as you can get roots in fall—usually late September or October, although now you can also get container-grown plants to set out in spring. Dig deeply and mix in a cup of balanced chemical fertilizer with peat or leaf mold. Then tramp the soil down to settle it. Put the peony root (which has three to five eyes or growing points if it's a good one) near the top of the hole so the eyes are covered just 2 inches deep. Fill in around with fine soil and water it thoroughly.

You may never need to divide a peony— but if one gets too big for its space or its blooms dwindle in size, that's the only answer. Wait until fall, and cut off the tops. Dig up the whole root system and wash off the soil. With a sharp knife cut the roots into sections so each has the required three

151

TWELVE GOOD PEONY VARIETIES

Chinese doubles

	Color	Bloom time
Festiva Maxima	White flecked at center with crimson; fragrant	Early
Kansas	Large, solid red	Midseason
Mons. Jules Elie	Medium pink with silvery sheen; large; fragrant	Early
Myrtle Gentry	Flesh pink, nearly white; fragrant	Late
Walter Faxon	Bright rose, deeper center; fragrant	Midseason

Singles
(yellow stamens at center)

Arcturus	Red	Midseason
Krinkled White	White, crepelike	Late
Pico	Blush pink	Early
Sea Shell	Deep lively pink	Midseason

Japanese
(with cluster of petaloids at center)

Ama-no-sode	Bright pink with center pink gold	Midseason
Charm	Deep red	Late midseason
Isani-Gidui	White with buff center	Midseason

to five buds. Each should also have 6 to 8 inches of single or branched root. Replant this as you originally did, taking the opportunity to add fertilizer and humus to the soil.

Only one serious disease mars the happy life of the peony—a blight called botrytis which makes buds dry up and the foliage look scorched. The remedy is to cut off the tops at ground level every fall and burn them; and spray the ground around the plant early each spring with Fermate spray. Botrytis is one reason why a peony may fail to bloom. Other possibilities are that it's planted too deeply, or in too much shade, or the root is still too small.

DAYLILY

By all odds, daylilies (*Hemerocallis*) are the easiest of perennials. They grow north to south, east to west—no region is without them. There is variety in color. Although most are yellow, you can get daylilies in red, wine, pink, apricot, lavender, and purple. Some have bars or eyes, and some are contrasting bicolors. Many of the newer ones are ruffled or waved and have unusual shapes—flat, bowl-like, or spidery. You can have them from iris time until the end of August or into fall by selecting the right varieties. In height there is a range from small, 18-inch kinds to those reaching 4 feet. You can have evergreens or deciduous ones in the South. Although the evergreens as a group are not so cold-hardy, a few will tolerate northern winters. They are as permanent as peonies and undemanding about their conditions. Each flower lasts only a day, but it is followed by another somewhere else on the scape, and the supply of new buds provides several weeks of bloom. If your garden is viewed in the evening, include some of the late day and evening bloomers, like 'Mrs. B. F. Bonner' or 'Friar Tuck.'

You will hardly ever have to stake daylilies, and spraying or dusting is only for the most particular devotees.

TWELVE GOOD DAYLILY VARIETIES

	Color	Height (inches)	Bloom time
August Pink	Rose-pink, small, much branched	34	August on
Colonial Dame	Light apricot with tan halo	36	June, July
Evelyn Claar	Salmon-rose turning orchid	30	June, July
Farewell	Buff-yellow	30	Mid-August on
Friar Tuck	Deep yellow, nocturnal	30	June, July
Garnet Robe	Dark red with yellow-green throat	36	July
Hyperion	Lemon yellow, fragrant, needs part shade	40	June, July
Little Cherub	Yellow, profuse	28	May, June
Mrs. B. F. Bonner	Light yellow, large, evening blooming	36	June, July
Pink Charm	Soft pink	30	Mid-July, August
Pink Dream	Pink, small, evening blooming	30	June, July
Salmon Sheen	Pink-salmon, broad-petaled	36	June, July

If you want to take their flowers into arrangements for the house, be prepared to replace them each day, for nothing you can do prevents them from closing when their time comes. On the other hand, the fresh blooms will last as well out of water as in it.

Daylilies carry the color load in midsummer while other flowers rest. If it doesn't get too hot for delphiniums where you live, combine yellow or pink daylilies with the Chinese or Pacific hybrids. Or put daylilies, especially clear pastel kinds, beside blue globe thistle, or with lythrum. The toasty colors are hard to combine with anything.

Plant daylilies in full sun or part shade and any good soil. See that they get moisture early while they're growing fast. You can transplant in spring, fall, or even while they are blooming. Put them about 2½ feet apart, with the crowns (where foliage meets root) at soil level. They will make large mounds of strap-like leaves. Tall growing kinds belong toward the back of a border. They fit well among peonies. Most modern varieties, although easy to establish and grow, are slow about increasing—which is a blessing. A new clump will go five years without dividing if it had room enough in the first place.

PHLOX

These are easy, dependable, adaptable perennials, rewarding you with lavish trusses of rose, coral, pink, purple, lavender, and white flowers in mid-summer. The new kinds, especially those from England, are so beautiful that it seems criminal to waste space on the ubiquitous magenta ("reverted") phlox that take over from seed in a neglected planting.

These flowers are for garden show—not for cutting. They fall too soon for that. But what a show they create! It starts with the perfect white 'Miss Lingard' as the irises fade, and continues with new ones chiming in right up until frost if you keep them from seeding. You will find all colors here but true yellows, reds, and blues, and heights from 18 inches to 3 or 4 feet.

They are good blooming companions for baby's-breath, veronica, coralbells, and delphiniums, but don't try mixing them with brick colored lilies or any but pale yellow daylilies. The white varieties, however, combine well with almost any plants. Most of them are of mid-border height, that is, 20 to 36 inches. Tallest growers like the white 'Mary Louise' belong in the background.

TWELVE GOOD PHLOX VARIETIES

	Color	Height (inches)
Charles Curtis	Bright cherry red	30
Columbia	Light rose pink	36
Fairy's Petticoat	Pale pink with darker eye, large	30
Leo Schlageter	Orange-scarlet	36
Lilac Time	Deep violet	42
Little Lovely	Violet with white eye	18
Mary Louise	White	36
Miss Lingard	White, early	24
Mt. Everest	White with pink eye	30
Reine de Jour	White with red eye, early	15
Salmon Beauty	Salmon pink with white eye, large	42
Sir John Falstaff	Salmon pink with darker eye, large	24

Put something low in front of these plants to hide their feet if you can't prevent lower leaves from yellowing and falling near summer's end—and you probably can't.

Give them a place in sun or light shade and soil rich in leaf mold, peat, or compost. Feed them at least once a year with a balanced fertilizer. They need regular moisture in the growing season and some protection from their worst enemies, red spider and mildew. Both of these pests can be warded off by regular spraying or dusting with a multipurpose combination containing a miticide like Aramite or malathion, and a fungicide like sulfur or Kelthane.

Set out new plants in early spring or in fall, with the growing point close to the surface of the soil—not covered more than an inch. Divide older clumps every three or four years. Save only the vigorous outer shoots. Replant them in freshly enriched, prepared soil.

In the summer keep bloomed-out heads cut off to prevent seed from dropping. Pull out chance seedlings you see. If you cultivate at all, do it very lightly, for the roots run nearly at the surface. Mulching is better.

ASTERS

Hardy asters are only a step from the aster of the roadside. In your garden they give a matchless soft enchantment as summer wanes. Another name for them is Michaelmas daisy, a tribute attached by the English, who were the first to appreciate and improve them. The new kinds appearing almost annually are making these a major perennial, where once they were obscure. They will grow everywhere. You'll find they fill a vacancy. They bloom when almost nothing else does. Just as the summer phlox begin to taper off in August, the asters begin—and they carry the color until chrysanthemums take it up in late September.

A size exists for any need—background, mid-border, edging. The small Pacific hybrids, ranging from 10 inches to 2 feet, start blooming a week or so earlier than the Michaelmas types. Try them in front of low shrubs and in the foreground of a border. Other kinds of asters may reach to 5 or 6 feet. They belong at the rear. Plants become mounds of small purple, lavender, pink, and white daisy-like flowers. You'll like them close to yellow helianthus, heliopsis, and gloriosa daisies, or the true blue leadwort (*Ceratostigma*). Against gray foliage of artemisia, or mixed with early blooming buff or

SIX GOOD ASTER VARIETIES

	Color	Height (inches)
Alaska	White	30
Bonny Blue (Oregon hybrid)	Blue-lavender	8
Harrington's Pink	Clear pink	48
Marie Ballard	Blue-violet	30
Persian Rose (Oregon hybrid)	Rose-red	15
Snowball (Oregon hybrid)	White	15

55 Creeping phlox or *Phlox subulata* nests in a rock crevice or hangs over a stone wall with equal ease and gives early spring bloom. *Roche*

56 In May, June, and sometimes through summer the fringed blooms of spicy pinks float above gray-green foliage. This is the fragrant soft pink 'Irene.' *Jackson & Perkins*

57 *Below* Lythrum or loosestrife offers airy spikes of upright flowers in rose and purple hues. It blooms through heat and drouth. *Roche*

58 *Left* Tolerating light shade, the columbine is graced with many-colored long-spurred flowers from May to July. 'Scott Elliott Hybrid' is shown here. *Genereux*

bronze chrysanthemums they make a lovely picture.

Give them a sunny location with good drainage and air circulation. Keep other plants from crowding them. During the growing season see that they get lots of water. Most varieties need dividing each spring or at least every other year. If you don't divide them, they decline and disappear. Save only the supple new outside shoots and reset them, two or three to each hole, at the level they were before. Space dwarf kinds 15 inches apart; tall kinds 2 feet apart. Tall growers like 'Harrington's Pink,' need staking. Use a stout rod. Set something in front of these to hide bare stems which are likely to develop as the season moves along.

Asters of the Michaelmas type sometimes fall victim to aphids. A quick all-purpose spray or dust controls them. The other threat is mildew which spoils the dark green foliage. Sulfur dust on a cool day is a good remedy for it.

CHRYSANTHEMUM

As the days grow cold these flaming colors end the garden year with high drama. You'll welcome the same warm blooms for cutting and taking inside. Everybody wants chrysanthemums, even though they are more work than other favorites like peonies.

Year by year chrysanthemums get better for more people. If you live in the North or in the gusty Plains, you are finding now that you can get kinds to bloom early, before your freezes come. Stress these in choosing what to grow. Every place has some chrysanthemums which will succeed. Find out which ones are for you. Otherwise, you're in for frustration. Your neighbors, nursery, and experiment station can help.

Get acquainted with the different types of mums: *cushion* which make hemisphere-shaped mounds, good in front of shrubs, walls, along drives, and in the foreground of large flower borders; *Koreans* or northland daisies, the single mums, loose-growing and informal, mixing well with other plants; *doubles*—buttons, pompons, and large garden types—the most important group for outdoor color. You'll also meet the spoons

(singles with spoon-shaped petals); spiders or fujis (semi-doubles with curled, thread-like petals—usually late and tender); and footballs (the incurved kinds especially grown and disbudded for large size).

You may rebel against giving all-season growing space to mums in your perennial border. Through spring and summer they stand there contributing nothing until all the other flowers are through. One solution is to grow them somewhere else, like a row in the vegetable garden, and move them to the spotlight when they are ready to bloom. Their shallow roots are easy to transplant any time if you water them well. Another solution is not to admit them at all to your border of mixed perennials, but make a special place for them—a planting along a walk, fence, wall, drive, or before shrubs.

At any rate, give them a place in full sun, and light, well drained soil. Space them 18 inches apart. If you're new at growing mums you'll be shocked at the small plants you start with. They are single divisions or rooted cuttings. Mums grow best from these. Pinch the tops out of them when they're 6 inches high, and again at 12 inches. This makes them branch so they won't need much staking, although some kinds like 'Purple Waters' will require stakes anyway. The cushion types are self-branching and never need staking.

Mums need dividing every spring; only occasionally will they perform for two seasons without division. April is a good time to do it. Lift clumps, pull off the husky outer shoots which have roots, and throw the old woody part away. Replant the single shoots. Water and shade them and soon they'll be flourishing. Undivided mums rapidly get weedy looking and the blooms dwindle to nothing. You wouldn't want them in your garden.

TWENTY-FIVE MORE PERENNIALS YOU WILL ENJOY

THESE BLOOM IN EARLY SPRING

Basket of gold (*Alyssum saxatile*). May-June, gold and yellow flowers above gray foliage. Height to 8 inches; tumbles grace-

TWELVE CHRYSANTHEMUMS WORTH GROWING EVERYWHERE

(Ask your state extension office about kinds especially recommended in your region.)

	Description	*Bloom time*
Apogee	Thirty inches, lavender, double 4-inch flowers	September 1
Apricot Sheen	Eighteen inches, cushion, buff-apricot	Mid-September
Avalanche	Thirty inches, white, double, large	October 1
Campaigner	Thirty inches, bronze-gold, double, large	Mid-September
Chiquita	Thirty inches, pompon, light yellow	October 1
Dr. L. E. Longley	Thirty inches, rose-lavender, double	September 1
Early Wonder	Thirty inches, pompon, pink	Mid-September
Mardi-Gras	Twenty-four inches, bronze to yellow, double, 4-inch flowers	Mid-September
Minnpink	Twenty-four inches, cushion, pink	Mid-September
Purple Waters	Thirty inches, dark purple, large-flowered, double	Mid-September
Tonka	Thirty inches, yellow, double	Mid-September
Yellow Avalanche	Twenty-four inches, yellow, double	Mid-September

fully over rocks, walls. Short lived. Give full sun, good drainage. *Citrinum,* a lemon yellow form, blends well with spring bulbs.

Bleeding heart (*Dicentra*). Blooms May-June, some kinds bloom again later, arching sprays of rose-pink to white heart-shaped flowers over fernlike foliage, plants to 24 inches. Long lived. Give partial shade, loose, humusy soil. Plant early spring or fall. Kinds: 'Silversmith,' hybrid, white flowering with compact, blue-green foliage. 'Bountiful,' spreading plants 10 inches high, pink blooms. *Spectabilis,* old fashioned species, large growing, red-pink flowers.

Candytuft (*Iberis*). May-June, snowy white flower heads above compact evergreen 6- to 12-inch plants. Choice for edgings, foregrounds. Give good drainage, full sun. 'Purity,' to 10 inches, dwarf, spreading with persistent flowers. 'Little Gem,' 8 inches, makes compact clump, flowers heavily.

Columbine (*Aquilegia*). May, June, July, graceful spurred flowers of white, pink, yellow, red, blue combinations on plants 2 to 3 feet tall. Attractive foliage. Tolerates light shade. Give light, humusy, well-drained soil. Not long lived, but self seeds. Control leaf miners by burning affected leaves and spraying plants with DDT. 'McKana Hybrids' have giant, long spurred blooms in many colors. 'Scott Elliott Hybrids' are not so large but easy to grow and in a wide range of colors.

Creeping phlox (*Phlox subulata*). Blooms in April-May, covering matlike 6-inch plants with pink, cerise, white, lavender-blue flowers. Give full sun, good drainage. 'Blue Hills,' strong growing, nearly evergreen, sometimes blooms again sparsely in fall. *Alba,* light green foliage, pure white flowers, vigorous.

Lily-of-the-valley (*Convallaria*). In April and May, forms tiny, white, arching, fragrant bell-shaped flowers. Plants under 8 inches. Foliage presentable most of summer. Plant in fall or early spring, in sandy, humusy soil, shade or semishade. A double variety and a pink flowering kind are also available, but the common white is most charming.

Meadow rue (*Thalictrum*). May-June, feathery blooms of white, cream, lilac, 3 to 4 feet. Plant in spring; humusy soil, good drainage. *Aquilegifolium* needs full sun;

purple or white flowers. *Dipterocarpum* needs light shade, protected site; lavender flowers in June, July, August.

Oriental poppy (*Papaver orientale*). In May-June, large crepe-paper cups of vivid crimson, orange, coral, pink, white, lilac, with contrasting centers, on 18-inch to 3-foot stems. Give full sun, light soil, good drainage. Foliage disappears after bloom, reappears in fall. Plant in August 2 feet apart, top of root covered 1 inch. Good kinds: 'Barr's White,' white with purple spots at base; 'Helen Elizabeth,' clear pink; 'Salmon Glow,' large, salmon-orange.

Pink (*Dianthus*). Flower in May-June; some kinds through the summer. Single and semidouble fringed and notched blooms of red, pink, white and combinations. Neat, compact blue-gray foliage. Give full sun, good drainage especially in winter. Shear in fall, divide after two years. *D. deltoides* (maiden pink), tight mounds to 12 inches covered with usually pink blooms on thin stems. *D. plumarius* (grass pink), to 12 inches, spicy, fragrant, single or semidouble flowers of red, rose, to white. 'Allwoodii' hybrids, 12-15 inches, mixed colors.

THESE BLOOM IN SUMMER

Baby's breath (*Gypsophila*). In June-July, a thin cloud of tiny pink or white flowers on 2- to 3-foot network of stems and leaves. Long lived. Give lime soil, full sun, good drainage. 'Bristol Fairy,' white, double flowered, 3 feet, repeat blooming. 'Rosy Veil,' 15 inches, double pink flowers on silver-gray foliage.

Balloon flower (*Platycodon*). Blooms in June, continues to August if no seeds form. Blue, white or pink balloon-shaped flowers on 30-inch plants. Hardy, long lived. Give sun, good drainage especially in winter and don't disturb roots with hoeing or digging. Comes up late in spring, so mark position well. 'Grandiflorum,' about 20 inches, has deep blue bells, sometimes semidouble. 'Grandiflorum album,' white form. 'Shell Pink,' pale pink form.

Baptisia (*Baptisia*). In June, indigo blue flowers above a 4-foot mound of pea-like foliage. Long lived, hardy, seldom needs dividing. Plant in spring in full sun, any good well-drained soil, allowing 2 feet of space from other plants.

Beardtongue (*Penstemon*). June to August, airy foxglove-like flowers on upright stems, purple, blue, lavender, pink, red, orange, white. Varied in size and form. Give full sun, light, well drained soil. Plant in spring. 'Rose Elf,' prolific rose-pink flowers on 15-inch spikes. 'Indian Jewels,' rose, pink, blue, white flowers on 20-inch stems. 'White Queen,' 30 inches, is stately pure white form of *P. digitalis*, best in rainy areas.

Bergamot (*Monarda didyma*). In June-August, attractive shaggy white, red or pink clusters of two-lipped flowers atop 2- to 3-foot stems. Shade tolerant, will grow anywhere. Plant in spring. Spreads. Stands drouth. 'Cambridge Scarlet,' bright red, attracts hummingbirds; 'Croftway Pink,' soft rose; *alba*, white.

Coralbells (*Heuchera*). In June to August, tiny pink, red or white bells on wiry stems to 20 inches, above mounds of rounded foliage. Plant or divide in spring. Separate old clumps every third year. Give sun or part shade, humusy soil, good winter drainage. Good for edgings. Kinds: *sanguinea*, red flowers; 'Rosamundi,' coral-pink.

Delphinium (*Delphinium*). Blooms in June, sometimes again in fall. Stately spikes of blue, purple, white or pink flowers, 3 to 6 feet high. Short lived and difficult in hot climates. Use for border, background. Give sun or part shade, humusy soil containing lime; protect from winter moisture around the crown. Cut down first bloom stalks before seeds set—encourages reblooming. Good kinds: Pacific Hybrids, 7-foot giants in all delphinium colors. Stake these. Chinese delphinium, about 2 feet. Clear light blue. Flowering starts in June. Repeats bloom in late summer if kept cut back. Short lived, self sows. *D. belladonna*, 3- to 4-foot spikes of true blue shades. Graceful, hardy and tolerant of heat. Longer lived than most.

Gas plant (*Dictamnus alba*). In June pink-white flowers on upright 30-inch stems. A volatile oil is produced by the flower, hence the name. Slow to establish but hardy, long lived, pest free. Give sun, lime soil, and don't disturb with digging, cultivating.

59 The garden phlox are a lovely sight blooming together with the azure echinops or globe thistle.

Grossman

60 The giant hardy hibiscus offers enormous blooms of white, pink, red, or blends. It renews them daily.

Grossman

61 The hostas in late summer shoot up spikes of pale lavender or white lily-like blooms above mounds of bold foliage.

Roche

62 A flower of the winter, the *Helleborus niger* or Christmas rose may bloom during warm spells from November to April.

Watson

Purple loose-strife (*Lythrum*). June to September, upright leafy spikes, 3 to 4 feet, producing rose or purple flowers. Carefree, long lived, hardy. Plant in sun or slight shade, any good soil. Seldom needs dividing. 'Morden's Gleam,' carmine, close to red, 40 inches. 'Morden's Pink,' rose colored, 36 inches. 'Dropmore Purple,' rich purple, 36 inches.

Shasta daisy (*Chrysanthemum maximum*). In June-July, daisylike white single or double flowers, 18 to 24 inches high. Hardy, easy. Give sun or slight shade, humusy soil, good winter drainage and moisture in summer. Divide clumps every other year. 'Alaska,' white, single. 'Mt. Shasta,' 4 inches across, double white.

Speedwell (*Veronica*). May to August, blue, white or rarely pink spike flowers on erect stems usually under 18 inches, depending on the kind. Give sun, good drainage, and water through dry weather, especially while blooming. Divide in spring every third year. 'Blue Peter,' navy blue flowers on 15-inch stems, blooms early summer; for foregrounds or edgings. 'Icicle,' white form of above. *V. incana* has gray matforming foliage, blue flowers to 10 inches, June.

THESE BLOOM IN LATE SUMMER AND FALL

Gayfeather (*Liatris*). August, September, purple or white flowers on stiff 24- to 50-inch spires, above grassy foliage. Give it full sun, any soil with good drainage. Tolerates drouth. Plant or divide in spring. 'September Glory,' to 6 feet, purple. 'White Spires,' similar but white. 'Cobalt,' red-purple on 2-foot spikes.

Helen's flower (*Helenium*). July to October, yellow, coppery, red composite flowers on 18-inch to 4-foot plants. Give full sun, plenty of water. Divide every spring. 'Chippersfield Orange,' to 4 feet, copper and gold blooms in August, September. 'Butterpat,' large pale yellow flowers, July to October.

Plantain lily (*Hosta*). July to October, white or lavender bell-shaped flowers on thin wands above or among strong mounds of attractive foliage, sometimes variegated or blue-tinted. Plants from 6 to 24 inches.

Flower stems may rise 3 feet or more. Trouble-free, long-lived, hardy. Give them part to full shade, average soil with humus added. Divide in spring. *H. coerulea* has large dark green leaves; lavender-blue flowers in July, August. *H. variegata undulata,* small growing, has leaves with wavy margins and marked with white; lavender flowers in July. 'Honeybells,' hybrid with light green leaves in 24-inch mound; spikes of fragrant lavender-pink bells on 3-foot stems in July, August. *H. subcordata grandiflora,* large grass green leaves; white fragrant trumpet flowers, largest of all hosta flowers, August.

Japanese anemone (*Anemone japonica*). September-October, papery blooms of white, pink or rose atop erect 2- to 3-foot stems. Glossy dark foliage. Give sun or partial shade and deep humusy soil. Plant in spring. Needs heavy winter mulch. Kinds: 'September Charm,' to 2 feet, pink. *Alba,* white with yellow center, easy, hardy, to three feet.

Yarrow (*Achillea*). July to September, white or yellow flowers in umbels above green or gray foliage, 2 to 4 feet. Give sun, any soil, plant in spring. Easy. Withstands drouth. *A. ptarmica* has white button-like flowers July, August, September, on 24-inch stems. Rampant, spreads by suckers, needs dividing every other year. Dark green foliage. *A. filipendulina* has gray-green foliage with long-lasting yellow flower clusters, June to September. Good for cutting, drying. 'Coronation Gold,' 3 feet. *A. taggetea* has lemon colored flat heads above 18-inch gray plants.

PRETTY PICTURES WITH GROUPS OF PERENNIALS

EARLY: Peony 'Myrtle Gentry,' iris 'Great Lakes,' iberis, heuchera.

MID: Phlox 'Mary Louise,' gypsophila 'Rosy Veil,' aster Frikarti 'Wonder of Stafa,' *Veronica spicata*.

EARLY FALL: Aster 'Harrington's Pink,' aster 'Bonny Blue,' lamb's-ear (*Stachys lanata*).

FALL: Chrysanthemum 'Apogee,' Echinops 'Taplow Blue,' *Achillea taggetea*.

FOUR THAT ARE BIENNIAL

In your perennial garden you'll want a few plants that are actually biennials. They spend their first year growing from seed, making a root and small top; and the second year they bloom and die. These often seed themselves and appear each year as regularly as perennials, if you don't hoe them out.

Canterbury Bell (*Campanula medium*). In May and June, blue, white, pink, lavender and purple upfacing bell flowers on 30-inch stems. Start seeds in special beds in July or August, protect over winter with light straw mulch and transplant to garden in spring, giving sun or light shade, good garden soil. You can even move them in full bloom.

Forget-me-not (*Myosotis*). April to June, sometimes again in fall, dainty sky-blue flowers on 6-inch spreading plants. You can also get white and pink forms. Place at the front of other flowers and among bulbs. Give half day shade and moist humusy soil. Sow seeds outdoors in July or August for bloom next spring. Once established they replant themselves and are permanent. Try 'Alpestris Blue Eyes.'

Foxglove (*Digitalis purpurea*). In June, elegant flowers appear on erect tapering 3- to 4-foot spires in a wide range of spotted white to rose colors. They do best in cool climates and are difficult where summers are hot. Give rich, humusy soil and partial shade. Plant seeds in August in special seed bed, moving seedlings to the garden in fall or spring. Try the Excelsior Hybrids, with large flaring flowers encircling the stem, and the Giant Shirley Hybrids.

Sweet William (*Dianthus barbatus*). In May and June, there are bright showy heads of scarlet, wine, pink, coral, and white, atop 18-inch plants. They are not fragrant. Sometimes they bloom the first year if you start seeds indoors in March or April and transplant them outside when soil is warm. To get bloom the following spring, sow seeds outdoors in June or July. If self-sown year after year, the colors will become dull, so start again with fresh seed.

EASY-DOES-IT IDEAS

Label your perennials. Labels identify plants while they are growing and guard their places while they are dormant. You can buy various kinds of labels. The most durable are those made of metal, with the name stamped or engraved on with a hard-tipped tool; or written on with a corrosive ink that can't wear off.

Avoid wiring labels tightly around stems of woody plants. As the stem grows the wire tightens, and may eventually strangle and kill that branch.

Make it a practice always to put labels in the same position with relation to the plant. For example, always in front, or always behind, or to the right, or to the left. This saves time when you're looking for the marker; and you know for sure which plant it identifies.

SIXTY FINE PERENNIALS FOR YOUR GARDEN

Name	Color	Height (feet)	Blooming time	Sun or Shade	Comments
Achillea Yarrow	Yellow, white	2-4	July to September	Sun	Drouth tolerant. *A. ptarmica* with white flowers spreads fast; plant where you can contain it. All are easy, hardy.
Aconitum fischeri *sparksi* *wilsoni* Monkshood	Purple Blue Dark purple	2-3 4-5 6-7	Sept.-October July-August Oct.-November	Shade	Not drouth resisting. Needs moisture, cool summers.
Alyssum saxatile Basket of gold	Yellow, gold	½	May, June	Sun	Give good drainage. Good for edging, top of walls. May be short lived.
Anchusa myosotidiflora (*Brunnera macrophylla*) Forget-me-not anchusa	Blue	1	May, June	Sun, light shade	Forget-me-not-like flowers; strong foliage accent, edging. Well drained soil.
Anemone japonica Japanese anemone	White, pink, rose	2-3	September, October	Sun, light shade	Needs heavy winter mulch in cold winters. Papery blooms sit atop erect stems; foliage is handsome, glossy. Give plenty of humus, and moisture.
Aquilegia hybrids Columbine	White, yellow, pink, lavender, blue	2-3	May-July	Sun, light shade	Not long lived, but self sows. Long-spurred flowers are graceful, and foliage is an asset. Give light, humusy soil.
Arabis alpina Rock cress	White, pink	½	April, May	Sun	Gray-leaf plants for blending. For walls, edgings, rock gardens; warm sandy soil.
Artemesia Silver Mound Silver King	Gray foliage Gray foliage	1 3	Flowers are inconspicuous	Sun Sun	Good for blending other colors. Takes poor, sandy soils.
Aster novae-angliae Hardy aster (Michaelmas daisy)	White, pink, blue, purple	1-6	August, September	Sun	Come in many sizes. Use dwarfs as edgings; tall kinds as backgrounds. Stake tall plants.

Name	Color	Height (ft.)	Bloom	Exposure	Remarks
Astilbe thunbergi Spiraea	White, pink, red	1½-4	June, July	Shade, sun	Handsome foliage; flowers are airy, fragrant. Give moisture.
Baptisia australis Blue indigo	Blue	4	June	Sun	Pea-like flowers on rounded plant. Hardy, tolerant, easy. For back of border.
Chrysanthemum	White, yellow, bronze, red, purple, lavender, pink	1-3	August-November	Sun	Divide every spring, or start new plants from cuttings. Pinch back tall growing kinds to make them branch.
Chrysanthemum maximum Shasta daisy	White	1½-2	June, July	Sun, light shade	Divide clumps every other year. Cut off spring blooms and flowers will appear again in late summer.
Convallaria majalis Lily-of-the-valley	White, pink	½	April, May	Semi- or full shade	Bell-shaped flowers on arching stems; fragrant. Makes good ground cover in shaded place.
Doronicum caucasicum Leopard's-bane	Yellow	1-1½	April, May	Sun or part shade	Daisylike flowers for cutting, border or bed. Does best in cool summers.
Delphinium	White, blue, pink, purple	3-6	June, sometimes fall	Sun, part shade	Short-lived and difficult in hot climates. Give humusy soil containing lime. Cut off first stalks after bloom for repeat flowering. Pacific hybrids are largest. Chinese delphinium is small, short-lived, self-sows.
Dianthus Pinks	White, pink, red combinations	1	May, June	Sun	Give good drainage, especially in winter. Compact blue-gray foliage needs shearing in spring. *D. deltoides* (maiden pink) has pink flowers; *D. plumarius* (grass pink) makes a spicy mixture.
Dicentra Bleeding heart	Pink, white	1-2	May, June; or later	Part shade	The old fashioned kind, *D. spectabilis*, blooms early and makes a large plant which dies down before fall; other kinds bloom in summer.
Dictamnus alba Gas plant	Pink, white	3	June	Sun	Long lived. Give lime in soil and do not disturb with digging. Takes time to establish.

SIXTY FINE PERENNIALS FOR YOUR GARDEN (continued)

Name	Color	Height (feet)	Blooming time	Sun or Shade	Comments
Echinops Globe thistle	Pale blue	3	July-September	Sun	Showy, prickly globe flowers with whitish foliage. Needs space. Dry for winter bouquets.
Gypsophila Baby's-breath	White, pink	1½-3	June, July	Sun	Takes limy soil. A thin cloud of tiny bloom on wiry stem network. Foliage makes a neat clump; plants live a long time.
Heliopsis Perennial sunflower	Yellow, orange	3-4	July-October	Sun, part shade	Needs space. Drouth resistant, carefree, for cutting or borders.
Helenium Helen's flower	Yellow, copper, red	1½-4	July-October	Sun	Give plenty of water. Divide each spring.
Helleborus niger Christmas rose	Pink, white	1-2	November-April	Shade.	Evergreen foliage. Cool, moist, humusy, well-drained site. Good by a wall.
Hemerocallis Daylily	Yellow, red, pink, lavender, mahogany	1½-4	May-September	Sun, light shade	Easy and tolerant of heat, drouth, neglect. Each flower lasts a day, is succeeded by others on the scape, giving a long bloom period. Transplant any time, even when in bloom.
Heuchera Coralbells	Pink, red, white	1½	June-August	Sun, part shade	Tiny flowers on wiry stems above clumps of glossy rounded leaves. Good edging. Give humusy, well-drained soil.
Hibiscus moscheutos Hardy hibiscus	Red, white, pink	3-5	July-September	Sun	Hollyhock-like 6-inch flowers. Needs space.
Hosta Plantain-lily	White, lavender	½-2	August-September	Part or full shade	Some kinds have variegated foliage. All are long-lived and trouble-free. Give average soil with humus.
Iberis sempervirens Candytuft	White	1	May, June	Sun	Foliage is evergreen in rounded clump. Give good drainage.

Name	Color	Height	Bloom time	Light	Notes
Iris kaempferi Japanese iris	White, orchid, pink, blue, purple	3	June, July	Sun, part shade	Need humusy, slightly acid soil and moisture during the growing season. Plant any time after flowering.
Iris sibirica Siberian iris	Blue, violet, white	3	May, June	Sun, part shade	May be planted spring, summer or fall. Fibrous roots seldom need dividing.
Iris spuria Butterfly iris	Yellow, white, blue, lilac	3-5	June, July	Sun, part shade	Tall and stately, good for arranging, corsage. Can tolerate much moisture.
Iris, tall bearded hybrids	Practically all	2-4	May, June	Sun	Plant or divide in midsummer, after bloom time. Stands heat, drouth; needs good drainage.
Liatris Gayfeather	Purple, white	2-4	August, September	Sun	Needs good drainage. Flowers appear in stiff spikes, above grassy foliage. Tolerates drouth.
Limonium latifolium Sea lavender (Statice)	Lavender	1½	July, August	Sun	Makes thin cloud of tiny blooms, good for drying. Takes well-drained, sandy soil. Resists drouth.
Linum perenne Flax	Blue	1½	May-August	Sun	Airy growth, carefree. Delicate blue flowers are poor for cutting but pretty in the garden.
Lythrum Loosestrife	Rose-purple	3-4	June-September	Sun, part shade	Airy spikes of upright flowers. Plants do best in moist spots, but take little care anywhere.
Mertensia virginica Bluebell	Blue, pink	1½	April	Part shade	Short blooming period, then disappears. Good under trees, edge of shrubbery and in borders.
Monarda didyma Bergamot	White, pink, red	2-3	June-August	Sun, shade	Tolerant, hardy, will grow almost anywhere. Tends to spread. Flowers attract hummingbirds.
Nepeta mussini	Lavender	1-2	April-August	Sun	Compact mound of soft gray, aromatic foliage. Thrives in hot, dry places.
Oenothera missouriensis Evening primrose	Yellow	1	June-August	Sun	Give sandy well-drained soil. Blooms fold in midday. Foreground of border, rock gardens. Drouth resistant.

SIXTY FINE PERENNIALS FOR YOUR GARDEN (continued)

Name	Color	Height (feet)	Blooming time	Sun or Shade	Comments
Paeonia Peony	White, pink, red	2-3	May, June	Sun, part shade	Double, single, Japanese and hybrids give variety, as well as species kinds and tree peonies. Not adapted in mild climates.
Papaver orientale Oriental poppy	White, pink, lilac, orange, crimson	$1\frac{1}{2}$-3	May, June	Sun	Give good drainage, light soil. Foliage disappears in midsummer. Plant or divide roots in August.
Penstemon Beardtongue	White, blue, lavender, orange, red, purple	1-3	June-August	Sun	Foxglove-like flowers on upright stems above thrifty leaves at the base. Sizes, colors, vary with the kind. Give well-drained light soil.
Phlox paniculata Garden phlox	White, pink, lavender, rose	$1\frac{1}{2}$-4	June-August	Sun, part shade	Need moisture during growing season; keep seed heads cut off to prolong bloom. Divide clumps every three or four years.
Phlox subulata Creeping phlox	White, pink, cerise, blue-lavender	$\frac{1}{2}$	April, May	Sun	Needle-like foliage is semi-evergreen. Plants form spreading mats.
Physostegia False dragonhead	White, rose, pink	$1\frac{1}{2}$-4	July-September	Sun, part shade	Good spikes for cutting, border. Protect from red spider in hot, dry weather. Spreads.
Platycodon Balloon flower	White, pink, blue-violet	$2\frac{1}{2}$	June, July	Sun	Comes up late in spring; avoid damaging new shoots. Give good drainage. Keep old flowers cut to prolong bloom time. Long lived.
Plumbago larpentae (Ceratostigma) Leadwort	Deep blue	1	August-October	Sun	Good edger, border, ground cover. Sometimes invasive. Well-drained loamy soil. Comes up very late in spring.
Polemonium reptans Jacob's ladder	Blue-lavender	1	May, June	Sun, light shade	Delicate edging plant. Fernlike foliage. Spreads. Carefree.
Primula vulgaris English primrose	Yellow	$\frac{3}{4}$	April, May	Shade	Give cool, moist, well-drained site, in edging or foreground.

Plant	Color	Height	Bloom	Exposure	Remarks
Pyrethrum roseum Painted daisy	Rose, red	2	May, June	Sun	Give well-drained soil. For cutting, border. Cut back growth for second crop.
Rudbeckia Cone flower	Yellow, gold, rose, white	3	July–October	Sun, part shade	Large daisylike flowers on erect stems good for cutting. Tolerates drouth. Some kinds spread.
Sedum sieboldi Stonecrop	Pink	1	September–October	Sun	Gray leaves, unusual foliage shape. A good blender or edging. Tolerates poor soil and lives long.
Stachys lanata Lamb's-ear	Purple	½	May	Sun	White woolly foliage, attractive all year. Use in edging or border. Give well-drained, sandy soil.
Thalictrum Meadow rue	White, cream, lilac	3–4	May, June, or later	Sun, light shade	Feathery blooms on *T. aquilegifolium*, petite lilac flowers on *T. dipterocarpum*; foliage is attractive. Easy to grow.
Thermopsis caroliniana	Yellow	5	June, July	Sun	Lupine-like plant, good with delphiniums. Don't transplant. Usually started from seeds. Takes little care when once established.
Valeriana coccinea Heliotrope	Red	2	June–August	Sun	Requires dry, limy soil. Good in border or rock garden.
Veronica Speedwell	Blue, white, pink, purple	under 1½	May–August	Sun	Needs moisture while blooming. Hardy and easy, but divide thick clumps every third year.
Yucca filamentosa Adam's needle	Green-white	6	June, July	Sun	Swordlike foliage makes sharp rosette to 2 feet high, evergreen. Makes a coarse accent; can take heat, drouth.

Chapter 11

ANNUALS ARE NEW EVERY YEAR

What can I grow for bright midsummer color?

For really high color that keeps on coming through summer's heat and into autumn, grow annuals. These are the yearly flowers. You plant them in spring, enjoy bloom that summer, and lose them to frost the same fall. A large garden of annuals is more work than perennials, since it starts from scratch each year. But dispersed among other flowers, annuals cost little extra effort—and repay it all. In this group, you'll find some of the brightest and most interesting of all flowers. They have many uses.

For quick color to cover a bare new yard, you can't beat them. Assuming you grow your own plants, you can landscape the whole place with annuals for under five dollars. Next year you'll have to do it over, naturally. If it's speed you want, buy greenhouse annuals in flats already blooming, and you'll have color the same day—and for the rest of the summer.

In a perennial border, use annuals to give midsummer color and to reserve space for things you'll add in fall. The glamorous new multiflora petunias, for instance, do a good fill-in of spots you're holding for chrysanthemums. See that annuals keep their distance from your permanent flowers, and don't smother them. Watch this especially around Oriental poppies which disappear for a summer nap.

Annuals, like portulaca, petunias, verbena, and sweet alyssum, set among fading tulips and daffodils, gracefully conceal the dying tops. Soon their spreading leaves and flowers cover the vacancy, and the roots are so shallow they never disturb the bulbs below.

For cut flowers to take inside, annuals offer some of the best possibilities. Perhaps for this you'll want to grow them in a picking plot or row in your vegetable garden.

If you're fascinated with the color uses of annuals you might like a special bed of them where you can combine shapes and hues to suit your artistic taste. Don't overdo this kind of gardening—but in small doses it's fun. Figure 38 gives some ideas for little annual patch gardens.

To make matters easier for yourself, stick to the simplest annuals to grow—the ones you plant right in the ground where they bloom. Zinnias, cosmos, marigolds, celosia, nasturtiums, Chinese forget-me-not, globe amaranth, annual phlox, and sweet alyssum, are some you can do this way. Next easiest are those that replant themselves when they drop their seeds. These come up all over the place in spring and you can either leave them where they are or lift and transplant where you want them. Some that are obliging this way are bells of Ireland, cleome, portulaca, gloriosa daisies, nicotiana, four o'clocks, and bachelor's-buttons.

If your favorites are not in these easygoing groups, more work is involved. Quite a number do *best* if started inside early, before it is possible to plant outside. They either need the long season they get this way, or special attention when they're tiny. China asters, ageratum, impatiens, lobelia,

63 A beautiful use of annuals—multicolor ribbons of verbena along a sweeping walk.   *Tatch*

snapdragons, petunias, verbena, periwinkle, torenia, all usually get this treatment. These you'll nurture in pots or boxes, probably transplanting them once before putting them out for the summer. Your neighborhood greenhouseman no doubt sells ready-started plants of most, so if you don't mind the added expense, you can get them from him and save all this fuss.

Where you live decides how much work some annuals require. If you have long mild summers you can plant in the ground certain seeds that northern gardeners would have to start inside, like snapdragons and stock. These need a prolonged cool growing season, so they can bloom before heat comes. For this reason, stock often fails in places where winter turns into summer without the formality of spring.

SIX IMPORTANT ANNUALS AND HOW TO GROW THEM

PETUNIAS

Here is a Cinderella! The modern varieties of glowing wine, pink, rose, red, blue-

purple, white or cream with ruffles, frills and flourishes—are a far cry from their sad sisters of a few years ago. If your back has been turned toward petunias recently, better look around and see what's happening.

For usefulness the petunia exceeds them all. It now has refined colors that fit well among perennials. It has a sturdy constitution that rises above drouth, heat and pests. Its sometimes winsome, sometimes bold flowers wear well in arrangements. Its growth habit is so flexible that you can let it cascade loosely from window boxes, or make it sit primly along edgings. Give it the spotlight in a planting to itself and it will perform gaily all summer and even after several hard frosts.

In the catalogs you will notice two petunia types, multiflora and grandiflora. The first describes early, profuse kinds with flowers $2\frac{1}{2}$ to 3 inches across. The grandifloras are plants of about the same size, but the flowers are an inch larger, not quite so numerous, and often frilled or ruffled. Either kind fits beautifully in any petunia purpose. Most of the new kinds are first

64   Coleus, a favorite for foliage effect, grows well in sun or shade.   *Downward*

65 *Left* Pansies are the earliest annual flower of the garden, especially pretty with tulips. *Roche*

66 *Above* Single dwarf marigolds make a dainty gold edging. *Denholm*

67 *Below* Petunias and sweet alyssum form a bright edging among shrubs.
All-America Selections

TEN HYBRID PETUNIAS YOU WILL ENJOY

Name	Type	Color	Height (inches)	Width (inches)
Calypso	Grandiflora	Scarlet and white, frilled	10	15
Cherokee	Multiflora	Rose-pink	12	24
Cherry Tart	Double multiflora	White and pink, fluffy doubles	15	24
Comanche	Multiflora	Scarlet-crimson	14	24
Coral Satin	Multiflora	Coral-rose	10	20
Maytime	Grandiflora	Salmon-pink	12	24
Neptune	Multiflora	Violet-blue	12	20
Paleface	Multiflora	White, smooth	14	24
Sabre Dance	Grandiflora	White star on dark crimson	14	24
Sugar Plum	Multiflora	Plum and purple	10	15

generation hybrids (F_1). This means, among other things, that if you let them go to seed their "children" will be a pitiful disappointment. The first lesson with modern petunias is never to give volunteers space in your garden. Start each year with new plants grown from the producer's seed.

Start the dustlike seeds in February or March. Prepare a box of sterilized soil or other seed-starting medium (see Chapter 28). Scatter seeds on top, and don't cover. Water from the bottom and keep moist until seedlings appear. Keep them growing, gradually giving fresh air and sunshine so they'll be hardened to outdoor conditions. When they have four leaves, thin the plants. When they have six leaves, transplant. Put them outside if frosts are over. Otherwise move them to a larger box until the weather is safe. Give full sun or light shade.

ZINNIAS

Justifiably popular, zinnias are easy, many-colored, and come in sizes from dwarf 8-inch mounds to 4-foot bushes. These stiff flowers are long-lasting in the garden or in bouquets. Try small ones as well as large. Among them are bold hues and the softest pastels, in every color except blue. Some like 'Peppermint Stick' are even striped and splotched. Others like the Fantasies have petals curiously twisted.

Some of the main groups of zinnias are

SIX ZINNIAS YOU WILL ENJOY

Name	Type	Color	Height (feet)	Flower size (inches)
Crimson Monarch	Dahlia flowered	Red	$2\frac{1}{2}$	6-8
Daffodil Queen	California giant	Canary yellow	3-4	5-6
Melody	Fantasy	Orchid-lavender	$2\frac{1}{2}$	3
Ortho Polka	Dahlia flowered	Multi—with stripes, streaks	3	4
Poly Pink	F_1 hybrid, California giant	Salmon pink	2	4-5
Snow Time	Cactus flowered	White	$2\frac{1}{2}$	5

172

OTHER MARIGOLDS YOU WILL ENJOY

Name	Color	Flower size (inches)	Plant size (inches)
Pot O'Gold	Gold-orange	4	12 to 20
Signet	Yellow or gold	1, single	6, spreading
Toreador	Gold-orange	5	36
Yellow Climax	Pure yellow	5	36

California Giants (5- to 6-inch flat smooth flowers, soft colors, on 3- to 4-foot plants); dahlia flowered (6-inch smooth, deep flowers, all colors, on 2½-foot plants); cactus flowered (fluffy 5-inch flowers, 2½-foot plants, curled petals); Lilliput (branching 1½-foot plants with button size blooms, all colors); Tom Thumb (4- to 6-inch plants with tiny flowers in all colors); Cut-and-Come Again (2½-inch flowers, all colors, on 2-foot branching plants); and Persian Carpet (sometimes called Mexican, 2-inch gold and mahogany blooms on 15-inch compact plants).

All zinnias grow amiably from seed dropped into warm soil outdoors. They are up and growing within a week. Thin or transplant them so they are 6 inches apart for the small kinds, 15 inches for the large ones. For cutting, try growing them in rows so you can cultivate. Make two or three sowings to get later flowers. Other good uses: for colorful summer hedges; for neat edgings; for accents in front of shrubbery; and in beds all to themselves or mixed with other annuals where the colors make patterns. The only disease that troubles zinnias is powdery mildew, which makes disfiguring white spots on the leaves and distorts them. This is less likely to start where air circulation is good. A protective spray or dust of sulfur or Karathane will keep the foliage looking presentable.

MARIGOLD

It is the gold of the garden. When midsummer comes you'll see it glow wherever you've dropped a few seeds or put in a plant. Right up to frost the color holds, so bright it lights up cloudy days.

Plant marigolds where you want them to bloom or start them somewhere else and transplant. Either way they are easy. Put them in full sun. The seeds will rot in cold, wet soil, so plant only in warm weather, covering with ¼ inch of fine soil.

For a dazzling edging, nothing equals dwarf doubles like 'Petite.' In beds where you need more height, but not too much, try 'Spun Gold,' a stocky 15-inch bush covered

SEVEN WILT-RESISTANT ASTERS

Name	Flower type	Bloom time	Height (inches)
Cactus flowered	Twisted pointed petals	Midseason	18
Dwarf Queen	Double	Early	10
Giant Crego	4- to 5-inch double	Midseason	36
Princess Improved	Crested center	Midseason	24
Queen of the Market Improved	Double	Early	20
Single Giants of California	Large single	Midseason	36
Super Giant	Feathery double	Late	36

with sunny puffs of flowers. If you go in for big flowers 'Cracker Jack,' with its 5-inch ones, is for you, but you'll probably have to stake it. Some coppery tones appear in the French single kinds like 'Naughty Marietta' —a good variety for a low edging.

CHINA ASTER

Annual asters are the queens of cut flowers because their stems are long and straight and they keep well. Choose early and late kinds so you can have them in bloom a long while. Among them are colors of orchid, creamy yellow, white, pink, bright rose, dark red and purple and all shades in between. In flower forms you can have large singles; cactus flowered kinds with twisted, pointed petals; fluffy Cregos; Princess types with central crests of quilled petals; and incurved kinds like 'Pink Lady.' You can get 10-inch dwarfs ideal for beds and borders. Early kinds like 'Queen of the Market' start blooming in July, although most wait until August and September.

For early bloom start seeds in the house. For later flowers sow them outdoors. Space the dwarfs for bedding 8 inches apart; large growers for cut flowers 12 inches each way.

Choose wilt-resisting kinds. Little can be done about this disease of asters except avoid it.

SNAPDRAGON

You'll want these clear colored flowers most of all for cutting. Their spires are unusually useful in bouquets. In your yard they have many other places. They get along well with perennials. In beds fronting fences, walls and shrubs, they are stately and colorful. Besides the tall kinds, you can get charming intermediates and dwarfs in all the right colors for bedding, edging, window boxes and rock gardens. Snaps come in every shade and blend imaginable except true blue.

Hot summers once were the undoing of snapdragons. This is still true with some, but new kinds like the Rockets are so heat resistant that they do well now in places where snaps used to be impossible outdoors. If there is a secret to growing them it is to start early in the house or greenhouse un-less you can buy started plants. Set well-developed seedlings out when hard frosts are over, in full sun. They bloom in early summer. Stake the tall kinds. Cut them down to 8 inches after the first bloom period and they will send up new spikes, a little smaller than the first, to bloom in fall. Where winters are mild, plants may live over and bloom a second year.

FOUR MODERN SNAPDRAGONS

Name	Flower description	Height (inches)
Giant Tetra	Large ruffled florets, thick texture	30
Panorama F_2	Strong flowers on base branching, profuse spikes	30
Rocket F_1 hybrids	Large, single, superior, vigorous	36
Tom Thumb	Compact and uniform	8

LARKSPUR

This is the annual delphinium. Where you can't grow the temperamental perennial kind well, it substitutes nicely. Scatter seeds in autumn and you will have blooms the next spring and early summer. These give one performance only—they bloom and then die. Although they reseed profusely, they are seldom as pretty the second year. Sow seed exactly where you want the plants. If you undertake to transplant, do it while plants are small and take a trowelful of earth so as not to disturb the taproot.

For bouquets, larkspurs are as good as delphiniums. In the garden, among pale yellow daylilies or beside a pink climbing rose, they are soul-satisfying indeed. Give them sun, soil containing lime, and one square foot of space.

A good type is Giant Imperial, which gives double flowers of white, blue, purple, lilac, pink, scarlet, and rose on 4-foot spires.

A DOZEN MORE ANNUALS YOU WILL ENJOY

Bachelor's-button (*Centaurea cyanus*). In early to midsummer, boutonierre-size blos-

68 *Above* Nicotiana is the foreground feature of this annual border. It flowers well in shade. *Downward*

69 *Below Left* Cosmos 'Mandarin' gives double orange flowers midsummer to frost. *Bodger*

70 *Opposite* Plume-like heads of scarlet, crimson, and yellow make celosia a bonfire of color. *Bodger*

71 *Below Right* Cleome or spider flower is a lacy pink or white background or bedding plant and sows itself from year to year. *Grossman*

soms of white, pink, blue and purple on long stems good for cutting. To 36 inches. Often self sows. Plant seeds in sunny spot, where to bloom, in early spring. Try the Monarch Giant strain for big flowers; Polka Dot for dwarfs.

Calendula (*Calendula officinalis*). Double daisy flowers in white, apricot to orange, 15 inches, on long cutting stems from early summer to frost. Choice for arrangements, and they look good in the garden. Northerners plant seeds indoors in March for transplanting out when frost is past. Give full sun. Try Pacific Beauty types for large flowers; 'Zvolanek's Crested' for those with a puff in the center.

Cockscomb (*Celosia*). Plume-like or crested heads of scarlet, crimson, yellow, or pink-buff, midsummer into fall, 8 inches to 3 feet. Dramatic as cut flowers, easy to dry for winter use. Colorful accents, edgings, bedding. Plant in warm soil outdoors, thin or transplant to 8 to 12 inches depending on size. Full sun. Many kinds self sow. Heat and dry weather don't faze them. Try 'Toreador,' (18-inch red crested type); 'Golden Feather, (yellow dwarf plume type); and the Gilbert crested pastel varieties.

Cosmos. Midsummer to frost, single or semidouble daisy blooms of white, orange, rose and crimson, on bushes that may reach 4 feet. Plant seeds where to bloom in warm soil; thin to 12 inches. Nothing bothers cosmos. Good for backgrounds and cutting, but the big kinds (all white, pink, rose hues called Sensations) take lots of space. The orange ones called Klondykes are smaller, to 3 feet. Of the last, try 'Mandarin,' for double orange flowers.

Gloriosa daisy (tetraploid *Rudbeckia*). From spring-sown seed, blooms by midsummer. Yellow or mahogany blends, single or double, flowers on 3-foot stems, long-lasting. They often survive winter, bloom following spring; self sow. Take heat and drouth. Excellent cut flower. Plant seeds outdoors in full sun.

Nasturtium (*Tropaeolum*). A month after you plant them, continuing to frost, you have fragrant yellow, red, cream, scarlet, salmon flowers above 12-inch mounds of pretty foliage. Prized for cutting, window boxes, beds and borders. Sow seed in sun, in thin, sandy soil, where they are to bloom. A rich soil makes them go to foliage. Try 'Dwarf Gem' for compactness; or Gleam Hybrids for large kinds.

Nicotiana. Starry white, pink, red fragrant flowers on graceful 3-foot wands, midsummer to frost. Some are only night blooming, therefore no good for cutting. All fit well with perennials, among shrubs or any place you'd want annuals. Often self sows. Plant seeds in warm soil outdoors where to bloom, or transplant if you like. For day and night bloom try the 12-inch 'Dwarf White Bedder'; or the 24-inch 'Daylight.'

Pansy (*Viola tricolor*). Little faces, some whiskered, some smooth, in every color, look up at you in spring from 6- to 12-inch plants that are ideal for bedding, edging, sprinkling among bulbs. The earliest annual, if grown right. Start them in August or September in a cold frame, protect over winter; and set out as your bulbs are popping up. Or buy plants in spring started by your greenhouse man. Keep faded flowers picked off. They take much cold—mature plants sometimes winter over in the garden. Give sun or semishade. Don't miss Roggli's Swiss Giants for color and size; Ellis' Oregon Giants for ruffles; Engelman's Giants for heat resistance.

Phlox (*Phlox drummondi*). Midsummer and fall, brilliant flower heads in all colors but yellow, many variegated. Plants grow 6 to 20 inches high. Sow seeds where to bloom or transplant them, whichever you like. Full sun, ordinary soil. Space 10 inches. Keep from seeding to get longer bloom. Sometimes self sow. Try 'Twinkles,' a dwarf star phlox, 8 inches; 'Glamour,' large-flowered salmon, 12 inches.

Sweet alyssum (*Lobularia maritima*). Four-inch spreading mats of white, pink or lavender flowers, midsummer to freezeup. The perfect plant for beds, edging, front of any planting; window box; hanging basket. Takes drouth, heat, neglect. Plant seeds in full sun where to bloom, or transplant into place. Space 12 inches. Try 'Carpet of Snow,' white; and 'Rosie O'Day,' non-fading pink.

Sweet pea (*Lathyrus odoratus*). Favorites for cutting because of their soft colors, several fragrant flowers to a stem. You can get vining kinds to grow on a fence, or low bush

72 Gloriosa daisy is a man-made improvement on the rudbeckia, often behaves as a perennial. *Burpee*

73 Tall marigolds give abundant yellow-gold blooms in late summer, spectacular for bouquets. *Burpee*

74 Torenia or wishbone flower, usually yellow and purple-blue, succeeds in part shade. *Roche*

75 Annual asters like these dwarf kinds provide bedding color and good material for bouquets. *Bodger*

76 Cape marigold (*Dimorphotheca*) has waxen daisy-flowers in warm apricot hues. *Downward*

kinds for beds and borders. To 8 feet. Sweet peas need an early start. Sow seed where they are to bloom, in full sun, as early as you can prepare soil. As they grow, feed and water to promote fast development. If you live where it gets hot early, use Cuthbertson's Floribunda varieties—they are most heat tolerant. For bush kinds, try 'Little Sweetheart'—8-inch mounds of ruffled flowers.

Verbena. In the hottest spot in your yard, these bloom with fragrance and unfading colors, all hues except yellow and true blue, from June until hard freeze. They make spreading mats 10 inches high, ideal to plant over bulb foliage, as edgings, borders, or in beds. Long-lasting cut flowers. Start seeds outdoors when soil is warm, or early indoors. They transplant easily. Space 12 inches. Can take drouth. Try 'Calypso' (light candy stripes on dark colors); 'Sparkle' (dwarf, warm blend colors often with white eye); and 'Firelight,' spreading bush with solid scarlet flowers.

TWELVE TALL ANNUALS FOR BACKGROUND

Name	Colors	Height (feet)
Amaranthus	Red flowers, maroon foliage	3-5
Castor bean (*Ricinus*)	Green foliage	6-12
Cockscomb (*Celosia*)	Red, yellow	2-4
Cosmos	Orange, white, pink, maroon	3-6
Fire bush (*Kochia*)	Green foliage turning crimson	3
Four o'clock (*Mirabilis*)	White, pink, yellow, red	3
Gloriosa daisy	Yellow	3
Marigold	Yellow, gold	2-3
Morning glory	Red, pink, white, blue	8-20
Spider flower (*Cleome*)	White, pink	3½-4
Sunflower (*Helianthus*)	Yellow	4-8
Torch flower (*Tithonia*)	Orange	4-6

TWELVE MEDIUM HEIGHT ANNUALS

(for borders, beds, and cutting)

Name	Colors	Height (inches)
Bachelor's-button	White, blue, pink, purple	24-36
Calendula	White to orange	15-24
China aster (*Callistephus*)	White, pink, crimson, purple	18-36
Cockscomb	Red, yellow	20-30
Gaillardia hybrids	Red, yellow	15
Larkspur	White, blue, rose	48
Nicotiana	White, rose, crimson	12-30
Nigella	Blue, white	18-24
Salvia	Red, pink, lavender	12-30
Snapdragon	All but blue	30
Stock	White, pink, lavender	12-30
Zinnia	All but blue	18-48

TWELVE LOW ANNUALS

(for edging flower beds, paths, and walks)

Name	Color	Height (inches)
Ageratum	Blue-lavender	6-12
Alyssum, sweet	White, pink, lavender	4-8
Calliopsis, dwarf	Yellow, red	8
Cupflower (*Nierembergia*)	Blue	6-8
Lobelia erinus	Blue	12
Marigold, dwarf	Yellow	6-12
Nasturtium	Cream to scarlet	12
Pansy	All colors	8-12
Petunia	All colors but true blue	10-18
Phlox drummondi	All but blue	12
Portulaca	All but blue	6
Verbena	All but yellow, blue	6-12

FORTY-TWO GOOD ANNUALS FOR YOUR GARDEN

Name	Use	Planting time	Bloom time	Flower color	Height (inches)	Space (inches)	Sun or shade	Comments
Ageratum houstonianum	Edging	Early spring*	Summer, fall	White, pink, blue	8	9-12	Sun or part shade	Remove spent flowers. In North start seeds indoors. You can propagate from cuttings. Plant out when frost danger is past.
Althaea rosea Hollyhock	Screen, background	Fall, early spring	Spring, early summer	White, red, pink, yellow	72	24	Sun	Singles self sow. Really biennials. Doubles are choice.
Amaranthus	Bedding, background	Spring	Summer, fall	Colorful foliage	12-48	18-24	Sun	Joseph's coat, low, has cream, green, red foliage. Molten Fire, tall, has red foliage.
Antirrhinum Snapdragon	Cutting, bedding, borders	Early spring*	Early summer, fall	All colors but blue	8-36	10	Sun	Start early in house or greenhouse. Stake tall kinds. Cut to 8″ after first bloom and they will send up new spikes to bloom in fall. In mild climate plants may live over and bloom next year.
Calendula officinalis Calendula	Cutting, bedding, borders	Early spring*	Early summer to fall	White, orange, yellow	15	15	Sun	Double daisy flowers for arrangements.
Callistephus China aster	Cutting, bedding, borders	Early spring*	Mid-to late summer	Purple, orchid, pink, yellow, white	10-36	8-12	Sun or part shade	For early bloom start seeds indoors. Choose wilt resisting kinds. Many flower forms: cactus flowered, singles, quilled and incurved. Dwarf forms available.
Celosia Cockscomb	Cutting, edging, bedding	Spring	Mid-summer to fall	Scarlet, crimson, yellow, pink-buff	8-36	8-12	Sun	Dramatic cut flowers. Use in dried bouquets. Tolerates heat and drouth. Many kinds self sow.
Centaurea cyanus Bachelor's-button	Cutting, bedding, border	Early spring	Early to mid-summer	White, pink, blue, purple	16-36	8-12	Sun	Boutonierre-size blossoms. Often self sows. Dwarf forms available.
Cleome spinosa Spider flower	Background, bedding	Early spring	Summer	Pink, white	48-60	12	Sun	Self sows. White 'Helen Campbell' is good. Spidery flowers, showy. Tolerates heat, drouth.

* In North, start seeds early indoors, set out plants when weather is warm.

Name	Use	When to plant	Bloom time	Color	Height	Spacing	Exposure	Remarks
Coreopsis drummondi or *tinctoria* Calliopsis	Bedding, border, cutting	Fall, early spring	Summer	Yellow, orange, mahogany	8-30	8-12	Sun	Sow where to bloom. Self sows. Blooms best where crowded.
Cosmos	Cutting, backgrounds	Spring	Midsummer to frost	White, orange, rose, crimson	36-48	12-18	Sun	Sensations take lots of space. Some dwarf forms are double.
Cynoglossum amabile	Edging, bedding, cutting	Spring	Early summer	Blue	15-24	10	Sun, part shade	Airy blue flowers. Cut back to get renewed bloom.
Delphinium (annual) Larkspur	Bedding, border, background, cutting	Fall or spring	Spring, early summer	White, pink, purple, red, blue	36-48	8	Sun	Needs limy soil. Grows where delphiniums fail. Sow where to bloom.
Dianthus caryophyllus Carnation	Cutting, bedding	Early spring*	Early summer	White, pink, red, yellow	18	12	Sun	Keep staked. Plants bloom in five months.
Dimorphotheca sinuata Cape marigold	Border, cutting	Spring	Summer	Orange, salmon, white, yellow	12	10	Sun	Flowers close at night. Tolerates heat, drouth.
Gaillardia hybrids	Cutting, bedding	Spring	Summer, fall	Red, yellow, combinations	15	12	Sun	Resists drouth. The doubles are choice.
Gomphrena Globe amaranth	Cutting, bedding, drying, edging	Spring	Summer, fall	Purple, white, rose	8-18	6-10	Sun	Tolerates heat, drouth. Has stiff clover-like blooms. Try 'Cissy' in edging.
Iberis Candytuft	Edging, bedding, cutting	Early spring*	Spring, early summer	White, pink, purple	10-24	12-18	Sun, part shade	Difficult to transplant. Do best in cool summers.
Impatiens balsamina Balsam	Bedding, borders, edging	Spring*	Summer, early fall	White, pink, rose, scarlet	6-24	18	Semi-shade or sun	Give well-drained moist soil. Pinch to produce bushy plants.
Lathyrus odoratus Sweet pea	Cutting, bedding, borders, vining on fence	Early spring	Early summer	All colors	8-96	5	Sun	Fragrant. Vining or bush kinds available. Feed and water to promote fast development. Cuthbertson's Floribunda varieties are the most heat tolerant.
Lobelia erinus Lobelia	Edging, window box, basket	Early spring*	Spring	White, shades of blue	4-10	6	Part shade	Mat-forming. Needs lots of moisture, can't stand much heat.

* In North, start seeds early indoors, set out plants when weather is warm.

181

FORTY-TWO GOOD ANNUALS FOR YOUR GARDEN (continued)

Name	Use	Planting time	Bloom time	Flower color	Height (inches)	Space (inches)	Sun or shade	Comments
Lobularia maritima Sweet alyssum	Bedding, edging, window box, basket	Spring	Midsummer to frost	White, pink, lavender	4	12	Sun	Mat-forming. Takes drouth, heat, neglect. Sow where to bloom or transplant.
Matricaria Feverfew	Bedding, cutting	Spring	Summer	Yellow to white	8-24	9	Sun or part shade	Often survives the winter.
Mathiola hybrids Stock	Edging, bedding, cutting	Early spring*	Spring, early summer	White, pink, purple	10-25	12	Sun	Start indoors, use 'Ten Weeks' kinds where summers come early. Fragrant.
Molucella laevis Bells of Ireland	Cutting	Fall, early spring	Spring, summer	White surrounded by green bracts	24	18	Sun	Self sows; often stems curve, better for arrangements that way. Plant seeds after frost.
Nicotiana	Border, bedding	Spring	Midsummer to frost	White, pink, red	36	15	Sun, part shade	Often self sows. Some are only night bloomers.
Nierembergia Cup flower	Bedding, edging, rock garden	Early spring*	Summer, fall	Blue-purple	6	12	Sun, semi-shade	A good combination with marigolds.
Nigella damascena Love-in-a-mist	Cutting, bedding, border	Spring	Early summer	Blue, white	18-24	8	Sun	Feathery foliage. Short blooming period. Sow where to bloom.
Papaver rhoeas Shirley poppy	Cutting, garden, bedding	Fall, early spring	Spring	White, pink, red	12	24	Sun	Not easy to transplant. Sow where to bloom, in sandy loam.
Petunia	Edging, border, bedding, box	Early spring*	Summer, fall	Red, pink, purple, white, lilac, bicolor, variegated	10-15	10-15	Sun, light shade	Make 2-3 sowings for later bloom. Tolerates heat, drouths. Multiflora, early and profuse. Grandiflora, larger, frilled, ruffled.
Phlox drummondi Annual phlox	Bedding, border	Spring*	Summer, fall	All but yellow; many variegated	6-20	10	Sun	Keep from seeding to get longer bloom.
Portulaca grandiflora Rose moss	Bedding, edging, rock garden	Early spring	Summer, early fall	All colors but blue	6	8	Sun	Self sows. Double kinds are choice. Drouth and heat tolerant.

* In North, start seeds early indoors, set out plants when weather is warm.

Plant	Uses	Sow	Bloom	Color	Spacing	Height	Light	Remarks
Rudbeckia (tetraploid) Gloriosa daisy	Cutting, background	Spring	Midsummer	Yellow, mahogany	36	15	Sun	Single or double flowers. Long-lasting. Self sows. Takes heat and drouth.
Salvia splendens Scarlet sage	Bedding, border, edging	Spring*	Summer, fall	Scarlet	12-36	12	Sun, light shade	Looks good with gray foliage plants.
Tagetes Marigold	Border, bedding, edging, boxes	Spring	Summer, fall	Yellow, orange, copper, mahogany	6-36	8-12	Sun	Plant only in warm weather. Stake big plants.
Torenia fournieri Wishbone flower	Bedding, border, boxes	Spring*	Summer, fall	White, yellow, purple	12	12	Sun, part shade	Foliage turns purple in autumn. Give moisture. May be propagated by cuttings.
Tropaeolum Nasturtium	Cutting, bedding, borders, boxes	Spring	Summer, fall	Yellow, red, salmon	12-18	10-18	Sun	Bloom a month after you plant them. Give thin, sandy soil.
Verbena	Cutting, bedding, border, edging	Spring*	Summer to frost	All colors but blue and yellow	6-12	12-18	Sun	For hottest spot in the yard. Fragrant. Mat-forming. Transplants easily. Tolerates drouth.
Vinca rosea Periwinkle	Border, bedding	Spring*	Summer, fall	White, rose, bicolor	20	18	Sun or part shade	Also try the creeping kind, 'Rose Carpet.' Endures dry or wet weather. Pest and disease free.
Viola cornuta Viola	Bedding, edging, rock garden	Early spring*	Summer	White, blue, yellow, purple	6	6	Part shade	Pick spent blooms to prolong flowering.
Viola tricolor Pansy	Bedding, edging, among bulbs	August	Spring	Purple, yellow, white, violet, brown-red	6-12	6	Sun, part shade	Pick faded flowers. Take much cold; mature plants sometimes winter over in the garden. Start seeds in boxes or cold frame; protect over winter.
Zinnia	Bedding, edging, border, cutting	Spring	Summer	Yellow, red, orange, pink, white, lavender	8-48	12	Sun	Single, double, cactus flowered, dahlia flowered. Need good air circulation to prevent powdery mildew. Make two or three sowings to get later bloom.

* In North, start seeds early indoors, set out plants when weather is warm.

SIX ANNUALS FOR FOLIAGE EFFECT

Name	Color	Height (feet)
Amaranthus	Maroon foliage	3-5
Basil, purple leaf	Dark purple foliage, aromatic	1-1½
Castor bean	Glossy green	6-12
Coleus	Vari-colored	2-3
Fire bush (*Kochia*)	Green turning to crimson	3
Kale, flowering	Purple and green, ruffled	1-1½

EASY-DOES-IT IDEAS

If you plant patches of self-sowing annuals like portulaca, cleome, and gloriosa daisy you will have them year after year without troubling to replant. When seedlings appear in the spring, either thin them in the same bed or transplant to a freshly prepared spot.

When you start some annuals on your windowsill early in spring, to get a head start on the season, put them in peat pots to grow on before time for the final transplanting to your garden. Then you set out, pot and all, and the plant suffers no set-back.

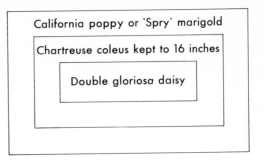

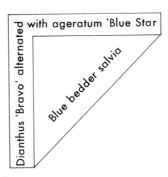

Fig. 38 Two little patch gardens of annuals. At their best in midsummer, they can be kept going until frost by trimming off spent blooms.

For edgings of sweet alyssum for your perennial borders, all you need to do is plant a pinch of seeds in softened soil every 10 inches or so. Should too many come up, thin to one or two plants per "hill."

Chapter 12

BULBS MAKE BEAUTIFUL PICTURES

How can I have very early flowers?

Plant bulbs, lots of them, for bloom from February on. Whether you realize it or not, many of your favorite flowers come from bulbs, corms, or tubers. The earliest little blooms of spring, crocuses and snowdrops, then the indispensable daffodils and tulips, lilies, gladiolus, lycoris, and dahlias—how could you do without this group of plants?

A bulb is a whole plant folded into a tiny receptacle. It has scales or layers, like modified leaves (which they are). Onions and lilies are bulbs. Corms are different because they are essentially thickened stems and therefore solid, not scaled or layered. Gladiolus and crocus are corms. Tubers are thickened underground stems or roots which the plant forms for food storage. If it is a stem tuber like the potato it has "eyes." If it is a root tuber, like the dahlia, it has none but grows instead from a bud on the stalk. For the sake of simplicity in our discussion, all of these are called "bulbs."

HOW TO SUCCEED WITH BULBS

All bulbs need good drainage. If they seem short-lived for you, check how well the water drains from your soil. If puddles stand around them, bulbs are in trouble. Beneath bulbs like lilies and daffodils, you can put a little mound of sand. This helps if your drainage problems are not serious. Or you can raise the level of the bed a few inches, a better solution.

The best soil is medium loam, not tight clay. Lighten heavy soil with peat moss and sand, both under and over the bulb.

Spring-flowering kinds like tulips have an awkward stage after they bloom. Their leaves very slowly sink to the ground and turn yellow. Don't follow your impulse to cut them off and get rid of them. The bulb is soaking up sun and nutrients for the next year, and making next year's flowers. If you interfere you will reduce the next crop. Wait until foliage turns brown and pulls away easily before you remove it. To conceal the yellow leaves, you can plant annuals like petunias or shallow-rooted perennials like chrysanthemums among them. Or dig the bulb, top and all, and with plenty of soil move it to a hidden part of the yard to finish ripening.

Try to keep seed pods picked off after your bulbs bloom. They rob strength from the plant. You'll have better bloom, too, if you feed bulb plantings. Use superphosphate, or slow-acting fertilizer like bone meal, but avoid fresh manures. A low-power chemical fertilizer like 5-10-5 is good. Fertilize the spring-flowering kinds like daffodils in early spring. Feed summer bulbs when you plant them, and again as they start to bloom.

You'll probably want most of your bulbs in the borders with other flowers. The hardy ones come up and bloom faithfully each year just like other perennials. Erect ones

77 A tulip assortment along a drive makes a gay welcome in May. *Roche*

like tulips, grape-hyacinths and Roman hya-cinths make orderly edgings along paths.

All the large spring-flowering kinds are best in sizable clumps of six to twelve bulbs. Of tiny bulbs like aconites or glory-of-the-snow you'll need at least fifty. Try

186

combining different sorts that bloom at the same time—early yellow tulips with grape-hyacinths, for example. Put perennials close to bulbs to bloom with them and complement their colors. Creeping phlox, *Alyssum saxatile*, myosotis and blue wood phlox or sweet william (*Phlox divaricata*) are good neighbors for tulips, grape-hyacinths, and daffodils.

Summer and fall flowering kinds that are replanted each year, like cannas and tube-roses, give good color among perennials. Some like gladiolus you may grow just to provide cut flowers. These you will probably want to put in beds to themselves. A few like tuberous begonias and achimenes are ideal for hanging baskets, planters and patio containers.

Hardy kinds, especially narcissus and the tiny bulbs, are good for naturalizing. Use drifts of *one kind* of narcissus over a hillside or at the edge of woods, to bloom with the wood phlox and the new green grass. 'Thalia' is a good kind for this. Fence rows are other good places to put these plantings. You can naturalize crocus on a smaller scale in a lawn. Choose a place where you don't want to mow until late May. Strew bulbs along in a natural way and where it falls slip each one under two inches of sod, pried open with a trowel. Try naturalizing crocus, scillas, chionodoxas and all other little earlies in unmowed spots at the bases of trees and posts, at the foot of walls and under shrubs. They'll do well under trees and leaf-shedding shrubs, since they bloom and are through before leaves come out to shade them.

SIX IMPORTANT BULBS AND HOW TO GROW THEM

NARCISSUS

Narcissus or daffodils bring the first big color of spring. Sometimes they lift their heads out of snow to smile at you. A few late

78 Daffodils bring the first big color of spring, here in a setting of white heather and birch bark.
Grossman

A DOZEN FINE DAFFODILS

Name	Height (inches)	Description
Carbineer	18	Golden perianth with large orange cup. Late.
Cheerfulness	19	Fully double, light yellow with dash of orange. Late.
Duke of Windsor	18	White perianth with large yellow-orange cup. Midseason.
Edward Buxton	20	Yellow perianth with small orange cup. Midseason.
February Gold	15	Small flowered, nodding, gold with large cup. Very early.
Geranium	16	Tazetta, four to six small flowers to stem, white with orange cups. Late.
Golden Perfection	22	True jonquil, two or three yellow flowers to stem. Late.
Mrs. R. O. Backhouse	20	White perianth with large light pink cup. Midseason.
Mt. Hood	20	Large cream-white trumpet above white perianth. Late.
Recurvus	17	Poeticus, single fragrant white flower with red center on tall stem. Late.
Texas	20	Full double, yellow mixed with orange-scarlet. Midseason.
Thalia	16	Triandrus hybrid, two or more large cupped flowers to stem, delicate white. Midseason.

varieties will still be blooming when the roses start. Most of them are basically yellow or white, but you can choose from hundreds of variations of shades, shapes, sizes and blooming times. Some like 'Mt. Hood' are white, some are pink, like 'Mrs. R. O. Backhouse'; some have contrasting trumpets, cups or eyes, some several flowers to a stem. Nearly all breathe a delicate fragrance like that of no other flower. Heights run from 6-inch miniatures to 20-inch giants.

Daffodils look best against a background —evergreens, wall, fence, tree trunk. In a border of perennials, put them in clumps in the middle of the bed, except the miniatures which belong at the front.

Daffodil varieties are slightly regional. Well adapted kinds usually outlast tulips, and will probably stay with you permanently. Find out what kinds are best in your area by taking notes at a local daffodil show. Blistering heat and long dry spells are hard on most daffodils. In places like the Great Plains and the Southwest, or in the North where winter freeze is deep, you can grow more kinds if you mulch above bulbs thickly with something like ground corn cobs. When spring weather is dry, give water both before and after they bloom. Don't be afraid to cut plenty of flowers for the house, and take stems as long as you like. But after bloom ends, spare the foliage. It will turn yellow, and after 6 or 8 weeks you can remove it. For the sake of appearance, plant something in front to hide it.

Plant narcissus bulbs as early as you can get them. This will probably be October. Give them a well-drained spot in full sun or part shade. Dig deeply and mix in a spadeful of sand, one of peat moss and a cup of bone meal for each clump. Set them so 4 inches of soil covers the bulb. In extra sandy soil put them a little deeper and in heavy clay soil, a little shallower. Cover the miniature kinds only 2 inches deep. Plant big bulbs 8 inches apart; small ones proportionately less.

"Daffodil" is the common English name for this whole group. Don't call them "jonquils" unless you really mean the sweet-scented species Narcissus jonquilla, or one of its hybrids.

TEN GOOD TULIP VARIETIES

Name	Height (inches)	Description
Astor (lily flowering)	25	Bronze-amber-pink, midseason.
Elmus (Triumph)	28	Cherry red, edged white; early midseason.
Good Gracious (Cottage)	25	Brilliant salmon-pink, midseason.
Kathleen Truxton (Breeder)	27	Coffee color with magenta sheen, yellow edge; midseason.
Mt. Tacoma (peony or late double)	22	Double white blooms, late.
Niphetos (Darwin)	29	Soft lemon yellow, midseason.
Orange Parrot (Parrot)	24	Big orange-gold petals heavily cut and waved; midseason.
Red Emperor (Fosteriana)	20	Dazzling red flowers, yellow base, 8 inches across. One of the earliest.
Red Matador (hybrid)	20	Orange-red large flowers, early, sturdy stems.
Scotch Lassie (Darwin)	25	Lilac-lavender with blue base, midseason.

TULIP

Tulips follow daffodils in blooming, although only by days. They usually appear together in your garden and in bouquets. From the earliest species tulip to the final late double kind, the season lasts a good six weeks. The whole time is filled with the cleanest, smoothest, boldest color of the year —everything in the rainbow except true blue.

Tulips need cold winters. If you live in Florida, the Gulf Coast and the frostfree parts of California, you will probably grow them like annuals, if at all. You'll replant every year, and then cool them first for six weeks in the refrigerator. Everywhere else, tulips are easy, but seldom as permanent as daffodils.

Use them wherever you need early color— among perennial flowers; in ribbons along walks; in clumps in front of shrubs or walls. Put them beside a step or door where they'll be seen and admired. A few tulips, like 'Dido' are fragrant—an extra advantage.

Plant them any time in fall, right up to December unless the ground is frozen. If your soil is average—not sandy on the one hand or heavy clay on the other, plant bulbs with 6 inches of soil above them. If you want annuals or shallow-rooted perennials to grow over the spot later, better plant bulbs deeper, even to 10 inches or so. The shallower you plant tulips, the oftener they need dividing. Make the soil mellow by adding sand and peat moss, and enrich it with bone meal—a cupful to each clump of six. Be sure they are where they get sun at least half the day. Space large bulbs 6 inches apart.

The two main groups of tulips are the earlies and the May or main-season kinds. Of the May-flowering, Darwins, breeders, and cottage tulips are the three big kinds. Darwins are the earliest blooming of the three. They have pure clean colors and stately, long stems. Usually the flowers have no streaks or mottles. Flower forms range from oblong with rounded bases to almost square. Breeders are the next to bloom, mostly with sunset colors, coppery or bronze tints, iridescence or rich deep shadings. They have stiff upright stems and grow vigorously. Cottage tulips are varied in size, color, shape and habit. In fact there seems little reason to put them in one group, except that they do not fit in the others. You'll find many unusual and good things among them.

79 The crocus is a bright harbinger of spring. Here the variety is 'Early Perfection.' *Burpee*

80 Lilies may be fiery as well as cool in color. Here is the hot and happy 'Fiesta' in a freckle pattern. *Wall*

81 Unusual and interesting blooms come from the alliums or flowering onions. This is the spectacular *A. albo-pilosum.* *Genereux*

82 For crisp texture and pure colors, the true lilies are unsurpassed. 'Black Dragon,' a recent hybrid, has flowers that are white inside and dark outside on towering spikes. *Fields*

TEN GOOD LILIES

Name	Description	Height (feet)	Bloom time
Black Dragon	White, purple-brown on reverse	5-7	June-July
Enchantment	Nasturtium red	4	June
Fiesta Hybrids	Straw, orange, maroon	4	June
Golden Chalice	Lemon to orange	3	May-June
Heart's Desire	White, orange center	5-7	June-July
Imperial Crimson	White, crimson markings	4	August
Madonna (*L. candidum*)	White	3	May-June
Olympic Hybrids	White	6	June-July
Pink Perfection	Fuchsia pink	6	June-July
Regal	White-ivory	4	June

Parrot tulips are a special group you'll prize for arrangements, because of their fantastic ruffled and fringed petals. They look well in the garden too, but don't use them where you want either strict formality or a woodland setting. Another variation, lily-flowered kinds, are more graceful than the classic shapes. They have pointed petals that turn back a bit. Finally, for a real thrill and something to show off, try the new tulip hybrids, like 'Red Matador,' for large size, brilliance, and sturdy long stems.

LILY

Lilies are so lovely, you might think they are hard to grow. Fortunately, that is not the case with some of the most beautiful, the hybrids created since 1950, nor with many older ones. For crisp shining texture, purity of color and markings, stately posture and fragrance—all points upon which they excel —they are the aristocrats of the garden. As cut flowers, they last many days and are easy to work with, especially if you nip off the anthers to prevent pollen from staining the petals.

Lilies bloom from tulip time to fall, but the main effect comes in early summer when the white and cream regals, Olympic hybrids and their pastel kin (like 'Black Dragon' and 'Pink Perfection') and the Aurelian hybrids are performing. The sight of these majestic 6-foot stalks, topped with graceful pyramids of fifteen or twenty large trumpet blooms, takes your breath away. In the quiet evening their fragrance perfumes the whole yard. Earlier, with the roses, you have the white purity of Madonna lilies, then the exuberant hot colors of Mid-Century and Fiesta Hybrids. Later when the garden is subdued by midsummer, the speciosums, auratums, and the hybrids between them called 'Imperials,' open exotic carmine-marked blooms. Finally the season closes with the white trumpets of the Formosa lily (*L. formosanum*) in August and September.

Lilies accept conditions in your perennial borders if they are well drained. Put them halfway back, not all the way, so you can inspect the flowers at close range. Around the base put shallow rooted plants like *Veronica incana,* dwarf hardy asters or cushion chrysanthemums, to shade the ground. Try lilies in the bays between tall growing shrubs like viburnum and forsythia or against screens of hemlock or yew.

Plant in fall as early as you can obtain bulbs. Treat them like live plants, for they are never really dormant. Choose a place in sun or afternoon shade. Take a few extra pains with the groundwork for lilies. Dig down 18 inches, mixing a half bushel of peat and a gallon of sand to the soil for each clump. Fill in and settle this soil mixture at the 8-inch level (shallower than this for small kinds), and put in a 1-inch layer of clean sand on which to stand the bulbs. Then add the mellow soil to ground level and gently firm it down. Mark the planting to protect it from the rake and hoe next spring. Finally, unless you catch a rain, water with the sprinkler to encourage quick rooting.

The exception to these planting rules is the Madonna lily (*L. candidum*). Plant it in August and never cover it with more than an inch of soil.

Through the season you'll have little to do for lilies except stake the tallest kinds. Spray them with the same multipurpose spray you're using on roses, to control aphids that might bring disease.

GLADIOLUS

Gladiolus you can grow are every bit as beautiful as those the florist sells, and you can have them in more colors and sizes. There are no real blues, but every other color, and a choice of florets smooth, ruffled, doubled or splotched—and stately spikes ranging from 12-inch miniatures like 'Star-

let' which have real garden value, to the man-sized 'Royal Stewart' for exhibition.

You'll use glads most for cut flowers. For this it is handy to grow them in garden rows easy to cultivate, water, feed or spray. Plant groups two or three weeks apart, to get flowers over a long span. If garden color and not cut flowers are what you want most, then spot the bulbs in wherever you want them to bloom. They look best placed behind lower plants so their low bare stems don't show.

Gladiolus can take cool spring weather. Plant as soon as you get the ground ready. March, April and May are good starting times, and you can plant as late as June and July for fall flowers. Set bulbs 6 inches apart and 6 inches deep, in full sun or a place with afternoon shade. As the spears shoot up, draw earth around them to hold them erect. Otherwise you may have to stake tall ones. Keep them watered while they grow— once a week is just right, whether by rainfall or by garden hose. This makes stems straight and prevents goose necks. If your ground isn't as rich as you'd like, when spikes begin to show sprinkle 5-10-5 fertilizer along the row, in a thin ribbon (1 cup to 10 feet) and water it in.

Thrips are the worst enemy of glads. They are so small you can hardly see them but they make conspicuous silver paths in the

TEN GOOD GLADIOLUS VARIETIES

Name	Color	Blooms after planting	Height
Burma	Rose	85 days	Tall
Friendship	Light pink	65 days	Medium
June Wedding	White	65 days	Medium
Little Pansy	Light violet with marks	70 days	Miniature
Lorelei	Cream	80 days	Tall
Salmon's Sensation	Blue	90 days	Tall
Salmon Crinkles	Salmon	75 days	Medium
Statuette	Yellow	65 days	Miniature
Tigertone	Orange	70 days	Medium
Zig Zag	Red	85 days	Miniature

83 Intense fragrance of tuberoses perfumes the whole yard in late summer.
Tiemann

84 Mexican shell flower, or tigridia, is a colorful midsummer bulb flower, handled like gladiolus.
Roche

85 Dahlias contribute late season color in all hues but blue, sizes from buttons to dinner plates. Small flowering kinds like these are as easy as annuals to grow.
Michajluk

TEN EXCELLENT DAHLIAS

Name	Type	Height (feet)	Color	Flower form
"A" size, 8 inches or more across				
Autumn Blaze	Informal decorative	5	Dark blend; red later turning gold-tipped	Irregular arrangement of slightly rolled petals
Five Star General	Formal decorative	5	Light blend; pink and yellow	Regular arrangement of flat petals
The Cardinal	Semicactus	6	Cardinal red	Petals flat at base with less than half of petals rolled or quilled
"B" size, 4- to 8-inch flowers				
Good Earth	Incurved cactus	5-6	Pink	Petals rolled their full length with tips curving back into the center
Nita	Straight cactus	4	Variegated orchid and red	Petals rolled for one-half their length or more with the entire length of petals straight or nearly straight
Windlassie	Informal decorative	5	Glistening white	Ball-shaped flower with very curled, twisted petals
Small flowered, 4 inches or less				
Betty Ann	Pompon	4	Pink	Double flowers almost round with tightly quilled petals
Daintiball	Ball	4	Lavender	Like pompon only larger
Ruby Charm	Miniature cactus	5	Red	Semicactus
White Fawn	Miniature decorative	4	White	Formal

leaves and discolor the flowers. Spray for them with malathion every ten days.

Cut for bouquets when the lowest one or two florets are open. The rest will unfold indoors, to the top.

After leaves begin to brown in the fall, harvest the bulbs. Dig each plant and cut off tops 2 inches above the bulb. Spread the crop out in the shade to dry for a week or two. Don't let them freeze. Finally shake off earth and loose husks, dust the bulbs with DDT to put an end to overwintering insects, and store in a cool airy place like your basement floor (but it must be dry).

Along with the big bulbs you'll find hundreds of little ones, called cormels. These make new plants. Scatter them thickly like peas the next spring in a shallow trench—some will bloom the first year.

DAHLIA

Dahlias contribute late season color almost equal to what you have earlier from tulips. They come in all colors but blue, and sizes from buttons to dinner plates. The little ones like Unwin Hybrids—which you can easily raise from seed like annuals if you wish—are gay bedding plants. They mix well among other flowers too, and are good for cutting. These bloom by midsummer and don't need staking, and from seed you can get a fine crop of tubers for next year. The whoppers coming at summer's end are the best bragging material from the garden all year. They are better for showing than arranging, because of their size. In between are shapes and sizes for every flower need. The American Dahlia Society recog-

86 Lycoris or hardy amaryllis sends up pink blooms in late summer, after spring foliage has disappeared.
Roche

nizes more than a dozen different types.

To get the greatest flower size from exhibition dahlias you have to disbud. This means to nip out with your fingernail all the side buds down the stem and let just the top one develop on each main stalk. Don't

195

87 Grow tuberous begonias where you can see them at close range. Each individual bloom is a masterpiece.

Baer

disbud small kinds where you want quantity not size. When you cut a dahlia it lasts longer if you burn the end in a flame before you put it in water. A cigarette lighter is handy for doing this in the garden.

Plant dahlia tubers outdoors at lilac time. Give them light rich soil that drains well, and a spot in sun or light afternoon shade. Sink a stake beside tall growers when you plant them. Lay the tuber flat in a 5-inch hole and cover it with only 2 or 3 inches—filling in the rest after it starts to grow. Keep your dahlias watered all summer, especially after buds set on. When the plant reaches a foot high, pinch the tip out to make it branch. Tie to the stake as it grows taller. You can keep frost from stopping the dahlia show for awhile in fall if you cover the plants with something light like cheesecloth. When the freeze finally falls, waste no time in cutting off blackened tops. Use loppers or your sickle, and cut just above the ground. Dig the clumps. Be careful not to break tubers. Turn the roots upside down for an afternoon to dry. Leave a little soil on them. Pack with peat or vermiculite in baskets, boxes or plastic bags and store them where they'll be cool but won't freeze. Your basement or garage is probably the best place unless you're lucky enough to have a root cellar. Next spring divide clumps into individual tubers, each with a little of the stem containing growth buds. Without a bud you'll get no new plant.

TUBEROUS BEGONIA

For protected places in cool open shade or light sun these plants give glorious bloom from summer to frost. They are more trouble than other tender bulbs, but worth it. Use them in planters, window boxes, hanging baskets, and shaded beds. The individual blooms are masterpieces. Have them where you can see them closely. The only colors you won't find are blue and purple.

Forms go from enormous singles to doubles resembling camellias, carnations, and roses—sometimes they are frilled, crested or fringed. Unless you live in a mild-winter climate, start tubers indoors in February in boxes of moist peat and sand. Nestle them *hollow side up* into the mixture. When

plants are two inches high, pot them. Use 8- to 12-inch pots and equal parts soil, leaf mold, peat and sand, covering tubers an inch deep. When the weather is warm and you can move plants outdoors, either sink pot and all or remove the pot and set the earth ball in the ground. A sand mulch around the base keeps off marauding slugs and snails. Water every two weeks with liquid fertilizer, and keep the soil moist. Their greatest need is plenty of water. Upright kinds need stakes (put them in when you are potting) and protect all of them from the wind.

In fall before a hard freeze lift roots, soil and all and set away from frost while foliage dries. Then remove tops and store tubers in peat, sand or vermiculite in a 50-degree place for winter. If you left them in pots, just lift and store as they are. The next spring, knock out the tubers, clean them and restart.

SIX LITTLE BULBS OF SPRING

On a blustery day in February or March, while the rest of the garden is still sleeping, you'll discover these wee ones looking up from the cold soil to greet you. And you'll appreciate them like nothing else in your yard.

Because they are so small you must stoop to see them well, they're best planted by the multitude. Use at least 50 to a drift of scilla, grape-hyacinth, snowdrop and glory-of-the-snow; 25 to a patch of each kind of crocus. With the larger Dutch hyacinths you can make a bright splash near a doorstep with six or twelve bulbs.

All except hyacinths are good for naturalizing—tucking into crannies beside a stone or tree, hiding among ground covers to give a spring surprise, and sprinkling along a fence row or anywhere about the yard you like to walk in early spring. Plant all of these in fall.

Hyacinths (Dutch). Their stiff 10-inch columns of red, pink, blue, purple, yellow, and white make good spring color where you want formality. They march along a path, and a group of them salutes you at a doorway. For effects like this use them in

197

ranks of two or three. They are better in beds and edgings than mixed with other bulbs or flowers, where their rigidity makes them seem out of place. Place bulbs 8 inches apart, and cover them, in average soil, 5 inches deep. Try: 'City of Haarlem'—yellow; 'King of the Blues'—rich indigo-blue, large; 'L'Innocence'—large white; 'Queen of the Pinks'—compact spikes of bright pink.

Crocus. Their bright cups of color—white, yellow, gold, purple, blue and mixtures, sit upon 3-inch tufts of grassy leaves in February and March. Crocus are at their best as drifts or spots of color, not whole beds. Their span is too short for that. You'll like them naturalized in a lawn or in a ground cover like *Vinca minor,* or snug in sunny corners where you don't mow or cultivate. Put them in warm pockets next to the house and you may see bloom in late January. Give them good garden soil, space 2 inches apart, cover 2 inches deep. Try: 'Early Perfection'—mauve purple with orange anthers; 'Little Dorrit'—blue, lilac, very large flowers; *chrysanthus* 'E. P. Bowles'—buttercup yellow, vigorous and early; 'Susianus'—bright yellow-gold, very

early; *biflorus* 'White Lady'—pure white throughout.

Grape-hyacinth (*Muscari*). You can have several degrees of blue, or white in this fragrant 10-inch flower. Don't be alarmed when you see these sending up foliage in the fall. This is natural, and the leaves will survive the winter. Use grape-hyacinths liberally in flower borders, at the edge of shrubs, in rock gardens. Or let them go wild under fences. They multiply so fast that in a few years you will have bulbs to plant far and wide. Give a sunny location, good garden soil, space 2 inches and cover 2 inches. Try 'Heavenly Blue' (*M. armeniacum*); *M. plumosum,* the feathery kind; and *M. botryoides album* for white flowers.

Snowdrop (*Galanthus nivalis*). These tiny nodding white flowers on slender stems brave snow sometimes to bloom in February and March. Give them a moist, drained slope under trees or high shrubs where they can spread themselves naturally. In fall lay a leaf mold mulch above them unless autumn's leaves make a blanket there. Plant bulbs in a humusy soil, 3 inches apart, 2 inches deep, and once they are established, do not disturb.

88 *Left* Agapanthus, or lily of the Nile, is hardy in mild climates and produces exquisite blue flowers in late summer. *Genereux*

89 Caladiums, potted or in the ground, add soft color to a terrace in partial shade. *Genereux*

FIFTEEN TENDER BULBS YOU WILL ENJOY

Name	When to plant outside	Depth (inches)	Height (inches)	Colors	Bloom time	Exposure
Achimenes	May	1 (a)	10	Red, violet, blue, white	Summer to frost	Shade
Acidanthera	May	5	20	Purple, white	Summer to frost	Sun
Begonia tuberosa (Tuberous begonia)	Spring when frosts end	Cover tuber	18	All but true blue, purple	Summer to frost	Shade
Caladium	Spring when frosts end	1 (a)	20	Foliage red, white, green	Colorful to frost	Shade
Canna	Spring when frosts end	2	to 60	Red, rose, yellow and combinations	Summer to frost	Sun
Colocasia (Elephant's ear)	Spring when frosts end	2	72	Foliage dark green	Interesting to frost	Part day shade
Dahlia	May	2	48-72	All but true blue	Late summer to frost	Sun, light shade
Gladiolus	Spring when frosts end	6	12-48	All but true blue	Summer, fall	Sun, part day shade
Gloriosa (Glory-lily)	Spring when frosts end	2 (b)	Vine to 72 average	Red-yellow	Summer, fall	Sun or light shade
Hymenocallis (Peruvian daffodil)	Spring when frosts end	4	24	White or cream	Summer	Sun or light shade
Oxalis bowieana	Spring when frosts end	3	10	Pink	Summer	Sun
Polianthes (Tuberose)	Spring when frosts end	3	30	White	Summer, fall	Sun
Tigridia (Mexican shell flower)	Spring	3	20	Red, white, yellow and combinations	Summer	Sun
Zantedeschia (Calla-lily)	Spring when frosts end	4	to 36	White, yellow, cream	Summer	Light shade
Zephyranthes (Zephyr-lily)	Spring when frosts end	2	to 10	White, pink, yellow	Summer	Sun

(a) Start early indoors. Nestle bulb in damp peat and sand until growth starts. Then pot or transplant to open ground, barely covering bulb with soil.

(b) Pot in February covering two inches deep. Set started plants outdoors from pot when frosts are over.

199

TWO DOZEN HARDY BULBS YOU WILL ENJOY

Name	When to plant	Depth (inches)	Height (inches)	Colors	Bloom time	Exposure
*Agapanthus mooreanus** (Lily-of-the-Nile)	April	1	20	Blue	Midsummer	Sun
Allium (Ornamental onions)	October	Twice their own depth	to 60; most under 24	Purple, yellow, blue	May, June, July	Sun
Anemone blanda	October	3	5	Pink, blue, white	April, May	Sun
Chionodoxa (Glory-of-the-snow)	October	2	4	Blue, pink, white	March	Sun
Colchicum (Autumn crocus)	August	3	to 8	Purple to white	September	Sun
Crocus	October	2	to 6	White, yellow, gold, purple, blue	February, March	Sun
Cyclamen neapolitanum	August-September	2	4	Pink	September-October	Shade
Eranthis (Winter aconite)	July-August	3	to 6	Yellow	Early spring	Part day shade
Eremurus (Foxtail-lily)	October	6-8	to 96	Yellow, white, pink	Summer	Sun, protected
Erythronium (Dogtooth violet)	August-September	3	12 average	Cream, white, yellow, (some pink)	Spring	High shade
Fritillaria imperialis (Crown imperial)	Autumn	6-8	34	Yellow, orange, red	April	Sun, midday shade
Galanthus nivalis (Snowdrop)	October	2	4	White	February-March	Sun, light shade
*Gallonia** (Summer hyacinth)	Spring	6	36	White	Summer	Sun
Hyacinth (Dutch)	October	5	10	Red, pink, blue, purple, yellow, white	Spring	Sun, light shade

Iris reticulata	September-October	3	7-10	Purple with yellow marks	March	Sun
*Ixia** (Corn lily)	September-October	3	12-30	Blue, pink, red, purple, white, yellow	Spring	Sun, protected
Leucojum vernum (Snowflake)	September-October	3	8-14	White tipped with green	March	Light shade
Lycoris squamigera (Hardy amaryllis)	August after bloom	6	24	Lavender-pink	August	Sun or light shade
Muscari (Grape-hyacinth)	Autumn	2	10	Blue, white	Early spring	Sun or light shade
Ornithogalum umbellatum (Star of Bethlehem)	Fall	3	10	White	Spring	Sun, light shade
Puschkinia libanotica (Striped squill)	October	2	6	Soft blue and white	March	Sun
Scilla campanulata (Wood hyacinth)	October	4	12	Lilac, blue, and white	May	Part day shade
Scilla sibirica (Scilla)	October	2	6	Blue, white	Spring	Sun
Sternbergia lutea	Early fall	4	6	Yellow	Fall	Sun, protected

* Not reliably hardy north of Washington, D.C.; best grown in North as pot or tub plant.

Glory-of-the-snow (*Chionodoxa*). Their dainty blue stars, sometimes pink or white, shine through departing snow the first warm days. Naturalize them along the south sides of shrubs, walls and woodlands. They need the sun they'll have there. Or put them at the edge of borders and among your rock garden treasures. Give them good garden soil, space 2 inches apart and 2 inches deep. Try: *sardensis,* gentian-blue; *luciliae alba,* white; and *luciliae rosea,* pink.

Scilla (*S. sibirica*). Of the many kinds of scilla this is the most vigorous and useful. Its vivid, nodding deep blue flowers follow the glory-of-the-snow, spreading by bulbs and seeds to make dense masses. Early bees love the flowers and seek them out. Plant this scilla in drifts where it gets sun, in good garden soil, 2 inches apart, 2 inches deep. You can also have it in white (*S. sibirica alba*) and sky blue (*S. azurea*).

EASY-DOES-IT IDEAS

Crocus are easy to naturalize around shrubs, rocks, bases of trees. You need not even prepare soil. Just lift a slab of sod with the trowel, slip in the corm, and replace the sod.

Naturalize little bulbs like scillas and glory-of-the-snow at the southern edge of shrubbery where grass doesn't grow and you aren't tempted to spade or hoe. They multiply and form colonies in such places, and bloom very early.

Caladiums and tuberous begonias are elegant and grown with ease in pots instead of directly in the ground. Sink pots in soil up to the rims. When winter approaches, lift pot and all to store undisturbed until the next season.

PART III

SPECIALTY PLANTS AND GARDENS

Chapter 13

EVERYBODY WANTS ROSES

Aren't roses hard to grow?

Wherever you live, Maine to California, Montana to Florida, you can grow roses. And what a variety of forms the family has produced! Midgets and giants, ground covers and climbers, singles and doubles, alone or in clusters, and the best of them marvelously fragrant. Some varieties like *Rosa gallica* date back to 2500 B. C. or perhaps earlier, and all before 1900 A. D. are called "old." There are new ones as modern as tomorrow.

You are pretty sure to want some roses, maybe a scented climber on a trellis by a bedroom window, a hedge of floribundas along a boundary, or a few big bushes in the shrub border. Maybe you will decide on a whole garden of roses or perhaps just a bed of six hybrid teas. Think about these possibilities in relation to your place and the time you can spend on your plants. Roses need more care than many other flowering plants. Most people think they're worth it.

ON CHOOSING ROSES

To get the most out of roses, select those that grow well in your locality and then cater to their needs. Let's take a look at the wonderful possibilities.

HYBRID TEAS

When you think of roses, this is the type that probably comes to mind, with slender pointed buds and radiant satin blooms of pink, salmon, red, yellow, or white, many of them perfumed. They bloom and bloom from June through October. Most stay under 4 feet except in California or the Northwest where they are shoulder high.

Uses: This is the best rose for flower arrangements; it is lovely in the garden, and fine for exhibiting. The American Rose Society recommends these varieties for growing anywhere in the United States: 'Charlotte Armstrong,' deep pink; 'Crimson Glory,' dark red velvet; 'Helen Traubel,' fragrant pink blend; 'Tiffany,' fragrant pink-gold blend; 'Dainty Bess,' pink single with crimson center; 'Picture,' light clear pink; 'Peace,' very large yellow blend, 'White Wings,' white single with purple center.

HYBRID PERPETUALS

These are the immediate ancestors of the hybrid teas. Several varieties are still much used, although these are no longer "modern" roses. Compared with hybrid teas, the plants are more vigorous, and the blooms are larger but on weaker stems and the growth is not so erect, and they are not really perpetual blooming. They flower in June and under good conditions produce another surge in the fall, with perhaps a scattering in between. Most of them are fragrant, and in height 5 feet is average.

Uses: They make informal hedges or backgrounds for low roses. Treat them as shrubs or grow them for cutting. Give each plant plenty of space, say 4 feet each way from neighboring plants. Some, like the lilac-pink 'Paul Neyron' reaches 6 feet in height. Other good kinds: 'Baronne Prevost,' rose-pink; 'Arrillaga,' light pink; 'General Jacqueminot,' red; 'Henry Nevard,' fragrant deep red.

FLORIBUNDAS AND POLYANTHAS

Historically, polyanthas are ancestors of floribundas, but as a practical matter the two kinds are usually thought of as pretty much the same. Typical floribundas are lower and bushier than hybrid teas, and flowers are less distinguished but more prolific. They look like miniature tea roses in clusters. Plants are hardy, tough, and vigorous, and bloom repeatedly through the season.

Uses: Good in arrangements, but most rewarding in the garden where they make colorful low borders or hedges, edgings to beds of tall roses, and accents in front of evergreens. A few grow tall—'Betty Prior,' pink, and 'Masquerade,' yellow-pink-red, but most are under 3 to 4 feet. Other good kinds: 'Spartan,' orange-scarlet; 'Fashion,' coral-pink.

Polyanthas usually have lower and bushier plants than floribundas. Flowers are individually smaller, in dense clusters. Except for boutonnieres or corsages they are not favorites for cutting, but they are good in the garden for low hedges, beds and mass effects. They bloom endlessly. Some good kinds are 'The Fairy,' light pink; 'Gloria Mundi,' orange-scarlet; 'Cecile Brunner,' pink-gold; and the very low, cream and orange 'Gruss an Aachen.'

GRANDIFLORAS

These are the newest class, a combination of floribunda with hybrid tea. Grandifloras bloom both singly and in clusters. Usually they grow strong and tall, and flower all summer. Stems are longer than on floribundas and flowers are larger, but not usually as large as a hybrid tea. Sometimes it's pretty hard to tell the difference. Grandifloras may take plenty of blue ribbons, but they seldom beat a hybrid tea for Queen of the Show.

Uses: Superb both for cutting and garden decoration. Some of the best: 'Starfire,'

bright sparkling red; 'Queen Elizabeth,' soft pink; 'Carrousel,' strong dark red.

SHRUB ROSES

In this group are a multitude of kinds, all self-supporting large bushes that you plant for the same reasons you would any flowering shrub. Every shrub border is the prettier for one or more. They may have either single or double flowers in many shades of red, yellow and white. Many of them are very fragrant. Some, like 'Fruhlingsmorgen,' yellow-pink, make mounds up to 8 feet high; some like the rugosas have showy red berries in fall; some, like 'Sarah Van Fleet,' pink, bloom repeatedly through the season. Other good kinds: Sweet brier (*Rosa eglanteria*), most valued for fragrant foliage; yellow 'Father Hugo' (*R. hugonis*); 'Stanwell Perpetual,' pink; and 'Bishop Darlington,' single pink and gold, fragrant.

CLIMBERS

These are strong growing, large-flowered roses with canes that become quite long. They usually bloom several times a season. You train them on fences, arbors, or trellises by tying them up—they don't climb as a grape vine does. A few, like 'Prosperity' (pink-white), are less vigorous than others and are called pillar roses. They are better for lamp posts than large climbers like the handsome 'New Dawn' (light pink) that can go up to the second story.

Uses: Depending on the size of the kinds you choose, they will do everything from festoon a fence to cover the side of a house. Good kinds: 'Don Juan,' dark red, tall; 'Climbing Peace,' yellow blend, tall; 'High Noon,' dark yellow, medium; 'Paul's Scarlet,' bright red, June-blooming; 'City of York,' white, tall; 'Dr. W. Van Fleet,' pink, tall.

TREE ROSES

Man, not nature, turned these out this way, with a bush at the top of a bare 3- to 4-foot stem. Tree roses are made by budding a top of some desirable variety on a stout long cane of another kind, which in turn

90 *Upper Left* Hybrid tea is the type of rose you think of first, the queen of all the many kinds. 'Memoriam' has the popular high style and many petals; it is delicate soft pink. *Peterson & Dering*

91 *Upper Right* 'South Seas,' another hybrid tea, is coral-pink and wavy-petaled.

Jackson & Perkins

92 *Lower Left* 'Queen Elizabeth' is a highly regarded example of the new group of roses called grandifloras—tall, vigorous, strong pink. *Roche*

93 *Lower Right* 'Sarabande' is a floribunda—low, compact, many bright red almost single flowers in each cluster.

Star Roses

94 A mixed garden of hybrid teas is a source of beauty for your yard and cut flowers for your table.

Genereux

95 Tree roses make striking accents. They come in many standard varieties, like this 'Spartan.'

Jackson & Perkins

may be budded to a root of yet another kind.

Uses: These make good formal accents. The blooms are fine for cutting, but the bush is more effective in the garden if you leave flowers on. Where it gets really cold, winter protection is a problem. Tree roses come in many varieties of hybrid teas or floribundas.

MINIATURES

Flowers, leaves and stems are all on a Lilliputian scale. Yet most miniatures are as hardy and easy to grow as floribundas.

Uses: They make charming edgings for flower borders or herb gardens, and as colonies in rock gardens. Plant them in containers, strawberry jars, window boxes. As cut flowers put them in miniature arrangements, boutonnieres, and corsages. Good kinds: 'Red Imp,' dark crimson; 'Baby Masquerade,' red, pink and yellow: 'Twinkles,' blush pink.

WHAT MAKES A ROSE BUSH WORTH THE MONEY?

As in everything else, you get what you pay for with roses, but the wide disagreement in prices may baffle you. Where the plant was grown is not so important as what it looks like. A dormant rose worth planting has at least three strong canes as big as your little finger, and a few smaller ones, all symmetrically spaced on the crown. It looks fresh and green, with swollen buds bursting with life. The roots are brittle, fat, and evenly distributed. The bud union (where root meets top) is healed smoothly without cracks. And this especially: The whole plant looks healthy—no warty nubs on root that might be galls; no gray-brown blots on stems that might be cankers. If you pay two dollars or more for a plant like this, you get your money's worth. For every such rose produced the grower has rejected dozens inferior to it. You'll sometimes find the rejects selling for sixty nine cents or so, in the supermarket. They might live and grow, but their chances of giving satisfaction are much poorer.

Roses from the nursery in early spring are apt to be bare root. Those you get by mail are, too. But those you buy later at your nursery will be potted up in cans or tar-paper pots and you take home pot, earth and all, along with a plant that is leafed out and maybe blooming. With them, you have to trust the man who pots them, since all you can see is the top. These are a convenience, for they lengthen the planting season—and you pay for this in a slight extra cost.

SITE, SOIL, AND HOLE

Give your roses a place in sun for at least half days, where drainage is good and tree roots do not intrude. The rest of the matter of locating them depends on your esthetic tastes and how you design your garden. Caring for roses is easier if you

96 You can train climbing roses on fences, arbors, trellises, and walls by tying them up. 'New Dawn,' climbers are usually vigorous and strong growing.
Gottscho-Schleisner

97 *Upper Left* To plant a rose, keep bare roots covered while you prepare planting holes. Trim off straggly or broken roots. Set the plant so bud union is at the proper depth for your climate. 98 *Upper Right* Carefully fill in soft soil under, around and over roots. 99 *Lower Left* Firm it down by treading. 100 *Lower Right* Finally, settle it with a bucketful of water and let water soak away before filling the hole.
Vance

group them together instead of scattering plants about. In a bed, range them in height so you can see the short kinds at the front, and they all get sunlight.

Roses need extra good soil, one that is firm and loamy, neither sandy nor all clay, so that water will enter it freely and remain long enough to benefit roots but not so long as to create a bog. It contains much humus, and does not bake to a brick in hot sun. Where soil does not meet requirements, add lots of peat moss, leaf mold, or both, and dig it in 12 inches deep. The more humus the better. You can't get too much. While you're at it, add fertilizer made for roses (sold at garden stores) at the rate suggested on the package. If rotted or dried cow manure is available, put that in, too. Do all this a week before you get plants, so soil can settle down.

Space floribundas, hybrid teas, and grandifloras 2 feet apart. The big shrub roses need 6 to 8 feet or more. Ten inches is enough between miniatures. When you are ready to plant, dig a *big* hole that accommodates the root spread, and unless it's a potted rose, pull up a mound of loose soil in the center of the hole to hold up the crown as you plant.

PLANTING THEM RIGHT

If roses are "bare root," unwrap them as soon as they arrive. If you can plant by the next day, soak roots overnight in a tub of water. Otherwise, moisten the packing and store in a cool place until you're ready.

Take plants out a few at a time and keep them covered with wet sacks until you come to planting them. Have pruners handy as you set out each rose, so you can trim off broken or straggly roots that won't fit without curling into the king-size hole you have dug.

How high or low to put the bud union (thickened place at base) is an international debate, but the truth is, it depends on where you live. If your winters freeze deep, put the joint an inch *below* ground-level to protect it. If your winters are less stern, and you seldom lose roses, put the joint just at *ground level* or even a little *above* to encourage good branching from the base.

With this in mind, hold the plant in the hole so the bud union is just above where you want it finally to be. Spread roots over the mound and fill in soft soil around them. Work it down. When the hole is half full, gently tread it with your foot. Pour in a bucket of water and let it soak in while you plant the next bush. After the water disappears, fill up the hole with soil. If you've done it right, the bud union will settle just where you intended. Mound soft earth 6 inches deep over the crown to keep the top damp. When you see growth beginning, remove this mound.

For potted roses prepare the hole just as

carefully but without a mound in the middle. Water them in advance so the soil sticks together and you can cut off the pot, without breaking the ball of earth. Look at what you can see of the roots. If they are coiled and jammed together, unjam them and spread them out. This is important, because roots stay where you plant them. Set the ball at the right level for the bud union, fill in around it and the roots, and water all copiously.

CARING FOR THE PLANTS

HOW TO FEED ROSES

People who grow lots of roses all agree that they need feeding, but there the agreement ends. The best advice for beginners is to follow a path of moderation. Use organic fertilizers like dried cow or sheep manure heavily (a spadeful to a bush) once a year in spring and dig it in *between* the plants. Then twice yearly (once when first buds show color, and again in August) give a dose of commercial rose food at the package rate. If you want to advance into more precise and scientific rose feeding, start with a soil test made by a professional at your state college, and follow the resulting recommendations as to what your soil needs to grow good roses.

MULCHING FOR SUMMER

Roses will grow without a mulch, but they seem to do better with it, and a mulch saves you time. It keeps down weeds and reduces the need for water and cultivation. Use mulches like buckwheat hulls, ground corncobs, cocoa bean shells, pine needles, cottonseed hulls, or chopped tobacco stems about one and one half inches deep.

Before applying a mulch in spring, level the bed, loosen the soil and work in the first feeding of fertilizer. Put later plant food on top of the mulch, stir it down and water it in. The mulch remains on top of the ground. If you hill your roses with earth for winter, remove the mulch and store it. Don't pile soil over it.

PROTECTING FOR WINTER

The need to protect plants in winter depends on your location and the kind of roses you are growing. You'd better protect your hybrid teas, and especially tree roses, if winters bring zero several times. If the temperature rarely hits zero, hybrid teas are probably as well off without protection. The hardiest roses are the shrubs and polyanthas, and they get less hardy in this order: hybrid perpetuals, floribundas, grandifloras, miniature roses, large-flowered climbers, hybrid teas, and tree roses (which are most easily damaged by cold).

To protect roses, hill them with soft soil 6 to 8 inches deep. Bring this earth in—don't scrape it up from between plants. Put it on in late fall *after a hard freeze stops all growth*. Fill in between mounds with loose oak leaves or hay. In the spring remove the protection after the ground thaws but before warm days start soft shoots growing inside the mound. Haul the extra soil away, so the level stays the same as before.

Where it gets even colder, make the mounds deeper, the hay and oak leaves higher, and enclose the bed with boards or plastic, and a cover to keep the mulch dry.

If you must protect tree roses, dig a trench on one side, loosen the roots on the other side and bend down the tree so you can lay it over into the trench. Then mound soil over top, stem and root. Even so, a tree rose may be short-lived in a harsh climate.

HOW TO PRUNE ROSES

Prune your roses in spring before growth starts. Don't prune them in fall except to cut off long tops that weave in the wind. You need both hand pruners and a lopper, and a small pruning saw is useful, too, especially for shrub roses and climbers.

First remove the mulch and mound (if there is one) so you can see all of the plant. Begin by cutting out dead wood, which you can identify by its light dry look. Leave no stubs. Next take canes that are diseased, showing stem cankers, for instance; and those that are deformed, in the wrong place, or obviously very old.

Now stand back for a good look, and see if you can make a balanced vase-shaped framework of three to five young husky canes free of twiggy growth at either top or base. Prune away everything that does not fit into this design.

How far to cut back tops? Winter usually decides this for you. Prune winter-killed canes back to live wood even if it means going to the crown. But hard pruning every year weakens plants, so if you can, leave canes as tall as your loppers. Prune tall growing kinds higher than you do low ones. To cut back canes, select a good leaf bud and make a slanting cut just above it. If you leave a long stub beyond the bud the stem dies. Top back young plants relatively less than older ones.

Remove suckers, the shoots that come from *below* the bud union. These are from the rootstock, which is a wild rose different from the upper plant. If you let a sucker go, it soon overwhelms the rest. When you find small pale flowers, or strangely different ones on a rose, don't think the bush has "reverted"—actually the rootstock has taken it over because you let a sucker grow.

It pays to cover all cuts thicker than a pencil with tree wound paint. This keeps the end from drying out and prevents stem borers from getting in.

On tall climbers and big shrub roses, retain most of the old wood. It produces much of the bloom. Prune climbers mainly to remove dead wood and keep the plant in bounds. Occasionally remove an old cane at the base to open up the plant for new growth. When you find diseased wood, like a cane with canker, remove it.

How to cut a rose. Roses are meant for picking. To encourage future blooms, cut stems just above a five-parted leaf. Here there is probably a growth bud that can develop a new stem to replace the one you are taking off. By cutting very close to it but not through it, you will leave no long stub to die back and possibly invite disease.

WHEN YOU ENTER A ROSE SHOW

Invariably those who grow roses want to show them. That's what will probably happen to you, and you will learn by doing.

Knowing a few fundamentals may make the start more encouraging. Prize-winning roses start with the good care that has already been described. Some varieties are frequent prize winners, for example, 'The Doctor,' 'Crimson Glory,' 'Mrs. Sam McGredy,' 'Countess Vandal,' 'Mojave,' 'Show Girl,' 'Tiffany,' and 'Symphonie.'

Two or three weeks before a show, when you see a likely end bud developing on a hybrid tea, remove small side buds. Take them off carefully so the scars do not show on the final bloom stem. Disbudding, as this is called, increases size and quality of the tip bloom.

The judges look at the form, color, stem, foliage, substance and size of your roses. Color is affected by the age of a flower. If you try to hold a bloom too long, the color betrays you. Stems need to be strong, straight and the right size for the flower. Foliage should be free of insect nibbles, disease or spray stains. You can wipe spray or dust residue off the leaves with a soft moist cloth, but don't wax foliage.

Cut your show blooms the afternoon before, put stems in a deep bucket of water and set in a cool place. This "conditions" them. Put plastic bags over the blooms to keep them prime. Before starting to the show, study your schedule and know exactly what classes you will enter. Have your varieties labeled in advance, to save precious time after you arrive.

KEEP YOUR ROSES HEALTHY

You may as well face it—many insects eat on roses, and many diseases spoil the plants unless you check them. But don't despair, new chemicals are making the job of control easier and quicker year by year. At the worst you won't spend over a half hour a week in this business, even with fifty roses.

Whether you spray or dust is something for you to decide (for help see Chapter 26). If you go in for rose growing in a big way, you will probably eventually do both. If you spray, do it early in the day so foliage dries soon. Dusting works best when air is still and foliage is dry, usually toward eve-

ning before dew begins to fall. If it looks like rain, get your spray or dust on *before the shower* so the fungicide is there to protect the leaves. Try to do one or the other, dust or spray, every seven to ten days through the summer. On the hottest days, however, give yourself and the roses a rest. Several common ingredients of sprays and dusts burn rose leaves when it's really hot. Sulfur, for instance, scorches things above 85 degrees.

The most practical remedies for rose pests —either as sprays or dusts—are combinations of chemicals that control blackspot, mildew and most of the insects that attack roses. Such preparations are sold ready to use under hundreds of trade names. A good multipurpose spray or dust contains phaltan, or zineb, or captan, or ferbam, or maneb (*for blackspot*); Karathane or sulfur (for mildew); malathion, or DDT, or lindane, or methoxychlor, or rotenone (*one or several, for most insects*); and sometimes aramite or Kelthane (*for red spider*).

STOP TROUBLE WHEN YOU SEE IT

Your regular 10-day spray or dust with a multipurpose combination will prevent most of these plagues. See also Chapter 26 for more on these unpleasant matters.

APHIDS

What they look like: Green or red lice swarm on tender stems and leaves, sucking the life out of them.

Remedy: Dust or spray with combination containing one of these: malathion, pyrethrum, rotenone; or spray with straight nicotine sulfate, $1\frac{1}{2}$ teaspoons to a gallon of water, with a tablespoon of liquid soap for a sticker.

BLACKSPOT

What it looks like: It starts on older leaves as fuzzy black spots which grow to one-fourth inch across. Then leaves turn yellow, soon fall off. Some varieties lose all leaves if not protected. This is a fungus and spreads by spores in drops of water.

Remedy: In early spring spray plants and soil around with lime-sulfur (a liquid sold for dormant spraying of many kinds of plants). After growth begins, spray or dust weekly with a combination containing one of these: captan, ferbam, maneb, zineb, or phaltan. Avoid overhead sprinkling.

BORERS

What they look like: First you see canes dying back, then notice holes in ends or sides of stems. Slit down and in the pith you find grubs of bees or wasps, or the adults, boring away or resting. They are especially busy in late summer.

Remedy: Remove cane down to sound wood and seal surface with tree wound paint or orange shellac. Don't leave pruning cuts unsealed.

CANKER

What it looks like: Spreading spots of red, tan, white, purple or brown sometimes circle stems and make them die back. This is a fungus that spreads by spores.

Remedy: Cut out diseased canes in spring; spray with lime-sulfur before buds break; avoid moist winter mulches.

CROWN GALL

What it looks like: Warty "tumors" near the crown or at bud union (sometimes under the soil) sap the strength of plants and they dwindle. This is a bacterial disease spread by cultivating and irrigating.

Remedy: Prevent it by inspecting new plants and burning any with gall. If you find gall in your garden, dig and burn the plant and remove surrounding soil. Replace with fresh earth.

JAPANESE BEETLES

What they look like: Metallic green oval $\frac{1}{2}$-inch beetles appearing in June and July,

devouring foliage and flowers. West to Ohio and maybe beyond these are a tough problem.

Remedy: Protect foliage each week with a combination containing one of these: DDT, methoxychlor, malathion, Sevin, or lead arsenate.

POWDERY MILDEW

What it looks like: Young leaves get distorted wrinkles and blisters, are covered with white powder, often turn purple. Buds and stems may be hit too. This is a fungus spread by wind.

Remedy: Before it starts use spray or dust containing one of these: sulfur, Karathane, phaltan or Acti-dione PM. (The last one, an antibiotic, is best applied alone and not combined with other chemicals).

THRIPS

What they look like: They are almost too small to see, but the damage they do shows in blighted flowers, or browned buds that won't open. They are speck-size, yellow, often found between petals of opening flowers, particularly light colored ones.

Remedy: Spray or dust with a combination containing malathion or DDT.

EASY-DOES-IT IDEAS

Set your roses in narrow beds that you can reach from both sides, so you can tend the plants without stepping into the beds. Three plants wide is a good width.

If you have had mildew on your roses, try to locate new plantings where they get good air circulation—away from walls and breeze-stopping hedges or tree rows.

Mulch your roses for a big saving of time. The mulch makes cultivating unnecessary, reduces watering, and it will probably cut down on disease troubles, too.

Chapter 14

CAMELLIAS ARE CHOICE

Can I have camellias in my northern garden?

Northerners look with envy on the camellia, the darling of the South, and no wonder. Now, happily, it is becoming apparent that these handsome flowering evergreens are hardier than most people imagined. And added to this, hybridizing is producing many camellias that are hardier than the older varieties.

Popularity rests on a unique combination of good qualities. First, camellias bloom in fall, winter and early spring when they have the spotlight virtually to themselves. Each bloom is a picture of perfection, suited to every use of a garden or cut flower. Furthermore, the bushes are superb broadleaf evergreens, glossy and attractive the year around, shapely and stalwart, 5 to 10 feet high. Even if your winters are too cold to permit bloom, the plants are worthwhile as evergreen shrubs. One final blessing—they are long lived. In the South, there are some camellias more than one hundred years old that bloom each year and seem to get more beautiful as time goes on.

FOR ZONE 7

As far north as Zone 7, they merit your consideration and experimentation. Take a look at this zone on the map. It includes part of Connecticut along Long Island Sound, and coastal sides of Rhode Island and Massachusetts out to Cape Cod. Swinging southeastward it takes in all of Long Island, southern New Jersey and the Phila-

delphia corner of Pennsylvania; then Delaware, most of Maryland, the District of Columbia, Virginia, the Carolinas and what is generally called the "Upper South." Going westward through part of Texas, the zone winds up on the seaward slopes of the Sierras and the Cascades.

All of the Southeast, the Gulf Coast, the warm Southwest, coastal sides of Oregon and Washington are in the range. Extreme south Florida has winters too warm to grow them well, since the camellia is definitely not a tropical plant. It needs cool but not frigid winters, and warm summers. If you have these plus a suitable planting site, camellias are possibilities for you. In Yonkers, New York, are camellias that have grown for thirty years and survived occasional temperatures of 5 below zero. They are found in gardens as far north as Toronto, Ontario, and a few reports of success have come from such unlikely climates as Missouri and Kansas. Sudden drops in temperature seem to be more devastating to camellias than cold itself. Chill that comes gradually hardens and toughens the tissues. Thus hardened, plants can take more cold than when they are struck suddenly after a period of warmth.

Best risks. It seems that midseason or late varieties that bloom at tulip time are better risks in the North than early varieties. On the other hand, in a few instances camellias on the northern frontier have succeeded because they were extra early and bloomed in November *before* the coldest weather arrived. Midwinter blooms outdoors in northern gardens are most unlikely.

The hardiest camellias apparently are

101   Northern gardeners can grow camellias by planting them in tubs which are moved to a protected spot or indoors for the cold weather. Everywhere they are spectacular porch and patio pot plants. In some cold climates they can also be grown outdoors.   *Whitland Locke*

found among the japonicas, and it seems that the singles and semidoubles are a little hardier than full doubles. Old plants are hardier than young ones, and long-established ones are hardier than newly set ones. Every now and then an enthusiast publishes an account of his successes in a northern area. At the end of this chapter is a list of kinds often mentioned in such reports.

TYPES OF CAMELLIAS

Flower form and color vary from simple singles with stamen puffs in the center to neat doubles with petals overlapping regu-

larly and in snow white, pink to crimson and countless blends, shades and combinations, even yellows now—all hues but blue. Plant size and shape are also variable. Get a color catalog and study it to help you select the varieties you want. Or go to a nursery and see plants in bloom.

Japonicas and sasanquas are the two main types of camellias, although six or seven other common species have been used in breeding. Of the two, japonicas are by far the favorites. There are some 1400 varieties from this species. They grow as shrubs or trees, and produce flowers 2 to 3 inches across—singles with nine petals or less, semidoubles, full doubles, imbricated (petals

102 'Flirtation,' a camellia hybrid, makes a shapely shrub that is pretty even when the single pink
blooms are gone.   *Armstrong*

overlapped), and some with irregular flower forms. In the South and in California, japonicas bloom over a long season and are classed as early, midseason and late, dates depending somewhat on location. Early blooming kinds perform from October to Christmas. Late December to February is midseason with the big surge of bloom. Those blooming from March on are considered late.

103   The double forms of camellias have petals in an overlapping pattern. Glossy foliage of japon-
ica camellias, like this one, is a year-round asset.   *de Gennaro*

104   'Brigadoon,' an example of the new camellia hybrids, is a cross of *C. saluenensis* and *C. japon-
ica*. It has fuchsia-pink ruffled blooms.   *Armstrong*

Ten good varieties of Camellia japonica.

'Adolphe Audusson,' semidouble, midseason, crimson with dark veins.

'Chandleri Elegans,' incomplete double, early midseason, rose-pink and white.

'C. M. Hovey,' formal double, late, red.

'Daikagura,' peony form, early, red and white variegated.

'Debutante,' peony form, early midseason, light pink.

'Herme,' semidouble, midseason, variegated rose-pink and white.

'Lady Clare,' semidouble, early midseason, rose-pink.

'Mathotiana,' double, with overlapping petals, midseason to late, red.

'Pink Perfection,' double, early to late, pink, upright, with fine foliage.

'Purity,' formal, double, late, white.

Sasanquas start to bloom mid to late fall in the South, and always before the japonicas. Most are single or semidouble, with only a few doubles. Fast-growing, the plants start to bloom young, and develop sprawling, compact or columnar bushes. Individual flowers are not long-lasting, but they keep coming for a long time and there are lots of them. The small foliage of sasanquas is very decorative. These are as good as japonicas for garden use, but for cut flowers and corsages they cannot compare. Sasanquas are probably not quite as hardy as japonicas for northern gardens, but because of their fall-blooming habit you might succeed in getting flowers from them where buds of other kinds would be killed by frost. As components in some of the new hybrids, sasanquas are increasingly important.

Five good varieties of Camellia sasanqua.

'Briar Rose,' single, soft pink, upright.

'Dawn,' single to semidouble, ivory tinted pink, upright.

'Jean May,' double, pink, upright.

'Lavender Queen,' single, lavender-pink, low.

'Sparkling Burgundy,' double, ruby-red, upright.

105 'Sparkling Burgundy' is a sasanqua camellia of ruby-rose color.   *Armstrong*

Other species. Reticulata camellias are still something of a rarity. They are less hardy, less easy, and less handsome in foliage than either japonicas or sasanquas; but they have enormous wavy-petaled blooms, some of them 7 inches across. You'll find reticulata influence in a few new camellia varieties, like 'Buddha.'

Camellia saluenensis is another species used to produce new hybrids like the single pink 'J. C. Williams.' This strong, hardy type freely produces 3-inch pink-and-white flowers on vigorous, attractive bushes. As a parent in hybrids it promises to help extend the camellia region northward.

WHERE TO PLANT CAMELLIAS

Camellias make ideal specimens if you place them where they have room to develop fully. The glossy foliage and elegant flowers look well near the house or on a terrace where you can enjoy them at close range. Remember that in time the plants will grow large, so avoid putting them in front of a window or too close to a path. They also do well in hedges, especially the small-leafed sasanquas. Foundation and doorway plantings, backgrounds, and borders mixed with other broadleaf evergreens are other possibilities, also as espaliers. Even in containers they espalier well against walls and trellises if you locate them out of bright sun.

All camellia colors are attractive. No other plants bloom at a time to fight with them except possibly azaleas. Magenta, orange and other strong shades of azaleas are therefore better not planted with a general grouping of camellias.

The ideal spot for camellias is in the filtered shade of high-branched evergreen trees such as pines, live oaks and large spruces and cedars. Don't place camellias in dense shade for they won't bloom well there and the plants will be thin; and don't put them in full sun or the foliage will burn. Kinds with variegated green and white foliage can take deeper shade than the others; and those with dark red flowers, as a rule, endure a little more sun than pink or white ones. Winter sun is especially hard on ca-

mellias in cold climates, so if you are trying them beyond their usual range, choose north or northwest exposures out of morning and noonday sun. A lath house might solve your problem for a good location.

Drainage is another prime factor—it must be good. If your soil drains slowly, raise the bed for camellias 6 inches or so. Like many other broadleafs, camellias need acidity, a pH of 5 to 6. Use acid peat, sulfur, or oak leaf mold to acidify the soil, unless it is already acid enough.

HOW TO PLANT CAMELLIAS

Nearby nurseries that grow camellias are your best source of good plants, because the soil they are balled or canned in is probably similar to what you have in your yard. This is an advantage, especially when it comes to watering, because earth in the ball absorbs water at the same rate as the soil around it. If no camellia nurseries are in driving distance, you can buy from a few firms that ship plants bare root, repacked in peat moss balls. You can set out container-grown camellias almost any time of year except in the very hottest or coldest weeks. If they're balled and burlapped, the best time is spring or fall. If you live where camellias are difficult, better plant them in spring.

Dig a hole twice as wide and twice as deep as the ball on the plant. Mix the soil removed with an equal amount of peat moss or leaf mold, and throw part of the mixture back in the hole and tramp it down so that the top of the root ball rests at least an inch above the surrounding ground. Fill in around the plant with the soil mixture; pack firmly. Water to settle the soil and then add more to bring the finished level up about 2 inches higher than the ground level. Finally, draw up a little dike to hold in water and top the area around the base with a 3-inch layer of loose mulch, like pine needles.

CAMELLIAS GROW WELL
IN CONTAINERS

In the North or on the upper fringe of the camellia belt, you may prefer growing camellias in large pots or tubs. In portable containers, plants are easily protected in winter by being moved to a cool porch. But container growing of camellias has exciting possibilities everywhere in the country, because the plant is admirably suited to it. In cans or tubs, camellias bloom earlier and even better than they do in the ground. They require less space and you can easily rearrange them in your garden, or on your paved patio. Feed and water tubbed plants regularly and move them to bigger containers when they outgrow the ones they are in, about every third year. Treated this way they stay healthy and handsome for many years. Metal cans, boxes, and wooden tubs are good containers if they have plenty of drain holes.

Use soil that is half peat. Feed potted plants in mid-March, May first, mid-June and August first, at the rate of one teaspoon of rhododendron-azalea-camellia fertilizer to each gallon of soil in the container, and water it in.

Watering should be thorough but not frequent. It is important each time to saturate the deepest roots. Once a week is enough except in very hot, dry weather; then twice a week. Never let the soil dry out entirely. In hot weather it helps to spray the leaves, too.

Eventually most camellias simply get too large for any practical container, and you will need to put them in the ground and start again with younger plants for your containers.

HOW TO FEED, PRUNE, AND DISBUD

Camellias need frequent feeding. The commercial preparations made for rhododendrons, azaleas and camellias usually consist of about 3 per cent nitrogen, 5 per cent phosphorus and 4 per cent potassium. Use two cups of such a fertilizer to each 3-foot plant. Feed once in late winter, once as new growth starts, again six weeks later as the second growth commences, then finally again in June. Always water fertilizer in well. You can also foliar-feed camellias with any of the soluble fertilizers diluted and applied according to package directions.

Where hardiness is a problem, stop fertilizing camellias by July first. Unless the season is extremely dry, pull back the mulch about the first of September so plants can dry off and mature. Letting them continue to grow soft leaves and stems late in fall makes them susceptible to cold damage.

Pruning camellias is simple. Actually, you don't need to prune at all. But it sometimes helps plants grow or look better. Shape them by removing stray shoots, cutting each time just above a leaf bud. Leave heavy pruning until spring, to save the next year's flowers. If light clipping is all you have in mind, any time of year will do. Pick flowers if you want to. It won't harm the bush and there should be plenty of other buds left to develop bloom for the next year.

Eventually you may want to enter camellias in a show. When you do, you will probably disbud them to get larger blooms. Where three or four flower buds appear in a cluster, leave only two or three. Break them off as soon as they are big enough to distinguish from leaf buds. Flower buds are swollen, but leaf buds are flat and pointed. A few varieties, like 'Pink Perfection' and 'Prince Eugene Napoleon,' do not respond with larger size even with disbudding, so there's no need to work on them.

WHEN FROST THREATENS BUDS AND FLOWERS

Buds come unscathed through frost of 28 degrees, unless they are far enough along to show color. Then they are damaged. Flowers that are open will surely be hurt. To save the flowers, use the direct method—cut them and take them indoors. To save buds, cover the bush with a sheet, using poles to hold it up off the foliage. This protects unless the mercury plunges far and stays down many hours. Or protect buds against a mild cold snap by hanging a wad of Spanish moss or sphagnum moss over them. If you anticipate trouble, try spraying plants in the fall with something like Wilt Pruf that leaves a thin protective coating on leaves, buds and stems. Where freezes are not too deep, this usually saves blooms.

KEEPING CAMELLIAS HEALTHY

Probably your camellias will never have troubles of any sort. But if they do, it is likely to be one of these three, and only the first is serious:

CAMELLIA FLOWER BLIGHT

Unknown in many camellia areas, but if you live in Georgia, Louisiana, the Carolinas, Virginia, California, and Oregon, watch out for it because it is real trouble.

What it looks like. At peak blooming time in February and March, tan spots appear on petals, particularly settling in the center of the flower. The blotch grows until the whole flower turns brown. Sometimes petals dry up, sometimes they get soft, depending on humidity. This fungus disease spreads by spores rising from infected mulch or soil beneath the plant where flowers fell the year before. It does not spread from flower to flower.

Remedy: Sacrifice flowers for a season. Pick *all* the flower buds off in the fall. Then starting in January and continuing to May, once a month thoroughly drench the ground and mulch under the plant with a solution of 1 pound of ferbam dissolved in 25 gallons of water. Cover the ground with this 10 feet out beyond each bush. Since fungus lives more than a year in the soil, do this monthly soil drenching a second season, too, although you need not sacrifice flowers the second year. When you buy plants in bloom, watch carefully to see that none show the symptoms. Whenever you find infected blooms, pick and burn them.

DIEBACK

What it looks like. Leaves suddenly wilt and twigs die back. This is a fungus disease.

Remedy: Cut affected twigs back to sound wood beyond blackened bark and burn the clippings. No more effective control is known.

TEA SCALE

What it looks like. Cottony or flaky looking specks appear underneath the leaves.

When there are enough together, yellow spots appear at the surface. Worse in humid areas than dry ones.

Remedy: Spray with an oil emulsion in spring or fall when temperature is over 45 and under 85 degrees, and seems likely to remain so for a week. Or spray weekly in spring and summer with a preparation containing malathion. Also treat nearby hollies and euonymus, which entertain the same scale.

THE HARDIEST CAMELLIAS

Red-flowering japonicas
  'Mathotiana'
  'Prof. C. S. Sargent'
  'C. M. Hovey'
  'Blood of China'
  'Tricolor Red'
  'Jarvis Red'
  'Flame'
Variegated japonicas
  'Lady Vansittart'
  'Tricolor'
  'T. K. Variegated'
  'Governor Mouton'
Pink japonicas
  'Magnoliaeflora'
  'Semidouble Blush'
  'Rev. Drayton'
  'Rev. Bennett'
  'Berenice Boddy'
White japonicas
  'Leucantha'
  'Triphosa'
Sasanquas
  'Sasan,' pink
  'Maiden's Blush,' pink
  'Totenko,' pink
  'Narumigata,' white and pink
  rosea, pink

EASY-DOES-IT IDEAS

A tub on wheels is just the thing for your camellia if you live in the North. In summer enjoy it outdoors on your shady terrace; in winter you'll have blooms at close range on a cool, light, enclosed porch.

223

On the north fringe of the camellia belt, for winter protection spray plants in late fall with an anti-transpirant like Wilt Pruf. It may save bloom and foliage damage during a cold snap.

Reed fencing is convenient and a not un-attractive winter protection for *new* plants. Tie it to stakes set away from the plant and leave an opening on the most protected side. But if camellias require such protection permanently in your area, better plant something else.

Chapter 15

YOUR GARDEN IN THE SHADE

What can I plant under my big trees?

Shade over your garden is a blessing if you take full advantage of it. Because sun-lovers like zinnias and marigolds produce no bloom in shade, you may have jumped to the conclusion that there are no flowers for the dim areas. You have not looked far enough. Not only are there annual flowers for shade, but there are perennials, shrubs, vines, and small trees, too. For foliage interest there are ferns and other plants not noted for flowers. You will prize your garden in the shade above all other places in your yard when you take refuge in it to rest and cool off on a hot sunny day. And the plants you can grow in shade have unusual freshness and charm, although they do not blaze with color.

STUDY YOUR SHADE SITUATION

If you have never analyzed your conditions of shade, spend a day with your watch and a notebook recording where the shadows fall and how long they stay over the places you are considering for your shade garden.

You will probably find about three degrees of shade. There is the dense shadow to the north of high walls or buildings where sun never reaches and even the open sky is obstructed. Similar to this is the place under low-spreading trees like beech and horse-chestnut where the ground is in semidark-ness as soon as the leaves mature in spring.

Next is the open type of shade you find to the north of a low building or wall where, true, the sun does not strike but the area is fully open to the sky. Somewhat like this is the place under or near high trees, or thin ones, where the sun filters through much of the day or there is up to two hours of intermittent sun a day.

Finally you have half-shade situations like those on the east or west sides of buildings, walls, trees or hedges, where in summer a plant gets as much as five or six hours of sun a day.

The list of what you can grow gets longer in places that get more sun. In dense shade, you can grow only a few plants, like money-wort, English ivy, creeping myrtle, and some ferns. Emerging to open shade you may add practically all plants ever recommended for shade. In the even brighter half-shade situation, you can plant many things normally grown in full sun but tolerant of some shade, and these include roses, irises, and lilies.

SOIL PROBLEMS IN SHADE

Consider always the kind of soil that exists in shade. You can find out something about this from the quality and vigor of plants that may already be growing there. If they are weak, thin, and hardly existing, you no doubt have a fertility or moisture problem—probably both—and probably caused by tree roots.

225

How to cope with tree roots. The roots of trees are the greatest obstacles to healthy gardens. The problem is worse if the trees are shallow rooted, like the Norway maple, elm, ailanthus, sycamore, linden, and beech that send out penetrating roots to use up all the available food and moisture. Turn a few spadefuls of earth, and you will soon know whether this is the situation. Under deep-rooting trees like oaks, hickories, ash, sweet gum, dogwood, and apple, your work will be easier and success more assured.

When you prepare soil for gardens in the shade of the trees, dig deeply so you can find and remove most of the roots. Push a sharp-shooter spade straight down in the soil to cut roots 8 to 10 inches deep. Mix extra large quantities of humus (compost, leaf mold, peat) in the soil for this shade garden and apply a balanced fertilizer too at the rate suggested on the bag.

It is dismaying to discover how fast tree roots will grow back into your garden. Every year you need to go around the edges of flower borders on the tree-ward sides with a sharp spade to cut roots back again as deep as you can reach. A more permanent way to keep roots out, although rather drastic, is at the start to open a narrow trench and install a root barrier like pieces of corrugated sheet-metal siding or roofing. Garden supply stores sell metal or plastic in rolls for this purpose. To be effective the barrier should reach down at least 2 feet.

Check acidity-alkalinity. Because so many of the woodland plants you might want to grow are acid-soil types, it pays to find out where your shade garden stands on this score. (See Chapter 3 for how to test soil.) Most likely you will find the existing condition acid enough.

106   Water and a wall make something special of this shade garden under high trees. Ferns, English ivy, and boxwood are the main plantings.
Roche

107 A garden in the shade may be simply a protected terrace with a few plants around it. *Tatch*

SOME SPECIAL MATTERS OF CARE

It's logical to think a shade garden needs less water than one in the sun. This is usually true to the north of walls and buildings, but under trees the case is just the opposite. Where tree roots mingle with those of your plants, it is the tree that has first call on moisture and food. You need to water more often, and also fertilize more than elsewhere in your garden. In dry weather, water heavily with a slow-running hose left for an hour or more in the same place. Do this at least once a week unless you have very good rains. Realize, too, that under trees a garden probably does not get nearly as much natural rain as in open areas because the tree holds it off. At least once a year, in spring or fall, add humus and fertilizer to the soil.

When you plant, allow for this rationing of water and food by spacing plants a little farther apart than you would in a sunny garden. Space also permits air circulation to ward off foliage diseases that might occur in cool, moist shade. And to conserve the soil moisture, use generous mulches of leaf mold, peat, pine needles, or buckwheat hulls.

WHAT KIND OF SHADE GARDEN WILL YOU CHOOSE?

Is it to be a shaded terrace with a few plants at the edge? Small-scale shrubs like camellias, azaleas, Japanese holly, pieris, and yews are good for such a planting. In these use pots and planters for accent. You will enjoy plants like tuberous or wax begonias, coleus, caladiums, achimenes, and patience plant. If there are nooks and crannies between flagstones or walls, ajuga, primroses, forget-me-nots, and little ferns are possibilities.

If you have a narrow area between walk and foundation on the north of your house, in open, high shade, you have a fine place to grow some charming shade plants. Consider any in the list of perennials marked for shade or part shade as possibilities (Chapter 10).

For a vine to clothe the north foundation or house wall, choose English ivy (or the hardier variegated *Hedera baltica*) and a variety of *Euonymus fortunei* like *E. f. vegetus* or *E. f. kewensis*. These are all evergreen. Among shade-tolerant vines that shed their leaves is the old favorite Boston ivy, *Parthenocissus tricuspidata*.

A ground cover garden. If low upkeep is what you particularly want in shade areas, cover them with ground cover plants. They will look restful, and be restful since you hardly need to lift a hand in caring for them. And you can have a variety of them.

In a grove of trees, you could have English ivy (*Hedera helix*) or Baltic ivy (*H. h. baltica*), and under this carpet, you could naturalize bulbs of wood hyacinths (*Scilla hispanica*) to give bloom in spring. Other possibilities are myrtle or periwinkle (*Vinca minor*), and Japanese spurge (*Pachysandra terminalis*).

The purple-leaf euonymus (*Euonymus fortunei coloratus*) is so versatile you can use it in ground cover strips that run from sun into shade. It does almost equally well in either exposure. Like English ivy, it will climb trees, but it makes a thicker carpet

than ivy so it is not easy to get bulbs started in it. You will have to clip off stray runners to keep it where you want it.

For narrow strips, small in scale, the moneywort (*Lysimachia nummularia*) makes a thin cover of bright green. It is more or less evergreen. In the spring, it has tiny starry yellow flowers along the creeping stems. This is a plant that seems perfectly happy even if it never gets sun, but you may find yourself picking it out of places where it is not wanted, for it spreads aggressively.

A SHADED FLOWER BORDER

Maybe you want simply to extend your flower border from the sunny region of your yard into the shade. Plan the sections in shade as carefully as you would lay out a garden in sun, choosing varieties for size and color, with the added requirement that they tolerate shade.

You may want to stress white flowers. They light dim areas especially well—flowers like astilbe, candytuft, lily-of-the-valley, and many of the hostas, especially the fragrant large-flowered plantain lily (*Hosta subcordata grandiflora*). Yellow flowers like primulas and daylilies, and light pink ones like hardy amaryllis, are pretty in shade too. Here is a good place for variegated white and green foliage, like that of some of the hostas, ajuga, or bishop's weed (*Aegopodium podograria*), but this is invasive, so don't put it where it can take over.

By all means include bulbs. They are the best way to get early spring color under trees and shrubs. Early-blooming bulbs survive in shade because their foliage ripens before tree leaves fully mature to hide the sun. Daffodils, crocus, scillas, and snowdrops are some that do well and live long in shade. Early tulips may do fairly well for you, but do not depend on the May-flowering kinds. They will last only a year or two and then dwindle away, unless you can give them at least a half-day of sun.

If you want shrubs to back up your shade garden your selections could hardly be called limited, either among evergreen or deciduous kinds. If rhododendrons and azaleas do well for you, they will probably be among your first choices because they offer flowers and in many cases evergreen foliage as well. Flowering dogwood and redbud are both superb in shaded surroundings, and you can grow plants under both of them. You will be especially delighted if you underplant them with daffodils, bluebells and ferns. The lists at the end of this chapter include many other shade-loving or shade-tolerant plants to choose.

NINE SPLENDID PERENNIALS AND A BULB FOR SHADE

Here are nine dependable perennials and a bulb you will enjoy in your border in the shade.

Bergamot (*Monarda didyma*). In spite of its one bad habit (it spreads too fast), this square-stemmed, rough-leafed plant is one of the best and most durable flowers for bright color in deep shade. Absolutely hardy, it does not even need any attention to soil or watering, but like everything it responds when you do give it good care. The red and pink varieties draw hummingbirds. The white kind is the most attractive in a shady location. Blooms come in June lasting until August, in crown-like clusters at the top of 2- to 3-foot stems. Put these plants midway or at the back of your planting plan. After bloom time you will probably want to cut down the stalks, so have something in front like hostas, to hide the bareness.

Bleeding heart (*Dicentra spectabilis*). High tree shade is ideal for this spring-blooming favorite, but don't let encroaching roots rob it of moisture and humus. The pink hearts hang along arching stems in May and early June. Of all the bleeding hearts this has the most graceful large colorful flowers, and is dependably long lived. Foliage often sinks down in late summer and disappears by fall. The fatty roots may be planted in fall as well as early spring, but once they are in place leave them alone. Mark the location well to protect early growth and the dormant root from cultivating accidents. Ferns and wood phlox make ideal companions.

Columbine (*Aquilegia*). The light colors and airiness of the blooms make these delicate May to July flowers seem most suited to a shaded location. They will succeed there if they can receive three or four hours of strong sunlight a day. The humusy soil you prepare for your shade garden suits them fine. It should be well drained to prevent rot at the crowns; see that you space plants far apart (two feet, at least) to permit light and air among them. At best, three years may be as long as a plant will live, but before it dies it spreads seed which germinates freely. Save a few seedlings for replacements. These usually differ from the parent in flower color, but are just as choice.

Daylily (*Hemerocallis*). You can grow these midsummer flowers in half-day sun or lightly dappled tree shade. The light yellow and pink kinds seem especially handsome there, for the colors are stronger than in full sun. 'Hyperion' is one yellow variety that does its best in light shade. In shade that is too deep daylilies crane their necks to the light unbecomingly, so locate them where your shade garden is the brightest. They will take almost anything in the way of soil, but do best in the same soft composty mixture you provide for other shaded flowers. Height of flower scapes ranges from 18 inches to 4 feet. Put tall ones near the back, and allow a square yard of space for the fountain of foliage the plant makes.

Hosta. This is both the common and botanical name for this group of plants so ideal for shade gardens. The white-flowered "plantain lily" is one of them, but there are many more—all with prominent leaves in round mounds. With some kinds the leaves are the whole attraction. Although different kinds vary in their light requirements, all can take some shade, and most will have sunburned leaves with more than two hours of sun a day. Hosta is so permanent it may outlast the tree it sits under. A clump can go for years with no attention at all, but it benefits from occasional lifting and dividing in early spring. What hostas need most is space to fit their large size. A mature clump of the plantain lily (*H. subcordata grandiflora*) will make a mound of foliage 4 feet across. These mix well with ferns, ajuga, and forget-me-nots.

229

Jacob's-ladder (*Polemonium reptans*). This is a willing plant with ferny foliage and light blue flowers. Sometimes called the "creeping" kind, it actually stays low but does not creep and is native, flowering in April and May. It can take much shade, needing sun only two or three hours a day. It is effective in masses under high shrubs. The little 12-inch clumps expand rather fast and need curtailing every couple of years. The larger-growing *Polemonium caeruleum* may go to 3 feet in height, and needs more sun. Give both kinds humusy loam and only average care.

Japanese anemone (*Anemone japonica*). These are worth every bit of the little extra effort you may put on them. The white or pink blooms that open in September and October are truly elegant. They sit sedately on slender, but strong 3-foot stems and belie their delicate look by standing up through cold rains and winds. Locate them where sun shines as much as four hours a day, and where soil is deep well-drained humus. In winter, mulch the crowns with a thick airy layer of oak leaves or hay. Put these anemones near enough to your garden path to permit a close look at the perfect papery flowers. Roots spread slowly by underground runners.

Lung-wort (*Pulmonaria*). Even when this spring bloomer is not in flower it is interesting in the shade garden because of its splotched foliage. The dark green leaves in a rosette are marked with light green. The opening flowers in April or May are rosy pink, but as buds open the blooms become more blue. *Pulmonaria* grows in deep shade provided it has plenty of humus and moisture. Never let it go dry. You'll like it combined with ferns in shaded nooks.

Primrose (*Primula*). High tree shade that permits sun four or five hours a day is best for these spring-flowering beauties. Primulas are best in cool locations and hardiest where they spend the winter under snow. If your summers are scorching and your winters cold and dry, you may have a struggle keeping them. The yellow, pink and white kinds of auricula and japonica primroses are especially pretty along a shaded path. Even the foliage rosettes are attractive in fall and spring. Give them soil much enriched with compost and peat; and be sure the place drains well. A stony slope is good if it has humus. In fall tuck the natural leaf mulch under the rosettes to prevent smothering them. The auricula primroses are among the hardiest, and have a fabulous array of colors. *P. vulgaris*, the English primrose, is another reliable kind, and so are the hybrid polyanthas grown by our Pacific Coast primrose specialists.

Wood hyacinth (*Scilla hispanica*). Unlike the earlier bulbs that can get by because they bloom before trees have leaves, this is a bulb plant that *thrives* in tree shade. In May it sends up 10-inch spikes of small nodding bell flowers, pink, lilac, and white. In a loamy well-drained soil, supplied with some humus, it will go indefinitely without attention. You will like these planted among ground covers of ferns or English ivy or in clumps at the foot of tree trunks or shaded walls.

A WILD GARDEN

This is a delightful place to have plants in a less cultivated and more carefree society, growing much as they would in the wild. They may not all be native plants, but most will behave as though they were. Take advantage of your natural opportunities—hillsides, native trees and shrubs—when you plan your wild garden, and use the knowledge you get from watching nature.

Some good wild gardens are created in space as small as the narrow strip between city houses. If the area is large enough to have a rambling path running through it, so you can walk there and see the flowers poking through the dead leaf carpet in spring, you will enjoy it more. If you have a bit of wilderness in your yard that has resisted attempts to tame it, perhaps a wild garden is what it should be. If there are rocks, native shrubs, a sloping bank with a brook below, and tall trees, so much the better.

Wild gardens are never a riot of color the way a cultivated garden may be. At times they may be simply green and brown. But in their brief seasons, the woodland plants have great charm, and part of their allure is

108 A good wild garden is an imitation of nature. It can be created in space as small as the strip between city houses. *Brilmayer*

109 In a shaded wild garden, ferns and variegated ajuga associate attractively along a winding path. *Genereux*

110 Certain annuals provide unexpected color in a shaded garden. Here are caladiums, *Impatiens sultani,* coleus, and wax begonias. *Roche*

the way they almost maintain themselves without attention.

Leaving things just the way nature did probably gives a result that is a little too wild for your taste. It is better to clear things out enough for the space to have some degree of organization. Locate your path through the trees, shrubs, and vines you'll leave (like bittersweet, wild cherry, sassafras, redbuds and dogwoods, and perhaps a grapevine in a tree), but don't hesitate to remove most of the boxelders, buckbrush, wild gooseberries or elderberries, and all the poison ivy. Thin out the rest to give room for some of the things you want—perhaps a red-stemmed dogwood, spice bush (*Benzoin aestivale*), witch hazel, clethra, or the deciduous *Azalea vaseyi* or pinkshell.

If you have a stream, put moisture-loving plants like blue flag (*Iris versicolor*), cardinal flower (*Lobelia cardinalis*), painted trillium (*Trillium undulatum*), yellow lady slipper (*Cypripedium parviflorum*), marsh marigold (*Caltha palustris*) and wood sorrel (*Oxalis montana*) there. Other suggestions for wild gardens are given at the end of this chapter.

It is a mistake to include tuberous begonias, hemerocallis and astilbes, that are identified with cultivated gardens and so rather out of place in the "wild," except perhaps at the edge where the wild garden joins the lawn and other cultivated areas.

Buy plants for your wild garden from a nursery; don't go to the woods and dig, for some plants are on conservation lists, never to be disturbed or taken from native sites. Your chances of successful transplanting are also best with plants from a nursery that specializes in wild flowers. Of course if bulldozers are going through the area soon anyway, go ahead and salvage whatever you can.

FERNS WERE MADE FOR SHADE

For whatever purpose—a ground cover in your wild garden, a planting beside a shadowed pool, a nook on the north of your house, or tucked into a tree garden with flowers—ferns are special. Mixed with daffodils or other early bulbs, they rise to cover the fading foliage. When they unroll their lusty new-green fronds or "fiddles," they speak of spring as nothing else does. Through the summer they make a garden look cool and inviting. A few are evergreen, to carry color over to winter. With only one or two obscure exceptions they are all better off in shade.

Most ferns are easy to grow. Give them a humusy soil and a light mulch, along with shade. They seldom require more, and even get along surprisingly well without extra moisture.

Early spring or late fall are the best times to move ferns—when they are dormant. The kinds that rise from a crown, like Christmas fern, are better in cultivated gardens than those that rise from a long invasive rootstock, like the hay-scented and lady ferns. These are better for naturalizing in a wild garden, where they act like ground covers and are not a nuisance coming up wherever they please. In transplanting, set crowns at ground level and not entirely covered, just as you see them growing.

EIGHT FERNS FOR SHADE

There are some six thousand species of ferns, many so much alike only experts can differentiate. In this group the maidenhair and Christmas ferns are the aristocrats.

Cinnamon fern (*Osmunda cinnamomea*). From 2½ to 5 feet. Grows in clusters, vigorously, good for backgrounds. The fertile fronds turn brown early. This likes a moist peaty acid soil, and grows in deep to light shade.

Ostrich fern (*Pteretis nodulosa*). May reach 6 feet. Has tall fronds that look like ostrich plumes. Makes a vase-like cluster of fronds, spreads fast by underground rootstocks. A dramatic fern for moist loamy soil in any but dense shade.

Interrupted fern (*Osmunda claytoniana*). Usually 3 or 4 feet high. Has large frond clusters, each with an interrupted space near the middle. Grows well in dry soil, any degree of shade.

Maidenhair fern (*Adiantum pedatum*). Beautiful fronds in wheel-shaped groups,

TWELVE ANNUALS FOR SHADE GARDENS

Name	When it blooms	Color	Height (inches)
Begonia, wax (*Begonia semperflorens*)	All summer	White, pink, red	18
Bells of Ireland (*Molucella laevis*)	June	Green bracts	24
Browallia	June on	Blue-violet	15
Coleus	All summer	Foliage chartreuse to maroon	18-30
Chinese forget-me-not (*Cynoglossum*)	June on	True blue	24
Balsam (*Impatiens balsamina*)	June on	White, rose, purple	24
Sultana (*Impatiens sultani*)	June on	White, red, cerise	12-30
Edging lobelia (*Lobelia erinus*)	June on	White, pink, blue	6-8
Baby blue-eyes (*Nemophila*)	June on	Blue	9
Wishbone flower (*Torenia*)	June on	White, yellow, blue	12
Periwinkle (*Vinca rosea*)	June on	White, pink, lilac	20
Viola (*Viola cornuta*)	April-July	White, yellow, blue, purple	6

EIGHT BULBS FOR SHADE

Name	When it blooms	Color	Height (inches)
Achimenes	July on	White, pink, blue, purple	10
Begonias, tuberous	July on	White, pink, red, combinations	18-24
Caladiums	All summer	Foliage red, white, green variegations	20
*Narcissus	May	White or yellow	15-20
*Crocus	March, April	White, yellow, lilac	6
*Scilla, many species	April, June	White, blue, lilac	12
*Snowdrops (*Galanthus*)	March, April	White	4
*Glory-of-the-snow (*Chionodoxa*)	March, April	Blue	4

* Tree shade only

TWENTY-FOUR PERENNIALS TO GROW IN SHADE

Name	When it blooms	Color	Height (inches)
Astilbe	June	White, pink, rose	30
Bishop's weed (*Aegopodium podograria*)	Juee	Foliage green-white	14
Bugle (*Ajuga*)	May, June	Blue, white, purple	12
Candytuft (*Iberis sempervirens*)	May	White	12
Christmas rose (*Helleborus niger*)	December-March	Pink-white	16
Coralbells (*Heuchera sanguinalis*)	June-August	White, pink, red	18
Dead nettle (*Lamium maculatum*)	May-July	White, rose	12
Euphorbia cyparissias	May, June	Yellow-green	12
False dragonhead (*Physostegia*)	July	White, pink, lilac	40
Forget-me-not (*Myosotis palustris*)	May, June	Blue	18
Foxglove (*Digitalis purpurea*)	June, July	White, pink, lavender	48
Globeflower (*Trollius*)	May, June	Yellow, light	24
Hardy amaryllis (*Lycoris squamigera*)	July, August	Pink	24
Iris, cristata	April, May	Blue	6
Japanese spurge (*Pachysandra terminalis*)	April, May	White	10
Lenten rose (*Helleborus orientalis*)	February-March	Purple-pink	12
Lilies, many kinds	June, July, August	White, yellow, red	to 60
Lily-of-the-valley (*Convallaria majalis*)	May	White	10
Meadow Rue (*Thalictrum dipterocarpum*)	July, August	Rose, lavender	36
Mistflower (*Eupatorium coelestinum*)	September, October	Violet-blue	36
Monkshood (*Aconitum*)	July-September	Blue, white, lilac	60
Myrtle (*Vinca minor*)	May	Blue	6
Snakeroot (*Cimicifuga racemosa*)	July, August	White	72
Spiderwort (*Tradescantia*)	May-July	Violet-pink	30

THIRTY-FOUR SHRUBS, TREES, AND VINES FOR SHADE

Name	When it blooms	Color	Height (feet)
Althaea (*Hibiscus syriacus*)	August	White, pink, blue	to 10
American holly (*Ilex opaca*)	June	White, small; foliage evergreen	to 45
Andromeda (*Pieris japonica*)	April, May	Cream white	10
Arrowwood (*Viburnum dentatum*)	May, June	White; red fall foliage	12
Azaleas, all kinds	March-June	White, yellow, pink, red	3-6
Barberry (*Berberis triacanthophora*)	May	White, small; foliage evergreen	4
Boston ivy (*Parthenocissus tricuspidata*)	Inconspicuous	Green foliage	to 50, vine
Burning bush (*Euonymus alatus*)	Inconspicuous	Foliage red in fall	8
Camellia	Winter, fall, spring	White, pink, red	to 20
Cornelian cherry (*Cornus mas*)	March, April	Yellow	15
Dogwood (*Cornus florida*)	May	White, pink	25
Drooping leucothoe (*Leucothoe catesbaei*)	April, May	White	3
Dutchman's pipe (*Aristolochia durior*)	May	Greenish-purple	to 30, vine
English ivy (*Hedera helix*)		Evergreen foliage	to 40, vine
Enkianthus	May	Yellow, red-orange; red foliage in fall	25
Heavenly bamboo (*Nandina domestica*)	June, July	Small, white; foliage semi-evergreen	to 6
Hemlock (*Tsuga canadensis*)		Needle evergreen foliage	to 60, tree
Honeysuckle (*Lonicera japonica halliana*)	July, August	White-yellow	15, vine
Japanese littleleaf holly (*Ilex crenata microphylla*)	May, June	Green, small; foliage evergreen	10
Japanese yew (*Taxus cuspidata*)		Needle evergreen foliage	to 35
Jetbead (*Rhodotypos*)	May, June	White	5

Name	When it blooms	Color	Height (feet)
Kerria japonica	May-July	Yellow	5
Mountain laurel (*Kalmia latifolia*)	May, June	Rose-white; foliage evergreen	6
Oregon grape-holly (*Mahonia aquifolium*)	April, May	Yellow; foliage evergreen	4
Redbud (*Cercis canadensis*)	April, May	Purple-pink	30
Red horsechestnut (*Aesculus carnea*)	May, June	Red	30
Rhododendrons, all kinds	May-July	White, pink, red	to 8
Rose acacia (*Robinia*)	May, June	Lavender-pink	10
Sassafras	April, May	Yellow; red fall foliage	50
Summer sweet (*Clethra alnifolia*)	July	White	10
Sweet shrub (*Calycanthus floridus*)	April-June	Brown-purple	4
Weigela	May, June	White, pink, rose	7
Wintercreeper (*Euonymus fortunei vegetus*)	June	White, small; foliage evergreen	to 25, vine
Witch hazel (*Hamamelis virginiana*)	October, November	Yellow	12

usually about 18 inches high. Spreads by rootstocks. Easily cultivated in rich humusy soil, any except dense shade.

Lady fern (*Athyrium filix femina*). A fern of 30-inch height, for moist acid soil and any but dense shade. Spreads from a long rootstock.

Christmas fern (*Polystichum achrostichoides*). One or two feet high, with leathery usually evergreen fronds, an especially good plant for shaded rocky nooks or to edge a woodland area. Grows from a crown. Little bristly teeth occur along the fronds. Takes a rich dry or moist loam in any degree of shade.

Hay-scented fern (*Dennstaedtia punctilobula*). Grows to about 3 feet, extending from a long rootstock. Is effective when allowed to take over a sizable area. Takes dry or well-drained moist acid soil in all but dense shade.

Bracken (*Pteridium aquilinum*). From 16 to 32 inches tall, this fern grows in rows along its rootstocks, making a large coarse background. Grow it in any sort of soil, moist or dry, in any degree of sun or shade.

EASY-DOES-IT IDEAS

Your garden in shade will be practically weed free if you spread a light mulch over the soil surface among your shaded plants. Pine needles are good for the purpose.

Plant ferns among roots of Virginia bluebells (*Mertensia*). As the bluebells finish their bloom and the foliage starts its yellow-

NINETEEN PLANTS FOR YOUR WILD GARDEN PATH

Name	When it blooms	Color	Height (inches)
Bellwort (*Uvularia*)	May, June	Yellow	18
Bloodroot (*Sanguinaria canadensis*)	April	White	6
Cardinal flower (*Lobelia cardinalis*)	July, August	Red	36
Columbine (*Aquilegia canadensis*)	May, June	Red and yellow	30
Dogtooth violet (*Erythronium*)	April, May	Yellow, cream, pink	10
Dutchman's-breeches (*Dicentra cucullaria*)	April, May	Cream	8
Jack-in-the-pulpit (*Arasaema triphyllum*)	May	Green	24
Liverleaf (*Hepatica americana*)	March, April	White, lavender	6
Mayapple (*Podophyllum peltatum*)	April, May	White	18
Rue anemone (*Anemonella thalictroides*)	May	White or pink	6
Solomon's seal (*Polygonatum biflorum*)	April, May	Greenish white	30
Spring beauty (*Claytonia virginica*)	March, April	Pink-white	8
Violets (*Viola* species)	April, May	White, yellow, purple	4-10
Virginia bluebell (*Mertensia virginica*)	April, May	Pink and blue	20
Wake-robin (*Trillium erectum*)	May	Brown-purple	12
White snakeroot (*Eupatorium urticaefolium*)	August-October	White	48
Wild geranium (*Geranium maculatum*)	May, June	Rose-purple	24
Wild ginger (*Asarum*)	May	Brown	10
Wood phlox (*Phlox divaricata*)	May	Lavender-blue	18

ing retreat, the fern fronds unfurl to replace them with another kind of beauty. Thus you will never have to "clean up" after your bluebells.

Forget-me-nots (*Myosotis*) seed themselves prolifically in shade. In August from the progeny of two or three plants, you will be able to transplant enough seedlings to edge all your shaded flower beds. You will be rich, too, with self-sown columbines. Save them, for they will bloom as beautifully as their parents but probably in different colors.

Chapter 16

HOW TO ATTRACT BIRDS

How can I bring birds to my yard?

Give birds safety, food, shelter, and water. These are your answers.

Perhaps you have practical reasons for wanting them in your yard, but most likely you simply enjoy them. It's a pleasure to watch the busy courting and nest-building that goes on in spring; the bumbling young as they face life on their own; and in winter the flashes of color as cardinals come to your feeder or waxwings plunder your hawthorn tree. And there's the lift you get from the wren's rippling song and the catbird's gossipy recital.

From the practical standpoint, you want birds because they help you keep a healthy place. They eat bugs. It's been said on good authority (by someone who kept count) that a chickadee eats nearly 140,000 cankerworm eggs in less than a month's time. A wren eats 500 or so insects a day, not to mention those she delivers to her brood in the nest. A warbler finding a colony of aphids may take an army of them in one meal. The foraging for food goes on winter and summer. In January when you see the brown creeper circling round and round the trunk of your elm tree, you may be sure he is cleaning up insect eggs and overwintering cocoons, preventing trouble for you next summer.

If it weren't for birds, scientists say, the earth would soon be overrun with insects—and all our powerful insecticides could not prevent this catastrophe.

Those birds not engaged in hunting down insects are busy with another pest of your garden—weeds. Although most make grubs and insects their diet in summer, especially in the nesting season, when fall comes they switch to seeds. The small seeds of most weeds are staples of their menu. It is hard to estimate the help of birds in keeping down weeds, but it is valuable.

Civilization brings many hazards upon birds—colliding with cars, encounters with cats, being shot at by little boys with air rifles, and occasional poisoning from insecticides, so it is up to man to protect these helpful creatures. The easy things you can do to make your yard popular with birds pay off in fewer insect pests and weeds to fight, and lots of life and interest, too.

FIRST MAKE YOUR PLACE SAFE

Birds won't come to your yard if there's danger. Put a bell on your cat, and on the neighbor's cat too if he prowls your grounds. On feeders and nesting trees, tack 10-inch wide flaring metal guards that cats and squirrels can't climb over.

A bird hazard worse than these ancient enemies has cropped up unexpectedly from the window-walls of modern architecture. Flying birds fail to see the glass and plunge headlong into it, killing themselves. They are especially likely to do this if they see light beyond the glass. They try to fly through it. The humane thing to do, if you have this problem, is to hang a light-colored drapery inside the glass so birds can recognize a wall. In Europe broad glass expanses have been protected against accidents to birds by hanging replicas of flying hawks or owls, on the theory that a bird seeing this will fly the other way. Although the theory works, surely the drapery is more pleasing for a home window.

HOW TO ATTRACT BIRDS WITH FOOD

In summer and winter the first thing that birds will come to your place for is something to eat. If they find food in abundance in spring they will look around for a suitable place to nest, and you will have them nearby the rest of summer. As fall comes, if food is still plentiful, some birds may decide to spend the winter with you instead of moving south.

WHAT BIRDS EAT IN SUMMER

In early spring when itinerant birds arrive, natural food is at the low ebb of the year. Insects are still hiding or unhatched; the new season has not yet produced berries or fruits, and seeds from the previous year are scattered and gone. This is the time when those few trees, shrubs and vines with long-lasting berries—kinds that have hung on all winter—may save the lives of birds. Hackberries, hawthorns, junipers, holly, Boston ivy, Virginia creeper, mountain ash, some dogwoods, and fruit-forming roses all help to fill in the food shortage early in the year.

Within a few weeks as spring advances, food becomes plentiful. Earthworms, moths, beetles, bugs and grubs and larvae of all sorts are there for the taking, and most birds gobble them up. At this season nearly all kinds are "meat" eaters, even though their habits change later on. If you have some open lawn, a few shrub thickets, and one or two large trees, you are almost sure to have the full range of insects that birds want.

Fruit in the diet. A little later birds look for fruit. Over one hundred different species —practically all the common kinds—eat raspberry-type fruits. If you own a raspberry patch or a cherry tree, you may be too well acquainted with this fact. Raspberries certainly draw a crowd to your yard, especially catbirds, cardinals and thrashers. The catbirds may be so bold as to take up house-

keeping in a raspberry bush and chase you off when you come near it. Keep in mind that before there were berries these same birds were cleaning up bugs for you—so don't begrudge them some of your fresh raspberries. One way to have birds and berries, too, is to plant a few extra bushes at a distance just for birds, and then protect your own berry crop with one of the age-old devices like scarecrows or blown-up paper bags dangling along a cord. Garden stores sell aluminum disks which you can string along a berry row or in fruit trees. They scare off birds effectively.

About this time the soft scarlet berries of the bush honeysuckle (tatarian) are just as alluring, especially to cardinals. This is the beginning of a procession of bird benefits offered by many members of the honeysuckle tribe. In July the Morrow honeysuckle (*Lonicera morrowi*) produces its berries; soon after that come those of the blueleaf honeysuckle (*L. korolkowi*) and in August, September and October the fruit of the Amur honeysuckle (*L. maaki*), making a long season succession of fruit. The middle of June, if you have permitted one mulberry tree space in your yard, you will see orioles, thrashers, robins, bluejays and catbirds stuffing themselves there in a shameless spree. They prefer mulberries even to cherries, which is reason enough for keeping one of these weed-trees on the place. (Don't put it over a driveway or clothesline, however.)

In July as elderberries ripen, birds turn to them for a month until August and September when the wild grapes begin to ripen. All through the season, if you have crabapples, cornelian cherry, barberry, yews (fruiting kinds), cotoneaster, serviceberries, or viburnums, there will be plenty of fresh summer fruit for all. You don't need to plant *all* of these of course, just a few will do.

Seeds in the diet. In May, the elms provide the first seeds of the year for birds. Goldfinches and purple finches make a feast on them. Seeds of the boxelder and ash trees are consumed by grosbeaks in summer. Indeed, many kinds of birds are seed-eaters, particularly goldfinches, purple finches, mourning doves, chipping sparrows, the song and other native sparrows and cardinals. They eat seeds of hundreds of kinds, wherever and whenever they find them—grass seeds, grain seeds, and fountain-grass seeds (*Pennisetum*). Then there are the seeds you consider weeds and don't want in your yard—like foxtail, ragweed, wild hemp, pigweed, thistles. If you have space, a meadow perhaps where seed crops can be left just for this group, here are some possibilities: clover, lespedeza, sunflowers, rye, oats, sorghum, vetch, soybeans, millet, and wheat.

Hummingbirds seek flowers. These fascinating, colorful little birds with the whirring wings feed on the nectar of flowers. Apparently the orange, pink, red and purple ones interest them the most. Plant some of these colors in your garden and you are likely to find these amazing birds darting and feeding among them on a summer morning: columbine, cannas, red horsechestnut, pink or red monarda, scarlet sage, trumpet vine (*Campsis radicans*), bouncing-bet (*Saponaria officinalis*), and red or pink flowering honeysuckles.

Hummers will come to feeders made just for them. The food consists of red-colored sugar water with perhaps a little honey or syrup added. The feeder is a small inverted jar with a bent glass "straw" in it in the center of an enticing red artificial flower (or a real one) to draw attention to the device. You can buy a feeder like this at garden stores, or contrive your own. Hang it on a fence post where you can watch.

WHAT BIRDS EAT IN WINTER

Most birds that stay north in winter go on a diet of seeds soon after frost. Favorite food of goldfinches, redpolls, and siskins comes from the "cones" of alders, birches and sweet gums that shake out seeds on the snow or the ground as the wind rattles them. Woodpeckers and jays, grackles, crows, and nuthatches all eat acorns for winter fare.

The small birds will accept seeds of these common flower garden plants—so spare a few from your fall cleanup: hardy asters, centaureas, cosmos, marigolds, sunflowers, portulaca, zinnias, California poppies, forget-me-nots. In the fence rows and fields, they find seeds of weeds and grasses, innu-

merable kinds. And they go after the berries and fruits hanging on late in fall on the hackberry, hawthorn, privet, juniper, holly, Boston ivy and Virginia creeper, mountain ash, dogwoods of all sorts, bayberry, flowering crabapples, sour gum, snowberry (*Symphoricarpos*), persimmon, red chokeberry (*Aronia*), viburnums (including arrowwood, nannyberry, blackhaw, American cranberry, and carlesi), winterberry (*Ilex verticillata*), sumac, and multiflora rose.

You can feed birds. Early fall is the time to stock your bird feeder so birds will begin eating from it before snow flies. Then when food is really scarce, they have your feeder located and know where to get a meal. Once you start to feed birds, keep it up through the winter. If you fail them in snowy subzero weather, they may starve. Vary the menu according to the kinds of birds you have around, or the kinds you would like to attract.

Juncos, finches, and native sparrows will come to scratch feed (the sort you'd buy for chickens), bread crumbs, wheat, millet and mixtures of small seeds. With cracked nuts, like walnuts and pecans, and whole or broken peanuts, you can attract titmice, chickadees, nuthatches, woodpeckers and jays. These same birds will also come to suet feeders (and so will starlings, which come to anything resembling food). For bluejays, blackbirds, cardinals, towhees, chickadees, nuthatches, and titmice the choicest item will be sunflower seeds. Whole or cracked corn might draw blackbirds, towhees, woodpeckers, jays, cardinals. With cut-up apples and oranges, raisins and currants you will help any beleaguered early spring arrivals among the catbirds, robins, thrashers, and mockingbirds. You might even induce cedar waxwings to take raisins and currants, especially if you soak them first.

Other possible foods for birds are chopped hard-boiled eggs, pork rinds, cracker and bread crumbs, crumbled cheese, popcorn, corn meal, hominy, rolled oats, and pumpkin, cantaloupe and squash seeds. If the temperature is above freezing you can put out things like cooked rice, potatoes, cottage cheese, and bananas. Avoid foods that are salty, like salted peanuts, but plain peanuts and peanut butter are acceptable. When

111 *Top* The highbush cranberry (*Viburnum opulus*)   *Roche*

112 *Center* A wren like this eats 500 or so insects a day and takes many more to her brood in the nest.   *Thomasson*

111, 113, and 114 show plants which form succulent fruits that are attractive to birds through the summer months.

113 *Below Right* The tatarian honeysuckle   *Michigan State University*

114 *Below Left* The cornelian cherry (*Cornus mas*)   *Michigan State University*

115 Red chokeberry (*Aronia*) *Michigan State University*

115, 116 and 117 show shrubs that furnish long-lasting berries relished by birds in winter.

117 Bayberry
Genereux

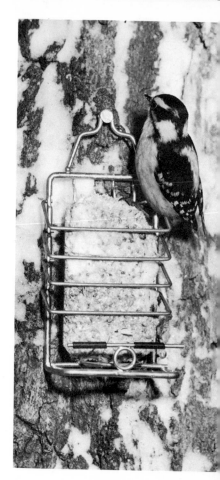

118 A suet and seed cake in a simple wire holder will tide over many kinds of birds during harsh winters. Here a downy woodpecker is having a feast.   *Hal H. Harrison, National Audubon Society*

116 Snowberry (*Symphoricarpos*)   *Roche*

snow covers the ground, it is a good idea to put out along with the food a saucer full of fine grit or sand, since birds need this for their digestive process.

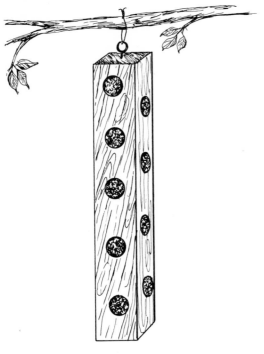

Fig. 39 Chickadee feeder stick stuffed with suet-seed mixture.

There are all kinds of feeders. A good feeder can be as simple as a platform or shelf raised above ground and put out of the wind and weather. Have a raised edge around it so food won't blow or slide off. For more protection from rain and snow you can get feeders made with a roof and sides. If the roof or sides are glass, you can watch the birds in action, which is part of the enjoyment of feeding them. Some feeders revolve with a weather-vane which keeps the entrance always turned away from the wind. Whether it is a fancy commercial redwood feeder or one you made yourself, is something the birds won't notice. Food is what they care about. For greatest enjoyment, locate the feeder in easy view from a window where you can pull up a chair and watch the show.

For feeders that are small and simple, you can have devices like the suet feeders made out of hardware cloth or onion sacks or soap shakers. Tack these to a board or hang them from a branch. Coconuts with a hole drilled in one side and stuffed with a mixture of suet and crushed peanuts will attract small birds like chickadees. When the suet is gone the birds will eat the coconut meat. Take big pine cones and stuff the cracks with peanut butter; then hang the cones with a wire beyond the reach of squirrels. Another feeder of this sort is the chickadee stick made of log sections or 2 x 2 lumber, with inch-size holes drilled as close to each other as possible and packed with a mixture of melted suet and bird feed. Hang these sticks from a screw-eye on one end.

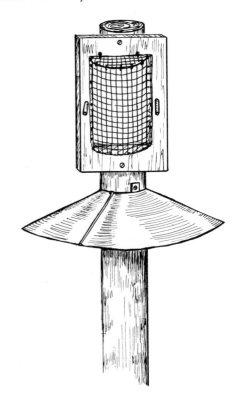

Fig. 40 Hardware cloth suet feeder, protected with a squirrel guard. This could also be mounted on a tree.

The very simplest way to feed birds is to toss out scratch feed on the ground. To keep snow from covering the spot, make a lean-to of boards, evergreen branches or corn stalks with the opening to the south. Scatter bird food underneath. This arrangement is popular with juncos, quail, and sparrows.

BIRDS NEED SHELTER, TOO

Birds need a safe and private place to build a nest and raise a family, and also a place to feed where cats can't pounce. In winter, and sometimes summer too, they need a dense thicket where they can get out of bad weather. If you have large trees, a row or two of shrubs of different kinds, and perhaps some vines, you can provide the necessary shelter for a wide variety of birds.

Different kinds of birds have different ideas about what they want. Robins look for large trees, where they perch a nest in the fork of two branches as big as your wrist. Not finding this, they accept substitutes—like the framework of an arbor or lath house, or even a shelf that you put up for them under the eaves. Robins also like lawns, large open spaces where six to eight at a time can congregate in a sociable quest for a meal.

Big trees are favorites of orioles as well. They hang their pouch-nests at the ends of arching branches of elms, maples and hackberries. The insects in the bark of such large trees are sought by vireos, warblers, titmice, chickadees and nuthatches. Woodpeckers, both redheaded and downy, like old trees too, especially if they have dead wood in them.

Catbirds, thrashers, mockingbirds, and cardinals like thickets of shrubbery and small trees. Bush honeysuckles are good nesting shrubs for all of these. In June and later when the red berries are there, the birds have things pretty nice, with food at the doorstep. None of these is in the habit of perching his nest very high, so cats and curious people are a constant menace. The thicker the shrubs, the better the birds like them.

Pines and spruces attract many kinds, especially bluejays and grackles. Ground birds like bobolinks, meadowlarks and quail need a place where you never mow the grass. Cedar waxwings are partial to wild cherry trees, hawthorns and bittersweet vines. Cardinals and towhees will flock to the native hornbeams (*Carpinus caroliniana*).

If you are planting your place with birds in mind, establish one or two thickets in your yard composed of these three general kinds of small trees or shrubs: (1) needle evergreens—junipers, pines or spruces; (2) thick shrubs with summer berries, like honeysuckles, elderberries or serviceberry (*Amelanchier*); (3) shrubs with long-lasting winter berries like Washington hawthorn, American or deciduous holly (fruiting kinds) shrub roses and viburnums. This combination provides year-round shelter and food.

Some birds will nest in houses. Wrens, bluebirds, and martins are three that take readily to birdhouses. Construct these (or choose them) with the top or bottom hinged or removable so you can clean out the box after each brood is raised. Place them where they are shaded in the heat of the day, and turn the entrance away from prevailing wind and weather. And don't put up too many. One or two martin houses are enough in your block. Wren houses are best spaced at least 75 feet apart. Bluebird houses (which belong only in open country) are best set 100 yards apart. Martins are the only birds that will live in "apartment" houses; all the others want single-family dwellings. Birds seem more attracted to houses on poles than those hung in trees where their enemies can reach them.

Bluebird houses. Make these 8 inches high, 5 inches square, with a 1½-inch entrance hole 6 inches up from the bottom. Hinge the top and fasten it shut with a hook and eye. Attach the house to a high fence post near an open area, 5 to 10 feet above the ground.

Wren houses. These can be of various sizes and shapes. A good standard is 6 inches high, 4 inches wide and 4 inches long. Whatever the other dimensions make the hole just the size of a quarter. This keeps bigger birds from invading. Locate it 2 inches up from the bottom.

Martin houses. Two-story affairs with six or eight apartments in the whole structure are the usual for these houses. Make individual compartments at least 6 x 6 x 6 inches with the entrance holes 2½ inches in diameter. Locate martin houses out in the open, if possible where they are shaded in the afternoon by a tree or house. They should be at the top of a cat-proof pole at least 12

245

FORTY SHRUBS AND TREES THAT FEED AND SHELTER BIRDS

Name	Zone	Height (feet)	Deciduous or evergreen	Growth habit	Food importance	Food season	Shelter importance	Comments
Amelanchier canadensis Serviceberry or shadblow	3	25	D	Large shrub or small tree	Red-purple berries	June	Nesting in summer	
Aronia arbutifolia Red chokecherry	4	8	D	Large shrub	Red berries	Fall	Nesting in summer	
Berberis thunbergi Japanese barberry	3	4	D	Low shrub, dense	Red berries	Fall, winter		
Celastrus scandens Bittersweet	4	to 15, in trees	D	Rambling vine	Orange berries taken by some birds	Fall, winter		Berries come only on female plants. Have male nearby for pollination.
Celtis occidentalis Hackberry	3	80	D	Upright tree	Blue berries eaten by at least 35 species	Fall, winter, spring	Nesting in summer	
Cornus florida Flowering dogwood	5	25	D	Small tree	Red berries	Fall, winter		
Cornus kousa Japanese dogwood	5	20	D	Small tree	Pink-red fruits	Fall, winter		
Cornus mas Cornelian cherry	5	15	D	Large shrub	Scarlet, cherry-like fruit	August	Nesting in summer	
Cotoneaster divaricata	5	6	D	Spreading open shrub	Red berries	Fall		
Crataegus phaenopyrum Washington hawthorn	5	25	D	Small thorny tree	Red berries eaten by many species	Fall, winter, spring	Nesting in summer	
Diospyros virginiana Persimmon	5	45	D	Upright tree	Soft orange fruits	Fall	Nesting in summer	
Ilex opaca American holly	6	75	E	Bushy or tall pyramidal	Red berries	Fall, winter, spring	Dense foliage gives winter protection	Berries only on female plants. Have male holly nearby.

246

Ilex verticillata Winterberry	D	3	8	Large shrub	Red berries	Fall, winter		Sometimes called black alder. Berries only on female plants.
Juniperus virginiana canaerti Canaert juniper	E	3	12	Upright dense small tree	Blue berries	Fall, winter, spring	Dense foliage gives winter protection	
Ligustrum obtusifolium regelianum Regel's privet	D	4	5	Dense, spreading shrub	Blue-black berries	Fall, winter, early spring	Twiggy growth gives winter-summer protection	
Liquidambar styraciflua Sweet gum	D	5	80	Upright tree	Seed pods provide winter seeds	Fall, winter	Nesting in summer	
Lonicera korolkowi zabeli Blueleaf honeysuckle	D	5	10	Spreading large shrub	Red berries	July-August	Nesting sites for cardinals, catbirds, brown thrashers	
Lonicera maacki Amur honeysuckle	D	3	12	Upright shrub	Dark red berries	August, September	Nesting sites for cardinals, catbirds, brown thrashers	
Lonicera morrowi Morrow honeysuckle	D	4	6	Spreading dense shrub	Dark red berries	July	Nesting sites for cardinals, catbirds, brown thrashers	
Lonicera tatarica Tatarian honeysuckle	D	4	8	Upright dense shrub	Red berries, a favorite of cardinals	June, July	Nesting sites for cardinals, catbirds, brown thrashers	
Malus species Crabapples	D	3-5	10-30	Small tree	Small apples	Fall	Nesting in summer	
Morus alba Mulberry	D	5	40	Small tree	Fruit usually purple, a bird favorite	June		Dropping fruit is messy. Locate far from house.
Myrica pennsylvanica Bayberry	D	4	7	Erect shrub	Waxy, gray berries	Fall, winter, spring		Leaves fall late.
Nyssa sylvatica Sour gum	D	5	70	Tall, cylindrical tree	Oblong blue-black berries	Fall	Nesting in summer	

FORTY SHRUBS AND TREES THAT FEED AND SHELTER BIRDS (continued)

Name	Zone	Height (feet)	Deciduous or evergreen	Growth habit	Food importance	Food season	Shelter importance	Comments
Parthenocissus quinquefolia Virginia creeper	4	75	D	Vining	Blue berries	Fall, winter, spring		Usually grows on buildings. Birds sometimes nest in vines.
Parthenocissus tricuspidata Boston ivy	5	40	D	Vining	Blue berries	Fall, winter, spring		
Picea Colorado and Norway spruces	3	50-75	E	Upright pyramidal trees	Cones contain seeds that are sometimes used for food	Winter	Evergreen foliage gives winter shelter	
Pinus Austrian, Scotch, White pines	3-4	40-75	E	Upright pyramidal trees	Cones contain seeds that are sometimes used for food	Winter	Evergreen foliage gives winter shelter	
Quercus palustris Pin oak	5	80	D	Upright pyramidal trees	Acorns taken by woodpeckers, nuthatches, jays	Fall, winter, spring	Persistent leaves give winter protection	
Rosa multiflora Multiflora rose	5 or 6	8	D	Dense spreading shrub	Orange-red "hips"	Fall, winter, spring	Nesting sites and winter cover for many species	
Rosa rugosa Rugosa rose	3	6	D	Dense spreading shrub	Orange-red "hips"	Fall, winter, spring	Nesting sites and winter cover for many species	
Rhus typhina Staghorn sumac	3	15	D	Stiff, upright shrub	Heads of crimson berries taken by some birds	Fall, winter, spring		Too large and coarse for small yard.
Sambucus canadensis Elderberry	4	10	D	Spreading shrub	Abundant purple berries	July, August		Considered too coarse for small yard.
Sorbus aucuparia Mountain ash	3	30	D	Pyramidal tree	Red berries	Fall	Nesting in summer	

Name			Type	Form	Fruit	Season	Wildlife	Notes
Symphoricarpos species Snowberry	3	2-4	D	Low shrubs	Red or white berries	Fall, winter, early spring		Grow in shade of other plants, space closely to make thicket.
Taxus cuspidata kinds Japanese yews	5	4	E	Small spreading upright tree or shrub	Soft red berries	Fall	Dense evergreen foliage gives winter protection	
Viburnum dentatum Arrowwood	3	10	D	Upright shrub	Blue-black fruit	Fall	Nesting in summer	
Viburnum lentago Nannyberry	3	20	D	Upright shrub	Blue-black fruit	Fall	Nesting in summer	Too large for a small yard.
Viburnum prunifolium Blackhaw	3	15	D	Heavy shrub or treelike	Red turning black fruit	Fall	Nesting in summer	Too large for a small yard.
Viburnum trilobum American cranberry	2	10	D	Spreading shrub	Scarlet fruit	Summer, fall, winter	Nesting in summer	

feet high. Martins usually arrive about the middle of April. To prevent starlings and sparrows from moving in have the floor removeable and don't put it in the house until this time.

WATER IS A NECESSITY

In the summer birds flock to water for drinking and bathing. In frigid winter weather open water may save their lives.

The best kind of birdbath is a shallow one with a gently sloping rough bottom like concrete or stone. The basin does not necessarily need to be raised on a pedestal, but usually it is as a way to protect birds from being ambushed by cats and dogs. Put your birdbath in the open, away from overhanging branches. The main thing is to keep water in it. If your yard is big, have more than one.

In the summer, you will see some birds, especially robins, bathing in the wet grass under your lawn sprinkler. If you can leave a hose running somewhere at a trickle, the robins and swallows take advantage of it in spring to find mud for plastering their nests.

In winter cold, try somehow to keep unfrozen water available to birds. One way is to add a little glycerin to the water to delay its freezing; another is to put out warm water and replace it daily.

If you have an inventive turn of mind you can rig a watering device with heat below to prevent freezing. One way to do this is to set an inverted shallow lid (this holds the water) over a bucket or number 10 can containing an electric light bulb. The bulb emits enough heat to prevent ice except in the coldest weather. If electricity is not available where you want the birdbath, you can accomplish the same thing with a kerosene lamp. Ventilate the can at top and bottom to provide a draft and set the lamp inside. Trim it to burn low. You will have to refuel the lamp every day.

EASY-DOES-IT IDEAS

Easy-growing tatarian honeysuckle is one of the best shrubs you can plant to attract songbirds. They feast on the berries in early summer and nest in the branches.

In winter make a suet feeder the simple way by merely putting a chunk of suet in a netted onion bag, tying the top and hanging it by a 2-foot wire from a tree branch. The wire is necessary to keep squirrels from looting the feeder.

Plant a crop of sunflowers to furnish winter fare for cardinals, native sparrows, and finches. They will harvest the seeds if you leave the plants in the garden.

Chapter **17**

HOW TO BUILD AND PLANT YOUR GARDEN POOL

What's the easiest lily pool to make?

You will always be glad you have a lily pool. It is a time-honored and worthwhile part of a garden. Its watery reflections of plants above and around it make restful patterns; the presence of water cools the atmosphere (or seems to, which is as good). But above all, pools let you grow some magically beautiful flowers possible in no other way.

The cost of water-gardening is up to you. If you like, you can start modestly by sinking an old washtub, bathtub or wooden keg in the ground and planting one or two of the smaller water-lilies in enriched soil on the bottom of it. At the other extreme is a reinforced concrete pool with two or three levels, and space for many plants.

REQUIREMENTS FOR YOUR POOL

Whatever size or shape it is, make it to meet these requirements:
(1) A location in full sun, if you expect to grow water-lilies in it.
(2) A site high enough so water drains away from, not into, the pool. There needs to be a lower place nearby to which you can drain the pool by siphoning.
(3) An average depth of 2 feet, for growing water-lilies.
(4) The rim raised enough above ground level to keep out surface water.

(5) The whole thing set absolutely level. A mistake about this shows in a hurry and spoils everything.

TUB POOLS ARE QUICK AND EASY

For ready-made convenience, use a pre-fabricated free-form pool of metal, Fiberglas or plastic. A variety of these is on the market. All you do is dig a hole to fit the shell, set the shell in it, and fill it with water. Some kinds have pre-cast planting depressions in the bottom.

The fastest kind of make-it-yourself water garden is a tub set in the ground. Old bath tubs are ideal for the purpose. You can make a nice long oval design if you use two tubs and set them end to end with a narrow dividing strip between. To accommodate each tub, dig a hole 25 inches deep, $5\frac{1}{2}$ feet long, and 3 feet wide. Spread a layer of coarse gravel over the bottom. Set the tub exactly level so the rim is 3 inches above ground. Fill in around it with gravel, and conceal the porcelain rim with an overhanging edge of brick or stone, laid in concrete. If you don't like the looks of the white interior, coat it with a dark-colored pool paint, a rubber-base compound sold by water-lily dealers. When you want to drain the pool, just pull the plug.

You can make similar pools out of stock tanks, wooden barrels, old iron kettles and metal barrels. But don't use anything made of copper, because the metal poisons fish.

119 A pool in a garden seems to cool the atmosphere. It provides a place to grow the magically beautiful water-lilies and many lovely waterside plants. *Genereux*

120 A garden pool may be as simple as an old washtub sunk into the ground. This provides room for one small-growing water-lily, a few small water plants and some goldfish. *Roche*

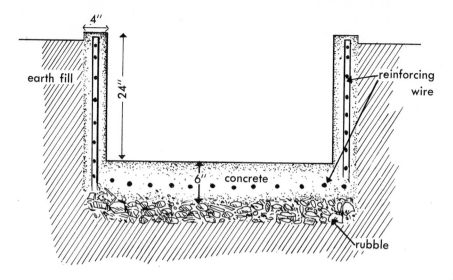

Fig. 41 Pool with straight sides, in cross section. Construct it with forms.

Barrels that once contained oils or chemicals are poor prospects too, because you can never clean them completely. Any material that might rust or corrode, like galvanized steel, lead or iron, needs painting with pool paint. Don't use oil or lead-base paints because they taint the water and soon peel off.

IF YOU WANT A CONCRETE POOL

For permanent garden pools of large size, there is only one material, reinforced concrete. Don't use concrete blocks or bricks—they are sure to crack and leak. It's all right, however, to use these materials for trim above the water level.

With straight sides. If you attempt a concrete pool as a do-it-yourself project, start by making or obtaining a set of careful plans. Decide if you want straight or sloping sides. If straight, you will need to erect wood forms; but a pool with sloping sides is possible without forms by laying concrete right onto the earth excavation, and this is much the easier way for amateurs. Use stakes and a string level to mark the level height of corners and edges, and recheck this to make sure that when water is in the finished pool it won't seem higher at one end than the other. Set the pipes you'll need for bringing in water; and if you plan a bottom drain or overflow drain, set those pipes too. Put in a layer of coarse gravel and smooth and tamp it over the bottom before you lay reinforcing material.

For a pool with straight sides, lay rein-

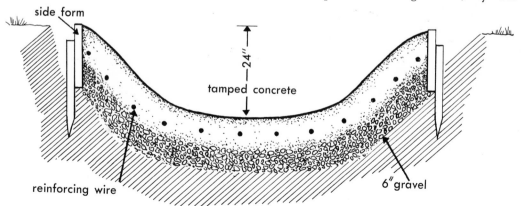

Fig. 42 Pool with sloping sides, in cross section. No forms will be needed.

121   The lotus is a dramatic plant for shallow water, tall and a good background for other plants. *Simpson*

122   The lotus flower reminds you of an enormous wide-open rose, and the center when dry resembles a salt shaker.   *Simpson*

123   'H. C. Haarstick,' an exotic night-blooming water-lily, grows large and needs space.   *Cutak*

124   The 'White Pygmy' water-lily is a hardy variety suited for tubs and small pools.   *Cutak*

forcing wire on the bottom and pour concrete 6 inches thick. Tamp it and smooth it. Set reinforcing wires in the side forms connecting with the bottom layer. Make sides at least 4 inches thick. Tamp this concrete too, to make a dense, leakproof job. Let the concrete cure slowly—put wet sacks or hay over it and keep them moist for ten days or so.

With sloping sides. A pool with sloping sides offers more freedom. You can make it any shape you want, and regulate the various depths by the depths you excavate. Make the excavation a foot deeper than the finished pool will be, and line it with a 6-inch layer of tamped gravel. Slope the sides gradually up to ground level with a slant of no more than 45 degrees. At the top make some sort of form around the outside for the rim. Take care to have it exactly level. Reinforcement is necessary. Lay this over the gravel and run it up the sides, and use plenty to prevent the pool from cracking and leaking. Start pouring the concrete in the bottom, tamping as you go. Gradually work around and around up the sides, tamping and smoothing up to the rim. The next day after the concrete has set, spread sacks or straw over it and wet it down. Keep it wet ten days or so.

If you like, you can cast planter boxes for lilies right in the pool. This has the advantage of being permanent—although for convenience in cleaning and replanting, removable tubs are better.

For a pool that's to have a fountain you can save water by installing a re-circulating water pump. This filters the out-flowing water and sends it through again. The only water you lose is what evaporates. Dealers in water-lilies and pool supplies sell these pumps. If you want to install one, do your planning and piping before you build the pool.

After you finish the cement work and before you plant lilies or put in fish, you need to "cure" the pool to neutralize the alkalinity of the concrete. If you don't do this, fish will die and nothing will grow. The treatment recommended by one of the big water garden companies is this:

Fill the pool and let it stand five days, then drain it.

Fill the pool and let it stand five more days, then drain it.

Scrub the walls and floor with vinegar solution (one part vinegar to ten parts water) using a broom or stiff brush.

Rinse with water from the hose.

Then you may safely put in plants or fish.

WHAT TO PLANT
IN YOUR POOL, AND HOW

Three broad classes of plants are possible in your lily pool, and you will probably want some of each. They are water-lilies, lotus, and the smaller submerged or floating plants used for variety or to make oxygen in the water. Besides these, there are some plants you may want for the pool side, at the edge of the water. And you probably intend your pool to be a home for fish.

Once you've planted water-lilies there is little else you need to do—no weeding, cultivating, pruning, watering or staking. When they begin to bloom you will get fresh enjoyment from the exciting colors of each new flower—and many are entrancingly fragrant. These are warm weather, warm water, sun-loving plants.

You can choose two types with dozens of varieties of each: (1) the hardies, which stay in the pool all winter, and (2) the tropicals, which you replant each year. Of these the hardy kinds are the least trouble, for they can go three or four years without replanting. But the tropicals are well worth extra care and cost because here you find the largest flowers, with the longest blooming seasons, and most gorgeous colors. Among the day-bloomers there are heavenly fragrances.

How many lilies can you have in your pool? This all depends. You can have many more small growers than big ones. Keep in mind the surface area of your pool, and balance it with the space requirements of the three main sizes:

(1) Strong growers, which need 12 square feet, (2) medium growers, which need 8 square feet, and (3) small growers, which need 4 square feet.

For looks, try to keep half the water surface of your pool unoccupied so it can mirror the sky and the plants around it.

Boxes and soil for planting. Plant all water-lilies in rich soil. Usually the soil is held in a submerged tub or box, but if you have a natural pond, you can plant hardy kinds right in the mud at the bottom of the pond, where water is about 2 feet deep.

Ideally, the container should be readily moveable so you can rearrange plants if you want to. Have it strong enough so it won't fall apart. Tubs or boxes of wood will do, except for redwood, which discolors the water. You can use metal containers like galvanized tubs and deep dishpans, but again don't use anything made of copper. Whatever the container, make it big enough to hold a bushel of soil, more or less, for an average water-lily. For pygmy varieties you can do with a little less.

Prepare a rich mixture. Four parts of good garden loam to one part well rotted cow manure is good. Never use fresh manure. If you use the dehydrated packaged product, use only one-fourth as much as you would of the natural rotted cow manure. Fill the tub or box with this mixture to within two inches of the rim.

It saves lifting and wading if you set the empty containers in place and plant them before you fill the pool in spring. Soak the soil mixture well before you plant the roots.

HOW TO PLANT
HARDY WATER-LILIES

If you live where there are winter freezes, the time to plant hardy kinds is from April 1 until July. If your winters are mild and free of frost, you can plant any time from February to October.

In the box of prepared soil, scoop out a shallow trench to fit the root-tuber and lay it in flat or slanted slightly with the growing point well out of the soil. Smooth soil over the rest of the root and lay a rock over it, to prevent washing when the pool is filled. This positioning of the root holds good for all the hardy kinds except Marliac varieties that grow more upright. You set them erect in the soil. Over all plantings spread an inch of clean sand to keep earth from muddying the water. Fill the pool by gradual stages, at first so the tops of containers have only about 6 inches of water above them; then after plants begin to grow, raise the level so there is 10 inches above them. Once a year feed these hardies by adding fertilizer to the soil. Put blood meal or a handful of a balanced fertilizer in a paper or cloth bag and bury it in the soil near the roots. Just wade in and do this—don't remove the pot from the pool. Every third year, repot and change soil.

What to do with hardy water-lilies in winter. These can spend the winter in the pool if their roots and crowns don't freeze. Where this might happen, go out after the first ice forms and cover the pool with plywood and then a thick layer of straw or leaves. This prevents ice from freezing deep. Or you can lift the containers with the plants and store them in the basement. There mound moist peat or leaves over them and dampen them from time to time. If any mice are around they are almost sure to get into them, so prevent this with traps or poison bait.

How to divide hardy water-lilies. If you don't divide these occasionally, say every third year, growth slows up and flowers are poor. Wash off the roots and look for growing points like sprouts on a potato. With a sharp knife, cut the root into 6- and 8-inch sections so each piece has one or two of these sprouts. If the plant is a Marliac type, the roots will be tangled and woody, but the procedure is the same. Find the tender growing points and cut, chop or saw the root so each section has one or two of them. Each growing point makes a new water-lily.

HOW TO PLANT
TROPICAL WATER-LILIES

Wait to plant until the water warms up to a steady 70 degrees. In most parts of the country this will be about the first of June. Tropicals usually come as growing plants. Sometimes they are blooming when you get them. Keep them in water or covered with a wet sack. Plant right away, and take care not to break the earth ball. Make an opening in the soil of the container big enough to hold the ball and set it in vertically. Let the growing tip reach out of the soil. Put an inch of sand over the surface to keep the water clear, and sink the container so it has 6 inches of water over the crown. Later as the plant grows, lower it to 8 to 10 inches. Tropicals grow a little shallower than the hardies.

What to do with tropicals in the winter. If your winters get the least bit chilly, remove tropicals from the pool. Wait until late fall when they go dormant, and dig the roots out of the soil. Put them in a big can of moist sand, and cover them completely with the sand. Store the can in the basement or some other place where the roots won't freeze and also where you won't forget to water occasionally, say about once a month. If the can has a lid, punch holes in it for ventilation and then put it on. It will keep mice away from the tender roots.

In southern California and the frostfree parts of Florida where the temperature of the water does not go much below 70 degrees, you can leave day-blooming tropicals outdoors all winter. Most of them will survive. The night-blooming kinds are too tender for this, so you'll need to store them indoors in sand.

Some people treat tropical water-lilies as annuals. All they expect is bloom for the summer, and they don't try to save them over. The gorgeous flowers over a long season justify the cost.

TEN GOOD HARDY WATER-LILIES

FOR TUBS AND SMALL POOLS

All of these stay small.

Nymphaea pygmaea alba. Small white flowers with yellow stamens, not over two inches across, and scented like tea.

Yellow pygmy (*N. pygmaea helvola*). Dainty, profuse, sulfur-yellow 2-inch flowers that ride on the water. Probably the best water-lily for a tub garden.

'Aurora.' Blooms open creamy-yellow, but change to red-orange and darken. Flowers and foliage are both miniature.

'Pink Opal.' Star-shaped delicate pink flowers, small, held erect above the water, deliciously fragrant. Recommended for cutting.

Nymphaea froebeli. Abundance of small crimson flowers.

FOR MEDIUM AND LARGE POOLS

'Marliac White.' (Also sold as *Marliacea albida.*) Large pure white blooms with yellow stamens at center, held just above the water, fragrant. Large size grower.

'Sunrise Yellow.' (Also sold as 'Giant Yellow.') Huge bright yellow blooms, 11 to 12 inches across, extending several inches above the water. Opens early in morning, and is probably the largest hardy water-lily. In addition to all this, it's fragrant. Large grower.

'Comanche.' A Marliac variety. One of the "changeables," this opens rose-apricot, turns to amber. Starts blooming early in spring and has largest blooms of all the changeable or "sunset" varieties. Large grower.

'Eugenia de Land.' Opalescent pink-rose blooms, up to 8 inches across, sit on the water unless too crowded. Grows vigorously and large, fragrant.

'Escarboucle.' A Marliac variety. Bright yellowish-red blooms up to 8 inches across deepening in color as they age. Stamens are a rich contrast of deep red with yellow tips. This variety is free blooming and grows large if it has the space.

A DOZEN FINE TROPICALS

FOR TUBS AND SMALL POOLS

'Patricia.' Small plants with petite but abundant crimson flowers. Medium size grower. Like many tropical water-lilies, this plant is viviparous—that is, it sends out from the center of older leaves baby plants that are complete miniatures of the parent, even to the tiny flowers. You can remove these and start new plants with them.

'August Koch.' Striking pale lavender flowers, up to seven inches across, with red-yellow stamens. It is fragrant; tolerates part shade. Flowers are prized for cutting. Plants viviparous. Medium size grower.

'Independence.' Rich pink blooms appear when plant is still small. Flowers are fairly large, but the plant seems to adapt itself to the space available; is suited in small areas. Plants viviparous. Medium size grower.

Nymphaea daubeniana. (Also sold as 'Dauben' variety.) Light blue flowers, rather small, does best in water shallower than average, around 6 to 8 inches. Plant is viviparous. Small size grower.

TROPICALS FOR MEDIUM AND LARGE POOLS

'Mrs. George H. Pring.' Pure white flowers, large (up to 12 inches), scented, with white and yellow stamens. Large growing.

'Golden West.' Color changes from the opening salmon tone to an apricot color, with deep yellow stamens. Foliage is spotted with maroon. Fragrant. Medium growing.

'General Pershing.' Cup-shaped blooms ten inches across, soft warm pink, with yellow-pink stamens. Flowers are fragrant, firm, and quite double. Large growing.

'Panama-Pacific.' Flowers open deep blue, change in a few days to purple, with yellow stamens at center. Intensely fragrant. Plants are viviparous. Large growing.

'Henry Shaw.' Sky-blue 8-inch flowers in shallow cups with yellow stamens; sweetly fragrant, opening early in the day. A medium size grower.

TROPICAL WATER-LILIES THAT BLOOM AT NIGHT

These are the aristocrats of the family, and the most tender of the lot. If your pool is seen after dusk, and particularly if you have it lighted, by all means have some of these glamorous beauties in it. They open at sundown and close near noon the next day. Usually a bloom will reopen for three days. Some varieties have enormous flowers, up to 14 inches. Many have unusual foliage, toothed or with striking variations. This group's only shortcoming is that few have any fragrance.

'Missouri.' Luminous white, full-petaled

blooms 14 inches across. Needs rich soil and lots of room. Foliage is mottled with maroon. Large growing.

Nymphaea omarana. Red blooms up to 12 inches across, with a thin light line along the center of each petal. The lily pads are bronze and heavily toothed. Large growing.

'H. C. Haarstick.' An abundance of large, clear red flowers with red-yellow stamens. Grows big and requires room.

LOTUS IS DRAMATIC

As easy as the hardy water-lilies, the lotus is a plant for the shallow area of your pool. You can even grow it in leakproof tubs or planters set on top of the ground. It is a good companion for water-lilies and is unlike them in leaves, flowers, and seed. The foliage reaches high above the water and the large and showy flowers look like enormous wide-open red, yellow, white or pink roses that are ethereally fragrant. When the flowers fall, seed pods are revealed—funnel-shaped giant shakers that when dried are prized for flower arrangements. Lotus makes a striking background for other water plants. You can probably leave it safely in your pool all winter. If ice does not reach the roots, it will bloom again next year more beautiful than ever.

Plant the root in May or early June in a tub filled with the same rich loam you use for water-lilies—four parts loam to one part rotted cow manure. Put a 2-inch layer of rotted manure in the bottom of the tub. Because the rootstock grows in a chain with each new link coming out of the one before, a round tub is better than a square one. Open a 2-inch trench in the soil and lay the lotus tuber in it horizontally with the growing tip sticking out. Cover the root lightly and weight it with a rock. Top the soil with an inch of sand, but don't cover the tip. Lower the tub into the pool and set it so the surface is under 4 inches of water. As the tip begins to grow, lower the container until 6 inches of water covers it.

When winter protection is needed. If you think water might freeze down to the growing tip, lift the tub after the foliage dies down, store it in a cool (40 degrees) place safe from frost. Remember to water the soil from time to time, every month or so, and again, watch out for mice.

Each section of the long chainlike root will produce a new plant. Every third year, in the spring, take the roots from the soil and carefully divide them. Use one new section to replant in fresh soil. The rest are surplus for planting somewhere else or giving away.

FIVE GOOD KINDS OF LOTUS

Only a few forms of lotus (*Nelumbium*) are sold commercially.

N. speciosum, also called Egyptian lotus, is the most familiar kind. Abundant blooms reach 12-inch widths, are strong rose color that fades by the third day to pink-white. Foliage is firm, upright, blue-green.

N. roseum plenum. Also called 'Double Dawn.' Flowers are double and huge; strong pink. Leaves look like parasols. Easy to grow.

N. album grandiflorum. Flowers are 12 inches across, white. Foliage is deep green.

N. luteum. Also called American lotus, as it is native. A good variety for naturalizing. Flowers are strong yellow, fragrant, 6 or 8 inches across; and held up strongly, along with the umbrella-size leaves. May take a few years to start blooming well in an open pond.

N. album striatum. Large white blooms have a touch of crimson at the tips of petals. Otherwise like *N. album grandiflorum.*

SMALL PLANTS FOR YOUR POOL

For a well-balanced pool you need some smaller plants too. They can serve as oxygenators for the fish and they provide spawning places. The floating kinds are interesting in their own right and sometimes colorful.

Most floating kinds need no soil. They grow even if they are just dropped into the water. Sometimes they become pests if not kept under control. But they make shade in the pool and help keep down the growth of algae. You will probably be satisfied to buy

these each spring and let them die with the freezeup in fall—although if you want to save them over you can put "starts" in an aquarium in the house, or in a tank in a greenhouse.

SOME FLOATING POOL PLANTS

Water lettuce (*Pistia stratiotes*). Blue-green leafy lettuce-like rosettes that float, and are prized for flower arrangements. Roots trail in the water, make good spawning place for fish. Thrives in heat and shallow water; part shade.

Water hyacinth (*Eichornia*). In some places this is a waterway weed and barred from shipment between states, but is no problem in the North because of freezing winters. Individual plants have bulbous leaf bases and hyacinth-blue flowers. It makes a good spawning bed for fish and is ornamental. It is one of the few water plants that does well in semi-shade.

Azolla (*Azolla caroliniana*). This makes crinkly little bean-size green rosettes that soon take over a pool unless you dip some of them out occasionally. Fish like to dine on the roots.

Salvinia (*Salvinia braziliensis*). Another small floater, but a little bigger than azolla. The hairy, bright green, heart-shaped leaves are arranged along a short stem. It seldom becomes a pest because the fish are too hard on it—they eat roots.

Duckweed (*Lemma minor*). Little clusters of tiny oval leaves make good fish food, but they spread so fast they are a menace in all but small pools and tub gardens.

Water poppy (*Limnocharis humboldti*). This is a floater but its roots go to the soil. Plant it like a water-lily, but near the edge of the pool where only 6 inches of water covers it. It has bright yellow three-petaled flowers about the size of a California poppy.

OXYGENATORS FOR YOUR POOL

These submerged plants seldom get to the surface, but their roots have a toe-hold on the bottom. In their living and growing activities, they put out oxygen in the water —a necessity to fish and the other animals living in the pool. In the same process they absorb carbon dioxide released by fish and help keep the water chemically balanced and healthful. Most of them are best planted in small pots of soil, several stems to a pot, and sunk into the shallow area of the pool. If you like, you can lightly weight one end of the stems of anacharis, cabomba, myriophyllum, and ludwigia with a short piece of wire and throw them into the pool. The weight will hold the end down until it roots in the bottom mud. These plants are hardy and unless the pool freezes solid they will still be there in spring.

Anacharis. This makes long stems with dark narrow leaves in whorls. If there is enough soil in the bottom of the pool, anacharis will spread soon over the whole area. Older growth turns yellow; just cut it off.

Myriophyllum. Leaves are dark green and hairlike, coming in tufts along the stems. Fish eat it and spawn in it. Free-branching.

Cabomba. This is similar to myriophyllum but the leaves are not so fine in texture; free-branching.

Ludwigia. Best for pool-edge and shallow water, this has shiny round leaves on the surface. In sunlight they turn reddish. New plants come up from a creeping root.

Vallisneria. Semi-transparent, ribbony leaves rise from the floor of the pool. Plant this in large pots that you sink at the bottom.

PLANTS FOR THE EDGE OF YOUR POOL

These are for the rim, usually with roots under water. They give the pool a natural look and are graceful and decorative. Some grow fairly tall. Set these plants in boxes big enough to hold 6 inches of soil, and sink them at the rim of the pool. If you want to naturalize them in a pond, just plant them in the mud at the water's edge.

Common arrowhead (*Sagittaria latifolia*). The leaves are arrow-shaped and rise up 2 feet on stout stems. In summer small white flowers appear on spikes. This is hardy (it is a native plant), and will grow beyond the rim of your pool if you keep the soil moist enough. Or you can plant it in water up to 6 inches deep. Thin it out now and then.

Cattail (*Typha latifolia*). Here is another easy-to-grow native. Plant it in containers to prevent it from getting out of hand. It grows in moist soil, or in water 1 to 6 inches deep. Besides this most common kind you can get (from some water-lily dealers) a dwarf kind (*T. minima*) and a narrowleaf kind (*T. angustifolia*).

Pickerel rush (*Pontederia cordata*). Another name is pickerel-weed. A handsome native plant, this is hardy and strong, but does not spread fast. The heart-shaped leaves are dark green and at the base of each one appears a spike of blue flowers. Mature height is about 2 feet. Plant it in water that is 3 or 4 inches deep.

Marsh marigold (*Caltha palustris*). Opening bright yellow flowers in March, April, May, this is perhaps the earliest blooming of the pool plants. Grow it at the edge where water comes up to the crown but not over it.

OTHER LIFE IN YOUR POOL

Even if it is only a tub garden, put a few fish in it. They make it more interesting, and take care of the mosquitoes. If you have goldfish, which are extremely hardy, you can leave them in the pool all winter without worry. They need no food while the water is frozen. There is plenty of air under the ice to supply them—no need to cut holes. If the pool is so small it might freeze solid, however, better remove the fish and winter them indoors.

The number of fish your pool will accommodate depends on the surface area. Figure this in square inches and allow one inch of fish to 20 square inches of surface. For example, if your pool is 4 by 6 feet (48 by 72 inches) it has a surface of 3,456 square inches; divided by 20 gives about 173 inches of fish you could put in it. If they are 3-inch fish (don't count the tails) you can include some 50 of them. If they are 5-inch fish, you can have only 30 or so. It's better to have fewer than the limit—because fish will grow. If there are too many for the size of the pool, they will suffocate for lack of oxygen.

In warm weather go easy on feeding. You can buy prepared fish food made for pools. Follow the directions on the package about how much to give. Be observant as you are feeding. If any food is left five minutes after you tossed it on the water, you are feeding too much. Feed only once a day, and perhaps only every second or third day. Your fish will be healthier if they are not overfed.

Besides fish, let a few snails make their home in your pool. These are the best scavengers you can get to clean your pool. You can buy snails in several fascinating varieties from the man who sells the goldfish. If they ever become too numerous, you can lure them to a head of lettuce tied to a floating board, and remove them.

The fish and snails appreciate shade in the pool where they can get out of direct sunlight. Water-lily foliage provides most of this, and if the tubs are set up on bricks the fish can hide under them.

HOW TO CARE FOR YOUR POOL

In the winter. Where you expect deep freezes, it is better to leave water in the pool than to drain it. If you have hardy water-lilies, leave them in the pool, too. Take out and store the tropicals as soon as the foliage dies. Where there is danger that ice will freeze solid, protect the pool after first ice forms, as already described. This is only needed, though, in the North where the temperature might go below zero and stay there for weeks. Ice as it forms exerts enormous pressures—enough to crack concrete pools. So it is a good idea in the fall to float a log in the water to absorb the pressure of expanding ice and save the concrete from taking the brunt of it. Pools with sloping sides are better off than straight-sided ones, because ice can easily expand up the sides to relieve the pressure.

Spring cleaning. In spring after ice melts and the water begins to warm up, it is time to clean the pool. Dip out some water in which to store your fish during the process so there's no shock of changing temperatures. Catch them with a net and put them in crocks or old washtubs in the shade. If you provided your pool with a drain, open the outlet. Otherwise, you can drain it by siphoning with the garden hose.

Do it this way. Put one end of the hose down in the pool and connect the other to the faucet. Turn on water so the hose is full. Disconnect from the faucet and hold your thumb tightly over that end, or cork it while you carry it to ground lower than any part of your pool. You might put it into a basement drain. Then release the stopper and the water will flow back through the hose, and out of the pool.

When the water is gone, clean out the leaves and other accumulation from last year; put fertilizer around the hardy lilies and other hardy plants in tubs; do any necessary dividing or replanting and see that containers are still in good shape. Cover the soil there with fresh clean sand. If the pool has any cracks, now is the time to repair them. You can seal tiny cracks with a coat of special pool paint, sold by dealers. Then refill the pool with fresh water from the hose, using the spray nozzle for a time so the water will contain ample oxygen to support your fish. Let the water warm up to what it was before, or warm it with a few buckets of hot water, before you put the fish back in. A sharp change of temperature might kill them.

Summer maintenance. If your pool is new and you have planted and filled it for the first time, the scum that soon rises will dismay you. This is almost sure to happen. Causes are too much food for your fish, bits of organic matter floating loose from the planting boxes, and microscopic plant life developing in the water. The best way to get rid of it is to skim it off with a broom. Once removed and after lilies and other plants begin to grow, it is not likely to come back.

An overpopulation of algae might make the water cloudy. One way to keep the water in balance is to put a few fresh-water clams in the pool. They will thin out the algae. Your goldfish will help too. Or you can treat the water with potassium permanganate. Use the fine form, not the crystals. You can get it at a drug store. Measure it carefully after you have figured the number of gallons of water. (To figure gallons, first figure number of cubic feet, then multiply by 7.48.) Use a half ounce to each one hundred gallons. This turns the water purple for a few days, and kills out most of the microscopic plants without harming fish or larger plants, *if you use the right dosage*.

Once the pool reaches a balance between fish, plants and microscopic life there is little maintenance. If lilies grow too freely and choke the water, you can trim them back by cutting stems close to the root. Remove all of the stem so no vegetation is left to decay and foul the water. Remove bloomed-out stems the same way.

FOR NATURALIZING IN PONDS

If you have a pond, the natural kind or one created by a dam, there are water plants you can grow with most pleasing results. Choose kinds that not only have blooms and foliage you like, but are well behaved and not likely to usurp the whole pond when given such freedom.

You can use any of the hardy water-lilies like the Marliac varieties because these have compact root systems that spread slowly. In catalogs of water-lily dealers these are identified as Marliacs. The name comes from a famous French hybridizer who produced these flowers early in this century. 'Comanche' and 'Escarboucle' are two large-growing lilies of this sort. A good way to set these in deep water is to plant them in bushel baskets of soil which you lower into the water with rope from a boat. If the basket falls apart in a year or so, no harm is done.

It is perfectly safe to use any of the tropical day-blooming or night-blooming water-lilies. They are so susceptible to cold that they can't survive the winter, so they couldn't possibly become pests. You will need to replant them each spring, however.

The several kinds of lotus are wonderful plants when naturalized; and they are hardy. These in time will cover a vast area if you permit them. The best way to contain them in the original space is to plant them in round tubs that restrict the roots. If you want to let them go free in the pond, wade in to a 4-inch depth and sink each tuber in the mud. The growing root-tip will find its own best depth and in autumn will reach to deeper water to escape freezing.

If you use durable tubs, you can have any of the other hardy water-lilies as well as the Marliac types. But without containers, plants grow so large that in a few years they cover the whole surface of a pond. You will need to lift and divide roots planted in containers every third year, the same as in a pool.

For shore plants, the cattail, arrowhead, and pickerel rush are hardy and desirable in every way. Plant them in the mud at the water's edge.

EASY-DOES-IT IDEAS

To keep water-lily blossoms wide open after you cut them, drop a bit of candle wax inside at the base of each unfolded petal where it meets stamens and sepal. When the wax hardens, it holds the flower open for three or four days. Otherwise blooms close toward evening.

If aphids appear on leaves or stems of water-lilies, knock them off with a blast of water from the hose. Your goldfish will finish the job of eradication.

The easiest way to light your pool for evening enjoyment is to use lighted lily-pads. These gadgets, available from dealers in water-lilies, consist of a light bulb in a water-proof socket beneath an artificial floating lily leaf. It makes a soft indirect light revealing fish and night-blooming tropical lilies.

Chapter 18

ROCK GARDENS
AND PLANTED WALLS

What can I plant on a rocky bank?

If you have a rocky bank you have something that is the envy of thousands of gardeners. Do you wonder what they would do with it? The answer is easy—they would turn it into a rock garden.

Here you can have plants that just won't grow on level ground or do much better among rocks and on slopes. Some of them are so winsome and lovely, so studded with color and charm, there is no need to explain why gardeners sometimes go to great extremes to grow them.

NATURAL SITES FOR
ROCK GARDENS

The slope that already *has* rocks, just as nature established them, is ideal for a rock garden. You may want to thread a path across the slope and set some steps in it. In any case, it is well along toward being ready for planting to a wide assortment of rock plants.

Almost as good, so far as potential is concerned, is a slope or bank without rocks. If you have a place like this, perhaps one that is desperately inhospitable to lawn or ground cover, you can make a garden of it by the proper placement of rocks so they look natural, improving the soil and setting out appropriate plants.

Dry stone walls (the kinds laid up without mortar to hold back terraces or banks) are also likely locations for rock plants. Whether walls face north, south, east, or west, certain plants will grow well in the crevices. Wall gardens are delightful, the most successful being planted as they are built instead of afterwards. If you have a slope to be terraced into descending levels, consider this dry-wall way of doing it and the opportunities this offers.

Old stone fences, the tumbling kind New England farmers laid up two centuries ago out of granite boulders heaved from the plow's path, make beautiful gardens if you fill their spaces with good soil and attractive rock plants.

IF THE GARDEN COMES FIRST

For some rock gardens, the rocks are really secondary. Maybe you have a situation flat as the parlor table, but you yearn for endearing rock plants that need gravelly soil, a slope, and stones to shelter roots. What you can do is to move in your own hill, or dig a valley, create slopes, set stones the way nature does so that the new rocky bank appears always to have been there. If well done, you have a place where rock plants grow well and a site pleasantly in keeping with the rest of your yard. The planning and hard work you do on a good garden of this sort are greater than for any other kind of rock garden. Consider that such an effort starts with the desire to grow the plants, not with the availability of slopes and rocks. Of course, a motley assortment of rocks, jutting up in knickknack display, does not constitute a garden and would be better not attempted at all.

HOW TO PLACE ROCKS
FOR A GARDEN

If nature placed the rocks on your bank, the problem of the site is solved and there is unlikely to be much you can do to improve it. But if you are to set the stones, start by studying nature's methods. First of all, notice that the outcrops you find breaking the sod of a meadow, or rimming the neighboring woods are made up of *the same kind of stone*—all limestone of the same sort, or all sandstone or all granite.

Here is nature's lesson number one: *Use all the same kind of stone, preferably a type you can find close to home.* This is cheaper and looks better than a rock collection you haul from far away. By all means avoid bizarre colors and shapes.

Next, notice how the natural stones lie in layers. They are probably horizontal or tilted a little. This, then, gives number two: *Arrange stones so they appear layered following the natural contour of the slope.* Make the "weave" run the same way. Don't stand some rocks on end, some on edge in a jumble. If stones are to follow one another along a slope, try to match the heaviest ridging, just as you find it naturally.

Finally, when you study a natural rock outcropping it probably occurs to you that you are seeing only a fraction of each stone, and the rest is buried. So lesson number three: *Select those rocks with the biggest part concealed* in the earth, only a small surface visible, and bury them the same way for your garden. This will also make your bank or other plantings more stable. Try to slant the stones so the surfaces *slant back into the slope,* rather than down it. Such a slant sends rain water back into the bank and prevents it from running off, leaving plants dry even after a shower.

If you are having rock delivered, try to obtain a variety of sizes. You will need a few large stones, as big as you can handle, and a great many smaller ones. The ultimate size of your rock garden is the determining factor, of course, but you will always need some relatively large rocks for emphasis. Sometimes you can get the same effect by placing several small ones close together to look like one big one.

TAKE THE COMPASS INTO
YOUR CALCULATIONS

If you are creating your own rocky bank, you can have something to say about what direction it faces. Natural or artificial, it will suit more plants if it faces east, west, or north, not full south. A southern exposure is hot and dry and takes constant attention to keep the little plants there from withering in the vicious glare. Suppose the rocky bank naturally slopes to the south—what can you do? Better plant trees to shade it for part of the day, and choose mainly heat- and drouth-tolerating plants, like the native verbenas (*Verbena bipinnatifida* and *V. canadensis*), sedums, and some of the evening primroses (*Oenothera*). Others are described in the next few pages, and ideas for planting a shady north-facing slope, too—as well as the "average" east and west ones.

WHAT KIND OF SOIL
FOR YOUR ROCK GARDEN?

Perfect drainage is the principal requirement for the plants you'll be growing. Because the ground slopes, surface drainage is naturally good, but drainage *through* the soil needs to be encouraged with liberal additions of peat moss or compost and sand.

A good soil mix for rock plants consists of equal parts of garden soil, coarse, gravelly sand, and peat moss or compost. Pack this in the pockets and nooks, or in the crevices of a dry wall to be planted. Sift it between the boulders of a stone fence garden. No fertilizer is required for rock plants; few need high fertility, and with their tight little planting holes, you do not want to encourage too much growth. The main thing is a fluffy soil able to hold air and moisture, and yet never soggy. A few plants may demand either a lime or an acid soil but in those cases, doctor the soil accordingly for each one.

HOW TO MAKE A SCREE

Some plants require a scree, that is, a layer of fine stones imitating the rubble of a true alpine rock slide. Water mainly runs right through it. A scree consists mostly of little rocks with humusy bits to catch a little water so plants can get a toe-hold. Develop a scree in an area that slopes slightly; at the bottom lay fist-size rocks, covered with a 2-inch layer of leaf mold or peat moss. Then make a mixture (by volume) of ten parts stone chips (bits of stone not over three-quarters of an inch across, most of them smaller) to one part garden soil, one part peat moss or leaf mold, and one part sand. Plants you might grow on a scree include drabas, saxifragas, and penstemons—all plants that need perfect drainage and suffer if water lingers at the crown. You are most likely to need a scree if your climate is humid and rainy.

UPKEEP IS DOWN
IN ROCK GARDENS

One of the best things about rock gardening is the low upkeep. It is heresy to hoe or fertilize them; plants are too low to need staking; and they are seldom afflicted with pest or disease, so you have little spraying. In drouth, you *may* have to water a few things, but not often because the stones themselves save moisture in the soil. To do an even better job of conserving water you can mulch the surface around plants with small stones.

The main job is weeding, and this can prove to be quite enough. Weedy grass that tries to come up beside a stone, seedlings of elm and oak that sprout in the crevices are the worst. With an asparagus knife, pry them out carefully while they are still small. Do the same with all weeds but be careful not to uproot your choice plants in the process. Keep watch for seedlings of plants like columbine, pinks, and penstemons that may

have planted themselves; let them stay in their self-selected spots.

Winter hardiness is a curious aspect of rock plants. Some weather harsh winters there better than in your level gardens. Nevertheless it is usually worthwhile to spread a fluffy hay mulch or evergreen boughs over plants you regard as slightly delicate—like some of the hypericums, helianthemums, and iberis. This is more to protect them from winter sun than from cold.

HOW TO BUILD A DRY WALL

An unmortared (dry) stone retaining wall is ideal for holding a steep slope. Divide the bank into a series of level steps, each faced with a long dry wall. Because this type of wall drains freely, it withstands pressures behind it that might send a solid wall tumbling down. Nevertheless, don't use a dry wall to hold back a bank over 4 feet high. Beyond that a solid mortared wall with plenty of drain holes is needed.

Dry walls are ideal for many plants, if you have planting in mind while you build. Use stone from a local quarry, broken or cut into roughly rectangular shapes and of various sizes. Give the wall a substantial base by excavating down to solid clay or firm subsoil. If the wall runs down a slope as well as across it, start at the low point and keep the foundation trench, as well as each course of stone, level as you work up in stairstep layers. "Batten," or slant, the wall backwards into the slope at an angle of 2 or 3 inches for each foot of height. As you set the lowest stones, start doing this by tipping them back just a little. Besides strengthening the wall, the batten makes rain run back into the soil behind, instead of down the stone face.

Use large stones at the bottom. *Select them so no vertical joints line up.* Leave as many V-shaped spaces between stones as you can—these are ideal for plants. Fill in between, under and behind each stone with the peat, sand and soil mixture and tamp it in with a thin stick, such as a piece of lath. Chink up each stone with chips to hold it where you want it.

125 A low stone wall filled with soft earth grows snow-in-summer, bleeding heart, sedums and dwarf irises. There are bulbs at the base. *Genereux*

If your wall plants are on hand, set them into the wall as you build. It's so much easier to plant now than afterward.

If you have done it well, your finished dry wall runs in level lines of evenly shaded stones, with a fairly regular face that tilts back toward the bank just a little.

PLANTING A ROCK WALL

If you plant the wall as you build it, you have no trouble inserting plants into crevices, because you can reach them from above. If the wall is already built, you will need to put in soil with each plant. Use small plants. Serious rock gardeners usually grow their own from seeds or cuttings, so they have a supply of small ones. Soak the roots free of soil and wrap them in wet sphagnum moss. Pry the rocks apart enough to let you slip in the flattened moss-wrapped roots; then tamp soil back into the crack with a flat stick or piece of lath until every possible pocket near the plant is filled. After you have planted the whole wall or a sizable portion of it, water your plants by laying the hose at the top and letting water run down over, into and through the stones.

PLANTS FOR ROCK GARDENS AND WALLS

It is difficult to define rock plants. Once they were mainly alpine plants, but now they include all kinds that look good together and grow well among rocks. Most of them are small. Typically they are cocky little tufts with colorful crowns, snuggled in the lee of a stone or spilling out through a crack. Some make dense mats that spread like a carpet, or cascade down a wall. In their seasons, rock plants have a way of turning to solid color. The rest of the year they may have foliage that is evergreen, gray or bronze but more likely it is herbaceous and disappears for the winter. Plants for shady walls and stony slopes of ravines and woods are often fernlike or shy kinds without much color but of a soft delicacy that is most attractive.

Because so many rockery plants come from alpine regions, they run heavily to early spring color. Things like the drabas, alyssum, phlox, and little irises are likely to be up and blooming quite early in the year, as soon as the last snow shrinks away and the strengthening sun warms the wet ground. It is not so easy to plan through-the-season color with rock plants as with perennials grown on the level, but if you choose carefully you can have some color from early spring till snow.

Most rock-garden plants are perennial, which is fortunate for this saves yearly replanting, but a good many annuals also look well among rocks. With annuals you can extend color through the summer.

Shrubs and trees for large rock gardens. If your garden is large, you may want to put some small trees and shrubs in it, perhaps some miniature evergreens just right for this purpose. Among spruces are such dwarfs as *Picea glauca albertiana conica, P. glauca densata, P. abies compacta.* The *Juniperus communis compressa* is a tiny upright kind; *J. horizontalis* 'Waukegan' and *procumbens* are low spreading sorts that hug the slope or the stone surface. The mountain pine (*Pinus mugho mughus*) looks weathered and appropriate. Some broadleaf evergreens, especially the Japanese hollies (like *Ilex crenata convexa* and *helleri*) appear at home in rock gardens; so do English ivies, especially small-leaf kinds. Although they have no winter foliage, the brooms (*Cytisus*) keep color all year and are suitable for growing among rocks.

Bulbs you'll want, too. A rock garden is ideal for bulbs which are never disturbed there by the hoe. Select species rather than cultivated varieties. Since a rock garden is a replica of nature, natural species look better, like the species crocus, miniature daffodils, the short early botanical tulips, many of the smaller flowering onions (alliums), also such low growers as the puschkinias, chionodoxas, and scillas. Don't try these in your wall garden, though, except at the top.

HOW TO ARRANGE PLANTS AMONG ROCKS

Informality is the keynote in this sort of garden. Avoid anything that looks unnatural. Plant the way you find things in the

126 Among annuals, a good one for rocks is sweet alyssum, which here drifts in the corners of steps, mingling with wild strawberry.
Baer

127 Along a stepping-stone path, carpets of dianthus, thymes, and sedums cover the ground.

Genereux

mountains—in little straggling colonies. Let two, three or more plants of each kind be together, just as though they had seeded themselves. Let columbine spill down a slope along a path that falling seeds might take. Fill a crevice of a rock with plants of one kind. Here and there set a few solitary gems, like a little gentian nestled under a rock or one saxifrage clinging to a ledge.

In arranging plants in a stone wall follow the same idea. Let plants of a kind follow one line of the wall for a distance. Let some spill down the wall in patches, and they may do this naturally, especially self-seeders. Repeat at intervals kinds with prominent foliage or flowers so your planting has theme and rhythm even though it is informal.

WHERE TO GET ROCK PLANTS

Unfortunately many of these plants are so offbeat that your local nursery may not have enough demand to stock them. The source for most of them is seeds, an easy and economical means. Seeds you can't find in catalogs of the larger dealers are probably stocked by specialists in rock plants or wild flowers and they may even be able to send you plants as well. Classified sections of garden magazines often carry advertisements of seed and plant specialists.

Another excellent source is the American Rock Garden Society, which each year sponsors a seed exchange (just a few cents per packet) for its members. And if you find rock-garden plants fascinating, you will enjoy this association with other enthusiasts, not to mention the seed exchange. Write for information to the Secretary, E. L. Totten, American Rock Garden Society, 1220 Everett Place, Hendersonville, North Carolina.

TWENTY-FIVE GOOD EASY PERENNIALS FOR ROCK GARDENS

These need no special soil formulas, and are hardy over a wide area. You will find other possibilities among the perennials described in Chapter 10.

Achillea tomentosa (Yarrow). Stems rise 8 or 9 inches above gray leaves to produce heads of yellow flowers, May into June. Foliage stays on all winter, spreads slowly into a wide ground-covering clump. Can take hot sun, a south bank.

Aethionema (Persian candytuft). Little shrubby hillocks of fine blue-green foliage, 8 or 10 inches high, topped in June with pink flowers resembling the other perennial candytuft, iberis. Tops may winterkill, but trim them off and they will rise again from the base. They can take heat and sun, including south slopes.

Aquilegia akitensis (Columbine). A tiny plant reaching 6 or 8 inches, with stems of dainty blue or violet columbine flowers, with a little touch of yellow, in mid-spring. Foliage makes a neat bush. For sun or part shade.

Armeria maritima (Thrift). Usually this appears as rosy pink flowers about 8 inches high, on stems above grassy clumps of foliage. It blooms in May and June. Give it a sunny spot in stony soil beside a path or atop a wall.

Artemisia frigida (Wormwood). Flowers are inconspicuous, but the silvery white foliage makes a lacy 10-inch mound that is attractive all season. It does well in any sunny place—hot walls or rocky slopes—and is ornamental against dark stones and with brightly colored flowers.

Aubrieta (or *Aubrietia*). Five-inch thick mats covered with pink, rose or purple flowers in spring. Foliage is spreading, dark gray, woolly, right for the top of a wall or rambling on a bank. Shear after blooming for good looks. Give sun or part shade.

Campanula carpatica (Carpathian harebell). You can get many forms of this. Typically it makes a mound of lilac-blue cup flowers, facing up in June, 8 or 10 inches high, on a wide-spreading plant. Foliage is fine and light green. Some forms are white or purple. Give sun or part shade.

Cerastium tomentosum (Snow-in-summer). A 10-inch gray mound of soft foliage, covered in April and May with starry white flowers. It spreads fast, so place it where it can cover up rocks or spread down a bank without smothering daintier things. Shear it back after blooming. Takes full sun, tolerates a south slope.

Delphinium nudicaule (Pink delphinium). This little larkspur grows loosely to 10 inches or so and hardly resembles any other delphinium. Its blooms are yellowish-pink and come in June. Plants tend to be short-lived. Give it shade, like the shadow of a cool stone, in the heat of the day.

Dianthus gratianopolitanus (Cheddar pink). In spring it makes 8-inch mounds of soft pink flowers, above blue-gray leaves. Flowers have a sweet fragrance. Plants spread gently, are good atop walls, in crevices, at the foot of rocks. Give them a moist but drained and gritty soil in sun or shade part of the day.

Draba aizoides. One of the tiniest and earliest. On a warm day in late winter you may find it blooming on a sunny ledge, a little yellow tuft of flowers on a 2-inch stem. The rosette at base is green and hairy. When these establish a colony they are showy, but place them where large plants won't overshadow them. Give it full sun, perfect drainage.

Gentiana septemfida (Gentian). Of the many kinds of gentians this is one of the least temperamental. In summer, trumpet flowers of spectrum blue bloom in clusters at the ends of 8- to 10-inch sprays. Give it a moist spot in sun or part shade, but not the hottest place in the garden. Shade it with a great, cool stone. It does best in a slightly acid soil.

Geranium sanguineum (Cranesbill). The rambling plant makes a mound of ferny foliage 1 to 1½ feet high, with wide white,

128 Sempervivums encrust themselves in crevices of stones and walls, wherever there is a suggestion of soil. *Genereux*

129 Armeria, also called sea pink or thrift, makes grassy clumps topped with rosy flowers. It is ideal in rock walls, as here with sempervivums nearby. *Roche*

130 *Primula sieboldi* is one of the primroses suited to rocky sites in light shade. *Genereux*

FIFTEEN PLANTS GOOD FOR DRY WALLS IN SUN

	Height (inches)	Bloom time	Color
Achillea tomentosa	8-9	May, June	Yellow
Alyssum saxatile	8	May, June	Yellow
Artemisia frigida	10	Flowers inconspicuous	
Cerastium tomentosum	10	April, May	White
Geranium sanguineum	12-18	June, July	Pink, lavender
Gypsophila repens	6	May, June	White, pink
Helianthemum	12	June	White, yellow, pink
Iberis sempervirens	6-12	May, June	White
Nepeta mussini	12-24	April-August	Purple
Oenothera missouriensis	12	June-August	Yellow
Phlox subulata (above wall)	6	April, May	White, pink, violet
Plumbago larpentae (Ceratostigma)	12	August-October	Blue
Saponaria ocymoides	5	May, June	Pink
Sedum cauticolum	8	August	Pink
Sempervivums	1-8	June-August	White, yellow, pink

pink or lavender flowers in June and July. After flowering, the long beaked seed pods appear, almost as interesting as the blossoms. Plants form a dense mat. Put them at top of walls and ledges, overhanging rocks, wherever drainage is good. They take full sun.

Gypsophila repens (Baby's-breath). From May or June on, the low silvery 6-inch mounds are covered with tiny white or pink flowers. You can use these dainty clumps in walls, steps, or atop ledges, wherever they are seen at close range. Give full sun. They tolerate south-facing slopes.

Helianthemum (Sun-rose). In early June the 12-inch plants are covered with papery white, pink, yellow or rose single blooms. Bushes are shrubby and spreading with woody stems. Leaves stay green all winter or most of it. Use these in wall gardens or on rocky slopes where they can anchor in good soil and tumble over a ledge. Full sun suits

them fine. They tolerate south walls and banks.

Iris chamaeiris and *pumila* (Dwarf iris). These two are much alike in that they send up tiny bearded iris blooms on stalks from 4 to 10 inches tall, starting in March or April. Colors may be purple, white, yellow or combinations and shades. Many hybrids are available now. Put them in a clump at the foot of a wall, or clustered over a stone, in full sun. They can take the hottest locations.

Lavandula officinalis (Lavender). This is hardy in Zone 6 and southward. More like a woody shrub, it makes a burst of gray 24-inch stems each topped in June with fragrant lavender long-lasting small flowers. The bush is handsome the year around, and needle-like foliage and flowers are good for sachets. Give lavender a warm sunny location at the top of a wall or above a big stone. It can take a south bank.

272

FIFTEEN PLANTS FOR NORTH OR SHADED WALLS

	Height (inches)	Bloom time	Color
Adiantum pedatum (Maidenhair fern)	10-20		Light green foliage
Ajuga	6-8	April, May	White, pink, blue
Aquilegia akitensis	6-8	May	Violet
Astilbe	18	June, July	White, pink, red
Aubrieta	5	May	Pink
Campanula carpatica	8-10	June, July	Blue-violet
Delphinium nudicaule	10	June	Coral pink
Dicentra eximia	12-15	June, July	White, pink
Gentiana septemfida	10	June, July	Blue
Heuchera	20	June-August	White, pink, red
Polymonium reptans	12	April, May	Blue
Primula	6-12	April-June	White, yellow, pink
Pulmonaria	10	May	Pink, blue
Sedums	12	June-September	Yellow, white, rose
Thalictrum dipterocarpum	24-36	June-August	Lilac

Oenothera fremonti (Evening primrose). In June the wide yellow 4-petaled flowers open and continue most of summer, along 10-inch stems that are rather relaxed and spreading. Flowers stay open most of the day. This can take the hottest bank, in full sun, in a wall or on a high bank.

Penstemon hirsutus (Beardtongue). In early June or late May this 12-inch plant produces airy wands of purple and white, sometimes pink, narrow bells. Foliage is deep green. Plants seed themselves freely, and may repeat bloom through the summer. Give them a place in full sun on a wall or rocky bank. They can take a south slope.

Phlox divaricata (Wood phlox). In April and May come graceful blue-violet blooms on 12-inch stems. Thin, narrow dark leaves make a low cluster which is hardly noticed the rest of the year. It spreads by rootstocks and seeds, but is not rampant. Grow it in full sun or light shade, in walls or on rocky banks.

Saponaria ocymoides (Soapwort). In May and June little pink flowers cover the spreading 5-inch plants. Leaves are dark green on meandering mat-making wiry stems. Shear plants back after blooming to make them tidy. Use this in rock walls, to droop over ledges, or any place in full sun. It tolerates south-facing slopes.

Sedum cauticolum. This little sedum blooms in August with deep pink flowers at the ends of 8-inch stems that droop. In winter the plant disappears, then returns in spring to make a sprawling cluster of dark gray-green fleshy leaves. Use it in full sun or partial shade. It is not particular. It looks good in rock walls, or hanging over a ledge.

Sempervivum (Hen and chickens). Many kinds are extremely hardy and they stay green and attractive all year. The little fat

273

TWELVE ANNUALS FOR ROCK GARDENS

	Height (inches)	Color
Ageratum, edging *Ageratum houstonianum*	8-12	White, pink, blue
Amaranth, globe *Gomphrena*	8-18	White, rose, purple
Calliopsis, dwarf *Coreopsis* species	8-15	Brown, red, yellow
Cup flower *Nierembergia*	6	Blue-purple
Dahlborg daisy *Thymophylla tenuiloba*	6-10	Yellow
Ice plant *Cryophytum (Mesembryanthemum)*	4-6	Rose
Marigold, dwarf *Tagetes signata*	8	Gold
Periwinkle, trailing *Vinca rosea* 'Rose Carpet'	5	Rose
Pinks *Dianthus heddewigi*	12	Red, pink, white
Portulaca *Portulaca grandiflora*	6	White, yellow, pink, red
Snapdragons, dwarf *Antirrhinum*	8-12	All colors but blue
Sweet alyssum *Lobularia maritima*	4	White, pink

rosettes of fleshy leaves look vaguely like miniature cabbages or artichokes. In summer mature clusters send up leafy columns topped with pink, yellow or white blooms. They reproduce by offsets and encrust themselves in crevices of stones and walls, wherever there is a suggestion of soil, in sun or semishade.

Thymus serpyllum (Mother-of-thyme). A flat mat of rooting stems and small dark aromatic leaves erupts in summer with a covering of white, red or pink-purple tiny flowers. Where it is well satisfied with soil and moisture it spreads and covers everything, so give it space to make a "lawn" far from dainty things that might be overwhelmed. It grows best in full sun.

Verbena bipinnatifida. One of the wild verbenas. In June, July and occasionally through summer, rounded heads of bright pink-purple flowers occur at ends of wandering 8-inch stems. Foliage is rather sparse and lacy and spreads slowly to make a mat. Grow it in full sun. It tolerates a south slope and drouth.

EASY-DOES-IT IDEAS

A sloping bank, awkward for lawn or flowers, may be an easy possibility for a rock garden. Once planted, this kind of garden requires little upkeep.

To set plants in a dry wall, use small ones with most of the soil soaked or shaken from the roots. Wrap roots in moist, sphagnum moss, and slide them into the crevices using a spatula to guide the way. Then tamp as much soil around the roots as the openings will hold.

Let seedlings of flowers like penstemons and columbines that sprout in your rock garden stay where they are—no need to transplant. They look natural in self-selected spots, and usually do well there. Just weed out extras to prevent one kind from taking over too great an area.

Chapter 19

FRUITS AND NUTS FOR THE HOME GARDEN

What are the most satisfactory fruit trees for my back yard?

Fruit from the market seldom compares in flavor with what you grow at home, so if you have the space—*and time and willingness to spray*—do have some fruit trees, some bush fruits too, and, of course, strawberries.

A small home garden on a 75- by 125-foot lot might well include a cherry tree, a dwarf peach, two dwarf apples, a 20-foot row of black or red raspberries, a parallel row of gooseberries for pies, and maybe mixed with your shrub plantings a clump of a half dozen or so blueberry bushes, which make such handsome plants. You can tuck in a strawberry patch in a corner or plant it in a pyramid.

Be forewarned that fruit trees take space and time. One standard apple tree, like 'Red Delicious,' needs an area approximately 25 feet across, and to obtain perfect fruit you will need to spray it eleven times through the season. Cherries and bush fruits like raspberries require much less attention; usually you don't have to spray them at all.

FRUIT TREES FOR YOUR YARD

Fruit trees pay for themselves three ways. Their flowers in spring are as pretty as those of any ornamentals; they furnish shade through summer; and they give delicious fruit. Standard sizes of apples, and sour and sweet cherries in time make fairly large trees with fine shade. Pears and peaches grow large too, but are less desirable as shade or ornamental trees because they are brittle and shortlived. Plums come in such variety they suit many ornamental purposes, but they seldom grow big enough for shade. They do make good shrubby backgrounds and are durable.

Dwarf fruit trees are the answer if your space is limited. Nurserymen produce these by grafting tops of standard kinds on dwarf root stocks. The restricting root keeps the top from getting big. You can pick fruit from these dwarfs without going up a ladder; prune and spray them with ease. Often they bear earlier than standard sizes. Flowers and fruit are as big as those of standards. You can now get dwarf versions of apples, pears, quinces, peaches, apricots, cherries, and plums. Apples and pears are the main kinds sold as dwarf trees.

Another space-saver from the nurseryman is the several-in-one tree. You can get five or six apple varieties grafted together. This means fruit over a long period and several kinds without taking much space. You can sometimes get peaches, cherries, and pears grafted with several varieties on the same tree, too.

The pollination problem. Something to consider when you choose fruit trees is the right combination for cross pollination. Some kinds set fruit only if another variety is nearby so bees can carry pollen to them. If none of your neighbors grows this fruit

131 Black and purple raspberries are favorite bramble fruits, luscious for fresh fruit and jelly, and easy to grow.   *Photographers Associated*

132 The Chinese chestnut serves both as a shade and nut producer, giving satisfaction both ways.
Hickox

133 Strawberry barrels are fun to build, plant, and maintain. This is an attractive way to grow a few berries in small space.   *Roche*

134 Dwarf fruit trees, like this 'Golden Delicious,' have fruits of normal size but the tree stays small—easy to spray and pick.　　　　　*Inter-State*

you either need to plant a pollinating tree of your own, or else have a variety that is self-fertile—that is, one that can pollinate itself.

Apple varieties that bear well alone include 'Golden Delicious,' 'Jonathan,' 'Grimes Golden' and 'Wealthy.' With plums, 'Green Gage' and 'Damson' are self-pollinating. With cherries it is 'Montmorency.' Almost all peaches except 'J. H.

Hale' are self-fertile, and among pears, 'Duchess' and 'Kieffer.'

But if you plant a 'J. H. Hale' peach, a 'Bing' or almost any other sweet cherry, a 'Bartlett' pear, or practically any plums, except those just mentioned, you will need a pollinator of another variety.

Where to place them. All fruit trees need a sunny, drained site. North slopes are especially good. Always prepare big planting

278

holes and give plenty of water. Where the wind blows hard, tie a young tree to a stout stake with soft twine or cloth. Plant dwarfs with the graft union slightly above ground to prevent non-dwarf roots from developing above the graft.

APPLES ARE FAVORITES

Plant apple trees in early spring. Only in the South or other mild areas can you safely plant them in fall or winter. Set them an inch deeper than they grew in the nursery. Cut back tops lightly and remove a branch or two if there is crowding. Water freely and cultivate the first season. Space standard trees 35 to 45 feet, dwarfs 8 to 12 feet apart. You can grow dwarf kinds between standard sizes for the first few years, then later cut them out.

Good early varieties. 'Yellow Transparent' ripens in July; a favorite sauce apple, it is yellow and juicy, hardy in New England and southern Minnesota. 'Lodi' is an improved, fire-blight resistant version of 'Yellow Transparent.' 'Beacon' is red, mild and extra hardy; in Minnesota it is a midseason instead of early variety.

Good midseason varieties. 'Wealthy' is a red fall apple, juicy, good for eating, cooking and cider. 'Melba' is another all-purpose, red-pink kind with rich flavor.

Good late varieties. 'Jonathan' is a great red winter keeper, prized for crispness, tart flavor, cooking, and eating qualities. 'Red Delicious' is another top keeper, red, large, with creamy flavorful flesh, fine for eating fresh. It is not hardy in Minnesota or northern Maine. 'Winesap' is popular for pies, jelly and eating, and it stores well. 'Golden Delicious' is a big yellow sweet variety best for eating fresh; it ripens in October and keeps all winter.

CHERRIES FOR PASTRIES AND SWEETNESS

Plant sweet cherries in spring; sour kinds spring or fall. Space sour cherry trees about 20 feet and sweet cherries about 24 feet; dwarf varieties can go 7 to 12 feet. Most dwarfs are simply small-growing kinds.

Good sour varieties. 'Early Richmond,' a sour pie cherry, is the earliest of all and hardy as far north as Maine and southern Minnesota. It has medium size, tart bright red fruits. It ripens in June. 'Montmorency,' a midseason red cherry, is sweeter than 'Richmond' when ripe and has tender yellow flesh, perfect for pies, preserves and cobblers. It makes a handsome low tree that is vigorous and hardy to Maine and southern Minnesota. Self-fertile, it pollinates itself.

Good sweet varieties. 'Kansas Sweet' has mahogany-red, sweet fruits fine for eating, cooking, and freezing. It's probably the hardiest sweet cherry and bears well through the Midwest and Southwest. Use 'Montmorency' with it for cross pollination. 'Schmidt's Bigarreau' is a large, black, sweet cherry, useful the same ways, but not so hardy. Don't attempt it as far north as northern Iowa or Maine.

For the northern states. There are no sweet cherries and few sour ones for the extreme North. 'North Star' and 'Meteor' are hardy sour kinds that originated in Minnesota. Both make small trees and are self-pollinating.

PEACHES ARE LUSCIOUS

These grow best in areas where temperatures are steady and spared from violent fluctuations. Quick freezes and thaws of late spring make some places out of bounds for peach trees. The flower buds are safest from frost on a north-facing slope that warms up late in spring. There are no peach varieties as yet for the coldest areas such as Zone 3 and the north of Zone 4.

Space peach trees 15 to 20 feet apart, and dwarf kinds 10 feet apart. Set them out in early spring. Prune back to leave only three or four side branches, the lowest a foot above ground, and cut each of these back halfway. Wrap trunks to prevent sunscald, and keep the trees cultivated.

Good early varieties. 'Starking Delicious' is an early ripening freestone peach, touched with red, large, sweet and juicy, with the 'Elberta' flavor. It is ideal for eating, canning, freezing, cooking. 'Red Haven' ripens in July. It is red with firm yellow flesh, freestone and hardy.

Good midseason and late varieties. 'Hale Haven' is a yellow-fruited freestone peach, large with strong skin, and self-fertile. 'Elberta' is gold with a red blush, ripening in August. For years it has been the standard freestone peach variety. 'J. H. Hale' is a late-ripening yellow freestone variety; plant it with some other kind to get pollination. 'Krummel October' ripens a month after 'Elberta,' large yellow fruits tinted red—sweet, firm, just right for eating and canning. 'Polly' is a white-fruited kind, hardy freestone and with the wonderful sweetness for which white peaches are famed.

PEARS ARE RELIABLE

Where it's hard to grow peaches, pears are a better choice. Plant in early spring and space standard kinds 20 feet, dwarf kinds 10 feet apart. At planting time, cut standard trees back to about 3 feet; on dwarf kinds, cut branches back halfway and take out one or two.

The main plague of pears is fire blight, which can be very destructive. Afflicted branches suddenly look burned and die. To avoid trouble, plant resistant varieties. If you see fire blight, prune it out, cutting at least 8 inches below affected wood. Two resistant kinds are 'Seckel' and 'Kieffer.' 'Seckel' is hardy enough for the northern states. It has small sugary fruits that ripen late in summer. 'Kieffer' is a healthy late-bearing kind, also hardy in the North, better for cooking than eating fresh, and a wonderful pollinator for other varieties.

Main season or late kinds. 'Bartlett' is an old-time favorite for eating and canning, but sometimes blights. 'Bosc' is a long-necked, late, juicy sweet winter pear that stores well. 'Duchess' has large flavorful fruit, fine for eating out of hand, and since it is a good pollinator for itself and other kinds it can be used all alone, or included with kinds like 'Bartlett' that need pollinators. 'Patten' is a large juicy rich flavored pear that bears in August and is hardy in the northern states.

PLUMS NEED POLLINATORS

Plant plum trees in spring at the same depth they grew in the nursery. Space them 18 to 22 feet apart. Keep them lightly cultivated. Most kinds need another variety nearby for pollinating.

The hardiest plums. These will grow in the coldest states. 'Mt. Royal' has large blue fruit, good for preserving and jam, extremely hardy, and needs no pollinator. 'Underwood' is a red freestone plum, delicious, bearing in July; for it 'Toka' is a good pollinator. 'Toka' which is such a good pollinator for other plums, bears well by itself, ripening in August large freestone fruits the color of apricots. 'Superior' has large red fruit in August and is another good pollinator for other plums; good for eating, canning, freezing.

Plums for milder climates. 'Green Gage' has greenish yellow, sweet, juicy oval plums in September, is hardy to central Iowa. 'Stanley' is a blue freestone prune type plum with large fruit good for eating and canning, hardy to central Iowa; it makes a rather small tree. 'Starking Delicious' has large red-fleshed fruit, glossy and hardy, with good flavor. 'America,' used in the Southwest, has golden fruit touched with red, sweet and juicy, ripe in July. It makes a large tree.

APRICOTS MAY BE RISKY

Usually where spring frosts damage flowers or buds of these earliest of flowering trees, they are considered unreliable. Two new varieties developed by the University of Minnesota, however, are worth trying in cold areas. They are 'Moongold' and 'Sungold.' Plant them together for good pollination. Both are good freestone fruits for sauce and canning; just fair for eating fresh.

In the Midwest your chances will be good if you plant 'Golden Giant,' 'Superb,' or 'Wilson.' In the mid-South two favorites are 'Chinese Early Golden' and 'Moorpark.' Other suggestions for the North are 'Scout,' 'Morden 604' and 'Manchu.'

NECTARINE, THE FUZZLESS PEACH

Like apricots, nectarines are poor risks where spring weather is cold and fluctuating, but if your warm-up comes gradually, you can have these luscious peach-flavored fruits. For the Northeast, suggested kinds are 'Garden State,' 'Lexington,' 'Cavalier.' For the Midwest you are likely to succeed with 'Stark Early Flame,' 'Burbank Flaming Gold,' and 'Fuzzless Berta.' In the mid-South popular kinds are 'Silverlode' and 'Pioneer.'

PRUNING FRUIT TREES

If you have dwarf trees, there's little pruning to do. With the large standards some pruning will be needed at the start and then every few years. But for fruits in a small yard, your objectives are different from those of an orchardist who grows to sell. The main idea is to keep trees thin enough so they don't break under the crop, high enough so you can mow or sit underneath, and open enough so fruit can ripen in sunlight.

With apples, keep the lowest branch at least $2\frac{1}{2}$ feet above ground. Let the central leader grow, but thin out side branches so they are evenly spaced, about 8 inches apart up the trunk. Start a two-year old apple this way and you'll have little pruning to do later. If a crop looks heavy enough to break the tree, remove some of the apples while they are small.

When you plant pears, cut the central tip at 4 feet to start branching. Permit only five or six well-spaced branches to grow, and remove the rest. It takes about two years to produce the right pattern. Thin out heavy crops in mature trees the same as you would apples.

With peaches and apricots you begin by cutting the main stem back to 3 feet; then when side branches come out, choose four or five well-spaced ones and remove the rest. Cut the chosen ones back halfway. As trees grow, prune lightly to keep centers thin and open.

With cherries nearly all you need to do is cut off secondary limbs that hang down inconveniently. Watch for the first few years to see that limbs are well distributed on the main trunk. If too many emerge from one place, thin some of them. Both sweet and sour cherries make nice bushy trees that need little attention.

BUSH FRUITS TAKE LITTLE SPACE

There are five excellent bush fruits for every home garden that can spare a small amount of space for them. Consider them if your yard is too small to permit fruit trees. From a 30-foot row of raspberries you can harvest all the fresh fruit a family of five can eat during the bearing season, and have some left for jam and jelly. Other good possibilities are blackberries, currants, gooseberries and blueberries. As a rule these are healthy plants, so you'll be free of the spraying that fruit trees require.

BLACK AND PURPLE RASPBERRIES

These start ripening in June. This type produces long canes in summer and fall. Where tips touch ground they root (called "tip layering"). Then there are the red and yellow raspberries that ripen two weeks later, stand upright and don't tip layer, but spread by underground runners that wander away from the row. It's best to plant all kinds in spring. Fix for them a trellis of two wires strung at ends of 24-inch cross arms on posts 4 feet high. Give a humusy well-drained soil in full sun. Your patch will produce more if you also provide a deep mulch of leaves or old hay.

Good black raspberry varieties. 'Cumberland' is an old-time reliable midseason favorite of good size and quality. 'Black Hawk,' a new kind from Iowa, is a heavy midseason producer of excellent fruit. 'Morrison' is a late ripening kind, large and relatively seedless.

Good purple varieties. 'Sodus,' a large, firm, purple, vigorous berry, ripens over several weeks. 'Burgundy Purple' is a high-yielding kind, strongly disease-resistant.

For black and purple raspberries, space rows 6 feet apart and plants 3 feet apart in the row. Dig a hole, spread out roots so the main growth bud is 2 inches below ground and refill with soil. Plants bear a full crop two years after planting. *Right after harvest, cut out at the ground all the old canes which bore the fruit.* They will die anyway.

To make them branch, pinch out the soft tips of new canes as they reach 30 inches

Fig. 43 Pruning black and purple raspberries. In early spring top the canes at about 30 inches and cut back all laterals to 8 to 10 inches.

in June and July. In late winter or early spring, while plants are dormant, *cut back all the side branches* (laterals) to 8 to 10 inches, and top at 30 inches any canes that were not pinched back the year before.

RED AND YELLOW RASPBERRIES

Good red varieties. 'Latham' is a hardy standard midseason variety; 'Indian Summer' is early and repeats again in fall with large red berries. 'September' is another repeat bearing kind, non-crumbling and flavorful.

A good amber or yellow raspberry variety is 'Golden Queen' which bears in June. Flavor is delicate and sweet, and the berries make delicious light-colored jelly.

Space rows 8 feet apart and plants 2 feet apart in the row. Set plants into holes so the growing points are an inch below the surface. These bear a full crop two years later. New shoots from the roots will fill in the row between plants. Permit this, but when they pop up a distance from the row, hoe them off or your patch will soon get out of hand. *After harvest, remove canes that bore the crop.* In winter or early spring, thin out weak canes at the base, leaving about four to a square foot. Shorten remaining canes by one-third, but leave them long enough to tie to the trellis.

How to pick raspberries. Use small containers so berries won't be crushed by their own weight. Grasp each berry gently be-

tween thumb and fingers and pull it from the plant leaving the white core on the stem. Don't wash berries until you are ready to eat them.

BLACKBERRIES

Fruit of blackberries and their kin (dewberries, boysenberries, loganberries) look like black raspberries but when you pick them the core comes too. You eat the core as well as the berry. They are less hardy than raspberries. In the cold northernmost states, winters will kill them. They need nothing special in soil or site—just sun and good garden soil.

Blackberries are of two types, bush kind and trailing. Trailing kinds are even less hardy and are grown only in the South and mild coastal gardens. They make sprawling limber canes, but the bush kinds have stiff thorny stems and spread by root suckers.

Good kinds of bush blackberries. 'Ebony King,' early, hardy, disease-resistant, produces a heavy crop of large sweet berries. 'Hedrick,' a late bearer, is dependable, makes high-quality fruit. 'Bailey' ripens after 'Hedrick' with heavy production of sweet, coreless berries.

Plant bush blackberries in rows 8 feet apart, spaced 3 to 4 feet apart in the row. Give them a two-wire trellis on cross-arms 4 to 5 feet high. They make a crop the second season. To induce branching pinch off new shoots as they reach 3 to 4 feet. In winter or early spring, prune these side branches back to about 12 inches. After harvest remove canes that bore the crop. Remove weak canes at the crown.

CURRANTS AND GOOSEBERRIES

Of all bush fruits these seem best for a small yard. They make neat bushes under 4 feet, and they do not spread. Unfortunately you seldom will eat them right off the plant, but sweetened in a pie, gooseberries take high honors, and for jelly and pudding, it's hard to equal currants. Both are adapted to cold climates where few other small fruits grow.

Currant variety. 'Red Lake' is outstanding, vigorous, hardy, reliable, and produces

282

large red berries in long heavy clusters.

Kinds of gooseberries. There are kinds whose berries turn yellow, pink or green when ripe. 'Pixwell,' from North Dakota, has medium size berries that turn pink. It is hardy, prolific, and has but few thorns. 'Downing' is a heavy-bearing kind with green berries; 'Welcome' is a hardy kind from the University of Minnesota with light green fruit turning pink when ripe; it has large fruit and few thorns.

Plant them in early spring or fall. Set them as you would any shrub, a little deeper than they were in the nursery. Space them 3 to 4 feet apart in the row with rows 6 feet apart. They will bear a crop the year after they are planted. Pruning is an insignificant job. *Every few years cut out at the crown the old branches that have slowed down in productiveness.* To make them branch, tip back the straight new shoots.

You can harvest the whole gooseberry and currant crop at one picking. Take currants you want for jelly just before they are fully ripe. Pick by removing the whole cluster from the bush. To pick gooseberries, wear leather gloves as protection from thorns. Strip berries from the branch into a large container like a bushel basket with a lining in it. Later clean the berries of chaff, stems and trash. Gooseberries will stay on the bush two weeks after they reach full size, and get sweeter the longer they stay.

Currants and gooseberries can be alternate hosts in the white-pine blister-rust cycle. This precludes their use in some of the white pine-forest areas as in parts of Minnesota. If you are in such an area, regulations may prevent nurseries from shipping plants to you. Your state extension office can give full information about this.

BLUEBERRIES

This berry has everything. You can eat it fresh right off the bush or put it in all sorts of baked goods—pies, puddings, even pancakes. Everyone enjoys the sweet mild flavor. And the bushes are also beautiful ornamentals.

If you live in the East where your soils are on the moist acid side and the air is humid, you can probably grow blueberries well, but not everywhere are they easy. Where summer temperatures are high, soils are dry and alkaline, and air is parching, they are a doubtful crop. If you live along the Gulf Coast or in an area of warm winters, the dormant season is not long enough for them. On the other extreme in the North, where winters are long and severe, plants are not hardy enough. The central bank of states from Maine to North Carolina, west through Michigan and Tennessee to Missouri, is the best area. A smaller blueberry belt is on the West Coast, in Washington and Oregon.

Blueberries make shapely shrubs. Foliage is good, and in May they produce pretty small white flowers. Plant in spring. Space plants in groups 4 to 6 feet apart. To get good cross pollination use more than one variety in a planting.

Good blueberry varieties. 'Earliblue' is an early variety with an upright bush, producing medium size, firm fruit in clusters. 'Weymouth' is older and one of the earliest; it has large fruit on a spreading, open bush. 'Bluecrop' is a midseason kind with tart but good large berries; it is cold-resistant and upright. 'Jersey' is a hardy late variety bearing extra large fruit on upright plants. 'Herbert' is a late and very hardy kind with large shiny dark berries, strong and productive. Of these kinds, those most likely to succeed throughout blueberry territory are 'Bluecrop,' 'Earliblue,' and 'Jersey.'

If your soil is not acid, mix it half and half with acid peat, sawdust or rotted leaf mold and add a sprinkling of sulfur ($\frac{3}{4}$ pound to one hundred square feet). Blueberries prefer a soil pH of 4 to 5. Choose a site that has porous soil and good drainage. Soak new plants in water an hour before planting, and cut off about half the tops. Set so upper roots are covered with only an inch of soil. Water well, pack soil firmly, and pull up a low dike to hold water around the plant so you can water frequently the first season. Put on a compost or sawdust mulch.

If foliage turns yellow, the soil is probably too alkaline. Acidify it by adding sulfur, as suggested; or feed plants with chelated iron obtained at a garden store—supply one tablespoon to one gallon of water. Spray this on the foliage and on the ground around the plants.

Prune yearly by thinning out weakest top growth and removing dead wood.

GRAPES FIT IN SMALL SPACE

Grapes are easy to grow and very rewarding. The handsome foliage will clothe an arbor for you in grand style if you choose to use the vines ornamentally. If you prefer to grow them for fruit on a trellis in your garden, you can have enormous production in little space. Except for spring pruning, they require almost no effort. For every part of the country there are at least a few kinds of hardy grapes.

Early settlers here found the American climate impossible for the European grapes to which they were accustomed, except in warm, dry California. The first good American variety, the Concord, was bred from a native grape, introduced in 1854, and is still the most popular variety east of the Rockies.

The kinds from Europe—viniferas, now called California grapes—need mild climates, dry soil, and dry air. They are prized for sweet flavor, eating fresh, cooking, wine-making. The American-developed kinds with the hardiness of the eastern native species are called Concord types. They have a "foxy" flavor and aroma and the skin slips off easily. In the South a third but minor kind is the muscadine or cluster grape; and in the far North where Concords are not hardy, a fourth minor kind is that bred from sturdy native species—'Beta' is a good example. Soon now there will be wide use of hybrids between California grapes and the hardy American kinds. These are already appearing, and they promise to bring the California type of grape, with its superb eating qualities, into the cool humid climates of the East and North. One of these, 'Seibel 9110,' is already widely available.

GRAPES ARE EASY TO PLANT

Plant grapes in early spring. Use one- or two-year-old plants. Dig a hole in your good garden soil, and spread the roots, refilling so the plant sets a little deeper than it was

in the nursery. Leave a depression and fill it with water, letting it soak in. Then finish filling the hole.

If you are growing grapes decoratively around an arbor, set them as close together as 4 feet. On trellises in your garden, put them 6 to 8 feet apart, and space the trellises 6 feet apart.

After you have planted the vine, cut the top off so just the two lowest leaf buds remain. Leaves and future stems will rise from these buds.

Grapes must have something suitable to climb on. Because the vines climb by tendrils, they can grasp only thin supports. For this reason, wire trellises are universally used. If you grow grapes as an orchard crop, make trellises of two wires strung on stout posts, the top wire 5 feet above ground, the second wire $2\frac{1}{2}$ feet above. Construct arbors on this principle, too.

GRAPES FOR EVERY CLIMATE

For cold-winter areas—New England, Northern Prairies, Great Plains: 'Beta' is a blue-black berry, tart, medium size, early, with heavy foliage, the hardiest of all. It makes a good screen on arbors. 'Concord' is disease-resistant, hardy, midseason, with flavorful blue berries hard to beat for jam, jelly and juice. You can get a seedless version of it. 'Fredonia' is a dark blue kind that ripens early, and is good in dry sections of the prairies and plains. 'Portland' is the earliest amber-white grape, sweet and productive, ripening before 'Fredonia.' 'Niagara' is a white, tangy grape hardy wherever you can grow Concords. 'Delaware' is a hardy red kind, slow growing but producing sizable clusters of medium large berries.

Where winters are cold but not extreme (with minus 10 degrees the usual minimum) you can grow all those named above plus these: 'Golden Muscat,' a late ripening golden grape with muscat flavor, needs extra long seasons; 'Interlaken Seedless,' a seedless golden grape, ripens early; 'Seneca' is a California type but hardy, early, sweet, white and with tender edible skin; 'Steuben' has distinctive spicy blue berries ripening fairly late, vigorous and productive; 'Seibel 9110' is a golden yellow hybrid of the California type, early and hardy; 'Alden' is a blue grape with plum sized berries in long clusters.

In the South, favorite muscadine varieties are 'Scuppernong,' a bronze medium, juicy, sweet and fairly early kind; and 'Hunt,' a black, berried kind, sweet, juicy and early.

PRUNING IS A YEARLY NECESSITY

Without pruning, the vine sets an enormous crop beyond its ability to mature, so your yield is almost nothing, and no new canes are formed for the next year's crop. Most people enjoy pruning grapes, once they understand the simple purpose—to make the vine much smaller, and leave avenues for future growth. It helps to realize that *grapes bear fruit only on canes that were produced the previous season.* You can scarcely expect a full crop until the fourth season after planting.

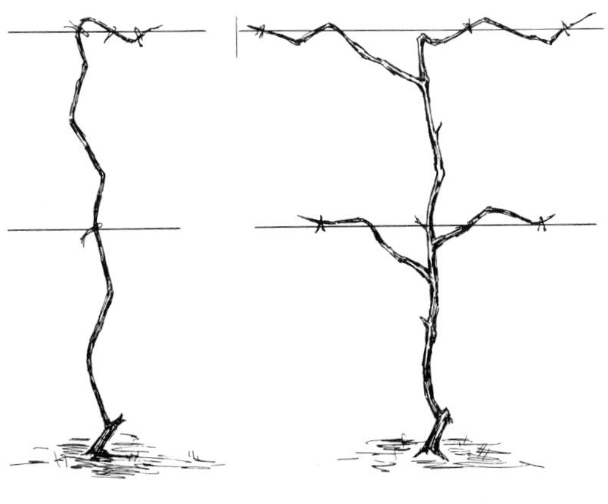

after first pruning
(second spring)

after second pruning
(third spring)

one long cane remains;
cut off beyond top tie

four side canes remain;
cut off the rest

Fig. 44 Pruning grapes by the Kniffin system.

Prune in February or March before sap flows. The easiest and best system for home gardeners is the Kniffin or four-cane method. Let's assume you start with new plants, which you have cut down to two buds when you plant them. By next spring there will be two long canes, possibly more. Select the strongest one and cut off the others. Train the selected one straight to the top trellis

wire and tie it there. If the cane reaches beyond, cut it off just above the wire.

The second summer, the upright cane will develop side branches. At next pruning time, the third spring, select two upper ones on opposite sides for the top wire, two for the lower. This makes a total of four side canes, two running each way. Cut off all the rest. Tie the four chosen canes to the wire, and cut them back to about 15 buds each. This year they will bear.

At next pruning time, the fourth spring, cut off those canes completely and select four more coming out near the same places on the upright trunk. Prune and tie as you did before. The "spurs" of former arms provide buds that become future arms. This is now the pattern that you maintain each year.

If you grow grapes ornamentally on arbors, prune them sharply each spring but don't cut them as much as you do orchard grapes. As a general rule, remove all dead wood and one-third of the live wood.

STRAWBERRIES FOR SMALL SPACE

If you don't have any other fruit, do have a strawberry bed or border. Your daily bounty of bright red berries is as pleasing and good eating as any fruit can be, especially since it comes as the first fruit harvest of the year. If you grow everbearing kinds, you can keep on picking these incomparable berries right up to frost. Where your space is limited, you can grow strawberries in pyramids, window boxes, flower pots, as a border to a perennial bed, or in a strawberry barrel.

June-bearing and everbearing are the two main kinds of strawberries. June-bearing are just that. You harvest a bountiful crop that month and then no more for the year. With everbearing kinds, which usually have smaller fruits, you get a crop in June, and a sprinkling through the summer with another surge in fall.

KINDS FOR YOUR REGION

Before you set out a large patch, put some study into selecting the right varieties. Each region has its own best kinds. Most states put out extension bulletins that recommend strawberry varieties; you can also get advice from your county agent and from gardeners around you. Here is a guide to kinds recommended in seven general regions:

Gulf South. 'Missionary,' 'Florida 90' (in Florida), 'Klonmore,' 'Blakemore,' 'Gem.' *
Mid-South. 'Tennessee Beauty,' 'Albritton,' 'Blakemore,' 'Dixieland,' 'Pocohontas,' 'Surecrop.'
Northern states east of the Mississippi. 'Catskill,' 'Sparkle,' 'Premier,' 'Vermilion,' 'Temple,' 'Empire.'
North Central states. 'Cyclone,' 'Ogallala,' * 'Sparkle,' 'Premier,' 'Dunlap,' 'Earlimore,' 'Chief Bemidji.' *
New England. 'Catskill,' 'Sparkle,' 'Premier,' 'Temple,' 'Vermilion.'
Central Midwest. 'Blakemore,' 'Premier,' 'Armore,' 'Tennessee Beauty,' 'Temple,' 'Midland,' 'Dunlap,' 'Robinson,' 'Ogallala.' *
Rocky Mountain states. 'Dunlap,' 'Robinson,' 'Catskill,' 'Gem,' * 'Superfection,' * 'Streamliner,' * 'Premier.'

Some strawberries are strictly novelties. Two such are 'Baron Solemacher' or the alpine strawberry, which spreads by seeds instead of runners and has sweet wild strawberry fruits; and 'Sonjana,' billed as a "climbing" strawberry. Actually it forms long runners with developing plantlets that can be trained up on trellises.

HOW TO MANAGE
JUNE-BEARING STRAWBERRIES

Plant in spring as early as you can obtain plants and prepare the soil. For one hundred plants a patch 8 by 75 feet will be fine and this is more than enough for an average family.

Choose a place that drains well and escapes late frosts. Gentle slopes are usually good, especially if they face north. If the soil lacks organic matter, spread compost, rotted manure or peat moss and turn it under. Put on commercial balanced fertilizer, such as 1 pound of 5-10-5 to 100 square feet, and work it in. Make rows 3 to 4 feet

* Everbearing varieties.

apart. Space plants 18 inches to 2 feet apart in the rows. Spread out the roots and *set crowns so they are slightly above ground level.* Then firm the soil down so the crown settles exactly at ground surface. Water the new plantings thoroughly.

The first season cultivate plants several times to keep down weeds and encourage runners to get started. Let runners take root to make a matted row up to 2 feet wide. Once you have this sort of bed, with individual plants averaging about 7 inches apart, hoe off any more runners that appear.

In late fall, after a hard freeze but before severe weather starts, scatter *seed-free* hay or straw loosely over the patch. Spread it 3 to 4 inches deep. The next spring pull it from directly above plants, but tuck it in around them to mulch the soil and keep fruit clean. You will have a fine crop the second year.

After you've harvested, harden your heart and hoe out all the oldest worn-out plants, so what are left are young ones standing about 12 inches apart. Spread one pound of a balanced commercial fertilizer, like 5-10-5, to 150 square feet, keeping it off foliage. Cultivate between rows, cutting mats back to 12 inches wide. Then let the plants grow again to renew the mat.

When you've picked the third big crop, use the runner plants to start a new patch in another spot, and plow up the first patch. It's easier than trying to keep the old bed producing.

HOW TO MANAGE
EVERBEARING STRAWBERRIES

Plant these the same way you do June berries. They don't make as many runners, so plant them closer, about 12 inches; and space the rows closer, $2\frac{1}{2}$ to 3 feet. You will get better fall crops of everbearers if you pick off blossoms until July 1. This sacrifices the spring crop and although late-season berries are hardly ever as fine as the early ones, this does lengthen the season.

Everbearing varieties are ideal for garden edgings, window boxes, strawberry barrels and pyramids, where space is limited.

Strawberry pyramids. These devices are sold prefabricated of metal, but if you like you can make your own of wood. They consist of a stacked series of progressively smaller square or circular tiers, usually three. You plant strawberries around each tier. In good rich soil, you can set them as close as 10 inches. The plants soon cover the whole affair and you can harvest a fair-sized crop the first year from everbearing kinds. Keep runners cut off after the soil is filled in with plants. Exposed as they are, the pyramids dry out fast, so keep them well watered.

Strawberry barrels are planters made out of wooden kegs or barrels with roomy holes cut in the sides to hold plants. These are ornamental novelties, rather than useful ways to produce berries, but fun to build and maintain. Make holes 2 inches across spaced about 10 inches apart. Insert a perforated drain pipe, filled with loose gravel, down the middle for a watering column. Use soil enriched with peat and rotted manure, and fill it in as you put in plants. Finish with a ring of plants at the top. Porous pottery strawberry jars are also planted this way, except that they have no watering column down the middle.

About disease-free plants. You will have to do little spraying on strawberries if you start with disease-free plants. The plague in the past has been hard-to-pin-down virus diseases that made plants "run out" after a while. Now nurserymen are producing virus-free stocks of most varieties: in advertising, they always stress if the plants offered are virus-free. When you buy, insist on these clean undiseased plants, so you don't get a virus started in your patch. If you already have a planting that seems diseased, avoid setting new virus-free kinds next to it, or soon they too will have the plague. Aphids spread viruses from place to place.

SHADE AND FRUIT FROM NUT TREES

Of all the trees you might grow for fruit, these are the best to give you shade as well. Allow them plenty of room because they become big trees, 75 to 100 feet high. For farm tree lots, windbreaks and fence rows, they are excellent. Walnuts, butternuts, pe-

cans, and chestnuts (Chinese) are the best for shade and production.

Black walnuts are probably the most valued. A selection called 'Thomas' bears fairly thin-shelled large nuts, starting when young. Another promising variety is the hardy English walnut called 'Carpathian,' an import from the Balkans. It looks like the thin-shelled walnuts grown in California, but is much hardier. It succeeds even in the northern Great Plains, where it is known to have survived temperatures of −30 degrees. It has shiny foliage and grows fast into a big tree. To get good pollination, plant two near each other.

Chinese chestnuts replace the practically extinct American chestnut, wiped out by disease. They are almost as hardy as our natives were, taking temperatures down to about −15 degrees. They grow fast, spread widely, and make good shade trees. Plant two in your yard, 40 feet apart, to get good pollination.

Pecans, although traditionally southern, come now in hardy varieties that will grow as far north as southern Iowa and Michigan. One for northern areas is 'Stuart,' hardiest of the southern types, which bears with regularity as far north as Kansas City and mid-Illinois.

The hican, a hybrid between hickory and pecan, grows even farther north. Its nuts resemble pecans in shell and flavor. Both pecans and hicans are self-fertile, so you need only one tree to get a crop. They make large shade trees.

Butternuts are a lot like walnuts. Some people call them white walnuts. Fruits are oblong, and the kernels are narrow and oily, delicious, and tops for candy, cookies and cake. The trees will grow in moist soils, and are as hardy as black walnuts.

HOW TO HAVE HEALTHY FRUIT

It would be nice if you could grow unblemished apples, peaches, plums, and other fruit without resorting to sprays or dusts, but these days that is unheard of. Too many insects and diseases are around to spoil the crop.

The horrifying list of things that can go

SPRAY (OR DUST) SCHEDULE FOR PERFECT HOME FRUIT

(Numbers refer to notes that follow)

When to spray	Apple	Pear	Peach, plum, cherry, apricot	Grape	Raspberry, blackberry	Strawberry	Blueberry	Currant, gooseberry
DORMANT SPRAY — before buds green at tips			(1) Spray					
GREEN TIP SPRAY — when buds break	(3) Spray	Spray			Buds (9) swelling	Buds swelling	Buds swelling	First leaves show
PREBLOOM SPRAY — buds colored but not open	(2) Spray	(2,3) Spray	Spray	Shoots ½-1" long	Shoots ¼" long	Shoots growing (3)	Just before bloom	Just before bloom (2,3)
BLOOM SPRAY — flowers open	Do not spray during bloom, or use captan, plus other fungicide only (4)			Shoots 4-8" long (3)	Shoots 4-6" long (3)	Just before bloom (4)	Petal fall	Just after bloom
PETAL-FALL — 90% of petals have fallen	(8) Spray	Spray	(2,3,8) Spray		As blooms open			Spray
1st COVER SPRAY — 10 days after petal fall	(5) Spray	Spray	Spray	Just before bloom		When berries half grown	Spray (3)	
2nd COVER SPRAY — 10 days after 1st cover	(5) Spray		Spray	Just after bloom (7)	Fruit growing	Fruit growing		Spray (5)
3rd COVER SPRAY — 10 days after 2nd cover	Spray (5)	Spray	Spray	Fruit pea-size (3)	Fruit ripening (5)	Berries ripening (5)	Spray (5)	
4th COVER SPRAY — 10 days after 3rd cover	Spray (5)		Spray	Fruit growing	Just after harvest (6)	Just after harvest (6)	Just after harvest (6)	Just after harvest (6)
5th COVER SPRAY — 10 days after 4th cover	Spray (5)	(5) Spray	(5,6) Spray	Fruit growing				
6th COVER SPRAY — 10 days after 5th cover	(5) Spray			Fruit growing (5)				
ADDITIONAL COVER SPRAYS — late maturing varieties	(5) Spray							

wrong with fruit trees is almost enough to make you give up growing them. Yet many people are satisfied with fruit they get after no spraying at all. Bush fruits especially, like raspberries, blackberries, and gooseberries hardly ever need sprays. Home cherries make good crops without spraying; so do strawberries, blueberries, and grapes.

But if it's perfection you are after, sprays are the way to get it. The table opposite shows what to spray through the season, and what with to get perfect home fruits. Where the direction is simply "spray," use a commercial multipurpose spray for fruit. These mixtures come under many trade names— they usually contain captan, methoxychlor and malathion. Mix according to directions on the container.

NOTES FOR SPRAY SCHEDULE

(1) Use ferbam—$2\frac{1}{2}$ tablespoons per gallon—on stone fruits as dormant spray to control *leaf curl, black knot* and *plum pockets*. Apply when outdoor temperature is 40 degrees or above.

(2) If *rust* is a problem, add ferbam, zineb or thiram—1 tablespoon per gallon.

(3) If *powdery mildew* is a problem, add Karathane—$\frac{2}{3}$ teaspoon per gallon—or wettable sulfur—2 tablespoons per gallon. Some fruits—blueberries, grapes and raspberries are sulfur-sensitive. Do not use sulfur on these.

(4) Do not apply a multipurpose spray during bloom; it will kill pollinating insects. To control *rust, brown rot, blossom blight* and *scab* which attack during this period, use a mixture of captan and either ferbam, zineb, or thiram—1 tablespoon of each per gallon. Spray just before rains if possible.

(5) Do not apply multipurpose spray within a week of harvest. Captan alone may be used right up to harvest to protect

against fruit rots. Use a mixture of captan and zineb ($1\frac{1}{2}$ tablespoons of each per gallon) for cover sprays on apples to control summer diseases.

(6) Spray cherry, raspberry, blackberry, strawberry, currant, gooseberry, and blueberry one to three times after harvest to protect growth for next year's crop.

(7) For *downy mildew*, add zineb or fixed copper to the multipurpose spray for grapes, in after-bloom sprays.

(8) To control *peach* and *apple borers*, spray or paint trunk three times, at twenty day intervals, using dieldrin—3 heaping tablespoons of 50 per cent powder per gallon of water.

(9) Use liquid lime-sulfur alone in the first two sprays for raspberries and blackberries to control *anthracnose* and *spur blight*—$\frac{1}{5}$ pint per gallon. Use multipurpose spray for all later applications.

EASY-DOES-IT IDEAS

In a small yard you can have a hedge that is both ornamental and useful if you plant gooseberries. They make low shrubs good for marking boundaries, and their thorns deter dogs and cats. They will be good for a few gooseberry pies in the spring.

A comely shrub fruit that fits well in foundation plantings is the blueberry. Use it as you do deciduous shrubs, with several close together. They'll provide pretty white flowers in May, berries a little later, good foliage all season long with fine fall color.

For ease in pruning, spraying, and picking—choose dwarf fruit trees. They are grafted on special roots that keep them from growing large, but the fruits are normal size and begin to set on while trees are still young.

Chapter 20

YOUR KITCHEN GARDEN OF VEGETABLES AND HERBS

What vegetables can I grow in a small space?

You don't need much space for a kitchen garden big enough to supply you with some wonderful fresh vegetables. In a small plot, say 10 by 20 feet, you can have salad sass in spring and fall; incomparable sun-ripened tomatoes, and plenty of peppers and a few egg plants; a surplus of seasonings and garnishes; and perhaps even a few staples like beets, chard, carrots and beans. Home-grown vegetables are superb, sun-filled, crisply fresh, young and clean; and the varieties are what you have chosen—not something rubbery enough to stand mass production and shipping to market.

START WITH A PLAN

Like the overall plan for your place and the detailed layout for your flower border, you need a plan for your vegetable garden with size and location thoughtfully considered. The best location will have:

full sun,
good drainage,
light humusy soil,
a place that warms up early,
space for rows to run north and south,
convenience for watering.

Permanent plants first. Plant the perennials, asparagus and rhubarb, along one or two sides where they will not interfere with plowing or spading. These come back year after year with little attention on your part. You will enjoy them for their earliness. Crinkly rhubarb tips breaking through soil are one of the small thrills of spring, but hardly equaling the big thrill a few weeks later when you have your first rhubarb pie or sauce. Asparagus gives the first harvest of greens, succulent spears from late April until late June.

Next the annual plants. Each year you start over with the annual part of your vegetable patch. Planning it is one of the pleasures of January, as soon as seed catalogs arrive. Take a piece of paper ruled off in squares, each square equaling a foot, and plan the garden row by row. Here are some general rules:

Leave rows far enough apart so your cultivator goes between and has room at the end to turn.

Put crops tall enough to cast shade—tomatoes and corn—to the north where they won't obscure low crops.

Run rows north and south if you can, unless your garden is on a slope—then let rows run across (contour) the slope.

Plan succession crops—early leaf lettuce succeeded by late lima beans; two quick crops one after the other, like consecutive plantings of bush beans.

Interplant early little plants with late big

ones—leaf lettuce, radishes or spinach between cabbage, tomatoes, or cucumbers.

To save space, use stakes or trellises for crops like cucumbers, vining squash, and tomatoes.

PLANNING A LITTLE GARDEN

In a tiny space, you'll especially want to use things that pay their rent. You can't afford lots of leafy stems without big yields. Investigate the small-growing vegetables. 'Tiny Tim' peas, for instance, make vines only 9 inches tall, but the 3-inch pods are packed and sugary. 'Morden' dwarf cabbage makes solid 4-inch heads. 'Faribo' dwarf sweet corn is a true miniature, making doll-size plants with tender 4-inch ears. These are only a few of the many possibilities.

Depend on interplanting and succession cropping to get the most yield, and give special attention to keeping the soil rich and humusy. You won't be going through a patch this size with power tractors, so you can put rows close together, even 12 inches for low growing kinds like spinach and lettuce. Leave just enough room to walk through.

Study the plan for a 15- x 17-foot garden with a big yield to see how early things come out to make way for the spreading tops of late crops, and how each inch of space gets long-season use.

PLANNING A BIG GARDEN

Where you have room and can manage the upkeep, you may have a big garden that not only puts a dent in the summer food bill, but yields plenty to can, freeze, and store for winter. In a large area, you can have hybrid sweet corn, lima beans, potatoes, squash, melons, enough peas for the freezer and enough cucumbers for pickling.

If you go in for vegetables on this scale, you will probably have machines to help

135 You don't need a lot of space for a kitchen garden that will pep up your summer menu. Here a small plot offers wide variety—strawberries (foreground), sweet peppers, cabbage, head lettuce, carrots, rhubarb, asparagus, and tomatoes trained against fence and wall. *Genereux*

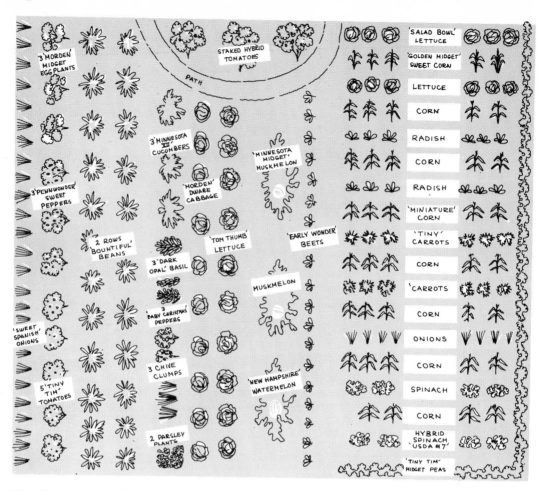

Fig. 45 A 15- x 17-foot garden with a big yield. It uses many small-growing kinds of vegetables, with early crops coming out to make way for later ones.

with the work. Plan the garden to accommodate them. Put rows far enough apart so the tiller goes between with room enough to avoid tangling plant tops. If the cultivator is a kind that straddles the row you'll still need to leave room for the wheels. Conserve space for between-row cultivators by making double rows—putting two rows close (10 inches), then leaving perhaps 30 to 36 inches for the cultivator. Snap beans, peas, beets, carrots, lettuce, spinach, onions —in fact any of the smaller plants—will grow in double rows.

If you include sweet corn, put it in a block of at least three adjacent rows to get good pollination. Save space for second or third plantings to give fresh ears over a long period.

Study the plan for a large 40- x 50-foot garden. Here again, succession plantings make the most of the space and crops are arranged for good growth and convenience.

PERENNIAL VEGETABLES AND HOW TO GROW THEM

Asparagus. Plant in spring, say eighteen plants for a family of four. 'Mary Washington' is a good variety. Choose a spot in full sun where water runs off or drains through quickly. Put on lots of rotted manure or compost, and spade or plow it all in, so soil is loosened 8 to 12 inches deep. Dig out a 12-inch wide trench, 6 inches deep, with a level bottom, unless you have clay soil.

292

136 These herbs from the Berkshire garden center will furnish all the garnishes, flavorings and aromatic plants you need. Sage, rosemary, and artemisia are prominent. Artemisia 'Silver King,' and sage, in the foreground, are interspersed with rhubarb. Tansy and nasturtium are beside the step. Marjoram, rosemary, and tarragon are some of the collection at left center. *Roche*

137 The garden begins with rows made straight along a stretched string and seeds sown sparingly in soft earth.
Henderson

138 Thinning permits seedlings to reach full development. Those thinned out of this lettuce row will make a tasty salad. *Hering*

139 The idea of succession crops works even in the tiniest gardens. These radishes and onions will be followed by the interplanted sweet corn. *Roe*

PLAN FOR A LARGE VEGETABLE GARDEN

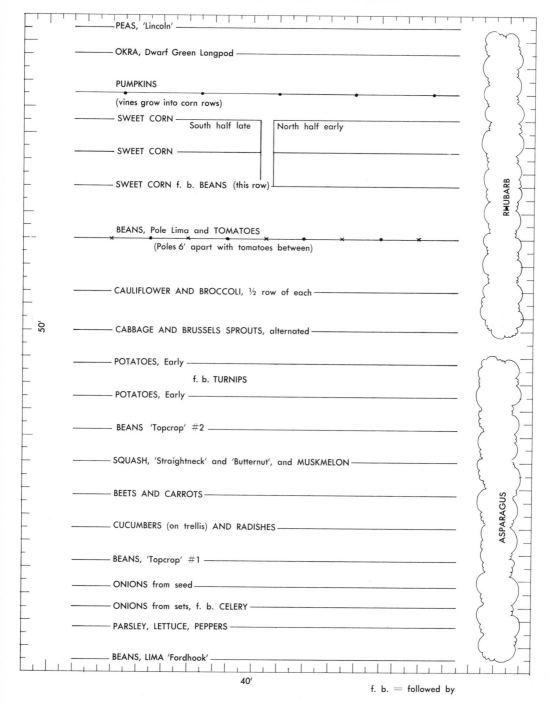

PEAS, 'Lincoln'

OKRA, Dwarf Green Longpod

PUMPKINS

(vines grow into corn rows)

SWEET CORN

South half late | North half early

SWEET CORN

SWEET CORN f. b. BEANS (this row)

BEANS, Pole Lima and TOMATOES

(Poles 6' apart with tomatoes between)

CAULIFLOWER AND BROCCOLI, ½ row of each

CABBAGE AND BRUSSELS SPROUTS, alternated

POTATOES, Early

f. b. TURNIPS

POTATOES, Early

BEANS 'Topcrop' #2

SQUASH, 'Straightneck' and 'Butternut', and MUSKMELON

BEETS AND CARROTS

CUCUMBERS (on trellis) AND RADISHES

BEANS, 'Topcrop' #1

ONIONS from seed

ONIONS from sets, f. b. CELERY

PARSLEY, LETTUCE, PEPPERS

BEANS, LIMA 'Fordhook'

RHUBARB

ASPARAGUS

50'

40'

f. b. = followed by

Fig. 46   Plan for a 40- x 50-foot garden, with succession plantings to make the most of the space.

Then make the trench only 4 to 5 inches deep instead of 6. Spread asparagus roots over this, spacing crowns 18 inches apart. Make rows 4 to 5 feet apart; or if you want, make double rows with the crowns laid zigzag, 18 inches each way.

Cover the growing points with 2 inches of soft soil and fill in the rest after plants start to grow. Add soil every few days until the trench is full. The first year let tops grow without any cutting. The second year, cut spears for the first two weeks, then let them grow. The third year, cut for three weeks. The fourth year, take a full crop, cutting until the middle or end of June. If you keep on harvesting too late you won't have as much next year. Cut spears at soil surface with a sharp asparagus or butcher knife.

To keep down weeds, cultivate the patch *thinly* in early spring before plants come up. At this time, put on fertilizer—something like 8-8-8, 2 pounds to 100 square feet—and work it in. If there are many weeds at the end of May, cultivate again—this will steal two or three days of harvest, but production soon catches up. After your last cutting of the season, cultivate once more and then let tops grow. Don't cut them down until after frost.

Rhubarb. Plant in spring, say six plants for a family of four. Good varieties: 'Canada Red,' with red-fleshed sweet stalks, and 'MacDonald,' a big kind with green flesh and red skin.

Plant in full sun where drainage is perfect. Start with fresh crown divisions that have a large growing bud and a sizable piece of root. Spread rotted manure or compost thickly (if it's compost enrich it with 8-8-8 fertilizer, 2 pounds to 100 square feet) and dig all this in 10 to 12 inches deep. Make a furrow and set crowns 3 feet apart, bud end up, with 2 to 3 inches of soil covering.

The first year let plants grow. The second season pull a few of the largest stalks. The third year take a full crop, harvesting the largest stalks as they develop over a six-week period. Keep seeds cut off. Harvest rhubarb by pulling, not cutting. The stalks break out.

Rhubarb is a cool-weather plant and won't thrive in the South. Performance is usually poor south of Zone 6. A disease called foot rot sometimes causes trouble in a rhubarb row, especially where weather is hot and humid. It causes stalks to rot at the crown. If you find this, dig the roots and

burn them. The next spring mix captan or terraclor in water according to package directions and pour a quart of solution around soil and crowns as they break through down the whole row. When you plant to replace losses, dust roots first with ferbam, sulfur or captan, and put fresh soil in that place.

Winter onions. Other names are potato and multiplier onions. They stay in the ground all winter. You can pull them for eating or flavoring any time they are not frozen. They never make bulbs, but long edible stalks, which grow in bunches. Each stem removed from the bunch is soon replaced by another. A dozen plants are plenty if you have other kinds of onions in summer.

Grow them from seeds planted in a $\frac{1}{2}$-inch row in fine soil in spring. Thin out seedlings to 5 inches apart. Mound loose soil around plants to blanch them at the base.

ANNUAL VEGETABLES AND HOW TO GROW THEM

Plant garden seeds when the soil is fine and crumbling, but moist underneath. Make straight rows by setting two stakes with a cord stretched between. Open furrows with a hoe blade, or if it is only a shallow row, with the tip of the handle. Scatter seeds into the row or drill at the spacing recommended in the "Planting Guide" in this chapter. Cover seeds with soil to the recommended depth and do be careful not to bury them—a cause of many failures. Cover seeds more thinly early in the season than later when soil is mellow and warm. If you have trouble with slow seeds like beets and carrots, mix a batch of equal parts peat, soil, and sand to cover seed. This will not crust over. Or cover the row with a board, and remove it as soon as sprouts appear.

Spring planting dates depend on the average date of the last hard frost. Your local weather bureau, county agent, or probably your gardening neighbor can tell you when this is likely to be. Also, consult the map in Chapter 1.

Bean, lima. They need a long warm season, which is why they are not much grown in northernmost states. Plant in soft warm

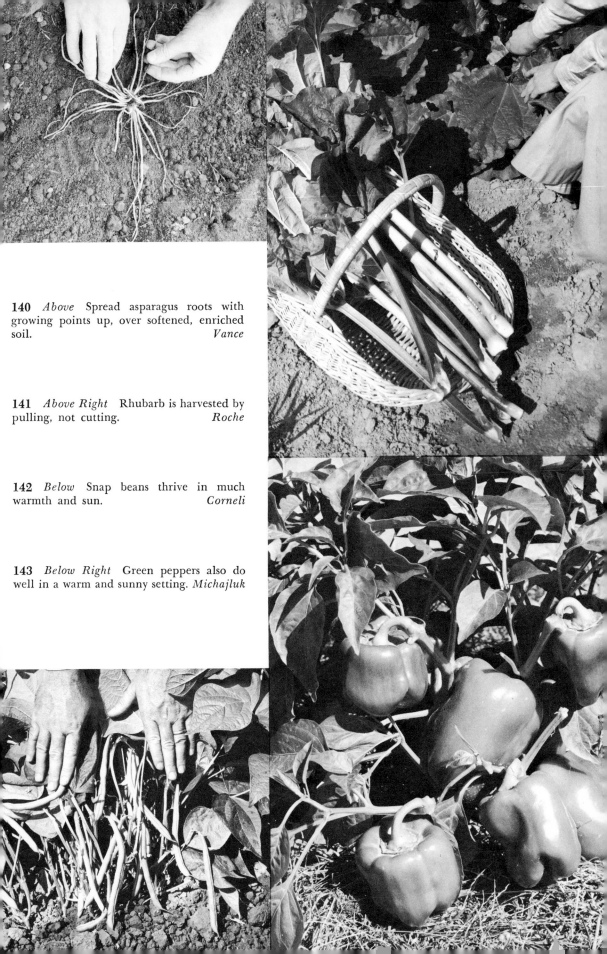

140 *Above* Spread asparagus roots with growing points up, over softened, enriched soil. *Vance*

141 *Above Right* Rhubarb is harvested by pulling, not cutting. *Roche*

142 *Below* Snap beans thrive in much warmth and sun. *Corneli*

143 *Below Right* Green peppers also do well in a warm and sunny setting. *Michajluk*

soil and if it crusts, shade or moisten until seedlings emerge. From seed to harvest is sixty-five to seventy-five days. Large seeded kinds like 'Fordhook 242' are easier to shell than small ones like 'Henderson's Baby Lima,' but the babies have fine flavor.

Bean, snap. Good kinds are 'Topcrop,' 'Tendergreen,' 'Tenderpod,' and for the South, 'Commodore.' They mature in fifty to fifty-five days. Grow shell beans the same way as snaps.

Bean, pole. Give these a trellis, post or fence to climb on—something at least 4 feet high. They need sixty-five days to mature. The standard and best variety is 'Kentucky Wonder.'

Beet. These will be eating size in fifty to sixty days from seed. Water and cultivate to keep them growing fast so they avoid becoming woody. Good varieties are 'Early Wonder,' 'Detroit Dark Red,' 'Ruby Queen.'

Broccoli. Green-sprouting kinds best for home gardens are 'Di Cicco' and 'Italian Green Sprouting.' Budded heads are ready to eat sixty to seventy days from the time you set out plants. Broccoli needs cool weather.

Brussels sprouts. 'Jade Cross,' and 'Catskill,' are two of the best home varieties. Pick these from the bottom upward, as new sprouts develop at the top of stalk. They need coolness to develop properly.

Cabbage. All of this family need cool weather, so start them early indoors or in coldframe. They will weather mild frosts if they are hardened off well. Give them fertile moist soil with much humus. Cabbage suffers a wilt disease called yellows. If you've had trouble with it, choose wilt-resistant varieties. 'Early Jersey Wakefield,' and 'Golden Acre' are good early kinds, available in wilt-resisting strains; 'Danish Ballhead' is a good later kind.

Carrot. For best results give carrots your sandiest soil, without much compost or manure in it. They will be eating size in sixty-eight to eighty-five days from seed. Plant in a new place each year to get away from soil insects like wireworms. Good kinds: 'Nantes,' 'Imperator,' 'Danvers Half Long.'

Cauliflower. Treat it like cabbage, but when it starts to head, pull the big base leaves up around and fasten with a string or rubber band. This makes the head white. You will have best luck with cauliflower if your summers are cool. Good kinds: 'Early Snowball,' 'Super Snowball.'

Celery. Unless your climate is mild and cool, this is only a novelty for you. It takes eighty to one hundred fifteen days between setting out plants and harvest. Start seeds in January or February and transplant outdoors about when you sow beets. Use plenty of water through the season to keep them growing. Two weeks before harvest, blanch stalks by wrapping with black paper, black polyethylene, aluminum foil, or by laying boards against stalks to keep out light. For home gardens good kinds are 'Summer Pascal,' and 'Tall Golden Self Blanching.'

Chard, Swiss. This grows much like beets, but is used for greens. Because it tolerates heat and has a long season, it is more practical than spinach in most places. Use outer leaves first. 'Lucullus' is a good kind.

Corn, sweet. Until you have this from your own patch, picked while the cooking water is already boiling, you haven't tasted sweet corn at its best. Open 4-inch furrows for the seeds, and as plants grow, gradually fill in soil with the cultivator. Put three or more rows together to get good pollination. If you make four successive plantings ten days apart you will harvest corn for six weeks or more. Ears are ready when the silks start to dry and kernels show milky juice if broken. To get a whopping crop, fertilize soil before planting with 5-20-20, 3 pounds per 100 square feet. Good home garden kinds: 'Golden Cross Bantam' (eighty days), 'North Star' (sixty-seven days), 'Iochief' (eighty-five days).

Cucumber. Plenty of fertilizer pays off with cucumbers. Use 2 pounds of 10-10-10, or something similar, to each 100 square feet and work it in before planting seeds. Good home varieties: 'Smoothie,' and 'Burpee's Hybrid' (for slicing); 'National Pickling' (for pickles).

Eggplant. This needs a long growing season, plenty of water, and warm weather. Good garden kinds are 'Black Beauty' (matures in eighty days after transplanting) and 'Black Magic Hybrid' (matures in seventy-two days). Use ground that has not grown other eggplants, tomatoes, or potatoes for several years. They all belong to the same family and get the same diseases.

Kohlrabi. This is a cool weather crop like cabbage but it's usually seeded where it's to grow. It tastes like cabbage, too. You can transplant seedlings thinned from your rows, if you like. Keep them watered and cultivated. Good kinds are 'White Vienna' (fifty-five days) and 'Purple Vienna' (sixty-two days).

Lettuce, leaf. Ten feet of leaf lettuce is enough for an average family. It does not last long because oncoming warm weather makes it go to seed, and then the leaves become bitter. Rather than a lot of one kind, plant a little of several, for variety in spring salads. Good kinds: 'Oakleaf,' 'Simpson's Curled,' 'Salad Bowl,' 'Ruby,' 'Slobolt.' They all mature in forty to forty-five days.

Lettuce, butterhead. This is the name for the small loose headed kinds. One head makes a delectable salad just as is. Leaves are smooth, tender, rich flavored, succulent. Heads are less than half the size of head lettuce. Where heat comes early, start seeds in coldframes or greenhouses or indoors six weeks ahead of planting time. If your summers stay cool, sow them where they are to grow. Good varieties are 'Bibb' (fifty-four days), 'White Boston' (seventy days), 'Sweetheart' (seventy-two days).

Lettuce, head. In hot summer regions this is the hardest kind to grow. Unless you have cool summers, start very early so round, firm heads can develop before hot weather. Good varieties: 'Mignonette' (sixty-five days), 'Great Lakes' (eighty-four days), 'Pennlake' (seventy-two days).

Muskmelon. Give these fertile, sandy soil. If you have long summers you can hardly fail with them. Most kinds take much room; they spread at least 4 feet each way. Melons are ripe when they part easily from the stem and when the blossom end indents slightly as you push on it. Good home kinds: 'Harvest Queen' (ninety days), 'Delicious 51' (eight-five days), 'Iroquois' (ninety days), 'Honey Rock' (eighty-eight days).

Okra. Indispensable in Creole sauces and good in soups and stews, okra is easy where summers are warm. Soak seed overnight before planting. A half dozen plants are ample for most families. Pick pods while young,

before seeds harden. Good kinds: 'Dwarf Green Early' (fifty days), 'Emerald' (fifty-five days).

Onions. You can grow onions three ways, from seeds, sets, or plantlets. Sets are favorites for spring eating onions. Grow from seed to get sets for next year and also to produce large bulb onions. For sets from seeds favorite kinds are 'Yellow Ebenezer' and 'White Ebenezer.' For bulbs from seeds good kinds are 'Elite,' and 'Yellow Sweet Spanish.' If you put out plantlets, you take what you can get from the garden store— probably they will be young seedlings of 'Yellow Sweet Spanish.' These are among the best onions for winter storing. Give onions light sandy soil; keep weeded but don't cultivate more than necessary. Throw soil up around spring onions with the cultivator to blanch the stems.

Parsnip. These roots improve with cold weather. Wait to dig until after several hard freezes. If you cover with a thick mulch you can leave them in the ground and use from the row all winter. Seed germinates slowly. To mark rows, scatter in a few radish seeds. Good kinds are 'All America,' 'Hollow Crown.'

Pea. The secret to raising prize peas is to harvest them before hot weather. Plant early and use quick maturing kinds. Good varieties: 'Alaska' (fifty-seven days from seed to maturity), 'Little Marvel' (sixty-four days), 'Laxton' (sixty-one days).

Pepper. These need warmth and a long season. Put them in a well-drained place in full sun. Good kinds are 'California Wonder' (matures in seventy-five days from transplanting); 'Ruby King' (sixty-eight days), and 'Yolo Wonder' (seventy-five days).

Potato. "Seeds" are blocky pieces of cut-up potatoes, each containing two eyes or growing points. Keep plants cultivated so soil is always loose. After tops turn brown, harvest by digging the hills with a spading fork. For small boiling potatoes, dig while tops are still green. Good kinds for using fresh are 'Irish Cobbler,' 'Triumph,' and 'Warba.' Good late kinds for storage are 'Green Mountain,' 'Katahdin,' and 'Kennebec.'

Pumpkin. See Squash.

Radish. You can grow delicious radishes

PLANTING GUIDE FOR THIRTY-SIX ANNUAL VEGETABLES

Name	When to plant seed	Seed depth (inches)	Distance apart (inches)	Distance between rows (inches)	TRANSPLANTS IN GARDEN			Remarks
					Distance apart (inches)	Distance between rows (inches)	When set out	
Bean, snap (bush)	After last frost date	$1\frac{1}{2}$	3	24-30				$\frac{1}{2}$ lb. seed to 50 feet of row.
Bean, lima (bush)	Week after last frost date	$1\frac{1}{2}$	4-5	30				$\frac{1}{2}$ lb. seed to 50 feet of row.
Bean, pole	On or after last frost date	$1\frac{1}{2}$	36	36-48				Needs trellis; 4 ounces seed to 75 feet of row.
Beet	3 weeks before last frost date	$\frac{1}{2}$	1(3*)	18-24				1 ounce seed to 100 feet of row.
Broccoli	(see Remarks)	$\frac{1}{4}$			18	30	4 weeks before frost-free date	Sow in coldframe or cool greenhouse 6 weeks before planting out time. Ounce of seed makes at least 4,000 plants.
Brussels sprouts	(see Remarks)	$\frac{1}{4}$			18	30	4 weeks before frost-free date	Sow same as broccoli; ounce seed makes nearly 5,000 plants.
Cabbage	(see Remarks)	$\frac{1}{4}$			18	24-30	4 weeks before frost-free date	Sow same as broccoli. Ounce seed makes nearly 5,000 plants.
Carrot	2 weeks before last frost date	$\frac{1}{4}$	$\frac{1}{4}$(1*)	18-24				$\frac{1}{4}$ ounce seed to 75 feet of row.
Cauliflower	(see Remarks)	$\frac{1}{4}$			18	30	4 weeks before frost-free date	Same as broccoli. Ounce of seed makes 4,000 plants.
Celery	(see Remarks)	$\frac{1}{8}$			4-6	30	2 weeks before frost-free date	Sow indoors 10 weeks before planting out time; $\frac{1}{16}$ ounce plants 100-foot row.
Corn	On or after last frost date	$1\frac{1}{2}$	12	30-36				Plant 3-4 seeds together, thin to 2 or 3 in each place; $\frac{1}{4}$ lb. seed sows 200-ft. row.
Cucumber	Week after last frost date	$\frac{3}{4}$	3(12*)	48-60				If in hills, 8-10 seeds thinned to 4, hills 3 feet apart. Ounce of seed plants 200 feet of row.

Eggplant	(see Remarks)	$\frac14$			30	36	1 week after last frost date	Sow indoors 8 weeks before planting out time; $\frac{1}{16}$ ounce plants 100 feet of row.
Kohlrabi	2-4 weeks before last frost date	$\frac14$	2(6-8*)	18-24				May also be started in coldframe and transplanted to garden; $\frac18$ oz. plants 100 feet of row.
Lettuce, leaf	4-6 weeks before frost-free date	$\frac14$	$\frac12$(2*)	16-20				$\frac14$ ounce sows 75- to 100-foot row.
Lettuce, head	(see Remarks)	$\frac14$	$\frac14$	18-24	8-12	20-24	2-3 weeks before frost-free date	Sow in coldframe 4 weeks before planting out time.
Melon (cantaloupe, muskmelon)	A week after last frost date	1	4(12*)	60-84				Or plant in hills of 3, spaced 5 feet apart; $\frac14$ oz. seed plants 100 foot row.
Mustard	2-4 weeks before frost-free date	$\frac18$	$\frac18$(6*)	10				Ounce of seed plants 100-foot row.
Okra	On or after last frost date	1	2(15*)	36				$\frac14$ ounce sows 100-foot row.
Onion (seeds)	2-4 weeks before frost-free date	$\frac12$	$\frac14$(3*)	18-24				$\frac14$ ounce sows 100-foot row.
Onion (sets)		$1\frac12$-2	3-4	18-24			4-6 weeks before frost-free date	1 lb. plants 50- to 75-foot row.
Parsley	4 weeks before frost-free date	$\frac14$	$\frac12$(2*)	18-24				$\frac14$ ounce plants 100-foot row.
Parsnip	4-6 weeks before frost-free date	$\frac12$	$\frac14$(3*)	18-24				$\frac14$ ounce plants 100-foot row.
Pea	4-6 weeks before frost-free date	1	2	30				8-12 ounces will plant 100-foot row.
Pepper	(see Remarks)	$\frac14$			15-24	30-36	1 week after last frost date	Sow seed indoors 6 weeks before planting out date; $\frac{1}{16}$ oz. furnishes enough plants for 100-foot row.

* thin to this distance.

PLANTING GUIDE FOR THIRTY-SIX ANNUAL VEGETABLES (continued)

Name	When to plant seed	Seed depth (inches)	Distance apart (inches)	Distance between rows (inches)	TRANSPLANTS IN GARDEN			Remarks
					Distance apart (inches)	Distance between rows (inches)	When set out	
Potato, Irish (tubers)	4-6 weeks before frost-free date	4	10	30				$\frac{1}{2}$ peck seed potatoes will plant 100-foot row.
Potato, Sweet	Week after last frost date				12	36	1 week after last frost date	
Pumpkin	On or after last frost date	1	6(24*)	72-120				Or plant in hills, 10 seeds thinned to 3 plants, space 10 feet apart; 1 ounce plants 100-foot row.
Radish	4 weeks before frost-free date	$\frac{1}{2}$	$\frac{1}{2}(1\frac{1}{2}*)$	12				$\frac{1}{4}$ ounce plants 50-foot row.
Spinach	4-6 weeks before frost-free date	$\frac{1}{2}$-1	$\frac{1}{2}(2*)$	18-24				$\frac{1}{4}$ ounce plants 100-foot row.
Squash, bush	On or after last frost date	1	6(24*)	48				Or plant hills of 10, thin to 3 plants, hills 4 feet apart; $\frac{1}{2}$ ounce plants 100-foot row.
Squash, vine	On or after last frost date	1	6(24*)	72-120				Or plant in hills like bush squash, space hills 6-10 feet apart; ounce plants 100-foot row.
Swiss chard	2-4 weeks before last frost date	$\frac{1}{2}$	$1\frac{1}{2}(3*)$	18-24				$\frac{1}{2}$ ounce seed plants 100-foot row.
Tomato	(see Remarks)	$\frac{1}{4}$			48	18-30, staked; 48 if unstaked	On or after last frost date	$\frac{1}{16}$ ounce plants 100-foot row. Sow seeds indoors 6 weeks before planting out date.
Turnip	4-6 weeks before frost-free date	$\frac{1}{2}$	$\frac{3}{4}(2-4*)$	18-24				Good fall crop. Sow in August; $\frac{1}{4}$ oz. plants 100-foot row.
Watermelon	Week after last frost date	1	6(24*)	72-96				Or plant in hills, 8 seeds thinned to 3 plants, 5 feet between hills; $\frac{1}{4}$ oz. seed plants 100-foot row.

* thin to this distance.

in spring and fall, but not in summer. A few feet of row is all you need at a time, but make succession plantings a week apart for three weeks in spring. White kinds are "hotter" than red ones. Fall varieties can take more heat, and grow slower. Good kinds: 'Scarlet Globe' (twenty to thirty days), 'Cherry Belle' (twenty to thirty days), 'White Icicle' (white, twenty-seven days), 'Chinese Rose' (for fall, fifty-two days).

Spinach. Plant as soon as you can work ground in an early part of your garden. Spinach does best if soil is slightly alkaline. Good kinds: 'Long Standing Bloomsdale' (ready in forty-two days), 'Early Hybrid 7' (thirty-seven days), 'America' (fifty days).

Squash. These and pumpkins grow alike; they need a long warm season and lots of space. Bush summer squash make fruits that you use fresh and can't store for any length of time. Pick them while they are immature and the skin is soft. You usually cook them skin and all. Good kinds: 'Seneca Prolific Hybrid' (yellow straightneck, fifty-one days), 'Early Golden Crookneck' (small, fifty-seven days), 'White Bush Scallop' (pie-shaped, sixty days), 'Black Beauty' (zucchini, cucumber-shaped, fifty-two days). Permit vine squash and pumpkins to ripen fully. They will store well into the winter, if they aren't permitted to freeze. Good vine or winter squash varieties are 'Blue Hubbard' (blue-gray oval, warty, 110 days), 'Butternut' (tan, bell-shaped, ninety-five days), 'Table Queen' (small green acorn, eighty-five days), 'Golden Delicious' (top-shaped marrow type, large, orange, one hundred days), 'Buttercup' (drum-shaped with knob at blossom end, one hundred days). The traditional pumpkin variety for home gardens is 'New England Pie' (110 days).

Tomato. When you transplant tomatoes to the garden, set them deep, to make heavy, thick roots. You can get large tomatoes earlier if you stake and prune vines, although pruning is not necessary to raise good tomatoes. Here's how to do it: Start when plant is 10 to 12 inches high and branches begin to develop. Select two or three stems low on the plant to keep. To remove the others, called suckers, pinch out each growth arising from the angle between main stem and leaf. These break out clean.

Don't confuse suckers with bloom stems which you want to keep. Continue pruning till midsummer, then let the plants go. Controlled this way, tomatoes are easy to keep staked and you can plant them as close together as two feet. Good varieties: 'Big Boy' and 'Burpeeana Early' (both hybrids), 'Rutgers,' 'Sioux' and 'Fireball' (for short seasons), 'Marglobe.' For novelty try cherry tomatoes—each plant makes hundreds of marble-size fruits.

Turnip. Usually a fall crop, planted in July or early August. If you plant in spring, start as early as you can stir the soil. Fresh new leaves are good for greens. Best kinds: 'Purple Top' (ready in fifty-five days), 'White Flat Dutch' (forty-six days), 'Just Right' (forty days).

Watermelon. These do well in warm, sandy soil, where the season is long and moisture is ample. To test a melon for ripeness, thump it with your finger. If it says "pink" it is still green—let it ripen a few more days. If it says "punk" it is probably ready to eat. Good kinds: 'Market Midget' (small, eighty-five days from seed), 'Sugar Baby' (small, eighty-six days), 'Kleckley's Sweet' (large, eighty-five days).

ELEVEN HERBS AND HOW TO GROW THEM

Among the delights of your kitchen garden are the herbs you can grow there. You need only a few to make cooking more adventuresome for the whole family. One row in the garden, or one small corner near the house is space enough with but one or two plants of most kinds. You can quick-dry the leaves of some for winter use, but the flavor is best if you use herbs fresh from the patch. For convenience, plant annual kinds separately from perennials. Most herbs grow well in poor, lime soil, in warm, sunny, dry places too barren for most other plants. Here are some of the most popular and easy to grow.

Chervil (*Anthriscus cerefolium*). Grow it as an annual, planting where you want it to be, in sun or part shade. Thin to 12 inches apart. It makes a small plant with flavor like mild licorice, and leaves are renowned for flavoring butter and cream sauces, egg dishes, stews, chicken, lettuce and potato salads.

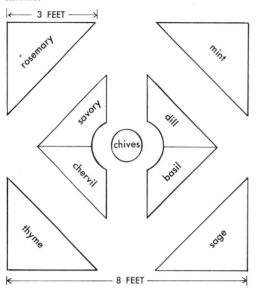

Fig. 47 An herb patch 8 feet square gives plenty of the basic herbs for flavoring, and is attractive besides.

Chives (*Allium schoenoprasum*). A hardy perennial, this has grasslike leaves 10 inches high with mild onion flavor. Mince the dark green tops into scrambled eggs, cheese dishes, salads, aspics, and sour cream. Slender stems form a dense clump. Propagate by dividing the clump. You can grow it easily from seeds, too. Flowers in May and June are little purple globes.

Dill (*Anethum graveolens*). Plant this annual where you want it, for it's hard to transplant. Afterwards it self-seeds. It has ferny foliage and umbrella-shaped flower heads, followed by seeds good for flavoring pickles. Minced fresh leaves are tasty in potato salad, soup, and cottage cheese. This is an easy herb and grows anywhere.

Mint (*Mentha* species). The one favored for mint jelly to serve with lamb is *Mentha spicata*. Use it also to garnish iced tea and other summer drinks. Propagate by divisions. It is an ultra-hardy perennial and tends to spread. Enclose it with a walk, or plant it in a tub or barrel to hem it in. It's one of the few "herbs" that will grow in semi-shade.

Parsley (*Petroselinum crispum*). For garnishes, salads and flavoring you need only about eight plants. Seeds may be slow to germinate. To speed things, soak them first overnight. In mild winters plants may live over to the second year. Good varieties are 'Paramount,' and 'Moss Green Curled.'

Rosemary (*Rosemarinus officinalis*). Although perennial, north of Zone 7 this is safest grown in a pot and wintered on a cool porch. The needle-like foliage is gray-green and pungently scented. Use leaves to flavor omelets and scrambled eggs, bread, bland soups, meat loafs, and vegetable dishes. Start it from seeds sown early indoors; transplant to light, dry soil in open sunny ground or pots. Propagate by seeds or cuttings or layer it. Seeds are slow to germinate.

Sage (*Salvia officinalis*). This is used to flavor sausage, veal, pork dressings, cheese and vegetable dishes, poultry, and stews. It is a gray-leafed slow perennial shrub, with blue or lavender flowers in slender spikes. You can grow it from seed or cuttings. Start seeds early indoors. Set plants about 8 inches apart. For flavoring use young stems and leaves, either fresh or dried.

Sweet basil (*Ocimum basilicum*). Annual with a tangy aromatic flavor. Leaves are good cut up in salads, soups, stews, and especially cooked tomatoes. 'Dark Opal' is a new purple leaf variety. Plants are 18 to 24 inches high, bushy, with small mint-like flowers in summer. Plant seeds in warm loamy soil, indoors or out, and separate to stand 12 inches apart.

Tarragon (*Artemisia dracunculus*). Perennial, with leaves that taste slightly like anise. Use them to flavor beef and pork, fish, salads and vinegar. Propagate it by cuttings which root readily, or by dividing the roots in early spring. Space plants 18 inches apart. Give it humusy well-drained soil. In moist soil it often winterkills. Where winters are cold pile earth over plants in fall and cover with straw; or winter them in a coldframe.

Thyme (*Thymus vulgaris*). This is a perennial but is slightly tender. It often winterkills. Sow seeds 8 inches apart in a special partly shaded and moist seedbed in April or May. Transplant to a sunny spot with 4-inch spacing. Light, limy soil is best. Use thyme in fish dishes, cheese, potatoes, chicken, stews, meats, soups, and sauces. Mulch the plant in December with evergreen boughs to prevent thaws from pushing it out of the soil. Give it perfect drainage.

HOW TO KEEP YOUR GARDEN GROWING

Once your kitchen garden is up and flourishing, try to keep it that way. *Follow a few easy upkeep methods.*

Thinning. Things like lettuce, radishes, beets, carrots, melons, turnips, always come up thicker than they should remain. You want them that way, to insure a good stand, but as soon as all are up, go through them with a hoe or use your fingers to remove extras. The thinnings of leafy crops like lettuce, spinach, and beets make tasty salads, so they are not wasted. Thinning is hard at first because you hate to pull anything up, but do it anyway. Only by thinning do you give little plants a full chance to become big and productive.

Watering. If rain fails to come about once a week in goodly amount, it's up to you to water at least parts of your garden. Everything suffers in drouth, but some plants like tomatoes are especially damaged if moisture is short when they are producing flowers and fruit. *The most efficient way to water is in trenches beside the rows.* Run the trench full of water and keep it that way two or three hours until the soil is saturated *at least 6 inches down,* and a few inches to each side. This works well only if the ground is fairly level or your rows are on a contour. In sloping rows, you can accomplish the same thing by using a canvas or perforated soil-soaker that distributes water gently. *The point is to water thoroughly each time, and then refrain from watering again for a week.*

Run the sprinkler to offset spring drouth that causes soil to crust on ground you've just seeded. Run a misty spray each day to keep soil soft while seedlings are emerging.

Fertilizing. Everything going out and nothing coming in depletes even rich soil. As soon as one season's garden closes, think about the soil for next year. If you concentrate on maintaining humus in the soil, the battle is nearly won. You can do this by spreading compost from your compost pile; or by putting on humus you buy (like peat moss). You can make compost right in the soil by digging in plant tops, grass clippings and even vegetable peelings and non-oily discards from the kitchen. Or spread leaves raked from your yard and plow them under in fall. By spring all of these will have broken down into soft humus. The finishing touch in spring is to spread a balanced fertilizer, like 8-8-8, 10 pounds to 1,000 square feet, just before you plow or spade the ground.

As the season goes along, fertilize crops that need it with light side dressings of the same kind. Tomatoes benefit from this sort of feeding in midsummer. Just scatter the fertilizer in a thin ribbon along the row, lightly hoe it in and then water.

HOW TO COPE WITH WEEDS

Weeds take the joy out of vegetable gardening, if you let them. They spoil the garden's looks, and by drawing on moisture and food, they cut down production. Aside from hand pulling and hoeing—the two most direct and reliable but time-consuming methods—the best way to cope with weeds is by cultivating and mulching.

Cultivating. This means loosening the soil surface—do it with blades fastened on wheel tools or on a handle like a hoe. Cultivating destroys weeds while they are tiny and also makes a loose soil layer that helps conserve moisture and lets rain sink in. In gardens of any size, cultivating is the preferred way to keep weeds down. It goes on all summer, after each hard rain, as soon as the soil dries enough not to ball against the blade.

Mulching. For a big garden with rows far apart and with large-growing crops like tomatoes, squash, melons and lima beans, mulching is a laborsaving method to keep down weeds, and it does great things for your soil, too. Put down a thick layer of spoiled hay, straw (seed-free), chopped cornstalks, grass cuttings, partially-rotted tree leaves, or ground corncobs. To smother weed growth, make the mulch 4 to 5 inches thick. Before applying, cultivate the soil and spread fertilizer, something high in nitrogen like 10-6-4, 1 pound to 150 square feet, to replace that absorbed by decomposition of the mulch. Heap mulch thickly in the centers of rows, but don't let it lie close to the growing stems or it may rot or smother them. Where rainfall is adequate or you water freely, an organic mulch like this both keeps down weeds and saves soil from drying out; and it makes the earth soft and humusy. You may not like the looks of a deep mulch in a small kitchen garden, and it's hard to handle in narrow rows. If your rainfall is naturally scanty, abandon the idea, for the mulch instead of the soil will take the little rain that falls.

Black polyethylene sold for mulch will keep down weeds, too. It also warms the soil for tender things like sweet corn, tomatoes and peppers. With transplants, lay the plastic first and cut holes in it as you set out the plants. For corn, lay the strip beside the row after plants are up.

HOW TO COPE WITH INSECTS AND DISEASES

Trouble control for vegetables is different from that on ornamental plants. For with vegetables your main concern is having food that is safe to eat; also vegetables have a somewhat separate set of problems.

Your greatest help is the multipurpose vegetable dust. This contains ingredients that take care of most insects and diseases. Such dusts are sold under countless trade names. Read the label to see what is included, what you can use the dust on, precautions to follow. Most such dusts contain malathion, methoxychlor, Sevin, rotenone and sometimes pyrethrum. These are all fairly safe for vegetable crops. If there is also included a fungicide like captan or zineb, so much the better.

Play safe with insecticides. Here are a few *don'ts* to observe with insecticides for vegetables:

Don't use sulfur on squash, melons, pumpkins, or cucumbers.

Don't use aerosol spray "bombs" on to-matoes—the propellant gas may injure foliage.

Don't use DDT on squash, melons, or pumpkins.

Some insecticides you use on lawn and ornamentals are not safe at all around home vegetables. Avoid these:

Dieldrin

Aramite

Heptachlor

Sodium selenate (better keep this out of your compost pile, too)

Use these only early in the season before food parts begin to form:

DDT

Chlordane

Lindane (or BHC)

Use these through the growing season, *except in the seven days just before the harvest:*

malathion

methoxychlor

Sevin

You can use these up to three days before harvest, *if you wash* the vegetables well before eating:

rotenone

sulfur

sabadilla dust

nicotine sulfate

pyrethrum

EASY-DOES-IT IDEAS

Mix a little radish seed in with the parsley when you plant. Radishes come right up to mark the row for the slow-starting parsley; and when you pull them, you automatically thin out the parsley row just right.

If some of your new tomato plants meet with disaster—cutworm or hail—replace them with "slips" from the survivors. Break off suckers 6 inches long, plant them shoulder-deep in the soil where you want them, drench with water and shade with paper caps. Three out of four will root and grow.

Plant pumpkins and vining squash hills in your sweet corn patch. The corn gets out of the way just in time to let the expanding squash take over.

COMMON VEGETABLE PESTS AND HOW TO CONTROL THEM

Host and pest	Damage	Control
BEANS, lima, snap, pole		
Mexican bean beetle	Underneath sides of leaves eaten away	Dust or spray with rotenone, malathion, Sevin or methoxychlor.
Bean leaf beetle	Holes eaten in leaves	Dust or spray with rotenone or DDT.
Leaf hoppers	Leaf tips turn brown	Dust undersides with methoxychlor, malathion, DDT.
BROCCOLI	See cabbage	
BRUSSELS SPROUTS	See cabbage	
CABBAGE		
Harlequin bugs (oval, black, red, and yellow)	Browned areas on leaves, plants wilt	Dust with sabadilla or hand pick.
Imported cabbage worm, cabbage looper	Eat holes in leaves	Dust with rotenone 1% dust weekly.
Cabbage yellows disease (wilt)	Plant turns yellowish, stunted, lopsided, won't head properly	Use resistant varieties; plant in new location.
CARROT		
Wireworms	Tunnels burrowed in root	Fumigate soil with commercial fumigant two weeks before planting, or apply 5% chlordane dust to soil, 2 lbs. to 1,000 sq. ft.
CAULIFLOWER	See cabbage	
CELERY		
Celery leaf tier	Leaves webbed together; hole tunneled into hearts	Dust young plants with 5% DDT. Near harvest use pyrethrum.
CORN, sweet		
Corn earworm	Tunnels eaten in tip of ear	Spray silks with DDT solution ($\frac{1}{2}$ cup 25% DDT emulsion to 1 gallon water) soon after they emerge.
European corn borer	Holes eaten in stalks, ears	Spray with DDT, 2 T. wettable powder per gallon of water.
CUCUMBER		
Striped and spotted cucumber beetles	Holes in leaves, roots, stem. Plant wilts, may die.	Dust weekly with 1% rotenone or 5% methoxychlor.
EGGPLANT		
Colorado potato beetle	Leaves eaten off	Dust with 5% DDT.
Aphids	Leaves curl, turn yellow	Spray with nicotine sulfate, or malathion.
Fruit rot	Brown, shrunken spots on stem, leaves, or fruit	Use resistant varieties.
Wilt	Plant gradually wilts, stunts, perhaps dies	Plant each year in new spot that has not grown eggplant, tomato or potato.

Host and pest	Damage	Control
KOHLRABI	See cabbage	
MUSKMELON Striped and spotted cucumber beetles	See cucumber	
Melon aphids	Leaves wilt and curl	Spray underneath of leaves with nicotine sulfate or malathion.
ONION Thrips	White blotches on leaves, tips wither and brown	Spray with malathion or 10% DDT.
PEA Aphids	Plants stunted, pods misshapen	Nicotine sulfate or 1% rotenone dust or malathion spray.
Fusarium wilt	Leaves yellow, plants wilt, die	Use resistant varieties.
PEPPER Cutworms	New plants cut off	Protect with paper collar or circle of chlordane dust.
POTATO Colorado potato beetle	See eggplant	
Blister beetle	Leaves are eaten	Hand pick (wear gloves) or dust with 5% DDT or 5% methoxychlor.
RADISH Flea beetle	Small holes eaten in leaves	Dust with 1% rotenone.
SPINACH Flea beetle	See radish	
Aphids	Leaves curled, distorted, yellow	Spray with nicotine sulfate or malathion.
SQUASH Striped and spotted cucumber beetles	See cucumber	
Squash bugs	Juice sucked from leaves, plants wilt and die	Hand pick the first you see; dust with sabadilla.
TOMATO Tomato hornworm	Foliage eaten away	Hand pick
Cutworms	See pepper	
Tomato fruitworm (same as corn earworm)	Holes eaten in fruit	Dust with 10% DDT starting when plants are young, stopping 10 days before harvest.
TURNIP Flea beetles	See radish	
Harlequin bug	See cabbage	
WATERMELON	See muskmelon	

PART IV

CARE AND INCREASE
OF YOUR GARDEN PLANTS

Chapter 21

WHY AND HOW TO PRUNE TREES AND SHRUBS

Isn't pruning a pretty complex business?

Pruning is not difficult nor mysterious once you get firmly in mind the purpose behind it. You prune for these purposes: To make a plant look better and bloom better, to keep it healthy, to limit its size to your space, to repair damage, to remove dead or extra wood, and in the case of a fruit tree, to make it bear better. You cut a limb off a tree if it is too low, or makes the tree lopsided, or threatens to break, or is diseased. You prune plants you are just setting out to get branches where you want them, and to reduce the number of leaves until roots are established to support them.

Except when you remove dead wood, think of pruning as a way to channel growth where you want it. All plants do most of their growing at the tips. This is because hormones (or *auxins*) produced there draw nutrients to the tips. If you remove these ends by pruning, the food flows to other points down the stem, to buds or smaller branches. They then begin to grow, or grow faster. Although methods vary, depending on kinds of trees and shrubs, on sizes and seasons, this one fact of plant growth guides almost all pruning operations. Don't be afraid to prune. Pruning helps plants in many ways. Just have a good reason in mind before you start cutting, and keep it uppermost as you proceed.

ESSENTIAL TOOLS FOR PRUNING AND HOW TO USE THEM

In pruning around your yard you are bound to need these five items:

(1) Hand pruners. Small enough to fit in your hand, these are for light pruning of roses, brambles, grapes and small shrubs. There are two types. One has a sharp blade which passes a hooked holding blade. The other has a sharp blade which comes against a flat "anvil." Both are good. Buy the very best quality. And don't ever lend them! Hide them between use. Properly treated, good hand pruners last for years. Mistreated, used on too large growth, they hardly last a season.

With either type, when you cut a small branch from a larger one, put the anvil or holding hook at the top, so the cutting blade moves up against it.

(2) Loppers. These are long-handled pruning shears that cut branches slightly over an inch through. The best kinds have long steel handles that won't break or spring out of line. These are better than wooden handles. Use the loppers for branches too big for hand pruners. When removing a branch, put the cutting edge below, and the hook in the crotch, so the blade moves upward. This avoids binding and tearing bark.

(3) Hand saw. Made for pruning, with coarse teeth that take a wide bite and don't

144 Hand pruners are probably the most used pruning tool—use them for small branches. This is the anvil type. *Smith*

145 Loppers will handle branches as large as one and a quarter inches thick. *Smith*

146 You'll need a pruning saw to cut limbs too big for the loppers. It is a coarse-toothed kind that does not clog or bind. *Smith*

clog, it should have a cutting edge on just one side. If it's slightly curved it gets into tighter corners. Use it to cut off limbs too big for your loppers. For small limbs, simply start cutting at the crotch where branch meets trunk and cut downward. If there is danger of tearing the bark, first make a short upward cut from underneath.

(4) Hedge shears. You need these to trim light growth of junipers, arborvitae and hedges, where you want an even sheared effect. They will not cut twigs over pencil thickness. Electric hedge shears are labor-saving for large trees or hedges. Hold shears parallel to the surface you are shearing and steadily move along it. Anything that sticks out gets cut off.

(5) Tree-wound dressing. You can apply this with a brush, or with a handy spray can. Don't use creosote or tar, which are toxic. Use this dressing to cover cuts bigger than a quarter. It prevents entry of bacteria and fungus. Apply it thickly and thoroughly.

SOME PRUNING WORDS

Thinning. Removing branches completely to larger branch, trunk or ground.
Heading. Cutting branches back to buds.
Leader. The longest central branch.
Suckers. Soft, straight, leafy, non-flowering growths from the base or lower part of plant, sometimes induced by too much pruning. Root suckers on grafted or budded plants like roses and dwarf fruits may look and grow differently from the tops.
Pinching. Removing soft young growth by snipping it off between your index finger and thumb nail.

PRUNING TREES

If your trees are ancient giants, call on a "tree man" to prune them. Without proper equipment, you take hair-raising risks and cannot do a proper job. Young trees, and small kinds, you can prune yourself. Remember that a limb once removed cannot be replaced. So think twice before you take

it off. When you are up in the tree, it helps to have someone stand back at a distance to guide the operation (but don't pick a screamer!).

After you've pruned a tree it is as sound as it was before if you do not leave places for disease or decay to enter. That is the reason you *always cut back to firm live wood,* and cover large cuts with a protective dressing to keep out insects and rot. Cuts less than an inch across will heal the first year and don't need dressing. Big scars take years to heal and need painting every year or so, especially if it's a really valuable old tree.

THE RIGHT TIME TO PRUNE

Prune most deciduous trees almost any time of year, with a few notable exceptions. Winter and early spring are good times to prune, because the leaves are off and you can clearly see the framework. Also you don't have foliage to contend with. But summer and fall will do too, unless you remove so much that the plant starts producing soft shoots that winterkill. Don't fall prune anything you think is slightly tender in your climate.

The big exceptions are maples, birches and walnuts. Prune these in late summer after the sap slows down. They bleed too much if you prune them in spring. Also, don't prune spring-blooming trees like flowering crabs and cherries in fall. Prune these right *after* they bloom so as not to reduce next year's crop of flowers.

Prune evergreens, both needles and broad-leafs, lightly in spring just before growth begins or soon after.

HOW TO CUT BACK A BRANCH

When you prune a branch look to its future. The buds or little branches along the sides *are* the future for that branch. In pruning it back, always cut *just beyond* a bud, or *just beyond* a smaller branch, to leave a way for it to grow. "Dehorning" of trees—the unselective topping of tree limbs —is not pruning, it is mutilation. The bare stubs that remain have no future at all, except to be concealed by the thicket of water-sprouts that usually rise from below.

HOW TO REMOVE A TREE LIMB

To avoid tearing bark when a heavy limb falls, make three saw cuts, not one: first, *a foot out* from where the limb joins the trunk, saw upward until the saw binds. Next, 2 inches beyond the first cut, saw downward until the limb falls, snapping off clean. Finally, remove the stub by sawing downward close to the main trunk. Support the stub with one hand so it can't tear bark. This leaves an oval-shaped cut which new bark will cover. Paint it with tree dressing. *Never leave a stub.* The tree cannot heal it over. Instead, the stump dies back into the tree, starting a pocket of rot.

HOW TO MEND BARK DAMAGE

Where bark has been torn or cut, reshape the wound so it can heal fast. Bark grows in quickly from the sides, but slowly from top or bottom. With this in mind, chisel edges back to unloosened bark and shape the exposed part like a tall oval, pointed above and below. Then paint it with tree-wound dressing.

HOW TO PRUNE TREES WHEN PLANTING

Small trees that are bare root—that is, without an earth ball—need cutting back of tops to compensate for roots lost. Take off about half the total length of all the branches. Cut out some side branches entirely. Leave remaining ones widely spaced and evenly balanced around the stem, and shorten them, cutting off one-third of their length. If it's a tree with a leader (central upright branch) don't cut that back unless you want to force out more branches below. If the upright piece is merely an unbranched whip, then do top it at the distance up the stem where you want branches to appear.

Watch young trees develop, looking for signs of trouble. If you see branches competing with the central leader, cut them out; branches too near the ground, cut them off; branches emerging too close to one another on the trunk, thin them; branches that rub, remove the weaker or less well-placed one.

PRUNE THESE WITH RESTRAINT

Dead or broken wood is all you should prune from magnolias, since the bark is unusually slow to heal. Never cut into it unless you have to. But it is all right to remove suckers from around the base. Flowering dogwood is another slow healer. Cut off only small branches.

Flowering crabapples, cherries and plums usually need little pruning except occasional thinning to improve their looks. After a year or two you may want to remove one or two low limbs so you can mow beneath, and also remove suckers from the center of the tree.

PRUNING NEEDLE EVERGREENS

Needle evergreens are of two kinds: those with whorled branches (pines, spruces and firs) and all the others (juniper, yew, arborvitae, chamaecyparis, hemlock) with growth of different patterns.

They all need pruning to keep them shapely, and the best time is early spring just before or soon after growth starts. New growth then soon covers your pruning cuts. If you prune a little every year, you will never need to do any drastic cutting.

Prune whorled evergreens by shortening the new shoots or "candles." This slows down upward and outward growth and makes the plant compact. You can do this pruning with your fingers in mid-spring, when new needles start to show on the candles, or new growth appears at the end of each branch. Don't pinch candles back to less than 2 inches. Select carefully which to shorten and which to leave—with the idea of making the whole plant symmetrical, filling up gaps and checking too-rampant branches.

You can cut back older side branches of these trees too, but not below the previous year's growth. On these whorled evergreens, buds for future branches do not break out except on nearly new wood. If you cut back too far into a pine, spruce or fir you will stop growth in that area entirely.

Needle evergreens without whorled branches are easy to prune because new

147 To remove a large limb, make three cuts in this order. Never leave a stub to rot.
Illinois Natural History Survey

148 Repair damaged bark by shaping the wound into a tall pointed oval, and painting it with tree wound dressing. *Illinois Natural History Survey*

growth comes from side buds as well as at the ends of twigs. If an upright juniper, arborvitae or yew has grown too tall, you

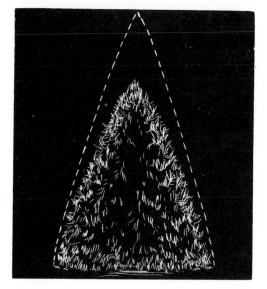

Fig. 48 If an upright juniper has grown too tall, cut off a fourth to a third of its height and shape remaining foliage to a point.

can top off a fourth to a third, shape the remaining top to a point or however you want it, and have a tree that looks much

younger. In a season the topped look disappears.

To save time, you can shear junipers, arborvitaes and even hemlocks with hedge clippers to keep them dense and in bounds.

Fig. 49 Shorten individual branches of juniper or arborvitae by cutting the main stem above one or two lateral branches.

Esthetic gardeners frown on this practice because it makes the trees look artificial, but it is better than no pruning at all. The ideal way is to use hand pruners to head back individual branches and keep plants looking natural. This is especially worthwhile on pfitzer junipers and yews whose charm lies in the feathery foliage. Don't shear them into boxy shapes unless you want a hedge. Leave some foliage on each branch of all needle evergreens. Cutting beyond the foliage may kill the branch. And don't remove lower branches unless you are really ready to settle for a high tree. The plant cannot replace lower limbs, and will ever afterward stand bare-legged, not always a pretty sight!

HOW TO PRUNE BROADLEAFS

Broadleaf evergreens, like the hollies, need less pruning than other shrubs. You can shear boxwood, euonymus and small-leaf hollies. American and English holly, azaleas, rhododendrons, camellias, pieris, leucothoe, and practically all the other broadleafs can stand a small amount of pruning. Don't cut branches back farther than there are leaves, or at least plump leaf buds. Cutting Scotch broom (*Cytisus*) back into brown wood will probably kill it.

When you cut American and English holly for Christmas greens you are trimming about all that is necessary. There is no harm in cutting these in winter, since blooms the next year, and subsequent berries, come on new wood. Avoid fall or winter cutting of rhododendron, pieris, azaleas or mountain laurel for you will lose bloom buds that are already formed for the next year. Prune these evergreens *after* they bloom except for any winter-killed growth.

Pinch off seed clusters that form after flowering on rhododendrons and azaleas, particularly on newly-set plants.

HOW TO PRUNE SHRUBS

In time, all but dwarf shrubs will overgrow their space, or old wood will make them look bad, so you will need to prune them occasionally. Prune those that flower in the spring, like lilacs, deutzia and beauty bush, right after blooming. Later pruning sacrifices the flowers of the next season, since you are removing new buds that form early in summer. You can prune late bloomers—althaea, pink and red spiraeas, peegee hydrangea, hydrangea 'Hills of Snow' and mimosa (*Albizzia julibrissin*)—in early spring before growth starts.

SPRING PRUNING FOR GRADUAL RENEWAL

With many flowering shrubs like Van Houtte spiraea, forsythia and mockorange, the best system is to prune for renewal. This means removing each spring, right after flowering, a few of the oldest and largest canes at the very base of the plant. Leave enough so the shrub keeps its form and has sufficient old or mature wood left to bloom

Fig. 50   To renew shrubs like spiraea and lilac, cut out oldest and largest canes at the base each spring, leaving the plant thinner and smaller. Before, above; after, below.

next year. Forsythia, for instance, blooms best on three-year-old wood. Head back long branches just above a side branch or good bud. Cut out suckers in the middle of the plant or coming out around the base, except strong ones you want to save to replace old branches you are discarding. Other shrubs to prune this same way are beauty bush, tatarian honeysuckle, weigela, caragana, kerria, ninebark, flowering almond, shrub roses, and viburnums.

Treat lilacs about the same except that in heading back tall lilac branches, take special care to save the most vigorous growers, for they will give the next year's bloom. Take off the weak and spindling growth. For good looks and if you have time, cut off dead flower heads—but only to their point of growth. Lilacs will go on blooming well even if seed heads remain.

DRASTIC PRUNING TO THE GROUND

Even with annual pruning, severe measures are sometimes called for with shrubs. Perhaps the most extreme is cutting them almost to the ground and letting them grow new tops. This succeeds with honeysuckle, philadelphus, Van Houtte spiraea and the pink spiraeas, deutzia, privet, tamarix, and red and yellow stemmed dogwoods. Give a shrub such treatment no oftener than once every five or six years, and *then* only if you think it is the only remedy, or if the shrub has outgrown its location and must be moved.

TO REMOVE DIE-BACK

Some shrubs often die back in winter. These include callicarpa, buddleia, vitex, kerria, caryopteris, abelia, and crape-myrtle.

Fig. 51 Kinds like caryopteris and buddleia that die back in winter need to be cut to the ground in spring.

They may be growing a little north of their range, and need heavy pruning in spring to remove dead wood. In some areas you may need to cut them to the ground as a routine part of spring cleanup. They swiftly grow a new top.

TOPIARY FORMS AND PLEACHING

Topiary work consists of clipping and training plants so they resemble sculpture —geometric shapes like globes or triangles or natural figures of animals. This ancient gardening craft has had its ups and downs. With the rise of patio-living, topiary trees are coming back again for use in pocket gardens. You can see good examples in the gardens at Colonial Williamsburg.

To make topiary forms, first determine the shape you want. Then work toward it by consistent trimming. Sometimes you may have to splint branches to grow in directions where they would not naturally go. Most topiaries are developed over a period of several years. The upkeep is never finished.

Plants best adapted are yew, boxwood, and privet. You can clip junipers into a rough sort of topiary, but thin spots often appear. Arborvitae is sometimes used. For miniature topiaries a good plant is rosemary. The bay tree (*Laurus nobilis*) is a favorite topiary subject in southern gardens.

Pleaching is a method of pruning and training trees into tall narrow interwoven hedges. You can even draw opposite rows together at the top to form an arch. This makes a pleasant covered walk, perhaps with a fountain or bench at the end, or a place to display statuary. Good pleaching makes a striking garden feature but requires years to develop. It is a feature for a large place and for someone who has plenty of time—or plenty of help.

Many kinds of trees can be pleached. Beech, privet and hawthorn are three. Plant them 2 feet apart, remove all front and back branches flush with the trunk, leaving only side branches. Weave these loosely together. As the plants grow, remove all branches except those parallel with the row. To form an arch pull the tops together and tie them loosely as soon as they are high enough.

317

Keep on with the weaving until you can re-move the ties and the arch supports itself. But if you have heavy snow in your area, prop the arch from below in winter to pre-vent breakage. Trim your arbor twice a sea-son to maintain it.

EASY-DOES-IT IDEAS

Take the lowest limbs from your pin oak while they are small enough to cut with loppers, and work upward gradually as the tree grows. You'll want to be able to walk under it.

Remove limbs too big for loppers but still fairly small with one saw cut instead of three. First make an upward slash through the bark from below to keep bark from peel-ing down.

Brush from your hedge and shrub prun-ing is useful in your garden. Stick short twiggy lengths along your row of peas to hold up the vines; or long branches for sweet peas to climb on; or place them to support baby's-breath in the flower garden. They can also be placed on the ground to mark off newly seeded areas. *Almost* every-one will see and respect such a barrier.

Chapter 22

HOW TO KEEP TREES IN GOOD CONDITION

Do I have to hire a specialist to take care of my trees?

Trees are the most important element in your garden picture. They add value and livability to your property; give you shade or color or both; and make your place look better in dozens of ways. They deserve good care.

If they are venerable giants, you may occasionally need a well equipped tree man to take proper care of them. This is certainly true for cabling of high limbs, repairing of bad breaks, or spraying for insects or disease. You can probably manage the care of young trees and small-growing kinds, and this does save you money.

Let's have a look now at the needs of trees large and small, aside from their pruning just discussed in Chapter 21.

HOW TO CARE FOR NEW TREES

New trees need staking. Practically all kinds need staking at first to keep the wind from loosening them in the soil. Stake when you plant the tree.

For trees more than 2 inches thick, use three guy wires. Anchor these to stakes driven in the ground around the tree at distances to make an equal-sided triangle. Where the wires touch the trunk (just above a lower limb) run them through a section of old hose. Then the wire won't cut into the bark. Tighten the wires so there is ten-

sion enough to hold the tree almost rigid in a gale.

For smaller trees, under 2 inches in diameter, thrust a tall stake into the ground

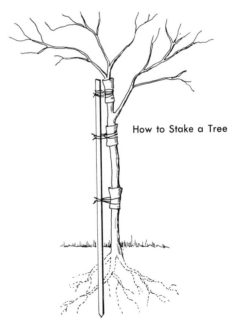

How to Stake a Tree

Fig. 52 Stake small trees by setting a strong stake beside the trunk and tying in two or three places.

close to the trunk. Get a stake stronger than the tree. A piece of 2 x 2 lumber will do. Make it long enough so you can sink it 2 feet deep and still have enough above ground to reach halfway up the tree. In two or three places, tie trunk to stake with

319

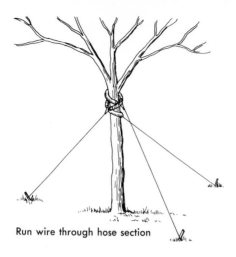

Run wire through hose section

Fig. 53 Large trees, newly planted, need guying three ways. Run wire through hose sections to prevent it from biting into bark.

strips of soft wide tough cloth. Let these circle the trunk several times to pad it.

Or, for a small tree, place two tall stakes on opposite sides, each a foot or so away. Then loop the tree in a piece of double wire stretched between the stakes and protected at the trunk by sections of old hose. If the tree is planted balled and burlapped, set the stakes outside the earth ball.

Wrapping protects tender bark. Young trees that lose their leaves in winter have

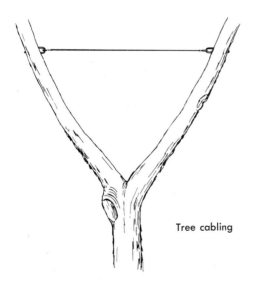

Tree cabling

Fig. 54 Tree cabling will save weak-crotched trees from splitting in wind storms.

thin bark—especially pin oaks, lindens and locusts. This is inclined to sun scald on the sunny side, so for the first two or three years it's a good idea to wrap the lower part of the trunk. Wrapping also discourages borers in birches and keeps mice and rabbits from nibbling bark. You can buy tree-wrap stripping in rolls at garden-supply stores.

Start at ground level and wrap spirally up the trunk to the lowest limb. Cut the wrapping off and fasten it there with a thumb tack, or tie it with a heavy rubber band. You can leave the wrap in place two or three years. By that time the bark should be thick enough to get by without protection.

New trees need watering. The first season after you plant a tree see that it has plenty of water. Unless rainfall is adequate, and it seldom is, water deeply every week. Don't give just a dribble but a real soaking that penetrates down 1 to 2 feet, depending on the size of the earth ball. Make a soil "dike" in a circle around the tree to catch the water; let a slow-running hose lie there for one to two hours.

HOW TO TAKE CARE OF OLD TREES

The older the tree the more valuable it is. You're fortunate if you have large trees. Neglecting them is a costly and irreparable mistake.

Feeding helps them. As a matter of principle, feed your trees occasionally. For average healthy trees, once every five years is a good frequency. What you scatter on the lawn is not enough. This is used by the grass before it gets to the tree roots. A tree reflects a need for feeding if its foliage seems small and thin. If it has met with weakening insect invasions, or several years of drouth, feeding and watering will help restore it to health. Small trees are easy to fertilize but large ones become a chore and you'll save blisters and backaches if you hire it done by someone with a power soil auger. Here is the method:

Drill or punch (with soil auger or crowbar) holes 18 inches deep, 24 inches apart, in concentric circles around the tree. Make the outer circle a few feet beyond the overhang of the tree's branches. This is about as far as the feeding roots extend. Let each inner circle come 2 feet closer to the trunk. For big trees—those with 2-foot trunks—allow 12 feet from tree trunk to the nearest ring of holes; for smaller trees, proportionately less.

Figure how much fertilizer the tree needs this way: Allow 2 pounds of 12-6-4 (12 per cent nitrogen, 6 per cent phosphorus, 4 per cent potash) or a similar mixture, for each inch of trunk diameter measured at chest height. Give young trees (those less than 6 inches through) about half as much. When you have arrived at the total number of pounds, count the feeding holes you've opened. Divide pounds by holes to see how much to put in each hole. After feeding refill soil in holes, and water the area long and hard.

A simpler way, and effective if you do it thoroughly, is to use a soil-feeding needle connected to your garden hose. These devices are called root feeders. They contain a chamber at the top for inserting fertilizer pellets which the water washes into the soil. Insert the needle as deep as it will go; let the water run until it bubbles up around the shaft. Then move the feeder to a new location a foot or two away. Section off the root area so you are sure to cover it thoroughly.

Mechanical repairs. Only occasionally can you do these yourself. Most times, it's best to have a tree man make them. But it helps to know what can be done to save trees that are in mechanical trouble.

Cabling and bracing. Keep your eye on trees developing weak V-crotches. The older and heavier the two sides become, the more likely they are to split apart in a wind and send one side crashing down. Before this happens, have the tree cabled. This consists of running a steel cable between the two limbs high up in the tree. The cable is fastened to eye-bolts run through each branch parallel to the direction of pull. Installing these is not expensive, and far cheaper than cleaning up the debris if the tree splits apart. Your tree man may think the crotch also needs bracing near the base. In this case, he drills through the major limbs or the trunk and inserts a long bolt

or two to draw the split together and hold it.

Tree cavities. On large trees this is hardly a do-it-yourself job, but on small ones it's within your capability. There are three reasons for filling tree cavities: (1) to stop decay; (2) to make a smooth surface that bark can heal over; and (3) to improve the appearance. It does little or nothing to strengthen a tree, and the job is expensive because it takes so much time. You can justify it only when you value the tree very highly and when its life is actually in danger.

These are the main steps in cavity filling: (1) Chisel out the decayed part back to reasonably sound wood, clean out the chips and chisel smooth the edge of the hole right up to live bark. (2) Shape the hole to points at top and bottom so it will heal faster. (3) Cover the inside of the cavity with tree paint. (4) Mix a stiff "filling" of two parts sand and one part cement with just enough water to stick it together. (5) Press the filling in firmly, a little at a time, inserting roofing paper dividers every 5 inches upward. (6) Smooth up the surface exactly to the base of live bark *but not over it.* (7) After cement dries, cover it with tree paint.

A tree is not a clothesline pole. Don't tie wires or chains around trees and forget to remove them. This causes a lot of trouble. Wire clotheslines, fences, chains for attach-

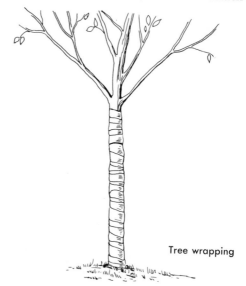

Tree wrapping

Fig. 55 Wrap trunks of thin-barked trees to protect against winter sun scald and gnawing by mice and rabbits.

321

ing swings and hammocks are some of the frequent offenders. As the tree grows the noose tightens. Many a tree is killed this way, for only the rare one has vigor enough to grow over the obstruction.

BE ALERT FOR PESTS AND DISEASES

These hit trees along with other plants, and can be a community disaster in an area where one kind, perhaps elm or oak, prevails. In such a situation you will need help from your city or neighborhood association, as well as doing what you can yourself.

Dutch elm disease. This is the killer that has made elms, previously one of our best shade trees, almost impractical to plant. Symptoms include wilting, yellowing, and falling of leaves during the growing season. If the disease hits early in summer, the tree may wilt and die within a week or two. Later in summer the progress is slower. Then only a branch or two will show yellow, wilted or dry leaves. For absolute diagnosis, you need a laboratory examination of affected wood. However, if you know Dutch elm disease is loose in your vicinity, you can be sure enough of the symptoms to start action. If you delay until your own trees are in trouble, you have generally waited too long. So far, there's no sure cure for affected trees, although scientists are at work developing injection treatments that seem promising.

What you *can* do is to control the beetles that spread the fungus. They are tiny insects that feed in twig crotches and tunnel under the bark. In the feeding process they spread the fungus spores picked up from diseased wood. To date, the best insecticide for the smaller European elm bark beetle (its full name) is DDT. If this is sprayed on before leaves come out, it is still effective months later, so it gets beetles when they begin to feed. A disadvantage to DDT is that it also harms birds, fish, pets and people so you need to be very careful when and how you put it on. Do it before nesting time, keep windows closed, people and pets out of the way, and fish pools covered. Let no pools of the poison accumulate. Your tree man will know how to mix the spray and have the equipment to put it on.

The second aspect of controlling the Dutch elm disease is to clean up completely and burn all dead or diseased elm wood that might harbor breeding beetles. Don't salvage a stricken elm as cordwood for your fireplace—you are just storing a source of infection for your other trees or your neighbor's.

To be effective, both the spraying of elms and the clean-up of dead trees must be handled by a community rather than by each home-owner alone. This disease is called Dutch because it apparently came from the Netherlands. It was discovered here in Ohio in 1930. Now it afflicts all the elm growing areas of the East, most of the Midwest, and it is expected almost any time to appear in the far West.

Oak wilt disease. Although not so devastating as Dutch elm disease, this is bad enough and becoming worse. It spreads over at least eighteen of the central states from Chesapeake Bay to just beyond the Missouri River. If you have many oaks, especially the red-oak type—scarlet, shingle, blackjack, pin or chestnut oaks—watch for it. It makes leaves wilt, turn yellow or bronze, and eventually fall off. Slice an infected twig lengthwise. If it shows dark brown to green streaks between bark and wood, the wilt is there. After one oak in a grove is hit, the disease spreads outward in a circle to other oaks whose roots touch the first tree. This wilt is a fungus, spread by spores, probably carried by insects and birds. White, post, bur, swamp and chinquapin oaks are affected too, but are slower to die.

You can prevent oak wilt by *not* pruning your oaks in spring or early summer when the fungus spores are spreading. When you do prune, cover *all* the cuts with tree-wound paint to keep the fungus from finding a place of entry.

If you find an infected oak or one you suspect, first get your county agent to come verify your diagnosis because if you are right, the remedy is drastic. To keep the disease from spreading through roots that touch, you have to cut down the affected tree and also any other oaks within 50 feet of it.

Tree banding. This is a time-honored way to keep insects from getting into trees, although now it has yielded in public favor to tree spraying. It consists of painting a wide ring of a sticky substance ("Tanglefoot" is one of the trade names) around the trunk well above the ground. The object is to entangle bugs as they travel upward. Probably the main one it helps to stop is the moth that makes elm canker worms. These moths crawl upward on the first warm sunny days of February so you need to apply the tree band early. Some moths are sure to struggle across, and later the worms will fly into your trees anyway on their silken threads blown by wind. So don't expect 100 per cent results. Tree bands do nothing to stop flying insects. In a grove of touching trees, you need to band every trunk or else you may as well save your trouble. The tree banding compound is harmless to mature trees but it might injure smooth-barked young ones. To avoid this, circle young trees with burlap and spread the compound on that.

CHANGING THE GRADE AROUND TREES

You don't expect a tree to survive if all the soil is scraped off its roots, but many people think they can dump on all the soil they want above tree roots. This is most harmful.

Although different kinds of trees vary in reactions, as a rule you cannot add more than 8 to 10 inches of soil without harming or probably killing the tree. This is because you are cutting off air, just as important to tree roots as food and moisture.

With a simple system to bring in air, you can have your new grade and the tree too. It's not expensive compared to the value of a large tree. First make a dry wall 18 inches thick, as high as your intended grade, in a circle with the tree as the center and a radius of at least 5 feet. Then lay lines of drain tile reaching as far as the branches and radiating out of the foot of the wall like spokes. Make at least six spokes. Haul in coarse gravel and spread it 6 to 8 inches deep over the whole root area including that around your tiles. Lay thick straw over the top of tile lines to keep soil from washing in, then put soil-fill on top of the gravel and tile. Air can penetrate now and the tree will go on thriving. There is one drawback, however—you will have to water the lawn above a tree-fill like this oftener than elsewhere.

Paving over tree roots. If you pave with asphalt or concrete over too much of the root area of a large tree, you are also very likely to lose the tree. "Too much" would probably be over more than half of the root area, depending on the tree and other circumstances. Again, roots are suffocated and also deprived of moisture. Bricks, patio blocks, wood sections or anything similar laid on a sand base and not as a *solid* covering do no harm whatever.

EASY-DOES-IT IDEAS

If you want to attach things to trees (like a hook for your hammock) use lag screws; or else drill through the limb and use a threaded bolt with a nut on the far side. This is safer than wrapping a wire or chain around the tree, which may eventually kill it.

Aluminum foil is a good temporary tree-trunk wrap to prevent winter sun from scalding thin bark; and it "foils" rabbits, too.

To reduce winter sunburn to a minimum, turn trees when you plant them so the lowest branches are on the south side. They will then break the sun's glare.

Chapter 23

PROPER WATERING
IS ESSENTIAL

Should I sprinkle my yard every evening?

When two weeks go by without a cloud to bring your garden a refreshing soaking shower, come to the rescue with water. Trees, shrubs, lawn, flower garden, vegetables, and fruits—all look and grow better with adequate moisture. If you can depend on rain for *all* the moisture your yard needs, you're one of the very fortunate few. Summer rains come erratically almost everywhere in this country, and in some sections they hardly ever come at all.

Watering is an art. People who are good waterers have the prettiest yards. But they are not the ones who take the hose for fifteen minutes of a summer evening to swish things off and sprinkle down the dust. If this is your practice, you'd do better not to water at all, for sprinkling does not benefit plants. The first, last, and almost only great rule about watering is "be thorough," and to this point many little rules pertain.

THE PRINCIPLES OF WATERING

Common sense and self-discipline are two traits that will help you be a good waterer. And if you have an analytical attitude towards your soil, climate and plants, that will help you understand better about watering needs. Also find out about the many different watering tools you can have, and select some good ones. They make

watering much simpler and more fun than it used to be.

HOW DEEP SHOULD THE SOIL BE MOISTENED?

Aim to wet the soil at each watering to a depth of at least 1 foot and preferably 2 feet. Plants need moisture in the soil around their deep roots. A few, such as cactus, can go long periods without it, but even they need some. Roots of most plants are concentrated at a level of 1 to 2 feet. Some go deeper, some are shallower, but that is a fair average. If you water to reach roots at the 2-foot depth, your garden will prosper. Since water sinks almost straight down from where you apply it, spread the water at the surface to cover the whole area. Water won't spread much after it starts its downward way.

HOW MUCH WATER DOES IT TAKE?

It takes an awful lot of water to moisten soil to 2 feet—how much depends on the texture of your soil (see Chapter 3) and how much moisture the soil may already have in it. Just as soil is moistened from the top down, it dries out from the top down too.

In dry sandy soil a 1-inch rain sinks down about a foot. In dry loamy soil, the inch of moisture penetrates only about 8 inches, depending on the fineness of soil particles. The finer the soil, the more water it holds. In a dry clay soil, the same amount of rain may reach down less than 5 inches. This sounds bad for clay soil, but it is not really, because clay holds water much longer, nearly three times as long as light sandy soil. Once you get it moist, you will not need to water again nearly so soon as on sandy soil.

Penetration of One Inch of Rain on Dry Soil

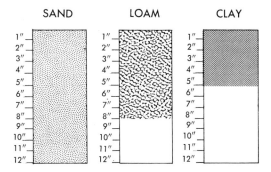

Fig. 56   The finer the soil, the more water it holds, and the more is needed to penetrate to a certain depth.

If your soil is an average loam, and it gets so dry that plants reach the wilting point, you will need to put on about $3\frac{1}{2}$ inches of water per square inch of surface to moisten it thoroughly to a 2-foot depth. This means about 20 gallons on a 10 square foot surface. In sandy soil it means 9 or 10 gallons; and in tight clay, nearly 30 gallons. If your hose puts out 5 gallons a minute (average), you would run it there two minutes for sandy soil, four minutes for loamy soil and six minutes for clay, and you'd need to build a dike around the area to prevent runoff. If you turn the water down to a slow stream to prevent runoff and washing, increase the time proportionately so you still apply as much water. For instance, if your hose is trickling out just a gallon every minute, then you'll need to run it twenty minutes to get the same amount needed to water that 10 square feet of average loam.

If the soil has not dried out completely from the last rain or the last watering, of course, it does not require such large amounts. It *is* possible to overwater, especially if your topsoil is underlaid by a dense layer of hardpan that prevents water from draining through.

HOW OFTEN SHOULD I WATER?

Let the soil become nearly dry before you water it again. With most established plants it does no harm to let them almost reach the wilting point. To check on soil moisture, dig down with the spade and feel the soil.

Places that hold moisture relatively long are: under heavy sods or ground covers, under mulches, and in areas of shade.

Places that dry out regardless of soil type are: lawns and gardens under shallow-rooted trees like elms and maples, windy spots in full sun, gardens with vigorous, actively growing plants like tomatoes setting on fruit.

In hot windy weather, soil dries faster than in cool springtime or fall. But even in winter, soil dries out. If this happens it damages evergreens, both broadleaf and needle kinds. These never go dormant but lose moisture every warm day through winter, so get out the hose again and deep-water them in late fall before freeze-up and if you can, also in any dry thaw periods through winter.

Keep an eye on plants to help you assess the dryness of soil. Wilting is not always caused by soil drouth. Sometimes on a warm summer afternoon soft leaves and stems wilt even in freshly watered soil. But if you see a wilter that doesn't straighten up by evening, then water it. Grass loses its springiness and sometimes the tips start to fire, as indications of dryness beneath.

Why alternate wet and dry? Why not keep the soil wet all the time? As soil dries out, air enters it, and this is almost as vital to plants as moisture. If watering is continuous, all air is driven out of the soil and plants stop growing and may die. Also, if you let soil dry somewhat between watering, roots are encouraged to grow deep in search of moisture. This is what you want, not just surface rooting.

Good average frequencies. Vary these according to weather and season. These approximations are based on thorough and deep watering each time: sandy soil every six to eight days, average loam every eight to twelve days, and clay soil every twelve to eighteen days.

Deep growers—trees and many shrubs—

can usually go at least twice as long before again needing moisture unless the weather has been hot, dry and windy.

Several light waterings do not equal one heavy one. This way you lose more in evaporation, and you lose in several other ways. A light sprinkling never penetrates past the top few inches, so roots tend to gather only in the upper layer where the moisture is. Plants need deep roots to tide them over in short drouths or when you go on vacation. It's best to start deep-watering in spring after heavy rains cease and you water for the first time.

New transplants are different. Newly planted things, whether they are woody plants like trees and shrubs or soft young plants like vegetables and flowers, need plenty of water *often* until they get established. For trees and shrubs this period lasts at least through the first summer and fall. For transplants like tomatoes, chrysanthemums, and zinnias it lasts until recovery seems complete and new growth starts. These have lost most of their roots in transplanting; what they have are all in the top layer of soil at first; if they dry out even briefly, the plant dies.

One experienced gardener in the East finds this a good program when watering is needed over a long period and for many plants: a slow-running hose beside new perennials or a small shrub for one-half hour, beside a 3- or 4-foot evergreen or a 5-foot birch for one hour, for larger trees and shrubs one to two hours. Lawn sprinklers are kept going from eight in the morning until about nine at night and moved every hour. It takes about a week to get over the place on this schedule which is maintained week after week until there is a really *heavy* rainfall. In a recent drouth of nearly eight weeks with only two light rains not a plant was lost of many new ones, and a considerable lawn area was kept green while other lawns in the area turned brown.

WHEN IS THE BEST TIME OF DAY TO WATER?

Probably the best time of day to water is in the early hours of daylight as the sun rises. Water then dries quickly on foliage

with the rising temperatures and sunlight; and you lose little by evaporation because the air is still damp. In many communities, water pressure in summer will be higher then than at any other time, because the neighbors are not yet up and using water.

Actually any hour of the day will do for watering, but because of possibilities of spreading leaf diseases, it's best to stop the sprinkler an hour or two before nightfall. Most leaf blights are fungus troubles that grow in water if timing is right for them. The object of sprinkling in daytime is to get foliage dry as fast as possible. Except with a few tender-leaf plants like African violets and gloxinias, no harm is done by watering while the sun is shining.

From the standpoint of conserving water, evening is a good time. Evaporation is low and all the water sinks in. Avoid wetting the foliage then—instead run water in trenches, flood basins around trees and shrubs, or use canvas or other soil-soakers that let water seep into the ground.

DEVICES TO MAKE WATERING EASY

Your garden store has dozens of devices for this purpose. They range high and low in price and quality, from the simplicity of a sprinkling can (still a useful item) to complicated "tractor" sprinklers that creep along the hose. First let's look at sprinkler devices made mainly for watering lawns.

LAWN SPRINKLERS

To find out what a new sprinkler puts out, get three or four coffee cans and space them evenly under the spray from close to the

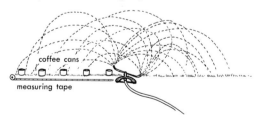

Fig. 57 How to test the spray pattern of a sprinkler. Space cans evenly from sprinkler to perimeter of watered area; let water run an hour; measure the amount falling in each can.

sprinkler to the outer reach of the water. Run the sprinkler for an hour at full pressure, and measure how much water falls in each can. You may find flooding close to the source, but only a trace of water farther out; or maybe all the water falls towards the rim of the circle (or square) leaving the middle comparatively dry. When you have this information you know better how to maneuver and overlap the sprinkling areas on your lawn to get even distribution. While you're making the test, use your watch and a measuring stick, to tell you just how much water this device delivers per hour. This way you'll know how long you need to run your sprinkler in each spot.

Ring or half-round sprinklers work by forcing water out through small holes. Some are brass, some aluminum, some galvanized iron. They have no moving parts, are cheap, and last a long time, but most of them throw more water to the periphery than to the center of an area. To get even coverage, you need to keep moving them a few feet at a time along the path to be watered.

Plastic sprinkler hoses with tiny holes along one surface of a flat tube distribute water in a similar way—concentrating it towards the outside of the spray reach with not so much near the center. The good things about these are flexibility and economy. Under good pressure they water a strip about 15 feet wide, and as long as the hose (usually either 24 or 40 feet). To get even coverage, move this device about 5 feet at a time across the area you are watering.

Pulsating sprinklers have jets that spurt in rapid order with a moving part that revolves the spray. You can get an adjustable kind that covers only part of a circle. Under good pressure such a sprinkler will water a 60-foot circle. Most of these give fairly even coverage but thinnest at the edge, indicating the need to overlap the watered circles several feet to get good distribution.

Oscillating sprinklers have a perforated bar that moves under water pressure to throw a spray slowly from one side to the other. They cover a rectangular or square area, usually concentrating a little more water in the center than at outer ends. Overlap the spray areas lengthwise to get even coverage.

Revolving sprinklers have two or more

Watering Tools

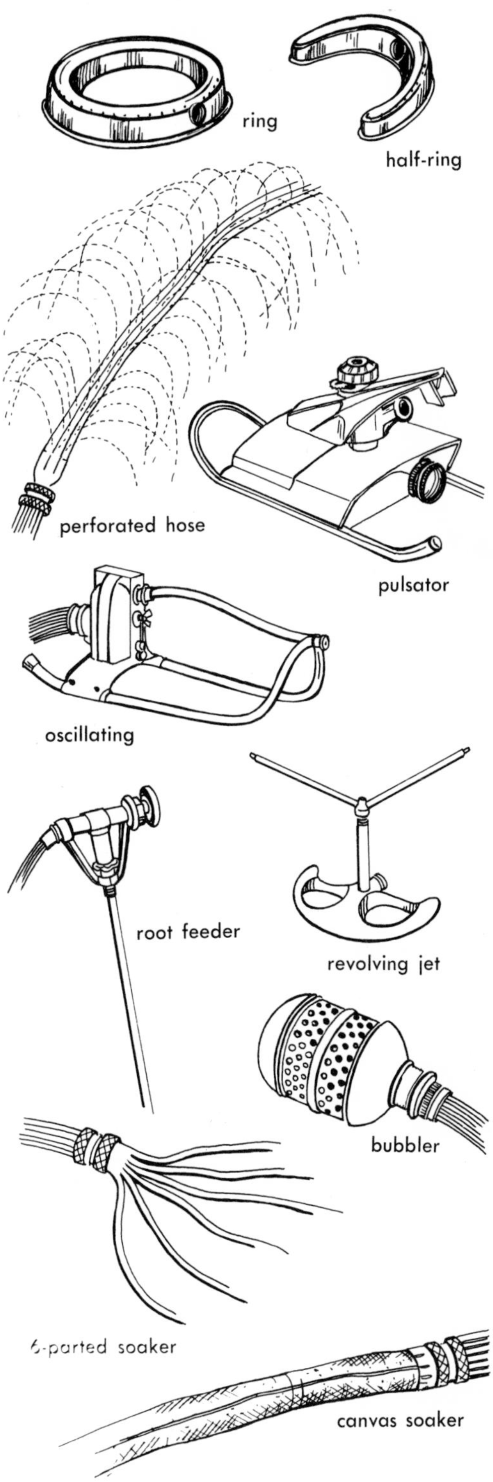

ring

half-ring

perforated hose

pulsator

oscillating

root feeder

revolving jet

bubbler

6-ported soaker

canvas soaker

Fig. 58 Your garden store has dozens of devices to make watering easy.

arms with water jets at the ends that cause the device to whirl slowly or fast. Although most of these give fairly even coverage, they vary widely, so it's worthwhile to make your coffee-can test to see what happens.

Round spray heads, stationary or pop-up, are typical of most underground sprinkler systems. They issue water in a fine spray or in small droplets. Most of them put the water closest to the spray head, the amount tapering off rather sharply toward the perimeter. If you use these, space sprinklers close enough to overlap them by at least half the radius of each circle.

Avoid sprinklers with a misty spray if you live in a windy climate. It's hard to get even coverage with them, and a lot of water is simply blown away.

OTHER TOOLS FOR WATERING

For watering plants, your selection is more limited.

The sprinkling can still has uses, and you can hardly do without one for watering transplants, for "touch up" watering in separated spots and for the big containers on terrace or porch.

Root-soakers and feeders. These are sharp, hollow spikes about 30 inches long with holes at the lower end and a hose connection and valve at the top. Stab the spike into the soil, push it down as far as you can, and turn on the water which will emerge far under the soil where the roots are. The Ross root-feeder has a chamber at the top for inserting fertilizer capsules, thus enabling you to root-feed when you water. This is a quick way to help trees, shrubs and other deep-rooting plants. Run the water in each place until it gurgles up around the shaft; then pull it out and insert it in another place close by.

Water-wands and bubblers. A water-wand is a bubbler with a no-stoop handle. The bubbler is a cylinder with holes and baffles that force water out in an airy gurgle instead of a spurt. Either device screws on the end of the hose. Water flows so gently that soil and mulches are not washed away. These are fine watering tools when you want to flood an area with slow penetration. The cane-length handle of the wand lets you

move easily from plant to plant for spot watering without wetting foliage.

Six-parted soaker. For slow soaking among roses or other flowers and shrubs, the six-parted "Soakeze" is convenient. Plastic tubes of various lengths are joined by one connection to the hose, so you can run a trickle of water at six different spots. By moving the tubes occasionally, you can water thoroughly a 15- to 20-foot section of flower bed without wetting foliage and without waste.

Canvas soaker. For watering a hedge, vegetables or anything in rows, this is ideal. Water seeps out through the porous canvas and goes right down into soil, with no run-off. Soakers come in 25-foot lengths and sometimes the end is removable so you can wash it out. Pick them up after use or they will rot.

About hoses. When you select a garden hose, get it with a big enough diameter, especially if you have a problem of water pressure. The largest size you can get, probably $\frac{3}{4}$-inch, gives the best flow. Other sizes are $\frac{1}{2}$-inch and $\frac{5}{8}$-inch. The smaller the hose, the more pressure you lose in friction. The rubber hose is still popular, but plastic hoses are much lighter and in most cases cheaper. Both kinds stand abuse, but they last longer if you don't leave them out in the sun, and drain and put them away in winter. You can buy them in lengths of 25, 50 and 75 feet.

WAYS TO MAKE WATERING MORE CONVENIENT

If you make things easy for yourself, success with watering is more likely. It's lugging awkward hose lengths and running back and forth to turn faucets on and off that wear you out (and make you mad). It pays to have a number of hose lengths that are easily disconnected for watering at short and long distances from the house, and a faucet on *each* side of the house is a joy. Connections at several places through the yard are also handy. Try to arrange them so you need no hose longer than 25 feet. Because of the digging and upheaval it takes to put in new connections, include these in your plans when you first lay out your yard.

149 With plastic pipes, the job of installing underground systems is within reach of do-it-yourself workers. *Philpott*

Get a plumber to help you decide on locations, pipe sizes, and length of lines.

Sprinkler systems. For the ultimate in convenience for lawn watering, install an underground water system with sprinklers that pop up and make it rain whenever you turn a valve. This device is also easier installed before the lawn is finished, although with new materials and methods you can now install one without ruining your grass.

Until the last few years, galvanized iron pipe (usually ¾-inch size) was used for underground sprinklers. The new trend is toward plastic pipe, which has proved to be so durable and easy to work with that it promises to replace the other kind entirely. Plastic has the advantages of low cost, freedom from rust and corrosion, and convenience. You yourself can connect fittings with a screwdriver. Plastic bends readily so you can take short cuts and avoid the square-corner system necessary with iron and this gives better water pressure, too. You can probably install a plastic pipe system yourself with just a little help from the dealer in planning it. Before you put it underground, lay the pipe out on top of the ground and run water through it to check spacing of sprinklers. Then all you need do is open a slit through the sod, 6 inches deep, usually, and set the pipe and sprinklers down in it.

Although plastic seems durable enough against freezing, particularly if water is drained out, it may break under extremely high water pressure, and if you accidentally hit it with a spade or fork it cuts easily. So sink it deep enough to be out of danger.

150 The pop-up heads may throw water in circles, squares, various rectangles, and other patterns. *Rain Jet*

When you go to inquire about underground sprinkling systems, take along an accurate map of your yard that shows the location, length and size of the water-line leading from the meter to the house, because somewhere along it you will want to tap in for your supply. This information about the supply line bears on the choice of pipe size and lengths. The larger the pipe, the less the loss of pressure. From the water company, get an idea of what the lowest pressure is likely to be. Pressure influences spacing of sprinkler heads and the number of valves required. You will need to use metal pipe (copper or galvanized iron) from the water source to the turn-off valves because this part of the system is subject to constant high pressure.

Another requirement in most communities is an anti-siphon valve to prevent ground water from being sucked back into the water system. And at the lowest point in the line, provide a drain that you control by valve, so you can drain out the water in the fall.

In planning a sprinkler layout, make use of various spray patterns—round, half and quarter circle, square, and even rectangular. These save wasting water along sidewalks and beside shrub borders.

If all this sounds too complicated for a do-it-yourself project, you can have the work done from start to finish by sprinkler system contractors. Most large cities have them.

IF YOU HAVE YOUR OWN WELL

You can save on the water bill if you can use water from your own well. Whether it works through the house system or is a separate unit just for outdoor use, you can get electric or gasoline pumps of a size to provide plenty of water and pressure for sprinkler systems. It is even possible to tap into ponds and streams for this use. Consult with a nearby pump dealer about this. The depth of your well, the size of the casing, and the distance to which you want to run water in your yard are all important considerations. Also, basically, whether your well is likely to supply *enough* water for liberal outdoor use.

PARTICULARS ABOUT WATERING

ABOUT WATERING LAWNS

Thoroughness and evenness are what you strive for in lawn sprinkling. You don't need to water often if each time you do it well. Always put on at least an inch of water for an average soil, and time the application according to how the weather has been and the nature of your soil.

Let's suppose you have a loamy soil, and it's been a week and a half since the last good rain. The weather has been hot and windy and since there's no rain in the forecast, you decide it's time to water. Maybe you investigate with the spade at the edge of the lawn, and find the soil dry about 6 inches down but below that still fairly moist. So you judge that an inch of moisture will be about right to replenish the top part and strengthen the store below.

Your sprinkler, let's say, covers a 40-foot circle—*you* be scientific and measure it to make sure. This is something you need to know. And assuming (again, *you* measure to be sure) that it puts out 5 gallons a minute, a little figuring shows you'll need 780 gallons of water which means running the sprinkler steadily for two and one-half hours. (How to figure this: the area of the circle, reduced to inches, divided by 231 cubic inches per gallon. And that divided by 5 gallons a minute to get minutes.)

If your soil is sandy you might decide on watering three to four days sooner and run the sprinkler only one and three-fourths hours.

If it is clay, you can put off the watering for several more days, say two weeks since the previous rain, but run the sprinkler a little longer—perhaps three hours.

Although this sounds like a lot of figuring, actually after you've worked it out once, you can depend pretty much on your own judgment to guide you and dispense in the future with figuring.

If you have a large lawn and one sprinkler, it takes several days to get over it at this rate, since you don't water at night. If you always proceed from area to area in the same order, you can get the whole place on your schedule.

Water may be slow to penetrate, making a runoff problem. To minimize this, aerate the soil with a spiker or aerator. Or shut off the hose when water begins running away, allow fifteen minutes for it to soak in, and then turn the hose on again.

ABOUT WATERING FLOWERS

You can water most of your flowers with a sprinkler. But there are a few—roses, delphiniums, zinnias, snapdragons, hollyhocks, dahlias and chrysanthemums—too susceptible to leaf diseases for watering from above. Use soil-soaking methods with them instead.

Some flowers seem to benefit from having their leaves washed, especially hardy asters, columbines and lobelias which may get aphids or red spiders. Some respond well to the increased humidity provided by sprinkling—ferns, azaleas, astilbes, helleborus, tuberous begonias. In a mixed planting it is generally all right to water with an overhead sprinkler.

On slopes and wall gardens especially, this is the best way to do an even job of watering. You can also water dry walls with a canvas soil-soaker laid along the top just back of the wall. Let it run for hours. Water soaks down behind the stones where the roots are. To water a rock garden, use a gentle misty spray at the top of the slope that lays water gently down on the stones and lets it seep away.

If you want to avoid the work of watering flowers, equip the beds with underground sprinklers, the same as for a lawn, sinking the pipes below spade depth. From the beginning, water deeply but not often, basing the frequency on the sort of soil you have.

ABOUT WATERING VEGETABLES

Although sprinkling is an acceptable way to water a vegetable garden, running water down furrows beside the plants is more economical and more likely to do a thorough job. When you know in advance that watering will be needed, make the furrow when you plant or soon afterward to avoid cutting roots. Remembering that water does not move to the side, put the furrow close to plants along one side of the row. This is a good system for irrigating corn, tomatoes, beans, in fact almost any plants except vines like melons that grow over the furrows. Water them with the sprinkler, or sink perforated large tin cans around them which you can fill from the hose.

331

Deep watering is necessary for plants like tomatoes; but most short-term crops like lettuce make shallow roots and will thrive if you keep moisture in the top 12 to 15 inches of soil.

The timing of water on vegetables depends somewhat on their stage of growth. They need water most urgently when they are blooming or fruit-setting (tomatoes and beans, melons, cucumbers, corn) or when they are forming heads (lettuce and cabbage). Beets, carrots, and leaf lettuce are most succulent if you keep them growing fast with timely watering from seed to harvest. Once a week is often enough.

ABOUT WATERING CONTAINER PLANTS

Use the drench-and-dry-out method for plants in tubs and large pots. Fill the container to the brim with water, let it sink in, fill it again and let sink in, until water runs out the drainage holes. Then wait until the touch test (your finger pressed into the soil), indicates the soil is getting dry.

Clay pots dry out faster than glazed, plastic, metal or wooden containers. To prevent too rapid drying, set pots inside larger pots or boxes, and pack the space around them with sphagnum, peat moss, vermiculite or perlite. Moisten this from time to time.

A hanging basket lined with moss is best watered by taking it down and soaking the whole thing in a tub of tepid water. Let it remain until bubbles stop rising. Then before replacing it on its hook, set it where water won't damage anything until the dripping stops. (See Chapter 35 for other ideas about watering and conserving water in hanging baskets.)

SOME USEFUL STATISTICS

1 inch of water per 1,000 square feet—620 gallons

1 inch of water per 100 square feet—62 gallons

1 inch of water per 10 square feet—about 6 gallons

231 cubic inches—1 gallon

How deep 1 inch of water or rain penetrates
Sandy, 10 to 14 inches, approximately
Loam, 6 to 10 inches, approximately
Clay, 4 to 6 inches, approximately

Hose capacities at 50 pounds pressure
$\frac{1}{2}$ inch—480 gallons per hour—$6\frac{1}{2}$ hours to apply 1 inch per 5,000 square feet
$\frac{5}{8}$ inch—720 gallons per hour—$4\frac{1}{3}$ hours to apply 1 inch per 5,000 square feet
$\frac{3}{4}$ inch—1200 gallons per hour—$3\frac{1}{8}$ hours to apply 1 inch per 5,000 square feet

Output of an average sprinkler
5 gallons per minute, 300 gallons per hour. Run your sprinkler 1 minute into a large container and measure the contents to see how this works out.

To penetrate soil 1 foot
Sandy, $\frac{3}{4}$ inch water or rain, approximately $4\frac{1}{2}$ gallons per 10 square feet
Loam, $1\frac{3}{4}$ inches water or rain, approximately $10\frac{1}{2}$ gallons per 10 square feet
Clay, $2\frac{1}{2}$ inches water or rain, approximately 15 gallons per 10 square feet

EASY-DOES-IT IDEAS

Take the guesswork out of watering with a rain gauge. Then you can tell if nature's watering (the best kind) is sufficient, or if you need to lend a hand. Place a rain gauge off the ground and out in the open away from trees and buildings.

For six dollars or so you can buy a timer to put on your outside faucet to be set for whatever length of time you want to run the sprinkler, or for whatever amount of water in gallons. It saves a lot of figuring and clock-watching.

Chapter 24

MULCHING YOUR SUMMER GARDEN

Would mulching my garden in summer save me work?

Summer mulching takes many forms and has many uses. Here is what a summer mulch can do:

Mulch helps control weeds. Annual weeds especially are easy to control with mulch if the layer is thick enough, say 3 inches. Tough perennial weeds like dock and milkweed, however, will come up through practically anything except possibly plastic or tar-paper.

Mulch conserves moisture. Mulching material on top of the ground prevents sun and wind from drawing moisture out of the soil, saving more for the plants.

Mulch keeps soil cool in summer.* This is important especially for rhododendrons, azaleas, mountain laurel, hollies, and lilies. Almost all ornamental plants benefit to some degree.

Mulch improves soil texture. In the complicated breakdown of humusy substances, tight soils tend to open up, and sandy ones become more absorbent. Either way it helps plants.

Mulch deepens the topsoil. Over a span of years you will notice that where you mulch, the dark layers gradually get deeper and richer.

Mulch peps up soil bacteria. Most organic mulches do this. The result is a healthier

---

* Except for black polyethylene used as mulch, which actually warms the soil and speeds up crops like corn and tomatoes.

---

condition for plant roots and better nutrient absorption.

Mulch curbs the spread of some diseases. Blackspot of roses, for instance, winters over in the soil. If you put on a clean thick mulch such as peat moss or pine needles in spring, the spores can't splash up out of the soil to start a fresh epidemic on the leaves.

Mulch prevents soil erosion. The right kind can hold even a steep slope from washing in hard rains, without loss of mulch or soil. Chopped leaves, compost and ground corncobs are three kinds that stay in place well.

Mulch saves cultivating. Aside from the time you save, the plants are probably better off too. Cultivating, no matter how carefully you do it, takes its toll of shallow plant roots.

HOW TO CHOOSE A MULCH

This depends pretty much on what's available. The chart on page 336 shows thirty kinds. A number of them are found only regionally. Needless to say, it's cheaper to buy kinds at hand than to have something shipped from a distance. On this account, you don't find much fir bark in the East or ground corncobs in the West. But wherever you live, there are various mulch materials available in good supply. The most economical is one grown right on your place, like tree leaves and grass clippings; but it will be surprising if you have enough of them once you discover the advantages of mulching. If you live where it is windy, use something that stays in place, such as wood chips or corncobs. If you live in a dry climate, avoid mulches like hay and wood shavings that catch fire easily from discarded cigarettes.

MANAGING YOUR SUMMER MULCH

As soon as spring clean-up and first weedings are finished, you'll probably want to put on a mulch or rejuvenate old ones. What is left from the previous year may be pretty well disintegrated. If it is, scratch it into the soil, taking this opportunity to apply a dose of balanced fertilizer (1 pound of 8-8-8 to 100 square feet). If the mulch is a 2-inch layer of pine needles or buckwheat hulls that have hardly begun to decay, or if it's non-organic like gravel, leave it alone. You may not even need to add to it, but you may want to push it aside temporarily to apply dry fertilizer, or you can pour a liquid fertilizer through it.

Mulches of shredded leaves, chopped hay, lawn clippings and leaf mold disappear fairly fast into the soil. After one season you can work them in and start over. Pine needles, buckwheat hulls, wood chips and peat moss are so durable they last several years before finally merging with the soil. The warmer your climate, the faster your mulches disintegrate.

If you want to hill up roses for winter protection and the bed is mulched with something long-lasting like pine needles, remove the mulch and store it in baskets or bags for the winter, before you bring in earth to mound over the crowns. Restore the mulch the next spring after removing the extra soil.

If you don't know just how much a mulch will settle, put it on a layer at a time, a few weeks apart, until it is thick enough. Spent hops, for instance, settle a surprising amount. With them you may need four applications.

WHERE TO MULCH?

Shrubbery beds, especially among shallow-rooted plants like rhododendrons and azaleas, camellias and hollies, are good places for a mulch. Since you won't ever remove or disturb it, something long-lasting such as wood chips or buckwheat hulls is practical. Or you can use sawdust, leaves, ground corncobs—any of the organic mulches.

Next mulch the rose bed. Peat moss seems to be especially good for roses, but many other things will do, too. Fir bark is an attractive color and rotted manure has a nutrient booster in it.

Mulch around the base of trees. This keeps grass and weeds from growing there and makes mowing easy and neat. Wood chips are good for this, also pebbles.

If you have lilies in special beds, lay a mulch on them to help control moisture and soil temperature. Here you may use fairly coarse but soft materials like chopped hay, oak leaves and pine needles. If you have a rock garden, spruce and fir needles make a fine-textured mulch that works in among stones and little plants; gravel makes a permanent well-drained mulch that stays in place on slopes.

Mulch perennial borders with something you can eventually work into the soil. With transplanting and dividing through the summer, you are certain to mix mulch with soil anyway. Peat and buckwheat hulls are attractive and ideal. So are chopped oak leaves. Ground corncobs work well but you may object to the color at first.

Mulch your fruit trees and berry patch. Straw, chopped cornstalks and hay are excellent for these; put down a 4-inch layer and stop worrying about cultivating and weed control there.

Mulch your vegetable garden. How deep is for you to decide. Mulch pays off quickly around large plants like tomatoes, cucumbers and squash, lima and pole beans. With small short-term, narrow-row vegetables like radishes and beets, you may find a mulch more trouble than it's worth. Leafy vegetables like lettuce and spinach stay cleaner when grown above a mulch.

Mulch your strawberries. Clean wheat or oat straw is the old standby for this and is as good as anything. This goes on in the fall after a hard freeze and stays on all the next season.

151 A pebble mulch is an attractive, permanent, and carefree ground cover among these plants beside a parking strip. *Tatch*

SOME MULCHING DON'TS

Don't put a water-holding mulch, like manure or peat moss, close to stems. Draw it back a little to avoid starting rots or cankers. This is especially important in winter.

Don't try to work a heavy straw, leaf, or hay mulch into the soil unless you work in at the same time a high-nitrogen fertilizer like 10-6-4, a pound to 100 square feet. This is to satisfy the extra nitrogen needs of plants due to increasing bacterial activity from the mulch.

Don't suppose a mulch makes it unnecessary to fertilize. Only a few mulches like rotted manure or alfalfa hay have any nutrient value—the rest offer humus and that's about all. Go right on with your fertilizer applications. Spread it on top of the mulch and water it in, or draw back the mulch and apply it direct to the soil. If you put it on top, use a little more to make up for that held back by the mulch.

PARTICULARS ABOUT TWELVE KINDS OF MULCH

Alfalfa hay. This is the best hay or straw for mulching, because of its high nitrogen content. It equals rotted manure in this respect. Sometimes you can get spoiled or rained-on hay from farmers for almost nothing, and it makes as good a mulch as any. For a commercial source of alfalfa hay, go to a feed store.

Buckwheat hulls. This is a luxury mulch unless you're in buckwheat country. But it is everything you could ask. It has the right color; it lasts and lasts; it won't blow or burn; and it never brings in weeds or diseases. Save this for your choicest permanent plantings where you'll not need to do much digging (although you could remove and store this mulch); a thick application lasts about four years.

Pebbles. This material gets more popular each year for mulching the circles between

THIRTY MULCH MATERIALS AND THEIR VIRTUES †

Scoring is from 1 poor, to 5 excellent. Local availability may affect your choice. * indicates that availability varies. ** indicates the mulch needs anchoring.

Materials	Won't crust	Color	Won't blow	Availability (cost)	Weeds; disease	Fire hazard	Length of effectiveness	Nutrients	
Pine needles	5	5	3+	3-5	5	2	5	1	Just about tops.
Peat moss	3	5	3	3	5	5	4	2+	Universally available. Use sphagnum, not sedge.
Coarse sawdust	4	3-4	4	5	5	4	3+	2+	Avoid fine grade. Add nitrogen.
Wood chips	5	3+	5	5	5	4	4+	3	Coarse texture preferred.
Leaves: oak, beech	5	5	2+	5	5	1-2	4+	2	Best if chopped or ground.
Leaves: maple, birch, elm	1	4+	4	5	4	1	2	2	Not recommended.
Ground corncobs	4+	2+	5	*	2-4	5	3	2	Use medium grind, not fine.
Buckwheat hulls	5	5	4	2-3	5	5	5	1	Long distance freight costs.
Hay, regular	4	3	3	3-5	1-2	1	3	2	For vegetables, fruit.
Hay, legume	4	4	3	3-4	2-3	1	2	4+	Much better than above.
Straw	5	1	2	2-4	1	1	2	1	For vegetables, fruits.
Well rotted manure (high straw content)	5	4	5	1-4	1-3	5	2-3	4-5	Smells bad, value varies, generally costly.
Lawn clippings	1-2	2	5	5	2-4	5	1-2	2	Not recommended. Too wet at times.
Spent hops	5	4+	3	1-5	5	5	3	?	Settles greatly. Bad odor initially. Few sources. Keep away from stems; it heats in hot weather.
Cottonseed hulls	4	4	4+	1-5	2-4	5	4	?	Increasing use in South.
Bagasse (sugar cane residue)	4+	4	4+	1-5	2-4	3+	3+	3	Increasing use in South.
Crushed peanut hulls	4+	3	5	1-5	4	4	3	2	Limited availability.

Spruce or fir boughs	5	5	5	1-5	5	2-5		0	Winter use and to anchor other materials.
Spruce or fir needles	5	5	3+	1-5	5	3	5	1	For seedling "acid loving" plants generally.
Excelsior	5	1	2	5	5	1	5	1	Not recommended.
Shredded tobacco stems	4	4+	4	1-5	3-5	3-4	4	2	Not widely available. Nicotine repels some insects.
Corn stalks	5	1-2	4-5	3-5	5	3+	4	2	Coarse and unsightly. Good for winter.
Wood shavings	5	1-2	1-3	3-5	5	1	4+	1-2	Generally unsatisfactory.
Leaf mold	4	5	5	3-5	2-5	5	1-2	3-4	Often home produced. Value varies with ingredients.
Salt marsh hay	5	4+	3+	1-5	4-5	4	4+	1	Normally only in winter.
Cranberry vines	5	5	4	1-5	5	4+	5	1-2	Normally only in winter.
Gravel, pebbles	5	3-4	5	3-5	5	5	5	0	Generally for alpines.
Coarse coal ashes	3-4	2	5	5	5	5	5	0	To cover crown of herbaceous perennials against winter moisture.
Aluminum foil	—	1	**	1-2	5	5	5	0	Not for ornamentals.
Black polyethylene	—	1	**	2-4	5	?	4+	0	Speeds berry, vegetable crops.

† This chart, by Dr. Fred J. Nisbet, was originally published in *Flower and Garden Magazine*

trees and lawns, little pockets around plants in terraces and parking strips and near doorways. It is pretty and permanent. The one disadvantage comes if there are children around—they can't resist playing in it. If pebbles are throwable size, there goes your mulch. Naturally you get none of the organic benefits from pebbles—just weed control, good drainage and good looks. Put them on 2 to 3 inches thick.

Ground corncobs. Except for the light color, these make a dandy mulch; they absorb and hold water well; last fairly long; stay in place. When they begin to break down, you may get a soil nitrogen deficiency, the same as with sawdust, so put on fertilizer then and water it in. You can tell nitrogen is lacking if plants show yellow leaves.

Oak leaves. Of all the leaves, those of the oak are stiffest and most lasting in summer mulches. They are especially good if put through a compost grinder, to make them into a fine-textured, crisp material. Lacking a grinder, pile them on the driveway and run your rotary mower through them two or three times. If you try to use them without chopping, they blow all over the yard unless weighted down with soil. Beech leaves are as good, but not as widely available. Use these leaf mulches among your shrubs, especially broadleafs, and in your flower garden where they contribute a small amount of nutrients as they decay.

Peat moss. The standard mulching material, peat moss, has some faults. For one thing, it is expensive. Some kinds cake and dry on the soil surface and draw too much moisture from it. If you decide on peat moss, get the fibery brown sphagnum peat, not the black, powdery sedge type. Sphagnum holds more air and water and lasts longer. When you buy a bale or carton of peat, it's a good idea to open the package and set it outside to be rained on. Or make a well for a slow-running hose to soak the peat moss before you spread it. Peat moss holds enormous amounts of water—and it's more successful as mulch if applied damp.

Pine needles. You can gather a supply of these in pine woods. They last several years, finally disintegrating into the soil and giving a slightly acid effect. Use pine needles especially for mulching under evergreens and under such acid-requiring plants as rhododendrons, azaleas, camellias, ericas, and hollies.

Polyethylene mulch. This differs from other mulches in making the soil beneath warmer. The commercial product sold for mulching is perforated so rain can run through. It is usually black and this has the effect of absorbing sun warmth and passing it to the soil to speed production of warm-weather crops like tomatoes, corn, and peppers. It is especially helpful in places with cool, short summers, but has been used successfully everywhere to get earlier crops. It completely defeats weeds. Have the soil well prepared, fertilized and moist before putting the mulch down, then plant through slits cut with a razor blade. Anchor edges with soil. With luck you can use the sheet a second season. Roll it up and store in the fall, after plants are cut down. It is not attractive enough for your flowers and shrubs, and the heat-gathering power makes it undesirable for most shrubs and perennials.

Rotted manure. Where available, this makes a dark colored, fine textured mulch that looks good in the garden and supplies some nutrients. If thoroughly rotted, it has no odor. Possible sources are stockyards, cattle sale barns, and feed pens for cattle along railroad lines. You run the risk of bringing weeds in with it. The dehydrated product sold in bags by garden stores is dusty and unpleasant to handle, smelly, and too expensive to use as mulch. But it is heat-processed to kill weed seeds.

Sawdust. Available nearly everywhere, this makes a satisfactory mulch only if you provide nitrogen along with it. It's best if it rots and weathers for a year or two in a compost pile, although this is not essential. Mix it with balanced fertilizer high in nitrogen (like 10-6-4), $1\frac{2}{3}$ pounds to a bushel, before applying it. A coarse grade is better than finer grades because it is not likely to crust. But you can use the fine by mixing it with something porous, such as ground corncobs. Oak sawdust is especially prized for acid-loving azaleas, rhododendrons, and blueberries. Pine sawdust seems to have a toxic effect on rhododendrons, but can be used safely on most other things. You need not worry at all if the sawdust has lain outdoors in the weather for a few years. Get it at sawmills, woodworking shops, or planing mills. Railroad yards often have the coarse kind—if there is an accumulation from what was packed around ice in refrigerator cars.

Spent hops. If there is a brewery nearby, it might be a source of this material. Except for the odor at first (it smells like beer for a week or so) it makes top-notch mulch. It sinks down rapidly, so you'll need to make more than one application to work it up to the right thickness; once established it lasts quite a while. A unique thing about hops is that they are practically fire-resistant.

Wood chips. In some areas (more all the time) telephone and electric line crews, tree companies and city park departments put tree prunings through chipping machines to get rid of them. The result is coarse wood chunks seldom bigger than 2 inches, with many smaller scraps of bark, twigs, buds and leaves. Because this material is larger and coarser than sawdust, it is less likely to cake and it lasts longer. When it does begin to decay, it has the same nitrogen-robbing effect on soil that sawdust does, so it pays to fortify it once a year by spreading nitrogen fertilizer (10-6-4) about 2 pounds per 100 square feet. As a mulch, wood chips are fairly attractive and they don't blow around, although they may float when surface water rises with hard rains.

EASY-DOES-IT IDEAS

In your vegetable garden when pea vines are through bearing, pull and make a summer mulch of them around tomatoes, green peppers, or cucumbers. They'll cut down on watering and weeding.

Hedge clippings are good mulch if they consist of thin twigs. Spread them in a berry patch or under tall shrubs, or even rake them against the hedge to make a mulch there.

Chapter 25

HOW AND WHY
OF WINTER PROTECTION

Do I have to cover my garden in winter?

The best winter protection of all is a thick covering of snow. If you live where you can depend on having snow on the ground from early winter until the last spring thaw, there is little need for you to protect plants with additional covering. If you live in a warm part of the country where plants come through winter unharmed without protection, you need not be concerned. But if your winters often go below zero, and you can't depend on snow, then do cover your garden or at least the most vulnerable plants in it. In a mixed planting where some plants are rather tender and some are hardy, you can cover them all. Certainly newly set plants benefit by protection.

If you are growing plants of doubtful hardiness in your zone, like hybrid tea roses, protect them as a matter of course unless you are willing to take the chance of having to replace them next year. See more about protecting roses in Chapter 13.

HOW TO PROTECT PLANTS
IN WINTER

Hardiness in winter is not a definite condition. Hardiness is influenced by many factors and combinations of them. The kind of garden you have, the plants in it, the exposure, the drainage, the built-in protection like trees, buildings and shrubs, the weather in any one year—especially snowfall, low temperatures and freak thaws—these are conditions that affect the winter hardiness of plants.

How you can make plants hardier. The hardy, woody plants, like trees and shrubs, take cold weather better if they have stopped making growth by fall and started thickening and hardening their stems. In the wild, plants naturally harden up when autumn dry spells parch the soil and fertility decreases from the season's use. In a garden you can kill plants with kindness if you keep on watering and fertilizing, especially with nitrogen, late into fall. Plants respond with new soft growth just as if it were spring; and this growth is too tender to resist cold. Pruning late in summer may also start growth. If autumn rains keep plants growing in spite of you, you can harden them with a special fertilizer, like 0-10-10, that contains *no* nitrogen but is strong in phosphorus and potassium. If you have plants that winterkill year after year, try this type of fall feeding. For a 4-foot holly you would use about a quarter cup.

If you keep a thick summer mulch around plants, this may also prevent proper hardening because so much moisture is conserved. Where there has been winterkill before, try pulling back some of the mulch in the fall to let the soil dry out. This is effective with *Pieris japonica* and Burford holly, for example. Even where shrubs have not been mulched you can improve their winter preparedness by cultivating lightly to improve drainage and dry the soil. Of course, do not cultivate soil under shallow-rooting shrubs like hollies, magnolias, azaleas, or rhododendrons.

Locate plants for greatest safety. Location for certain plants has much to do with hardiness. Broadleaf evergreens like azaleas and rhododendrons will be better off on the cold shaded side of your house rather than in a sunny place. Avoid planting in low spots or wind channels, as between buildings or at a wind-swept corner.

What you protect against. The actual physical damage that comes to plants over a hard winter takes various forms:

(1) breakage from ice and snow,
(2) sun scald from direct or reflected sun,
(3) drying out from wind and sun,
(4) cell damage to stems and roots from actual freezing,
(5) exposure of roots and crowns by frost heaving,
(6) drowning of roots from ice or water standing in poorly drained spots, and
(7) chewing by mice and rabbits.

Let's consider how to prevent this destruction.

HOW TO PROTECT AGAINST ICE AND SNOW BREAKAGE

Heavy snow, and particularly wet snow, on needle evergreens like arborvitae, junipers, yews, and others, may bend or break them. Late in fall, you can protect sheared junipers and arborvitae by winding twine spirally up and down the trees. Make it firm but not tight. This strengthens them against bending under weight of the snow. Protect spreading junipers and yews that might be crushed under snow (especially if they are where sidewalk or street snow is piled on them) with one or more sturdy props under the boughs most likely to be weighted down.

Go right out after a heavy snow and before it hardens, *gently* sweep or shake snow from tree branches to relieve the load. But do this carefully or you may break branches or knock off tips. When trees are frozen they are brittle.

Icicles are a menace when they form on foundation evergreens under overhanging eaves that dam up and then drip. Sometimes trees become solid ice columns. When this happens, try to melt off the ice with water from the hose when the temperature is above freezing. Or arrange some temporary winter shelter over plants to divert the drip from the eaves. Best of all, avoid the problem by placing trees out beyond the roof overhang.

If you see an avalanche of snow forming on the roof and threatening to bury your foundation trees, make a lean-to of boards over them during the crisis. Ice storms coating branches are likely to break down some deciduous trees like Siberian elms. The only way you can avoid this is to keep trees pruned so the branching is strong, and there is less twiggy growth at ends of branches.

HOW TO PREVENT SUN SCALD ON YOUNG TREES

Covering with tree-wrap is the surest protection. Trees most in need of this are young deciduous specimens with smooth skin—lindens, oaks, maples, horsechestnut, beeches, apples, and London planetrees. When leaves fall, the full force of the sun strikes the parts facing south, especially the lower sections of the trunk that present the broadest surfaces. With snow, reflected sunlight makes matters worse for it dries out exposed areas and thus kills the tissues which curl and peel. The whole tree may not die but one side of it can be damaged for several years. If these trees stand to the north or northeast of tall buildings, within the winter shadow, they need no protection.

Instead of commercial tree-wrap, you can improvise with aluminum foil pressed around the tree trunk, gunny sacks, a flat board tied on the south side, or a cover of tough wrapping or building paper tied around the trunk.

HOW TO PROTECT FROM DRYING

Drying out in winter causes major damage to woody plants. Evergreens, both needle and broadleaf kinds, suffer particularly. While moisture-supplying roots are locked in frozen soil, wind and sun on the foliage continue to draw out water. The supply is exhausted and branches become parched, unless you come to the rescue.

Spray on an anti-desiccant. This is simply a soluble plastic coating you put on leaves to check water loss from drying wind. "Wilt Pruf" is one trade name. Spray it on in fall just before freezing and renew the coating during the winter in a warm spell. Rhododendrons, azaleas, hollies, pieris, pyracantha, boxwood, and euonymus all benefit from this treatment, as well as arborvitaes, yews and young hemlocks.

Keep up watering in winter. Don't water if ground is frozen, but when it is open, seize the opportunity to water your evergreens, both needle and broadleafs. Run water slowly so it can sink in deep.

Erect sun and wind screens. This is the last resort and a most unsightly one. However, unless your very tender shrubs, especially broadleaf evergreens, are in a protected place, you may have to consider putting around them a canvas, burlap, plastic, or lath screen. Of course, these shrouds don't have to stay on long, and two sections are usually all you need for sun screens. Face one southeast, one southwest, with the corner to the south. If a third side is needed to block north winds, add it on the northwest, leaving the northeast side open. Low shrubs like azaleas can be protected with lath screens tilted over them from the south. They may thus be saved but are certainly no ornament to the winter landscape.

HOW TO PROTECT AGAINST DAMAGE FROM FREEZING

Mounding and mulching are your two best methods. Some plants cannot take such intense cold as others, but you can grow many slightly tender plants if you ease the climate a little for them.

A mound of soil over the crown of a rose or crape-myrtle keeps it a little warmer. Even though the mound freezes, the temperature inside it is more moderate than outside. So the crown and base, the parts most important to save for next season's growth, are safe even though tops are killed. The colder your winters, the deeper you bury the crown.

Warmth rises from below in the soil. If you put a mulch like dry hay above the mound, you add an insulation that keeps this comparative warmth from escaping and the intense cold of the air from penetrating. When you turn a leaf-filled bushel basket over the mounded crown (an old-fashioned method that has merit) you accomplish the same thing. When there is deep snow, it provides insulation. Wherever you put a thick dry mulch, the ground below stays warmer and freezes less deep.

HOW TO PREVENT HEAVING FROM FROST

Mulching is again the best method. In this case you use mulch to keep the cold *in*. Heaving occurs when the ground thaws briefly at the surface, but remains frozen below. The damage comes when crowns or roots of small plants like phlox and dianthus are pushed out of the soil by this action and exposed to wind and further freezes. A thick loose mulch shades the frozen ground and insulates it against the brief unseasonable warmth, so plants stay secure until spring really arrives.

Kinds of winter mulch. A dry, airy mulch is safer around plants than matted material that holds water.

Branches of pine, juniper, spruce, fir and Douglas-fir are excellent. They shade the ground but are so springy and woody they can't mat down. And they are available from your holiday decorating or Christmas tree. Right after Christmas is a good time to put them on, too, to be ready for January and February thaws. If you don't have enough from your own decorations, on the twenty-sixth of December go to a place that sold Christmas trees and you'll get all you need for a pittance, if not free.

Other good winter mulches are fresh oak leaves, which are crisp and don't compact easily, and corn stalks. Grain straw, generally used for strawberry beds, is acceptable for your perennial garden too if you inspect it first to be sure it is free of seeds. Otherwise you'll be fighting wheat, oats, or whatever next summer among your flowers. Prairie hay is just as good if it also seems clear of weed tops. Straw and hay are unsightly on flower beds, so you'll want to remove them after winter. Oak leaves are

342

something you can dig in or leave on the surface, come spring. *Put all these mulches on after the ground is frozen hard.* Mice might take cover in a deep leaf or hay mulch, and eat on plants there through winter. To prevent this, scatter a little poisoned wheat before applying the mulch.

Avoid covering the tops of plants that stay green all winter—oriental poppies, creeping phlox, candytuft, hollyhock, penstemons and primulas. Iris and daylilies, when established, need no winter mulch.

Managing your winter mulch. If you have windy winters you may have trouble keeping mulches in place. One drastic but secure way is to unroll chicken wire over them and fasten down at ends and here and there in the middle. Another way is to lay tree branches over the mulch; or unroll netting like that sold for sweet-pea trellises or erosion control.

When the calendar and the groundhog tell you that spring is just around the corner, open a few peep-holes in the mulch to see what's happening. You want to time the removal just right—not too early, not too late. If tulips, crocus and daffodils are poking through the ground, remove mulch from around them. In early spring they can stand even a hard freeze. Watch for other plants to appear, and gradually as you find them, lift off the leaves to let in light and air. Most early shoots have built-in frost resistance—they will surprise you by the cold they can take. Remove as much mulch as necessary to let them green up properly.

HOW TO PROTECT AGAINST STANDING ICE AND WATER

The best prevention is good drainage. Some plants are especially touchy about spending the winter in icy soil—chrysanthemums, some lilies, delphiniums, oriental poppies and many of the rock garden plants. This is probably the reason they so often grow well on slopes where drainage is assured. Even irises that can stand almost anything resent cold wetness around their crowns.

Try to plant all these where water can't gather into icy pools. For some of them you can improve conditions in a level bed by putting a spadeful of dry sand, coal ashes or fine cinders over the crowns in fall. This leads water away. But don't cover the foliage of oriental poppies or delphiniums. Your prized chrysanthemums are safer if you lift them with a clump of earth and store them in the coldframe. Lacking a coldframe, simply dig them with a big spadeful of soil and set them on top of the ground beside the hole. If you have a row, set clumps close together and lay boards along the row to keep the soil from washing off. You can winter the Frikarti aster this way, too, although a coldframe is better.

HOW TO PROTECT FROM MICE AND RABBITS

When snow lies long and deep, the mice and rabbits in your yard may be driven by hunger to eat on young shrubs and trees. Tender bark of fruit trees may be gnawed away at the snow line. If the tree is completely girdled it will die. Other victims frequently are raspberry bushes, roses, and viburnums. Where this is likely to happen, a collar of screen or hardware wire encircling trunk or stems from ground level to well above snow depth will keep the rodents away and prevent damage. Although it may not seem practical to guard every shrub, tree or berry bush this way, it is certainly worthwhile on the very valuable ones.

EASY-DOES-IT IDEAS

Your old Christmas tree, cut up into separate branches, makes extra good winter protection for perennial flowers, and right after Christmas is a good time to spread the evergreen pieces over the garden.

A bushel basket filled with dry oak leaves and turned over slightly tender plants like tritomas is an easy way to protect them through frigid weather. Set a brick on top to keep wind from upsetting it.

The lath screen you use in summer to shade transplants is handy too for winter protection of young broadleaf evergreens like azaleas and hollies. Stand it upright or lean it against a post on the south side of them to break the drying winter sun.

343

Chapter 26

YOUR PRIVATE WAR
ON PEST AND DISEASE

How much do I have to spray to have a good garden?

You will have only a small war to wage, or none at all, if you choose certain kinds of plants. You can't have roses or fruit trees if you aren't willing to spray or dust, but you could have a multitude of other plants. Either nothing much bothers them or they are too tough to be affected.

For instance, among trees you can have some oaks, tulip tree, goldenrain tree, redbud, juniper, or flowering crabapple, to name a few. Among shrubs, you might choose kinds of euonymus, spiraeas, kerria, common lilac, forsythia, or honeysuckle. For perennials, you could have daffodils, tulips, all the little bulbs like scilla and crocus, sedums, hostas, Siberian irises, bleeding hearts, hardy candytuft, coralbells, daylilies, artemisia, ornamental grasses, and hardy ferns. For annuals, you would have petunias, marigolds, salvias, larkspurs, portulaca, and dozens of others.

A CLEAN GARDEN IS A HEALTHY GARDEN

No matter what you grow, you can avoid most troubles if you maintain a "clean" garden, and you'd do this anyway just to keep things looking good. For instance, keep down weeds around your flowers, shrubs, and vegetables because many insects breed among weeds, and then move from them to your choice plants. In the fall when frost has killed plant tops, cut them off and dispose of them, either by burning or composting so that bugs or diseases that might overwinter in them go elsewhere. Don't compost anything that looks diseased; the spores may live over. Burn it instead.

Get rid of old boards, cans, brush piles— all possible shelters for insects. If you want evidence of them, lift a board that has lain in the same place a while and see what a variety of slugs, sowbugs, crickets, and centipedes have been living under it.

If you're a vegetable gardener or have a patch of annual flowers, you'll want to have the garden plowed in the fall. This brings to the surface slumbering insects or their eggs or pupae where winter disposes of them. Relocate your crops just as a farmer does. Don't grow cabbage or tomatoes in the same place two years running. Do the same with certain flowers, like China asters, that might build up a disease hotspot if they stay long in the same place, and select disease-resistant varieties of these and other plants whenever they are available.

Space plants far enough apart so there can be air between them. They not only grow better, but diseases are less apt to start and spread in uncrowded plantings. Curb your impulse to go out on a warm evening and sprinkle everything with the hose. Besides being a bad way to water, this practice encourages foliage diseases.

Then make friends with the natural enemies of insects. These creatures are your allies. At the top of the list are the birds. Most kinds, even sparrows, eat insects and eggs of insects. Encourage birds to stay in your yard by providing nesting places, water, shrubs for shelter. (More ways to encourage birds are suggested in Chapter 16.) Take a kindly attitude towards your garden toads; every good garden needs a family of them. Insects are almost all toads eat. Two *beneficial* insects to know and respect are ladybugs and praying mantis. You can even buy these in quantity to police your yard (although you are powerless to keep them in it). Wheat farmers use ladybugs by the millions to clean up aphid attacks.

Depending on how much time, help and area you have, you can control some large insects—Japanese beetles, blister beetles and potato beetles—just by watching for them and hand picking. Carry a tin can half full of kerosene with you and knock them into it. To be effective with this approach, seek out and destroy the early insects before they have had time to propagate new generations. Wear gloves for collecting blister beetles.

You can protect young transplants of asters, zinnias, and marigolds from cutworms and armyworms with paper collars. A paper milk carton with top and bottom out and cut in two will do the trick.

When you see early evidence of disease, like rose blackspot or chrysanthemum leaf spot, remove the affected leaves and burn them. This slows down the spread of the epidemic.

Harden your heart and destroy by burning any plants you find hopelessly diseased, like lilies with mosaic and dahlias with stunt. In this way, you protect other plants that are still healthy.

YOUR CHEMICAL ARSENAL

Beyond these more or less peaceable means, you will have to declare war, and rely on chemicals to help you conquer insects and diseases. If you grow fruit trees, roses, or specialize in something like iris or lilies you're almost sure to have problems that can hardly be solved any other way.

It is important, when you're growing plants you know will need protection, to give it in time. It is far easier to prevent trouble than to cure it. Go after aphids, for instance, as soon as you see the first one—not after you see a mob of them. For diseases like blackspot of roses that spread in water, dust or spray ahead of rains, not afterward. Using chemicals protectively, you'll probably make it routine to go over everything lightly each ten days or so—an excellent practice, for it usually prevents any serious trouble.

SHALL I DUST OR SPRAY?

This is a question without an answer. Spraying is cheaper and gives better control. But many gardeners consider it messy and more trouble. Dusting is faster, more convenient and has no clean-up afterward. A little rotary duster kept filled with a multipurpose mixture is handy indeed. Dusting, however, works best only when the air is still, and in some areas such a condition seldom exists. To dust or to spray is something for you to decide, based on your own needs and circumstances.

A good sprayer and a good duster cost about the same, but the duster will probably last longer. Whichever you get, make it a good one. Cheap kinds are frustrating.

MULTIPURPOSE COMBINATIONS ARE A BOON

When you do dust or spray, the whole business is simplified and much time is saved if you use a multipurpose preparation that takes care of most insects and diseases with one material. You can buy these under hundreds of trade names. Or if they are to be used as sprays, you can make them up yourself. (Making your own dust mixtures is more trouble than it's worth.)

Read the label before you buy. A good multipurpose spray or dust combination for a flower garden contains at least:

one chemical (like malathion) that kills some insects when it hits them,
one chemical (like methoxychlor or DDT) that has a lasting effect, and poisons certain insects when they come upon it,
one good fungicide (like zineb or ferbam) that prevents the spread of fungus diseases.

Some materials go a step further and include something like Aramite to control red spiders; and if it's a spray particularly for roses it ideally includes something like Karathane to prevent mildew.

If you want to mix your own spray (a considerable saving in cost) here is one recipe:

2 gallons of water
2 tablespoons 50 per cent methoxychlor wettable powder
7 tablespoons ferbam
2 tablespoons malathion (50 per cent liquid emulsion)

Stir enough water into the dry materials to make a thick paste. Then add them to the larger quantity of water. Finally add the malathion. Stir out the lumps, add a capful of liquid soap or detergent for a sticker, and strain the spray through a cheesecloth or fine sieve into your sprayer.

This mixture controls pests like aphids on shrubs; flea beetles on petunias and sweet alyssum; scale insects on lilacs; thrips on gladiolus, leaf spot on chrysanthemums, blackspot on roses, and botrytis on peonies.

When you spray, hold the nozzle low and aim it up so the mist hits the undersides of leaves. Then spray from the top down.

When you dust, also hold the spout low so dust rises through the foliage. Wear long sleeves to keep your skin covered—and wash your hands with soap when you get through.

SPECIFIC REMEDIES

When you have severe and specific trouble, like aphids all over your snowball bush, you might select a chemical designed just for aphids. In such cases, it pays to know something about the main chemicals and what they will do. Here is a guide to twenty-four of them:

FOR INSECTS

Aramite. Kills red spiders and spider mites but not other insects. As a 15 per cent wettable powder, 1 tablespoon to 1 gallon water.

Chlordane. Kills grasshoppers, ants, grubs, chinch bugs, weevils. As a 50 per cent wettable powder, 2 tablespoons to a gallon.

DDT. Kills most beetles, cankerworms, iris and lilac borers, and sowbugs. As 50 per cent wettable powder, 2 tablespoons per gallon.

Diazinon. Kills many insects including spider mites, thrips, flea beetles. As $12\frac{1}{2}$ per cent concentrate use 1 tablespoon per gallon.

Dieldrin. Kills practically all soil insects. Use 2 tablespoons 5 per cent wettable powder per gallon.

Lead arsenate. Kills anything that chews foliage; especially good for bagworms. Use 3 to 6 tablespoons to a gallon.

Malathion. Kills most small thin-skinned insects. As 50 per cent emulsion, use 1 teaspoon per gallon.

Methoxychlor. Gets many kinds of small beetles. As 50 per cent wettable powder, 2 tablespoons to a gallon.

Nicotine sulfate. Black Leaf 40. Kills aphids and other soft bodied insects. Use 1 teaspoon per gallon.

Rotenone. Kills many small insects and is safe to use on food. As 5 per cent wettable powder, use $3\frac{1}{2}$ tablespoons to a gallon.

Sevin. Fairly safe short term control for Japanese beetles, bagworms, many other insects. As 50 per cent wettable powder, 2 tablespoons per gallon.

Sulfur. Both an insecticide (kills mites) and fungicide (controls mildew). Use 4 tablespoons to a gallon, or use as a dust.

FOR DISEASES

(Follow package directions for mixing.)

Arasan. Controls diseases borne on seeds and corms.

Bichloride of mercury (Mercuric chloride or corrosive sublimate). A powerful disinfectant to be poured on the soil to control crown and rhizome rots. Use glass, ceramic, or enamel container, dissolve one 7-grain tablet to each pint warm water. Corrodes metal and is *highly poisonous.*

Bordeaux mixture. Made of lime and copper sulfate, controls cankers and blights. Follow package directions.

Karathane. One of the best things for powdery mildew. Sold as Mildex.

Acti-dione PM. Antibiotic, perhaps the best

remedy for powdery mildew. Acti-dione RZ is formula for turf diseases.

Captan. For fruit rots, scab diseases, rose blackspot.

Ferbam. For fruit rots, rusts, botrytis blights, leaf spots.

Lime-sulfur. Usually a cool-weather spray, controls cankers, leaf spots, blights, on woody plants.

Maneb. For downy mildews, rose blackspot, several kinds of anthracnose diseases.

Phaltan. For rose blackspot, mildew, rots, leaf spots.

Terraclor. Soil fungicide, poured on soil around living plants, for crown and stem rots, and club roots. (Same as PCNB.)

Zineb. For peony botrytis, rose blackspot, snapdragon rust.

In buying these chemicals, you will find that they are put up in various forms. You can get chlordane, for instance, as a liquid "emulsion" (this means it will blend with water) of different strengths; as a wettable powder (this means you can dissolve it in water) usually at 50 per cent strength; and as a dust (usually at 5 per cent strength).

Certain chemicals you can combine, and certain ones you can't—for the simple reason that one of the substances may neutralize another making it useless, or else cause a reaction that harms the plant. Bordeaux mixture, lime-sulfur and oil sprays are kinds best used alone.

Sulfur, either alone or in a combination, may burn foliage at high temperatures. Don't use it or a combination containing it when the thermometer is above 85 degrees. Avoid using it on pink snowball (*Viburnum carlesi*) or on any cucumber or melon vines—it harms the foliage.

DDT may harm melons, squash, or cucumber vines; and sometimes camellias. Choose another insecticide for these.

Oil sprays put on when plants are dormant may be harmful if temperatures are below 45 degrees. On the other hand, summer oil sprays may burn in bright sun or when the temperature is over 85 degrees.

Lead arsenate may harm foliage of cherry, peach or plum trees.

Most of the newer garden chemicals (and many old ones, too) are powerful enough to harm people, pets, and birds. *Always follow the directions and warnings* on a package of insecticide or fungicide. Remember that you are handling poison. Store it out of the reach of children; burn or get rid of old containers; and leave no buckets of mixed spray sitting around where youngsters or pets can get at them.

Here is a list of *possible* troubles and what you can do about them. Be comforted —your plants may never have any of these, or very few of them, especially if (1) you keep a clean garden, and (2) you spray or dust with a multipurpose mixture *before* trouble starts.

SLUGS AND SNAILS

Although not insects, slugs and snails are worse than most in the damage done —eating ragged holes in leaves. One way to keep them away from choice plants is to encircle the area with a ribbon of sand, cinders, or lime. They seldom will cross these materials. You can also buy baits (Snairol is one trade name) to place where slugs and snails congregate. These contain poisons which will harm birds or pets that eat them, so scatter them under dense foliage or boards where these animals are not likely to find them.

HOW TO COPE WITH MOLES

Perhaps moles do not really eat bulbs and roots, but are after grubs and other soil insects. But the results are the same as if they were eating everything. They raise ned in a flower border or a lawn. If you use insecticide on your lawn (see Chapter 4) you will not have much trouble there with moles. In flower beds you have three possible methods of control—trapping, poisoning, or gassing. Trapping is surest, if you are patient and a good trapper. Watch runs daily to see which are in use. Press down the earth over one that is, and set the trap over it. You can also buy poisoned peanuts to drop into runs. They might get the mole or at least kill a few mice that use the run. For gassing runs you can buy "smoke bombs" to light and poke into the hole. These are very effective. As a last resort you

SOME POSSIBLE INSECT AND DISEASE TROUBLES ON ORNAMENTALS

Host and pest	Damage	Control
AJUGA Crown rot	Plants turn black, wilt.	Take out plants and soil. Treat area with Terraclor (PCNB).
AQUILEGIA Red spider	Worst in hot weather. So small they are seldom seen. Identified by the trouble they cause. Suck juices, cause yellowing or whitening of foliage, sometimes loss of leaves, decline of plants.	Dust with sulfur. Strong stream of water. Malathion spray. Aramite dust or spray.
ARBORVITAE Bagworm	1-inch brown worm inside a silky debris-covered bag which moves with him. Devours foliage.	Hand pick and destroy bags. Spray affected plants with lead arsenate 2 oz. to 3 gallons water in May to early June just after caterpillars hatch. Or spray with diazinon.
ASTER, CHINA (*Callistephus*) Aster wilt	Plants wilt, roots seem to rot.	Grow wilt-resistant varieties. Do not plant where asters recently grew. Burn infected tops. Spray with captan or zineb.
Aster yellows	Yellowish plants, stunted.	Spray weekly with DDT to control leaf hoppers.
Leaf hoppers	$\frac{1}{8}$-inch active wedge-shaped pale green or tan insects that fly when disturbed. Suck juices, whitening and curling leaves, tender tips. Some transmit diseases.	5% DDT dust or 50% methoxychlor WP*, 2 T. in 1 gallon water.
Striped cucumber beetle	$\frac{1}{4}$-inch yellowish green beetles with three black stripes on wing covers. A spotted kind, similar, has 12 black spots on back. They eat holes in buds, flowers, leaves, stems, deform flowers. Plants wilt, sometimes die.	1% rotenone dust or DDT 50% WP*, 2 T. to gallon water, or 5% methoxychlor dust, or Sevin 50% WP*, 2 T. in 1 gallon water. Repeat weekly.
BEGONIA, TUBEROUS Powdery mildew	White spots on leaves.	Spray with Acti-dione PM or Phaltan.
CALENDULA Leaf hoppers	See ASTER	
Tarnished plant bug	Brassy flat $\frac{1}{4}$-inch bugs with yellow and black marks. Common in late summer. Puncture leaves and sting tissue of leaves and buds causing flowers to be deformed.	DDT 50% WP*, 2 teaspoons per gallon or 5% DDT dust.
CARNATION (Pinks or Sweet William) (*Dianthus*) Leaf spots, branch rot	Lower branches and stems die from leaf base rot. Ashy-gray spots with dark brown, moldy center.	Spray with zineb, maneb, captan or ferbam.

* WP = wettable powder form

Host and pest	Damage	Control
Downy mildew	Irregular purplish areas on leaves and stems. Downy mold (white) may develop on undersides of leaf spots if humid.	Spray with zineb, or maneb.
CHRYSANTHEMUM Bud and ray blights	Buds may be one-sided, brown-black, fail to develop rays, may rot. Flowers show pinkish spots, later become brown or straw-colored.	Spray with zineb or captan.
Leaf spots	Gray, dark brown or black spots on leaves. Leaves may shrivel, die and fall prematurely, starting at base of stem.	Hand pick and burn affected leaves. Spray plants with zineb, captan, maneb or ferbam.
Stem and stalk borer	See IRIS	
Striped cucumber beetle	See ASTER	
Tarnished plant bug	See CALENDULA	
COLUMBINE Crown rot	Rotting of stems near ground line results in death of plant.	Remove infected plants and soil as soon as noticed.
COSMOS Tarnished plant bug	See CALENDULA	
COTONEASTER Bagworm	See ARBORVITAE	
DAHLIA Mosaic, stunt	Yellow-green areas in leaves, with margins often uprolled; plants short, bushy; disease transmitted by aphids.	Pull out and burn infected plants. Control aphids.
Powdery mildew	Gray-white mold patches on leaves and petioles. Leaves may wither and curl.	Spray with Karathane, sulfur, or Acti-dione PM.
Stem and stalk borer	See IRIS	
Leaf hoppers	See ASTER	
Striped cucumber beetle	See ASTER	
Tarnished plant bug	See CALENDULA	
DELPHINIUM Crown rot	Plants rot at crown, with reddish mustard-seed-like bodies (sclerotia) and white fungus mycelium; spreads fast in warm humid weather.	Remove diseased plant and surrounding soil. Drench area with Terraclor solution or bichloride of mercury, one 7-grain tablet to a pint of water.
DOGWOOD Leaf spot	Brown leaf spots with purple borders.	Spray with maneb or captan starting when buds break.

349

Host and pest	*Damage*	*Control*
EUONYMUS Scale insects	Grayish, whitish or brownish and flat, rod-shaped, pear-shaped or shell-shaped circular encrustation on stems or leaves. Weaken or kill plants by sucking sap.	Spray in crawling stage in late spring with malathion, $1\frac{1}{2}$ teaspoons 50% emulsion to 1 gallon, or during dormant season with white oil emulsion spray, $\frac{1}{2}$ cup to a gallon.
FERN Scale	See EUONYMUS	
GARDENIA Scale	See EUONYMUS	
GERANIUM Aphids	Green, red or black $\frac{1}{8}$-inch soft-bodied insects, found in large colonies. Some have wings. Suck juices from stems or leaves deforming foliage or flowers. Sometimes even on roots.	Nicotine sulfate spray or malathion spray each week until controlled.
Blackleg	Cuttings get black rot at base of stem.	Start cuttings from healthy plants in vermiculite or sterilized sand.
GLADIOLUS Dry rot	Brown spots on corms, husks, with small black sclerotia. Plants are yellow, die early.	Dust corms before planting with Arasan. Select unblemished stock.
Leaf hoppers	See ASTER	
Thrips	Tiny insects seldom seen, brown with light feathery wings. Active. Feed on leaves and buds—cause silvering of leaves and bleaching plants or splotching of flower parts. Sometimes foliage browns and dies back.	Dust 5% chlordane dust weekly; or 10% DDT dust; malathion 50%, $1\frac{1}{2}$ teaspoons to 1 gallon. Dust glad corms in storage with DDT. Keep down neighboring grassy weeds.
Yellows, basal rot	Soil fungus infects plants through roots. Plant turns yellow, wilts, and dies.	Use resistant varieties. Change location.
GRASSES Armyworm	Fleshy, $1\frac{1}{2}$-inch green to black with light streaks. Feeds at night on foliage.	5% dust DDT or spray with 50% DDT WP*—3 T. to 1 gallon at edge of garden.
HOLLYHOCK Leaf hopper	See ASTER	
Rust	Yellow to orange pustules on underside of leaves; yellow spots on upper side. Leaves die.	Spray with zineb. Remove diseased leaves as they occur. Cut down and burn old stalks in fall.
IRIS Leaf spots	Oval brown spots with reddish borders on upper portions of leaves.	Spray with zineb or bordeaux mixture; clean up in fall.

WP = wettable powder form

Host and pest	Damage	Control
Soft rot	Vile smelling soft rot with yellow ooze in rhizomes and at base of leaves, often follows borer injury.	Prevent borers. After division soak rhizomes 30 minutes in mercuric chloride solution, 7-grain tablet to 1 pint water. Plant in fresh soil.
Iris borer	A clue to their presence is sawdust on leaves or ground under plants, and hole tunneled into base of leaf. Usually seen as soft pale larvae working through rhizome.	Burn dead iris leaves in fall; in spring, spray new leaves every two weeks with 50% DDT WP*, 3 T. per gallon of water.
JUNIPER Bagworm	See ARBORVITAE	
Cedar-apple rust	Brown galls put out orange horns in spring; spores infect alternate host (apples, hawthorn).	Remove galls in winter or spray in spring with Acti-dione to prevent spore horn formation.
LILY Botrytis blight	Especially serious on madonna lily. Oval orange spots grow together; leaves darken and droop in wet weather.	Start spraying early with bordeaux mixture, repeat every 7-18 days.
Mosaic and other virus diseases	Leaves mottled dark and light green; plants are stunted, lack vigor.	Buy virus-free bulbs if possible; do not plant in infected soil or near diseased lilies or tulips. Destroy plants that seem diseased. Control aphids.
MARIGOLD Tarnished plant bug	See CALENDULA	
MIMOSA Mimosa wilt	Serious in the south; soil fungus enters via roots and kills tree.	Resistant varieties have been developed. Ask nurserymen for them.
NARCISSUS Basal rot	Brown rot at base of bulb scales.	Discard and burn bulbs.
Mosaic, streak	Mottling, streaking, deformation.	Dig out and destroy diseased bulbs.
PANSY Botrytis blight	Gray mold develops on plants that are too crowded or kept too moist.	Remove diseased plants. Spray others with captan, zineb.
PEONY Botrytis blight	Buds turn black or flowers blast; young shoots rot with gray mold; large irregular brown spots appear on leaves.	Cut stalks at ground level in fall; burn tops. In spring spray with zineb, ferbam, or bordeaux mixture, starting as shoots appear.
PETUNIA Tobacco mosaic and other virus diseases	Foliage mottled, leaves crinkle and plant dies.	Pull out and burn diseased plants. Do not smoke while handling plants, especially while transplanting seedlings.

* WP = wettable powder form

Host and pest	*Damage*	*Control*
PHLOX Leaf blight (physiological)	Lower leaves turn brown, die, from base upward on stem. Not a true disease.	No real control. Believed caused by reduced water supply in old stems. Cut old stalks at ground to encourage new growth.
Powdery mildew	White felty coating on leaves and stems.	Dust with sulfur or spray with Acti-dione PM or Karathane. Cut and burn old stalks in fall.
PHYSOSTEGIA Red spider	See AQUILEGIA	
PINES (especially Scotch and Austrian) Pine tip blight	Young tips are blighted, brown.	Cut out infected parts; spray trees with ferbam.
PRIMROSE (*Primula*) Botrytis blight	Gray mold forms on leaves and flowers in moist weather.	Pick off fading flowers; spray with captan or zineb.
ROSES	(See Chapter 13)	
SNAPDRAGON Rust	Powdery brown spots on undersides of leaves, yellow above.	Choose resistant varieties or spray with zineb.
SWEET ALYSSUM Club root	Mature plants wilt; root system a mass of distorted swellings.	Treat soil with Terraclor before planting, if this has occurred in previous years.
SWEET PEA Anthracnose	White spots on leaves, stems, flowers and pods about flowering time. Later leaves and shoots wilt and dry up.	Spray with zineb. Do not plant near apple or privet.
Powdery mildew	Disfiguring white coating on leaves.	Spray with Acti-dione PM or Karathane.
TULIP Botrytis blight or fire	White patches on leaves, plants stunted, buds blasted. Shiny black sclerotia form on rotting leaves and on bulbs.	Discard bulbs showing black spots. In early spring spray with ferbam or zineb. Burn dead tops.
Lily mottle virus	Broken flower colors, mottled foliage.	Isolate such plants from tulips or lilies. Control aphids.
VIOLET Red spider	See AQUILEGIA	
ZINNIA Leaf hopper	See ASTER	
Powdery mildew	White coating on foliage in late summer.	Spray with Karathane, Acti-dione PM or dust with sulfur.
Striped cucumber beetle	See ASTER	

can drive the mole away at least temporarily by flooding the run with water from the hose.

EASY-DOES-IT IDEAS

A multipurpose garden dust combination is the handiest remedy to keep ready for garden insect or disease emergencies. Puff it on at the first signs of trouble.

Save cardboard milk cartons in spring. With ends removed and cut in two, they make good collars around tender young transplants like marigolds, tomatoes, and peppers, to fend off cutworms.

A stitch in time saves nine when you're controlling insects. Wipe out the first generation you spot in the spring, and you'll have fewer insects all summer long.

Chapter 27

HOW TO HANDLE PLANTS FROM THE NURSERY

When should I plan to set out new plants?

The proper planting time depends both on region and plant material. It also depends somewhat on your method. The most practical time to set out the majority of plants is fall or spring. But almost any time is possible if you transplant with care.

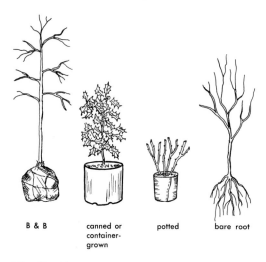

B & B   canned or   potted   bare root
         container-
         grown

Fig. 59   Four ways nursery plants are sold.

When you talk with nurserymen, you will hear words like "balled and burlapped" (sometimes they abbreviate it to "b and b"), "canned," "potted," and "bare root."

Balled and burlapped means that roots are enclosed in an earth ball just as they grew; the nurseryman has dug it with care

and wrapped, pinned, and tied the burlap to prevent soil from cracking and falling off. Most large needle evergreens and many deciduous trees, like dogwoods and pin oaks, come this way.

Canned usually means the same as "container-grown" with plants already growing in all sorts of metal cans—lard cans, large food tins, and whatever else the grower could find to put them in when small. He uses these for hard-to-transplant things like pyracantha, holly and dogwoods. They have grown up in the can instead of the field. All the roots are inside. Remind the nurseryman to cut the can before you take it home, or you'll have a tussle getting the plant out. The nursery has a special can-cutter that does it with ease. Plants bought in cans are almost fail-proof.

Plants in pots are like "canned" ones except that they are smaller. Today pots are usually something disposable of tar paper or plastic-coated cardboard, and the plants —perennials, roses or small evergreens— have grown there only a season or so.

"Bare root" is just what it says. The roots have been dug and the soil shaken off; you can see every inch of them. This is the way you'll buy most *dormant* shade and fruit trees, flowering shrubs, early spring- or fall-planted roses, and hedge plants.

Why nursery-grown plants stand a better chance. The quality of the plant you get depends on the skill and industry of the nurseryman. To make roots close to the trunk, the nurseryman root-prunes plants by deep, close cultivating, or transplants them several times. Small trees put out many more roots back of each big one that is cut off, thus making a fine dense mass. A plant so grown is more likely to survive transplanting than its counterpart from the woods, where it probably developed one or two long rangy roots, part of which you had to cut off in digging.

The nurseryman also fattens the plant, feeding it heavily the summer before he digs it, so it is loaded with stored nutrients. The tree from the woods, on the other hand, has competed with others of the forest and is lean and half-starved.

BEST PLANTING TIMES

PLANTING EVERGREENS

Evergreens obviously have foliage the year around so they are never completely dormant. In fall, winter, and early spring they slow down most, and that is when transplanting them is best.

Needle kinds like pines, junipers, arborvitae, spruces, and yews—if balled and burlapped or canned—are best moved from early fall (August, September) to late spring (April, May). Don't move them in midwinter if you live in the North where the ground is frozen and you can't prepare a good planting hole. As soon as spring opens up you can begin setting out this type of nursery stock. In the South, you may be planting in January and December.

If you are setting out quantities of plants for a hedge or shelter belt, buy little bare-root evergreens. A high percentage will survive provided you never let roots dry for even a minute as you plant. Keep them covered as you work. The best time for setting these out is early spring as soon as you can prepare ground properly and as the soil begins to warm up.

Broadleaf evergreens. If you live where winters are mild in the South and West, you can plant broadleafs in fall or spring, the same as needle kinds. If your winters are long, dry and cold, better wait until spring. Occasionally you can get broadleafs bare root instead of b and b or canned.

When you do, you will have better luck transplanting them in spring than in fall, no matter where you live.

PLANTING DECIDUOUS TREES AND SHRUBS

Maples and lilacs are examples of plants that stay dormant from the time they lose leaves in fall until they put them out again in spring. Transplant any time during this dormancy. For most kinds whether you do it in fall or spring depends on the kind of winter you have.

If your average winters bring plenty of moisture; if the temperature does not take prolonged plunges to zero so soil is never frozen deep; if you have many cloudy days with high humidity and few sunny ones; and if strong wind is a rarity—then you should be able to plant most trees and shrubs including roses in fall. If your winters are long, frigid, deep-frozen, sunny, windy, dry—better wait for spring to plant all deciduous trees and shrubs.

As a general geographic rule, fall planting is safer on the East and the West coasts and in the South, than it is in the Midwest. In the northern tier of states and in the Great Plains, losses from fall planting are too high to justify it.

Where fall planting is safe, it is to your advantage to plant then, because nursery stock is then fresh-dug, food-packed and full of vitality from the growing season just completed. In spring the stock you buy has probably spent the winter in storage, where it has lost some of its vitality, even though held perfectly dormant.

A few kinds are always better planted in spring, so root damage can mend in a hurry. These always-in-spring kinds are:

birch	magnolia	sweet gum
dogwood	redbud	tulip tree
hawthorn	scarlet oak	walnut
hornbeam	sour gum	white oak

To be on the safe side, add fruit trees, flowering fruit trees, and London plane-trees to the spring list, although fall is also sometimes a successful planting time for them.

Where you think fall planting is risky

and you do it anyway, increase the odds by starting as early as you can get the stock; and by keeping plants well watered until freeze-up to get quick rooting. Shield and mulch such plantings extra well. See Chapter 25 for ways of winter protection.

PLANTING PERENNIALS AND BULBS

Herbaceous perennials (the kinds that die back to the roots each year) transplant best during their dormant or underground stage, usually just before growth appears. For most kinds this is fall or spring. With numerous exceptions, the rule is to plant in spring kinds that bloom in summer and fall, and to plant in fall kinds that bloom in earliest spring and summer.

Two big exceptions are iris and daylilies, or hemerocallis. Irises have a slowdown right after they bloom in June and July. This is the best time to plant or transplant them. Hemerocallis are so amicable, you can plant them any time from early spring to fall, even while they are blooming. The big sales season for them is in June and July. Another exception is the oriental poppy. This disappears in midsummer, making August or September the best time for transplanting the roots.

Some perennials for spring planting are chrysanthemums, hardy asters, shasta daisies, delphinium, campanulas, phlox, iberis, achillea, Japanese anemone, echinops, dianthus, baby's breath, helleborus, hostas, balloon flower, plumbago (leadwort), and astilbe.

Some to plant in autumn from mid-August on are lilies, tulips, daffodils, and other spring-flowering bulbs, mertensia, old-fashioned bleeding hearts, peonies, foxgloves, and hollyhocks.

Because of the disappearing trick done by many bulbs, mertensia, oriental poppies and bleeding hearts, you may prefer to dig and replant those when the foliage begins to turn yellow. Otherwise you may lose or forget them. This timing seems just as successful as fall transplanting.

The small group of autumn blooming bulbs—lycoris and belladonna-lily, chiefly—those that make foliage early in the year and blooms much later—transplant best in August and September right after they bloom. Reset colchicums, however, after the foliage dies down and before blooms appear, probably July or August.

Some that you can plant with almost equal success either spring or early fall are columbines, ferns, lily-of-the-valley, and creeping phlox. By using container-grown rather than bare-root plants, you can set out almost any perennial whenever you please, even peonies and lilies, but don't forget to keep them well-watered and shaded the first two weeks.

OUT-OF-SEASON PLANTING

Don't let these "rules" about planting times scare you. You'll be surprised how you can stretch them. After you get used to transplanting, you'll be moving things almost all year around, but do:

Save all roots you can, even if it means moving much soil.

Work fast to avoid drying.

Cut back leafy tops to compensate for roots that have also been cut off.

Water the roots freely at planting time and later.

Protect tops from drying by shading, spraying with water or covering with an anti-desiccant like Wilt Pruf.

It helps also to choose a cloudy day for planting. If the cloud brings rain, you are in luck. The smaller and younger the plant, the easier it is to transplant. If you use container-grown, canned or potted plants, you can set them out when you please—and let the rules go.

About container-grown plants. These are a boon when you're busy, because they let you plant all season long, whenever plants are available. Another advantage is that after you get the plants you can postpone planting for days or even weeks without harm, provided you water them. Because of the weight of a can of soil and costs of shipping, your selection is limited to what you can find at nurseries within driving distance.

152   June or July is the best time to plant iris rhizomes. The root is barely covered with soil.   *Ross*

153   *Opposite*   September or October is an ideal time for planting peonies. Good root divisions come from husky clumps like this one.   *Kohl*

154   *Below Left*   Difficult-to-transplant things, like these melons, may be started in peat pots and transplanted pot and all without difficulty.

George J. Ball

155   *Below Right*   When you buy nursery plants by mail, they usually arrive as bare root dormant plants. Often they are packed in plastic bags, which keep them fresh.   *Inter-State*

TRANSPLANTING

Whatever you transplant, prepare a good soil mixture for it. Whether it is an oak to last a lifetime or a tomato plant just for the summer, you get more for your money and quicker, surer results if you dig in humus like compost, peat moss, or rotted manure. This lightens the soil and makes it hold more water. And humus encourages quick root formation on a young plant—a process vital to survival. If you enrich the soil with fertilizer, put it low in the soil so it *does not touch roots or stem.*

HOW TO SET OUT BALLED AND BURLAPPED PLANTS

Let's say you have been to the nursery and brought home a young juniper, perhaps a spreading Pfitzer, to plant beside your front walk. It is balled and burlapped and seems to weigh 80 to 100 pounds (which it probably does!).

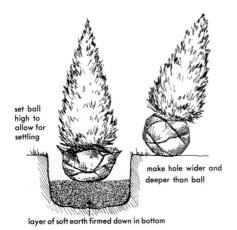

set ball high to allow for settling

make hole wider and deeper than ball

layer of soft earth firmed down in bottom

Fig. 60 Planting a balled and burlapped tree. Fold back burlap from around top of ball, but do not remove it.

For a 1-foot-wide ball, dig a hole about 2 feet wide and 6 inches deeper than the ball. Pile the earth on a canvas or burlap bag to keep it off your walk or lawn. When the hole is big enough, put 6 or 7 inches of the soil back in the hole, and tramp it down. You want to avoid much settling.

Maneuver the soil ball into the hole. You may need someone to help lift it. Or

you can use a plank for leverage to lower the plant. Handle the earth ball gently so you don't crack it. The top of the ball should be just a little above the surface of the ground to allow for a half-inch of settling. Lay a yardstick across the hole to show for sure where ground level is. Turn the plant so its best side is where you want it, and it stands straight.

Throw soft soil into the hole, and with your fingers or a stick, poke it under and all around so the tree is firm and doesn't rock. Put in more soil until the hole is half-full. Press or stamp this down. Fill with water and let it soak in.

Unpin the burlap around the top of the plant, fold it back a little and work in some soil. Leave the burlap. It will disintegrate and not harm the plant. Add soil to the top of the hole and press it gently with your foot. Away from the trunk, pull up a ring of soil to make a saucer, and fill it with water. Let it soak away. Refill two or three times to be sure of a good watering job, and then leave the tree alone for several days.

Water every four to seven days unless you get heavy rains. As the burlap disintegrates in the moist soil, the tree roots reach out into the earth. Your watering saucer won't be needed after the first month or so. Then put on a 3-inch layer of compost, leaves or other mulch to preserve moisture.

HOW TO SET OUT BARE-ROOT TREES AND SHRUBS

Let's say you have bought a flowering crabapple to plant on a fine spring Saturday. First unwrap the tree in the shade and lay the roots in a tub of water to keep them fresh until the hole is prepared. Or you can cover roots with wet gunny sacks and take the tree to the yard with you. Estimate the depth and spread of the roots. Dig the hole wide and deep enough so roots won't curl against the sides or bottom. If there is one long root, make a special channel at the side of the planting hole for this. Don't cut off a big side root.

Make a mound of loose soil in the bottom of the hole to help steady the plant while you fill in soil around it. Set the plant so the dividing line between top and roots (smooth bark indicates top, roughness and lighter color shows root) is an inch above ground level. Spread roots so they run downward and outward over the mound, and begin to fill in soil. Poke it down with your fingers all around the roots. If the plant seems to be descending into the hole draw it gently up again and fill in more soil underneath. The idea is to work the earth firm with no air spaces left to dry the roots or let the plant settle later.

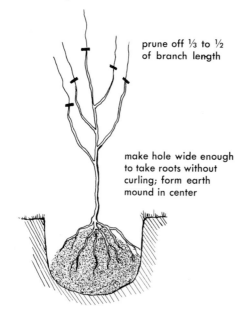

prune off ⅓ to ½ of branch length

make hole wide enough to take roots without curling; form earth mound in center

Fig. 61 Planting a bare-root tree.

When the hole is half full, pour in water to the top and let it soak down. Then finish filling with soil, and finally make a saucer of soil around the top to hold the water you will be careful to give for the next month or so.

The nursery may already have pruned the plant for you. You can easily tell if there are pruning cuts. From a third to a half of the branch area should have been cut off. If the nursery did not do it, then it's up to you. Use hand pruners and leave no stubs. This cutting back of the top compensates for roots the tree has lost, and almost guarantees survival. After a season the tree grows back what you cut off, and then goes beyond it. This need for pruning extends to all bare-root trees and shrubs. You can prune difficult-to-move trees like hickories and walnuts to one single stick.

First aid for distressed transplants. If as time goes on your bare-root tree or shrub shows no signs of life, try to save it and waste no time. With pruners cut the tree back to one main stem; and cut that down to two-thirds of its height. Don't do this operating piecemeal—do it all at once. The object is to bring the size of the top quickly down to balance what the injured roots can support. Wait to see what happens, watering the root occasionally and also moistening the top. Put on a compost mulch and pour water through it, so humusy water reaches the root. Don't abandon hope until at least two months have gone by without growth.

Planting depths for different plants. Plant dwarf fruit trees high enough so the bud union or graft (swelling or jog between root and stem) comes at ground level. These are standard varieties grafted or budded on dwarfing roots. If you set the root section of this combination too high, it may send up a top of its own, which is a nuisance. On the other hand if you plant the graft too low, the top may form roots of its own with the result that the tree loses its dwarfness.

Plant roses so the bud union is near ground level (see Chapter 13) but not high enough to encourage root suckers to sprout. Roses are budded on a vigorous root, and if any of it reaches above ground it is likely to send up canes that soon overshadow the desirable kind budded on top.

Plant lilacs and viburnums (all grafted kinds) 2 inches deeper than they stood in the nursery. In this case, the purpose is to encourage the grafted-on tops to form their own roots. Such roots assure a longer life than the existing grafted-on roots, which are often short-lived and merely there to provide a strong start.

How to "heel" plants in. If your bare-root plants arrive before you are ready to set them out, "heel" them in in a shaded spot. Heeling in is simply temporary planting. It involves digging a shallow trench, laying roots in it, and throwing soil over them. This is not true planting—only a way to store stock safely until you can plant properly. At most, leave plants heeled in for only a few weeks.

HOW TO SET OUT CONTAINER-GROWN PLANTS

These are easiest of all, but prepare soil just as carefully as for any other kind of planting. Make the hole about a foot wider and 6 inches deeper than the earth in the can. Fill soft earth into the bottom of the hole and push it down firmly.

If you had the nurseryman slit the can, it is easy to remove the plant. Otherwise, cut the can top to bottom with a tin snipper so as to slide out the soil ball in one piece. If you water the plant a few hours beforehand, the ball is less likely to break. Inspect the roots. Sometimes plants sold as "container-grown" have not really been grown there long, and you can see roots that were jammed and crowded to get them into the can. Let's hope you don't find this, but if you do, straighten these roots out, drawing them away from the ball toward the sides of the hole. Quickly turn the plant with its best side forward, set it level at the depth it was in the can, or perhaps a little deeper, and fill in soil. When the hole is half-filled, pour in water and let it soak down. Then finish filling, and give one last watering from the top.

HOW TO SET OUT SMALL PLANTS

Annual vegetables and flowers. Perhaps you have bought a market-pack full of 4-inch petunias. The roots are tangled. Starting at one end of the box, pry them apart and lift them out one by one as you plant. A table fork is a good tool. If some soil adheres, leave it. In the bed you have prepared, make a roomy hole for each plant with a trowel. Set roots into the hole so none are twisted, and seed leaves (the first little leaves on the plant) are at ground level or covered a little. However, stem-rooting tomatoes, marigolds, cosmos, and zinnias can go quite deep, right up to the first set of adult leaves. Fill in soil from the sides; add a cup of water and finish filling. Then pour another cup of water around the crown.

Pinch out tips of plants like tomatoes, peppers, petunias, marigolds, zinnias, sal-via, phlox, and cockscomb to reduce leaf surface and make up for roots that may have been lost. Cabbage, cauliflower, and lettuce seedlings and very *small* plants of all kinds recover quickly without pinching. Set a shade (shingle, paper cup, or milk carton) to keep sun off; and go on to the next plant.

Despite your care, the plants will wilt a little. See that they don't dry out. In two days they should be erect again. In the evening or while the sun is overcast, remove the sun shade, replacing it sometimes in the morning and leaving it for the day. This is the planting method for all sorts of easy annuals.

Your percentage of success will probably increase if, instead of water for transplanting, you use a mild liquid fertilizer. Instructions on a package of soluble fertilizer will tell how to make a transplanting solution.

Some annuals are difficult. You will usually find these grown in individual plant bands or peat pots so you need not disturb the roots in moving them to your garden. They include portulaca, annual candytuft, nigella, poppies, and larkspur. If any of these volunteer in your flower beds, you can transplant them safely only if you do it while they are still tiny, and if you take a big enough chunk of soil with each to get almost the whole root system.

When you plant something grown in a peat pot, don't try to remove the pot. Dip it in water to wet it, and plant pot and all in a hole deep enough to cover the rim. Soak the ground around each plant to encourage roots to penetrate the peat and make the pot decay.

When you plant something grown in a wood or paper band, remove the band. If a staple fastened it, break that first. There should be enough roots to hold soil together in an unbroken cube.

How to set out perennial plants. When you buy perennials by mail they often come bare root and dormant. Because they *are* dormant, nurserymen ship them safely far and wide with only the protection of a polyethylene bag or a paper wrapping with a little damp sphagnum over the roots. Unwrap and inspect plants as soon as they arrive to see that they are not dry. Moisten

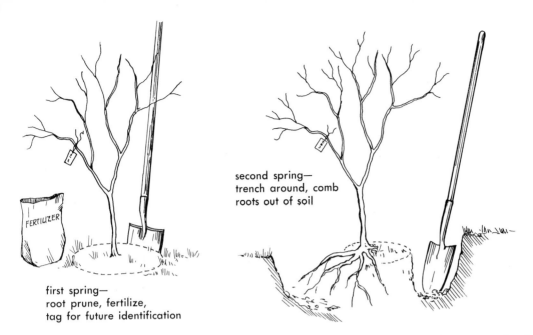

second spring—
trench around, comb
roots out of soil

first spring—
root prune, fertilize,
tag for future identification

Fig. 62   Moving a tree from the woods. If it is a good-sized plant, start preparations a year ahead of time.

the moss if need be, and set plants in a cool place while you prepare a place for them in your yard.

Make generous planting holes in soil you mix to suit whatever type of plant goes there. Spread roots carefully and water them in. Firm soil around the roots, setting crown at the level it was before.

Place things like baptisia, phlox, balloon flower, lythrum, gas plant, hosta, and lily-of-the-valley with the pointed buds or growth tips covered an inch or less. You won't need to shade these. Japanese anemone, hellebore, and delphinium usually have leaves, either a trace from last season or thrifty new ones to show you how deep to plant. The right level is where the stems meet the roots. Shade the plant tops for a few days until new leaves appear. Others to be handled this way are hardy asters, daylilies, heuchera, Siberian irises, creeping phlox, baby's-breath, shasta daisies, chrysanthemums, veronica, and achillea.

HOW TO TAKE TRANSPLANTS FROM THE WILD

Only in a few cases are you justified in transplanting trees, shrubs and flowers to your yard from the wild. They will probably grow better where nature put them; and besides, stealing from the wild violates good conservation practices, not to mention the ethics of the case involved.

However, if an area is doomed to the bulldozer anyway, you are certainly entitled to try to save some of the wildlings growing there if you have permission to go on the land. And if it's your woods that contain an overabundance of some kind, perhaps shadblow or sassafras—things hard to find in nurseries that you covet for your yard—then go ahead. If you can, make advance preparations to guarantee success. These same preparations are needed if you merely wish to move a tree from one place to another in your yard.

With woody plants like shadblow, start one year ahead in the spring unless you intend to take only tiny trees. You'll need a spade and $\frac{1}{2}$ pound of fertilizer, and something for marking the trees so you can find them again. Choose specimens that are rather small and preferably growing in sunny locations—they will be stronger than shaded ones.

If the tree is 6 feet tall, make a circle around it with an 18-inch radius (about

361

one-fourth of the height). Just outside this circle, thrust the spade full depth and draw it out again, following the outline of the circle. The idea is to cut the roots, forcing the tree to make more of them near the trunk. For large trees it's best to dig a trench around so as to reach deeper. Cut all roots you encounter. Sprinkle a cupful of fertilizer over soil inside the circle, and depart.

The next spring, when the ground thaws, dig your tree. Make a trench around it and undercut as far as you can. Comb the soil out of the roots, saving all the roots you can. You'll find many fibrous roots inside the circle because of the root pruning you did the year before. Finally with slanting downward cuts sever the lowest roots and lift out the plant. Safeguard roots by covering with wet sacks as you expose them. Wrap them for the trip home so they won't dry out.

Plant as you would a nursery tree, and prune off at least a third of the branches when you finish. Follow this method with deciduous trees up to 4 inches in diameter.

Advance root pruning helps in transplanting anything, but is extra important with difficult trees like dogwood, sassafras, and hawthorn. These are most likely to succeed if taken quite young. Move broadleaf and needle evergreens this way too. Always get a ball of earth with sweet gum (*Liquidambar styraciflua*), even while it is dormant.

To dig a plant with an earth ball, plan to save a soil mass eight times the thickness of the trunk. (A 1½-inch trunk needs a 12-inch ball.) Dig a circular trench around the plant and undercut it as far as you can. Fasten a corner of a burlap square, an opened gunny sack, around the trunk. Draw the burlap down one side to the base, tuck it under the tree as far as it will go, and push it into a tight roll.

Working from the opposite side, shove a sharp spade under the plant to cut the lowest roots and tilt the ball away from you. Then you can pick up the burlap from the bottom and finish the wrapping. Use nails to pin edges together. You'll probably need a second piece of burlap to wrap the ball completely. Finally loop heavy twine around and under the ball and tie it firmly.

Slide a stout plank under the plant as far as you can, for a lever to lift and pull the ball out of the hole. This is a strenuous job, so you'll probably need help. A 12-inch earth ball weighs about 85 pounds.

Transplanting wild flowers. Plastic bags, the kind you use for frozen foods, are a boon for moving wild flowers. Dig them with all the root possible, and slip root, plant and all into the bag. This way you don't need to take much soil, or worry about water. Plants stay fresh in the bag for several days. If you are moving kinds that have peculiar soil requirements, like bird's foot violets, take a supply of soil at the same time, to use in the relocation in your garden.

PLANTING AND TRANSPLANTING LARGE TREES

By paying extra, you can get nursery trees bigger than average transplanting sizes. These make quick effects for people who can't stand waiting the few years while little trees grow up. On the whole, these oversize trees are a headache. In the first place, they are difficult to move. They are so big they require special equipment, so you need to have the nursery plant them for you.

But the main drawback is that they are not really much quicker. Most times you'll find that small trees transplanted the same year as large ones will catch up in a few seasons and finally outstrip them. The only time for buying and planting unusually large trees is when you demand a well established look immediately.

You can make small trees grow fast by careful watering, fertilizing, and protecting from sunscald and insects.

How to transplant big trees. Some day you may want to transplant a fairly large tree, or have it done, more likely. This might happen if the tree is blocking some building project and seems too valuable to cut down. Moving it will be costly, because it takes two or three men and a truck with a winch. Tree services usually perform this work.

To save your lawn, save money, and do a good job with the tree, have it moved in midwinter. If you like you can start yourself in the fall by digging completely around the tree, carving out a root ball. Have the tree man advise how big to make it. At the same time dig the hole where you intend to plant the relocated tree, and cover the earth removed to prevent freezing. After freezing weather arrives, water the tree ball with the hose so it freezes into a hard chunk of ice. Then the movers can cut it loose from the bottom, lift it with the winch and take it to the new location. Frozen this way, the earth ball is safe without wrapping, so you save labor. The truck can come over your frozen lawn without hurting it, and best of all, the tree hardly knows it has been moved. Prune off some branches in spring to compensate for roots lost.

EASY-DOES-IT IDEAS

Paper cups from dispensing machines make ideal shades for tender little annual transplants; they deflect sun and keep plants cool; they also keep cutworms from getting at your plants.

The handiest and quickest way to see what you're doing when dividing tangled roots of chrysantheums, shasta daisies, or asters is to dunk the whole clump in a tubfull of water so the soil falls away. And the plants profit from the soaking.

If you have to plant bare-root trees or shrubs after summer arrives—later than the usual deadline for transplanting this way— you can still succeed if you spray the tops with Wilt Pruf to prevent drying, and mulch deeply over roots (to save moisture and keep soil cooler).

Chapter 28

GROWING PLANTS FROM SEED, CUTTINGS, AND LAYERS

Isn't it hard to start your own plants?

Growing your own new plants is easy. As many gardeners have discovered, it's also fascinating. If you want more of some plant without buying it, you can reproduce it by seeds, start new plants from cuttings of the old one or layer the branches of some kinds to make them root.

GROWING FROM SEED

For the cheapest, fastest and often best way to get new plants—and incidentally the most interesting—grow them from seed. Kinds commonly planted outdoors in a vegetable garden like beans, lettuce, peas, squash, radishes, and corn are all easy. Their large food-packed seeds get plants off to a strong start. So they make a crop despite poor weather, planting too deep, and crusty soil.

Not so with fine seeds like those of snapdragons, geraniums, pansies, petunias, begonias, and many of the perennial flowers, trees and shrubs. Starting them right means planting in your greenhouse, coldframe, or at a window where you can control conditions. Because some require long growing seasons you also need to start them early. But even these fine seeds are not difficult. It's mostly a matter of making the right preparations. Spring is a better time for seed starting than fall because days are getting longer, and this is a powerful influence on how things grow. But some perennials like columbine and delphinium do just as well if sown in August, so they have the cool autumn in which to get established.

Seed-starter kits. If speed and convenience are important to you, get preplanted seed-starter kits. Dozens of these are on the market now, with all the most popular kinds of seeds. Usually all you do is take off the lid and start watering. Some kits are even planted with house plants.

WHAT TO PLANT SEEDS IN

If you want to grow unusual seeds, or perhaps those you collected yourself, the process is more complicated. To begin with, get a container—pot, flat, coffee can or whatever —with holes in the bottom so water can drain out. Have it clean—no old soil clinging to it from last year. If you are *very* particular, first sterilize your clay pots in boiling water.

Put broken crockery or a wad of sphagnum moss over the drain holes to prevent soil from falling out. Then fill the container with something in which to plant seeds. This can be garden soil, sand, peat moss, sphagnum moss, vermiculite, perlite, leaf mold, or combinations of these. Whatever it is, it is

364

156 Fine flower seeds need special starting care, are best planted in flats or pots. Start with a shallow drainage layer in the bottom. Fill the container with a fine soil mixture that has had the large lumps sifted out of it. *Michajluk*

157 A sterile soil topping of something like sphagnum moss, peat or vermiculite (as here) prevents seedlings from damping off. *Burpee*

a big factor in success or failure. A good planting medium, as this is called, should be:

(1) dense or fibrous enough to anchor developing roots,

(2) free of weed seeds,

(3) free of undesirable fungus spores and bacteria, and

(4) filled with enough nutrients to keep young seedlings growing.

Sphagnum, peat moss, sand, vermiculite and perlite are all practically sterile—that is, they contain no weed seeds, bacteria, or fungi. Seeds planted in them do not "damp off" unless spores causing this fungus come from elsewhere. But these four are not the whole answer because they contain no nutrients—plants cannot grow long without food. So you add nutrients, either by mixing something into the planting medium beforehand, or by watering with a soluble fertilizer after seeds germinate and you can see the little plants. Preplanted seed-starting kits often consist of vermiculite fortified with chemical nutrients.

Garden soil or leaf mold from the woods or compost pile would be good for seed starting if they didn't almost always contain harmful fungi. Seeds planted in them are too likely to "damp off." Damping off is a disease that makes young seedlings suddenly fall over and die. It often kills almost every plant. Seedlings too thick, soil too moist, or air too still and humid are conditions that encourage this disease. To avoid it, drench soil before and after planting with a liquid fungicide like Pano-drench. Or get rid of the worst fungus and bacteria pests, and also soil insects, by pasteurizing it.

Soil pasteurization. Get a Fahrenheit thermometer that registers up to about 200 degrees. Sift crumbly moist loam through quarter-inch hardware cloth and dump it loosely into a clay pot that fits into your largest canning or soup kettle, one with a lid. Place a rack in the kettle, add a couple of inches of water (not quite touching the bottom of the pot which you set on the rack), put on the lid and set the kettle over the fire. Keep hot water handy to replenish what boils away. Insert the thermometer into the center of the soil. Check it occasionally. When it reaches 180 degrees, keep it at that

temperature for ten minutes. Then lift out the pot and dump soil on a workbench so it cools quickly. This process kills most harmful soil organisms but leaves some of the beneficial ones.

Another way, less precise but satisfactory for most purposes, is to put a covered dishpanful of damp loose earth in the oven and heat it to 180 degrees for an hour. Do not turn the heat up high or you will kill everything in the soil. This is always a smelly business, so if you have a stove in your basement or utility room, it's better to do it there than in your kitchen.

Large quantities of soil are best pasteurized by steam. Some greenhouse operators are equipped for this. Perhaps you can persuade one to sterilize soil for you or sell you some he has already sterilized. Or you can buy a bag of soil for African violets and this is always sterilized.

Here are formulas for seed-starting mixtures:

Pure fine sphagnum moss. Most seeds germinate successfully in this, but seedlings need feeding with liquid fertilizer soon after germination. Don't let them grow more than four to six weeks in this or roots will become a tangled mass that you can't get apart for transplanting.

Half-and-half sand and peat. This seems to be fairly free of weed seeds and fungus spores, and seeds germinate well in it. You might want to spread it an inch thick as a disease-free topping over regular garden soil, to encourage rooting and prevent tender seedlings from damp-off. With this "clean" mixture on top, seeds germinate, then send down roots into the soil below for nourishment. Plants will grow a long time this way without need for fertilizer or transplanting. It's an inexpensive method for large plantings.

Pure vermiculite. This material is expanded mica, a mineral product, and is sterile. You find it in preplanted seed kits, and garden stores sell it in horticultural grade by the bag. Plants make good root systems in it and they pull apart readily for transplanting. To keep them growing in vermiculite, add liquid fertilizer every week. In time, vermiculite tends to become waterlogged so don't use it over and over.

366

North Platte mix. This is 1 part fine-screened sphagnum and 2 parts each of perlite and vermiculite. This mixture for seed starting originated at the University of Nebraska North Platte experiment station. Seeds germinate well in it, do not damp-off, and you can easily pick out the seedlings for transplanting. Add liquid fertilizer every few weeks to maintain growth, because there are no nutrients in this. Perlite is a white mineral product sold in bags by garden stores. If you don't find it there, the supermarket may stock it as a fire base for outdoor barbecue grills.

Equal parts soil, peat, and sand. This is an old-time combination of available materials. Most seeds do well in it. For tricky seeds like begonias it pays to pasteurize the soil for the mix.

John Innes seed-starting compost. This standard mix is used by English gardeners, giving phenomenal results with practically all seeds. It consists of 2 parts medium loam (pasteurized), 1 part peat moss and 1 part coarse sand (particles up to $\frac{1}{8}$ inch). To each bushel of this mix add $1\frac{1}{2}$ ounces granulated 20 per cent superphosphate and $\frac{3}{4}$ ounce of hydrated (builder's) lime. This is more effort to prepare than any of the others, but worth it—especially if you are dealing with difficult or expensive seeds like fancy hybrid petunias, and can't afford a failure.

THE PLANTING PROCESS

Avoid starting too early the seeds of tender things you plan to transplant outdoors after frost. If you are sowing petunias, zinnias, marigolds, snapdragons, tomatoes, and green peppers, the right time is about six to eight weeks before the time you will set them out. If you try to hold them indoors longer, they get weak and spindly, more or less worthless for planting out when the time finally comes.

Fill your planting container to within a half-inch of the rim with whatever seed-starting medium you have chosen. Thump the pot or flat on the table to settle the mixture, and smooth the surface. If you are planting more than one kind of seed, use a separate pot or flat for each to prevent mix-ups, and also to let you give each kind what it needs. Sow seeds thinly. Young plants develop better if not crowded. If seeds are large, cover them with a sprinkling of your soil mixture. The larger the seeds, the deeper you cover—a good rule is to cover twice the diameter of the seed. This is never very much. If seeds are tiny and powdery like those of begonias, African violets, and petunias, don't cover at all. Just sprinkle them on the surface and firm them in with the flat of your hand or the bottom of a jar.

To water a newly seeded pot or flat, set it in a tub of shallow tepid water until moisture glistens on the surface. Then cover the container with a piece of clear plastic held with a rubber band or slip the whole thing into a plastic bag. You probably won't need to water again until you take the cover off when the first little plants come up.

If seeds come up too thick despite your efforts to plant sparsely, better thin out excess plants. Tweezers are the best tool for this. As soon as seedlings get their second leaves, you can safely transplant the extras to another box.

SOME HINTS ON SEEDS AND THEIR NEEDS

Some seeds have such hard coats they need softening to sprout. This process is called stratification. Use it on seeds of plum and pear, rose, hawthorn, holly, mountain ash, and hickory. What you do is simply place them between layers of moist sand in a pot. Sink the pot in the ground in fall, and leave it there all winter so that rain, snow, freezes and thaws will soften and break the tough seed coats. Next spring remove them from the sand and plant them like other seeds. Hawthorn and holly seeds need stratifying longer than just over winter—usually a whole year.

Delphinium, hellebore and mertensia seeds need freezing before you plant. A good way is to freeze them into an ice cube in the refrigerator. Then "plant" the ice cube after a few days. Old delphinium seed is worthless. Plant the freshest you can get (which means buy from a dealer you trust) and preferably in August or September.

367

158 When plantlets have their second set of leaves they are big enough to transplant to another box where they have more room. The coleus seedlings in this box will grow up in a hurry.   *Roche*

Walnuts, acorns, and chestnuts are worthless as seeds if they dry out. Plant them while they are fresh—in the fall of the year you harvest them.

Larkspur, poppies, lupines, stock all have sensitive roots that transplant poorly. Sow these seeds in separate small pots to avoid having to transplant.

Canna, morning glory, and moonflower seeds need softening in tepid water before you plant them. Soak them for at least a day.

Columbine seeds need time to germinate. Give them a month.

Iris, peony, gladiolus, hemerocallis. There are various ways to handle these, but this is what most fanciers do: for iris and peonies, plant outdoors in coldframes in the fall, soon after seeds ripen. For gladiolus, plant indoors in early spring in 6-inch-deep boxes; then set the boxes outside after frost. Harvest the new corms in late summer. For hemerocallis, start seeds indoors in early spring and transplant them outside when the weather warms up.

Old seeds. Seeds left from the year before may still be good or, more properly, viable. Much depends on the kind of seeds and how they have been stored. Before planting, test them for viability. Count out fifty or one hundred seeds and place them on a moist blotter in a saucer. Cover the saucer with a light piece of clear plastic to keep the blotter from drying out. After about two weeks, count those that have sprouted against those that have not. Thus you can get the percentage of germination and know if the seeds are worth planting.

Many kinds of seeds make almost as good a crop the second or third year as they do the first, but they take longer to come up. So allow old seeds plenty of time before giving up on them. If you want a general rule, three years is about the limit for most seeds and it's not worthwhile to keep them longer.

TRANSPLANTING SEEDLINGS

When you start plants from seeds, you usually have to transplant them, often more than once, before you put them outdoors. Transplanting gives room for growth, and thickens root systems. Start shortly after seedlings show their second set of leaves— the true leaves rather than the first little pair (or single leaf) sent up by the seed.

159   For speed and convenience, try the pre-planted seed starters sold commercially. The device at left is an electric propagating box.   *Philpott*

Lift or prick out the tiny plantlets with any small, flat blade (like a nail file or a paring knife) saving all the roots you can. Set plants 2 inches apart in a freshly prepared flat or planting box containing a mixture of two parts soil, one part sand and one part peat or sifted compost.

Choose a shaded, cool room to do this job, and work fast. Carefully firm out air spaces around the transplanted roots, and when you finish a box water it well with a fine spray and set it in the shade until the plants straighten up. Then return them to a place in the sunny greenhouse or window.

Let transplants grow along until a week or two before time to reset them in their permanent places. If they are to go outdoors, they will need hardening off. This means gradually exposing them to cooler temperatures, air and strong sunlight. Start about two weeks before setting-out time. Begin by carrying the pots or flats outdoors on warm days and leaving them there fifteen to thirty minutes. On each occasion leave them out a little longer until you can let them stay out safely from dawn to dusk.

Two or three days before you do final transplanting, score the soil between rows of plants each way with a sharp knife and water plants heavily. This makes root systems more compact. On transplanting day, soil should be fairly dry so it separates in neat blocks. Start at one end to lift out plants.

INCREASING PLANTS BY CUTTINGS

Cuttings are small sections of a plant which you can induce to form roots and eventually make new plants. Stem cuttings are sections of stem, usually with a few leaves attached. Leaf cuttings are just leaves, often with a part or all of the leaf stem or petiole left on and sometimes with a "heel" of stem as well. Root cuttings are small lengths of root capable of sending out growth buds.

You can propagate many plants by cuttings. Commercial growers take cuttings instead of sowing seed when they want new plants to be *exactly* like the parent.

Cuttings, dividing and layering are methods of "vegetative" reproduction. If you have a good kind of perennial phlox, for instance, and you want more of it, you can easily make twenty new plants from root cuttings of the old one, and they will all be like the parent. But if you save seeds from the phlox and plant them, you get a hodgepodge with probably not one plant like the parent or as good. Many plants, like philodendron, don't set seeds under normal conditions, so cuttings are practically the only way to get new ones of these.

HOW TO TAKE STEM CUTTINGS

Geranium (*Pelargonium*) might be something you would propagate with stem cuttings. Here is how to do it: With a thin steel blade—a razor blade or a sharp knife, not scissors or a dull knife that would bruise tissue—cut off pieces of stem about 4 inches long, not counting the leaves. Make each cut a quarter inch below a node, the little swellings on the stem, and remove all but three or four topmost leaves. Select medium-soft stems—not watery young or tough old wood.

Dip the base in a rooting hormone like Rootone, and shake off the excess. Insert the cutting $1\frac{1}{2}$ inches deep in a hole made with a pencil in a box of clean, moist vermiculite. Press down around it. After all cuttings are inserted in the box, water them three times and let the box drain. Then set it where the temperature is between 60 and 70 degrees and the light is plentiful but not in direct sun. The cuttings will need water every ten days after that, or oftener if the air is dry.

In about three weeks, the cuttings will be rooted. Pot them up as soon as you find, by pulling one out, that bunchy roots have developed. Don't wait too long or roots will be so tangled you'll have to break them, and this will set plants back.

In general, then, take stem cuttings this way; some need longer time to root than geraniums:

cut straight across the stem below a node,
remove lower leaves,
dip into rooting hormone,
insert fairly shallow,
set in good light out of direct sun,

keep the rooting medium and air around fairly moist.

Poinsettias have hollow stems, so cut these right at the node (where stems are solid) rather than below.

Sand alone is good for rooting some cuttings, especially those of plants with thin stems, as coleus, Christmas begonias, wax begonias, peperomias, ivy and African violets, phlox and pinks. Many of these will also root in water. But sand and vermiculite are preferred because the new roots spread out in these and transplant more successfully. In water, roots cling together and when you transplant, they tend to knot.

Keeping cuttings moist. Choose boxes or pots that are at least 4 inches deep. The larger the container, the easier it is to keep moisture and temperature constant. To preserve humidity for cuttings, cover the box or pot with a piece of glass or plastic or set it in a terrarium. To keep moisture constant, use the pot-in-pot method. Take a large clay 10-inch bulb pan, and a small 3-inch one. Cork the hole in the small pot. Hold it in the center of the large pot so the rims are even, and fill in around and under the small pot with vermiculite or other planting medium. Water the vermiculite and fill the center pot with water. As moisture penetrates the porous wall of the small pot, it moves into the vermiculite around it. All you do is watch to see that the "well" in the middle never goes dry. Insert cuttings in the vermiculite circle around the center pot.

Besides geraniums, you can propagate many house plants and perennials by stem cuttings—iresine, Joseph's coat (*Alternanthera*), tradescantia, zebrina, impatiens, wax begonia, tuberous begonia, dieffenbachia, philodendron, pothos, rubber plant (*Ficus elastica*), poinsettia, cissus, *Vinca major,* coleus, ivy, chrysanthemums, nephthytis, santolina, dusty miller (*Artemisia*), penstemon, hardy candytuft (*Iberis*), phlox, pinks, *Vinca minor,* hardy and tender hibiscus, gaillardia, *Alyssum saxatile,* lythrum, evening primrose, platycodon, lavender, salvia, teucrium, flowering maple, and lantana.

Woody plants from stem cuttings. With these the method is the same as for softer-stemmed plants but the process is longer. If you make cuttings in spring, May or June,

they are called softwood cuttings because they are new twigs. You can start lilac, forsythia, viburnum, rose, and azalea cuttings then. Put them in a moist, sand-peat mixture under glass jars in the shade.

More mature growths taken in summer and fall are called hardwood cuttings. You can start euonymus, holly, mahonia, junipers, boxwood, yew, arborvitae, and chamaecyparis from these. Dip these in a stronger rooting hormone than you use on soft-stemmed plants, insert in boxes of sand-peat, and take them in before a hard freeze, to finish rooting under fluorescent lights, on your windowsill, or in a greenhouse. Keep them moist and humid.

To start deciduous trees and shrubs from cuttings, take 6-inch lengths in early winter, using a razor blade or sharp knife. Tie them in little bundles and bury them in a box of moist sand. Set the box in a place that stays cold but not frozen—like a root cellar or unheated garage. Or bury box and all outdoors deeper than frost can reach. Next spring, uncover the cuttings and set them in your garden in rows covering all but the top inch with one growth bud. A high percentage will form roots and grow. Grapes, forsythia, privet, roses, weigela, althaea, are easy kinds to do this way.

HOW TO TAKE LEAF CUTTINGS

Handle leaf cuttings like stem cuttings, by inserting the petiole or leaf stem in sand or vermiculite, preferably sand. When you insert African violet, peperomia, or Christmas begonia leaf stems, avoid setting them too deep, because new plants come from the base of the petiole. If these are too deep, plants will have a struggle to reach the light.

Sedums and echeverias root if you simply stand the leaves on end in sand. Slit rex begonia leaves across the main veins in four or five places, daub them there with rooting hormone powder, and pin them face up on moist sand, with the stem covered. New plantlets will grow at the slits.

Cut sansevieria or snake-plant leaves into 4-inch sections, insert them base down in sand, vermiculite or ordinary soil (that is, the lowest part of the piece as it grew on the plant, goes in first). A new shoot soon arises beside each cutting. If you have a gold-stripe sansevieria, however, propagate it by dividing the original plant, because you lose the gold color when you root from cuttings.

Other easy subjects for leaf cuttings are gloxinia, bryophyllum (air plant), Christmas cactus, epiphyllum, kalanchoe, crassula and heuchera. Most of these will root in water as well as sand, but are not so easy to transplant that way.

If you take leaf cuttings of rhododendron with a "heel" or wedge of stem attached so it includes the growth bud in the leaf axil, you may be able to get new plants from them. Dip them in rooting hormone and insert in peat moss and sand—keep them moist and in a humid enclosure like a terrarium.

HOW TO TAKE ROOT CUTTINGS

This is mainly for perennials but it works with a number of woody plants too. For convenience take the cuttings and start rooting them in fall. First fill a 4-inch-deep flat about three-fourths full with a half-and-half mixture of garden soil and sphagnum peat moss. Firm it down.

To get root cuttings, either lift the parent plant completely out of the ground, or thrust a sharp trowel or spade down on one side to get at a few roots without taking up the whole plant. Select heavy vigorous roots. With oriental poppy and globe thistle, these will be fat and thick, the size of a lead pencil. With phlox and Japanese anemone they will be more like grocery string. Cut both kinds into 2- to 4-inch lengths and lay them out 3 to 4 inches apart on the soil mixture in the flat. Label, if you have more than one kind, and cover with a half inch of sand.

Water the flat well and set it in a cold-frame. After the first hard freeze, pile on a 6-inch leaf or straw mulch and close the frame. When the weather warms up in spring, remove the mulch. Before long new plantlets will appear above each section of root. You will find thrifty root systems already formed. Transplant them directly to your garden, or in the case of woody things like wisteria and bittersweet, put them in a

nursery row somewhere out of the way, and let them grow for a season.

Perennials to propagate by root cuttings include phlox, Japanese anemones, bleeding heart, baby's-breath (single kinds—doubles are grafted), anchusa, oriental poppy, sea lavender (*Limonium*), globe thistle (*Echinops*), and dictamnus. Woody plants to try are bittersweet (*Celastrus*), rose-acacia, wisteria, trumpetvine (*Campsis*), and mimosa (*Albizzia*).

NEW PLANTS BY LAYERING

If a few new plants are all you want, simple layering offers an easy way to get them. Some plants tip-layer themselves. You see this when a forsythia branch touches the ground and takes root. Black raspberries make nuisances of themselves because of this habit. Cut loose the parent branch and you can move the new plants wherever you please.

When something takes root along the branch instead of at the tip, it's seldom accidental. To achieve this, you need to lend a hand. Most shrubs will root along the stem if you bend down a branch and fasten it firmly in contact with soil kept moist for two or three months. This is what the process of layering is.

Start this in midsummer. Select a branch that is long and low, and will readily bend down. Mix a batch of moist peat moss and soil, equal parts, and spread it under the branch. Dig out a little depression for the mixture but save two quarts to heap over the top. Invert two U-shaped wires over the branch to hold it to the ground. It helps to score the bark lightly on the lower side with a sharp knife—but don't cut deeply. Treat the cuts with a rooting hormone. Cover the bent branch with the peat-soil mixture at the place where you have pinned it down, usually about half to two-thirds of the way out on the stem. Let the tip of the branch protrude. Put a brick on top of the layered portion to be sure it stays down.

Then give the layer time, probably a year. The next season, if investigation shows that roots have formed, take pruners and cut the new plant loose from the parent but don't dig it up. Wait until fall or the following spring to transplant it to a new site, and cut the top back proportionately to the size of the roots.

These are easy subjects for layering: rose, dianthus, hardy candytuft (*Iberis*), daphne, clematis, grape, magnolia, wisteria, rhododendron, euonymus, pyracantha, azalea, and dozens of other shrubby plants and perennials with stems limber enough to bend to the ground. Choose branches that are neither immature nor woody, but sound and young. The method takes longer than stem or root cuttings but you have a larger plant when you finish.

How to air-layer. Air-layering is a way to make a plant grow new roots on stiff stems too high to bend to the ground. A favorite subject is the rubber plant (*Ficus elastica*) both because it is easy to do this way, and also because it solves the problem of what to do when your plant reaches the ceiling.

Select a place about 18 inches below the tip and between leaves. With a razor blade, slash halfway through the stem. Insert a piece of toothpick into the cut to hold it open, and work some rooting hormone into the gash. Tie two short "splints" at opposite sides of the stem to keep it from falling over. Tongue depressors make good splints. Soak a bunch of springy sphagnum moss in water, and squeeze out the excess. Then wrap a big handful evenly around the cut stem. Wind string loosely around to hold the moss in place. Finally cover it completely with a sheet of polyethylene. Tie this tight at the bottom and top of the layer with a strip of rubber. This keeps the moss from drying out. Even so, watch closely and if it seems to be dry, add water through the crack at the top.

If your wrap is working, you will soon see roots forming under the plastic. When roots seem adequate to support the top, cut through the stem just below the wrap, remove the plastic and carefully pot the new plant. Keep it in a cool (60-65 degrees), humid and shaded place, and water it well until it seems safely established. If roots seem inadequate and the plant is obviously in trouble, cut back the top halfway.

This same system will work with many other plants. It is easier to air-layer house plants and greenhouse plants than those outdoors. Nevertheless if you can keep them from drying out (the main reason for failure) you can air-wrap branches of pussy willows, magnolias, maples, hollies, forsythias, flowering crabapples, cotoneasters and privets. Dracaena is another easy houseplant for this method. The advantage of air-layering is the speed with which it gives you a sizable new plant. But it is a time-consuming and impractical system if you want more than one or two plants.

EASY-DOES-IT IDEAS

The pussy willow branch you cut for a bouquet in March might make a batch of new trees for you. Strip off the pussies, cut the stem into 6-inch sections, and sink the sections 4 inches deep in a big pot of peat moss and sand. Keep it moist and in the light and by May you'll have a young forest.

Glass canning jars, quart size, make dandy individual "greenhouses" for single cuttings of rose, forsythia and lilac. Mix a thin paste of mud and swirl it around on the inside to make the jar give shade. Then invert it over the cutting. A plant under it can even spend the winter safely there, the jar piled high with leaves.

You can root chrysanthemum cuttings in a trench outdoors in the shade. Make it 4 inches deep, fill it with peat moss and sand, and insert your 3- to 4-inch cuttings with lower leaves removed and ends dusted with Rootone. Water once or twice, thoroughly. In about three weeks you'll have a crop of rooted mums.

Chapter 29

HOW TO HYBRIDIZE, GRAFT, AND BUD

Where do all the new varieties come from?

Backyard gardeners like you have produced some of the fine roses, irises, daylilies, peonies and other plants you see around you. New varieties are not all the work of plant scientists, far from it. Despite the increased knowledge of heredity, much of plant hybridizing still seems to depend on chance, so the more gardeners there are who attempt to cross plants, the better the total chances of finding those hoped-for "breaks" that bring new colors, sizes and forms.

Although commercial breeding has developed into a complicated science, the principles are so simple anyone can understand and use them. Basically hybridizing consists of taking pollen from one flower and putting it on the stigma of another. The seeds that result are a cross of the two flowers. You haven't finished the job, however, until you plant these seeds and see what the progeny are. It is only in this final step, and your records of it, that you go the bees one better.

If you start hybridizing a certain plant, iris perhaps, you will want to work out some system of record keeping. Then your pollen daubing that goes on from year to year can follow an organized pattern, with logic behind it and a goal ahead. Your records will be like a genealogy. When you finally arrive at the iris of your dreams, your records will tell you how you got there. You will know the mother, father and grandparents and what they looked like. Studying this line may suggest to you your next breeding project for this is a fascinating pursuit, always luring you farther on. It's said that suicide is unknown among plant breeders; they are too eager to see next year's seedlings to contemplate ending it all.

HOW TO CROSS-POLLINATE TWO FLOWERS

First learn to recognize and locate the reproductive parts. In the iris and most other flowers, the male and female parts are both in the same flower. The male ones include anthers and stamens that carry the pollen or male reproductive cells. The female ones are the pistil, with the stigma at the top and the ovary at the base containing the ovules which, when fertilized, develop into seeds. To cross-pollinate, you merely put pollen from one flower onto the stigma of the other. That's basically all there is to it. Natural processes take care of the rest.

Let's locate the various parts on a lily, where they are easy to see. The long greenish tube in the center of the flower is the pistil; the three part cushion at the tip, often shining with moisture, is the stigma. The ovary is at the base of the tube, but almost concealed from your surface inspection. In it the seeds will form. The six long slender wands daintily balancing oblong "buns" at their tips are the stamens. The buns, colorful and pollen-laden, are called anthers.

All flowering plants are equipped much

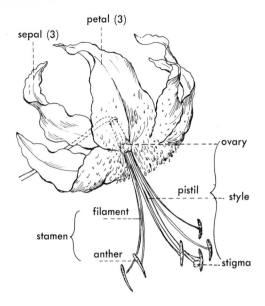

sepal (3)

petal (3)

ovary

pistil

style

filament

stamen

anther

stigma

Fig. 63   The reproductive parts of a lily flower.

in this way, although they may disguise or hide the parts. Some, like pines, may have male flowers in one place and female in another on the same plant, which is called monoecious. Hollies and yews have the sexes separated on different plants and are called dioecious. When a flower has all the reproductive organs in it, it is called a perfect flower—and the majority are formed this way.

When you work at pollination, you'll probably choose a fine brush, your fingertip or a pipe cleaner to transfer pollen to stigma; or simply touch the pistil tip with the anther.

In nature it's the bee or another insect that takes pollen from anther to stigma. These creatures do it inadvertently on their real mission, which is to gather pollen and nectar. Wind also plays a part in spreading pollen, for some kinds float far and wide on currents of air.

How to keep out unwanted pollen. Both before and after you make the cross, be sure that the mother plant or pistil parent is safe from pollination from some other source. It can even get pollinated with its own pollen. There are various methods to prevent contamination and insure a pure cross. To keep out bees and other insects, slip a plastic bag over the flower *before* it opens. After it opens but before pollen matures, you can

snip out the anthers to prevent self-pollination, and then re-bag the flower. After you have made the intended cross you can protect the pistil by wrapping aluminum foil around it, if it is large enough, as it is in most lilies. In gladiolus you can discourage visits from bees by removing the parts of the flower on which they light. In fact, you can remove nearly all of the flower—petals and stamens—and leave just the pistil which in this state of solitude is safe from visits of insects, and is no longer exposed to its own pollen. Use this method, called emasculation, also with the small flowers of penstemon and snapdragon.

Timing is important. The pollen you use can be days or weeks old. In fact you can dry and store it in the refrigerator for months, and in this way cross early-blooming kinds with late ones. But the flower you put it on should be newly opened, with the stigma just mature enough to be receptive. If it looks moist and expanded, it is probably ready.

HYBRIDIZING WITH IRIS

Let's say you are fascinated with iris, and would like to make a few crosses with the tall bearded varieties in your yard. First, become acquainted with the reproductive parts of this flower, which look a little different from those of the lily. Here's how to find the stigma and stamens, which may elude you on first glance: First, locate the beard, the colorful hairs at the base of each of the lower petals or falls. Over the beard is a wide arm called the style branch, finished at the top with little ears or crests. Hold this by the ears and tip it back to find the stigma, in this case called the stigmatic lip, a little shelf just below the crests. There are three of these in the iris flower, one with each set of petals. Now lift the style branch still further and you find, below it, the paddle-shaped anther which bears the pollen.

For the mother plant, select a variety you know is a good seed-setting kind. If you have seen it bearing seedpods, perhaps accidental ones, that is all the evidence you need. Look for a recently opened flower on this plant.

For the father, which will contribute the

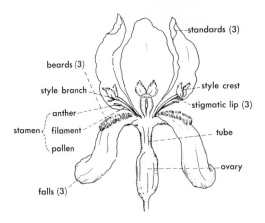

Fig. 64 The reproductive parts of an iris flower.

pollen, select a variety that has characteristics you'd like to see repeated in the seedlings. The pollen needs to be ripe—mature enough so it drops freely from the anther. With tweezers pick the anther, take it to the seed-parent flower and touch it to the three stigmatic surfaces.

For your records tie below the flower a tag that shows, first, the name of the seed parent and second the name of the pollen parent. If the pod is to be on 'Snow Flurry' and the pollen came from 'Chivalry,' for instance, write 'Snow Flurry' x 'Chivalry.' This tag should stay with the pod, the seeds that come out of it, and later with the seedlings that grow from it.

All that's left to do now is watch for the development and ripening of the pod, and then harvest and plant the seeds. Two springtimes later, you may have from each pod dozens of young irises in bloom. Some will not be as good as either parent; some will probably look much like one or the other of the parents; and others may be decidedly different and perhaps, you hope, better.

WHAT FLOWERS ARE POSSIBLE MATES?

Widely different plants will not cross with each other. You can't, for instance, hope to mate a dandelion with a larkspur. The mother plant needs to be closely related to the father or no seed develops when pollen

falls on the stigma. If it is a lily, for instance, it may cross with other species of true lilies, but if you put on pollen from a hemerocallis (called a daylily) nothing happens because the hemerocallis is not a true lily.

Crossing between different species of the same genus is fairly common, but two parallel species will not always cross. The *pallida* and *variegata* irises will cross, for example, but not *I. pallida* and *I. spuria* (at least no instances are known). Crosses between two different genera are rare. The *Fatshedera,* one of the very few examples, is supposed to be a cross of *Fatsia* with *Hedera.* To have crosses from plants belonging to different family groups is unheard of, which effectively dismisses the proposed affair between dandelion and larkspur.

Easy for home hybridizing. Hemerocallis, iris, and lily are the three most popular flowers for amateur cross-breeding. Each of them has a flower that is large and simple to work with, unlike the more difficult composites or daisy types of zinnia and chrysanthemum, or the tiny flowers of snapdragons. Each of the three is also fairly reliable about setting seeds. The seeds grow to blooming size in two years, a reasonable length of time. If you choose to work with peonies, flowering shrubs or fruit trees, you will wait many years to see results of your first cross.

WHAT IS A HYBRID?

This word is used so loosely it has almost lost meaning. A true hybrid results from the crossing of two or more different species or pure strains. The two tall bearded irises you cross are probably members of the same species or the same genetic "line," so what you get is not really a hybrid but just a new variety. But when you cross an auratum lily with a different species like the speciosum, then the result really is a lily hybrid. 'Jillian Wallace,' that fabulous beauty, comes from just such a cross. True hybrids in the first generation often show dramatic changes from the parents, and are usually large, more vigorous and the crop is more uniform. This is the principle behind the use of hybrid corn by farmers; and is the secret of the F_1 (first generation) petunias you prize for your yard.

OTHER KINDS OF PLANT BREEDING

There are other ways to get new plants. For ages past selection has been the means to new plants. Seeds from the best plants are saved for sowing the next crop. Many modern varieties have been obtained this way, and such selection still goes on. Professional seed growers follow this method to produce the uniform seed strains of many of your favorite vegetables and flowers. You can select in your garden, too, although to get important improvements, you need to grow great quantities of each kind of plant.

Changes through colchicine. Treating the fertilized ovary with colchicine will cause changes in plants. This powerful drug, derived from the colchicum or autumn crocus, is put up in kits for experiment in the home garden. If you apply it to the ovary soon after fertilizing the flower, cell division in the developing seeds will be greatly affected; at a certain stage the chromosome contents of two cells are merged into one. Then each succeeding cell of the new plant, as it divides, has twice the normal number of chromosomes. Since these are the tiny units governing characteristics of plants (and animals) the seedling that results has more of everything. Greater size and stamina are two of the most evident new qualities. Plants with double the normal number of chromosomes are called tetraploids. The new flower named gloriosa daisy is a tetraploid version of the old brown-eyed susan, *Rudbeckia.* Other flowers you can buy in tetraploid forms are snapdragons, marigolds, zinnias, and phlox; probably many more are soon to appear from this process.

Irradiating seeds. Another fascinating field of plant breeding for home experimenters is with radiation. This work has taken a boost since easy sources of radiation have become available as by-products of atomic industry. But for a long time, scientists have known that short waves of ultra-violet, X-ray, and gamma ray would induce changes in plants. Radiation speeds up the rate of mutation. Mutations are spontaneous changes that occur naturally in plants, but they are normally fairly rare. When you bombard the plant cells with radiation, you vastly increase the rate of mutations. How? By knocking the genes (heredity factors) on the chromosomes out of their orderly line-ups. Unlike colchicine which merely doubles the number, radiation radically mixes things up. Results may be weird rather than worthwhile. In fact, few changes to date have been improvements.

You can buy packets of seeds that have been irradiated, but don't expect to get a useful crop from them. Germination will be low, and what comes will be crippled plants, mainly interesting for what has happened to them. In the second generation, obtained by sowing the seed of these strange plants, you may see more practical changes and they will not be so extreme. It is also feasible to radiate the pollen you use in cross-breeding. You can do this yourself by placing the pollen 6 inches below your ultra-violet sun lamp for different lengths of time—a few minutes at most.

Research laboratories expose growing plants in various stages to radiation, and have produced significant mutations this way. But it takes complicated and dangerous equipment for such work so it is beyond the scope of home experiment. The usefulness of this line of study is still questionable. Some day it may prove valuable.

HOW TO GRAFT AND BUD

The nurseryman propagates woody plants by grafting and budding, especially kinds that can't be produced as well from seeds or cuttings. The techniques are simple enough for you to follow them successfully at home with the roses, shrubs and trees, especially the fruit trees, in your yard.

Grafting and budding are surgical ways of joining the root system of one plant to the top of another. For the root select a kind closely related to the top, or the combination won't "take." The root is usually from a more vigorous, earlier, or better adapted species or variety than the natural roots of the variety you want for the top. For instance, vigor is the quality of the multiflora

377

rose that makes it acceptable as the root-stock of your hybrid tea roses. However, it may be that you want a special root that you know will dwarf the top. Nurserymen employ a venerable English rootstock called Malling No. 9 to develop dwarf apple trees for them.

Here are some combinations that have worked well: almond, apricot and plum will unite with peach but not with apple. You *can* graft almond on plum. You can graft rose acacia on black locust, pear on quince roots, pyracantha on hawthorn, lilac on privet, and Christmas cactus on prickly pear or on practically any other kind of cactus. You can put a tree peony top on the root of a herbaceous peony (in fact, you usually buy them this way). If you have a rare apple variety, you can graft it on roots of any apple seedling. The same is true of pear on pear, and cherry on cherry. And you can always graft any plant to another part of the same plant.

WHAT IS GRAFTING?

The term grafting is used when the top for the new plant, the scion, is a short twig. Budding is the term used when the scion is a single bud with only a tiny slice of wood attached. With either method the root end is called the *stock*. The work of grafting goes on during winter and early spring while plants are dormant. Budding is carried on in summer.

How to make a graft. Let's say you want to have plants of a rare kind of apple tree that is old and seems about to die. First, get some seedling apple trees for rootstock. You may have to start a year ahead by planting seeds unless you can find volunteers under your old apple tree. One-year-old rootstocks are big enough to work with.

Next on a warm day in March, when stems are *not* frozen, cut off a supply of pencil-size twigs that were new growth last year. Cut at least as many twigs as you now have seedling plants for rootstocks. Put the twigs in a plastic bag, fasten with a rubber band, and store in the refrigerator, not the freezer, for four or five days. When the ground is thawed, dig up your seedling rootstocks with as much root as

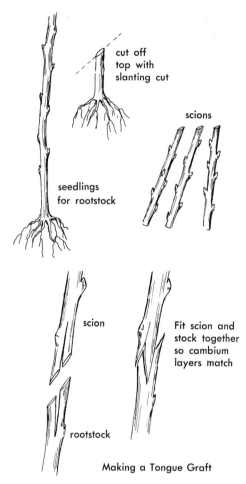

How to make a Graft

cut off top with slanting cut

scions

seedlings for rootstock

scion

Fit scion and stock together so cambium layers match

rootstock

Making a Tongue Graft

Fig. 65 How to make a graft. This particular type is called a tongue graft.

you can and cover them to prevent loss of moisture.

Indoors at a work table in a cool place where you can keep them moist, cut off the tops of rootstocks on a long slant 2 inches above the root. Use a razor blade or very sharp knife to make sure of a smooth cut, about $1\frac{1}{2}$ inches long. The longer the cut surface, the stronger your graft will be.

Now take the scions from the refrigerator and make a similar cut at the lower end. Without turning the twig make a straight cut up to form a "tongue." Cut a matching tongue on the rootstock. Then fit stock and scion together so the pieces interlock. See to it that on one side at least the green or cambium layers of the two parts touch. These are the only places that can grow together.

To keep the two parts firmly together, wrap them with raffia, cord, adhesive tape, or thin strips of rubber. To prevent drying out, cover the graft with warm, but not hot, paraffin or grafting wax. Also coat the top with the wax to keep it from drying, and place completed grafts under moist moss until you finish the whole lot.

Finally plant them in a row in your garden where it will be handy to watch and water them. Set them deep enough to cover the grafts. Water as they need it and wait for developments.

All your grafts will not live and grow, especially the first time you try this, but if you get only two or three out of a dozen, you will be doing pretty well. This is why it is a good idea to attempt a number and not just one or two. In a year, the successful grafts will be ready for transplanting to permanent places.

The method just described is called a whip or tongue graft. The tongue is simply to hold the two parts together while they are wrapped. It is the usual method when top and bottom twigs are nearly equal in size, but there are other ways. The object of them all is to keep the cambium layers together until growth starts on at least one side. It is important that both root and scion be in similar phases of activity, not roots dormant and tops leafing out, for instance.

How to graft on large trees. With grafting you can work all sorts of magic. You can put a new top on an old tree, for example, a 'Golden Delicious' on your old 'Winesap' apple. You can put five or six different varieties of apple or pear on the same trunk. You can even conceivably put more than one kind of fruit, as plums and apricots, on the same tree. If you like, you can graft a branch of a good pollinating variety on apples or plums to avoid planting a second tree for the purpose.

Suppose it's an apple tree you want to topwork with new varieties. In late fall, cut a supply of pencil-size scions from the varieties you want. Store them where they are damp and cold but not frozen. You

How to graft a new top on an old branch

Fig. 66 How to graft a new top on an old branch. With this method you can put several varieties of apple or pear on the same trunk.

might tie them in a bundle and bury them in a coldframe.

In early spring, with a saw or sharp pruners, prepare for grafting some tree branches a little bigger than a broom handle. Cut them squarely across. Remove any growth farther down on the branches. Sharply split the end of each stub for a short distance, and wedge open the cut with a chisel inserted at the center of the branch. Cut the lower ends of the scion wood into long, narrow V-points. Insert two of these pieces in the split, one at each end, so that on the outer edge the cambium of the scion touches the cambium of the stock. Draw out the wedge so the wood closes on these scions to hold them in place. Cover all exposed wood—the stub ends, around the grafts and the tips of the scions—with warm paraffin or grafting wax.

So treated, a branch won't bear for a few years. How long depends on how far you have had to cut it back—the farther, the longer it takes. If you have a big tree you want to work over, it's best to deal with just a few branches each year and watch closely so as to remove any new branches or suckers arising *below* your grafts. These will be from the original variety, and take strength from the grafted-on branch tips.

First aid with grafting. If one of your fruit trees (or any other kind) is girdled at the base or at the snow line by rabbits or mice, you can save it by prompt "bridging" early in spring before the sap rises. Bridging is a type of grafting which forms arches to carry life-giving water and nutrients up into the tree. For the bridges, look for long unbranched growth the thickness of a pencil, perhaps water sprouts or suckers growing from the base of the trunk, or long sucker wood up in the tree or from another tree of the same kind. Cut this in lengths to reach from below the wound to above it, with an inch or two left over. With a sharp knife, taper the suckers smoothly at each end so they will lie firmly against the trunk. Make pairs of vertical slits in the bark of the tree, one above the girdled area, the other below, to receive the ends of these bridges. Cut just deep enough to expose the cambium when you lift the top layer of bark.

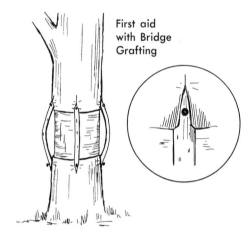

Fig. 67   First aid with bridge grafting. This is a way to save trees that have been girdled by rabbits or mice.

Insert ends of the bridge pieces into the slits so they lie flat against the cambium and each piece has a slight bow in it. Tack the ends to keep them in place, fastening the lower end first. Smooth grafting wax or warm paraffin over both ends of each bridge. If the tree is as large as six inches in diameter, you will need five or six bridges, and add another for each added inch of diameter. If you have done your job well and in time, the rising sap, turned from its normal channels by the girdling, will find a new path across these scions and the tree will be saved.

380

WHAT IS BUDDING?

In budding, you use for the scion a small slice of wood containing a growth bud, instead of a piece of stem. The work goes faster and results are a little surer than with grafting. You can do this work in warm weather—July, August, and September—and you need not dig the roots to work on them. You need a very sharp knife with a rounded point, and some stout rubber bands cut into strips.

Budding suits some plants better than grafting, and for quantity this is the best method, since it yields as many new plants as your stem of scion wood has buds on it—many times what you could get from grafting. This is why in commercial production roses are budded instead of grafted. You can bud the same combinations of plants that you can graft; in fact, budding is technically one type of grafting.

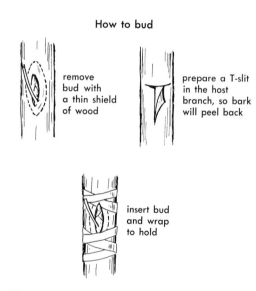

Fig. 68   The main steps in budding.

For your budding rootstock, select seedling plants with the diameter of a pencil. Remove lower leaves and rub off buds that are close to the ground. Take the buds from the variety you wish to propagate. You will find the buds in the leaf axils all the way up and down the stems. Be sure to get a leaf bud and not a flower bud. You are almost sure of the right kind if you take them from twigs of the current summer's growth. Start cutting the bud a quarter inch below the leaf stem, upward to get a shallow slice of stem under it, and bring the blade out on the upper side. Remove the leaf, leaving $\frac{1}{4}$ to $\frac{1}{2}$ inch of the leaf stem or petiole for a handle. The sliver of wood underneath the bud slice does no harm, but for roses some growers prefer to pick it off leaving only the bark, bud and petiole.

On the shaded or north side of the rootstock, just above the ground, lightly cut the bark in the shape of a T, just big enough for the bud shield and only deep enough to expose the cambium. Draw back the corners and slide the bud down inside. Smooth the flaps of bark back over the bud. Wrap a rubber strip around the stem to hold the bud in place. Make several turns above and several below. Then tuck the ends of the band under the first and last loops to fasten them. There is no need to cover edges with wax, since the fit is almost perfect.

If the bud "takes," it stays plump. Early the next year it will begin to grow. As soon as you see this, prune off the entire top of the parent plant just above the bud. From the one bud the whole new plant will develop.

A variation of budding is possible with plants like roses that root readily from cuttings. Insert the buds in upper branches that are a size and age you would choose for hardwood cuttings. Allow two or three weeks for the buds to establish themselves, and then make the branch into cuttings with an inserted bud at the upper end of each. Dip the base of cuttings in Rootone and set them in a peat-sand mix in a shaded coldframe, or with a jar over them. Leave them over winter. Next spring as they start to grow, cut off any growth above the bud (also any side branches below it) and transplant the rooted cutting to your yard.

PART V

GARDENING WITH SAW AND HAMMER

Chapter 30

HOW TO CONSTRUCT WALKS, STEPS, WALLS, AND PATIOS

How can I make my own garden walks and walls?

You can add to the beauty and usefulness of your property with a few well-constructed features like walks and walls. Walks provide a solid footing to take you from place to place in all kinds of weather. Steps are part of this transportation system, easing the ups and downs. Walls help mark off the different areas of your yard, emphasize the design or guard your boundaries. And a paved terrace or patio surface is the first thing you'll need for your outdoor living and dining area.

Constructing all of these is well within your capabilities if you select simple plans and take on just a little at a time. They all entail hard work. In this chapter you can find out how to make them, with a minimum of time, effort and materials.

BUILDING WALKS AND PATHS

Study the overall plan for your yard to decide on best placement of walks. You need a walk for visitors arriving at your front door; one from kitchen to service area; and the design of your garden may call also for walks or paths to increase your enjoyment and access in all kinds of weather.

In locating and designing a walk, keep in mind that:

(1) Curved lines are more inviting than squared-off ones, but a curve in a path must have a purpose. It should curve *around* something. Stake out the walk first or mark it with a hose length to visualize its position and be sure it is usefully placed.

(2) Be generous with width; make it wide enough for two people to walk side by side, a minimum of 4 feet.

MATERIALS FOR WALKS

Bricks are favorites. They look wonderful in a garden, are smooth enough for easy walking, are one of the simplest materials for do-it-yourselfers. Whether you put them on sand or mortar them, you can hardly fail. Bricks make a cool, quiet surface and they don't absorb or reflect much heat.

There are four standard designs with many variations and improvisations. These four are running bond, basket weave, herringbone and jack-on-jack—the first two the best for beginners. Slight variations in brick size make less difference with these two than with the others. For long walks with curves, running bond is most practical.

But don't be misled about the ease of brick-laying. If you do a careful job, you will be amazed at the time consumed in preparation before you come to the actual process of laying brick.

Concrete is the most durable; also it's fairly economical. A good concrete walk

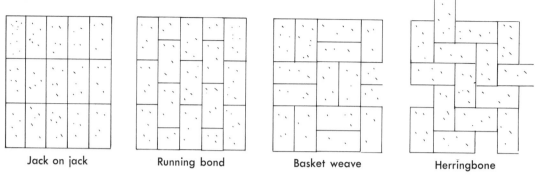

Jack on jack   Running bond   Basket weave   Herringbone

Fig. 69   Four standard patterns for bricks.

lasts for years, is safe, smooth and easy to clean—but a big expanse of it is uninteresting and glaring. And some think it looks too utilitarian for a garden. There are refinements that make it more acceptable. For instance, use pre-cast slabs with imprint designs; alternate concrete and brick panels; pour concrete in divided stepping-stone patterns; or scrub it to expose the pebble aggregate. You can even lay in sorted pebbles to make mosaics.

Flagstones, quarry-cut or naturally flat and laid as stepping stones, belong in a gar-

den. They are not so easy to navigate as a continuous walk, but if you space them closely (from 6 to not more than 15 inches apart), they are fairly convenient. *Set them at ground level so you can run the mower wheel over them* and avoid hand-trimming. Besides stone, you can make stepping stones of concrete shapes cast in place or laid in, or select cross sections of logs. For a very fine walk, lay carefully fitted flagstones on a concrete base and mortar them together. This is a big project and takes considerable skill.

160   Concrete finished with the pebble aggregate exposed has a beautiful texture that fits well in a garden.   *Alpha*

SOFT MATERIALS FOR PATHS

These cushion footsteps and absorb rather than shed moisture, so are nice close to your house or in heavily traveled places. But don't put them where you have to shovel snow in winter, for you are bound to remove the walk surface with it. The soft yielding materials look neater and are more practical if you hold them in place with edging strips of wood. These strips need a wood preservative, of course.

Tanbark, by-product of tanning leather, consists of loose soft chips of oak bark. It is available only at tanneries or at some nurseries that use it to pack plants. To get drainage, apply it above a 2- to 3-inch layer of fine gravel. Although it lasts several years, it does disintegrate eventually, and needs renewing after about five years.

Shingle-tow is similar, but consists of cedar slivers and shavings; once plentiful around nurseries, it is now scarce. Substitutes are coarse pine wood sawdust, pine needles, and wood chips from tree-care companies. These make fairly durable paths, but weeds will come up through all of them. You can keep weeds down with a spring sprinkling of weed killer that does not harm deep-rooted plants nearby.

Gravel is not easy to walk on but does make a clean surface and lasts several years. It is best screened so pieces are about $\frac{1}{2}$ inch in diameter. Smaller than that they are too easily tracked around. Larger, they are uncomfortable for walking. Of course gravel is never a favorite for women in open-toe or high-heeled shoes. Lay gravel about 2 inches deep. Rake and roll it occasionally to keep it presentable. After a few years it tends to work into the soil, so you need to replenish it. Natural gravel is screened out of sand; crushed rock, which serves the same purpose, is reduced to this size at rock quarries. It usually is crushed limestone, very light in color and attractive.

MATERIALS FOR PAVING A PATIO

All the solid materials good for paving walks are also good for patios and terraces, and there are also a few other possibilities. Because of the living requirements of this area—there will be furniture and much traffic, and children will probably run wheel

161 Sawed rounds from tree trunks make a distinguished patio floor with a pleasant feel. They are especially practical in mild dry climates. *Tatch*

162 *Left* Curved lines are more inviting than straight ones. *Tatch*

163 *Below* Flagstone walks, when set flush with the lawn as here, are easy to mow over. *Genereux*

164 Bricks are a favorite material for walks, ideal in garden surroundings. The running bond pattern, used in this Williamsburg garden, is easy to adapt to curving walks. *Roche*

toys there—you want a surface that is hard, smooth, and *easy to clean*. It's impractical to use soft gravel or tanbark.

Besides bricks, poured concrete, flagstones and asphalt, consider wood blocks or boards, precast commercial patio blocks and quarry or ceramic tile.

Wood surfaces of sawed blocks, rounds from a tree trunk or squared-off sections of railroad ties have a pleasant look and feel. Lay them as you would bricks with grain side up. Be sure to treat any wood you use with a preservative, because at best wood surfaces are less lasting than earthy kinds like brick. Lay wood blocks on a sand base and with mortar or sand to bond them together and fill the cracks. Wood blocks or slabs are most practical in dry climates or places sheltered from rain by roof or awning. If your winters are wet and cold, wood

paving may split and warp under climatic pressures.

Patio blocks are popular, cheap and available almost everywhere. They make one of the quickest pavings you can put down. Sold by firms making concrete blocks, they come in various shapes, sizes and colors, enabling you to work out patterns. Lay them like bricks over a pre-designed pattern. Excavate at least a 4-inch base and fill in at least 3 inches of sand, tamping, leveling and smoothing it before laying blocks. To finish edges, place redwood strips anchored with stakes, bricks or blocks on edge, or pour concrete. Should some blocks crack after a few years, you can easily take those out and replace them.

Tile is hardly a job for a do-it-yourselfer, but it has been done. It makes such a spectacularly beautiful and appropriate surface for a patio or terrace close to the house, that it merits consideration especially if the house is still in the planning stage. Sometimes you can plan a tile terrace as an extension of an indoor floor. When skillfully laid, tile is so durable it may outlast the house itself. It resists stains and is easy to keep clean.

HOW TO LAY MATERIALS

BRICK PAVING ON SAND

First divide the work into sections small enough to finish in a weekend or one work session. Otherwise the size of the project defeats you at the start. Determine the dimensions and location of what you want to pave, and lay it out with stakes and cord. If

you can, make a width that uses bricks without cutting. Common bricks measure about 8 x 4 x 2½ inches, but there is variation. To be sure, lay out a sample pattern on the ground. If it's a large project, all you can do is start at one side or end and cut bricks as needed to make the design come out right. If you plan open joints between bricks (the easiest way, especially if the bricks are slightly irregular or you need to make curves), allow ¼ to ½ inch between. At outer edges make a header strip. This might be a course of bricks set on edge or end, or a narrow strip of poured concrete or a well-anchored 2 x 4 redwood board.

With absolute dimensions established, excavate at least 4 inches of soil, or if it is poorly drained clay, go an inch or so deeper and spread coarse rubble over the bottom.

Next install forms at the sides to help

165 Bricks set on sand make an easy-to-lay patio surface. *Tatch*

you achieve a level surface. A patio should be level across both width and length; a sidewalk across the width if possible. Use a carpenter's level and straight-edge board long enough to reach across. Adjust side forms until they are exactly the right height, nailing to stakes to keep them firm. If you are paving a patio and it is so wide you can't reach across it, put a temporary leveling strip down the middle and square the edges with that.

Lay the outer row of bricks against the side forms, either on edge or on end. On end is stronger but takes more bricks and deeper excavation. Hold them with wet mortar. Next fill sand into the center, smooth and tamp it until it is less than a brick's width from the top. To smooth and level the sand, make yourself a "screed." This is a straight-edge board just the width of the sand bed with short extensions nailed on at the right depth at each end so when you scrape it along it grades the sand to the right level. In judging how deep to set the screed, allow $\frac{1}{4}$ inch for sand to settle.

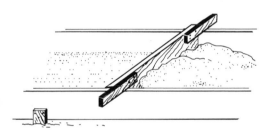

Fig. 70 A screed for leveling sand.

Start laying bricks at one end, smoothing sand as you go, and move down the length of the area. Put boards over bricks already laid to prevent your weight from tipping them. Where cut bricks are to be fitted, leave them until last and cut all at once. To cut brick, lay it on a solid base, score with a brick set, and then give the set a hard blow to break the brick.

When you finish laying bricks, it remains to fill in between them with plain sand or a dry mix of sand and cement. With sand, simply dump some on and sweep it into the cracks.

The sand-cement mixture is more trouble but gives greater stability. Mix one part cement and three parts practically dry sand. Spread a thin layer over the bricks and tamp it down in each crack with a small board or a trowel blade. Sweep off any excess. Set a fine misty sprinkler to water the surface. Let it run slowly an hour or two to moisten the sand-cement thoroughly. Smooth off or fill any uneven joints with a trowel. Soak bricks again the next day to cure and solidify the concrete filling.

HOW TO LAY BRICKS IN WET MORTAR

If soil settling or freeze-thaws often ruin brick walks in your locality, use the wet-mortar method, even though it's more work. First spread a 4-inch drainage layer of rubble. Then pour a 2-inch layer of concrete and let it harden. Finally lay the bricks, buttering each with mortar as you place it. Tamp and level carefully, tooling out joints with a spoon or the trowel-tip as you go along.

CONCRETE FOR DRIVEWAYS, WALKS, AND PATIOS

Excavate 6 inches below the final desired surface where you want to pour concrete and put in side forms, using strong stakes and boards so heavy concrete can't budge them. Fill the bottom of the excavation with 2 inches of tamped rubble, rocks or coarse gravel. For a driveway, excavate deep enough to make the rubble 3 inches thick and the slab 6 inches. The slab in sidewalks and patios can be $3\frac{1}{2}$ to 4 inches thick.

Estimate how much concrete you will need. If the slab is to be 4 inches thick, you will need $1\frac{1}{3}$ yards of mixed concrete to cover 100 square feet. Mixing it yourself you will need 8 sacks of cement, about 18 cubic feet of sand and 24 cubic feet of gravel for each hundred square feet of area. If your project is where a ready-mix concrete truck could back in to deliver without damaging your sidewalks, lawns or shrubs, it certainly saves backaches to have it delivered. Ready-mix companies usually will not bring less than a cubic yard at a time. The cost is not much greater than when you mix it yourself.

If you do mix your own, tackle small areas

166 Tile makes a spectacularly beautiful surface. It is often planned as an extension of indoor flooring.

Mosaic Tile

at a time. Wherever you can, install wood or brick dividers to give convenient stopping places. Level these carefully. If they are wood, nail them to stakes set low so concrete will cover them. Where they join, toe-nail them together. To make them bond with the concrete and not pull away, drive in spikes part way.

The right proportions for concrete in driveways, walks and patios:

1 part Portland cement
2 parts sand
3 parts gravel or crushed rock
Enough water to make a mix that is plastic but not soupy.

To mix, put sand and cement together and blend first; then add gravel and blend; finally pour water a little at a time into a depression in the middle of the pile. Depending on the moisture content of sand

167 Closely fitted quarry flagstone makes a terrace floor that is almost indestructible. *Genereux*

and gravel, you will probably need about $2\frac{1}{2}$ gallons of clean water for each batch containing a half-sack of cement.

If the batch is not enough to fill one section, spread it thinly and bring the level to the top with the second or succeeding batches. Leave the surface rough each time to make a good bond with the next layer. When the concrete reaches the top, smooth it with a straight-edge board worked across the forms, and remove excess. Fill in any depressions. Let the cement stand until surface moisture disappears, then quickly smooth it with a wood float which is a smooth board with a handle. If you want a slicker finish, wait until concrete starts to stiffen and polish it with a trowel. To make a glare-free, slip-free surface, brush the surface right after you smooth it with a broom or whisk broom.

Make expansion joints every 4 feet in walks or patio slabs. In driveways, put large contraction joints at 10-foot intervals, and in wide drives, also put one down the middle. Where winters are hard with many freezes and thaws, put down reinforcing wire for large stretches of poured slab.

How to make a pebble finish. This gives a textured look free of the glare of smooth-finished concrete, also good traction in icy weather and the prettiest cement finish for a garden. On the other hand, it may be a bit tipsy for furniture, and may skin the knees of children who play on it. To finish concrete this way, scrub it with a wire brush before it dries completely, to expose the aggregate. Aggregate is the course stuff like gravel that gives it bulk. Most attractive for the purpose are pebbles of graded sizes and different but soft colors. The supply of colored gravel, gray, pink or buff, depends on locality. You will probably have to settle for a mixture. Mix and pour the concrete as you would any. Let it set five to six hours, then scrub it with a wire or stiff bristle brush dipped in water. The cement and fine sand particles scrub out, letting the larger particles show. Wash away loose sand and cement. Don't wait more than twenty-four hours to do this scrubbing or you will never be able to work the concrete down to the pebbles. When cement hardens quickly, as in hot weather, it resists scrubbing. In such a case, scrub with a solution of 1 part

393

muriatic acid to 6 parts water. This softens the cement. Be sure to use rubber gloves and a bristle, not a wire, brush for this.

How to cast concrete stepping stones. First decide on size and shape. If the stones are to be bigger than 4 square feet, better cast them in place. You may devise ways to cast circles, hexagons and trapezoids but the simplest shape is square or rectangular. With 2 x 4's, three hinges and a hasp lock, make a form that may be opened. Mitre and hinge three corners. Fit the fourth with a lock to hold it shut. Cover the inside of the form with axle grease.

If you are working in a garage or on a sidewalk, spread building paper to keep the concrete off the floor. Mix and pour concrete into the form, tamping to work out bubbles. Let it set a day or two. Then open and remove the form. Keep the slab moist for three or four days before you set it in place.

How to make pebble mosaics. It takes patience to work out designs with pebbles. Use restraint with mosaics—save them for the really choice spots where decoration will be seen and appreciated, and not look fancy. Designs are easiest when enclosed with brick, concrete or wood dividers. First decide on pattern and colors, preferably muted ones. Then collect pebbles to work it out. Be sure to have plenty. The best are smooth flat ones from a stream bed, the kind you can stand up on the sides. Sort them by colors. For practice, lay out the design first on sand, a sidewalk or big sheet of paper. Then you'll know how many pebbles you need. Divide the design into small sections that you can complete in about an hour and a half.

First pour a concrete slab, bringing it up to within an inch of the surface, leaving it chopped and rather rough. Moisten it when you are ready to place your design. Mix a batch of mortar consisting of two parts sand and one part cement, with just enough water to make it spread. A bucketful at a time is enough. Spread this on the slab about $\frac{3}{4}$ inch deep.

Start putting in pebbles in the planned design. Insert so that about two-thirds of each is embedded in the concrete. When you finish, tamp with a board lightly over the tops of the pebbles to settle them into a level surface. Let the cement set five to six hours. Then with a whisk broom lightly brush off any loose concrete and carefully clean the surfaces of the pebbles with a moist sponge. Lay a wet sack over the whole thing and let it cure several days. If cement film dulls the sparkle of your pebbles, clean it off after two weeks by scrubbing with muriatic acid, 1 part dissolved in 2 parts of water in a glass jar or crock, not a metal bucket. Wear rubber gloves and goggles and don't get any acid on you. Rinse off the acid-treated surface immediately with plenty of clear water.

HOW TO BUILD GARDEN STEPS

Steps help you go easily from one level in your garden to another, and they are an attractive feature for your yard. When you plan steps:

Make the riser or vertical part less than 7 inches.

Make the tread, the part you step on, at least 12 inches wide.

To get good proportion within these limitations, let width of tread times width of riser equal at least 72. For example, if the riser is 6 inches, let the tread be at least 12 inches; if the riser is 5 inches let the tread be at least $14\frac{1}{2}$ inches. Outdoor steps are generally more ramplike and take their slopes more gradually than indoor stairways.

Where you possibly can, make steps 4 or 5 feet wide so two people can go up and down side by side.

Provide a hand rail where there are four or more relatively steep steps.

To have steps in harmony with your yard, use the same materials as those of the walk or path leading up to them. If they are part of a brick terrace, for example, make them of bricks also.

Steps can be made of concrete, brick, stone, wood combined with concrete, wood combined with brick, wood risers combined with sod, gravel or tanbark treads, all wood in various designs, wood combined with asphalt treads, flagstone or tiles.

Where you have a steep long bank to

168 Carefully planned and well placed garden steps improve the looks of your yard. Here heavy timbers form the risers; packed earth makes the treads. *Baer*

climb, consider breaking one steady flight of steps with a landing, to provide a little rest between climbs.

To determine how steep to make the steps, first measure the distance they are to cover. Stand a post at the foot of the slope

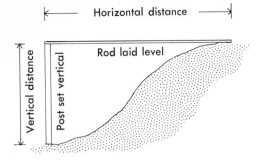

Fig. 71 Finding the horizontal and vertical distances of a slope.

and lay a horizontal rod across to it from the top of the slope, making sure it is level. The distance from top of slope to top of post is the horizontal distance; the distance from top of post to ground at the foot of the slope is the vertical distance. Divide the vertical distance by some practical riser height—4, 5, 6 or 7 inches. This will indicate how many steps you need. In turn, divide this number into the horizontal distance to find the width for each tread. It is easy to make small changes in slopes to improve the proportion of steps. For instance, if the angle is too steep for good looks, start the steps back farther and let them cut into the bank at the top. Move earth from the top to fill in below.

For masonry steps of brick or stone, first excavate deep enough to put in an under layer of gravel for drainage. At the base of the stairway, dig down and put in a large concrete footing that reaches below the deepest penetration of frost. This will support the whole stairs.

If wooden steps are what you will have, you can set the whole structure above ground and build it with cut-out stringers just as you would an indoor stairway. If the steps are to touch soil, protect them from rot and insects by treating with a wood preservative.

HOW TO BUILD GARDEN WALLS

Walls can be both ornamental and useful in your yard. They can emphasize your design, make a front for a raised flower bed, provide a place to sit, tie together separate areas of your yard or make a background

for a pool or a rose garden. For a wall instead of a fence along your boundary, construct it of materials that lift it out of the forbidding class and make it something light and beautiful that your neighbor can enjoy too. If a steep earth bank is to be held back, a wall can serve this functional purpose, yet add interest with its own attractive form.

If you are fairly experienced, with plenty of time and a penchant for exactness, you can build almost any kind of wall yourself. But the easiest are those of concrete blocks and bricks. Stone walls are more difficult and perhaps best left to specialists. Walls of poured concrete, if they rise more than a foot or two, require so much form-building, concrete mixing and heavy lifting that you are sure to need help, and any wall over 6 feet offers problems beyond the ability of one man working alone.

Walls of stone, blocks, or bricks are very heavy and require a deep footing under them, deeper than frost ever goes. If the wall crosses a filled area, piers are needed to reach solid clay or subsoil. Otherwise cracks, humps and hollows develop to ruin the beauty of your wall and demand constant repair.

Before you build, check local ordinances. In some places you need official permission to erect a wall. Many cities have requirements that will affect your plans. If there is a question about your property boundaries, start with a survey if a wall is to run close to the line. If you build it well, your wall will be permanent and immovable.

BUILDING FREESTANDING BRICK AND BLOCK WALLS

Concrete blocks make wall-building go faster than bricks. On the other hand, blocks may look too cold and commercial to you for your home grounds. If you want the speed and economy of blocks and good looks too, with thought you can get this also. For instance, choose from the wide variety of available blocks a combination of shapes and sizes to give a stonework effect; turn some on the side to get an openwork pattern; combine with bricks for a decora-

396

169 A high wall of screen blocks around this terrace provides privacy without stopping the breeze. A low brick retaining wall handles the change of levels.
Dorian International

tive effect. You can also improve block walls by painting them.

The many styles of concrete blocks offer corner possibilities. For example, you can get bullnosed blocks that have smoothly rounded corners; or rounds to make a graceful curve. "Screen" blocks, ornamental concrete precast in geometric shapes, offer possibilities where you want a wall to conceal a view but not block the breeze. You can use different kinds of construction tile in the same way.

Start brick or block walls from a footing that goes at least 18 inches deep in the ground. Make it as thick as the wall and twice as wide. If it is to be a fairly high wall of concrete blocks, say 4 feet, put upright reinforcing rods in the footing every 4 feet. Set them so they stand up 2 feet through the block cores. Then as you lay each new course of blocks, fill in around these rods with concrete. This makes a wall that resists buckling and does not move out of line.

You can make a straight brick wall one 4-inch brick thick only if it is to be under 18 inches high and will have no particular stress put on it. Curved or serpentine walls tend to brace themselves, however, and can go as high as 5 feet with single-brick thickness. When walls go high or need strength, as they do if they support a seat, hold back soil in a planter box or get jolts from chil-

dren playing, then make them at least two bricks thick.

Free-standing walls 5 feet or more high need bracing every 10 to 15 feet with a square pillar twice the thickness of the wall. Walls close to plants may block air movement on frosty nights and cause cold damage. Prevent this by making lattice-like openings in your brick walls. Many patterns will suggest themselves to you. Do experiment beforehand to determine upon a good design.

If your wall is to climb a slope, keep the courses level and let it ascend in a series of

170 To prevent brick walls from stopping air movement, you can give them a lacy openwork pattern such as this. *National Concrete Masonry*

WORKING WITH CONCRETE

Recipe for mortar mix—to lay bricks, stone or blocks

1 part Portland cement
1 part hydrated lime
5 to 6 parts sand

Water added gradually until mix spreads, but does not run

Recipe for poured concrete—for walks, patios or driveways

1 part Portland cement
2 parts sand
3 parts gravel or crushed rock

Water added gradually until mix spreads, but is not liquid

Vital statistics for home masons

1 sack Portland cement makes about 4 cubic feet of concrete
Standard bricks measure about 4 x $2\frac{1}{2}$ x 8 inches
Standard blocks measure about 8 x 8 x 16 inches
Slab depth for walks and patios, $3\frac{1}{2}$ to 4 inches
Slab depth for driveways, 6 inches
Minimum width for driveways, 8 feet; if curved, 3 feet wider than straight

steps. This holds true for both block and brick construction. With a wall on a slope, start at the high point and work down. When you have the footing in level steps, the rest follows easily. For any laid-up masonry wall, start at the corners. Get the corner true with a plumb bob or level and stretch a tight line from one corner to the next to keep the wall straight and level. When you come to the top, finish the job with a cap layer of some kind. For a brick wall, turn the bricks a different way. For a block wall, make the cap layer of bricks if you like, or cap it with mortar rounded or peaked. Some cement block styles are suitable for capstones, too. It helps if the cap extends an inch or two over the sides as protection from rain.

BUILDING RETAINING WALLS

Where a wall must hold back a high bank of soil, it needs special construction. Water must be able to get through the wall—otherwise it accumulates with such pressure that the wall may tumble down on a tide of wet earth. To let water through a wall, put holes in it.

For these retaining walls, use solid poured concrete, concrete blocks, bricks or heavy timbers like railroad ties or telephone poles. Natural stone also makes a good retaining wall when it is mortared, but it is hard for amateurs to lay.

Unlike the dry wall of unmortared stone (described in Chapter 18) a true retaining wall presents a solid face and you cannot plant in it, only over it with vines.

Provide a deep, strong concrete footing for any such wall. If you feel extra strength will be needed, pour an "apron" at the front of the footing to resist tilting. Dig out soil back of where the wall will be and lay drain tiles along the base to lead off water. After you complete such a wall, dump gravel behind to cover the line of tile. Also, as you put up the wall, provide "weep" holes at intervals through it, one for every 12 square

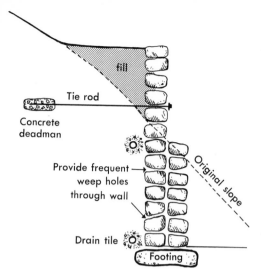

Fig. 72 Method of bracing a high retaining wall.

feet of wall surface, more at the base than near the top. For extra strength, make the wall thicker at base than top, adding the extra thickness on the bank side if you want the face to appear vertical.

Sections of drain tile make good "weep" holes through a brick or concrete wall. With concrete block walls, all you need do is turn the block on its side so water can drain through the core holes. Where wetness and weight are a threat to stability, put a second line of drain tile behind the wall halfway up and parallel to the line laid along the base. As a further safeguard, tie the wall into the bank by burying heavy concrete "deadmen" several feet back and connecting them with steel tie rods that pass through to the face of the wall.

When you have a very high bank, it is much easier and safer to make two or more low retaining walls than one big one. Four

feet is about as high as you should make a home-constructed retaining wall.

EASY-DOES-IT IDEAS

You can cast concrete stepping stones in place. Make a movable form (like sketch)

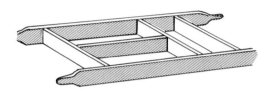

Fig. 73 A form for casting stepping stones in place.

that casts three at a time. Grease the form and fill it with concrete. Let set. Then lift off the form, turn it over to reverse the pattern, and pour again. In easy stages, you can pour a walk this way in a week's time.

Fill cracks between bricks in sidewalk or patio with a dry sand-cement mixture, tamp down, then water it thoroughly. When it sets, the bricks will be solidly bound in concrete.

Lay a narrow ribbon two bricks wide at the edge of flower beds to give a walking surface. Make it low so the mower can run over it, and you will save yourself many an edging job.

Chapter 31

HOW TO BUILD
A GOOD FENCE

What is the best fence for my place?

You probably have reasons for wanting a fence but stop to think what they are. It may be to keep children, dogs, and passersby out. It may be to keep your own children and pets in. Perhaps you want privacy in your back yard—so you can escape the eyes of neighbors. Or maybe you need to block out a view in your own yard or next door, or provide a pleasing background for your plantings. You may want a fence to slow down the wind. Your reasons for building a fence determine your choice of material.

Something else to consider is cost. The fence you finally decide on may be a compromise between what you can afford and the purpose you want served. If you do the work yourself, any fence costs less.

Let's look at various fences and see what they will do. To check on costs, see the table at the end of this chapter.

MATERIALS FOR FENCING

FENCES OF WIRE

Of the dozens of wire fences, three good kinds for your yard are welded wire, woven picket, and chain link. All are unclimbable. Welded wire is made of wires welded together in 2- x 4-inch up-and-down rectangles. Woven picket or double woven picket with an overlapping pattern near the bottom is an old-style decorative wire fence that is still popular and useful. Chain link is a more recent development, made of steel or aluminum wire with diagonal 2-inch mesh. Often there is a metal rail along the top.

Any of these fences, galvanized to resist rusting, will last fifteen years or more if you set them right at the beginning. The aluminum chain link, of course, never rusts but it is weaker than steel and more likely to be damaged by impacts. Any wire fence gets most of its strength from the posts to which it is attached, so use durable kinds of wood or round or channeled steel. Set them with proper bracing and anchoring.

Wire fences are one of the best kinds to keep children and pets in the yard and trespassers out, because wire is hard to climb. Low in price, they are also easy to install except that they require fence-stretching equipment. You will need a\ helper if you tackle this yourself. A disadvantage is the functional, institutional look that is out of harmony with a garden unless planted with vines or shrubs. Wire gives no privacy and is useless as a windbreak.

FENCES OF WOOD

There are many excellent types of wood fencing.

Fences of sawed pickets. The classic picket fence is well suited to traditional houses, Cape Cod or Williamsburg types, and is perfectly adapted to practically all

171 Post and rail fence is a country type easily brought to the suburbs. It is long lasting and pretty in informal settings.

Tatch

older homes. With so many designs, they harmonize with almost anything except contemporary styles.

Pickets make a practical fence, holding in children and pets and keeping out intruders. With a little maintenance they last twelve to fifteen years, perhaps longer. Maintenance consists of replacing pickets now and then, possibly splicing a broken post or putting in a new one, and painting every four or five years. The initial cost of picket fencing is fairly high, especially if you count the time you spend making it or if you hire this done. This fence has little value as a screen or windbreak.

In long fences, pickets tend to look monotonous. You can relieve this effect by making slight departures in the pattern, such as raising or lowering the height in certain sections where there is justification,

or inserting posts with finial designs. Three to 4 feet is height enough for average pickets. Width of boards and spacing is up to you. When you have pets to keep in, space pickets closely enough to prevent their squeezing through. If you want to keep dogs from burrowing under, fasten a strip of chicken wire along the inside base buried a few inches in the soil.

Fences of rustic pickets, sometimes called stockade fences, never need paint. If pickets are close-set and the fence is high, they give complete privacy and wind control. Instead of the neat formality of painted pickets, these are informal and look at home in almost any situation. They have a rough texture and after a few years become weathered gray, blending well with flowers, trees, shrubs, old bricks, and stone.

Usually rustic pickets come prefabricated

401

in sections. The prevailing material is white cedar, or on the West Coast, redwood, which is also used for grapestake pickets. Cedar pickets come with bark or peeled. They

172 A board fence looks less utilitarian and more decorative with simple cutouts like this flower pot design. *Western Pine Association*

may be woven tightly in wire so you can't see through, or nailed to cross-pieces like ordinary pickets. Close-set kinds are available in fences up to 8 feet that make un-

climbable, longlasting privacy screens. Some designs look finished on both sides.

These are comparatively high in cost and unavailable in some localities. You may have to order from a manufacturer. Grape stakes, where you can get them, are not prefabricated and you can assemble them yourself. The rough finish of all these pickets is a splinter hazard if children play close to them.

Fences of board on board. This fence design consists of matching boards alternated and slightly overlapped on opposite sides of the framing piece they are nailed to. You can run the boards, usually 1 x 6's or 1 x 8's, vertically or horizontally. Either way you get almost complete privacy without entirely stopping circulation of air, and the fence looks finished from both sides. If made with boards set vertically, it is a good barrier for children. If you run boards horizontally, almost any three-year-old can, and will, climb over. Cats and pups can struggle through either style, since there is almost 4 inches of space between the two surfaces. You can make this fence of economical lumber, but it requires a lot of it. If you set boards horizontally, use vertical supports about every 4 feet to prevent warping and sagging. This fence has the advantages of louvered fencing but is easier to construct. Tricky to paint, it is best stained or allowed to weather naturally.

Fences in basket-weave. Good screens with an interesting shadow pattern, basket-weave fences are economical if you can get half-inch rough-sawed lumber, strong, and easy to construct. Unfortunately children and cats find them simple to climb over once they get a toe-hold in the weave. But they make a good barrier for dogs and adult intruders. In long stretches the zigzag shadow pattern overwhelms the eye—so much so that basket-weave is attractive only for short distances.

Fences of posts and rails. This old-fashioned country fence also suits the suburbs for an unobtrusive boundary or to enclose livestock. Children, grown folks and pets can easily get through or over it, so it is no barrier. It has no screening qualities and offers no wind protection, but is fairly economical and a well-built one lasts many

173 Fences made of rustic pickets have the advantage that they never need paint.

Habitant

years. Variations include post and board fences and split-rail zigzag fences. Construction methods range from nailing rails to posts, wiring them, doweling them, or using mortise joints.

Fences of boards. This Tom Sawyer type fence gives complete privacy and is a good barrier against people and wind. Its great disadvantage is that it may look too utilitarian to suit you, and as Tom discovered, it occasionally needs paint. To relieve its plainness, you can dress it up with cutouts where the boards meet. Any symmetrical design like diamonds, pinetree shapes, ovals, circles, half-moons, tulip shapes, hourglasses, or hearts lend themselves to cutout decor on a board fence and lift it out of the ordinary. The fence pictured shows one idea. The sketch suggests more.

Use any kind of lumber and almost any grade, although boards with knotholes are detracting and weakening. A board fence lasts as long as a picket type, to fifteen years.

FENCES OF OTHER MATERIALS

Besides wire and wood, fences are being made of so many new materials, we do not yet know how they will hold up.

Plastics make colorful boundaries and screens. One type that you can mount in wood frames is corrugated or plain Fiberglas panels of various translucent hues. Plastics screen off a view and protect you from wind, but allow light to come through. They are ideal for patio or poolside. Another plastic product for a fence is webbing. You weave this between wood framing into

403

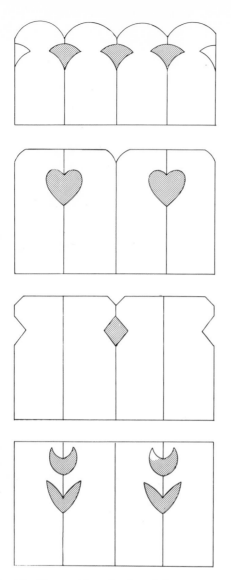

Fig. 74   Cutout ideas for board fences.

a basket design. It makes a good, quickly erected screen and windbreak, but after a season's exposure to wind and weather it tends to sag, and needs frequent tightening. None of the available plastic materials for fencing is what you could consider cheap.

Reed and bamboo. Whether woven between fiber or wire, or tacked to a frame, these make good light fences and screens. They are superb as backgrounds or portable panels that you can move at will. More of a visual than a real barrier, they are easily broken by pressure and hard knocks—so don't use one to backstop your ball game.

Rain and hot sun soon make them look weathered and gray. To keep them new-looking, coat with spar varnish every couple of years.

SCREENS ARE A SPECIAL TYPE OF FENCE

You put screens up mainly to block a view, perhaps of your trash burner or compost pile. Or you may wish to separate your patio from the service yard, conceal it from the neighbor's windows, or even make a background for some chosen plant. Screens are not child- or pet-proof barriers. Usually you want them only in short sections. Such limited uses are possible with many new materials.

To eliminate or filter the view, select redwood, fir, white pine, plywood, tempered waterproof hardboard, asbestos board, aluminum panels with an enamel finish, or corrugated sheet metal mounted on wood frames, Fiberglas and plastic panels mounted in wood or metal frames, awning canvas stretched on wood or pipe frames, masonry screens of concrete or tile, woven rattan panels, reed or bamboo mounted in wood frames, or ornamental iron grillwork.

One use for a transparent screen is to block wind instead of a view. If you live in the mountains or at the seashore, or on a high windy hill with a vista, this might be your greatest need. Beside a swimming pool a transparent screen will admit the warm sunlight but keep out the chilly wind. Glass is the most appropriate, and practically the only, material for this sort of screen. Unfortunately it is fragile, so you have to devise ways to protect it from hard knocks. Wire glass with fine wire strands embedded in it is the least accident prone.

If you work with wood, you can invent all sorts of attractive screens. A favorite is the louvered wood panel, because it permits good air circulation. Such screens are beyond the carpentering ability of most do-it-yourselfers, and best left to skilled craftsmen. Swiss cheese or other cutouts from plywood panels make interesting designs, and basket-weave panels of redwood are attractive and permanent. Tempered hardboard

174 Fiberglass panels set into redwood frames make a good screen that blocks the view but lets light through. *California Redwood Association*

175 *Right* Plywood has possibilities for privacy screens. Cutouts give interest.
Douglas Fir Plywood Association

176 *Below* Woven plastic webbing makes a basket weave fence used with redwood supports. It is easy to construct.
Dow Chemical Company

177 The post and rail fence has many refinements and variations. This one, made of pine lumber in a herringbone pattern, gives a degree of privacy without shutting out air and sun.

Western Pine Association

makes practical screen panels but requires close cross supports to prevent buckling, especially if you use $\frac{1}{8}$-inch thickness. You can paint it to give it color. Use the tempered hardboard that is smooth on both sides. This comes in 4- x 8-foot panels.

THINGS TO DO FIRST

Before you erect a fence, check to see if there are regulations in your community about height, materials, and location. It's best to have all this in mind when you begin rather than have to change your plans, or maybe your fence, later on. Also, do consult your neighbor. Sometimes good neighbors cooperate in putting up a fence, and share the cost. If you can work out such an agreement, locate the fence right on the property line. If your neighbor declines to go along, then put the fence entirely on your side, about 6 inches inside the line so there can be no arguments about it.

Maintaining it is then entirely up to you, but you also have the right to plant vines on it or paint it any way you like with no criticism acceptable from the other side. Where a fence goes in front of or behind your house, along street or alley, it is also all yours. When a division fence is joint property with a neighbor, it is wise to put your agreement on paper, so you can remember your rights and obligations and they are definitely understood in case the property on either side is sold.

HOW TO BUILD A FENCE

BUILDING A WIRE FENCE

A wire fence starts with the posts, usually of metal for a chain-link type. For woven and welded wire, posts can be of metal or wood. The kind of posts you choose and how well you set them affect the durability of your wire fence and how satisfied you will be with it. You may have to take what your lumberyard can supply in wooden posts. Here are some of the best kinds:

redwood—usually rough sawed, as 4 x 4's

cedar, white or red

black locust, durable but hard to find

yellow pine, the commonest kind

Osage orange or hedge, durable but hard to find.

Treat all wood posts before you put them in the ground unless you buy them pre-treated. Fill an oil barrel with creosote or pentachlorophenol, called penta for short, and soak the lower 30 inches of each post for a day or two. But avoid creosote on posts you expect to paint, for creosote stains paint. You can paint over penta preservative unless it was diluted with something greasy like fuel oil. The most damaging rot comes on wood posts just at soil level so be sure to cover that area with preservative. If you bevel the tops of wooden posts or cut them to an inverted V-point, they shed rain and last longer.

Metal posts come as round tubes or channeled in U, H or sometimes T shapes. Set round posts in concrete. You can drive the channeled types into place with a sledge hammer and driving cap, and you don't usually need to set them in concrete.

To get posts in a straight line, set the two corners first. Stretch a cord between as a guide for the other post holes. Set posts 8 to 10 feet apart but no more. For wooden posts make holes 6 inches or more in diameter and 2 to 2½ feet deep.

To make the holes, use a post-hole auger or clam-shell digger. The auger makes the neatest hole but the clam-shell works better where ground is stony. Make the hole a few inches deeper than needed, and dump gravel in the bottom to bring the post up to the right height. Digging post holes is hard work, so you may want to hire someone with a postholer rig on his tractor to do this for you. Set posts about 24 inches deep.

Whether concrete is needed around them depends on the soil you have and the stress on the posts. Ordinarily you set round metal posts in concrete, although kinds are sold now with spreading angle-irons that anchor them. If your soil is firm, wooden posts will probably stand solidly without concrete. Dump gravel 10 inches deep around the base and top it with tamped earth. Check to get posts exactly perpendicular; a carpenter's level helps.

Corner, gate and end posts need diagonal bracing. It is always wise to set these and the braces in concrete. Brace corners both ways; ends only on the fence side. To set the brace, dig a hole a foot deep where the

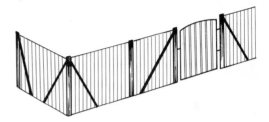

Fig. 75 Corners, ends and gate posts need diagonal bracing.

brace enters the ground. Fill it with wet concrete and push the brace down into it, having already fastened the other end of the brace to the post. To give concrete time to harden, set all posts and braces two days before attaching the fence.

Wire fences need stretching. First you need a stout rod or a pair of 2 x 4's to clamp on the end and give an even pull over the whole width of the fence. Attach a chain to the clamp and hook it to a tractor, jeep, car or truck. Some tool-supply firms rent fence clamps and block and tackle sets to stretch wire. Or you might borrow them where you buy the fence.

It takes at least 200 to 400 pounds of pull on a 100-foot fence to prevent sagging. To use block and tackle, attach the free end to a tree or truck, or anything solid you can place there, *but not to another fence post.* On wooden posts use staples, on metal posts use tie wire. If the post has metal lugs, hammer these shut over the wire. Stretch the fence and fasten it to each post down the line. Put a staple or tie every 12 inches up and down each post.

Where a fence turns a corner, stretch and fasten it to the corner post, letting it just overlap. Cut and reattach the fence on the

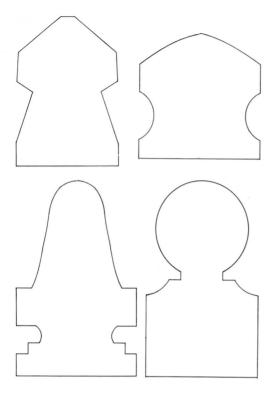

Fig. 76   Four designs for picket tops.

other side of the post, and move the puller to stretch the new way. Don't try to pull the fence around a corner. Where it rounds a curve, stretch one straight section at a time. Up and down hills, set the puller at the top of the slope until all posts are attached; then move the stretcher to the bottom for the down slope.

HOW TO BUILD A PICKET FENCE

First decide upon the design of your fence, the height and spacing of pickets. At some lumber yards you can buy pickets already cut, or you can have pickets cut to order at a woodworking shop. This saves time, although you can easily saw your own in a home shop. Have all the posts, rails, and pickets cut out before you start to assemble them.

The post that joins consecutive sections is an important part of a picket fence. This usually is a 4- x 4-inch post from the lumber yard, dressed to a peaked, rounded or sloped cap. Any but a square top will help the post shed water and last longer. If you want a

turned ornamental top on posts, you'll need a lathe to do it.

Be exact when you set posts. Space them perfectly, face them properly at the right height and truly vertical both ways. Use a carpenter's level on each face to check position. If posts are not exactly true all your construction will be more difficult. Space posts 8 feet apart.

Use pine, cedar, redwood or fir for pickets. They need not be clear grade but should be free of open knotholes.

To join rails to posts. You need two 2 x 4 rails, one for the top, one for the bottom. Attach the top rail by lapping it over the posts and nailing it there. Or you can attach both top and bottom rails by butting them to the post and toe-nailing in place.

To space pickets. Decide on the distance and cut a spacer out of scrap lumber. Make it long enough to reach from top to bottom rail. Nail on a cleat at the top so you can hang it over the top rail. Then you can lay each picket against this without bothering to measure every time. To prevent rust streaks use galvanized or aluminum nails. Set pickets high enough to clear the ground by 2 inches.

What to do with slopes. Decide whether

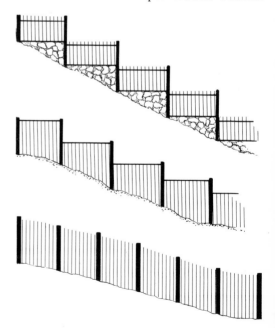

Fig. 77   What to do with slopes—stepped down or sloped down.

to keep your fence sections horizontal and step them down a slope or let them curve, following the ground contour. Tilting the sections with the slope is probably the easiest way and just as desirable, but you will need to do a special fitting job where rails butt against posts. Of course, the pickets, all

Bolt action latch

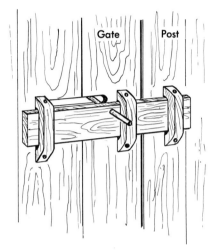

Thumb latch action

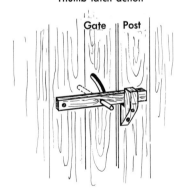

Fig. 78   Two types of gate latches you can make yourself of wood.

the same length, go on vertically just as if they were over level ground. The stepped-down system is better if the pickets are to go above a brick or stone wall that also steps down the slope.

Some ideas for picket tops are shown in Figure 75. You can make your own design by taking paper the width of the picket, folding it lengthwise and experimentally cutting into the edge until you get a prac-

tical, pretty pattern. Transfer it to stiff cardboard to follow in cutting out pickets.

To make picket fence last longer, treat boards and posts with wood preservative and a prime and finish coat of paint before you assemble them. Later you can go over the fence to touch up nail heads and bruises. White is classic for pickets but pink, yellow, light gray, dark green and brown have been successfully used. Keep the color light if you want to emphasize the attractive design of rounded, pointed or dart-shaped cutouts at the top. Whether you make pickets or buy them, store a few extras to replace any that break or get lost.

Types of hinges for gates

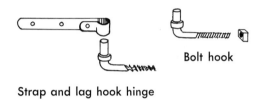

Strap and lag hook hinge

Bolt hook

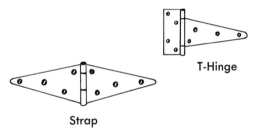

Strap

T-Hinge

Fig. 79   Types of hinges for gates.

It is claimed that a white fence makes your yard look smaller unless the fence is built with strong horizontal lines. However, you will hardly notice any shrinking effect with a low white picket fence. Gray, brown and dark green on the other hand are receding colors and tend to make a yard look more spacious.

GATES FOR YOUR FENCE

You will need gates to let you pass through your fence and gates do offer opportunities for making pretty garden pictures, so plan them with care.

178 This gate is a modern plywood cutout design set solidly in a concrete wall. *Tatch*

A gate probably comes with a chain-link or woven wire fence. It is a practical but not beautiful affair and you can't really do anything more with it. But you can design an attractive gate for picket, board, basketweave and board-on-board fences, or brick, block, or stone walls.

First decide how to latch it, for this may make a difference in how to build it. Thumb latches and bolt-action locks are favorite hardware latches. With wood you can invent your own version of either of these. The drawings offer two ideas. For either to work properly, be sure the gate and latch post edges are even.

Next consider the gate post on the hinge side. To prevent sagging, make the hinge post strong and firm. Anchor it if possible to the house or other building, or set it deep in concrete and brace it diagonally. If you can, hang the gate before you set the latch post. Then anchor this heavily in concrete, taking care to position it just right for the latch to work.

Get large strong hinges in keeping with the style of your gate. Use strap hinges if there is a strong wide wood area on which to fasten them. Large strap hinges are too long for a 4-inch post, so you might use big T-hinges there. If the gate has only a small solid area, perhaps just a wood frame with a wire or plastic inset, then use butt hinges. With any of these hinges the gate swings only one way. If you want it to swing both ways, consider a set of bolt (or lag) and strap hinges. The bolt or lag goes right into the post, hook end up, and the strap loop rests on the hook. This makes a strong hinge and the whole gate just lifts off if you want to remove it for painting or any other reason. Provide three hinges instead of two if gate is solid, heavy and large.

179 Gates can be interesting. This one, using bamboo nailed to a wood frame, is an entry to a side yard. *Tatch*

How to brace gate frames

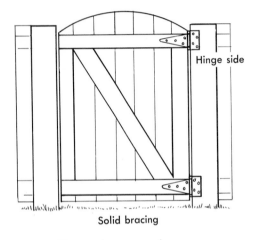

Hinge side

Turnbuckle and wire bracing

Hinge side

Solid bracing

Fig. 80   How to brace gate frames.

Brace the gate frame diagonally to prevent sagging. If you use wood, run it from the bottom hinge side diagonally up to the top on the latch side. Cut it carefully for a perfect fit. If you use a wire and turnbuckle brace, run it the opposite way, from the upper hinge side down to the lower corner of the latch side.

Leave a little space—$\frac{3}{4}$ of an inch or so—between gate and latch post, so there will be no binding in wet weather or after posts settle.

EASY-DOES-IT IDEAS

Slant tops of wooden fence posts to make them shed rain and last longer. Or cut them to points.

When you include gates in your fence, hang the gate before putting up the post it will latch against. This helps you make the latch work properly.

To save painting time on picket or board fences, spray-paint the parts before assembling them. Lay pieces together on a covered floor and spray them all at once. Let dry, then turn to do the other sides.

COSTS OF POPULAR FENCING MATERIALS

	Description	Cost (approximate)	Comment
Wire fences			
Chain link	11-gauge steel, 4 feet high	75¢	Per running foot, including posts and rails
Double picket wire	11-gauge steel, 4 feet high	35¢	Per running foot, posts not included
Welded wire	11-gauge steel, 4 feet high	36¢	Per running foot, posts not included
Peeled pickets (stockade)			
White cedar	4 feet high	$1.45	Per running foot, assembled in sections
Picket, board fences			
Pickets	1 x 4 inches x 4 feet, No. 2 yellow pine	15-20¢ each	
Lumber	No. 3 yellow pine	11¢	Per board foot
	Common redwood	17¢	Per board foot
Miscellaneous materials			
Exterior fir plywood	$\frac{1}{2}$-inch, 4 x 8 feet	$6.50	Per section (21¢ per square foot)
Tempered hardboard	$\frac{1}{4}$-inch, 4 x 8 feet exterior type	$5.40	Per section (17¢ per square foot)
Corrugated Fiberglas	40- x 96-inch panels in colors	$15	Per section (about 55¢ per square foot)
Reed screening	Peeled, woven in wire, 6 feet high	60¢	Per running foot
Posts			
Yellow pine	6 feet long	60¢	
Tubular steel	2-inch, 6 feet long	$2.10 to $2.50	Anchor in concrete
Pressed or angle steel	6 feet long	60¢ to $1.20	Drive into ground
Redwood	6 feet long, surfaced on 4 sides	$1.35	

Chapter 32

HOW TO BUILD COLDFRAMES, HOTBEDS AND WORKSHOPS

Is a coldframe or hotbed necessary for a garden?

As your interest and experience in gardening increases, a coldframe can be very useful to you for propagating with seeds and cuttings, for growing things somewhat out of season and for protecting doubtfully hardy plants in winter. Suppose you want bibb lettuce or cherry tomato plants and your greenhouseman has none. You can get your own plants from seed sown in the coldframe and have them at a fraction of the cost. Perhaps in fall you yearn for garden-fresh lettuce and radishes. In October, sow the seeds in your coldframe and you can have them from Thanksgiving up to Christmas. You may enjoy the beautiful Fuji mums in your garden but find them too delicate to spend winter there. If you have a coldframe, you can lift them in a clump and store them safely there until spring. And these are only three possibilities. In the section of this chapter called "Calendar for Your Coldframe," many more suggestions are given.

WHAT YOU NEED FOR COLDFRAMES AND HOTBEDS

Coldframes and hotbeds are built the same but a hotbed is heated and a coldframe is not, except for the warmth of the sun. Either is basically an enclosure set in the ground with a glass or plastic cover. The purpose is to trap light, warmth, and humidity for the benefit of the plants inside.

The best location. To insure warmth, select a protected site. South of a building is ideal. The frame needs sun, so set it beyond any shade and let it face south in a place where rain will run off and not into it. Good drainage is essential. Try to place your coldframe where you can tend it conveniently, preferably near a faucet so you can water it easily. If you plan some day to put in a heating cable to convert it to a hotbed, locate near a source of electricity.

The best size. If you use glass for the cover, you can get 3- x 4- and 3- x 6-foot sash units already assembled. It's easiest to build your coldframe to fit one or more of these units. Generally speaking, a frame consisting of two 3- x 4-foot units is large enough to grow all the seedlings and cuttings most people want, and this allows ample space for winter storage. If you need more room, just add more units at the sides. Figure 81 shows how to construct a coldframe. The front to back width measures 4 feet on the outside. The end-to-end length is 6 feet plus the 1 inch center-spacer for the sash, making a total of 73 inches. Above-ground height at the front is 6 inches and 12 inches at the back. About 12 inches extends into the ground.

You can make a coldframe to fit any glass

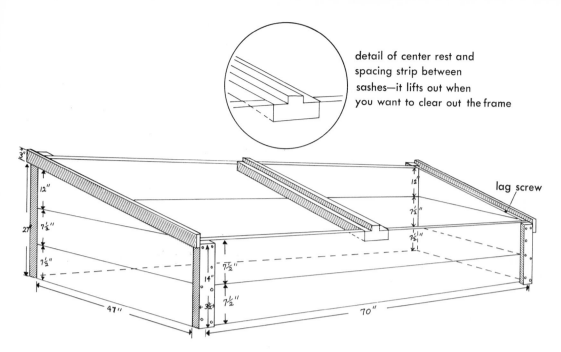

detail of center rest and spacing strip between sashes—it lifts out when you want to clear out the frame

lag screw

Fig. 81 Plans for a small coldframe. A good material is 2-inch redwood. It is made to use standard commercial coldframe sash units.

you have, perhaps an old French door or storm sash. If you use polyethylene, vinyl or Mylar to cover the frame, any size or shape will do. Here are some dimensions that give good results:

3 x 4 feet is a practical minimum; if any smaller, the frame cannot hold enough heat for cold nights.

slope the cover at least 1 inch for each 12 inches of width to get plenty of light.

make front height at least 6 inches above soil level to give seedlings headroom. Make the front much higher to grow large plants or hold pots.

run sides at least 12 inches *below* ground level, to allow for drainage layers and special soil.

The best materials. The frame can be of brick, concrete blocks, or wood. Bricks and blocks are the most durable and the best insulated, but they are harder to work with. If you use wood, redwood or cypress has the most durability, and any wood lasts longer if first treated with a preservative like pentachlorophenol or Cuprinol. So treated, even pine and fir will last a few years. Don't use

creosote; in such close quarters the fumes injure plants. To make a wood frame substantial and to insulate it properly, use 2-inch thick boards. To keep out air, line the frame with building paper. To keep your coldframe snug and airtight, take care with the wood sill at the top, on which the sash rests.

As for the covering, glass is by far the most satisfactory and lasting unless there is a bad hail storm or somebody throws a rock through it. Plastic films (vinyl, polyethylene, and Mylar) are cheaper than glass but not so durable, and with full exposure to sun they disintegrate in one to three years. They offer less insulation from cold than glass, but transmit just as much light—perhaps more. If there is likely to be heavy snow weight on your plastic coverings, better underlay them with wire mesh.

To hinge or not to hinge. If your sashes are large, say the 3- x 6-foot size, you don't need hinges. In fact, they're easier to handle if you can slide them up for ventilation, and when you are sowing seeds or inserting cuttings, you can remove the sash entirely. In midsummer you'll probably set a big sash aside. If it is only a 3- x 4-foot sash, then

415

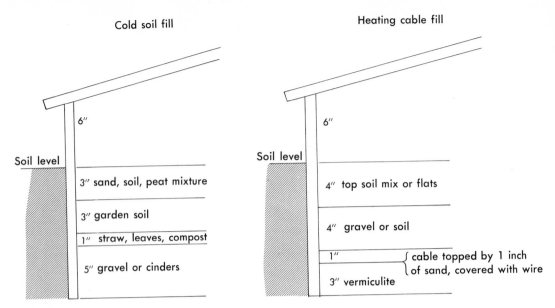

Cold soil fill

6"

Soil level

3" sand, soil, peat mixture

3" garden soil

1" straw, leaves, compost

5" gravel or cinders

Heating cable fill

6"

Soil level

4" top soil mix or flats

4" gravel or soil

1" { cable topped by 1 inch of sand, covered with wire

3" vermiculite

Fig. 82   The soil and drainage layers in a coldframe, at left, and with the minor variations for an electric hotbed, at right.

hinging is practical. You can prop it open for ventilation by placing blocks of various sizes under the front edge.

Details about building. If you make the frame of wood, construct the whole thing in your shop or on top of the ground. Then dig the excavation, lower the frame into it, set it level, and fill in around it with soil you removed to make the hole. On the inside fill in the necessary drainage materials and the soil mix.

If the frame is of brick or concrete blocks, excavate about 12 inches deep, or deeper to go below possible frost penetration, and begin the wall at that level. Footings are unnecessary. Finish the top with a smooth edge, and cement in a wood sill all around to hold the sash.

For a close fit between sash and frame, tack weatherstripping along surfaces that meet the sash. Bank soil from the excavation on the outside of the frame, making it higher on the north. To get extra light reflection, cover the inside back of the frame with white or aluminum paint.

Soil for the frame. If you do not intend to heat the frame and plan to sow seeds right in it, fill in the excavation in this order: 5 inches of cinders or crushed rock; 1 inch of straw, coarse leaves, or partly-rotted compost; 3 inches of good garden soil; a 3-inch

topping of a mixture of equal parts sand, soil, and peat moss.

If you plan to plant in flats or pots, put on a surface layer of sand, fine gravel, or vermiculite instead of soil. Water the fill and let it settle before planting seeds.

If you are heating the frame with a soil cable, make the layers like this: 3 inches of vermiculite, then the cable; then 1 inch of sand; a piece of hardware cloth or mesh divider; and finally 4 inches of gravel or garden soil. Set flats or pots on top of this, or if you want to plant directly in the soil, top with 4-inch mixture of peat, sand, and soil.

HOW TO OPERATE A COLDFRAME

In spring and summer, your main concern is to keep plants growing along, so watch the temperature, light and moisture. In early spring when the sun is still to the south, keep the glass clear and unshaded to get all possible light. Later as the sun moves above the frame, shade it against too much heat. Whitewash the glass, drape white muslin over it or cover with a lath screen.

If the frame still heats too much, raise the sash in midmorning to let in cool air.

Open the side away from the wind if the sash will work that way. Towards evening, close the sash to hold the warmth of the day. Your aim is to keep the temperature acceptable without losing too much humidity. How you manage this aspect of your coldframe makes the difference in how well plants grow in it.

When a cold snap threatens your seedlings, close the frame tight to hold in ground warmth. You might even cover the top with an old rug for extra insulation.

A thorough watering once a week is ample unless you leave the sash open so much that soil dries out. By all means avoid overwatering.

In winter your prime concern is to make the frame safe for the dormant plants there. Let them harden off gradually in fall by giving just enough water to keep them alive but not enough to promote soft new growth. Keep the frame cool. After the first cold freezes the topsoil in the bed, mulch everything with a fluffy layer of dry leaves or hay and close the frame.

Insulate the walls with hay or soil. You can even tack a piece of polyethylene over the glass for added protection without loss of light. Keep a rug handy to put over the top in bitter weather. This is usually advisable around Christmas, just before you expect the coldest weather of winter. Remove the protection as the days begin to lengthen late in February, before time to start planting seeds again.

HOW TO OPERATE A HOTBED

The purpose of putting heat in a coldframe, that is, making it into a hotbed, is to let plants start earlier in spring and give bottom heat for rooting cuttings. The old way was to get heat from a thick layer of fermenting fresh horse manure in the bottom. This way has been abandoned in favor of soil heating cables thermostatically controlled. These are cheap to operate, and they heat soil efficiently and evenly. You can get cable sheathed in lead or covered with vinyl. The lead costs more but lasts longer. You need 30 feet of cable (180 watts at 115 volts) for each equivalent of a one-sash hotbed (3 x 6 or 3 x 4). Place the cable over a layer of vermiculite in a series of snaking loops. Lay each loop over about 7 inches

180 This coldframe, electrified with a heating cable so it can be used as a hotbed, is constructed of two-inch redwood lumber and uses a standard coldframe sash. *Philpott*

beyond the previous one; do not let the wire cross over itself. Install an electrical receptacle at the back of the frame for plugging the cable into.

Also install a thermostat to control soil temperature. This has a bulb that you bury in the soil; it reads the temperature of the soil, not the air, and turns the electricity on or off as needed to maintain the heat you have set for it. Install the control box for the thermostat beside the electrical receptacle in the back of the frame. Put a thin layer of sand over the cable. Then to prevent accidentally cutting the cable when digging, lay a piece of hardware cloth above it. Put 4 to 6 inches of soil over the cable.

In the hotbed late in February you can start seeds of cabbage, head lettuce, cauliflower and petunias. The steady bottom warmth brings plants along faster than in a coldframe. As soon as the sun is warm enough to heat the frame, disconnect the cable.

Mild bottom warmth promotes the rooting of cuttings. If you take softwood or hardwood cuttings early in fall, use your heated frame as a propagator to stimulate growth. Keep soil temperature about 5 degrees warmer than the air.

CALENDAR FOR YOUR COLDFRAME

January, February. Use good days this month to finish preparations for a new frame. Put in drainage and soil layers. Install heating cable if you want one. Go over the glazing of sash and have everything shipshape. Get some straw and an old rug on hand to throw over the frame in case of cold wave.

March. Early this month start seeds of cabbage, broccoli, cauliflower, head lettuce. Sow them directly in the soil of the coldframe or in pots or flats. Toward the end of the month, you can plant all the seeds from which you want transplants as soon as frost danger is over—tomatoes, peppers, asters, zinnias, marigolds, and salvia, to name a few.

April. If cabbage or other seedlings are big enough to transplant, do it now to give each more room, setting them in idle space in the frame. In a corner insert cuttings of chrysanthemums and hardy asters in sand. At the end of this month if your tomato and pepper plants are well grown, transplant them to larger space in the frame. Set tender plants you started indoors in the frame to harden off.

May. Most of your seedlings can move outdoors this month, vacating much of the frame. The chrysanthemum and other cuttings remain. Soon these too will be rooted and ready to set out. You can start seeds of most perennials in the frame now.

June. Insert cuttings of perennial *Alyssum saxatile,* dianthus, clematis, and heuchera in sand. Shade the frame so the plants have diffused light and do not get too warm. Start boxwood, forsythia, lilac, and daphne cuttings this month. Ventilate the frame enough to keep it cool, but not too much or you will reduce the humidity that keeps cuttings alive.

July. Put down more cuttings of azaleas, roses, and barberries. Plant seeds of columbines, verbascum, delphiniums, lupines, Canterbury bells, foxgloves. This may be the time to remove the sash entirely and replace it with a lath screen or muslin cloth. Do not let soil dry out in hot weather.

August. Transplant the perennials you started from seed in July. They will probably spend the winter where you place them now in the frame. Insert cuttings of yews, arborvitae, and junipers in a peat and sand mixture. Start seeds of hollyhocks, pansies, and violas.

September. Put down hardwood cuttings of euonymus. Transplant pansies or violas to give them more space. If you are dividing primulas and phlox, set the smallest starts in the coldframe to guarantee winter safety. Put root cuttings of oriental poppies and bleeding hearts in flats in the frame.

October. Move to the coldframe clumps of doubtfully hardy chrysanthemums, frikarti asters, dianthus, foxgloves, Canterbury bells, and anything else you want to safeguard for winter. Put the sash back on. Plant seeds of lettuce and radishes for a final kitchen crop before winter. Late this month pot up daffodils, crocus, and small bulbs for spring forcing and store them in the coldframe.

418

November. Pot up tulips, hyacinths, and any remaining daffodils you want for later forcing and store them in the coldframe. Sow penstemons, iris, and peonies. Water as necessary so plants do not dry out.

December. After several hard freezes, mulch plants in the bed with straw or leaves, close the sash and heap straw and soil around it for insulation. Spread old rugs over the frame when temperature goes below zero but don't leave these on longer than necessary or plants inside will turn yellow and spindly from lack of light. Open the frame every week or so when the cold moderates, to let in fresh air.

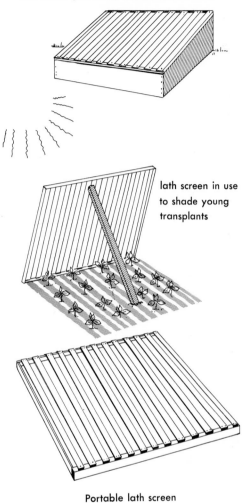

lath screen protecting coldframe in summer

lath screen in use to shade young transplants

Portable lath screen

Fig. 83 A portable lath screen will find many uses around your yard.

LATH SHADES AND THEIR USES

In places of very high summer heat, lath shelters are invaluable. A movable lath screen or shade:

reduces transplanting shock

keeps a coldframe cooler

protects sun-sensitive azaleas, camellias, house plants, tuberous begonias and tiny seedlings

shades new seedbeds against heat, drying out.

A simple portable screen might be 3 x 6 feet, and made to fit one unit of your coldframe. This size can also be set on temporary posts to shade a bed of transplants or in an emergency protect them from hail. Or you can prop it on its side to shelter newly planted shrubs.

Plasterer's lath was the original material used for portable screens. For better looks and a longer life, make yours of redwood lath, or batten strips which are about $3\frac{5}{8}$ inches, twice as wide as lath.

First build a rectangular frame of 1- x 2-inch wood; then nail lath or battens across. If you want 50 per cent shade, make the spaces as wide as the lath; for 75 per cent shade, leave just half the width of the lath between, and so on. The 50 per cent plan is the usual one.

A lath screen is one of the easiest garden helps you can build, and one of the most useful. When not shading plants, it can be a temporary fence or an emergency screen; in off seasons it is easily stored.

YOUR GARDEN WORKSHOP

This is the place to store your tools, sprayers and dusters, fertilizer, pesticides, peat moss, vermiculite, potting soil, hose and sprinklers, flats and pots, even your garden shoes—all the trappings of your garden work. A workshop is also a fine place for potting, transplanting, seed sowing in flats, flower arranging and general puttering. You may want to make it just a storage yard with

419

181 A redwood bench becomes an adequate work center in a small space. It was built to be the right height for potting, and fitted with four bins underneath to store sand, vermiculite, soil and peat moss. *California Redwood Association*

no roof—the minimum place where you can corral your tools and hide them from view. Or you may want a haven sheltered from rain and sun for doing quiet jobs. These areas often evolve—beginning as simple storage yards and growing into work centers as your gardening interests expand.

Where to locate a work center. When you plan your yard, put this among the work features. Make it easy to reach but out of sight of the living area. If you have a vegetable garden, perhaps it should go close to that. If you do a lot of flower arranging, have it near the house. If you have a cold-frame or hotbed, put the workshop near that. A corner or side of the garage or part of the utility room are possible places for a workshop. Or you can build a shelter just for the purpose against a back or side fence or along an outside wall of the house or garage. It helps to have water and electricity there.

As a storage center. The essentials for storage are protection from wind and rain for tools, fertilizers and pesticides; some bins

for potting materials—soil, peat, sand; shelf space for storing pots, labels, stakes and all the rest.

You might list what you have to store. If you have a riding lawn mower, a wheelbarrow or garden cart, a rotary tiller, a lawn sweeper and a gasoline edging machine, you will need to design a pretty roomy place. Or you may decide to leave them in the garage and store smaller things in your workshop. Spades and shovels, sprinkling cans, rakes, pitchforks, hoes, loppers, hedge shears, and pruners can all hang on the walls. Perhaps you can make a rack to hang your fertilizer spreader, sprayer and duster. The garden hose loops nicely over hooks on the wall.

Trowels, dibbles, grass shears, and hand cultivators take the least room on a shelf or in a drawer. You can put garden gloves there, too, and labels and pencils. Save a high shelf for pesticides, weed killers and everything you use when mixing spray. If children are around, better put a locked door on this cupboard. Provide lots of shelf space for containers—flower pots, flats, and whatever else you use to hold plants. Provide roomy bins for soil, peat, sand, and fertilizer. These are a wonderful convenience. Or you can use metal garbage cans for the soil, peat, and sand, but not for fertilizers. For these use wood or plastic.

A wood frame like an umbrella rack is fine for stakes, but make it roomy. Have a tightly closed place where you can store seeds safe from mice and moisture. And you will need more shelf space for some miscellaneous essentials—twine, Twistems, butcher knives (every workshop needs one), pliers, screwdriver, hammer, measuring spoons and cups, scissors, soil sifter, plastic bags, gunny sacks, and the oil can. Provide a hook for your rubber boots and slicker, if you like to plod around in the rain. Whatever kind of workshop you make, be sure it will shed rain and that snow can't find a crack to enter, or the fertilizer and pesticides stored there will be ruined. The moisture will damage your tools, too.

As a work center. If you plan to spend pleasant hours working here yourself, design it for comfort and convenience. Make the work surface wide and at an easy height. Have something to sit on, and arrange for good lighting. If propagating interests you, include a closed frame for that, and perhaps display shelves for plants you are proud of.

If you want a flower-arranging center, include shelves for containers and supplies of clay, holders, and wire, and a wastebasket for trimmings. You will need a wide working surface and a sink with a drain.

If you decide on a free-standing structure in your yard, find out about building permits and restrictions as to the height and size allowed for a separate building or whether you can have one at all. There may be a requirement about location.

EASY-DOES-IT IDEAS

If space is at a premium in your yard, bolt your coldframe or hotbed together so it can be easily taken apart for storage when the seed-starting season is over.

182 The interests of the owner are obvious in this well-organized work center. There is a display for a pot collection of succulents, a bathtub to facilitate watering, a wall rack for hand tools, and a spacious workbench. *Harlow*

183 The workbench corner includes a pegboard for small implements and a closed cabinet for insecticides. The bins below hold potting materials. *Harlow*

Use wall space efficiently for tool storage. Hang spades, rakes, hoes, sprinkling cans, and hand tools on pegs or nails. Label their places so you can remember where they go. Even large equipment like a garden cart, fertilizer spreader, or lawn sweeper can be suspended from a sturdy hook.

Provide yourself with a puttering place where you can sit down to repot, sow seed in flats, divide perennial clumps, and the like. Make it a convenient height and have supplies of water, labels, pots, trowels, and soil handy. All this makes gardening more fun.

PART VI

PLANTS AND FLOWERS FOR THE HOUSE

Chapter 33

PLANTS FOR YOUR HOME

What are the best plants to grow indoors?

To be successful with plants indoors, select kinds that grow well under conditions you can offer, or else improve your conditions a little to suit the ones you want to grow. Plants need:

Light in great or small amounts, but all need some

The right daytime temperature, warm or cool depending on kind, with about a 10 degree drop at night

Water, much or little, depending on the plant

Humidity in the air

HOW TO IMPROVE CONDITIONS FOR PLANTS

Fortunately, what is comfortable for people is also healthful for a vast number of plants, but some like the cyclamen need it to be somewhat cooler. None need it warmer, and the African violet goes right along with you at a cozy 72 degrees.

Where light is too dim, supplement with artificial light. The bulb in a reading lamp will keep a philodendron or pothos in fair condition for several years and fluorescent lights work magic. Install a unit over a bookcase planter, for instance, or hang a shelf under a fluorescent wall unit in kitchen or bathroom. Where light is too bright for shade-loving ferns or begonias, just set the plants back a little from the window or filter the sunshine through a thin curtain.

Where temperatures are unfavorable, as over a radiator at your "best" window, cover the radiator with a layer of insulating material or place a wood or glass shield over it to deflect the heat. A board on top and pebble filled trays with water in them to increase humidity where heat is high make it possible to have a flourishing indoor garden even above a radiator. When sills or floors are cold, you can install a cheap heating cable under pots or trays. This uses little electricity and adds just enough warmth to reduce the chill. Drafts from a window or air conditioner can be checked with a drapery, a screen or even a piece of cardboard or glass.

You can increase humidity, so vital to plants, by placing them, as already suggested, on shallow metal waterproof trays filled with nugget-size gravel or pebbles. Your plumber can make these to fit your window sills or window shelves. Very heavy aluminum foil can be molded into temporary trays to hold pebbles or gravel. Pour on water until it shows just at the top of the pebbles, and maintain that level. Set pots on top of the gravel, but do not push them down so as to stand in even a little water. Moisture evaporates from the tray and envelops the plants.

Another way is to set small glasses of water among the pots. They increase humidity a little but not nearly so much as the pebble trays. If you have many plants grow-

425

184 For a place at a dim window or on a coffee table, this collection of variegated plants would do well. It contains a variegated ivy, chlorophytum, sansevieria, and *Neanthe bella*.

Photographic Arts

185 Homes have more places for plants than they used to, since modern architecture has included many built-in planters. *Gaynor*

PLANTS UNDER FLUORESCENT LIGHTS

ing in one place, they raise the humidity for themselves by moisture transpired from the leaves—so group your plants if you can. You can also buy an inexpensive hand-misting device. You squeeze the handle and out comes a very fine fog. Used once or twice a day, this increases humidity considerably and the mist is so fine that properly directed it does not harm furnishings. You can also buy a portable or built-in humidifier to raise air moisture in one room or the whole house. It is an electrical device that evaporates water with a fan, is good for both people and plants and even makes your furniture last longer by preventing drying out of glue and finishes.

For plants like orchids that need higher humidity than is practical in a living room, provide a terrarium. This is a glass enclosure with a lid to prevent moisture from escaping. An aquarium with a piece of glass on top makes a good terrarium, also large bell jars and brandy snifters. Little jungles of delicate tropicals flourish inside these glass houses, and are most decorative. You can grow the plants in pots or plant them directly in the soil of the terrarium.

Fluorescent tubes have opened a houseplant frontier and have proved to be an admirable substitute for daylight. They are

186 At a windowsill, this pretty collection contains a thriving caladium, miniature bulrush, dwarf tangerine, ornamental pepper, and geranium. *Photographic Arts*

187 Ivy geranium, with trailing branches and waxy leaves, is fine in a hanging container.

Genereux

188 Another colorful geranium is the Lady Washington type. Here it is with a rose-scented geranium for a background and a pot of English ivy 'Fan' at the base. *Grossman*

189 When a plant seems to have outgrown its space, as revealed by the binding roots of this geranium, give it a new pot one size larger and fresh soil. *Roche*

190 *Philodendron hastatum* is a foliage plant that can take it. *Walker*

economical to run. If house plants are your hobby, fluorescents will increase your space and opportunities. With them, plants will grow in closets, basements, or otherwise unlighted corners and often results are better than with sunlight. It has been discovered that under fluorescents, plus humidity, orchids will bloom just as freely in a converted coal bin as they do in the jungle. In fact, practically all plants bloom well under fluorescents.

Arrange tubes in any practical way that suits you. Install them in special stands or racks, in bookcases, tiered shelves, underneath benches or tables, or simply suspend them over any flat surface that will hold plants.

Provide 15 to 20 watts of fluorescent light for each square foot of plant space. A 24-inch tube gives 20 watts. A 48-inch tube, 40 watts, a 96-inch tube, 74 watts. If you have a shelf 10 inches wide and 28 inches long, one 20-watt tube will give enough light. Where you can have several tubes, use half cool white and half daylight types. If you have only one tube, use a cool white.

Sylvania has recently marketed a new tube type called Gro-Lux, designed for plants. Tests show these new tubes to have a light spectrum promoting better growth than any tubes previously available.

When you garden under fluorescents, let plants have a nighttime rest as in nature. A fourteen to sixteen hour day is long enough for most of them—lights on at 7 A.M., off at 11 P.M. at the latest. A timer that costs about ten dollars will automatically switch lights on and off and is a convenience, especially when you are away.

Keep plants fairly close to the lights. If you are building a rack for plants, make a way to raise or lower either the shelf or the lights. Chains and small pulleys are practical for this. Adjust the height as plants grow. Try for an average of about 12 inches between leaf surface and tube.

The behavior of plants indicates whether lights are at the proper distance. When plants bloom poorly and leaves turn pale and spindly, they usually need more light. So move them closer by lowering the light or raising the shelf. If neither is adjustable, stand pots on inverted pots or boxes, to bring them closer to the lights.

191 The showy gloxinia grows from a tuber and lives on from year to year.

Genereux

Tubes lose power as they get old. New tubes give approximately 40 per cent more light at 1 foot distance than tubes used for two hundred hours or more. To keep plants growing well, replace tubes every 5,000 hours or when dark rings show at the ends—whichever happens first.

SOIL FOR HOUSE PLANTS

You can buy potting soil in a sack at a garden store or mix it yourself. Plants differ in their requirements. Some need a lean and gritty soil, some a soft, rich, humusy mixture. A few grow best in various types of well-drained humus.

When you make your own potting mixture, it is well to pasteurize the soil in it by steaming (see method in Chapter 28) or by heating a dishpan full in a 180- to 225-degree oven for thirty to sixty minutes. This is especially good insurance with disease-prone plants like African violets and gloxinias. Crown rots, fungus troubles and soil insects perish under this treatment.

Mix No. 1—*For most flowering plants and general purposes*
　　2 parts loamy soil
　　1 part peat moss or leaf mold
　　$\frac{1}{2}$ to 1 part sand, depending on nature of soil
To each gallon of the mix add
　　2 tablespoons dried sheep manure

　　2 tablespoons bone meal
　　2 tablespoons hydrated lime

If you are potting acid-loving plants like azaleas omit bone meal and lime; if cactus, double the amount of sand.

Mix No. 2—*For foliage plants and other kinds needing humus*
　　1 part loam
　　1 part peat moss
　　1 part leaf mold
　　$\frac{1}{2}$ part coarse sand
　　$\frac{1}{2}$ part rotted cow manure (or substitute $\frac{1}{4}$ part dried packaged cow manure)

Mix No. 3—*For bromeliads, orchids, anthuriums*
　　Osmunda fiber, *or*
　　Shredded fir bark with a little broken charcoal, *or*
　　Sphagnum moss with a little Perlite added

You may need to vary the basic potting mixes in small ways to suit needs of individual plants. Those with fine roots like begonias do better in a lighter more humusy soil than those with heavy roots like sansevieria that can stand more loam.

ABOUT CONTAINERS

The standard house plant container is an unglazed clay pot. It is cheap, porous and

429

192 African violets come in many colors and forms. This is 'Orchid Sunset,' a double.   *Genereux*

193 Fluorescent lights offer new possibilities in plant-growing space. This portable cart has room for a large collection of African violets. The plastic cover helps hold in humidity.   *General Electric*

194 The calamondin is a citrus with bright fruit and glossy leaves. *Philpott*

well drained. Plants dry out in them more quickly than in ceramic pots. Even tin cans, old kettles and pans with holes in the bottom make practical containers in emergencies, but they are not the prettiest things to use.

Fancy ceramic or metal planters are attractive and give plants a dressed-up look, but most of them have no hole for drainage, so you have to provide a drainage layer in the bottom when you are potting. Put a layer of broken clay-pot pieces, or gravel or small stones and sand in the bottom adding the soil mixture above this. Then be *very* careful not to overwater. Or you can fit the ceramic container with an inner pot that does have a drain hole, and put your plant in the inner pot.

For large plants the best containers are redwood or cypress tubs or boxes. These usually come with drain holes—if there are none, then drill some. It helps if these have a protective pan under them, to keep drips

off the floor, and casters to facilitate moving the plants.

THE PROCESS OF POTTING

First have the container clean. If it's been used before, scrub it with soapy water; if it's a clay pot, you can set it in a pan of boiling water for a few minutes, then let dry. At the bottom put a layer of drainage material —broken flower pot, coarse gravel or charcoal chips—to keep soil from washing out through the hole. Fill the pot part way with the desired soil mix. Holding the plant so its crown is a half inch or less below the pot rim, fill soil in around and under it, spreading roots as much as you can. Thump the pot on the table to settle the soil, and leave it a half inch lower than pot rim. Finally water three times and let each drenching soak through.

Most house plants, especially flowering

431

kinds, do better if slightly pot bound. When one outgrows its space—stops growing and has roots matted out to the pot wall—give it a new pot just one size larger.

WATERING AND FERTILIZING

Watering is the most attention-requiring part of caring for house plants. Indoor plants dry out faster than those in the ground outside, and need water comparatively often. Actively growing in porous pots, they may require it daily. In winter when growth is slow and temperature cooler, you can water less than in spring and summer. The best way to tell if a plant needs water is to feel the soil with your finger. Take into account the plant's requirements and the time of year. Some kinds like geraniums do best if they become nearly dry and then are drenched thoroughly. Others, like African violets, need more steady moisture. Hardly any do well kept constantly wet. Here are five watering rules:

Use water at room temperature
Water small pots more frequently than large ones
Water more often in hot weather
Water more often when the plant is growing actively
Water plants in porous clay pots more often than those in glazed or metal containers.

Fertilizing house plants. Frequent watering washes many of the nutrients out of house plant soil, so you need to replace them with regular feedings of liquid fertilizer. Many commercial kinds are available, most containing all the essential elements and formulated especially for indoor use. Follow package directions for dissolving in water and applying to plants. Substitute the feeding for one of the regular waterings, but avoid putting liquid fertilizer on when soil is markedly dry.

WHAT TO DO ABOUT HOUSE PLANT PESTS

Most house plant pests are prevented by good housekeeping—cleaning leaves with a

weekly spraying or dunking in mild soapsuds. Inspect plants often and if you see any that are harboring pests, separate them from the others. Use a house plant aerosol spray each week or two on affected plants to bring pests under control. Here are some of the worst house plant insects and specific remedies for them:

Red Spiders. Too tiny to see, they show in yellowing leaves, a mealy texture or fine webbing on undersides. Ivy, dracaena, aphelandra and cacti are some of the victims. Control by washing foliage every week or two with a brisk water spray.

Mealybugs. These cottony insects cluster in corners of leaves and stems, likeliest on African violets, begonias, cacti, poinsettias, fuchsias. Adults sit unmoving, like a patch of wool. Control with a house plant spray bomb, nicotine sulfate and soap spray, or touch each with a tooth pick swab dipped in alcohol.

Aphids. Green, white or brown plant lice may get on begonias, ivy, chrysanthemums and other plants. Use controls suggested for mealybugs.

Cyclamen mites. On African violets, cyclamen, geraniums and others, this microscopic pest makes leaves turn dark, deformed, curled or stunted. Fight them with cleanliness and quarantine, destroying infested plants. Arrange pots so leaves don't touch. Wash hands and tools with soap after touching a plant suspected of harboring mites, to prevent spreading them. There is a systemic insecticide, one absorbed into plant tissues, to control mites, called sodium selenate. Sold by house plant suppliers, it is dangerous and needs careful handling. If you use it, abide by *all* the package directions and cautions.

Scale. Immobile little warts appear on stems or leaves of cacti, ferns, rubber plants, many others. Control by scrubbing with soapy water, spray with Volck or use the aerosol spray.

Earthworms. An earthworm tunneling in a pot breaks off roots and disrupts growth. If you can find him, pull him out. Otherwise drive him out by watering with lime water—made by stirring a tablespoon of hydrated lime into a quart of water and letting it stand twenty-four hours. Pour off and use only the top part of the solution.

Springtails. Wiggly gray $\frac{1}{8}$-inch insects scurry busily over soil. Actually they are harmless to plants, but a nuisance in your house. Water plant with lime water as suggested for earthworms.

HOW TO CARE FOR GIFT PLANTS

These are the ones the florist brings, sent by someone dear to you to mark an important occasion. Of course you would like to keep them if you can.

Azalea. Kinds sold by florists are usually tender. Keep them in cool west, east or south light; and sprinkle leaves with water each day to raise humidity. Never let the soil, probably peat moss, dry out. When weather warms, sink pot and all outdoors in dappled shade and continue watering. Before a hard freeze in fall store the plant in your coldframe, cool porch or garage or other frost-protected place. In February or March take it to a cool sunny window indoors, begin watering and spraying, and buds will soon open.

Calceolaria. A beautiful gift but impossible as a house plant. It will die after it blooms. To make it last longer, keep it cool (60 degrees), out of direct hot sun, and water it whenever it begins to get dry.

Cineraria. Another beauty, but useless to try to keep. For longest life treat it like calceolaria.

Christmas begonia. Difficult as a house plant, but possible if kept in fresh, moist, cool air and bright diffused light. Start new plants from cuttings to replace the old plant if it dies.

Chrysanthemum. Give these copious water until the last bloom fades. Then cut down the stems, remove rootball from pot, and set outdoors in the ground. In winter, however, leave plant potted and set it on the floor of basement or garage, or in the soil of a coldframe until spring when you can plant it outside. A few florist mums are hardy enough to take cold winters; but usually severe cold will kill them, so lift and store clumps in the coldframe.

Cyclamen. You can keep this plant only if you have the right conditions. Give it your coolest, most humid room, preferably 50 degrees, out of bright sun. To water, set the pot in a pan of water; never let it go dry while blooming. Later let it die down, watering only every three or four weeks, and rest it outdoors in the shade until August. Then repot (use Mix No. 1), and in fall bring it indoors to a cool sill.

Hydrangea. Water this every day. If you live in Zone 7 or southward, transplant it outdoors after flowers fade. It will probably be hardy there. Elsewhere cut tops back to two buds per stem, repot in soil Mix No. 1, sink pot outdoors for summer in partly-shaded ground. After frost, store pot under mulch in a coldframe until January, then bring gradually to warmth, finally returning it to a sunny sill and 65 to 70 degrees, watering daily.

Easter lily (Lilium longiflorum). This bulb's usefulness is over as a house plant, but after blooms fall and spring frosts end, remove from pot and set the plant in the ground in your garden. It is hardy and will bloom again the next spring; and possibly even that autumn.

Poinsettia. Give it your sunniest window, keep it watered and out of drafts. When leaves begin to fall, stop watering, let the soil dry, and store pot in the basement, garage or a cool closet. In April cut stems back to 6 inches, repot (use Mix No. 1), water, and when weather is warm, set pot outdoors in soil in a sunny place. In fall, bring the plant indoors, keep up watering and fertilizing, and see that it gets only natural daylight but lots of that. Artificial light at night prevents bloom.

HOW TO MAKE BULBS BLOOM IN WINTER

You get a real splash of color in January and February from tulips, hyacinths or daffodils planted in pots in autumn and forced to bloom early.

Select good forcing varieties: Tulips, 'Prince of Austria,' orange-scarlet; 'Clara Butt,' pink; 'Zwanenburg,' white. Daffodils, 'February Gold,' 'Cheerfulness,' and 'King Alfred.' Hyacinths, 'L'Innocence,' white; 'Etna,' red; and 'Queen of the Blues,' blue.

Use 6-inch bulb pans, clay pots that are shallower than the standard kind. You can plant about six tulip bulbs per pot, about three daffodil or hyacinth bulbs. Do this in October. Put chips over the drain hole and half fill pot with a mixture of one part loam, one part peat, and one-half part sand, with a half cup of bone meal added to each two potfuls. Plant tulip bulbs broad-end down with tops just covered. Plant daffodils and hyacinths with the necks slightly exposed. Have only one kind to a pot, otherwise they will bloom irregularly. Water each pot until the water runs through and store in a cold place for rooting, perhaps an unheated garage, unheated root cellar or coldframe. Slight freezing does no harm but prolonged freezing slows up rooting and may break the pot. Water them occasionally, about every two weeks.

When the pot is full of roots, bring it indoors to start top growth. To see if roots have grown enough to permit forcing the top, invert the pot and tap the ball out in your hand. Replace it after your inspection. The longer you wait, the more sure your success. If you wait until mid-January, good results are practically assured. First bring pots to a fairly cool place. After a week, move them to a warmer spot, light but not bright, and keep on watering. When tops are 2 inches high, move pots to a sunny window and they will soon explode into bloom. Get flowering pots into a cool room at night so flowers last longer. Don't use forced bulbs again for forcing, but planted outdoors in your garden they will probably revive enough to bloom there in a year or two.

SIXTY HOUSE PLANTS AND HOW TO GROW THEM

Culture and methods of propagation for each plant are given by numbers at the end of the description. To interpret the numbers, see the section on "Code to Culture" in this chapter.

Abutilon (Flowering maple). An old-fashioned shrubby plant grown for its small hollyhock-like white, yellow, salmon or red flowers. Soft green leaves resemble maple,

are sometimes variegated. For a cool sunny porch or terrace. Culture: 1; 5; 8; 12; 14; 18.

Acalypha hispida (Chenille plant). Long drooping red flower spikes look like strips of chenille. Leaves are oval, bright green, hairy, on large plants. For a heated porch in winter, patio in summer. Culture: 1; 5; 8; 12; 14; 18.

Aechmea fasciata (Billbergia). Makes a whirl of horny stiff green and white leaves. Blue-rose flowers come in a rounded head and last a long time. The cup-shaped base holds water. Fine for warm homes, apartments, dim windows. Culture: 2; 6; 8; 11; 16; 19.

African violet (see *Saintpaulia*).

Aglaonema modestum (Chinese evergreen). Fine for modern desks, coffee tables, indoor planters. Large, shiny, slender leaves are dashed with white, gracefully pointed. Culture: 3; 6; 8; 11; 14; 19.

Airplane plant (see *Chlorophytum elatum*).

Aluminum plant (see *Pilea*).

Amaryllis (see *Hippeastrum*).

Aphelandra squarrosa. Large broad dark leaves have silver, white or cream variegations along veins; attractive yellow-red flowers on tight spikes. Good in moist planters with other foliages. Culture: 2; 6; 8; 12; 15; 18.

Aralia (see *Fatsia japonica*).

Artillery plant (see *Pilea*).

Asparagus sprengeri (Sprenger fern). Lacy, small, light green needle-like leaves on arching, twiggy stems. Roots have round tubers. For hanging baskets or planters on windowsill or sunny porch. Culture: 2; 5; 8; 12; 14; 17 or 19.

Aspidistra elatior (Cast iron plant). A modern looking old-timer with leathery long dark glossy leaves, sometimes variegated, and purple flowers at ground level. Ideal for dimly lighted coffee tables or planters. Culture: 3; 5; 8; 11; 14; 19.

Baby's tears (see *Helxine*).

Begonia. A huge clan, of which these are the best house plants: B. *feasti* (beefsteak begonia)—round, large, dark green lacquered leaves, red-hairy underneath, with creeping rootstalk, pink flowers. B. *semperflorens* (wax begonia)—small glossy leaves, sometimes bronze, on rounded plants; profuse small white, pink or red flowers. The angel-wing group of which 'Lucerna' is typical—cane-stemmed, tall, with long wing-shaped leaves, sometimes potted or streaked, and red, pink or white hanging flowers. All are good for sunny sills on east, west or south. Culture: 2; 6; 8; 12; 15; 17; 18.

Beloperone guttata (Shrimp plant). Sparse plants, grown for long-lasting spikes of red or chartreuse brown flower bracts. Interesting on a cool porch or patio in summer. Culture: 1; 5; 7; 12; 14; 18.

Bird of paradise (see *Strelitzia*).

Boston fern (see *Nephrolepis exaltata bostoniensis*).

Cactaceae (Cactus). The prickly, leafless desert kinds are those usually thought of, and there are hundreds you might have—pincushion, bunny ears, rattail, peanut. All are perfect for sill collections and dish gardens in warm homes. They will bloom in good light. Culture: 1 or 2; 5 or 6; 7; 11; 14 with added sand; 17; 18.

Cape jasmine (see *Gardenia jasminoides*).

Capsicum annuum (Christmas pepper). Although you must start it from seed each spring, it makes a colorful plant for a warm south window, or patio in summer. Peppers turn scarlet in fall and stay on through winter. Culture: 1; 6; 8; 12; 14; 17.

Carrion flower (see *Stapelia*).

Cast iron plant (see *Aspidistra*).

Ceropegia woodi (Rosary vine). Heart-shaped mottled olive-green leaves and lavender flowers dangle on thread-like stems. Pretty in small wall planters and hanging containers. Little stem tubers make new plants. Culture: 2; 5 or 6; 7; 11 or 12; 14 or 15; 17, 18.

Cestrum parqui (Jasmine). Fragrant, tubular green-white flowers in early spring above glossy, willowy leathery green leaves. A large plant, decorative on a warm humid porch, or patio in summer. Culture: 1; 6; 8; 12; 15; 18.

Chenille plant (see *Acalypha*).

Chinese evergreen (see *Aglaonema*).

Chlorophytum elatum (Spider plant, airplane plant). A fountain of narrow white striped recurving leaves, with starry white flowers on long wands, followed by plantlets. Good in hanging planters. Culture: 2 or 3; 5 or 6; 8; 11; 14; 19.

Christmas cactus (see *Schlumbergera bridgesi*).

Christmas pepper (see *Capsicum annuum*).

Cissus rhombifolia (Grape ivy). Three-parted smooth glossy brown-veined leaves on winding stems with tendrils. Handsome for hanging planters, or trellis at window's edge. Culture: 2; 5 or 6; 8; 11; 14; 18.

Citrus (Lime, Lemon or Orange). Buy started plants of small varieties bred to bear edible fruit. All have glossy oval leaves, fragrant white flowers, and ideal for porches, patios. Culture: 1; 5; 7; 12; 14; 17.

Clerodendrum thomsoniae (Glory Bower). Long-lasting clusters of white flowers with crimson centers, come in spring above vining dark green leaves. Put in a large pot on a warm humid sun porch, and give it a trellis. Culture: 1; 6; 8; (10 after blooming); 12; 14; 18.

Codiaeum (Croton). Thick, parchment-like highly colored and veined green, yellow, red leaves, sometimes lobed, flare from woody straight trunk. Striking in large containers with other foliage plants. Culture: 1; 6; 8; 12; 14; 18.

Cordyline (Hawaiian ti plant). A foliage plant for planters in warm dim corners. Large long glossy dark leaves with sizable stem and thick trunk. Many varieties. Culture: 2 or 3; 6; 8; 12; 14; 18.

Croton (see *Codiaeum*).

Crown of thorns (see *Euphorbia splendens*).

Crassula argentea (Jade plant). Fleshy small oval jade-green leaves on fat stems, woody in old age. Older plants bear pink flowers. Reliable for window gardens and planters under lamps or in part sun. Culture: 1 or 2; 5 or 6; 7; 11; 14; 18.

Dieffenbachia (Dumb cane). A tolerant tropical plant with bold white splotched or banded green leaves. There are many varieties, all upright, some tall, ideal for planters. Culture: 2; 6; 7; 11; 14; 18.

Dracaena. Some look like young corn with long leaves, others have oval leaves—most streaked or mottled with white or yellow. Suited to dim corners. Culture: 2 or 3; 6; 9; 11; 14; 18.

Dumb cane (See *Dieffenbachia*).

Epiphyllum (Orchid cactus). The long,

flat, wavy-edged, stem-leaves bear exotic, colorful fuchsia, pink, cream, or white flowers. Most kinds grow large, are good on light porches, bright sills and terraces in summer. Culture: 2; 5; 8; 12; 14; 18.

Episcia (Flame violet). Clambering stems and crinkled, hairy variegated coppery or pink leaves. Produce red, orange, white, pink, lavender, sometimes spotted flowers. Stems cascade from baskets or a shelf, good under fluorescents. Culture: 2 or 3; 6; 8; 12; 15; 18.

Euphorbia splendens (Crown of thorns). Thin, gnarled thorny stems with a few small leaves, produce scarlet bloom bracts in clusters. Interesting for a pot collection in a south window. Culture: 1; 5 or 6; 7; 11, 12; 14; 18.

Fatsia japonica (Aralia). Leathery, palm-shaped large shiny leaves on tall plants; white flowers. For cool entryways, planters away from intense sun. Culture: 2; 5; 8; 12; 14; 18.

Ficus elastica (Rubber plant). A dramatic tall, erect, plant with thick glossy dark long-oval leaves and reddish stems and midribs. A good tub plant for doorways and window walls and as a focus in large planter groups. Other good Ficus are fiddle-leaf fig (*F. lyrata*); and creeping fig (*F. pumila*). Culture: 2; 5 or 6; 8; 11; 12; 14; air-layer or 18.

Fittonia. Low-growing with shiny, oval leaves strikingly marked with white, pink or red along veins. Best with other plants in large containers (for humidity), terrariums, or bathroom planters. Culture: 2 or 3; 6; 9; 12 or 13; 15; 18.

Flame violet (see *Episcia*).

Flowering maple (see *Abutilon*).

Fuchsia. Small shrubs grown for the summer tear-drop red, carmine, blue-purple, rose, white flowers, and varied forms. Try them on cool north porches or spare east or north rooms that do not freeze. Culture: 2; 4 or 5; 7 in winter, then 8; 12; 15; 17 or 18.

Gardenia jasminoides veitchi (Cape jasmine). Glossy-leaf woody plant produces fragrant white waxen flowers in spring and summer. Large-growing, an ideal tub plant for a bright porch, or patio in summer. Culture: 1; 6; 8; 12; 15; 18.

Glory Bower (see *Clerodendrum thomsoniae*).

Gloxinia (see *Sinningia*).

Grape ivy (see *Cissus rhombifolia*).

Gynura aurantiaca (Velvet plant). The velvety-hairy oval purple leaves are the main reason for growing it. Put it in a south window. Culture: 1; 6; 8; 12; 14; 18.

Hawaiian ti plant (see *Cordyline*).

Hedera (ivy). There are small and large leaf, variegated creamy yellow, deep lobed, rounded, heart-shaped, curled, dwarf, tall —and many more variations of this vine. Good for pots, planters, or even a bowl of water on a coffee table. Culture: 1 or 2; 4 or 5; 8; 11; 15; 18.

Helxine (Baby's tears). A low, creeping plant with light green tiny round leaves blanketing the soil, it is best where it has humidity, as in a large planter or terrarium. Culture: 2 or 3; 5 or 6; 8; 12 or 13; 14 or 15; 19.

Hibiscus rosa-sinensis. Tender, erect woody shrub with bright green sometimes variegated leaves, and spectacular single or double mallow-like rose, scarlet, orange, crimson blooms. Superb tub or pot plant in a south porch or window, and patio in summer. Culture: 1; 2; 6; 8; 12; 14; 18.

Hippeastrum (Amaryllis). An easy-to-grow bulb with strap leaves and flaring white, pink, coral, crimson, lilac or striped flowers. Needs annual dormancy. For sunny windows. Culture: 1; 5 or 6; 8 (10); 11 or 12; 14; 19.

Hoya carnosa (Wax plant). Thick leathery leaves sometimes splotched silver yellow on cord-like stems that climb or hang. Waxen fragrant pink flowers come in clusters. Give lattice or hanging basket beside bright window. Leave on old bloom stems—they flower again. Culture: 1 or 2; 5 or 6; 7 in winter, 8 summer; 11; 14; 18.

Hypoestes sanguinolenta (Pink polkadot plant). Soft green leaves have rose splotches, lavender flowers. Put it among other small plants in a pot collection or planter. Culture: 2; 6; 8; 12; 15; 18.

Inch plant (see *Tradescantia*).

Ivy (see *Hedera*).

Ivy geranium (see *Pelargonium*).

Jacobean lily (see *Sprekelia*).

Jade plant (see *Crassula argentea*).

Kalanchoe. These easy succulents have many forms, such as the air plant (*Bryophyllum*) that forms plantlets on leaf margins. All have curious leaf shapes, and impressive yellow, red, orange, violet, white flowers. For sunny warm sills. Culture: 1; 5, 6; 7; 11, 12; 14; 17, 18.

Lady Washington geranium (see *Pelargonium*).

Maranta leuconeura kerchoveana (Prayer plant). Small-growing soft oval leaves with dark purple spots; fold together in evening. For pot or planter, set in the shade of taller kinds. Culture: 2; 6; 8; 12; 15; 19.

Mimosa pudica (Sensitive plant). The ferny compound leaves close at the slightest touch. Flowers are interesting but not showy pink puffballs. Good on a warm sun porch or summer patio. Culture: 2; 6; 8; 12 or 13; 14; 17.

Monstera deliciosa. Commonly called split-leaf philodendron, with huge dark green leaves developing sizable perforations. Withstands dim warm corners, becoming very large. Culture: 2; 6; 8; 11; 14; 18.

Moses in the bulrushes (see *Rhoeo discolor*).

Neanthe bella (Palm). One of the smallest of the many palms. Slow growing, making a graceful spray of dark, leathery fronds, ideal for low planters, dish gardens, coffee or lamp tables. Culture: 3; 6; 8; 11; 14; 19.

Nephrolepis exaltata bostoniensis (Boston fern). A common house fern, requiring same conditions as most others; ideal for a shaded porch or set back from a bright window. Culture: 2; 5; 8; 12; 14; 19.

Nephthytis (see *Syngonium*).

Nerium oleander (Oleander). A large growing shrub with lance-shaped glossy leaves on woody stems, and rose, pink or white blooms in groups at ends of branches. Give a large pot or tub in a cool window; porch or patio in summer. Culture: 1; 5; 8; 12; 14; 18.

Oleander (see *Nerium oleander*).

Orange (see *Citrus*).

Orchid cactus (see *Epiphyllum*).

Palm (see *Neanthe bella*).

Pelargonium (Geranium). All of this huge tribe have showy flowers and fine foliage. Zonal geranium, *P. hortorum,* has leaves often marked with darker or lighter colors, and bold flowers of white, pink or red. Lady Washington kinds, *P. domesticum,* have lush foliage and are delicately marked, ruffled, or doubled flowers. Ivy geraniums, *P. peltatum,* have trailing branches, waxy leaves, usually pink flowers. Others, like *P. gravolens* (rose) and *P. odoratissimum* (apple) have scented leaves. For sunny sill collections where you want color. Culture: 1; 5; 7; 12; 14; 18.

Peperomia. A large, varied group, all with distinctive leaves, variegated or plain, some crinkled, but most smooth and small. For dish gardens or small planters on well lighted tables or stands. Culture: 2 or 3; 5 or 6; 7; 12; 15; 18.

Philodendron. Perfect for modern decorating—planters, pots, hanging baskets, or plain water. Many, but not all, climb and need totem pole support. Some, like *P. hastatum,* make large upright plants, good for sizable pots or tubs. Culture: 2; 6; 8; 11; 15; 18.

Pickaback plant (see *Tolmeia menziesi*).

Pilea. P. microphylla is the artillery plant —tiny, dense, watery leaves and flowers that pop out pollen when moved. *P. cadierei* is the aluminum plant, with silver-splotched, oval, stitched leaves. Both are good for table gardens, sill collections. Culture: 2; 6; 8; 11; 12; 15; 18.

Pink polkadot plant (see *Hypoestes sanguinolenta*).

Pothos (see *Scindapsus*).

Prayer plant (see *Maranta leuconeura kerchoveana*).

Rhoeo discolor (Moses in the bulrushes). Dark, long strap-shaped leaves, purple on lower sides with white "boat" flowers clustered at base. Ideal in planters where light is dim. Culture: 2; 5; 8; 12; 14; 19.

Rosary vine (see *Ceropegia woodi*).

Rubber plant (see *Ficus elastica*).

Saintpaulia (African violet). The charming white, pink, blue, purple, doubled, ruffled, fringed or single flowers sit above neat low mounds of leaves. A stand beside an east window is a perfect location. Culture: 2; 6; 8; 11, 12; 15; 17, 18.

Sansevieria (Snake plant). The common upright kind (*S. trifasciata*) has flat spear-like mottled leaves rising in a cluster. A vaselike rosette is made by *S. hahni*. There are many other kinds, all unbeatable for planters in dark dry places. Culture: 1, 2 or 3; 5 or 6; 7; 11; 14; 18 or 19.

Schlumbergera bridgesi (Christmas cactus). Chain-like branches of flat leaf sections produce showy cerise flowers in November, December. For bright sills or porches; patio in summer. Culture: 1 or 2; 6 and 8 (except in fall: 4 and 7); 12; 15; 18.

Scindapsus aurea (Pothos). An incredibly tough foliage plant with slender heart-shaped leaves, mottled with cream. Stems are more fleshy and vigorous than those of philodendron with which it is often confused. For coffee tables, wall planters, hanging baskets. Culture: 2; 6; 8; 11; 15; 18.

Sensitive plant (see *Mimosa pudica*).

Shrimp plant (see *Beloperone guttata*).

Sinningia (Gloxinia). Hybrids have showy bell- or slipper-shaped white, pink, crimson, royal purple flowers, also spotted, bicolors, and doubles. Velvety leaves are often large. Will bloom in light, not sunny windows. Culture: 2; 6; 8; (10 after flowering); 12; 15; 17, 18.

Snake plant (see *Sansevieria*).

Spider plant (see *Chlorophytum elatum*).

Sprekelia formosissima (Jacobean lily). A bulb plant with strappy leaves, crimson spidery orchid-like flowers in spring, summer. Colorful in windows or on porches or patios. Culture: 2; 6; 8; (except 10 and 4 in fall and winter); 12; 14; 19.

Sprenger fern (see *Asparagus sprengeri*).

Stapelia variegata (Starflower, carrion flower). The cactus-like long soft green stems produce yellow-green, spotted star-shaped flowers with a vile odor. Interesting and easy on sunny sills. Culture: 1; 5; 7; 12; 14; 18.

Starflower (see *Stapelia*).

Strelitzia reginae (Bird of paradise). Long, oval, stiff, blue-gray leaves at base of exotic orange, blue, red flowers ascending on strong stems. Large growing, excellent for tubs on porches or patios. Culture: 1; 5; 7; 12; 14; 19.

Syngonium podophyllum (Nephythytis, tri-leaf wonder). Arrow shaped usually three-parted leaves are light and dark green, contrasted along margins, veins. Fine for coffee tables and planters in medium light, city apartments. Culture: 2; 6; 8; 11; 15; 19.

Tolmeia menziesi (Pickaback plant). Grown for the interesting hairy leaves, which produce baby plants at the base. Suited for hanging baskets, table tops or sills where larger plants dominate. Propagate by rooting the plantlets. Culture: 2; 5; 8; 12; 14.

Tradescantia (Wandering Jew, inch plant). Leaves are on clambering fleshy stems and are usually banded lengthwise with white, purple or yellow. White or purple flowers are not showy. Perfect for hanging baskets, wall planters, as ground covers in indoor planters. Similar are the many zebrinas. Culture: 2; 5; 11; 12; 14; 18.

Tri-leaf wonder (see *Syngonium*).

Velvet plant (see *Gynura aurantiaca*).

Wandering Jew (see *Tradescantia*).

Wax plant (see *Hoya carnosa*)

Zonal geranium (see *Pelargonium*).

CODE TO HOUSE PLANT CULTURE

Match numbers with those at the end of the preceding descriptions of house plants to find the conditions and care each plant requires.

Light requirements

1. Full sun or strong light many hours a day.
2. Medium light—2 hours of sun or strong light daily, or filtered sun.
3. Tolerates north light, or places with no sun but good open light.

Temperature requirements

4. Cool—as low as 45 degrees at night, 60 in daytime, especially in winter.
5. Medium cool—as low as 50 degrees at night, up to 70 in daytime.
6. Warm—no lower than 65 at night, up to 80 in daytime.

Water requirements

7. Allow to become nearly dry between waterings, then soak thoroughly.

HOUSE PLANTS FOR SPECIAL CONDITIONS

These can take dim light:	*These can take dry air:*	*These can take it hot:*
Aglaonema	Aechmea	Aglaonema
Aspidistra	Aglaonema	Aphelandra
Chlorophytum	Aspidistra	Crassula
Cissus rhombifolia	Cactus (desert kinds)	Codiaeum
Cordyline	Chlorophytum	Cordyline
Dracaena	Crassula	Dieffenbachia
Episcia	Dieffenbachia	Dracaena
Fittonia	Dracaena	Episcia
Hedera	Ficus	Fittonia
Helxine	Hedera	Gynura
Monstera deliciosa	Hoya carnosa	Maranta
Neanthe bella	Monstera deliciosa	Monstera deliciosa
Peperomia	Neanthe bella	Philodendron
Philodendron	Philodendron	Pilea
Scindapsus	Sansevieria	Saintpaulia
Syngonium	Scindapsus	Sansevieria
Tolmiaea	Syngonium	Scindapsus
Tradescantia		Syngonium

8. Keep nicely moist most of the time, but not wet.
9. Water it often and well—drenching, then letting it become just moderately moist, and never drying out.
10. Needs dormancy with watering reduced.

Humidity requirements

11. Tolerates a fairly dry atmosphere, as in most houses and apartments.
12. Prefers moderate humidity, as you would find among a large collection of plants or under humidified conditions.
13. Needs high humidity as in a terrarium.

Soil requirements

14. All-purpose mix—2 parts loam, 1 part peat moss or leaf mold, $\frac{1}{2}$ to 1 part sand.
15. Humusy mix—1 part loam, 1 part peat moss, 1 part leaf mold, $\frac{1}{2}$ part sand, $\frac{1}{2}$ part rotted manure.
16. All humus—osmunda, fir bark, sphagnum moss, or peat moss. Plants in these need regular feeding with liquid fertilizer.

Propagation

17. Plant seeds.
18. Root cuttings in vermiculite, sand, or peat-sand mixtures.
19. Divide the old plant or take offsets.

EASY-DOES-IT IDEAS

Grow house plants together to increase humidity around them, and stand a few glasses of water among the pots to release moisture into the air.

Give house plants an occasional shower bath under the spray at the kitchen sink. This cleans the foliage, washes off pests like red spiders and aphids, and provides a pleasant interval of humidity.

To get more space for house plants, consider a shelf in your bookcase, lighted with a fluorescent tube. All plants grow well in the artificial sunshine furnished by fluorescents.

Chapter 34

GARDENING IN WINDOW BOXES, PLANTERS AND TUBS

What shall I plant in sunny garden boxes and shaded terrace tubs?

Container-growing gives your yard another dimension and an opportunity to grow well a great variety of interesting plants. In the city, if *terra firma* is all paved over or more than one story below you, boxes and tubs may be your only way to grow things. Whatever the circumstance, you will enjoy this kind of garden in which plants can be appreciated close at hand and from all sides, while you are in a relaxed, appreciative mood. And they are more beautiful because it is easy for you to give container plants special watering and fertilizing.

Be selective in the containers you choose —tubs, planters, boxes—and in the plants you put in them. If you want color, you can have a rainbow of bright annual petunias and marigolds. If striking form and texture appeal to you, you can grow some wonderful foliage plants—dracaena, fatsia, yucca, and sempervivums.

When you garden outdoors with moveable containers, you need not be restricted by climate. Even in the cold north you can grow camellias, hibiscus, bamboo, or oranges on your own patio; and when frost threatens, trundle them inside to a sunny window, cool porch, even your basement or garage if there is light there.

If you like miniatures, you can have a complete landscape in a trough or box de-

signed with Lilliputian material. Such a garden stirs the imagination and interests both of children and grownups.

CONTAINERS AND WHERE TO USE THEM

Containers for plants outdoors are generally of three kinds: (1) flower boxes usually but not always hung at windows; (2) built-in planters of wood or masonry that stay in place the year around; (3) tubs, urns, and various containers adapted for plants on terrace or patio.

Their main need is good drainage, with not just one but several holes in the bottom, although exceptions can be made. The other need is protection against rotting or rusting. If containers are of wood, use a rot-resistant type and preservative paint like penta or Cuprinol. If containers are metal or masonry, coat them with moisture-proof asphalt or waterproof paint to make them last longer.

Flower boxes at windows are traditional in some places and pleasing because you see the flowers from both inside and out. They improve the appearance of many houses, and this is pronounced when a building itself is quite plain—no shutters, awnings, or painted trim. Boxes usually look best if painted to match the house, but not always. Some woods like redwood or cypress look as

195 Flower boxes at windows are traditional in some places. Geraniums and double petunias here mix agreeably, with inch-plant trailing from the edge. *Roche*

196 Grown in tubs kept close at hand, plants come into sharp focus as individuals, as this perfect azalea demonstrates.
California Redwood Association

197 Petunias in boxes here give distinction to a doorway. *Gaynor*

good and last as long if stained instead of painted. The idea is not to let the box dominate the flowers. The same type of box you hang at a window might also decorate other places. For example, three stepped-down flower boxes look well on a bare garage wall, or you can place one atop a sturdy porch railing.

Built-in planters are permanent, so plan them carefully. An appropriate place for these is along the front wall of a house or around a front corner, where you want to break a vertical line and give color. Size should be in scale with house or yard. Make a planter high enough for convenience but not so it appears obtrusive. Sitting height is about right.

Planters are also attractive along a terrace or patio, a fence or wall, or flanking low steps, wherever you need an architectural accent to divide or add interest to an area that is much lived in or near foot traffic. You can make planters of wood or masonry, whichever suits the style of your house. Masonry lasts longer than wood.

Then there is the little pavement pocket —an opening in a paved surface thoughtfully placed to give an accent of color or texture. These pockets are usually put in when the house or patio is built, but they can be afterthoughts, too.

Tubs, urns, and other patio containers give the most pleasure. Usually portable, they are often used for plants you take indoors in fall. Possibilities here are limitless. You can use relics from the past, old churns or apple-butter kettles, or good replicas of classic containers from Greece or Rome. Perhaps you will want some modern boxes or pots designed by Japanese craftsmen. Select whatever suits your outdoor decoration. A visit to a junk yard will turn up all sorts of possible containers—copper wash boilers, large pickle crocks, kegs, barrels. If you don't entirely like the container but the shape is good, perhaps you can change it with paint, rope wrapping, or tile overlays.

Your primary purpose, of course, is to grow plants well, so a container needs to be large and deep enough to hold considerable soil, and preferably of a material that can be drilled to provide drainage, though a coarse layer of stones in the bottom can serve if plants are not overwatered. Commercial wooden tubs usually come with enough drain holes. They may also have a false bottom with a pan underneath to protect the floor from drips important when you move plants indoors for winter. These same tubs sometimes come with casters, which make it easy to roll heavy plants from place to place.

You can rearrange tubs and urns as you wish. If you have several of matching style or shape, combine them for a special purpose, like end to end for a long screen or boundary, grouped at a corner for an accent, or spaced out for a rhythmic effect.

PLANTS FOR FLOWER BOXES, PLANTERS, AND TUBS

Plants for containers differ little from those you grow elsewhere. For window and porch boxes they are usually small subjects since tall ones obscure the view and make the relatively small container seem top-heavy. Larger plants, even small trees, look well in sizable tubs and urns or in raised beds or pavement pockets. Trailing plants are excellent for window and porch boxes or at the edge of raised planters where there is room for them to cascade over the edge. Ordinarily there are too few opportunities to grow the graceful hanging plants.

If you plant spring bulbs, you can have two seasons of bloom in flower boxes. Species tulips and hyacinths look lovely there. Pot these in fall and store them in a cold place while roots form. When weather warms up toward the end of March, bury the pots with tops just showing in the flower box soil. Fill in between with pansies or violas for an early show of color that lasts until summer. Then take out pots of bulbs and put in heat-enduring petunias, coleus, or lantana. In large built-in planters, bulbs can remain through the year, the same as in flower beds.

Harmonious color combinations can be worked out for flower boxes. The gray foliage of dusty miller (*Cineraria*), and fragrant white or lavender sweet alyssum are good blenders. Either used with a plant of bold color, like 'Comanche' petunia, for instance, is pleasing. Of course, the color

198 *Above* A row of movable tubs, all planted with bright flowers, puts a colorful edging on this patio. *Tatch*

199 *Below Center* Pavement pockets are a special type of planter. This one features heat-tolerating sempervivums, pinks, sedums, and a young pine. *Grossman*

200 *Below Right* A masonry planter at a front entrance brings a welcome with pink geraniums and variegated *Vinca major*. *Genereux*

201 *Below Left* Under overhanging eaves a brick planter box offers a chance to grow a vine (here clematis) on an architectural trellis. *California Redwood Association*

of your house is a factor. The red petunia is striking against white or gray, but not agreeable with red brick. Blue ageratum with variegated green coleus foliage would then be a better choice.

For fall emphasis. Plants that give wonderful fall color are only practical if grown to maturity elsewhere and put in when budded in the fall. The low-growing hardy asters, chrysanthemums, and Christmas peppers can be brought along elsewhere in your yard. As color develops, you can transfer them to patio containers, planters or window boxes. You can grow asters and Christmas peppers from start to finish in pots, the asters in fairly large ones. Grow chrysanthemums in open ground and put them into tubs when they begin to bloom. Supply plenty of water and there will be no setback.

In tubs and urns on your patio, you will like some taller, bolder plants, including the tender kinds that spend the winter indoors. What you select depends on your facilities for wintering them. A banana plant, for instance, would undoubtedly be a problem because of its size. But you may have space for a camellia, hibiscus, or gardenia in a tub. Unless your winters are mild, you will be able to carry over but a few patio plants outdoors, even though they are hardy kinds. The small amount of soil around the roots is too responsive to freezing, thawing, and drying.

When you have a single plant in one pot, an orange tree, perhaps, cover the bare earth with a ground cover like sedum. If you have a sizable patio container that will hold a group of plants, select a tall one for vertical accent and the others for contrast in size, foliage texture or color—for instance a tall dracaena, Sprenger fern (*Asparagus sprengeri*), and at the base plants of English ivy, perhaps one variegated type, to grow over the rim.

LOW PLANTS FOR WINDOW BOXES AND SMALL PLANTERS

Preferably you want plants that stay under 10 to 12 inches high, although you may have to pinch them back to keep them there. This will increase bloom and thicken the plants. You will want plants to cascade over the edge of the box or trail down. When you select these plants, check catalog or packet descriptions carefully to be sure of getting low growers. Among marigolds, for instance, there are the midget 'Petites' and the giant 'Sahara.'

These do best in full or at least half-day sun; C indicates cascade type; T, a trailer; and Te, a tender house plant type.

Ageratum	Blue, lavender
Alyssum, sweet	White, pink, lavender (C)
Begonia, wax (*B. semperflorens*)	White, pink, red (Te)
Browallia	Blue, purple (C)
Calliopsis (dwarf)	Yellow, mahogany
Cockscomb (dwarf)	Red, yellow
Coleus	Foliage maroon, chartreuse (Te)
Dahlborg daisy (*Thymophylla tenuiloba*)	Yellow
Dusty miller (*Cineraria*)	Foliage gray
Fescue, blue (*Festuca ovina glauca*)	Foliage blue-gray
Geranium, ivy	White, pink, red (C) (Te)
Geranium, zonal	White, pink, red (Te)
Ground ivy (*Nepeta hederacea variegata*)	Foliage variegated (T)
Hyacinth	White, cream, pink, red, purple
Joseph's coat (*Alternanthera*)	Foliage red, green, white (Te)
Lantana, trailing	Yellow, white, orange (C) (Te)
Lobelia, trailing	Blue, purple (C)
Marigolds, signet and dwarf French	Yellow, mahogany (C)
Moneywort (*Lysimachia nummularia*)	Foliage green (T)
Nasturtium	Yellow, brick, red (C)
Nierembergia	Blue
Pansy	White, yellow, violet
Pepper, Christmas	Scarlet pods

Periwinkle, trailing (*Vinca rosea* 'Rose Carpet')	Rose (C)
Petunia	White, pink, purple (C)
Phlox, annual	White, pink, red, purple
Portulaca	White, yellow, pink, purple (C)
Rose, miniature	White, yellow, pink, red
Sedums	Foliage light or off-green
Sempervivums	Foliage usually off-green
Snapdragon, dwarf	White, yellow, orange, red, purple
Sprengeri fern	Foliage green (C) (Te)
Strawberry	White flowers, red fruit
Torenia	Yellow, purple
Tradescantia (or *Zebrina*)	Foliage variegated (T) (Te)
Tulip (species)	Yellow, red
Verbena	White, pink, red, blue-purple (C)
Vinca major	Foliage variegated (T)
Viola	White, yellow, violet
Zinnia, dwarf	Red, yellow, white, orange, pink, purple

These do well in deep or part shade, but you can also use practically any foliage house plant in a shaded exposure—rex begonias, philodendron, pothos, cissus, sweet potato vines, nephthytis, pilea, and fittonia, to name a few.

Achimenes	White, pink, blue, purple (C) (Te)
Begonia, tuberous	White, pink, yellow, red (Te)
Begonia, wax (*B. semperflorens*)	White, pink, red (Te)
Caladium, dwarf (like 'Candidum, Jr.')	Foliage variegated white, red (Te)
Coleus	Foliage maroon, chartreuse (Te)

Ferns, many (like *Pteris ensiformis victoriae*)	Foliage green
Ground ivy (*Nepeta hederacea variegata*)	Foliage variegated (T)
Hosta, variegata	Foliage variegated
Impatiens sultani, dwarf	White, pink, red (Te)
Iresine	Foliage red (Te)
Ivy, English or Baltic (like 'Goldheart,' 'Glacier')	Foliage green, variegated (T) (Te)
Ivy, German (*Senecio mikanioides*)	Foliag green (T) (Te)
Lobelia, trailing	Blue, purple (T)
Spider plant (*Chlorophytum*)	Foliage variegated (T) (Te)
Sprengeri fern	Foliage green (C) (Te)
Tradescantia or Zebrina	Foliage variegated or colored (T) (Te)
Vinca major	Foliage variegated (T) (Te)

TALL PLANTS FOR TUBS AND LARGE PLANTERS

Plants 15 inches or taller look well as specimens or in combinations where you need height and size. Choose some for color, some for form and texture.

Annual marigolds, datura, nicotiana, periwinkle, petunia, and salvia are annuals started each year from seed. Hardy asters, pennisetum, mint, yucca, and chrysanthemums (hardy types) usually live over winter outdoors if they are in large enough containers. Don't let them dry out completely and give extra protection with a covering of sand or soil.

These do best in full or at least half-day sun; Te indicates that they are tender house plant types and must be taken in for winter.

Agapenthus africanus	Blue
Asters, hardy (dwarf and medium, like 'Snowball')	White, pink, blue, purple

Avocado	Foliage green (Te)
Bamboo (*Bambusa nana*)	Foliage green (Te)
Banana, dwarf (*Musa nana*)	Foliage green (Te)
Bird of paradise (*Strelitzia regina*)	Red, yellow, blue (Te)
Boxwood	Foliage green
Canna, dwarf (like 'Pfitzer's')	Yellow, orange, pink, red
Chrysanthemums (cushion types like 'Knockout')	White, yellow, bronze, red, pink, purple
Citrus (orange, lemon, lime, calamondin)	White flowers, colorful fruit (Te)
Coleus	Foliage maroon, chartreuse (Te)
Crape-myrtle	Pink, lavender
Daiura metel	White
Four o'clock	White, yellow, red
Gardenia	White (Te)
Geraniums, scented	Foliage aromatic (Te)
Geraniums, zonal	White, pink, red (Te)
Hibiscus, tender (*H. rosa-sinensis*)	Scarlet (Te)
Jade plant (*Crassula arborescens*)	Foliage green, pink flowers (Te)
Lantana	White, yellow, pink, red, lavender Te)
Marigold, low (like 'Spun Gold')	Yellow
Mint (*Mentha piperita*)	Foliage peppermint-flavored
Nicotiana ('Dwarf White Bedder')	White
Oleander (*Nerium oleander*)	White, pink, red (Te)
Ornamental grass (like *Pennisetum ruppeli*)	Showy seed heads
Periwinkle (*Vinca rosea*)	White, pink
Petunia	White, pink, red, purple
Pineapple (*Ananas comosus*)	Foliage gray-green (Te)

Rose, floribunda (like 'Fashion')	White, pink, yellow, red
Rose, hybrid tea (like 'Crimson Glory')	White, pink, yellow, red
Rose, polyanthus (like 'The Fairy')	White, pink, red
Rose, tree form	White, pink, yellow, red
Rosemary	Foliage for flavoring (Te)
Salvia, scarlet	Red
Sweet olive (*Osmanthus fragrans*)	White flowers, glossy leaves (Te)
Yucca	White, foliage blue-green

Plants for deep or partial shade (all of these are tender).

Begonia, angel-wing	White, pink, red
Begonia, tuberous	White, yellow, pink, orange, red
Caladium	Foliage white, green and red
Camellia	White, pink, red
Clivia	Orange-red
Dracaena	Green or variegated foliage
Elephant ear (*Colocasia esculenta*)	Foliage green, large
Euonymus japonicus (variegated forms)	Foliage green and white
Fatsia japonica	Foliage green
Ferns (like Birdsnest, Boston)	Foliage green
Fuchsia	White, pink, red
Impatiens sultani	White, pink, orange, red
Palms (like *Chamaedorea elegans*)	Foliage green
Sansevieria	Foliage green and yellow

WINTER SALVAGE

To get a start for next year from many of the tender plants in the foregoing groups, follow these methods:

Take cuttings of wax begonias, coleus, nepeta, impatiens, iresine, English and German ivy, spider plants (save the stem plants), tradescantia, *Vinca major,* geraniums, lantana, Joseph's coat.

Lift and store in a cool, not freezing, garage or attic, the roots of cannas, tuberous begonias, caladiums, elephant ear, achimenes.

Overwinter indoors, in greenhouse, bright porch or window, such plants as Sprenger fern, pineapple, avocado, angel-wing begonia, palms, banana, camellia, citrus, jade plant, fuchsia, bird of paradise, hibiscus, sweet olive, fatsia, oleander, bamboo, rosemary, clivia, agapanthus, dracaena and any other house plants you may have used.

Take containers of roses, boxwood, crapemyrtle and *Euonymus japonicus* to a sheltered place and heap sand or earth over them, covering the crowns well. Turn a tree rose on the side and cover the whole thing with soil, or else move it to a window in your cool garage and keep it watered over winter.

The moneywort, sedums, strawberries and sempervivums will probably survive winter outdoors. Most other plants may as well be started over each spring from seed.

SHOW OFF YOUR TOPIARY AND ESPALIER

If you succeed in espaliering a plant or developing a topiary tree, you can indeed be proud, so why not display them on your patio? Place the trellis or frame for training an espalier in the tub with it. Pyracantha, dwarf fruit trees, forsythia, althaea, and camellias make good espaliers. Set the portable planters against a wall or screen where the pattern will show. But if they ever need spraying, move them away from the clean wall and do the job where the spray can do no harm.

Topiary trees of juniper, yew, boxwood and privet—sheared into formal shapes—take a lot of doing to create and maintain, so the intimate surroundings of your terrace or patio are a nice stage for them. If they are in tubs, you can stand them in protected corners for the winter.

MINIATURE GARDENS ARE A WORLD OF THEIR OWN

All ages fall under the spell of well laid-out miniature gardens. If you live in a city where your landscaping is confined to a rooftop or patio, you will particularly enjoy these diminutive replicas of nature. They usually are rock gardens scaled down to show-case size, with miniature plants in a wooden, concrete or stone container. These landscapes with trees, shrubs, flowers, rocks, hills and paths make a delightful alpine picture.

The English prefer old stone troughs for containers, something hard to find here. You can cast your own of concrete or make a box 12 inches deep, about 2 feet wide and 3 feet long, using heavy planks, at least 2-inch stock. Where you expect severe winters, provide a galvanized sheet metal lining, perforated for drainage. You can then lift out the garden and store it in a coldframe or sink it in the ground during the cold months.

To prepare a box for your miniature garden, spread a 3-inch layer of gravel over the bottom and fill in a soil mixture of equal parts loam, sand and peat. Place stones on the surface to create a natural little plateau, put the plants among them, and mulch the surface with pebbles or stone chips. Give your little landscape full sun and keep it nicely moist. Protect from driving rains and hot, drying winds. Your terrace will probably afford such shelter. Most of the suitable plants are for rock gardens, and you may have to order them from a specialist. Here are some plant possibilities for a miniature garden:

Bar Harbor juniper, young plants
Dwarf spruce, young plants (*Picea nidiformis*)
Creeping Japanese yew, young plants (*Taxus cuspidata nana*)
Dwarf heather (*Calluna*) 'J. H. Hamilton'
Drabas, like *D. aizoides, D. fladnizensis*
Aubretia deltoidea
Arabis sturi
Silene acaulis or *alpestris*
Aquilegia akitensis
Artemisia glacialis

447

Antennaria dioica
Cerastium alpinum lanatum
Iris cristata
Sempervivums of several kinds, like *S. arachnoideum*

BUILDING YOUR OWN CONTAINERS

If you build your own containers, you can get the size and design you want. Redwood, cypress and exterior grade plywood are the best woods for flower boxes and planters, for they resist rot longer than most other woods. Pine and fir are for short-term boxes. Treat any wood with a preservative, non-injurious to plants, like pentachlorophenol or Cuprinol, which you can buy at the lumber yard.

CONTAINERS MADE OF WOOD

Make window boxes fairly small, keeping in mind that they are to hang on the side of your house. When they are filled with soil and watered, even small boxes get heavy. A good size is 8 inches deep and 10 inches wide with a length to suit the situation but not longer than 6 feet or a box becomes unmanageable. To prevent rust stains, use aluminum nails or screws. Make the top wider than the bottom so when soil freezes it can expand upward instead of bursting outward. In the bottom make $\frac{1}{2}$-inch drainage holes 10 inches apart, along the outer edge so water can't run down toward the house. Fasten flower boxes to the wall with strong bolts or lag screws anchored in the studding, not with nails or small screws. Or support the boxes with wood or metal brackets fastened to the wall. Then you can set the box an inch or so out from the house, discouraging rot and termites. A box so constructed is easily taken down for cleaning, planting, or storage.

Planter boxes are made about the same as window boxes except for shape, and they can be heavier since they are almost on the ground. Put wooden cleats on the bottom to raise them an inch or two for good drainage and longer life. Allow about five $\frac{1}{2}$-inch drainage holes for a box 16 inches square. A pair of handles helps in moving.

If you live where summers are hot, windy and dry, you may need to provide planters and window boxes with double walls to reduce heating and drying out. To accomplish this, build two boxes, one bottomless and small enough to fit inside the other, with a half inch space all around. Stuff the space with vermiculite or sphagnum moss, and keep it moist. This will cool the inside soil.

When you use boards (not plywood) for the sides of planters and boxes, turn them so end grain or rings of the wood curve in. When boards warp, they curl in the direction of the rings. With the grain curving in, warping can be controlled.

CONSTRUCTING MASONRY PLANTERS

These are bigger projects than planters of wood. To keep walls from cracking, base them on a slightly wider concrete footing that extends below frost line. Concrete blocks, bricks and stone are possible materials, the brick and stone more suitable than blocks and better looking in a garden.

Unless you are building atop an existing slab, leave the bottom open for natural drainage into the soil. On a slab, provide a number of openings about 18 inches apart along the bottom for drainage. Where winters get so cold that soil may freeze solid, allow for expansion to avoid cracking the wall, perhaps a wooden liner to absorb pressure. If the planter is so large and low it is unlikely it will freeze clear through, don't bother about this.

If the walls rise 10 inches or less, make them single-brick thickness based on an 8-inch footing. Higher walls need at least two-brick thickness. A planter wall the right height for sitting will certainly be used for that, and this is a joy when you tend flowers in a planter. Give it a smooth surface of wood or concrete to make it comfortable. Walls too low or high for sitting also need flat tops for you to set pots and tubs on.

To protect the inner face of the wall from water seepage that might cause freezing and cracking, cover it with a thick coat of asphalt paint, or plaster it with cement paste. Let the coating dry completely before filling in soil. If the back of the planter is a

448

house wall, fence or other unprotected surface, better give it a waterproof coating too, or line it with building paper.

HOW TO PLANT OUTDOOR CONTAINERS

First cover drainage holes with arching pieces of broken flower pots to hold in the soil. Add a layer of gravel—for a window box 1 inch, for a large built-in planter 5 or 6 inches. If the container has no drainage holes, put in an extra thick bottom layer of coarse pebbles, 4 or 5 inches in something like an iron kettle. Then fill in the remainder, to within an inch of the top, with a mixture of one part loam, one part sand, one part peat. If you can get rotted manure, add one part of that, too. Otherwise use one-third part dried cow manure obtainable by the bag at garden stores. The soil will settle in large planters, so plan to add more later. Wait until soil has settled—a week or two for large planters—before you plant.

Whatever the varieties, select stocky, well-branched plants even though they are not yet in bloom. They will soon surpass spindly plants that have a flower or two. In a 10-inch-wide window box set a staggered double row with tall plants at the back and trailers or low kinds in front.

When all plants are placed, water them thoroughly. Then cover the soil with a half-inch of sand to hold in moisture and prevent splashing and washing out when it rains. The smaller the container, the more often you need to water it, in hot dry weather perhaps more than once a day.

Pinch back petunias, geraniums, and coleus to keep them low, and promote blooming by picking off dead flowers.

When winter comes, you can dress up bare window boxes with branches of pine, spruce or fir stuck into the soil. At Christmas you might wire in silvered cones, and add berried bittersweet or holly for color.

For window-box in sun: Blue ageratum, dusty miller (*Cineraria*), and *Vinca major;* Christmas pepper, sweet alyssum 'Carpet of Snow,' and inch plant (*Tradescantia* or *Zebrina*); pink wax begonia (*B. semper-florens*) chartreuse coleus, and moneywort (*Lysimachia nummularia*).

For window-box in shade: Achimenes 'Purple King,' hanging blue lobelia, and small-leaf variegated English ivy; impatiens 'Scarlet Baby,' Sprengeri fern, German ivy.

For redwood patio tub in sun: Pfitzer's dwarf scarlet canna, and Dahlborg daisy; hardy dwarf aster 'Snowball' and tagetes marigold 'Ursula.'

For footed iron kettle in shade: Dracaena deremensis warneckei, chlorophytum, and philodendron or pothos; caladium 'Candidum,' and variegated English ivy 'Glacier.'

EASY-DOES-IT IDEAS

To fill mid-season vacancies that may appear in a box of petunias, you can start cuttings from other petunias. Break off a six-inch stem, insert lower half, stripped of leaves, in the soil where you want it to grow, and keep well watered.

To get early color in window boxes pot up bulbs of species tulips or hyacinths in the fall and store them for winter where it's cool. Plunge them into the soil of your window boxes in March where they will grow and bloom. In May, replace faded foliage with new transplants of petunias or dwarf marigolds.

You can transplant chrysanthemums and dwarf hardy asters right from your garden in fall to a patio tub to furnish bright autumn color close at hand. Choose bushy low kinds just coming into bloom, and give them lots of water after you move them.

Chapter 35

PLANTS FOR BASKETS, BOWLS, JARS, AND BONSAI

How can I use the decorator's touch with plants?

Living plants in beautiful containers are decorative for many places in and around your home—hanging in a basket beside a window, in dish compositions on a desk or breakfast table, in glistening jar and bottle gardens for bright sills. The fascinating and somewhat mysterious bonsai dwarfs raise interest and admiration wherever they are displayed. These special ways to use growing plants are becoming more popular day by day.

PLANTING IN BASKETS

Trailing or cascading plants in suspended containers are attractive indoors and out. Hang them for welcoming accents beside your entrance, porch or carport, from trees, fences, even the eaves of the house. Suspend them above pools, where their beauty is reflected, or arrange them in a pattern across a blank wall, but take care not to let them interfere with foot traffic.

Use them indoors beside bright windows; suspended under fluorescent lights in bathroom or kitchen, and decorating plain walls of sunrooms and breezeways. Provide stout hooks, and strong wire or chains, since well-watered baskets become heavy. And locate

them away from direct all-day sun and windy corners if your climate is hot and dry.

The best containers. You can use any attractive container that suspends easily and preferably has drainage holes, or at least a separate liner inside to hold the plant. Utility wire baskets, merely 8- to 18-inch half-spheres with three hanging hooks on the rim, grow plants well because they provide aeration. On the other hand, they dry out fast, so they are not practical outdoors in dry climates.

Redwood or cedar baskets in squares, half-spheres, kegs and other shapes, are better than wire in dry weather and are more attractive. You might contrive hanging containers from kettles, gourds, coconuts, bowls, bean pots, strawberry jars, willow and reed baskets with metal liners, or even an old straw hat turned upside down. Indoor hanging plants, which are usually smaller than those outdoors, do well in the brass, copper, pewter and pottery containers found at gift counters and flower shops.

How to line. If you use a wire or openwork wood log basket, line it to keep the soil in. Two good lining materials are either sheet moss, like that found in the woods, or moist unscreened sphagnum moss. One thickness is enough sheet moss if it covers every opening. Make a lining of sphagnum moss about 2 inches thick. Inside either type of moss put an inner lining of burlap cut

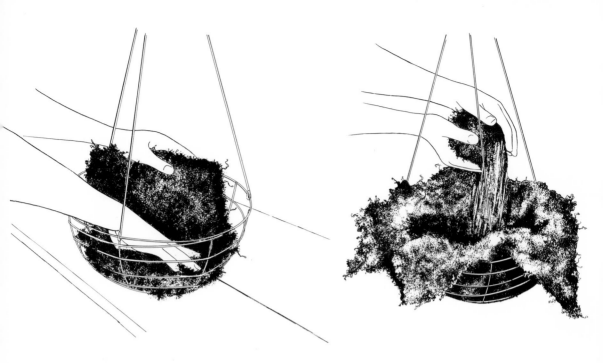

202, 203, and 204 Planting a wire hanging basket. *Top left* a thick layer of sphagnum moss is spread as a lining. *Top right* soil mixture is filled in, nearly to the top. The surplus moss will be removed.
Below the plants — here caladiums and pothos — are removed from pots and set in place. The whole thing is watered by soaking it in a tub of water. **205** Planting completed with several caladiums, pothos, and gold dust aucuba which will trail over the edge. *Philpott*

from a gunny sack, or perforated aluminum foil to keep soil from washing through the moss.

Soil to fill the basket. Mix equal parts peat moss, leaf mold or compost, loam, and sand, with a cup of dried cow manure to each peck of mixture. Fill this into the container nearly to the top of the moss, setting in plants as you go. Plant them either directly in the soil, or embedded pot and all. If removed from the pot they grow large, so avoid overcrowding. Have at least one vertical plant like a geranium in the center, with trailing kinds like *Vinca major* or petunias near the edge.

Watering hanging plants is different. Water when soil feels practically dry and the basket is light. Possibly the best and easiest way with moss-packed wire or wood baskets is to soak them in a tub of tepid water until they are thoroughly wet. Then hang them to drip where the runoff does no harm, and return them to their hooks when dripping stops.

You can water without removing the basket from its hook by pouring water slowly in at the top, permitting each sip to soak in. It helps to insert a funnel in the middle of the soil surface as you plant the basket, and pour water into that so it enters the soil without runoff. It is nearly impossible, however, to prevent a well-watered hanging basket from dripping, so either put a protective paper or plastic under it or take the basket outdoors. A plastic bowl cover over the base of small baskets does a fairly good job of catching the drip.

With undrained metal or pottery containers you may have the problem of too much water. In drainless containers first put in an extra thick layer or charcoal chips and gravel, before adding soil. Water these just enough to penetrate soil without saturating it. If moisture still shows after a few minutes, lay the container on its side to drain.

Feed hanging plants every two weeks with liquid fertilizer like Hyponex or fish emulsion. Clip off withered leaves and flowers, and prune too vigorous growers that obscure shy types.

WHAT PLANTS TO USE

Flowering kinds in the following groups are usually, but not always, grown outdoors because they need much light. Except possibly the Sonjana strawberry, the foliage group will do as well indoors as out. Start each year with new plants for outdoor hanging baskets. Meaning of symbols: su—sun; sh—shade; T—trailing or cascading.

Twenty flowering plants for baskets in sun or shade:

Achimenes	(sh)	(T)	White, pink, violet, purple
Ageratum	(su)		Blue, lavender
Alyssum, sweet	(su)	(T)	White, pink, lavender
Begonia, tuberous (hanging basket)	(sh)	(T)	White, yellow, pink, red
Begonia, wax	(su, sh)		White, pink, red
Browallia	(su, sh)	(T)	Blue, purple
Campanula isophylla	(sh)	(T)	White, blue
Fuchsia, trailing kinds	(sh)	(T)	White, pink, red, purple
Geranium, ivy	(su)	(T)	White, pink, red
Geranium, zonal	(su)		White, pink, red
Impatiens sultani	(sh)		White, pink, orange, red
Lantana, trailing	(su)	(T)	White, yellow, orange, pink, red
Lobelia, trailing	(sh)	(T)	White, blue, purple
Marigold, tagetes or dwarf French	(su)	(T)	Yellow, mahogany
Nasturtium, vining	(su)	(T)	Yellow, orange, red
Periwinkle, trailing (*Vinca rosea*)	(su)	(T)	Pink

452

Petunia, balcony or dwarf	(su)	(T)	White, pink, red, purple
Portulaca	(su)	(T)	White, yellow, pink, purple
Torenia	(su, sh)		Yellow, purple
Verbena	(su)	(T)	White, pink, red, purple

Twenty foliage plants for baskets in sun or shade:

Caladium, dwarf (like 'Candidum, Jr.')	(su, sh)		Foliage variegated red, white
Chlorophytum	(sh)	(T)	Foliage variegated white
Coleus 'Trailing Queen'	(su, sh)	(T)	Foliage variegated purple
Crassula marginalis	(su)	(T)	Foliage red-margined
Creeping fig (*Ficus repens*)	(sh)	(T)	Foliage green
Dracaena	(sh)		Foliage often variegated
Fern (like Boston)			Foliage green
Ground ivy (*Nepeta hederacea variegata*)	(su, sh)	(T)	Foliage variegated white
Iresine	(su, sh)		Foliage red
Ivy, English (like 'Gold Heart', 'Glacier')	(sh)	(T)	Foliage sometimes variegated
Ivy, German (*Senecio mikanioides*)		(T)	Foliage green
Philodendron, vining kinds	(sh)	(T)	Usually green foliage
Pothos	(sh)	(T)	Foliage variegated white
Rat tail sedum (*Sedum morganianum*)	(su, sh)	(T)	Foliage green, rope-like
Sprengeri fern (*Asparagus sprengeri*)	(su, sh)		Foliage green, lacy
Strawberry begonia (*Saxifraga sarmentosa*)	(sh)	(T)	Foliage slightly variegated
Strawberry (Sonjana)	(su, sh)	(T)	Foliage green
Tradescantia or Zebrina (inch plant or wandering jew)	(su, sh)	(T)	Foliage variegated purple, yellow, white
Vinca major	(su, sh)	(T)	Foliage variegated white
Wax plant (*Hoya carnosa*)	(sh)	(T)	Foliage sometimes variegated

PRETTY GROUPS FOR HANGING BASKETS

In 16-inch wire or redwood baskets.

In the sun: Salmon-pink geranium 'Salmon Supreme,' Sprengeri fern, and either *Vinca major* or chlorophytum; white petunia 'Pale Face,' coleus 'Trailing Queen,' and sweet alyssum 'Rosie O'Day.'

In the shade: Hanging basket type tuberous begonias, any color, pothos (*Scindapsus aureus*), and English ivy 'Glacier.'

PLANTS FOR BOWLS

These are the little gardens you want as close as your dining table, desk, coffee table or top of your television. Plants used in them come under the heading of house plants.

A traditional bowl garden is the pot of paper-white narcissus, forced into winter bloom in a low bowl of colored pebbles and water. Something newer is the dish landscape, composed of several plants in a tiny imitation of nature. Two essentials for bowl gardens are a pleasing container and suitable plants.

To force paper-white narcissus in a bowl, first select the right kinds—*Narcissus tazetta* varieties *lacticolor, papyraceus, panizzianus, polyanthos,* or *canariensis,* all white with several fragrant small-cupped blooms to a stem. 'Paper White' is the standard named variety, but yellow kinds, like 'Soleil d'Or' are available that force just as well.

Started in November or December they

take four or five weeks to bloom. Planted in late January they take only three or four weeks. For continuous flowers start some bulbs every two weeks from December to the end of February.

A blue pottery low bowl about 8 inches wide is pretty for the purpose. In it you could have eight to twelve bulbs of the kinds mentioned, preferably all alike. Pour about $1\frac{1}{2}$ inches of small pebbles or coarse gravel into the bottom of the bowl. Space bulbs $\frac{1}{2}$ inch apart and add more pebbles until they cover the bottom third of the bulbs. As bulbs swell they will move upward until they are practically on top of the pebbles. Bring water just to the bottom of the bulbs and no farther. Store the bowl in a dark place where the temperature is about 50 degrees, while roots form—perhaps on the lowest shelf of the refrigerator, under a cake pan on a cool windowsill, or on the basement floor. See that the bowl does not dry out, and when leaves are 4 inches high, move it to a sunny window, where good color will soon develop. Turn the bowl

every few days so all sides get equal light. When leaves are 6 inches high, buds will begin to show, and blooms in two or three more weeks. The spent bulbs are useless for forcing again and too tender to survive in an outdoor garden in the North; but Southerners may plant them outside.

Dish gardens in low bowls. Like a flower arrangement or fruit centerpiece, these are intended to please the senses and stimulate the imagination. They are fine gifts for shut-ins, with their illusion of being a miniature of the natural world. Size may vary from little living landscapes on top of a button, using tiny cacti and succulents, to sizable gardens in bread trays. Containers for these gardens—low plastics, china and pottery bowls, basketry and wood containers with waterproof metal pans inside—generally lack drainage, so you can set them on polished surfaces without worrying about water stains.

A visit to a local greenhouse or even the supermarket may yield a good supply of plants. Bear in mind the general conditions each needs, to avoid planting cultural opposites in the same bowl. Sun-loving cactus, for example, would be a poor combination with shade-requiring ferns. First make a trial arrangement while plants are still in their pots. In the bottom of the bowl put a thick drainage layer of coarse gravel mixed with charcoal chips. Fill in potting soil of equal parts loam, peat, leaf mold and sand, or use a commercial packaged soil. Then unpot your plants and set them in the predetermined design. It might picture a miniature woodland with a path and a mossy forest floor, or a castaway island of white sand and tropical "trees"—or anything else your fancy creates. With plants and soil in place, water just enough to settle the roots. Thereafter keep the soil nicely moist, but no more. For a clean topping add a layer of sand, gravel or granite grit sold at the feed store or pet counter, or a dark carpet of bacterial peat. Perhaps you will want to include paths of stream-bed stones or tiny tiles, ceramic or wood figures or other accessories—or you may leave the landscape simply as is.

Dish gardens need water and light, like any plants. In winter they do best in a sunny east, south or west window, but when days are longer, set them farther from direct sun. After about two months begin applying diluted house plant fertilizer every other week, in small doses so plants will not outgrow the limited space. You may have to prune to keep them in bounds; At best, plants in bowls do not last long and need occasional replacement, perhaps even entire replanting every six months or so. But the magic of these gardens deserves some extravagance in cost and care.

Plants for dish gardens. Here are twelve types and three specific varieties of plants good for dish gardens—tolerant enough to take warm dry apartment air, and even neglect in watering. They do best in at least two or three hours of sunlight a day.

Aloes
Cacti—pincushion, echinos, or opuntia
 (bunny ear) types
Crassulas, like *argentea* and *falcata*
Dracaenas, young or small kinds
Echeverias like *coccinea, haageana, gigantea*

English ivy, miniature and variegated-leaf
 kinds
Gasterias
Haworthias
Kalanchoes, like 'Tom Thumb' and *pumila*
Peperomias, small kinds like 'Pixie' and
 'Little Fantasy'
Sedums, like *dasyphyllum, multiceps, sieboldi*
Sempervivums, like *tectorum* and *arachnoideum*
Acorus gramineus pusillus
Chlorophytum elatum variegatum
Neanthe bella

In the dish garden on page 454, the bold clump is chartreuse-green *Costus igneus,* an easily-grown ginger. The delicate dark "tree" at right is *Dizygotheca* (aralia) *elegantissima.* In the left foreground, grass-like spears of *Acorus gramineus variegatus* stand behind a tiny *Sedum multiceps,* sometimes called "little joshua-tree," and to the right of that is *Gasteria liliputana,* a miniature succulent which may even bloom. White granite sand covers the hillock and a path of water-washed stones winds across the miniature strand.

PLANTS FOR JARS

As distinguished from bowls, jar gardens have more depth. In a pottery strawberry jar you can plant from top to bottom. This is a pretty way to display African violets or an ivy collection, and on your patio planted with strawberries it is a tantalizing attraction.

Other jars—made of glass with tall sides and perhaps lids—are good humidity- and moisture-holding containers, letting you grow plants impossible elsewhere in your house.

How to plant a strawberry jar. The larger the jar the better it is for strawberries or miniature roses on your terrace. Smaller kinds having only four or five pockets are good for ivy collections, miniature African violets and parsley. Always put in a bottom drainage layer of coarse gravel mixed with charcoal chips, up to the lowest pocket. Fill in above with a mixture of equal parts loam, peat, leaf mold, sand and rotted manure, or substitute for this last a half part of heat-dried manure. Place plants as you add soil. For a parsley jar, merely fill it with soil and plant a pinch of seeds at the back of each pocket.

Other plants for strawberry jars are sedums, echeverias, and sempervivums for sunny locations; maidenhair fern for a shaded outdoor spot; and ground ivy (*Nepeta hederacea variegata*) for either sun or shade.

If your house is too dry for your plant favorites, you may be able to grow them in a glass jar. This moist, bright enclosure gives good growing conditions and makes a striking garden for a table, stand or north window. Large and small brandy snifters, apothecary and bell jars, bubble bowls, bottles—anything of clear glass large enough to hold plants—are possible containers. A glass pickle jar 14 inches in diameter laid on its side and planted becomes a ready-made terrarium large enough for a number of plants.

Bottle gardens are as attention-getting as a ship in a jug, and much easier to achieve. Start with the jar or bottle sparkling clean and dry inside and out, so no soil will stick to the sides. Use a humusy soil mixture, either bought in a package or home-mixed of equal parts loam, peat, leaf mold and sand, with the loam and leaf mold pasteurized to prevent fungus diseases (see Chapter 33). Have the mixture *slightly* damp. At bottom put for drainage a layer of gravel mixed with charcoal chips to keep the soil sweet, and over this spread the soil mix just deep enough to grow plants well. For example, in a 1 gallon cider jug put an inch of gravel and 2 inches of soil. If plants have been potted, remove soil from around their roots by shaking them gently or if necessary by soaking in water.

To plant in jar, simply use a long-handled spoon to open a hole, lower the plant into it and hold it with a fork, then spoon soil back around it. A spatula or long stick helps to firm down the soil when you finish. Start with small plants around the sides and end with the large ones in the middle. Arrange shapes and colors to blend well.

Planting in a bottle takes a bit more doing. Put in the soil through a funnel. With bendable wire, like 9-gauge aluminum clothesline wire, make a tool with a small hook at one end to open a planting hole and guide the plant, root down, through the neck of the bottle. Another long wire used chopstick-style helps. Even fairly large supple-stemmed plants like pileas, peperomias, and dracaenas go through easily. Wrap those with delicate foliage spirally with tissue paper for protection, then remove the tissue with the hook when the plant is in place. If a plant falls where not intended, nudge it to the right location and cover the roots with the wire. Set small outer plants first, and the large ones in the center last.

If color is lacking, add small accessories—animal figures perhaps, or a sprinkling of colored pebbles over the soil. Give one light watering to moisten foliage and soil.

A jar or bottle garden needs good light, but direct sun would overheat plants and burn the foliage. Open jars like brandy snifters need watering more often than narrow-necked bottles, but none of these needs frequent watering because what evaporates condenses and runs back into the soil. You can tell by the appearance if the soil is dry. Then give it only a light sprinkle. Avoid fertilizing, so as not to encourage fast growth. Do not close up a jar or bottle permanently with a lid or cork—some ventilation is needed to keep condensed moisture from obscuring the plants.

207 *Opposite* Bottle gardens are as attention-getting as a ship in a jug, and much easier to achieve. *Photographic Arts* **208, 209, and 210** *At bottom* Planting a bottle garden. The soil mixture, slightly damp, is put into the clean dry bottle through a funnel. Soil is removed from the plant's roots, and the plant is guided through the mouth of the bottle with a wire tool. The plant is tamped into place with the wire. Set outside plants first. *Philpott*

Plants for jars and bottles. Here are a dozen relatively tall plants for the center:

Acorus gramineus variegatus
Boxwood, young plants
Citrus, young plants of orange, lime, lemon
Cordyline terminalis, 'Baby Ti' variety
Dracaenas, many kinds, like *D. sanderiana*
English ivy, many kinds, like 'Glacier,' 'Curlilocks'
Euonymus japonicus varieties, like 'Yellow Queen'
Ferns, like *Polypodium aureum mandaianum*
Golddust plant (*Aucuba japonica*)
Neanthe bella palm
Nephthytis (*Syngonium*) like 'Tri-Leaf Wonder'
Osmanthus illicifolius variegatus

Here are a dozen spreading kinds for medium height:
African violets, especially compact ones like 'Baby Helen,' 'Little Geneva Princess'
Aluminum plant (*Pilea cadieri*)
Begonias, like *B. boweri,* and rex 'Dew Drop' and 'Baby Rainbow'
Cryptanthus, like *bromelioides tricolor*
Episcias, all kinds
Ferns, like *Pellaea rotundifolia* and *Adiantum bellum*
Fittonia vershaffelti argyroneura
Grape ivy, miniature (*Cissus striata*)
Inch plants and wandering jew (*Tradescantia* and *Zebrina*)
Peperomias like 'Emerald Ripples,' 'Little Fantasy,' 'Blackie'
Prayer plant (*Maranta leuconeura kerchoveana*)
Wax plant, variegated (*Hoya carnosa variegata*)

Here are a half-dozen small plants for ground covers, or for tiny containers. The dwarf gloxinia will thrill you with perfect blue-white flowers the size of a dime.
Artillery plant *Pilea microphylla* or *depressa*)
Baby's tears (*Helxine*)
Clubmoss, spreading (*Selaginella kraussiana*)

Creeping fig (*Ficus repens*)
Dwarf gloxinia (*Sinningia pusilla*)
Strawberry geranium (*Saxifraga sarmentosa variegata*)

PLANTS FOR BONSAI

Bonsai is an ancient Japanese craft of dwarfing woody plants. These potted trees or shrubs are not only small, but also twisted, as though they have lived on a mountaintop. Their graceful form, interesting foliage and often colorful flowers make them prized for indoor and outdoor decorating. Needing part-day sun, fresh air and humidity, they are especially suited as patio or porch plants, not house plants.

Although bonsai is time-consuming, it is within the ability of amateurs. The dwarfing principle consists of systematic starving and pruning of both tops and roots, over a period of years. To shape the plant you prune and ply branches with wires.

Well-cared-for bonsai specimens often live hundreds of years, becoming more beautiful as they age. Don't let this alarm you— a good bonsai tree can be grown in much less time, perhaps five years, and it is fun to do.

Plants and containers for a start. Begin either with seeds or small plants. Nurseries sometimes have year-old seedlings, first year grafts or rooted cuttings that are excellent. If you prefer seeds, easy subjects are ginkgo, zelkova (an Asiatic tree resembling small-leaf elm), short-needle pines, bald cypress, junipers and flowering crabapples. Dealers in rare seeds sell these by mail through classified ads in garden magazines. If you start from young plants or cuttings, easy possibilities are hardy azaleas (such as the *kaempferi* hybrids), small-leaf Japanese maple (*Acer palmatum*), flowering quince, peach or apricot, Sargent's juniper, spruce and sweet gum.

Among tender plants those best suited as year-round house plants are gardenia, dwarf pomegranate, boxwood and rosemary.

Bonsai containers are small and quite shallow, with at least one drain hole in the bottom. Neutral colors are better than bright ones, and heavy pottery is better than porous clay which dries out fast. You can launch a 6-inch juniper for bonsai in a pot 2 inches deep and 4 inches in diameter. Increase the size slowly from year to year, depending on the progress of the plant, until you stabilize it at the mature size you want to keep.

Soil and potting. The best times for potting and repotting are autumn and early spring. Spread pea-size gravel in the bottom of the container. For pines and junipers use a soil mixture of equal parts humusy loam and sand. For deciduous trees like maples and zelkova include one part sand, three of loam, two of rotted shredded manure.

211 A collection of bonsai trees, effectively displayed, is an addition of interest and beauty to your yard. *Masonite Corporation*

For rotted manure you can substitute a half part of dried packaged cow manure and one and one half parts leaf mold. For fruiting and blooming plants omit sand and use two parts loam and three parts rotted manure (or if it's the heat-dried kind, only three-fourths part, and two and one-fourth parts leaf mold). Screen the soil into coarse and fine, and spread a layer of the coarse over the gravel.

Put the little tree in the container, perhaps tilting it for artistic effect. If the bowl is oblong, set the tree closer to one end than the other, but if it is round, set it in the center. Fill in fine soil around the roots but leave it loose and unpacked. After filling the container, water branches, trunk and soil with a soft spray, let drain, and then spray again. Set the plant in the shade until it is established, and water it this way each time it is dry, probably daily in the summer.

Molding the shape. After growth starts, determine how you want to develop it. You will need copper wire strong but soft enough to be workable in your fingers. If none other is at hand, burn medium gauge copper wire in a fire to soften it. Wind 1-inch spirals up the stem to be trained, and gently bend wire and stem together to the angle you want. You may need to remove some of the branches, cutting clean at the main stem, to emphasize growth in one direction. Cut back tips of twiggy trees like maple and zelkova as they grow, whenever new shoots are an inch long, leaving only one or two leaves on a branch. Tip back new shoots on junipers and pines also, cutting even individual needles if it helps the appearance. Do not prune crabapples and other flowering kinds this way, however, or you will remove bloom buds.

How and when to root-prune and repot. Every few years in early spring, bonsai trees need repotting—zelkova every other year,

212 Use dish gardens as you would flower arrangements. At top, a long-stemmed hen-and-chickens in a miniature Italian marble birdbath. Lower left, a similar container planted with coleus, ivy, and a few sedums. At right, a variegated crassula trimmed to tree form resembles bonsai. A small cluster of budded kalanchoe is on the ground below it. These arrangements by Mrs. Ralph Spence, Garden Club of Toronto.
Panda

other leaf-shedding kinds at least every third year, pines and spruces every three to five years. If a plant does not seem pot bound, leave it alone.

Before repotting permit the soil to become fairly dry. Remove the plant from its container and set it on a table in a cool room. With a stick work soil away from the lower and outer half of the roots. Using sharp scissors, trim off about one-third of the upper roots and about half of the lower ones. Protect those remaining with a damp cloth while you prepare to replant. If you will use the same pot again, wash and dry it and replace the drainage layer.

Mix fresh potting soil. Set the tree back in the container and tamp soil around the roots with a small stick, working slowly and carefully, solidly filling every empty space. Although this takes time, it is necessary, for pressing with your fingers is not enough. Keep on working with the stick and adding soil until the pot will take no more. Brush off excess, leaving the surface just below the pot rim.

To keep the tree in position, tie it to the container, either with wires previously inserted through the drain hole, or with cord looped around the outside of the pot. Set pot and plant rim-deep in a pan of water to soak. Then drain it and finally water gently from overhead with a water spray, repeating this each day. After a week you may release the ties or wires.

Care in winter. A cool season is essential to pines, junipers and deciduous trees and shrubs, so you cannot overwinter them in a warm house. Because of watering problems and possible pot breakage, however, it is just as bad to expose them to hard freezing weather. So the thing to do is put them in a cool, light, frost-free place—an unheated sun porch or a deep coldframe—where you can heat and ventilate when necessary and water regularly.

Tender plants like pomegranate and rosemary can spend the winter on a cool windowsill with other house plants.

EASY-DOES-IT IDEAS

If your hanging basket is hard to take down, water it in place from the top but protect the carpet or floor beneath by covering the lower part with a plastic bowl cover. Even a shower cap may do to catch the drip.

To ease the watering job for hanging baskets, insert a small funnel top center when you plant the basket, and pour water into that. Then it sinks in instead of running off over the sides.

For a start with bonsai, look around your yard for seedling trees of maple, elm, peach, or apple. They are good material on which to practice the methods of dwarfing and training to interesting shapes.

Chapter 36

FLOWERS
FOR THE HOUSE

What shall I grow for bouquets?

By planting well-chosen flowers, trees and shrubs, you can have blooms and foliage for bouquets in your house all through the year.

In January and February, you might cut and force branches of forsythia, flowering crabapple and quince or choose the attractive buds of magnolia, maple or grape, or the early blooms of witch hazel. English ivy, holly, pyracantha, pines, junipers, spruces all offer green foliage for winter bouquets, and from some you also get color from berries or cones. The seed pods of the lotus and the coneflower, preserved leaves of nandina and magnolia are a few other materials you might enjoy in winter.

In March, spring bulbs begin to furnish cutting material—tiny crocus, scillas, galanthus, anemones and chionodoxas, early daffodils and eranthis. Dwarf iris and Lenten roses will furnish blooms about this time too; and to combine with them you'll have pussy willow, cornelian cherry or hazel branches in bloom, or the evergreen foliage of camellia, pachysandra, or *Euonymus fortunei*.

The main bulb season, opening in April and continuing through May, gives glorious bouquets of daffodils and tulips. Good material to put with them in arrangements includes *Phlox divaricata*, lilacs, viburnums, crabapples, spiraea, dogwood, redbud, plum and peach. For smaller bouquets there will be the grape-hyacinths, forget-me-nots, basket-of-gold, and creeping phlox, pansies and violets.

Mid-May till July, you are sure to have an abundance of blooms for cutting if your garden contains peonies, Darwin tulips, oriental poppies, large-flowered clematis, irises, or lilies. These make bold arrangements. For daintier creations there are candytuft (*Iberis*), pinks, bleeding hearts, and veronicas. The white shasta daisies and mock-orange will be blooming then too, and these bring out the colors of other flowers. At this season you'll get interesting foliage effects from ferns, broom, hostas and magnolias. Gray leaved artemisia and English lavender are good all season.

From midsummer to frost the brightest color for bouquets comes from annuals—zinnias, marigolds, petunias, gladiolus, snapdragons, annual phlox, celosia, gaillardia, cosmos, and later the China asters. Bells of Ireland spikes are a fascinating green touch in summer bouquets, as is the foliage of ornamental kale or cabbage. Count on some summer and fall perennials for late color—the garden phlox, liatris, Japanese anemone, and of course, hardy asters, and chrysanthemums which furnish whole baskets of blooms. Some trees and shrubs—the ginkgo, sweetgum and Japanese barberry—have gay foliage in fall as pretty as flowers for bouquets.

Roses make superb arrangements. Good to put with them in late summer are globe

213 This spring arrangement is composed of plum blossoms, daffodils, mullein leaves, and a light colored rock in an Oriental-style walnut container placed on two bamboo rafts. By Mrs. Eric Bax van Werald.

Nelson

214 Here a day's harvest from the spring is arranged in a somewhat French, somewhat Victorian manner. The yellow rose buds, basket-of-gold, heliotrope, sage, veronica, clover, daisies, mockorange and pansies, are in a French bronze sweetmeat urn. By Mrs. Chester M. Way.

Gustav Ekman

thistle (*Echinops*), sweet autumn clematis, baby's-breath, tuberoses, and variegated hosta foliage.

As winter draws near you can still have colorful bouquets from the berries of the hawthorn, bittersweet, and pyracantha, and the red leaves of the Mentor or Japanese barberry or burning-bush euonymus (*E. alatus*).

MATERIAL FOR BOUQUETS

Most of the flowers for your arrangements can come right out of your perennial and shrub borders. The cutting of blooms actually benefits most plants, and you can remove a great many without detracting from the color that remains. When you go in for arranging in a big way and know that you will want lots of certain blooms, plant a generous supply in rows in a special cutting garden. Cultivate, water and weed them just as you would a vegetable crop. Then you can take flowers by the armful and not worry about robbing your landscape of its beauty. Here are some kinds you might plant especially for cutting:

For spring bloom:
tulips—red, white, yellow, pink, orange, lavender, purple
daffodils—yellow, gold, white, pink
larkspur from ball-sown seed—white, pink, rose, blue

For summer bloom:
bells of Ireland—green
coreopsis—yellow
cosmos—white, pink, yellow, purple
gladiolus—white, pink, yellow, red, orange, lavender, purple
gloriosa daisy—yellow, mahogany
hemerocallis—yellow, pink, scarlet, lavender
marigolds—yellow, orange
snapdragons—white, yellow, pink, red, purple, orange and blends
tuberoses—white
zinnias—white, pink, yellow, red, orange, purple and blends

For fall bloom:
china asters—white, pink, yellow, red, purple

chrysanthemums—white, pink, yellow, bronze, red, purple and blends
dahlias from seed—white, pink, red, yellow, orange, purple and blends

You may also want some flowers especially for your church. Stress white or light kinds with fairly large flowers—they show up well at a distance and are appropriate for most occasions. A cutting garden to supply church flowers might include:

April, May	Narcissus, especially 'Thalia,' 'Mt. Hood'
May	Peonies
May	Tulips, especially white varieties
June, July	Regal and Olympic hybrid lilies
June to September	Delphiniums in light shades
July, August	Calla lilies
July to September	Zinnias, large-flowering kinds
July to October	Marigolds, large-flowering kinds
July to October	Gladiolus in consecutive plantings
September to November	Chrysanthemums

A fruiting holly, a patch of ferns, a bed of English ivy, and a pine tree could all be used for foliage. Some flowering trees and shrubs, especially lilac, mock-orange, viburnum, and magnolia will be helpful in their seasons.

TO MAKE FRESH FLOWERS LAST LONGER

It pays to "condition" flowers before arranging them—they last longer. Pick kinds that are fresh and newly opened. Cut them in early morning or toward evening, not at noonday. Take a can of tepid water with you to the garden and put cut stems immediately into it. You may need several cans or buckets. Cut with a sharp knife or razor blade, taking slightly longer stems than you will need, and set the flowers without delay in a basement or cool room for a few hours to condition. Strip off foli-

215 These yellow rose buds are in an ancient copper and brass bowl. The dark bronzy green rose foliage is important to this arrangement. By Mrs. Fred J. Hay.   *Carolina Studios*

216 This is a graceful design with camellias. The blooms are faintest blush pink; the porcelain cat is white with pink touches; the container is white ceramic. Foliage in this simple arrangement is that of *Camellia sasanqua,* and the bases are Oriental. By Mrs. Fred J. Hay.

Carolina Studios

217 Summer blossoms from a Southern garden—hydrangeas of vivid pink touched with blue create a strong massed effect in this French pressed brass container. By Mrs. C. E. Martin.   *Skvirsky*

age along the sections that will be in water and have the containers and water sparkling clean. These measures greatly extend the life of flowers. You can also buy chemicals for the water that prolong life even longer.

Hard-stemmed plants—peonies, lilacs, chrysanthemums, mock-orange, forsythia—take up water better if you split stems with a knife or crush them with a hammer. Kinds with milky or sticky juice—oriental poppies, poinsettia, dahlia and euphorbia—are best charred in a flame before being put in water. You can use a lighted candle in the garden as you cut or hold stem ends over the flame of the gas stove as soon as you come in.

MECHANICAL HELPS FOR ARRANGING

Acquaint yourself with the many devices for supporting flowers in bases and bowls particularly the popular pin or needle-point holder. This is a clump of pins held in a metal base. You can fasten it to the base of a dry container with a wad of floral clay. Secure the flowers by pressing their stems down onto the pins. These holders come in many sizes and shapes. Those of brass with close-set points last longest and are easiest to use.

Crumpled chicken wire is a good holder for slender stems, especially in tall containers; cage-type holders anchored with clay are excellent for thick branches; glass blocks are good in shallow bowls for small stems like those of pansies tied in bunches; hairpin holders are especially recommended for daffodils. You can also support branches with pebbles, vermiculite, Oasis and Snopak.

Lead spiral holders attach to the rim of a vase and have flexible "arms" which hold long stems any place you want them. Plumber's sheet lead in narrow strips pressed over the rim will hold single stems. You can even make your own holders with green twigs, split at one end into a Y and wedged in across the top of the vase to keep stems from leaning.

Other tools for bouquets. Wire and floral clay are necessities. The florist can supply these. Use clay to anchor holders in the containers. Use No. 18 or No. 19 wire to strengthen or shape weak stems or make "legs" for short ones. You can even run wire up a daffodil stem to stiffen it. Thread, rubber bands or spool wire are best for tying blooms into clusters. By all means conceal these mechanical aspects of your arrangements.

HOW TO FORCE WINTER BRANCHES INTO BLOOM

In February and March the flower buds swell on forsythia, dogwood, pussy willow, flowering quince, azaleas, rhododendrons, and many other shrubs and trees. It is then fairly easy to force branches into premature bloom. Cut forsythia, azalea and daphne from the end of January on. Cut pussy willow, andromeda (*Pieris*), cornelian cherry, Japanese quince and rhododendron from mid-February on. Take spiraea, redbud, deutzia, flowering fruit trees, dogwood, honeysuckle, lilac, magnolia, leucothoe, philadelphus, and wisteria from mid-March on, always making certain the branches you select contain flower buds. These are more round than leaf buds.

Year-old branches at least 2 to 3 feet long are usually best. Cut them on a slant with a sharp knife or razor blade, ideally on a mild day after a gentle rain.

Crush the ends if branches are thick and to hurry them soak tops and all in a bathtub of tepid water for twenty-four hours. Move them to a deep vessel of water in a dark room and leave until buds begin to open, then take to a sunny window where the flowers will expand. Or condition them like cut flowers and put them in a deep container in a sunny window. This takes longer but may seem to you less trouble. Colors of forced flowers will seldom be as dark as normal, but rather delicate pastels.

The longer you wait before cutting branches to force, the sooner they open indoors. Forsythia cut in January may take three weeks or more to bloom, but if cut in late February it flowers in about two weeks. Lilac, dogwood, philadelphus, rhododendron, and wisteria take four or five weeks to open, and their forced blooms are usually small.

HOW TO PRESERVE BY DRYING

Dry some of your garden flowers for winter bouquets. With new techniques they look so real that at a casual glance you think the blooms are freshly picked. There are three favorite means of preserving: with borax and sand, silica gel (sold in commercial preparations like Flower-Dri) and air drying.

To dry flowers in borax and sand, make a mixture of two parts powdered borax and one part dry sand, sifted together. A convenient amount is 4 pounds of borax and $3\frac{1}{3}$ cups sand.

Cut the flowers—perfect specimens, of course—in the morning after the dew has dried, as they near the full-open stage. Except for strong woody kinds like roses, remove stems to within a half-inch of the flower. Make a substitute stem with wire (23-gauge, available from florists) inserted through the lower part of the flower from front to back. Just before pulling the wire through, bend a $\frac{1}{4}$-inch hook at the upper end and draw it into the center, anchored but invisible. For kinds that easily lose petals, like large-flowered clematis, reinforce with Elmer's glue, a drop under each petal.

Put the prepared flowers in the drying box—perhaps a shallow carton, cigar, shoe or dress box—in positions suggested by their shape. Large-flowered clematis, for instance, are best face down on a quarter-inch layer of the mixture. Spoon more mix over them until it is an inch and a half deep. Set the box in a well-ventilated place. Flowers will dry in about five days. Place daffodils face up and work the mix gently between petals and into the cup. They dry in three or four days; roses, marigolds, and Queen Anne's lace in five; silver-lace vine in three. Flowers dry faster in warm weather than in cool rainy periods. Most garden flowers are easy to preserve by this method.

When they are well dried, remove them carefully from the mixture and store until you are ready to make bouquets. A good way is to support blooms with cotton or tissue in a roomy suit box into which you have sprinkled a drying agent like De-Moist, and a few moth crystals to discourage mice and insects.

Other ways to dry flowers. Silica-gel works basically the same as borax and sand, but is faster. Imbed the flower in it and distribute it among the petals. The absorbent substance draws moisture out, leaving the flower colors nearly as bright as originally. When in the course of reuse the gel becomes too damp to work well, dry it out in the oven.

Air drying is good for celosia, achillea, strawflowers, globe amaranth, blue salvia, sea lavender (limonium), and goldenrod. First strip off foliage. Then tie in loose bunches and hang upside down in an airy place that is dark, to keep colors from fading. Flowers dried this way usually shrink, so preserve plenty.

How to preserve foliage. Methods vary depending on the type of foliage. Preserve soft fern fronds by wiping them with salad oil and pressing between weighted newspaper layers for three weeks. They will be fairly pliable when removed.

Glycerine and water treatment is good for leaves of beech, aucuba, Scotch broom, magnolia, pear, forsythia, dogwood, Siberian iris, aspidistra, plum and hawthorn—and they stay flexible. Wash them first, and crush hard stems by pounding. Mix one part glycerine in two parts water, pour about 2 inches into a glass jar and stand the stems in this mixture for two weeks or longer. You can hasten the penetration of glycerine by swabbing the leaves, or even immersing individual leaves entirely in the mixture. Leaves cured with glycerine can be used in fresh arrangements as well as in dried ones, since water does not harm them. By replacing water that evaporates, you can use the same glycerine mixture over and over from year to year. A commercial preparation called Perma-Dip is similar to this.

Some foliages—beech, leatherleaf viburnum, and maple leaves—preserve well if pressed between weighted newspapers. Mullein, canna, and artemisia can be hung upside down in loose bunches. If you want them curved, dry them over a rounded surface as a bowl. Colorful fall leaves of ginkgo, maple, and oak are easy to preserve by dipping them in warm paraffin and ironing between newspapers.

To make the arranging of preserved foliage easier, attach wire stems. Because of its fragility, dried material is a little harder to handle than fresh, but otherwise arranging it is the same as with fresh flowers and leaves. Use sand or Styrofoam instead of mechanical holders to keep stems in place. Hide any wires by wrapping with green or brown floral tape. You will also need Scotch tape, glue and clay to hold dried leaves, stems and flowers where you want them.

Use pods and berries to give form and color to winter arrangements, also fountain grass, wheat, broom corn, and sorghum. For pods, select those of catalpa, baptisia, castor bean, teasel, honesty (lunaria), yucca, honey locust, poppy, and milkweed; for berries consider bittersweet, holly, barberry, bayberry, and nandina.

How to skeletonize leaves. Only the midribs and veins remain after this process. Good subjects are magnolia, oak, maple, avocado, holly, and ivy leaves. In a quart of water, put two tablespoons of Clorox and soak leaves in the solution slightly more than an hour. Then rinse in clear water and gently wipe each surface with a soft cloth to remove any fleshy tissue remaining. Then press leaves for a day and night between weighted layers of newsprint, blotters, or paper towels.

EASY-DOES-IT IDEAS

Remove most of the leaves from stems of chrysanthemums and mock-orange, so flowers last longer.

Moisten your fingers when working with gardenias. It will prevent bruising them.

Your cupboard may yield pretty flower containers you didn't know you had—bean pots, sugar bowls, cream pitchers, and gravy boats are some of the utilitarian dishes that look good with flowers in them.

PART VII

USEFUL MISCELLANY

USEFUL MISCELLANY

A. THE TOOLS YOU NEED

Tools are now available to ease the work of gardening, no matter how large your project. Using these modern tools gives you more time to enjoy your garden.

ESSENTIAL HAND TOOLS

Spade for digging, root pruning, transplanting, excavating. A good spade has a curved or straight tip, a sharp edge, a broad surface for your foot which pushes it into the ground, and a strong handle.

Digging fork for lifting clumps of lilies, iris, potatoes, dahlias without cutting roots. It is light and easy to use for digging jobs.

Hoe for cultivating and chopping out weeds. In your vegetable garden, you'll use it to make rows and cover them.

Wheel hoe for cultivating vegetables. Faster and easier than hand hoeing, it does as good a job except in high weeds.

Bow rake, the steel-tined tool for smoothing out freshly tilled ground for planting, and gathering up debris.

Wire or bamboo leaf rake, to use with a sweeping motion on lawns to gather grass or leaves.

Pronged cultivator to loosen thin soil crusts and do light weeding. For these jobs this is better than a hoe.

Trowel, for small planting jobs. Kinds with rounded wood handles, firmly joined to a curved steel blade, are less likely to raise blisters or bend out of shape than trowels stamped out of one piece of metal.

Garden cart for carrying loads, the modern successor to the wheelbarrow. It can haul as much without so much lifting.

Spreader, essential to cover a large lawn with chemical fertilizer. Get one with a bin big enough to allow you to cover the lawn with only a few refillings. Use the spreader also for distributing grass seed, peat moss and soil conditioners like lime, sand, and vermiculite.

SPRAYERS AND DUSTERS

With sprayers and dusters, the question is which to get first. Eventually you need both. For only a few plants, start with the duster, which is lighter to carry, less effort to use and needs no cleanup afterward. For a big yard and lots of plants, start with a sprayer and get the duster later, for spraying is cheaper than dusting and does a better job of insect and disease control. If you have both, you'll probably use the sprayer for routine pest control, but dust when you're pushed for time or don't want to bother with spray. *Keep a separate sprayer for weed killers* that are nearly impossible to clean out of a spray tank, for their residues will kill plants.

If you use as much as ten gallons of spray at a time, consider a power sprayer. The engine compresses the air. On non-power sprayers of this type you do the compressing yourself with a hand pump.

Hose-end sprayers use water-system pressure to propel the spray. With this type, be sure the nozzle has a good metering device to control the dilution rate. Well-made ones are reliable. Hose-end sprayers have enough pressure to spray small trees and large areas.

Dusters come in many sizes and shapes. For orchards and large gardens, select a knapsack duster which propels the dust as you turn the crank. Crank or bellows-operated hand-dusters are adequate for average gardens. For small plantings, plunger types are large enough.

POWER TILLING

Garden tractors come in riding, walk-behind, plowshare and rotary tiller types. A large garden justifies the riding kind. The pull-blade plowshare is more practical for soil preparation if you have heavy crops or weeds to turn over. After plowing, you need to disk or harrow the ground before you can seed it.

Rotary tillers do the best job in ground fairly free from weeds or other surface growth, and rocks, and they will complete soil preparation in one operation. Their revolving blades sometimes loosen the ground as deeply as a plow. Some models go only 4 to 5 inches, however, and are intended for cultivating. If you want to dig deep, buy a tiller engineered to do so. Unlike pull-blade plows and cultivators, rotary tillers don't straddle crop rows but go between them, so leave space enough between rows, usually 3 feet, for the machine. In a small area, light rotary tillers can handle soil preparation plus all-season cultivating. Those with tines in front will turn in less space than those with rear tines.

For flower gardens, shrubbery borders, fence rows, greenhouse benches and other tight corners, you can have a still smaller power tiller, an electric tool with a rotating blade at the base of a handle. It requires an electrical outlet near the work area.

POWER MOWING

Rotary mowers, powered by a gasoline engine, do a good job of mowing almost any kind of grass, including fairly tall weeds. Treat yours with respect because the whirling blade striking metal, glass or stone can propel them like bullets; and it can whip off fingers or toes. Whether it is a riding rotary or one you push, observe these safety rules: (1) use it only when grass is dry; (2) clear the lawn first of toys, tools, wires or other obstructions; (3) wear substantial shoes while you are mowing; (4) keep pets and children away while you are at work; and (5) don't attempt steep banks.

Reel mowers, self-propelled and gasoline powered, are recommended for fine lawns, especially those that require close clipping

—bermuda, bentgrass, dichondra, centipede, zoysia and bluegrass in areas where close cutting is recommended.

If you don't like noisy gasoline engines on lawn mowers, you can get quiet kinds powered electrically. One type connects to an outlet by a long cord which follows you around. Another kind carries its own rechargeable battery.

To clip around sidewalks, curbs, trees and flower beds, use an edger or trimmer. Power-driven types are usually electric. Push them along the edge of a walk and a whirling blade cuts off the grass that hangs over. For bigger jobs, use self-propelled gasoline models that literally "saw" grass edges off clean. These work best on straight level surfaces.

POWER RAKING

A mechanized lawn sweeper has a revolving brush that whisks up leaves or clippings and throws them into a catcher. You can get sweepers that are either hand-pushed or engine powered. Either one drastically reduces the time you spend raking. In a half hour you can finish what takes all day to rake by hand. These are cumbersome tools needing a big area to maneuver in, so lawn sweepers are not practical for small yards.

POWER PRUNING

Electric hedge trimmers rank close to lawn sweepers as blister- and time-savers. Their one disadvantage is that they are followed by the electric cord, which limits the distance you can go from the outlet. A recent model plugs into a battery-driven lawn mower, so you can go anywhere with it.

B. HOW TO TAKE CARE OF TOOLS

Tools with gasoline engines require upkeep like your car, but they are so simple you can do the servicing yourself. Instructions are probably on a plate fastened to the engine, showing the weight of crankcase oil to use and how often to change it.

Before storing a four-cycle engine (the

usual kind on good lawn mowers and tillers) for winter, drain out the gasoline to save rust and corrosion in the tank and line. Remove the spark plug and scrape off carbon accumulated on it. While the plug is out, put a few drops of motor oil into the cylinder, and turn the engine over two or three times to spread the oil, then replace the spark plug. Drain out crankcase oil and replace it with clean oil of the weight you will need next spring. Take off the blower housing and wipe out dust and grass stuck there and in the cooling fins. If there is an air-vane governor, clean it of dirt and grease so it works freely. Leave the carburetor alone, unless you are an expert, but if you are, take it off and clean it too.

Rotary mowers. Scrape off all the matted grass clippings underneath. Before tipping up a gas-powered rotary, remove the air cleaner from the engine or all the oil will spill out of it. Before touching the blade always disconnect the spark plug to prevent the engine from starting accidentally. Remove the blade, sharpen it, coat it with rust-preventing light oil, and put it back on in the original position. Oil the wheels.

Tillers. Put away clean. Scrub off soil and coat the tines and exposed metal parts with rust-preventing oil. Fill oil up to the proper levels in differentials and gear boxes.

Fertilizer spreaders. These take a beating from the chemicals you put in them. After use, always empty out every bit of fertilizer. Open spreader to its widest setting and hose it out. Scour the agitator and bin with a blast of water. Turn it over in the sun to dry, then oil it. Light lubricating oil in a pressure spray can is ideal for protecting metal parts.

Compression sprayers. These need cleaning after *each* use. Empty out the spray and fill the tank with clean water. Remove the nozzle and take it apart, washing the screens and strainers in water or kerosene. Pump up the air and run water through the sprayer while nozzles are off. Then reassemble the sprayer without closing it tight. Before winter storage, clean it even more thoroughly by adding a half cup of ammonia to the water. With parts cleaned and put back together, pour a teaspoonful of light oil into the tank, add water, pump up pressure and run this oily water through to leave a light coating inside tank, hose valves and nozzle. Then empty the tank and store it wide open on its side until dry. Rubber parts and leather plungers wear out fast and may need replacing each year. Garden supply stores sell these parts. You can install them yourself with ordinary wrenches, pliers and a screwdriver.

Hose-end sprayers. These are simpler to clean and maintain. All you do is run clear water through to flush out the spray.

Dusters. These are almost maintenance free. Before winter storage, merely empty and blow them out.

Hand tools. Spade, hoe, rake, trowel, hedge clippers, pruners, grass snips serve better if kept clean. After each use, clean off soil by running them up and down in a bucket of sand, rubbing with a scouring pad or wiping with a handful of grass clippings. Oil them before winter to retard rust. Clean and sharpen tools with cutting edges and oil them before putting away. Keep wood handles shiny and smooth and out of the rain. Rub rough places with sandpaper and raw linseed oil.

C. WHERE TO SEND FOR EXTENSION BULLETINS

(Write to the office in your state; here are the addresses)

Alabama
Coop. Extension Director
Auburn University
Auburn, Ala.

Alaska
Extension Director
U. of Alaska
College, Alaska

Arizona
Extension Director
U. of Arizona
Tucson, Ariz.

Arkansas
Extension Director
U. of Arkansas
P.O. Box 391
Little Rock, Ark.

California
Director Ag.
Extension
U. of California
349 University Hall
Berkeley 4, Calif.

Colorado
Extension Director
Colorado State U.
Ft. Collins, Colo.

Connecticut
Extension Director
College of Agriculture
U. of Connecticut
Storrs, Conn.

Delaware
Mailing Room
School of Agriculture
U. of Delaware
Newark, Del.

Florida
Ag. Experiment Station
U. of Florida
Rolfs Hall Annex
Gainesville, Fla.

Georgia
Director Ag. Extension
U. of Georgia
College of Agriculture
Athens, Ga.

Hawaii
Coop. Extension Director
U. of Hawaii
Honolulu 14, Hawaii

Idaho
Ag. Extension Director
Ag. Science Bldg.
U. of Idaho
Moscow, Idaho

Illinois
Information Office
College of Agriculture
U. of Illinois
Urbana, Ill.

Indiana
Extension Director
Purdue University
Lafayette, Ind.

Iowa
Extension Director
Publications Dist. Office
Iowa State U.
Ames, Iowa

Kansas
Distribution Officer
Div. of Extension
Umberger Hall
Kansas State U.
Manhattan, Kans.

Kentucky
Extension Director
College of Agriculture
U. of Kentucky
Lexington, Ky.

Louisiana
Ag. Extension Director
Louisiana State U.
Knapp Hall
Baton Rouge 3, La.

Maine
Coop. Extension Director
U. of Maine
Orono, Me.

Maryland
Extension Director
U. of Maryland
College Park, Md.

Massachusetts
Extension Director
U. of Massachusetts
Amherst, Mass.

Michigan
Coop. Extension Director
106 Agricultural Hall
Michigan State U.
East Lansing, Mich.

Minnesota
Bulletin Room
Institute of Agriculture
U. of Minnesota
St. Paul 1, Minn.

Mississippi
Ag. Extension Director
Mississippi State U.
State College, Miss.

Missouri
Extension Director
Whitten Hall
U. of Missouri
Columbia, Mo.

Montana
Extension Director
Montana State College
Bozeman, Mont.

Nebraska
Ag. Extension Director
College of Agriculture
U. of Nebraska
Lincoln 3, Nebr.

Nevada
Extension Director
U. of Nevada
Reno, Nev.

New Hampshire
Coop. Extension Director
Thompson Hall
U. of New Hampshire
Durham, N. H.

New Jersey
Associate Director
Ag. Extension Service
College of Agriculture
Rutgers University
New Brunswick, N. J.

New Mexico
Extension Director
College of Agriculture
New Mexico State U.
University Park, N. M.

New York
Mailing Room, Extension Serv.
Stone Hall
College of Agriculture
Cornell University
Ithaca, N. Y.

North Carolina
Extension Director
P.O. Box 5157
State College Station
Raleigh, N. C.

North Dakota
Extension Director
State University Sta.
Fargo, N. D.

Ohio
Ext. Office of Information
Ohio State University
2120 Fyffe Road
Columbus 10, Ohio

Oklahoma
Ag. Extension Director
Oklahoma State U.
Stillwater, Okla.

Oregon
Bulletin Room
Printing Dept.
Oregon State U.
Corvallis, Ore.

Pennsylvania
Extension Director
102 Armsby Bldg.
Pennsylvania State U.
University Park, Pa.

Rhode Island
Ag. Editor's Office
16 Woodward Hall
U. of Rhode Island
Kingston, R. I.

South Carolina
Director Extension Serv.
Clemson College
Clemson, S. C.

South Dakota	Virginia
Extension Director	Extension Director
S. D. State College	Virginia Polytech.
College Station, S. D.	Inst.
	Blacksburg, Va.

South Dakota
Extension Director
S. D. State College
College Station, S. D.

Tennessee
Dept. of Informa-
tion
Ag. Extension Serv-
ice
Box 1071
Knoxville, Tenn.

Texas
Coop. Extension Di-
rector
A. and M. College of
Texas
College Station,
Tex.

Utah
Extension Service
Director
Utah State U.
Logan, Utah

Vermont
Extension Service
Director
Morrill Hall
U. of Vermont
Burlington, Vt.

Virginia
Extension Director
Virginia Polytech.
Inst.
Blacksburg, Va.

Washington
Extension Director
Washington State U.
Room 106, Wilson
Hall
Pullman, Wash.

West Virginia
Extension Director
West Virginia U.
Morgantown, W. Va.

Wisconsin
Extension Director
U. of Wisconsin
240 Agricultural
Hall
Madison, Wisc.

Wyoming
Bulletin Room
P. O. Box 3354
University Station
Laramie, Wyo.

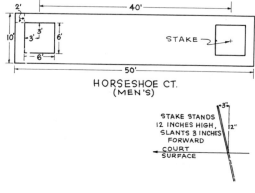

SHUFFLEBOARD

HORSESHOE CT.
(MEN'S)

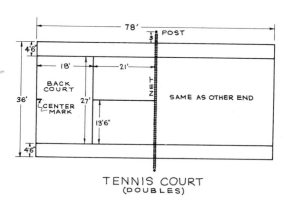

BADMINTON

D. OFFICIAL DIMENSIONS FOR GAME COURTS

Croquet, badminton and horseshoe courts are commonly laid out in lawn areas. Tennis may be played on a lawn, too, but is better if the court is surfaced with smooth compacted earth, clay, or asphalt. A croquet court, not illustrated, is officially 30 by 60 feet, but more often than not is played in a much smaller space.

E. PLANTS FOR THE SEASHORE GARDEN

Conditions by the sea put plants to a test. They must endure salt spray and fog, glaring light, wind and sandy soil. To buffer the wind you can erect windbreaks—fences, walls or a dense row of Scotch pine. To im-

TENNIS COURT
(DOUBLES)

Fig. 84   The dimensions of game courts.

prove the soil use lots of compost and other humus, but much of it will run through. For low upkeep and greatest satisfaction,

475

select tolerant plants. Here are some that do well there:

ANNUAL FLOWERS

Ageratum (*A. houstonianum*)	lavender, blue, pink
Bachelor's buttons (*Centaurea cyanus*)	pink, rose, white, blue, purple
Calendula (*C. officinalis*)	yellow, orange
Gaillardia (*G. pulchella*)	red, yellow
Globe amaranth (*Gomphrena globosa*)	purple, white
Marigold (*Tagetes*)	yellow, orange, maroon
Nasturtium (*Tropaeolum*)	yellow, orange, salmon, red
Petunia hybrids	white, pink, red, purple
Phlox (*P. drummondi*)	pink, red, white, violet
Sweet alyssum (*Lobularia maritima*)	white, pink, lavender
Verbena (*V. hortensis*)	purple, lavender, pink, red, white
Zinnia (*Z. elegans*)	white, yellow, red, pink, purple

PERENNIAL FLOWERS

Adam's needle (*Yucca filamentosa*)	white
Artemisia (dunesilver) (*A. stelleriana*)	silver-white foliage
Baby's-breath (*Gypsophila paniculata*)	pink, white
Baptisia (*B. australis*)	blue
Basket-of-gold (*Alyssum saxatile*)	yellow, gold
Daylily (*Hemerocallis*)	yellow, pink, lavender, red, mahogany
Gaillardia (*G. aristata*)	yellow, red, mahogany
Globe thistle (*Echinops*)	blue
Goldenrod (*Solidago*)	gold
Hollyhock (*Althaea rosea*)	white, pink, yellow, red
Iris (especially *pumila* and tall bearded varieties)	white, yellow, blue, purple, red
Lythrum (*L. salicaria*)	rose, pink, lavender
Peony (*Paeonia*)	white, pink, red
Primrose, Missouri (*Oenothera missouriensis*)	yellow
Santolina (*S. chamaecyparissus*)	gray foliage
Snow-in-summer (*Cerastium tomentosum*)	white
Statice (*Limonium latifolium*)	lilac, lavender

TREES FOR COLD SHORES

Black oak (*Quercus velutina*)
Eastern larch (*Larix laricina*)
Honey locust (*Gleditsia triacanthos*)
Junipers, such as Keteleer or Canaert (*Juniperus chinensis keteleeri* or *J. virginiana canaerti*)
London plane (*Platanus acerifolia*)
Northern red oak (*Quercus borealis*)
Pines (*Pinus sylvestris, P. mugo, P. thunbergi, P. banksiana*)
Russian olive (*Elaeagnus angustifolia*)
Shadblow (*Amelanchier canadensis*)
White poplar (*Populus alba*)
White willow (*Salix alba*)

TREES FOR MILD SHORES

Australian-pine (*Casuarina* species)
Cabbage palm (*Sabal palmetto*)
Cajeput tree (*Melaleuca leucadendron*)
Dahoon (*Ilex cassine*)
Eugenia species like Sea Apple (*E. grandis*)
Karo (*Pittosporum crassifolium*)
Live oak (*Quercus virginiana*)
New Zealand Christmas tree (*Metrosideros tomentosa*)
Norfolk Island pine (*Araucaria excelsa*)
Southern magnolia (*Magnolia grandiflora*)
Sweetgum (*Liquidambar styraciflua*)

SHRUBS FOR COLD SHORES

American holly (*Ilex opaca*)
Amur privet (*Ligustrum amurense*)
Arrowwood (*Viburnum dentatum*)
Barberry (*Berberis thunbergi*)
Bearberry (*Arctostaphylos uva-ursi*)
Bayberry (*Myrica pensylvanica*)
Chokeberry (*Aronia arbutifolia*)
Junipers, low, such as Pfitzer, Waukegan, Andorra
Leatherleaf viburnum (*V. rhytidophyllum*)
Scotch broom (*Cytisus scoparius*)
Sea buckthorn (*Hippophae rhamnoides*)
Tamarix (*T. parviflora*)

SHRUBS FOR MILD SHORES

American holly (*Ilex opaca*)
Bottlebrush (*Callistemon* species)
California privet (*Ligustrum ovalifolium*)
Cherry laurel (*Prunus laurocerasus*)
Crape-myrtle (*Lagerstroemia indica*)
Euonymus japonica
Oleander (*Nerium oleander*)
Rock cotoneaster (*Cotoneaster horizontalis*)
Trifoliate orange (*Poncirus trifoliata*)
Yaupon (*Ilex vomitoria*)

F. PLANTS FOR A WINDBREAK

High wind makes gardening a trial. It is one of the main problems in the Great Plains and the Southwest, where it blows winter and summer almost without ceasing. One remedy is to plant a windbreak of ultra tough, hardy trees and shrubs, to lift the air currents and cause them to pass above your yard. In winter these same windbreaks may save fuel and perhaps bring your yard extra moisture by causing snow to dump on the lee side of them. Plant windbreaks on at least two sides of your property in an L, choosing the sides from which the prevailing winds come.

LOW SHRUBS AND TREES FOR OUTER ROWS

Northern Great Plains
(Nebraska northward)

Lilac (*Syringa vulgaris*)	8 feet
Red cedar (*Juniperus virginiana*)	50 feet
Rocky Mountain juniper (*J. scopulorum*)	35 feet
Russian olive (*Elaeagnus angustifolia*)	25 feet
Serviceberry (*Amelanchier canadensis*)	25 feet
Siberian peashrub (*Caragana arborescens*)	20 feet
White willow (*Salix alba*)	40 feet

South and Central Plains
(Kansas southward)

All the above except Siberian peashrub, plus:

Honeysuckle (*Lonicera tatarica*)	8 feet
Multiflora rose (*Rosa multiflora*)	8 feet
Osage orange (*Maclura pomifera*)	50 feet

TALL TREES FOR CENTER ROWS

Northern Great Plains
(Nebraska northward)

American linden (*Tilia americana*)	100 feet
Box elder (*Acer negundo*)	70 feet
Cottonwood (*Populus deltoides*)	80 feet
Hackberry (*Celtis occidentalis*)	80 feet
Green ash (*Fraxinus pennsylvanica lanceolata*)	60 feet
Siberian elm (*Ulmus pumila*)	50 feet
Silver maple (*Acer saccharinum*)	100 feet
White poplar (*Populus alba*)	80 feet

South and Central Plains
(Kansas southward)

All the above plus:

American sycamore (*Platanus occidentalis*)	120 feet
Russian mulberry (*Morus tatarica*)	35 feet

EVERGREEN TREES FOR INSIDE ROWS

Northern Great Plains
(Nebraska northward)

Black Hills spruce (*Picea glauca densata*)	40 feet
Colorado spruce (*P. pungens*)	40 feet
Douglas-fir (*Pseudotsuga taxifolia*)	50 feet
Foxtail pine (*Pinus balfouriana*)	40 feet
Limber pine (*P. flexilis*)	50 feet

South and Central Plains
(Kansas southward)

All the above except Black Hills spruce, plus:
Western yellow pine (*Pinus pon-*   100 feet
    derosa)

G. HOW TO STORE HOME-GROWN VEGETABLES AND FRUITS

The surplus from your vegetable garden stored for winter makes fine nutritious eating, and if you don't count the time involved, it's economical, too. These are the five main methods of storing home-grown vegetables and fruits:

Cool dry storage—dark, dry and safe from frost but with temperature under 50 degrees—perhaps a walled-off part of the basement.

Cool moist storage—frost-free, humid, with temperature under 50 degrees, perhaps a root cellar, earth floored bomb or tornado shelter, or a specially dug and lined pit outdoors.

Warm dry storage—dark and dry with temperature between 50 and 65 degrees. Most basements will qualify.

Canning—hardly needs explanation. Companies that sell jars and lids have excellent canning cookbooks.

Freezing—a freezer chest, refrigerator compartment, or locker in a cold storage plant are where you store frozen foods. Many vegetables and fruits taste better frozen than canned. You can obtain freezing cookbooks from freezer manufacturers and companies that make freezer bags and boxes.

Here are preferred methods for each of thirty vegetables and fruits:

VEGETABLES

	Cool dry	Cool moist	Warm dry	Canned	Frozen	Comment
Asparagus				x	x	Freezing gives best flavor
Beans, dried	x					
Beans, lima, fresh				x	x	
Beans, snap, fresh				x	x	Canning gives best flavor
Beets		x		x		
Broccoli				x	x	Freezing preferred
Brussels sprouts		x			x	
Cabbage		x				Or make into sauerkraut
Carrots		x		x	x	
Cauliflower				x	x	Freezing preferred
Celery		x		x		
Corn (sweet)				x	x	May be frozen on the ear
Muskmelon					x	Freeze as small balls or chunks
Onions	x					
Parsnips		x		x		
Peas				x	x	Freezing preferred

	Cool dry		Cool moist	Warm dry	Canned	Frozen	Comment
Potatoes	x	or	x		x		You can obtain a chemical dust to prevent sprouting
Potatoes, sweet				x	x		Heat-cure before storing
Pumpkin	x			x	x		Leave on 3-inch stems if storing
Rhubarb					x	x	Freezing preferred
Spinach					x	x	Freezing preferred
Squash (winter)	x			x		x	Leave on 3-inch stems if storing
Tomato					x		
Turnips			x				
FRUITS							
Apples			x		x	x	Also make sauce
Cherries					x	x	Freezing preferred
Peaches, apricots					x	x	
Pears					x		
Raspberries					x	x	Freezing preferred
Strawberries					x	x	Freezing preferred

H. THE pH PREFERENCES OF FIFTY PLANTS

SHRUBS

Abelia, 6.0-8.0
Arctostaphylos, 4.5-5.5
Azalea, 5.0-5.5
Buxus, 6.0-8.0
Camellia, 5.0-6.0
Chaenomeles, 6.0-8.0
Cornus florida, 6.0-6.9
Daphne cneorum, 6.0-7.5
Deutzia, 6.0-8.0
Euonymus, 6.0-8.0
Fraxinus, 6.0-7.5
Hydrangea, blue, 4.5-5.5
Ilex, 4.0-5.5
Magnolia, 5.0-6.0 (grandiflora, soulangeana and stellata)

FLOWERS

Alyssum, 6.0-7.5
Aquilegia, 6.0-7.5
Aster (perennial), 5.5-6.9
Astilbe, 6.0-6.9
Begonia, 5.5-6.9
Calendula, 5.5-6.9
Chrysanthemum, 5.5-7.5
Delphinium, 6.0-7.5 (annual and perennial)
Gladiolus, 6.0-6.9
Gypsophila, 6.0-7.5
Heuchera, 6.0-6.9
Iberis, 6.0-6.9
Iris, 6.0-6.9
Narcissus, 6.0-6.9
Nasturtium, 5.5-6.9
Pansy, 5.5-6.9
Peony, 6.0-8.0

Mahonia, 6.0-8.0
Pieris, 4.0-5.0
Pyracantha, 6.0-8.0
Rhododendron, 4.5-5.5
Roses, 5.5-6.9
Skimmia, 5.0-6.0

Primula, 6.0-6.9
Saintpaulia, 6.0-6.9
Tulip, 6.0-6.9

VEGETABLES

Asparagus, 6.0-7.5
Beans, 6.0-6.9 (snap, lima, pole and soy)
Cabbage, 6.0-7.5
Celery, 5.5-6.9
Cucumber, 5.5-6.9

Lettuce, 6.0-6.9
Peas, 6.0-7.5
Potato, Irish and Sweet, 5.0-6.0
Rhubarb, 5.5-6.9
Tomato, 5.5-7.5

I. THE MEANING OF PLANT NAMES

Advanced gardeners may seem to you to be the worst of name-droppers as they roll out the many-syllabled scientific name of some common plant, as *Lysimachia clethroides* for loosestrife. What you may be too dumbfounded to appreciate is that the scientific name is actually the easiest way out. At least three other plants are called "loosestrife." By the time you explain which of the four you mean, you have used more brain power than if you had said *Lysimachia clethroides* in the first place.

Scientific names are logical and meaningful, once they are understood. Most of the credit for them goes to a Swede named Linnaeus who in the 1700's thought of giving plants two Latin names, the first to indicate the genus to which it belongs, and the second for the species. This is like the two names of a person, except that the plant's surname comes first. Because the names are in Latin, they are understood throughout the world.

Linnaeus also outlined a system from which the present method of classifying plants has been derived. Under it, each plant has a group, class, order, family, genus, species and variety. Perhaps you learned this kind of classification in a biology class—for much the same method is used to name all living things.

The family is a large group. In actual use, you seldom go farther back in thinking about a plant than its family. Scientists who specialize in classifying plants look for similarities that set one group apart from the others. *Family* traits are more general than the similarities in the next smaller group, the *genus.* Latin plant family names end in *ae* or *aceae.* For example, the rose family (which includes such different plants as strawberries, hawthorns, apples and raspberries) is *Rosaceae* (pronounced ro say' se ee).

Genus is more exclusive. Only the plants you know as roses are included in the genus called *Rosa,* for example. They have prickles, basically five petals, compound leaves, and hard seeds enclosed in a "hip." The differences between members of this genus are limited, compared to the wide variety found in the whole rose family.

The species is the next step down, with a description of characteristics shared by no other plants, not even by other species of roses. *Rosa rugosa* is a species with straight thorns, rough leaflets, and large flowers. No other rose has just the same characteristics.

Rosa rugosa and every other plant species is unique. No one knows how many different species there are in the plant kingdom but the number goes to hundreds of thousands.

Variety is the finest distinction. One step beyond the species name is the plant's varietal name. This accounts for all the *small* differences within a species. Rugosa roses may have red, pink, white, single or double flowers, each type being a different variety with a name. Here you depart sometimes from Latin with such names as 'Sarah Van Fleet' and 'Grootendorst,' or you may retain a Latin varietal name like *alba.* In the latest usage, non-Latin varietal names are indicated by single quotation marks.

Going back to genus and species names, when you use these two together to describe a plant, you are being exact. Take, for instance, *Chrysanthemum,* a prominent genus. There are many different kinds or species. When you put the species name with the genus name, you pinpoint a precise one. When you say *Chrysanthemum maximum,* you narrow the possibilities from more than one hundred different kinds down to the one single sort known popularly as shasta daisy. *Maximum* is its species name, and as such, always comes after the genus name. In writing the words, capitalize the genus name but not usually the species name in modern usage. Italicize both words.

WHAT THE NAMES MEAN

As you learn the scientific names of plants, you will notice that they offer more vivid descriptions than common names. Genus names are nouns; they are often historic and frequently use Greek root words. Species names are adjectives and they are usually descriptive. Perhaps they tell you something about the uses of the plant, its origin or culture. These clues make names easy to remember. If you have studied Latin or Greek, the interpretations are easy. Or you may notice a connection with English words you know. Let's translate a few botanical names to show the pattern.

Chrysanthemum maximum—Chrysanthemum means gold (*chrys*) flower (*anthemum*) —"gold flower." Don't take it literally—but doesn't it suggest the sort of plants you know in this big group? The species name *maximum* means big. It refers to flower size, since the shasta daisy has individual blooms characterized by large size. In *Chrysanthemum coccineum,* the *coccineum* means scarlet, so the combination means "scarlet chrysanthemum" which describes accurately this plant known commonly as pyrethum or painted daisy.

Mertensia virginica—Here the genus name honors a German botanist named Mertens. Virginica indicates this flower, the bluebell, was first found in Virginia.

Gypsophila paniculata—The genus name *Gypsophila* means lime-loving, which is literally true for this plant. *Paniculata* means panicled or having flowers in loose pyramidal racemes, describing the arrangement of the airy blooms of the common baby's breath. *Gypsophila repens* indicates by *repens* that it is a creeping form.

When writers deal with many species of the same genus, they abbreviate to avoid repeating the genus name. So in the previous paragraph *"G. repens"* would have meant gypsophila, since it was the genus beginning with G already referred to.

Prefixes and suffixes are full of meaning. If you recognize elements of combination words you can construe what many botanical names mean. Number prefixes are among the most common—like uni- or mono- for one; bi- (two); tri- (three); tetra- or quadri- (four); and so on. Here are some other common prefixes:

brevi- (short)	micro- (small)
grandi- (large)	multi- (many)
hetero- (various)	oxy- (sharp)
lati- (broad)	platy- (broad)
longi- (long)	poly- (many)
macro- (large)	sub- (under, almost, somewhat)

These are common suffixes:

-florus (flower)	-iensis or -ense (from
-foliatus (foliage)	the vicinity of)
-oides (like, or resembling)	-petalus (petals)
	-phyllus (leaf)

Species words. Some descriptive words are found over and over in species names. These are common ones:

alatus–winged	mollis–soft haired
alpinus–growing above timber line	niger–black
	nitidus–shiny
arborescens–like a tree (woody)	ovatus–egg-shaped
	pallidus–pale
barbatus–bearded	pedatus–bird foot-like
campanulatus–bell-like	
	plumosus–feathery
caerulea–blue	pumilis–small
coloratus–highly colored	radicans–stem rooting
cordatus–heart-shaped	scandens–climbing
	semperflorens–ever-flowering
cornutus–horned	
deltoides–triangular	sempervirens–evergreen
discolor–two colored	
edulis–edible	speciosus–showy
elatus–tall	spicatus–spike shaped
floridus–free flowering	
	tenuifolius–slender leaved
glaber–smooth	
guttatus–spotted	vegetus–strong growing
hirsutus–hairy	
humilis–dwarf	vernalis–of the springtime
lanatus–woolly	
luteus–yellow	vulgaris–common

J. GLOSSARY OF NAMES AND TERMS

A

acid–soil low in lime (see alkaline)

alkaline–soil containing available lime

annual–a plant that grows from seed, blooms and dies in one season

axil–angle where leaf or branch meets stem

B

B & B–balled and burlapped, refers to trees and shrubs dug with an earth ball wrapped with burlap

beard–hairlike growth, found on lower petals of some iris and other flowers

bicolor–two-colored

biennial–a plant that requires two years from seed to bloom, and dies the second year, after blooming

blanch–to cause stems or leaves to turn yellow or white by shutting out light; done with celery and endive

blast–refers to flower buds that dry up without opening

481

bole–the central trunk of a tree

bract–a modified leaf resembling a flower petal. The showy parts of dogwood and poinsettia blooms are bracts.

C

callus–a hard surface that grows over an injury or cut

calyx–the covering of flower parts, consisting of sepals

cambium–layer of cells in trees between bark and wood

catkin–flower spike with scaly segments, usually applied to willows

chlorophyll–green coloring in plant cells

chlorosis–condition causing green parts of plants to turn yellow or white

clone–group of plants derived vegetatively from the same parent plant

compost–vegetation that has decomposed

compound leaf–one that consists of a number of separate leaflets

conifer–tree bearing seed-cones

corolla–usually the showy part of flowers consisting of petals

cotyledon–the first leaf (leaves) of a plant, contained in the seed

crown–place on a plant where tops join roots

D

deciduous–describes plants that drop their leaves in winter

dioecious–plants with pistillate (seed setting) flowers on one plant, staminate (pollen producing) on another

disk flowers–in composites like daisies, the small close-set centers as distinct from ray flowers around the edge

E

ecology–the study of plants in relation to environment

embryo–baby plant enclosed by the seed

emulsion–a liquid in which fats or oils are suspended

epiphyte–plant anchored on another plant but taking sustenance from the air, like certain orchids

espalier–system of pruning and training plants to grow in one place as on a wall

eye–a growth bud, especially on roots like peonies

F

falls–three lower "petals" or sepals of an iris flower

flat–a shallow box for growing seeds or cuttings

flora–collective term for all plants growing in the place referred to

floret–individual small flower, of a many-parted cluster

force–to cause growth or bloom to develop earlier than normal

frond–leaf blade of a fern

G

genus–plant group including species that are alike in certain distinguishing characteristics

germinate–begin to grow, as a seed

glabrous–smooth

glaucous–covered with a powder-like "bloom" (seen on Concord grapes)

graft–process of joining a bud or stem of one plant with a root of another

H

harden off–expose gradually to more difficult conditions such as cold or dry air

hardy–able to withstand adverse conditions, especially cold, without special protection

heave–refers to the action of soil freezing and thawing that pushes plants out of the ground

heel–a base piece of parent stem taken with young wood cuttings

heel in–cover plant roots temporarily with soil in a trench, awaiting permanent planting

herbaceous–with fleshy stems, not woody

hill up–to mound soil around plants to support, as with gladiolus, or protect for winter as with roses

hip–seed-fruit of a rose

humus–decomposed vegetable matter in soil

I

imperfect flower–one lacking either pistil or stamens

inflorescence–part of the plant containing the flowers

L

laterals–side branches

layer–to cause a branch to form roots without cutting it from the parent plant

leach–to wash out nutrients from soil with repeated influx of water

leader–the central upright branch of a tree

leggy–stems are abnormally long and with few leaves, usually caused by too little light, overcrowding, or undernourishment

legume–a member of the pea family (*Leguminaceae*)

M

miscible oil–one that will mix with water in a spray

monoecious–plants with pistils (seed-setting) and stamens (pollen-producing) in separate flowers on the same plant

mulch–a soil covering intended to afford winter protection, conserve moisture, prevent overheating or keep down weeds

mutation–a sudden change in some part of a plant, or a variation of seed or cutting-grown offspring from its parents

N

native–growing naturally in the wild in a given area

naturalize–to adapt a plant to grow in a space as though it were native

neutral–applied to soil, neither acid nor alkaline

node–swellings on stems where leaves may develop

nutrients–with plants, minerals or other substances that nourish growth

O

organic matter–plant or animal refuse, the term usually applying to decomposed forms in soil

ovary–place at the base of the pistil containing ovules which develop into seeds

P

peat moss–partly decomposed organic matter, often fibery and moisture retentive

pedicel–individual flower stem

perennial–a plant that lives more than two years

perfect flower–one with both pistillate and staminate parts in the same bloom

petal–one section of the corolla, usually the showy part of the flower

petiole–a leafstalk

pH–symbol indicating the acidity or alkalinity scale on which 7 is neutral, over 7 alkaline, under 7 acid

pinch–to remove growth tips

pistil–pollen-receiving organ of a flower

plicata–in iris, a color pattern having dark stipples on a white or light background

pollen–the male reproductive cells which when applied to the pistil begin the process of seed production

pot bound–describes a plant whose roots are crowded in the container

proliferation–an offshoot of a plant that can be used for propagation

propagation–the process of increasing the numbers of a plant

R

raceme–a flower cluster in which pedicels are all the same length, as in lily of the valley

ray flower–in composites like daisies, the long narrow petal-flowers around the outside of the flower, as distinct from disk flowers in the center

rhizome–a thick rootstem, as in iris

rogue–to weed out undesired plants

rosette–a circular cluster of usually basal leaves

runner–a thin trailing shoot that takes root, as in strawberry

S

scape–a flower stalk rising from the crown without leaves

scion–in grafting or budding, the piece that is to form the new plant top

scree–a bed of stones with little earth, for rockeries

sepal–one of the separate sections of a calyx, at the outer base of the flower

sessile–without a stem or stalk

set–a small seed-grown onion used for spring planting

shear–cut off branches in an even plane

shoot–a developing new branch

slip–a cutting; or, to take a cutting to be rooted

sphagnum–undecayed water-retentive moss used for packing or in seed starting mixtures

spike–long flower cluster with florets radiating evenly from it, like hosta and delphinium

spore–reproductive body of non-flowering plants like ferns and fungi, capable of producing a new plant

sport–another name for mutation

stamen–the pollen-producing part of a flower

sterile–with flowers, one that cannot set seed; with soil one that has been treated to rid it of most harmful fungi or bacteria

strain–a race of similar plants produced from seeds

stolon–a runner that will take root

stratification–process of softening hard seeds by embedding in sand and exposing to moisture and freezing

sucker–fast-growing shoot from root, or base of trunk or branches

T

tap root–a central heavy root that goes down, as in carrot

tendril–a twining branch that enables a plant to climb, as in grapes

thin–to cut out some plants (or blooms) reducing the number

trenching–a system of soil preparation involving unusually deep digging and addition of bottom humus

trumpet–in daffodils, the long center tube of the flower

tuber–a thick underground stem usually containing growth buds

U

umbel–an umbrella-shaped flower cluster

V

vein–the line in a leaf, smaller than a rib

W

whorl–circular cluster of leaves around a stem

INDEX

(Italic numbers refer to illustrations)

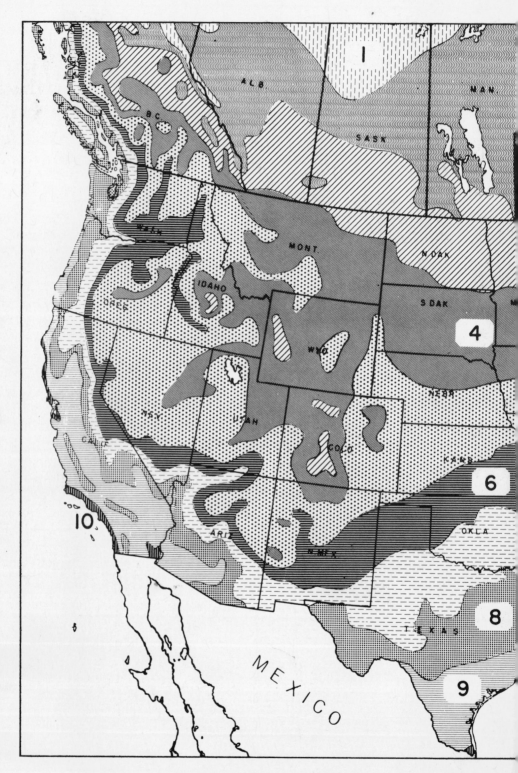

PLANT HARDINESS ZONE MAP